TRUMP
TWITTERVERSE

THE CAMPAIGN

TRUMP
TWITTERVERSE

THE CAMPAIGN

MALEVOLENT BOOKS
Santa Monica, California

Cover design by Mischief
Typeset in Times New Roman, Garamond and Big Noodle Titling

FIRST EDITION

Library of Congress Cataloging-in-Publication-Data is available on file.

Hardcover ISBN: 978-1-936573-19-6
Trade Paperback ISBN: 978-1-936573-20-2

Malevolent Books, in association with Global ReLeaf, will plant two trees for each tree used in the manufacturing of this book. Global ReLeaf is an international campaign by American Forests, the nation's oldest nonprofit conservation organization and a world leader in planting trees for environmental restoration.

10 9 8 7 6 5 4 3 2 1

ACKNOWLEDGEMENTS

INTRODUCTION

The 2016 United States quadrennial Presidential election was remarkable in its embrace of technology. While candidates had previously used emerging social networking platforms, none used social networking so pervasively and effectively as Donald J. Trump used Twitter and Facebook. Twitter became the candidate and subsequent President-elect's mode of choice for his approach to circumventing traditional modes of communication and media outlets.

It was proven to be a highly effective tool for targeting and galvanizing an audience with effectiveness being assessed with near immediacy. While at times using very provocative language (which has been the subject of much debate from both sides of the political aisle), Mr. Trump's ability to use the platform to persuade and reach a mass audience in an immediate and cost effective manner has been of no debate.

To be used as a reference, policy topics of note during the campaign as well as various then current topics were included in the index. In addition, individuals and corporations that were cited were also included. We did not include pervasive slogans such "Make America Great Again" or hashtags such as #MAGA in the index. Emojis may have been removed only for purposes of layout. We have attempted to identify all individuals cited as some are cited by first name alone.

We did not editorialize, selectively include or exclude any tweets. We chose to refrain from offering a personal viewpoint or commentary on the contents of this book, but rather have it stand as a record which may be discussed and commented on by others.

Jim Strader – Publisher

TRUMP
TWITTERVERSE

THE CAMPAIGN

June 16, 2015

The Announcement

- Jun 16, 2015 02:04:03 AM "@realJoeMurray: Hopefully tomorrow is the day we start to make America great again! Looking forward to it, @realDonaldTrump. #Trump2016
- Jun 16, 2015 02:04:19 AM "@brentcfritz: Today is the day America becomes great again. @realDonaldTrump has some huge news that will shock the world #Trump4President"
- Jun 16, 2015 02:28:37 AM "@insuraider: @realDonaldTrump is going to make Hillary's head spin tomorrow morning. Presidential Debate? Yes, please. #Trump2016"
- Jun 16, 2015 02:28:54 AM "@DONJUBBER: @realDonaldTrump Shock the world!#Trump4President"
- Jun 16, 2015 02:29:11 AM "@PianoBecca: @realDonaldTrump No Amercian, really, can impact such staggering influence. Stay True! Great and savvy bizman! America: GREAT!
- Jun 16, 2015 02:29:34 AM "@isabelsimon80: @realDonaldTrump @brentcfritz Donald has as good of a chance as anyone else.. People like him...NO MORE POLITICIAN'S..."

- Jun 16, 2015 02:29:50 AM "@Knight276: @realDonaldTrump @realJoeMurray America can be great again with trump at the helm. Confidence counts."
- Jun 16, 2015 02:30:05 AM "@_Snurk: @realDonaldTrump Love it! Always respect FIGHTERS over overrated loser POLITITIANS!! Inspire GREATNESS! #TRUMP #2016"
- Jun 16, 2015 02:32:41 AM "@rg_radical99: Counting down the hours to @realDonaldTrump announcement! Ready for America to become great again. Supporting you Mr. Trump.
- Jun 16, 2015 02:33:52 AM "@Rhumeey: I really would want to see what America would look like...with @realDonaldTrump at the helm of affairs. https://t.co/zfvJpyjVoH"
- Jun 16, 2015 02:34:01 AM "@NickyFlash2: #Trump4President #Trump2016 @realDonaldTrump"
- Jun 16, 2015 02:34:14 AM "@Jarod_Pitmon10: I am a full supporter of #Trump2016 @realDonaldTrump is a guy that will help this country"
- Jun 16, 2015 02:34:57 AM "@premuse: @realDonaldTrump Let's take this country back. #TrumpLeeds2016"
- Jun 16, 2015 02:35:30 AM "@Desheay: @realDonaldTrump Your twitter banner is awesome. Cant wait for tomorrow.....TRUMP 2016.."
- Jun 16, 2015 02:35:40 AM "@DavidSBaldwin: @realDonaldTrump today's the day #Trump2016! Good luck!"
- Jun 16, 2015 03:15:59 AM "@jaketapper: DonaldTrump in Iowa says "I have a Gucci store that's worth more money than Romney" Fact check: true http://t.co/xvDVHmntvR"
- Jun 16, 2015 07:20:40 AM Big time in U.S. today - MAKE AMERICA GREAT AGAIN! Politicians are all talk and no action - they can never bring us back.
- Jun 16, 2015 07:24:41 AM Thanks. https://t.co/eZfgrOy1Hn
- Jun 16, 2015 08:00:39 AM "@AppSame We are going to listen @realDonaldTrump If you are really running & if you keep to your word You really have a great chance to win
- Jun 16, 2015 08:04:05 AM It is almost time. I will be making a major announcement from @TrumpTowerNY at 11AM. Follow on social media! #MakeAmericaGreatAgain

- Jun 16, 2015 08:07:50 AM Make sure to follow me on @periscopeco #MakeAmericaGreatAgain
- Jun 16, 2015 09:01:13 AM In one hour I will be making a major announcement from Trump Tower. Watch it live on Periscope! https://t.co/kYOHIpBzan
- Jun 16, 2015 09:31:51 AM Make sure to follow me on @periscopeco. I will be streaming my announcement at 11AM.
- Jun 16, 2015 09:48:26 AM 11AM #MakeAmericaGreatAgain https://t.co/445bOdp6QY
- Jun 16, 2015 09:51:37 AM Thanks Geraldo, you're a champion. https://t.co/APfc0PThCP
- Jun 16, 2015 09:58:14 AM LIVE on #Periscope: Major announcement! #MakeAmericaGreatAgain https://t.co/XW3PqHemNq
- Jun 16, 2015 10:57:23 AM I am officially running for President of the United States. #MakeAmericaGreatAgain https://t.co/Ct0lNu7kz0
- Jun 16, 2015 12:23:59 PM #MakeAmericaGreatAgain https://t.co/JguVmqXqWA
- Jun 16, 2015 12:59:15 PM Thanks Eric. https://t.co/phUbaTvq8d
- Jun 16, 2015 02:15:54 PM Today I officially declared my candidacy for President of the United States. Watch the video of my full speech- https://t.co/gonTk0o9Dt
- Jun 16, 2015 07:22:01 PM Dear @kimguilfoyle, Thank you so much for your nice words today on @TheFive. Will not be forgotten! In Iowa now. Packed house!
- Jun 16, 2015 07:28:59 PM @ericbolling, watched you on my flight to Iowa. Will not be forgotten.
- Jun 16, 2015 08:13:33 PM Thanks @greggutfeld. Really nice! I'm glad I did your show. @GregGutfeldShow
- Jun 16, 2015 08:55:59 PM @ericbolling, in addition,no doubt you would have been amazing on @ApprenticeNBC! Keep up the great work.
- Jun 16, 2015 10:37:30 PM Enjoyed watching @MonicaCrowley's analysis of my @BillOreilly interview. Great points! Thank you, Monica.

- Jun 17, 2015 08:51:33 AM "@Gabigayle @FoxNews @realDonaldTrump He doesnt need anyone's money and can speak the truth because of it! Go Donald!"
- Jun 17, 2015 09:53:22 AM Thank you Sarah--Let's have pizza in New York soon with you & your great family https://t.co/SQ6LsNZ6UC

- Jun 17, 2015 10:54:34 AM Only a fool would buy the @NYDailyNews. Loses fortune & has zero gravitas. Let it die!
- Jun 17, 2015 11:05:58 AM We need someone with experience to rebuild America. #MakeAmericaGreatAgain https://t.co/Y5Wq9LuCT0
- Jun 17, 2015 12:43:36 PM Heading to New Hampshire. #MakeAmericaGreatAgain https://t.co/qTMiYoR9wu
- Jun 17, 2015 05:56:57 PM Speaking to great patriots @MCC_CT. My first visit to Granite State since declaring my candidacy! #FITN https://t.co/HfdDwzjOf0

- Jun 18, 2015 10:52:15 AM Thank you. https://t.co/cTB9G0sAl0
- Jun 18, 2015 11:35:52 AM Trump Int'l Hotel & Tower, Chicago, has received accolades for design, service & our signature restaurant, "Sixteen" http://t.co/4oJj9nQnUH
- Jun 18, 2015 11:58:49 AM The tragedy in South Carolina is incomprehensible. My deepest condolences to all.
- Jun 18, 2015 12:35:19 PM Watch my appearance on @Morning_Joe - great interview! http://t.co/ZVftDka774
- Jun 18, 2015 01:52:48 PM Trump Nat'l Golf Club Philadelphia, 360 beautiful acres as designed by Tom Fazio with views of the Philly skyline. http://t.co/jha0m0W4Kk
- Jun 18, 2015 03:58:51 PM "@JustinBorges1 Trump 4 president...has a nice ring to it. About time someone who isn't afraid to say/do what's necessary took the reigns"
- Jun 18, 2015 08:09:26 PM "@megliq: Ive been saying "Donald trump for preZ" since 2nd grade.I AM YOUR BIGGEST FAN LOOK I MET U @realDonaldTrump http://t.co/LrJujtXbFJ

- Jun 19, 2015 06:55:49 AM "@AndyBran: @JoeNBC Mr. Trump nailed it! Wow: After Doubts, Economists Find China Kills U.S. Factory Jobs - http://t.co/bzYPJ5bWSo""
- Jun 19, 2015 06:58:26 AM "@MrInsaf: @realDonaldTrump @AndyBran @JoeNBC @keichri I believe Donald Trump will always make the best deal for his people"
- Jun 19, 2015 06:58:34 AM "@CliffShep: @realDonaldTrump You've got my vote!!"

- Jun 19, 2015 06:59:00 AM "@hufseyg: I've waited to vote for @realDonaldTrump since I was little. I can't wait for 2016"
- Jun 19, 2015 07:01:04 AM "@elizwatkins: @realDonaldTrump So how many more days until you are in office? #PresidentTrump #Letstalkbusiness"
- Jun 19, 2015 07:03:14 AM "@HolySelena: @realDonaldTrump You are such a bright man. You have my vote!!"
- Jun 19, 2015 07:05:51 AM "@hollyammon: @AndyBran @JoeNBC DONALD TRUMP has been telling anyone who would listen about the Chinese currency manipulation." So true.
- Jun 19, 2015 07:07:36 AM "@dcfoodsafety: Mr. Trump you're the candidate that we have been waiting for you tell it real and you will get it done you have my vote!"
- Jun 19, 2015 07:08:21 AM "@ChaddRyann: Keep doing what you're doing! You're attracting attention and people are talking more then they were before! #Trump2016"
- Jun 19, 2015 07:10:18 AM "@SMW5683: @realDonaldTrump Donald trump will do this country good! He is a businessman & will know how to grow our economy"
- Jun 19, 2015 07:53:20 AM Just watched Brian Williams on @TODAYshow - very sad! Brian should get on with a new life and not start all over at @msnbc. Stop apologizing
- Jun 19, 2015 07:56:36 AM "@williamonlyrent Why is government run by politicians? It's a huge business and needs a businessman to run it successfully! #Trump2016"
- Jun 19, 2015 08:04:01 AM "@theHickMan33 Let's get the Trump trending #MakeAmericaGreatAgain #TheDonIsComing #TrumpCard #Vets4Trump"
- Jun 19, 2015 08:41:05 AM "@llambert0207 I've always said the Country needs to be run like a Major Corporation it takes a Brilliant Businessman #power #donaldtrump"
- Jun 19, 2015 09:27:59 AM Goofy political pundit George Will spoke at Mar-a-Lago years ago. I didn't attend because he's boring & often wrong—a total dope!
- Jun 19, 2015 09:34:04 AM George Will was a big Iraq fool. $2 trillion, thousands of lives lost -- & we got nothing! Dummy.
- Jun 19, 2015 09:35:44 AM Has Charles @krauthammer ever apologized for being so totally wrong on Iraq? I called it right in every way—Make America Great Again!

- Jun 19, 2015 09:42:45 AM Hillary Clinton reaches new low. #TrumpVlog https://t.co/kgmQ2jVF6b
- Jun 19, 2015 11:30:25 AM Stop saying I went bankrupt. I never went bankrupt but like many great business people have used the laws to corporate advantage—smart!
- Jun 19, 2015 11:30:50 AM People buy deals & immediately put them into bankruptcy in order to make better deals. It's a very effective & commonly used business tool.
- Jun 19, 2015 11:31:27 AM Almost every major dealmaker has used the bankruptcy laws as a business tool. Icahn, Black, Zell—but nobody says they went bankrupt!
- Jun 19, 2015 11:32:02 AM Out of hundreds of deals & transactions, I have used the bankruptcy laws a few times to make deals better. Nothing personal, just business.
- Jun 19, 2015 01:42:55 PM Via @WashTimes by @CharlesHurt: "Donald Trump declares war on lying, street-hustlers of Congress" http://t.co/IonH0WEDEs
- Jun 19, 2015 03:31:45 PM Our country is in a major crisis of incompetent leadership. We cannot continue to go on with these politicians who do nothing but talk.
- Jun 19, 2015 03:44:37 PM "@stevenkirk @realDonaldTrump @PatrickBuchanan great article .. At least #thedonald is finally saying what us average working people know!"
- Jun 19, 2015 08:03:05 PM Why did @DanaPerino beg me for a tweet (endorsement) when her book was launched?
- Jun 19, 2015 08:15:22 PM I like Mexico and love the spirit of Mexican people, but we must protect our borders from people, from all over, pouring into the U.S.
- Jun 19, 2015 08:54:25 PM Mexico is killing the United States economically because their leaders and negotiators are FAR smarter than ours. But nobody beats Trump!
- Jun 19, 2015 09:22:29 PM Druggies, drug dealers, rapists and killers are coming across the southern border. When will the U.S. get smart and stop this travesty?

- Jun 20, 2015 03:42:16 PM "@bobbybnews: The only person running for President that will not betray America for money is Donald Trump. Fox is cutting him down=Reagan!

- Jun 20, 2015 06:09:29 PM "@andrewwagner29: Its pretty clear that @realDonaldTrump would absolutely destroy HillaryClinton in a debate & i really wanna see it happen.
- Jun 20, 2015 06:11:55 PM "@Tea_Alliance: @realDonaldTrump @bobbybnews The establishment fears Trump!" They are afraid to make America great again.
- Jun 20, 2015 06:37:49 PM "@njoh1234: @realDonaldTrump Trump speech is on C-span right now...f.y.i."
- Jun 20, 2015 06:48:43 PM My speech is right now on C-SPAN 1
- Jun 20, 2015 07:25:21 PM Thank you @AnnCoulter for your nice words. The U.S. is becoming a dumping ground for the world. Pols don't get it. Make America Great Again!
- Jun 20, 2015 07:28:29 PM "@BreitbartVideo: .@AnnCoulter: Trump Has Best Shot in General Election http://t.co/Vf6c5kvrcn via @IanHanchett http://t.co/GOQTWZhjAM"
- Jun 20, 2015 07:32:07 PM "@SenzuLean: America should be so lucky to have @realDonaldTrump even consider leading our nation" Thank you.
- Jun 20, 2015 07:57:54 PM Who would you rather have negotiating for the U.S. against Putin, Iran, China, etc., Donald Trump or Hillary? Is there even a little doubt?
- Jun 20, 2015 08:52:07 PM "@Riggs101: Carl Icahn: Donald Trump Is Completely Correct That "We Are In A Bubble Like You've Never Seen Before"

- Jun 21, 2015 05:36:02 AM "@sugarhoney157: @realDonaldTrump He really is a great business man and gets the job done right." So true!
- Jun 21, 2015 05:40:56 AM "@NishantAgg23: Donald Trump is the only hope for a crumbling American economy. Hope my American friends choose Trump"
- Jun 21, 2015 05:43:04 AM "@I_Dont_Know_Her: @realDonaldTrump you are the best candidate for president in a long time. Hope you win" Thanks.
- Jun 21, 2015 05:57:18 AM "@nytimes: If you're a betting man, it's time to start believing Donald Trump http://t.co/YGeFcDz6Vo"
- Jun 21, 2015 10:41:29 AM Via @nypost by @JonathonTrugman: "Donald Trump's resume backs his run for president" http://t.co/mDKEOW9vrf
- Jun 21, 2015 12:14:23 PM Happy Father's Day to all! I had a wonderful and loving father. https://t.co/SdrRctSxhu

- Jun 21, 2015 01:38:29 PM Via @BreitbartNews by @ASwoyer: "Exclusive: Trump Slams Obamatrade, Stands Up For American Jobs" http://t.co/kE5pjagvtq
- Jun 21, 2015 05:28:29 PM .@KarlRove, who spent $430 million in the last cycle and didn't win one race, said I'm not a candidate until I file papers. Next week Karl!
- Jun 21, 2015 05:35:05 PM "@BK00023: Donald Trump's resume backs his run for president http://t.co/KXJPyRPK67 @realDonaldTrump #greta @ThisWeekABC" Thank you, so true
- Jun 21, 2015 05:39:55 PM "@CandyThomas3583: @realDonaldTrump I tend to vote for democratic candidates, but I feel excited about you in the presidential race. "
- Jun 21, 2015 05:41:28 PM "@utwey: @realDonaldTrump @KarlRove can't wait for debates! DT will crush them" Could happen!
- Jun 21, 2015 06:12:02 PM .@MarthaRaddatz was so unprofessional and biased when discussing me on This Week. @GStephanopoulos should not allow this conduct!
- Jun 21, 2015 06:50:55 PM The great Mike Wallace covered me in a much more professional manner than his son, Chris Wallace of @FoxNews. Mike was a total pro!
- Jun 21, 2015 07:37:58 PM "@JakeKonczyk: @realDonaldTrump @KarlRove The best candidate! #GotMyVote #MakeAmericaGreatAgain"
- Jun 21, 2015 07:38:27 PM "@fackinpeter: @realDonaldTrump @KarlRove theyre all jealous of your success #Trump2016 #MakeAmericaGreatAgain" Thanks.
- Jun 21, 2015 07:38:52 PM "@Auburnfan2155: @realDonaldTrump @KarlRove Karl Rove destroyed the Republican Party. Time to rebuild it." True!
- Jun 21, 2015 07:46:35 PM .@KarlRove stated clearly that he wants to repeal the 2nd Amendment. I thought @FoxNews was going to fire that jerk after his Romney fiasco?
- Jun 21, 2015 07:49:56 PM "@MrBrentAllen: @realDonaldTrump @KarlRove @FoxNews I watched the @KarlRove interview. He sounds like an unpatriotic dolt. Trump 2016!"
- Jun 21, 2015 07:50:45 PM "@TeamBobbyEwing: @foxnews @karlrove I am stunned that Rove would suggest repealing the #2A! That will not solve the problem, IMO!"

- Jun 21, 2015 07:54:13 PM .@KarlRove still thinks Romney won! He doesn't have a clue! @FoxNews
- Jun 21, 2015 07:55:16 PM "@shawncrazyshawn: I have Loved you since Wrestlemania when I was kid. I grew up & see what you're all about. I am behind you ALL the way!"
- Jun 21, 2015 07:58:33 PM "@hyannis1952: @realDonaldTrump @FoxNews Believe they are worried you may win!
- Jun 21, 2015 08:00:00 PM "@JPJAC: @realDonaldTrump @FoxNews Why is it that FOX loved you until you declared as a candidate???" Good question!
- Jun 21, 2015 08:05:22 PM "@bdckool: I do believe that Trump has the intestinal fortitude to set right all the wrongs of the current administration. #Trump2016"
- Jun 21, 2015 08:06:07 PM "@joncford: @realDonaldTrump @TeamBobbyEwing @FoxNews @KarlRove I'm just about done with Fox news!"
- Jun 21, 2015 08:08:01 PM "@IsaacNewYorker: Finally somebody with real intelligence & leadership is runnig for president Mr @realDonaldTrump. #MakeAmericaGreatAgain"
- Jun 21, 2015 08:08:32 PM "@pbstwo: @realDonaldTrump @hyannis1952 @FoxNews The Donald owes NOTHING to lobbyists. He could restore our Republic." True.
- Jun 21, 2015 08:10:37 PM "@Alaskan_Gypsy: @FoxNews @seanhannity indicated he would support you if you ran. Let's see if he puts his money where his mouth is!
- Jun 21, 2015 08:11:12 PM "@kirkcameronfan: @realDonaldTrump @FoxNews Because they're AFRAID of you! #Trump2016 #American"
- Jun 21, 2015 08:12:50 PM "@lauralynn1955: @realDonaldTrump - @oreillyfactor loves you. It was obvious to me when you were on the day you announced." Bill O is great.
- Jun 21, 2015 08:13:22 PM "@IsaacNewYorker: I said when Trump ran for president i was gonna be the happiest man on earth,when he wins,all Americans will be #Trump16"
- Jun 21, 2015 08:13:59 PM "@sallyvp: @realDonaldTrump Mr. Trump tell America they are fired! Bring some respect and balls back to the USA."

- Jun 21, 2015 08:18:46 PM "@JakeAwK: Donald Trump is the ONLY candidate that is incorruptible and he will get rid off all of the incompetence ruining our country.
- Jun 21, 2015 08:19:34 PM "@Jessyandcandy: Trump, you got my vote. With your proven resume os success. People would be nuts not to vote for you. Trump2016"
- Jun 21, 2015 08:21:31 PM "@cota2012: @realDonaldTrump @hyannis1952 @FoxNews it's amazing how people fear a change for the better"

- Jun 22, 2015 05:31:26 AM Sadly, I will no longer be doing @foxandfriends at 7:00 A.M. on Mondays. This is because I am running for president and law prohibits. LOVE!
- Jun 22, 2015 05:39:21 AM I want to thank Elizabeth, Steve, Brian and all of the great folks of @foxandfriends for the long and successful run we had together. NICE!
- Jun 22, 2015 08:15:31 AM "@williamonlyrent @realDonaldTrump Only a fool will underestimate #Trump2016. Trump will surprise everybody and America needs him."
- Jun 22, 2015 08:50:01 AM .@deneenborelli Thank you for your nice words-- greatly appreciated.
- Jun 22, 2015 09:10:27 AM Thank you. https://t.co/l4g1VmXsCn
- Jun 22, 2015 09:23:06 AM "@SovAdjEast The USA is like Wollman Rink or Ferrypoint before DJT. You came you saw and built a masterpiece. Now it's the USA' s turn."
- Jun 22, 2015 09:32:37 AM "@carsonbonner @realDonaldTrump A businessman that understands the world's business/politics. #Trump2016"
- Jun 22, 2015 09:39:02 AM "Hillary Clinton Dominates the Pack in Fake Twitter Followers" http://t.co/e16f6FM8uQ
- Jun 22, 2015 09:55:10 AM .@JordanSpieth Great job--you are a true champion! See you soon.
- Jun 22, 2015 11:24:15 AM "@AbishurPrakash My latest piece on @realDonaldTrump winning the foreign policy race. #Trump2016 https://t.co/vzLZgJOEQC …"
- Jun 22, 2015 11:35:39 AM It's time for government to stop picking winners & losers. Let's make sure everyone can achieve the American dream! https://t.co/u25yI5T7E8

- Jun 22, 2015 11:42:24 AM Who do you want negotiating for us? #MakeAmericaGreatAgain https://t.co/WASlyxbG1j
- Jun 22, 2015 12:16:55 PM Flashback – Jeb Bush received a $4M tax payer bailout in 1990 http://t.co/R2bpNbRQRX Guess who was POTUS then?
- Jun 22, 2015 01:09:50 PM The Senate must NOT pass TPA! Any Senator who votes for it is disqualified for being POTUS. Protect the American worker and manufacturer!
- Jun 22, 2015 01:43:16 PM Entrepreneurs: Negotiation is an art. Treat it like one.
- Jun 22, 2015 01:46:14 PM Entrepreneurs: Be tough, be smart, be personable, but don't take things personally. That's good business.
- Jun 22, 2015 02:03:04 PM Entrepreneurs: Brainpower is the ultimate leverage. Don't underestimate yourself or your possibilities.
- Jun 22, 2015 02:40:19 PM .@DanaPerino Have you released a copy of the beautiful thank you card you sent me? Would you like to see it? @ericbolling @kimguilfoyle
- Jun 22, 2015 02:59:42 PM "@nojoed: @realDonaldTrump @KarlRove Karl, why don't you sit this election cycle out, we had enough losers to last us a life time." True.
- Jun 22, 2015 03:47:04 PM True. https://t.co/wjffOyAxZM
- Jun 22, 2015 03:54:33 PM "@MalachiNorris: Donald J. Trump is the very definition of the American success story. Through Trump we can bring back the American dream."
- Jun 22, 2015 03:55:49 PM "@luckydoginwesty: @realDonaldTrump @FL_GIRL979 I'll be voting for Mr. Trump"
- Jun 22, 2015 03:58:23 PM "@troubic I'm definitely voting for @realDonaldTrump I would love to see what a real businessman can do for our economy!"
- Jun 22, 2015 04:38:56 PM Today I filed my Statement of Candidacy with the FEC. Let's #MakeAmericaGreatAgain https://t.co/DB4q4J2gKn
- Jun 22, 2015 05:49:01 PM Via @bpolitics by @emtitus: "Defying Doubters, Donald Trump Makes Presidential Bid Official" http://t.co/Cjz7p3hFPX
- Jun 22, 2015 06:18:28 PM "Donald trump files statement of candidacy" http://t.co/uiMCfHmtMU via @CBSNews

- Jun 22, 2015 09:12:50 PM "@MeaganShamy: .@ScottFordTVGuy @BrandenHarvey I was at @TrumpLasVegas when @realDonaldTrump announced president bid. He's got my vote.
- Jun 22, 2015 09:14:04 PM "@WGinetta: WE ARE GONNA NEED @realDonaldTrump IN 2016 TO UN-NEGOTIATE EVERYTHING OBAMA SAID HE NEGOTIATED #MakeAmericaGreatAgain" True.
- Jun 22, 2015 09:15:55 PM "@_bri: This is the first election I'll be able to vote, and my vote goes to Trump because I want to live in a great country! #Trump2016"

- Jun 23, 2015 08:35:48 AM "@williamonlyrent So sick of politicians sugar coating problems and issues. It will be so great to have #Trump2016 say it like it is!"
- Jun 23, 2015 09:32:56 AM "@WordgirlSmith @realDonaldTrump Please keep telling all of America that jobs, jobs, jobs are important to us because YOU ARE RIGHT!!!"
- Jun 23, 2015 10:24:30 AM "@CWilliams_Rltr @realDonaldTrump. I am so happy you are running for President. You have my vote."
- Jun 23, 2015 10:34:50 AM Via @WSJPolitics by @reidepstein: "Trump Surges in Popularity in N.H." http://t.co/Iw6O3qhquR
- Jun 23, 2015 12:37:57 PM "@Stevenfclifford @realDonaldTrump thank you for running. You have my vote and I'm spreading the word. We need you there to fix this mess."
- Jun 23, 2015 01:25:43 PM My @gretawire interview on @FoxNewsInsider "Trump: 'Last Person I'd Want Negotiating for Me Is Obama'" http://t.co/DCIhNlGmdT
- Jun 23, 2015 03:50:28 PM "@kolbytraveller #Trump is more than just talk. I hope he wins the election and gets something done for once in this country. #Trump2016"
- Jun 23, 2015 05:24:08 PM Via @fitsnews:"Donald Trump Surges In New Hampshire Poll: MOGUL, REALITY STAR EMERGES AS GRANITE STATE'S 'ANTI-BUSH' http://t.co/TqFBtG9PHc
- Jun 23, 2015 09:49:46 PM Speaking at the Red, White and Blue Dinner in Maryland- https://t.co/TzuXN715fQ

- Jun 24, 2015 07:12:37 AM The highly respected Suffolk University poll just announced that I am alone in 2nd place in New Hampshire, with Jeb Bust (Bush) in first.
- Jun 24, 2015 09:16:48 AM Politician @SenatorCardin didn't like that I said Baltimore needs jobs & spirit. It's politicians like Cardin that have destroyed Baltimore.
- Jun 24, 2015 10:20:52 AM "@tryeye @realDonaldTrump Very strong start, Mr. President!" Thanks.
- Jun 24, 2015 10:25:37 AM Thank you. https://t.co/H8ZxLh6NCd
- Jun 24, 2015 02:20:03 PM My daughter, Ivanka, will be representing me today at the opening of our campaign office in Manchester, NH #MakeAmericaGreatAgain!
- Jun 24, 2015 03:52:20 PM .@Neilyoung A few months ago Neil Young came to my office looking for $$ on an audio deal & called me last week to go to his concert. Wow!
- Jun 24, 2015 04:01:34 PM For the nonbeliever, here is a photo of @Neilyoung in my office and his $$ request—total hypocrite. http://t.co/Xm4BJvetIa
- Jun 24, 2015 04:04:19 PM .@Neilyoung's song, "Rockin' In The Free World" was just one of 10 songs used as background music. Didn't love it anyway.
- Jun 24, 2015 06:39:36 PM "@barbgee68: @realDonaldTrump Excellent! I still can't believe voters have Jeb in front of you. Haven't Americans learned anything?" NO!
- Jun 24, 2015 06:39:55 PM "@MarkAGiarrusso: @realDonaldTrump Go get 'em Donald."
- Jun 24, 2015 06:40:23 PM "@LionsTrinityCap: @realDonaldTrump UNMATCHED PRESIDENTIAL CAMPAIGN...Trump RESTORES America's credit rating to AAA in 3-4 yrs.
- Jun 24, 2015 06:40:47 PM "@adeeasthope: @realDonaldTrump I'm voting for #trump for CEO of these United States, time to haul ass #Trump2016" Great.
- Jun 24, 2015 06:41:22 PM "@_laurenharding: @realDonaldTrump not to mention that there's a whole lot of people who never got asked (me included)!!! #Trump2016" Cute.
- Jun 24, 2015 07:36:14 PM Uncomfortable looking NBC reporter Willie Geist calls me to ask for favors and then mockingly smiles when he is told of my high poll numbers

- Jun 24, 2015 07:48:24 PM Just out, the new nationwide @FoxNews poll has me alone in 2nd place, closely behind Jeb Bush-but Bush will NEVER Make America Great Again!
- Jun 24, 2015 08:00:32 PM I am really beginning to respect Mark Halperin and John Heilemann as political reporters - they truly get why "Trump" poll numbers are high.
- Jun 24, 2015 08:55:14 PM The ratings for The View are really low. Nicole Wallace and Molly Sims are a disaster. Get new cast or just put it to sleep. Dead T.V.
- Jun 24, 2015 09:07:53 PM .@WhoopiGoldberg had better surround herself with better hosts than Nicole Wallace, who doesn't have a clue. The show is close to death!
- Jun 24, 2015 09:11:01 PM My daughter Ivanka did great tonight in New Hampshire. The sold out crowd loved her, and she loved them. Thanks Ivanka!
- Jun 24, 2015 09:16:38 PM My message, MAKE AMERICA GREAT AGAIN, is beginning to take hold. Bring back our jobs, strengthen our military and borders, help our VETS!
- Jun 24, 2015 10:07:11 PM "@MunichEleven: Baseball, Hotdogs, Apple Pie and a vote for @realDonaldTrump in 502 days! On 11/08/2016 we make our country great again!"
- Jun 24, 2015 10:08:31 PM "@DanielaMarino: @FoxNews enough with #Bush #Clinton and the same faces every damn year. We need fresh new ppl that r not greedy. U r d one"
- Jun 24, 2015 10:08:59 PM "@TaraHollyFigure: @realDonaldTrump we are counting on you, Mr. Trump. I believe you are the answer to #MakeAmericaGreatAgain"
- Jun 24, 2015 10:13:06 PM "@nickcokley: @realDonaldTrump my first vote ever will be for one of the most historic businessmen in history.
- Jun 24, 2015 10:17:46 PM We have to bring back and cherish the middle class - once the backbone and true strength of the U.S.A. It can happen!
- Jun 24, 2015 10:31:18 PM "@_GOLD4MONEY: @ThePatriot143 @realDonaldTrump Trump is as Honest as they come. He wants a border and doesn't hide it. #Trumpforpresident"
- Jun 24, 2015 10:34:28 PM "@Mitestarossa: Jeb Bush should support Donald Trump for President" I agree!

- Jun 25, 2015 07:19:39 AM I hear that dopey political pundit, Lawrence O'Donnell, one of the dumber people on television, is about to lose his show-no ratings?Too bad
- Jun 25, 2015 07:23:49 AM "@gneumann_wkow: New national 2016 GOP poll from @FoxNews - @JebBush leads field, @realDonaldTrump second. http://t.co/qRW1iWucRu"
- Jun 25, 2015 07:29:09 AM Governor Rick Scott of Florida did really poorly on television this morning. I hope he is O.K.
- Jun 25, 2015 08:17:26 AM "@nanaelaine7 @realDonaldTrump only YOU can make it GREAT again. Your plan is the only one inside reality. MAKE AMERICA GREAT with TRUMP"
- Jun 25, 2015 08:23:01 AM "@JWCesare I appreciate @realDonaldTrump and his straight talk. Our country needs this."
- Jun 25, 2015 09:26:52 AM Mexican gov doesn't want me talking about terrible border situation & horrible trade deals. Forcing Univision to get me to stop- no way!
- Jun 25, 2015 09:27:20 AM Univision wants to back out of signed @MissUniverse contract because I exposed the terrible trade deals that the U.S. makes with Mexico.
- Jun 25, 2015 09:27:45 AM I love Mexico but not the unfair trade deals that the US so stupidly makes with them. Really bad for US jobs, only good for Mexico.

- Jun 26, 2015 09:06:22 AM Once again the Bush appointed Supreme Court Justice John Roberts has let us down. Jeb pushed him hard! Remember!
- Jun 26, 2015 09:07:44 AM Anyone who wants strong borders and good trade deals for the US should boycott @Univision.
- Jun 26, 2015 10:13:06 AM .@Univision cares far more about Mexico than it does about the U.S. Are they controlled by the Mexican government?
- Jun 26, 2015 11:38:33 AM If I win the presidency, my judicial appointments will do the right thing unlike Bush's appointee John Roberts on ObamaCare.
- Jun 26, 2015 03:11:09 PM Letter to @Univision - Re: @TrumpDoral https://t.co/6mauCmg6uO

- Jun 27, 2015 03:37:36 AM "@Bass705: @realDonaldTrump Thank you Mr.Trump for standing up for America" My great honor!

- Jun 27, 2015 09:36:24 AM "@RobRucker: "The greatest social program is a job" -Donald Trump"
- Jun 27, 2015 09:50:19 AM When somebody challenges you unfairly, fight back - be brutal, be tough - don't take it. It is always important to WIN!
- Jun 27, 2015 09:52:12 AM When you are in a war, or even a battle, losing is not an option!
- Jun 27, 2015 10:49:48 AM .@billmaher: Bill, you are really beginning to understand what is going on with "Trump" - actually, you always knew!
- Jun 27, 2015 12:17:08 PM Only very stupid people think that the United States is making good trade deals with Mexico.Mexico is killing us at the border and at trade!
- Jun 27, 2015 12:20:20 PM The leader and negotiators representing Mexico are far smarter and more cunning than the leader and negotiators representing the U.S.!
- Jun 27, 2015 12:41:33 PM I'll be in Iowa tonight making a speech to a record setting crowd. The word is getting out, MAKE AMERICA GREAT AGAIN!
- Jun 27, 2015 12:55:05 PM "@tonyewen: @ReaganWorld @realDonaldTrump is the real deal! When was the last time we had someone with true conviction for US?
- Jun 27, 2015 12:56:25 PM "@Chris_D2: @realDonaldTrump go get em!! How does it feel to be the "next" POTUS? #Trump2016" Thanks for the spirit!
- Jun 27, 2015 12:59:02 PM "@TheReaLJuiCe88: I'm working real hard Mr Trump getting you votes in Boston/Rhode island area! #IBelieve #MakeAmericaGreatAgain #Trump2016"
- Jun 27, 2015 03:09:25 PM A great article by @NolteNC spelling out the truth on Mexico, trade, the border & illegals. Thank you @BreitbartNews http://t.co/oJnV2OXcEc
- Jun 27, 2015 03:40:55 PM Must read article via @fitsnews: "DONALD TRUMP VERSUS MEXICO" http://t.co/tdjtvtB6NB
- Jun 27, 2015 07:50:53 PM Addressing record crowd @ Madison County Iowa GOP Dinner. We can bring common sense to DC & Make America Great Again! http://t.co/mI7j7XDzOY

- Jun 28, 2015 07:35:17 AM "@incorrectpoliti: Establishment Government, Media, and Hollywood are killing America. MAKE AMERICA GREAT AGAIN ! @realDonaldTrump

- Jun 28, 2015 07:36:08 AM "@rtoneff25: @realDonaldTrump just kicked ass on Fox News. Guy is a winner" Thank you!
- Jun 28, 2015 07:38:27 AM "@GovtsTheProblem: The appeal of Donald Trump to people is that he's a fighter, not a Republican surrender monkey."
- Jun 28, 2015 07:41:02 AM "@joseangelSP500: @realDonaldTrump Trump for President! TRUMP2016!"
- Jun 28, 2015 07:42:02 AM "@DeanDesign101: Why not @realDonaldTrump? He knows how to create wealth, jobs and is not a wimp. #DonaldTrump #foxandfriends"
- Jun 28, 2015 07:43:45 AM "@johnmarzan: @RubenNavarrette Trump is right. Giving illegals the right to vote will destroy the GOP and turn dems into dominant party"
- Jun 28, 2015 07:45:59 AM "@GZervs: @realDonaldTrump is Americas only chance. He will #MakeAmericaGreatAgain"
- Jun 28, 2015 07:46:31 AM "@bucwaas: @realDonaldTrump please get elected! Be the next Reagan! You can do it!" Thanks!
- Jun 28, 2015 07:47:32 AM "@StephPrichard1: @RealDonaldTrump GOP: Trump's Fearless War with Univision Only Increases His Appeal - Breitbart http://t.co/oJnV2OXcEc"
- Jun 28, 2015 08:07:08 AM "@davidco71875026: @realDonaldTrump @GovtsTheProblem You say what the working people are thinking. Proud to support you. Don't back down !"
- Jun 28, 2015 08:07:29 AM "@oates_tom: @realDonaldTrump congrats on running! You tell it like it is.....which is rare."
- Jun 28, 2015 08:07:54 AM "@jamesgo31991021: @realDonaldTrump @johnmarzan @RubenNavarrette Donald trump is the man" Thanks.
- Jun 28, 2015 08:08:56 AM "@NYCStadsliv: @realDonaldTrump @StephPrichard1 You have my vote Mr. Trump, give 'em hell. I will.
- Jun 28, 2015 08:11:17 AM "@mjh811: @realDonaldTrump @oates_tom You are the only one with guts. We need that!! Have my vote!" Great.
- Jun 28, 2015 08:44:14 AM "@JasonKoster17: In @realDonaldTrump we trust.. #MakeAmericaGreatAgain"
- Jun 28, 2015 08:45:16 AM "@FreedomHaawk: @realDonaldTrump Don't let them try to school you, or try to rearrange you, you have a mind of your own.STAY SHARP." I will!

- Jun 28, 2015 08:47:39 AM "@WGinetta: @CNNSotu THE @realDonaldTrump & @BernieSanders ARE DOING WELL CUZ THE PPL R DISGUSTED WITH #CORRUPT POLITICIANS
- Jun 28, 2015 08:51:01 AM "@trapman2000: RT @Deaf_Dwayne: @realDonaldTrump Thanks for not being politically correct! America needs the truth.
- Jun 28, 2015 08:52:59 AM "@DattiJulia: @realDonaldTrump I did not like you before but watching your interview on CNN, you are the man."
- Jun 28, 2015 02:42:26 PM "@Samstwitch: Bill O'Reilly's interview with Trump:Q&A over what Trump would do as President!Definitely has my vote! https://t.co/tDGDGUJLs2
- Jun 28, 2015 02:43:11 PM "@usplaymoney: DonaldTrump @beny_benson He would be a leader because he is used to being the boss. Wont be bought like politicians either"
- Jun 28, 2015 02:48:21 PM "@HCannonball: Everybody get on the Trump Train!! It's a First Class One-Way ticket to the White House with @realDonaldTrump #Trump2016"
- Jun 28, 2015 02:48:40 PM "@tonyschiano: Unlike #Obama....he can think outside the box! #Trump2016 ~ @usplaymoney @realDonaldTrump @beny_benson"
- Jun 28, 2015 02:49:31 PM "@incorrectpoliti: Oh My are they starting to WAKE UP. MAKE AMERICA GREAT AGAIN! We must save America ELECT @realDonaldTrump
- Jun 28, 2015 02:49:42 PM "@itsEmilyshine: @realDonaldTrump would be the best president #DonaldTrumpforPresident"
- Jun 28, 2015 03:06:14 PM "@Knight276: @realDonaldTrump @HCannonball not being a career politician is an asset. I'm on board trump can make America great again.
- Jun 28, 2015 03:06:44 PM "@TadBoikins: @dabeard @realDonaldTrump He's firing up the GOP base. #crushingit"
- Jun 28, 2015 03:21:51 PM Will be in Chicago tomorrow for a record setting (by far) luncheon.
- Jun 28, 2015 04:06:23 PM Via @thehill by @martinmatishak: "Trump: 'We look like we're beggars' in Iran nuclear talks" http://t.co/z8RpCnuGN1
- Jun 28, 2015 04:12:37 PM See story in Fusion and Huff. Post about rape at the border. Beyond terrible! Isn't Fusion owned by Univision?

- Jun 28, 2015 04:28:54 PM "@RSan: Donald Trump's Polling Looks too Good to Be True.
- Jun 28, 2015 06:23:25 PM .@NYDailyNews, the dying tabloid owned by dopey clown Mort Zuckerman, puts me on the cover daily because I sell. My honor, but it is dead!
- Jun 28, 2015 06:34:33 PM Univision apologized to me but I will not accept their apology. I will be suing them for a lot of money. Miss U.S.A. contestants are hurt!
- Jun 28, 2015 08:18:49 PM .@jorgeramosnews Please send me your new number, your old one's not working. Sincerely, Donald J. Trump

- Jun 29, 2015 05:59:02 AM "@DynamyteBeats: @realDonaldTrump is the only choice for 2016. #MakeAmericaGreatAgain" Thank you.
- Jun 29, 2015 06:02:15 AM "@Jaguar11d: @realDonaldTrump Have a great time in Chicago today. You are the best person for the job"
- Jun 29, 2015 06:05:36 AM "@KEEMSTARx: Mexican criminals coming into USA? YES Did Trump say we need to stop them? YES Did he say Mexicans are good? YES Racism? NO"
- Jun 29, 2015 06:10:19 AM "@KEEMSTARx: Wait Mhndz, you have 5 mins to prove to me that @realDonaldTrump " doesn't support the latinos " if u do i'll paypal u $1k."
- Jun 29, 2015 06:11:26 AM "@KevinGalyon: @realDonaldTrump i support donald trump for president. He is a great leader" Thank you.
- Jun 29, 2015 06:12:52 AM "@MalachiNorris: I sure don't trust any other politicians running to be President except @realDonaldTrump #MakeAmericaGreatAgainThroughTrump
- Jun 29, 2015 06:14:05 AM "@agirland3boys: @icenycbx @realDonaldTrump @POTUS disagree a leader takes a stand. Putin would be scared of him. Peace through strength"
- Jun 29, 2015 06:14:55 AM "@MalachiNorris: I know @realDonaldTrump will be the best President that ever has or ever will walk into the Oval Office. #Trump2016
- Jun 29, 2015 06:19:49 AM "@jjhrkel: @realDonaldTrump don't ever back down from these clowns! fight the good fight!!" I promise!

- Jun 29, 2015 06:21:35 AM "@MollyCBS2: @realDonaldTrump will speak @ #Chicago city club today; Reports claim 2,000 people are on the WAITING LIST to get in!"
- Jun 29, 2015 06:26:55 AM "@hollyammon: @realDonaldTrump @MalachiNorris Mr. Trump is the ONLY one who tells the truth, no matter how politically unpopular it may be.
- Jun 29, 2015 06:40:38 AM Saudi Arabia should be paying the United States many billions of dollars for our defense of them. Without us, gone! @AlWaleedbinT
- Jun 29, 2015 06:50:49 AM "@MalachiNorris: Just over a year before everyone hears DonaldTrump say "I Donald Trump do solemnly swear that I will protect America""
- Jun 29, 2015 06:52:09 AM "@BrittainShannon: @realDonaldTrump @AlWaleedbinT Or at least give it back in oil"
- Jun 29, 2015 06:54:39 AM Remember, Univision apologized!
- Jun 29, 2015 06:55:38 AM "@JoylynBest: @Maryannzfoster @Morning_Joe Don't care about #GOP or Trump but he's the best #GOP running and should win the Primary"
- Jun 29, 2015 11:24:15 AM Via @JNSworldnews by @JacobKamarasJNS: "Donald Trump says he is no apprentice when it comes to Israel" http://t.co/O4yHtwCzbm
- Jun 29, 2015 12:38:39 PM Speaking at the City Club of Chicago. Sold out in minutes with thousands on the wait list!… https://t.co/7SKav05hnA
- Jun 29, 2015 03:14:37 PM Statement on Relationship with NBC- https://t.co/BpczGaIGWq
- Jun 29, 2015 06:57:45 PM "@imprimis310: @NBC is the bigot. @realDonaldTrump and @SenTedCruz only speaking the truth about ILLEGAL immigrants"
- Jun 29, 2015 07:01:44 PM "@ghostofnicky: @OutFrontCNN @CNN @realDonaldTrump Donald is the only candidate that speaks the truth!!!!"
- Jun 29, 2015 07:05:34 PM "@MARGIE352: @realDonaldTrump I believe Donald Trump is the only one that can do this. He has no skin in the game. Just his Country.
- Jun 29, 2015 07:08:59 PM "@amstaffbru: Pull out the heavy artillery, buy every liberal network and flush them in the toilet. You,Mt.T, have my Vote hands down"

- Jun 29, 2015 07:10:11 PM "@jamalwms45: @HowardKurtz @johnnydollar01 @megynkelly For the remark Trump made on dumping NBC, I'll vote for @realDonaldTrump"
- Jun 29, 2015 07:11:59 PM "@slucch24: @AnnCoulter don't worry... we clearly don't have an illegal alien criminal problem. #AdiosAmerica http://t.co/2LKr8zoSwy"
- Jun 29, 2015 07:16:25 PM "@jacobmathews: @realDonaldTrump @jamalwms45 @HowardKurtz @johnnydollar01 @megynkelly I like Donald for his no fear tell the truth attitude.
- Jun 29, 2015 07:17:05 PM "@susanadana432: lDonaldTrump @amstaffbru Keep telling it lIke it is. You have the recipe for making the USA great again. You have my vote
- Jun 29, 2015 07:19:30 PM "@TheHolyBreadcat: @realDonaldTrump Vote for Trump, he's making America to where we won't worry about illegal immigrant problems."
- Jun 29, 2015 07:20:05 PM "@KristyWillams79: @realDonaldTrump I've waited years for you to run for president! You are going to fix America! We Need a businessman.
- Jun 29, 2015 07:21:31 PM "@Knight276: @realDonaldTrump @amstaffbru I have confidence trump can turn a negative into a positive. Trump can make America great again!
- Jun 29, 2015 07:22:20 PM "@RickysPlace1: @realDonaldTrump @slucch24 @AnnCoulter It is so blatantly obvious! Why do people refuse to see it?"
- Jun 29, 2015 07:22:56 PM "@MARGIE352: Listen to what he says. You will know in your heart it is the truth. We are in a bad way. he is the only one who gets it."
- Jun 29, 2015 07:31:51 PM "@C_Archaeology: @realDonaldTrump is our only hope @littlebytesnews #tcot"
- Jun 29, 2015 08:37:37 PM "@echump: @megynkelly @realDonaldTrump if what everyone says is true Trump will score huge if this is for publicity. i'd trust Trump"
- Jun 29, 2015 08:41:10 PM "@ChipB: Like him or not @realDonaldTrump says EXACTLY what he thinks and doesn't beat around the bush. And that's admirable. #Election2016"

- Jun 29, 2015 08:42:37 PM "@KristenCWard: Great statement and it's finally nice to have someone who stands by what they say! #GotMyVote https://t.co/qsi68qgat4"
- Jun 29, 2015 08:44:41 PM "@Einsteinrevisit: @megynkelly @GeraldoRivera @realDonaldTrump LOVE the TRUMP!"

- Jun 30, 2015 07:35:44 AM We MUST have strong borders and stop illegal immigration. Without that we do not have a country. Also, Mexico is killing U.S. on trade. WIN!
- Jun 30, 2015 07:57:28 AM I love the Mexican people, but Mexico is not our friend. They're killing us at the border and they're killing us on jobs and trade. FIGHT!
- Jun 30, 2015 08:44:06 AM "@kingjersey1 @realDonaldTrump #MakeAmericaGreatAgain they can't stand that you are speaking for the American people"
- Jun 30, 2015 08:45:15 AM "@WILDMANBS It says a lot about @NBC when they fire @realDonaldTrump but keep Brian Williams and @TheRevAl on the payroll. #tcot"
- Jun 30, 2015 08:51:36 AM Thank you Ted. https://t.co/MVUzSAn6ru
- Jun 30, 2015 11:30:19 AM "@Figlo7 @realDonaldTrump Apologize to the press for not being a politician - because you haven't learned to LIE yet. Go Donald!"
- Jun 30, 2015 11:31:32 AM "@melsthemom @realDonaldTrump NBC=censorship. I'm done with them"
- Jun 30, 2015 11:32:57 AM "@yankeeworshiper thank you to Donald Trump for standing up for what you believe in.leave the B.S.and lies for Hillary and Barack."
- Jun 30, 2015 11:35:42 AM "@woofeous @realDonaldTrump Everyone loves Donald because he'll tell it like it is without any political "sugar-coating" & double-speak."
- Jun 30, 2015 03:17:31 PM @tedcruz, now I know you're smart! See you soon. http://t.co/vzVHbA1TAr #TCOT #MAKEAMERICAGREATAGAIN!
- Jun 30, 2015 03:51:17 PM Watch me on the @oreillyfactor tonight at 8PM.
- Jun 30, 2015 03:53:59 PM "@webster07 @realDonaldTrump wish there were more people in the public eye with this attitude. It's only way 2 defeat political correctness"

- Jun 30, 2015 04:44:42 PM My just filed lawsuit against Univision. Always fight back when right. #MakeAmericaGreatAgain https://t.co/ies96YzSeG
- Jun 30, 2015 05:21:55 PM Via @THESHARKTANK1: "Donald Trump's Controversial Mexican Comments Are Accurate" http://t.co/nYL2QQMwKZ
- Jun 30, 2015 05:52:18 PM Get ready for @Oreillyfactor tonight at 8- always interesting!

July, 2015

- Jul 1, 2015 10:21:53 AM My recent statement re: @macys -- We must have strong borders & stop illegal immigration now!… https://t.co/HLCboRmTbl
- Jul 1, 2015 11:59:51 AM Those who believe in tight border security, stopping illegal immigration & SMART trade deals w/other countries should boycott @Macys.
- Jul 1, 2015 12:00:19 PM For all of those who want to #MakeAmericaGreatAgain, boycott @Macys. They are weak on border security & stopping illegal immigration.
- Jul 1, 2015 02:33:55 PM .@andersoncooper Anderson—Thank you for being so fair with your reporting & story last night. Greatly appreciated!
- Jul 1, 2015 02:45:29 PM "@tixxannatrix @Lrihendry: Now this is the @RealDonaldTrump we have come to know At least Trump speaks his mind. Doesn't cower to PC."
- Jul 1, 2015 03:14:37 PM "@phxladydi @realDonaldTrump I truly believe you can bring America back to great. You don't cower to the media, lobbyists or anyone else."

- Jul 1, 2015 04:09:35 PM .@GovernorPataki was a terrible governor of NY, one of the worst -- would've been swamped if he ran again!
- Jul 1, 2015 04:09:53 PM .@GovernorPataki couldn't be elected dog catcher if he ran again—so he didn't!
- Jul 1, 2015 04:10:58 PM Interesting that @Macys criticized me but just paid $650,000 in fines for racial profiling. Are they racists?
- Jul 1, 2015 04:11:30 PM Who is @Macys to pretend innocence when they "racial profile" all over the place? Paid big fine!
- Jul 1, 2015 04:57:12 PM Look what the President of NBC sent me recently about his stay in my Las Vegas hotel. Very loyal guy. https://t.co/J9bsbc1WEN
- Jul 1, 2015 05:27:55 PM Make our borders strong and stop illegal immigration. Even President Obama agrees- https://t.co/OcKfUFgSPU
- Jul 1, 2015 07:30:31 PM "@JohnRiversToo: @instapundit Macy's sales are declining, their stock is downgraded - maybe not the best time to spit on half of America."
- Jul 1, 2015 08:45:31 PM "@ehShaun: @realDonaldTrump knows what he's talking about. Please don't give us another Bush as president."
- Jul 1, 2015 08:48:00 PM "@David_A_Hurd: @realDonaldTrump Fight the good fight Mr. PRESIDENT TRUMP! You are the only one fighting for America! #Trump2016"
- Jul 1, 2015 08:48:40 PM "@ftimewifenmomma: I am really liking @realDonaldTrump. We NEED someone who will tell the TRUTH. "

- Jul 2, 2015 06:40:03 AM "@JewNamedLew: @realDonaldTrump @Macys to pay $650,000 settlement over racial profiling... http://t.co/bT6S8F9NnK" Boycott Macy's.
- Jul 2, 2015 06:40:59 AM "@JimStaricha: Mr. Trump, I truly hope you are elected. I strongly believe you have more than the skills required. We need a professional."
- Jul 2, 2015 06:42:01 AM "@ibleedcoffee: Just deleted the @Macys app off my phone. It's a shame, We used to spend thousands there a year. No more. #BoycottMacys"
- Jul 2, 2015 07:55:06 AM "@JulUSN: @realDonaldTrump They look bad. @Macys screwed up BigTime!They are so hypocritical,YOUR Right & they know it!"

- Jul 2, 2015 07:55:56 AM "@soupman227: @Karentalk @ForAmerica @realDonaldTrump #WakeUpAmerica the media has shown its true colors.
- Jul 2, 2015 07:58:18 AM "@TeresaWageman: @realDonaldTrump @Macys Stick to your guns Mr. Trump. You are telling the truth that too many are afraid to."
- Jul 2, 2015 07:58:43 AM "@Sheriapple: @realDonaldTrump Thought ur interview w @donlemon was inspiring. U speak the truth.
- Jul 2, 2015 07:59:09 AM "@muireb_tpnd: @realDonaldTrump You have Lib media scrambling..I just freak'n love that! Thank you for your leadership and patriotism!"
- Jul 2, 2015 08:02:48 AM "@TickerCandy: @realDonaldTrump @Macys Ah yes, so many people I know are cancelling their Macy credit cards. #YouJustGotTrumped" Great.
- Jul 2, 2015 08:03:03 AM "@DagnyRed: @Karentalk @ForAmerica @realDonaldTrump ? #'m Latina/ Legal & fully support you speaking the TRUTH! Don't back down!"
- Jul 2, 2015 08:03:20 AM "@JimStaricha: @eastevens54 @cvpayne @tonykatz @realDonaldTrump Watch what he said, yes maybe a bit kinder, but a fact is a fact."
- Jul 2, 2015 08:03:50 AM "@BettyeBear: @realDonaldTrump Every working class (every color) knows Trump & wants to be rich like him - faces light up @macys"
- Jul 2, 2015 08:05:40 AM "@AnnCoulter: Yes, strange that Trump is surging in the polls for saying what other GOPS too stupid to say. https://t.co/fgmgLjQAeE"
- Jul 2, 2015 10:09:03 AM .@Macys stock just dropped. Interesting. So many people calling to say they are cutting up their @Macys credit card. Thank you!
- Jul 2, 2015 10:09:42 AM Why doesn't somebody study the horrible charges brought against @Macys for racial profiling? Terrible hypocrites!
- Jul 2, 2015 10:37:36 AM "@lafrana @realDonaldTrump @Macys I will not shop at Macy's. I am with you Mr Trump!"
- Jul 2, 2015 11:34:43 AM "@racheljoycowley I'm done with Macy's. Apparently, they follow the trend of trying to force legislation on every American freedom. Done!"
- Jul 2, 2015 12:47:07 PM "Trump Gives 'Em Hell" http://t.co/dD53I0PeXw via @limbaugh

- Jul 2, 2015 12:59:12 PM "NBC FIRES TRUMP, KEEPS SHARPTON: The bigots of the NBC executive suite look the other way" http://t.co/EfQk8cbbTR via @AmSpec by @JeffJlpa1
- Jul 2, 2015 01:14:23 PM "@RealNinjetta @ErinSiegal @AppSame @Univision http://t.co/QNOuFlufaS My many MEXICAN friends fly to visit Mexico because UNSAFE border"
- Jul 2, 2015 01:20:10 PM Via @trscoop: "Mark Levin DEFENDS Trump: Hillary Clinton is a CROOK and a FRAUD and she's not treated this way!" http://t.co/MdU0pvTThi
- Jul 2, 2015 01:24:26 PM Via World Tribune "The elites' problem with Donald Trump: He's not for sale" by Jeffrey T. Kuhner http://t.co/ez08iprQH1
- Jul 2, 2015 01:29:04 PM Via Huffington Post "Congrats, America! Donald Trump Is Now A 2016 Presidential Front-runner" http://t.co/X1YYz7x002 by Igor Bobic
- Jul 2, 2015 01:35:45 PM "@onesoldiersmom @ArtNGonzalez @earredondo If you would listen to his words, you will hear that he was slamming our gutless politicians."
- Jul 2, 2015 01:38:20 PM "@mstrbass2000 @DashMan18 @AppSame taking a stand against stupid companies over reacting to free speech, nothing trump said wasn't true"
- Jul 2, 2015 01:39:54 PM "@Neilleon_ @realDonaldTrump sir! Thanking you for speaking your mind and or having your very own opinion on certain issues."
- Jul 2, 2015 01:41:26 PM Great article by @RichLowry on @POLITICOMag : "Sorry, Donald Trump Has A Point" http://t.co/5irmxJjPWk
- Jul 2, 2015 01:45:08 PM "@RunPureMichigan Macy's stock drops after coming out in support of #illegals dust up with @realDonaldTrump and public #BoycottMacys"
- Jul 2, 2015 01:47:17 PM "@NeilECollins @Macys only interested in sales and could care less about America. Veterans and Military will be with Trump."
- Jul 2, 2015 01:49:27 PM "TRUMP DECLARES VICTORY ON IMMIGRATION AS OBAMA ADMITS SOME ILLEGALS ARE 'GANG BANGERS'" http://t.co/e0HLxf1dS2 via @BreitbartNews @ASwoyer
- Jul 2, 2015 01:59:58 PM New jobs report: 432,000 left workforce, manufacturing & durable goods go - http://t.co/RD1blUZyRn We need leaders who understand business.

- Jul 2, 2015 02:12:19 PM Via @RedState by @EWErickson: "Always Play On Offense" http://t.co/mF3OjUMjp3
- Jul 2, 2015 02:17:31 PM New orders for manufacturing down 9/10 months http://t.co/RD1blUZyRn Time for fair trade. Stop TPP!
- Jul 2, 2015 02:24:12 PM A country must enforce its borders. Respect for the rule of law is at our country's core. We must build a wall! https://t.co/u25yI5T7E8
- Jul 2, 2015 02:26:59 PM "@KosloffM I really admire your straight talk and not bowing down to the drive by media and special interest groups say what you mean" Thx
- Jul 2, 2015 02:28:33 PM "@rebamoreland you must be doing something right, cause the left has circled the war wagons. Stay strong in your convictions, WE LOVE IT!!"
- Jul 2, 2015 02:31:17 PM "@BackOnTrackUSA @JulUSN @Macys Donald, I love your ties. Just set up a website online & millions of us will continue to buy your products."
- Jul 2, 2015 02:35:27 PM "@LepleyAmanda @realDonaldTrump @DagnyRed @Karentalk @ForAmerica amen honey honest is honest dont back down support the truth!"
- Jul 2, 2015 02:41:00 PM Obama once again just missed a self-imposed deadline with Iran. Our leadership is weak & ineffective. Double the sanctions!
- Jul 2, 2015 02:47:31 PM It is time to bring competence to Washington. It is time get results. Let's Make America Great Again! https://t.co/u25yI6aIvG
- Jul 2, 2015 05:17:07 PM "@chipman88 @realDonaldTrump @DavidDCarpenter @lafrana @Macys I didn't know Macy's was still in business. Oh well, still not going there."
- Jul 2, 2015 08:03:59 PM "@Highlander6700: @realDonaldTrump @Macys: Seems 1 or 2 lines of Mr. Trump's comments about immigrants are continuously taken out of context
- Jul 2, 2015 08:07:07 PM "@MARGIE352: @Highlander6700 @Macys They were taken out of context. Trying to make him look bad to the American Hispanic community."
- Jul 2, 2015 08:07:44 PM "@tonyarolandtr: @Youxia88 @tedcruz @realDonaldTrump @Macys The American ppl are taking a stand! We are fighting back!!!"

- Jul 2, 2015 08:08:43 PM "@clew136:DonaldTrump your charisma, confidence, leadership, and record of incredible success is exactly what this country needs #Trump2016"
- Jul 2, 2015 08:09:22 PM "@PerryJames778: @Highlander6700 @Macys The media Loves to twist words, and so do the politicians. @realDonaldTrump will set it straight!"
- Jul 2, 2015 08:10:02 PM "@GroverWindham: @realDonaldTrump @Highlander6700 @Macys #obama called them gangbanger & criminals"
- Jul 2, 2015 08:13:15 PM "@michell33841372: Donald keep speaking the truth! The media has printed your words out of context. You will make America great again!"
- Jul 2, 2015 08:13:56 PM "@SaveAmerica15: @MrBiggles12345 @tonyarolandtr @Youxia88 @tedcruz @Macys Trump just might be the savior of America! Better than Reagan!"
- Jul 2, 2015 08:14:39 PM "@jeanne_mazzotta: @Macys @realDonaldTrump shame on you Macy's. Whatever happened to freedom of speech #cancelingmycard"
- Jul 2, 2015 08:14:49 PM "@MellysModern: So ready for @realDonaldTrump to do this! Keep it up, you've got 'em scared!"
- Jul 2, 2015 08:16:25 PM "@PatrickJLavin: @realDonaldTrump @GroverWindham @Highlander6700 @Macys Donald Trump for President 2016! America, let your voices be heard."
- Jul 2, 2015 08:16:48 PM "@DHarley187: @vdare @claramarks @AnnCoulter @realDonaldTrump you tell em trump! Trump speaks the truth"
- Jul 2, 2015 08:19:20 PM "@TheUSALifeStyle: @AnnCoulter TO #MakeAmericaGreatAgain VOTE FOR DONALD TRUMP. #Trump2016 #Eleccion2015 #USA #GOP http://t.co/KMDUXI1IDJ"
- Jul 2, 2015 10:09:43 PM "@HoustonGunn: My Grandma from #Seattle and Mom in #Nashville just said they won't shop at @Macys again. @realDonaldTrump
- Jul 2, 2015 11:10:49 PM "@yeswecandeport: @realDonaldTrump @Macys I am sure rocketing up to polls at the cost of losing a place to sell his ties is killing him."
- Jul 2, 2015 11:19:53 PM As Governor of Texas, Rick Perry could have done far more to secure the border - but that's O.K., I like him anyway! @GovernorPerry

- Jul 2, 2015 11:22:03 PM "@jharwood14: If Reagan, a Hollywood actor, was president, then your chances are strong. It sure would be nice to have an "honest" POTUS."
- Jul 2, 2015 11:25:42 PM "@2014_vince: @realDonaldTrump only our Donald will save Christianity..Christ bless our land"
- Jul 2, 2015 11:26:53 PM "@Non_PC_Guy: @HoustonGunn @Macys In Chicago we're still mourning loss of once great Marshall Fields, to mediocre Macys. Screw Macys!"

- Jul 3, 2015 04:13:31 AM "@TheguhMantap: @realDonaldTrump you are next President USA" Make America Great Again!
- Jul 3, 2015 04:18:54 AM "@Spen_A_John: @realDonaldTrump @TheguhMantap hey you're the man Trump. Fight the fight"
- Jul 3, 2015 04:21:20 AM "@Numerologynow: In my 37 years of Life U are the 1st person I have Ever Supported Running 4 the White house U WILL MAKE AMERICA GREAT AGAIN
- Jul 3, 2015 04:23:26 AM "@babyylissa: Obama calls immigrants gang bangers&criminals but Trump gets attacked for calling SOME illegals from SOME countries bad people
- Jul 3, 2015 04:24:12 AM "@KingRollinZonez: @realDonaldTrump never voted but your getting my vote"
- Jul 3, 2015 04:24:31 AM "@bperez733: @realDonaldTrump @Numerologynow Yes In Deed!! #TrumpforTriumph"
- Jul 3, 2015 04:26:53 AM "@frankdimauro: @realDonaldTrump Keep speaking the truth. The media elites cannot stop you from telling it as it is. #Trump2016"
- Jul 3, 2015 04:27:39 AM "@JUSTTHETRUTHTV: @WFinchner @realDonaldTrump @Macys So? How does that change that very bad people are coming over the boarder?"
- Jul 3, 2015 04:28:51 AM "@Iceman0921: I support @realDonaldTrump and I as well will no longer give my business to @Macys . #Trump2016" Great!
- Jul 3, 2015 04:36:50 AM "@kobuck12: @realDonaldTrump Donald Trump runs to help America become great again. You know he's not doing it to enrich himself like Clinton
- Jul 3, 2015 04:37:27 AM "@james_artherton: @realDonaldTrump full respect from a British guy. I wish I could vote for you! Trump for president!"

- Jul 3, 2015 04:38:05 AM "@seanbarakett: @realDonaldTrump id rather have a businessman in the White House than a politician. You've got my vote"
- Jul 3, 2015 04:39:39 AM "@PizzaPartyBen: @realDonaldTrump thank you for standing up for America let's make this country great again!"
- Jul 3, 2015 04:41:04 AM "@jazztheelf: @realDonaldTrump you're the only reason I'm registering to vote & first president I'm donating to!! US" Thanks.
- Jul 3, 2015 04:41:29 AM "@davidrwoods: @realDonaldTrump is 100% correct! You have so far made the most sacrifice! Thankfully."
- Jul 3, 2015 04:41:50 AM "@BigGstory: @realDonaldTrump is not a politician, he's the leader that America needs"
- Jul 3, 2015 06:09:51 AM Mexican leaders and negotiators are much tougher and smarter than those of the U.S. Mexico is killing us on jobs and trade. WAKE UP!
- Jul 3, 2015 06:22:38 AM Wow, Huffington Post just stated that I am number 1 in the polls of Republican candidates. Thank you, but the work has just begun!
- Jul 3, 2015 11:18:55 AM "A nation that cannot control its borders is not a nation." - President Ronald Reagan
- Jul 3, 2015 01:43:58 PM Via @DailyCaller by @rpollockDC: "NYC Mayor Action Against Donald Trump Is 'Not the American Way'" http://t.co/SnV1yXVs4P
- Jul 3, 2015 01:48:17 PM We need jobs & we need them fast. I am a job creator. None of the pols can or will. Let's Make America Great Again! https://t.co/u25yI5T7E8
- Jul 3, 2015 04:14:38 PM Via @NRO by @JOELMENTUM: "Matchless Name Recognition and Deep Pockets Make Trump a Threat in Iowa" http://t.co/Wg3eBcDypo
- Jul 3, 2015 05:08:09 PM Our Southern border is totally out of control. This is an absolutely disgraceful. situation.http://t.co/ujz3jENIYo We need border security!
- Jul 3, 2015 05:12:24 PM Our Southern border is unsecure. I am the only one that can fix it, nobody else has the guts to even talk about it. http://t.co/ujz3jENIYo
- Jul 3, 2015 05:39:46 PM My heartfelt condolences to the family of Kathryn Steinle. Very, very sad!

- Jul 3, 2015 05:44:54 PM Where are the other candidates now that this tragic murder has taken place b/c of our unsafe border http://t.co/amaV7tqgAR We need a wall!
- Jul 3, 2015 06:15:38 PM "@_fly_on_wall_: sucks when @realDonaldTrump says what most of us think and gets punished for it. scares us"
- Jul 3, 2015 06:16:55 PM "@BonnieKit: Thank you America Ferrara for supporting lawless criminals from Mexico. One more needless death. 2 innocent lives taken"
- Jul 3, 2015 06:17:04 PM "@bzocash: @realDonaldTrump that speech was inspiring Trump I'm with you"
- Jul 3, 2015 06:26:22 PM .@marcorubio what do you say to the family of Kathryn Steinle in CA who was viciously killed b/c we can't secure our border? Stand up for US
- Jul 3, 2015 06:29:08 PM .@TheJuanWilliams you never speak well of me & yet when I saw you at Fox you ran over like a child and wanted a picture. Please share pic!
- Jul 3, 2015 09:59:15 PM Via @CNNPolitics by @teddyschleifer: "Trump: San Francisco killing shows perils of illegal immigration" http://t.co/WJ872PRCO5
- Jul 3, 2015 10:38:47 PM "@CNNPolitics: Trump: San Francisco killing shows perils of illegal immigration http://t.co/aiBnAOhYup (via @TeddySchleifer)"
- Jul 3, 2015 10:47:46 PM "@funtravel777: @RoniSeale @usplaymoney @marcorubio Donald Trump can't be bought, bullied, or intimidated. He is a strong leader."
- Jul 3, 2015 10:48:31 PM "@myGianLuca: @CNNPolitics @teddyschleifer Say it LOUD & PROUD @realDonaldTrump! *** ILLEGAL IMMIGRATION *** Is an Attack on Our Country!"
- Jul 3, 2015 10:49:10 PM "@KsRedbirds13: @realDonaldTrump for president. No better candidate than Mr Trump. http://t.co/Z3ICtUXDh2" Thank you.
- Jul 3, 2015 10:50:03 PM "@RoniSeale: The American people deserve a wall to protect our jobs, economy and our safety. I am the only candidate who would build it."
- Jul 3, 2015 10:50:11 PM "@omgnastygirl: @realDonaldTrump Make our country great again.. TRUMP FOR PRESIDENT !"
- Jul 3, 2015 10:51:44 PM "@Reveretoo: @realDonaldTrump @CNNPolitics @teddyschleifer Absolutely. All the American people need is a leader to rise up #DonaldTrump"

- Jul 3, 2015 10:53:16 PM "@mikescintoshow: @realDonaldTrump He says what others are too afraid to say; the truth!"
- Jul 3, 2015 10:57:30 PM "@mikescintoshow: This is why we need @realDonaldTrump He tells it like it is! https://t.co/4bxhrMDPNw"
- Jul 3, 2015 10:59:41 PM "@KingAmory: Cta driver just tweaked I'm voting for @realDonaldTrump"

- Jul 4, 2015 07:05:49 AM I will be on @foxandfriends this morning at 8:30. Enjoy!
- Jul 4, 2015 07:58:27 AM "@roparsons: @realDonaldTrump @foxandfriends It is so refreshing to see a candidate with a backbone. Mr. Trump you have my vote!"
- Jul 4, 2015 08:16:44 AM HAPPY 4TH OF JULY TO EVERYONE! MAKE AMERICA GREAT AGAIN!
- Jul 4, 2015 08:17:57 AM "@usclarry: Mr @realDonaldTrump is the only candidate that hits my three main topics, Border Security, Economy and National Defense."
- Jul 4, 2015 03:51:45 PM "@rodsandguitars: @danaperino just lied about DonaldTrump - Dana, Trump Did NOT say "ALL are criminals & rapists" .. #ProudAmerican#NoLying"
- Jul 4, 2015 03:55:09 PM "@mariclaire81: @justdoit377 @realDonaldTrump @marcorubio I do not yet who I will vote for but can assure you it will not be Rubio"
- Jul 4, 2015 05:15:01 PM What about the undocumented immigrant with a record who killed the beautiful young women (in front of her father) in San Fran. Get smart!
- Jul 4, 2015 05:19:24 PM "@airforce2100: @Macys This 4th of July lets also remember the thousands of American citizens killed by illegals. http://t.co/vsdiL1Z6oZ"
- Jul 4, 2015 05:20:58 PM "@SharNeal: ANY conservative candidate who disses DonaldTrump's stand on illegals will not get my vote-he stands for US first over Illegals.
- Jul 4, 2015 05:21:15 PM "@MikeG_Beats: @realDonaldTrump #Trump2016"
- Jul 4, 2015 05:28:56 PM Why would Republican candidates want the support of Mitt Romney. He lost an election against Obama that should NEVER have been lost!

- Jul 4, 2015 05:29:37 PM "@zengadfly: .@VRWCTexan @JebBush @marcorubio @realDonaldTrump @gatewaypundit More than a few voters may #PlayTheTrumpCard! #backlash"
- Jul 4, 2015 05:30:44 PM "@nanaelaine7: I can't wait for your inauguration!! The beginning of the end to these criminal immigrants. MAKE AMERICA GREAT AGAIN" Thanks.
- Jul 4, 2015 05:33:39 PM "@BradSaidWhat: @realDonaldTrump NEVER GIVE UP. You're our last hope!"
- Jul 4, 2015 05:35:15 PM "@VeneziaMatthew: Trump is the only real candidate. He is only saying what we all know. Much crime comes from illegal immigrants. Fact!"
- Jul 4, 2015 05:37:07 PM "@Lauren_Nann: @realDonaldTrump @BradSaidWhat STAND WITH TRUMP 2016"
- Jul 4, 2015 05:38:18 PM "@mckee16365: @realDonaldTrump I registered to vote yesterday when renewing my driver license. #Trump2016"
- Jul 4, 2015 05:39:00 PM "@Nick_Da_Slick: #Trump2016 #MakeAmericaGreatAgain @realDonaldTrump"
- Jul 4, 2015 05:39:22 PM "@FrankieEMT_B: @realDonaldTrump You have my vote already! We don't need another Obama, it's time for someone who knows how to lead!"
- Jul 4, 2015 05:39:49 PM "@markg0077: @NeBonnie @realDonaldTrump But still, we put our trust in @MittRomney and he FAILED us."
- Jul 4, 2015 05:40:55 PM "@StephPrichard1: You never give up Hope you win. @realDonaldTrump you're my #1 choice #Trump2016 #ProudAmerican"
- Jul 4, 2015 05:42:10 PM "@_Tsac_: I'm probably going to vote for @realDonaldTrump simply because he has the balls to speak his mind. And half of America agrees."
- Jul 4, 2015 05:42:21 PM "@TJeeyy: #MakeAmericaGreatAgain #Trump2016 #TrumpNation #TrumpForPresident @realDonaldTrump"
- Jul 4, 2015 05:42:32 PM "@DCnumerology: @realDonaldTrump @VeneziaMatthew TRUMP IS THE MAN"
- Jul 4, 2015 05:44:00 PM "@KMoriconi: @realDonaldTrump Waiting for the day we can call you Mr. President!"
- Jul 4, 2015 05:48:38 PM "@Darci51: @realDonaldTrump the blue! I don't care WHAT @nbc says or @Macys Screw them! I'm voting 4 you, Mr. Trump! #trumpforpresident"

- Jul 4, 2015 05:48:59 PM Via @BreitbartNews: "GAME ON: TRUMP RESPONDS TO JEB" http://t.co/whpR1m7FFz
- Jul 4, 2015 05:49:53 PM "@judiejudyjudy: @Macys I will never shop in your store 4 the rest of my life because of how quickly U turned on DonaldTrump.U have no spine
- Jul 4, 2015 05:50:13 PM "@bdean1468: @JebBush & @marcorubio couldn't carry @realDonaldTrump 's gym bags. #Trump2016"
- Jul 4, 2015 05:51:00 PM "@BooBooBear4U2: #Trump keeps comin back like Bruce Willis in RED! Trump is hard hitting PATRIOT! TRUTH TRUMPS ALL! https://t.co/KE614fyAPW"
- Jul 4, 2015 05:52:05 PM "@nolehace: @DCnumerology @VeneziaMatthew #Trump #thedonald 3M followers, ck the other candidates-do the math. #trump echoes Americans"
- Jul 4, 2015 05:52:32 PM "@catisbetter666: @realDonaldTrump I'm voting trump bc we need a real man to lead the country not that socialist Obama"
- Jul 4, 2015 05:56:08 PM "@Karentalk: @realDonaldTrump @BreitbartNews America will be restored under Mr. Trump.. https://t.co/zFm0OOkkH0 God Bless America."
- Jul 4, 2015 05:56:42 PM "@realmarkjackson:Trump has them on the run and they are scared as hell that finally the pyramid scheme is about to be exposed. #truthhurts"
- Jul 4, 2015 05:57:28 PM "@marita1j: Praying @realDonaldTrump continues 2 keep the Repubs honest! It w/b so great 2 hv another Reagan 2 rebuild respect 4 USA!"
- Jul 4, 2015 06:01:06 PM "@ReillyCarole: @realDonaldTrump .We all need to get out and vote for Donald . We need a change and he is the man to bring it ." Thank you!
- Jul 4, 2015 06:50:13 PM "@mdavis22569: : @realDonaldTrump How is it possible @Macys is having a 4th of July sale, when it's against Freedom of Speech?
- Jul 4, 2015 09:35:25 PM "@eastonelliott22:@_Tsac_ More than half of America agrees with Trump- everyone I talk to loves Trump&respects blunt truths- God Bless Trump
- Jul 4, 2015 09:36:18 PM "@wizHether: DonaldTrump Keep it up! They're attacking you because they're afraid. You're winning! We who love our country have your back!"

- Jul 4, 2015 09:36:45 PM "@PeritusTraining: @realDonaldTrump Don't worry Democrats, Donald will make America great again for you too http://t.co/lyenc4gXNx"
- Jul 4, 2015 09:37:24 PM "@futureicon: @GOP Trump is correct Hear about a young woman who was shot to death in San Francisco by a Mexican who'd been deported 5 times
- Jul 4, 2015 09:40:12 PM "@NeBonnie: @markg0077 @helendhughes @realDonaldTrump @MittRomney I agree! Romney needed #Trump's cajones - all I'm saying!"
- Jul 4, 2015 09:43:04 PM "@jackie4545890: @realDonaldTrump good for you Mr. Trump for speaking up for America you're the only one that's real"
- Jul 4, 2015 09:43:32 PM "@spankemewanke18: #MakeAmericaGreatAgain @realDonaldTrump #2016"
- Jul 4, 2015 09:44:25 PM "@MichaellW56: @tedcruz Saw where you supported @realDonaldTrump on @meetthepress to be aired tomorrow AM. Thank you." Thanks Ted!

- Jul 5, 2015 03:35:10 AM "@eva_rider: Ted Cruz Backs Trump about securing the borders. Nothing has been done for decades. http://t.co/abD8GMDthl via @Newsmax_Media"
- Jul 5, 2015 03:35:28 AM "@GarettWadekempe: Donald Trump for President! He has my vote come elections!"
- Jul 5, 2015 03:57:17 AM Miss Universe, Paulina Vega, criticized me for telling the truth about illegal immigration, but then said she would keep the crown- Hypocrite
- Jul 5, 2015 04:31:12 AM "@thedemonking18: Late night confessions: I think Donald Trump would be a good president"
- Jul 5, 2015 04:36:45 AM "@pdxnancy: Donald Trump and 2015 / 2016 Considerations... http://t.co/BRwt2jWxsH via @thelastrefuge2~ I just signed up to support Mr. Trump
- Jul 5, 2015 04:41:04 AM "@MichaellW56: @tedcruz Saw where you supported @realDonaldTrump on @meetthepress to be aired tomorrow AM. Thank you."
- Jul 5, 2015 04:42:25 AM "@futureicon:DonaldTrump continues to move up in the presidential polls as his message begin to resonate with the 'fed-up' American people."

- Jul 5, 2015 09:44:31 AM Rick Perry failed at the border. Now he is critical of me. He needs a new pair of glasses to see the crimes committed by illegal immigrants.
- Jul 5, 2015 09:51:42 AM I appreciate the GOP candidates who remain strong on border security. They know I am right. A nation without borders cannot survive.
- Jul 5, 2015 10:02:22 AM Jeb Bush will never secure our border or negotiate great trade deals for American workers. Jeb doesn't see & can't solve the problems.
- Jul 5, 2015 10:23:20 AM Flashback – Jeb Bush says illegal immigrants breaking our laws is an "act of love" http://t.co/p8yFzVuw8w He will never secure the border.
- Jul 5, 2015 10:33:38 AM It is time to create jobs for Americans, not D.C. We need a bold new direction. Let's Make America Great Again! https://t.co/u25yI5T7E8
- Jul 5, 2015 07:27:15 PM Thank you @loudobbsnews, I will be trying very hard to prove you right - great show!
- Jul 5, 2015 07:47:54 PM I said simply that the Mexican leaders and negotiators are smarter than ours and that the Mexican gov't is pushing their hard core to U.S.
- Jul 5, 2015 08:01:32 PM "@BabyPhatRox: @realdonaldtrump The huff post pollster has @realdonald trump in first place ahead of jeb bush"
- Jul 5, 2015 08:01:49 PM "@shoegoddesss: @realDonaldTrump Will definitely vote for you. Breath of fresh air. America needs you!"
- Jul 5, 2015 08:02:14 PM "@bdean1468: @realDonaldTrump DONALD! DONALD! DONALD!!! #MakeAmericaGreatAgain #Trump2016 #trumpforpresident"
- Jul 5, 2015 08:02:27 PM "@LendonDonna: @realDonaldTrump BC our government are spineless. We need someone who will stand their ground. You have my support"
- Jul 5, 2015 08:03:36 PM "@2big2bereal: @realDonaldTrump donald I don't have to tell you , your doing something right"
- Jul 5, 2015 08:21:58 PM "@Virginia4USA: @ArtistdeeDd @HowardKurtz As do I, Diana.Saw Mr. Trump in Manchester & crowd was energized & hungering 4 real leadership.

- Jul 5, 2015 09:55:08 PM "@tiffyluck: @realDonaldTrump God bless America and DonaldTrump. You have all of my support and that of all those who are fed up with DC."

- Jul 6, 2015 12:14:42 PM Thx to all the people who called to say they are cutting their @Macys credit card as a protest against illegal immigrants pouring into US
- Jul 6, 2015 02:14:43 PM "@absabella Mr.Trump speaks the TRUTH And Will NOT Back Down!! That's why he will be our next President!! #MAKEAMERICAGREATAGAIN"
- Jul 6, 2015 04:00:31 PM "@fernandocarnal @realDonaldTrump @Macys not shopping there again!"
- Jul 6, 2015 07:30:47 PM "@DavesBigWife:@Macys I have a Macy's store I used to love to shop at until they turned on Americans @realDonaldTrump #MakeAmericaGreatAgain
- Jul 6, 2015 07:31:08 PM "@Retrogirl01: @AP Mr. Trump is right! BUILD THE WALL! @realDonaldTrump"
- Jul 6, 2015 07:36:28 PM "@ericbolling: The "Establishment" GOP out in force tonight trying to discredit @realDonaldTrump Congrats Donald you've got them nervous.
- Jul 6, 2015 08:24:28 PM "@CoachJMan: If the majority will bind together and support Trump we will reverse the downward spiral the US is on. http://t.co/J1FEV8eHg1"
- Jul 6, 2015 08:25:00 PM "@thegre8_1: @SenTedCruz In addition to the criminals among the illegal aliens what about all the infectious diseases they brought to US"
- Jul 6, 2015 09:48:36 PM We have got to take our country back. It's time!
- Jul 6, 2015 09:52:54 PM "@Brainbow_Bite: @realDonaldTrump I AGREE WITH PAT BUCHANAN THAT YOU SIR ARE A MAN OF ACTION!" Thank you!
- Jul 6, 2015 11:08:08 PM "@bdean1: If I had a dollar for every time a politician lied, i'd be as rich as @realDonaldTrump I'm happy as hell he's running! #Trump2016"

- Jul 7, 2015 08:51:29 AM "@hallmarkm1 @realDonaldTrump is the only Presidential candidate that TRULY is fighting to #MakeAmericaGreatAgain"

- Jul 7, 2015 10:33:19 AM People rarely say that many conservatives didn't vote for Mitt Romney. If I can get them to vote for me, we win in a landslide.
- Jul 7, 2015 10:35:14 AM .@AnnCoulter U were great last nite @ericbolling on FOX. Our country has become a dumping ground for the world--I'll get it to stop & fast!
- Jul 7, 2015 11:16:35 AM "@lolabigirl I'm not sure why people are mad @realDonaldTrump he really speaks the truth. Sir, I support you for #President."
- Jul 7, 2015 04:11:43 PM "@DanScavino Illegal Immigrant Deported 6 Times Charged in Felony Hit & Run of Family. @realDonaldTrump is not wrong. #Trump2016"
- Jul 7, 2015 05:00:23 PM Wow! I hear that thousands of people are cutting up their @Macys credit card. That's great. #MakeAmericaGreatAgain!
- Jul 7, 2015 05:49:37 PM MUST READ-"It's time people listened to Trump,' says mother of gunned-down teenage football star" http://t.co/7hs5RN8Qb7 SECURE THE BORDER!
- Jul 7, 2015 06:15:37 PM "RUBIO'S GANG OF 8 BILL WOULD HAVE REWARDED SANCTUARY CITIES HARBORING ILLEGALS" http://t.co/on0rUCv4MG Marco is a politician-he flip flops!
- Jul 7, 2015 06:25:53 PM Via @limbaugh: "See, Trump Told You So" http://t.co/ATsX4mdcGl
- Jul 7, 2015 06:29:50 PM We must restore the entrepreneurial spirit of our country. A small business boom. Let's Make America Great Again! https://t.co/u25yI5T7E8

- Jul 8, 2015 06:22:53 AM I will be in California this weekend making a speech for Clint Eastwood. Then to Arizona and Vegas. Big crowds. Discussing illegals & more!
- Jul 8, 2015 08:30:35 AM Via @Newsmax_Media by @ChrisRuddyNMX: "Donald Trump and the End of Free Speech" http://t.co/XU36opl7ZL
- Jul 8, 2015 08:53:54 AM .@ronsirak Thank you for being so fair this morning on @GolfChannel—greatly appreciated.
- Jul 8, 2015 08:54:17 AM .@natalie_gulbis Thank you for your support this morning on @GolfChannel. Even more importantly, play well this week! Say hi to all.
- Jul 8, 2015 08:59:29 AM "@KelliKM @realDonaldTrump stay strong D. The last thing America needs is the same old politician."

- Jul 8, 2015 09:09:34 AM "@MilitaryRosary @Scully64 @KarlRove @GOP most people like Trump because he speaks honestly and hopefully and we know he cannot be bought."
- Jul 8, 2015 09:21:31 AM Dear @MaraLiasson, I greatly appreciate your fairness. My history shows I never disappoint. Looking forward to meeting you soon.
- Jul 8, 2015 09:30:30 AM "@MARCMODE @CNNPolitics @realDonaldTrump @mj_lee now I know where not to watch or shop @Macys account closed"
- Jul 8, 2015 09:34:08 AM Via @Ammoland by Fredy Riehl: "Donald Trump Talks: Gun Control, Assault Weapons, Gun Free Zones & Self Defense" http://t.co/eLAVFVs6Zm
- Jul 8, 2015 10:29:44 AM "@jimlibertarian @ronsirak @GolfChannel Donald our forefathers would be proud of you, you are displaying A love of country like Reagan did"
- Jul 8, 2015 10:54:06 AM "@CrystalPrebola @realDonaldTrump @MARCMODE @CNNPolitics @mj_lee @Macys Me too. No more shopping at Macy's."
- Jul 8, 2015 11:14:16 AM "@CaseyBierer America needs to hear the truth. Keep it up, Mr. Trump. You can help us make America great again. Never give up."
- Jul 8, 2015 12:31:33 PM Via @businessinsider by @hunterw: "TRUMP UNLOADS: Hillary Clinton was 'the worst' and is 'extremely bad'" http://t.co/lPGSlczakP
- Jul 8, 2015 02:26:15 PM "@greta just read @realDonaldTrump going to Phoenix to give speech on illegal immigration on Saturday" That is correct. I look forward to it
- Jul 8, 2015 02:26:29 PM Thank you @BrentBozell --- As you know I have been saying this for a long time http://t.co/4UcpdSS8qK
- Jul 8, 2015 02:37:09 PM Via @mrctv by Ben Graham: "Border Reports Back Up Trump's 'Rapists' Claim" http://t.co/4UcpdSS8qK
- Jul 8, 2015 04:13:35 PM Via @DailyCaller by @samsondunn: "Pastor To Hispanic Congregation Speaks Out On Trump Immigrant Crime Statement" http://t.co/rfWcQ7wcjf

- Jul 9, 2015 06:14:56 AM Do you believe that highly overrated political pundit @krauthammer said this is the best Republican field in 35 years. What a dope!
- Jul 9, 2015 06:25:43 AM Jeb's brother George insisted on a $100,000 fee and $20,000 for a private jet to speak at a charity for severely wounded vets. Not nice!
- Jul 9, 2015 07:09:13 AM You mean George Bush sends our soldiers into combat, they are severely wounded, and then he wants $120,000 to make a boring speech to them?
- Jul 9, 2015 07:10:03 AM "@tranerofmonstrs: @krauthammer He is an openly declared traitor to this nation as are the execs of @Univision and @Macys #LETSDOTHISAMERICA
- Jul 9, 2015 07:11:26 AM "@williamonlyrent: @realDonaldTrump @krauthammer Only good candidate in this GOP field is you sir! Go Trump. #Trump2016" Thank you.
- Jul 9, 2015 07:12:05 AM "@mcgranejt: @realDonaldTrump @krauthammer @ChuckLane1 both fools & out of touch with reality! We need Trump # 45 #MakeAmericaGreatAgain"
- Jul 9, 2015 07:12:44 AM "@DavidBougs: @krauthammer Krauthammer sold some books, now "His Pomposity" thinks he knows US Pres politics....just another DC insider!"
- Jul 9, 2015 07:15:25 AM "@KBrocking: @realDonaldTrump @krauthammer The Donald is the only good Republican candidate, in my opinion. Rubio, Perry, etc??? Um, no."
- Jul 9, 2015 07:15:56 AM "@bdevil89: @krauthammer & rest of pundits r scared of truth teller like @realDonaldTrump - #immigration affects everything in society.
- Jul 9, 2015 07:16:22 AM "@RossMahan1952: @realDonaldTrump @krauthammer Like Harry Truman, you tell them the truth and they think it's hell. Give em hell Donald"
- Jul 9, 2015 08:25:11 AM Totally false reporting on my call with @Reince Priebus. He called me, ten minutes, said I hit a "nerve", doing well, end!
- Jul 9, 2015 08:31:38 AM "@_JoshBishop @ppppolls gop or dem, you have to love Trumps blunt honesty. So many things wrong most won't point out. Borders big problem"
- Jul 9, 2015 08:34:48 AM "@SharNeal @ericbolling @TheFive a lot of us support Trump because of his support to stop illegals from killing anyone else"

- Jul 9, 2015 08:40:48 AM "@rbern11162 @SharNeal Donald Trump , keep it up you only get flack when you are close to the target, I support you completely"
- Jul 9, 2015 11:36:24 AM Watched chief negotiator for Iran on @charlierose last night. He is far smarter than our reps—increase sanctions and walk!
- Jul 9, 2015 11:45:36 AM Via @EWErickson: "Stop Complaining About Donald Trump" http://t.co/CWx8gA5DTz
- Jul 9, 2015 11:49:44 AM "@customwww @Clare_OC @Forbes Again ..not news.. news is.. he leads NC & will have NH on next true poll.. stop attacking the truth."
- Jul 9, 2015 11:50:54 AM "@gomrunner @realDonaldTrump keep up the tempo and don't listen to the RNC! You are correctly presenting what people want."
- Jul 9, 2015 12:10:50 PM Dummy writer @Clare_OC from failing @Forbes magazine works so hard to make such trivial license deals look important…
- Jul 9, 2015 12:11:06 PM Dummy @Clare_OC from failing @Forbes magazine: NASCAR deal was 1 nite ballroom, ESPN was small golf outing...
- Jul 9, 2015 12:11:40 PM Dummy @Clare_OC @Forbes: Tiny fragrance deal with Parlux means nothing. Still sold at Trump Tower...
- Jul 9, 2015 12:12:11 PM Why does a failed magazine like @Forbes constantly seek out trivial nonsense? Their circulation way down. @Clare_OC
- Jul 9, 2015 12:23:04 PM "@rdbrewer4 Trump: Keep throwing those giant hand grenades into the amnesty debate. You're pissing off all the right people in the GOP."
- Jul 9, 2015 12:48:57 PM "@limbaugh: 'Trump Has Changed the Entire Debate on Immigration'" http://t.co/894aXjRXDn via @Newsmax_Media by Jason Devaney
- Jul 9, 2015 01:18:24 PM Via "TRUMP: HILLARY PRESIDENCY WILL CAUSE 'CRIME WAVE LIKE YOU'VE NEVER SEEN'" http://t.co/cTnLLwl1z4 via @BreitbartNews
- Jul 9, 2015 01:23:44 PM "@ErinEdwards001 @realDonaldTrump thank you for telling it how it is, no one else will address these issues. You have my vote."
- Jul 9, 2015 01:32:55 PM "TRUMP BATTLES THE NEW TOTALITARIANS: GOP elites join with leftists at Media Matters in targeting threat to both" http://t.co/Vd9FaOVcjr
- Jul 9, 2015 01:40:36 PM Thanks. https://t.co/ewjfWYic4c

- Jul 9, 2015 01:42:47 PM "@tommyz63 @Reince let Trump speak. He is only saying what the rest of us, including you, already know #Illegals are a huge problem!"
- Jul 9, 2015 01:45:35 PM True, thanks. https://t.co/k0IxFL6NxK
- Jul 9, 2015 01:54:25 PM The elites want Common Core so they can take education out of parental control. NO! Let's Make America Great Again! https://t.co/u25yI5T7E8
- Jul 9, 2015 02:02:12 PM Obama and Republicans are hollowing out our military. Now want to cut troop levels. Lowest level in over 20 years.
- Jul 9, 2015 04:01:44 PM Via @BreitbartNews by Katie McHugh:"POLL: DONALD TRUMP LEADS THE PACK AS GOP FRONTRUNNER" http://t.co/QHP8CZpM5q
- Jul 9, 2015 04:14:43 PM "EXCLUSIVE — DONALD TRUMP ON THE GOP PRIMARY: 'IF I WIN, I WILL BEAT HILLARY'" http://t.co/wlz13nYels via @BreitbartNews by Katie McHugh
- Jul 9, 2015 04:29:52 PM Via @CNNPolitics by @JDiamond1: "Trump: RNC call was 'congratulatory'" http://t.co/9ZhIKiBqw5
- Jul 9, 2015 04:59:25 PM I'm on @CNN's @AC360 tonight @8pm & @FoxNews' @seanhannity @ 10PM discussing immigration and lots of other things.#LetsMakeAmericaGreatAgain
- Jul 9, 2015 08:55:07 PM BREAKING - Border 46 rally in Phoenix, AZ at 2PM MST has been moved to @PhoenixConvCtr! Build a wall! Let's Make America Great Again!

- Jul 10, 2015 04:31:56 AM Via @trscoop: "WHOA: Trump changing venues for Saturday rally in Arizona due to OVERWHELMING RESPONSE" http://t.co/nryPS8aPxA
- Jul 10, 2015 08:25:34 AM Iran continues to delay the nuclear deal while doing many bad things behind our backs. Time to WALK and double the sanctions. Stop payments!
- Jul 10, 2015 09:04:49 AM "@kpmck63 Stay the course Mr. Trump! It's easier for others to attack you because you are saying the things that they won't. #Truth"
- Jul 10, 2015 09:48:37 AM "@alarae37 @realDonaldTrump keep speaking truth!! There are many of us who want America great again! Thank you!"

- Jul 10, 2015 09:51:31 AM Jeb Bush just announced he raised over $100M. Everyone of those people who contributed are getting something to the detriment of America!
- Jul 10, 2015 10:59:21 AM I want to #MakeAmericaGreatAgain https://t.co/sRePS1nvIq
- Jul 10, 2015 12:14:56 PM Via @nypost by @GeoffEarle: "Polls show 'President Trump' may not be so far-fetched" http://t.co/C3v63rb9pD
- Jul 10, 2015 01:21:36 PM Laura--Massive crowd, had to move to Phoenix Convention Center. https://t.co/76fQCecDBd
- Jul 10, 2015 02:28:59 PM "@Mitestarossa Please follow @realDonaldTrump ...We already know what all the other politicians will do. #Trump2016 #MakeAmericaGreatAgain"
- Jul 10, 2015 06:18:29 PM http://t.co/PtViAyrO4A
- Jul 10, 2015 06:49:38 PM Our biggest problems are solved by growth. We need a President who is a job creator. Let's Make America Great Again! https://t.co/u25yI5T7E8
- Jul 10, 2015 08:47:00 PM Standing with Jamiel Shaw, Sabine Durdin, Don Rosenberg, Lupe Moreno, Brenda Sparks, Robin Hvidston & their spouses. http://t.co/X67CF765jQ

- Jul 11, 2015 12:03:50 AM Look forward to being in Phoenix tomorrow at 2:00 P.M. Hottest ticket in entire country. Was supposed to be 500 people, now many thousands!
- Jul 11, 2015 12:08:12 AM I love that thousands of people are boycotting @Macys and cutting up credit cards. No guts no glory. This really backfired - love it!
- Jul 11, 2015 03:20:39 AM "Tone it down? No way! Donald Trump needs to crank up the volume" http://t.co/3qSUVRaf6f via @FoxNews by @toddstarnes
- Jul 11, 2015 03:21:32 AM A strong military will stop wars. Peace through Strength! Let's Make America Great Again! https://t.co/u25yI5T7E8
- Jul 11, 2015 03:22:02 AM Via @CBNNews by @TheBrodyFile: "Donald Trump To Brody File in 2011: People Send Me Bibles" http://t.co/5QWk3GgBiB
- Jul 11, 2015 03:23:29 AM The Republicans who want to cut SS & Medicaid are wrong. A robust economy will Make America Great Again! https://t.co/u25yI5T7E8

- Jul 11, 2015 06:37:59 AM "@hamishjoy: There's no republican field at all. When the @realDonaldTrump is in play, the others all kinda fade away. Trump2016
- Jul 11, 2015 06:38:47 AM "@mcgranejt: @realDonaldTrump @krauthammer @ChuckLane1 both fools & out of touch with reality! We need Trump. #MakeAmericaGreatAgain"
- Jul 11, 2015 06:44:39 AM Has anyone seen the financials of @Univision. They are doing really badly. Too much debt and not enough viewers. Need money fast. Funny!
- Jul 11, 2015 06:46:36 AM Boycott @Macys and @Univision. MAKE AMERICA GREAT AGAIN!
- Jul 11, 2015 06:49:38 AM "@TheVotingVenue: @realDonaldTrump when Fox News tries to push Jeb on their viewers, remind them of this article: http://t.co/x1RqZcMn6q"
- Jul 11, 2015 06:51:11 AM "@DannyBo4455: @hamishjoy Mr Trump I have never been so excited to vote for somebody in my life .I'm literally hanging on your every word"
- Jul 11, 2015 06:52:22 AM "@WayneDupreeShow: Aren't U angry how the media has turned DonaldTrump SLAM against "illegal immigration" into him hating "all immigrants
- Jul 11, 2015 06:54:04 AM "@Pg1493: @realDonaldTrump I love what you want to do with this country!!"
- Jul 11, 2015 06:54:34 AM "@DannyBo4455: @mcgranejt @krauthammer @ChuckLane1 The establishment Republicans and the Democrats are absolutely 100% terrified of you !!"
- Jul 11, 2015 06:55:07 AM "@frank_lemoine: @realDonaldTrump The competition tries to fake it till they make it. Trump the REAL deal!"
- Jul 11, 2015 06:55:44 AM "@PHATWHODAT: @realDonaldTrump Trump 2016 yard signs. Where can we get them?" Everywhere!
- Jul 11, 2015 06:56:25 AM "@gump6363: I always said I will not vote until I truly believe in a good leader, you sir will get my vote! #MakeAmericaGreatAgain"
- Jul 11, 2015 09:49:40 AM Getting ready to go to Las Vegas (Freedom Fest) - great crowd. Then on to amazing Phoenix - that will be a total happening! Love America.

- Jul 11, 2015 09:50:48 AM "@Eugene_Scott: "I want people to come into the country. Let it be legal," @RealDonaldTrump http://t.co/NfTFsp1zBn via @CNNPolitics"
- Jul 11, 2015 11:37:38 AM Via @CNNPolitics by @mj_lee: "Father of murder victim to introduce Trump in Phoenix" http://t.co/JZuIg1cmEB
- Jul 11, 2015 11:48:29 AM Today I will be rallying with with 15,000 patriots in Arizona for border security! Let's Make America Great Again! https://t.co/u25yI5T7E8
- Jul 11, 2015 11:55:19 AM Today I am standing with patriots in Arizona for border security! Build a wall! Let's Make America Great Again! https://t.co/Ve6IxqXqfb
- Jul 11, 2015 02:00:20 PM Great @ANHQDC segment with @CharlesHurt: "Breaking Down the Trump Factor" http://t.co/PIo4YHPJlP Let's Make America Great Again!
- Jul 11, 2015 02:06:50 PM Legal immigrants want border security. It is common sense. We must build a wall! Let's Make America Great Again! http://t.co/I5CybmR0MF
- Jul 11, 2015 07:56:56 PM I will not be able to attend the Miss USA pageant tomorrow night because I am campaigning in Phoenix. Wishing all well!
- Jul 11, 2015 10:43:13 PM Via @BreitbartNews by @AWRHawkins: "TRUMP PREACHES PEACE THROUGH STRENGTH IN PHOENIX" http://t.co/HCu2T8TFP2

- Jul 12, 2015 08:18:21 AM Convention Center officials in Phoenix don't want to admit that they broke the fire code by allowing 12-15,000 people in 4,000 code room.
- Jul 12, 2015 08:21:24 AM Phoenix Convention Center officials did not want to have thousands of people standing outside in the heat, so they let them in. A GREAT day!
- Jul 12, 2015 04:03:19 PM Mexico's biggest drug lord escapes from jail. Unbelievable corruption and USA is paying the price. I told you so!
- Jul 12, 2015 04:08:52 PM Sleep eyes @ChuckTodd is killing Meet The Press. Isn't he pathetic? Love watching him fail!
- Jul 12, 2015 07:25:37 PM Can you envision Jeb Bush or Hillary Clinton negotiating with 'El Chapo', the Mexican drug lord who escaped from prison? ....
- Jul 12, 2015 07:29:05 PM ...Trump, however, would kick his ass!

- Jul 12, 2015 07:36:25 PM I hear that sleepy eyes @chucktodd will be fired like a dog from ratings starved Meet The Press? I can't imagine what is taking so long!
- Jul 12, 2015 09:10:23 PM Now that the Mexican drug lord escaped from prison, everyone is saying that most of the cocaine etc. coming into the U.S. comes over border!
- Jul 12, 2015 09:14:13 PM .....but that's what I've been saying. Very unfair treatment by the media!
- Jul 12, 2015 11:05:42 PM The U.S. will invite El Chapo, the Mexican drug lord who just escaped prison, to become a U.S. citizen because our "leaders" can't say no!

- Jul 13, 2015 05:47:36 AM El Chapo and the Mexican drug cartels use the border unimpeded like it was a vacuum cleaner, sucking drugs and death right into the U.S.
- Jul 13, 2015 05:53:14 AM ....likewise, billions of dollars gets brought into Mexico through the border. We get the killers, drugs & crime, they get the money!
- Jul 13, 2015 05:59:19 AM When will people, and the media, start to apologize to me for my statement, "Mexico is sending....", which turned out to be true? El Chapo
- Jul 13, 2015 10:55:50 AM "@bdean1468 @jlangdale @realDonaldTrump @HillaryClinton @CNN SAY IT LOUD & SAY IT PROUD - - WE WANT TRUMP!!!!!!"
- Jul 13, 2015 11:14:01 AM Isn't it interesting that now that I'm #1 in the polls, the networks show polls that are a month old!
- Jul 13, 2015 11:14:16 AM .@McLaughlinGroup Greatly appreciate yr wonderful comments this weekend. People of "great accomplishment" should easily quality for prez.
- Jul 13, 2015 11:20:39 AM The joke around town is that I freed El Chapo from the Mexican prison because the timing was so good w/ my statements on border security.
- Jul 13, 2015 11:21:40 AM Mexico's totally corrupt gov't looks horrible with El Chapo's escape—totally corrupt. U.S. paid them $3 billion.
- Jul 13, 2015 11:24:01 AM El Chapo comes to the U.S. often thru our border—it's been revealed he has CA drivers license. http://t.co/E7UA3eyP5O
- Jul 13, 2015 12:04:06 PM Have some fun with this- https://t.co/J59RW8tqQX

- Jul 13, 2015 01:54:41 PM Rush Limbaugh: "Trump Has Changed the Entire Debate on Immigration" http://t.co/894aXjRXDn
- Jul 13, 2015 02:00:12 PM "@SaintPetersblog Part of me really, really likes @realDonaldTrump. The man is breathtakingly honest. Have to give him credit."
- Jul 13, 2015 02:15:40 PM I absolutely support Kate's Law—in honor of the beautiful Kate Steinle who was gunned down in SF by an illegal immigrant.
- Jul 13, 2015 02:18:57 PM Very nice - @HuffingtonPost @pollsterpolls has me in first place at 18% and Bush second at 14% http://t.co/IXCbCtDUIp
- Jul 13, 2015 04:16:56 PM I am so happy that people are boycotting Macy's http://t.co/qtmaEbeVy8
- Jul 13, 2015 11:27:44 PM "@greta: Huffington Post has @realDonaldTrump in first place in the polls http://t.co/wAEAsWY5u8"

- Jul 14, 2015 06:13:40 AM Let Pete Rose into the Baseball Hall of Fame. It's time, he has paid a big and very long price!
- Jul 14, 2015 06:16:47 AM "@Marta_AQT4U: Obama - just retire I'm ready for a real Leader !! #Trump2016 @realDonaldTrump Please Hurry up and Get to The WHITE House !
- Jul 14, 2015 06:18:15 AM "@LeeEllmauerJr: LEGAL Latino Immigrants talk to me in factories & warehouses. Want to know why OBAMA to give AMNESTY? They did it RIGHT!"
- Jul 14, 2015 06:18:23 AM "@NorthStarMF: @realDonaldTrump love you, please fix america!"
- Jul 14, 2015 06:18:41 AM "@Zimbo251: @realDonaldTrump @greta Go Donald! Show them what a real man is!"
- Jul 14, 2015 07:55:59 AM Ford is MOVING jobs from Michigan to Mexico AGAIN! http://t.co/TgVQ1458AJ As President, this will stop on Day One! Jobs will stay here.
- Jul 14, 2015 08:23:46 AM Matt Harvey @Mets -- Don't let the @NYDailyNews get you down---nobody reads it. Play well.
- Jul 14, 2015 08:40:19 AM A nation without borders is no nation at all. We must build a wall. Let's Make America Great Again! https://t.co/u25yI5T7E8
- Jul 14, 2015 09:06:38 AM I can't believe that President Obama isn't able or willing to make just one phone call to the family of Kate Steinle.Come on Pres-MAKE CALL!
- Jul 14, 2015 09:42:03 AM Response to Hillary Clinton- http://t.co/nzYfehyURa

- Jul 14, 2015 10:00:11 AM Who do you want negotiating for us? https://t.co/WASlyxbG1j
- Jul 14, 2015 10:09:02 AM Getting ready to land in Charlottesville, Virginia, at Trump Vineyards, another job producing development that I bought and made AMAZING!
- Jul 14, 2015 10:10:51 AM "@kavemanrj @realDonaldTrump Amazing work trump! I believe you will do the same for our country."
- Jul 14, 2015 11:31:59 AM We are no longer silent. We are energized & ready to take our country back. Let's Make America Great Again! https://t.co/u25yI5T7E8
- Jul 14, 2015 11:57:11 AM "@Britinnv @realDonaldTrump Would the people of US prefer a liar @HillaryClinton or a man that speaks the truth and facts!! No Brainer hey!"
- Jul 14, 2015 03:37:38 PM Via The Hill: Trump Tops National Poll for Second Straight Week http://t.co/s6nxfqdSQs
- Jul 14, 2015 07:59:48 PM "@AProudRebel: @realDonaldTrump HIGH NUMBERS SHOW DONALD TRUMP IS BEATING HIS RIVALS IN THE POLLS, GO TRUMP, TRUMP NATION."
- Jul 14, 2015 08:21:55 PM "@AnnCoulter: I think DonaldTrump has struck a cord! 30,000 MACY'S CUSTOMERS RETALIATE IN SUPPORT OF DONALD TRUMP http://t.co/0QNLGESdju"

- Jul 15, 2015 01:11:40 AM "@ben_techpro: It's way worse than we know.Just read @AnnCoulter #AdiosAmerica-be educated!! #MakeAmericaGreatAgain https://t.co/atRmfrr6lZ"
- Jul 15, 2015 01:13:25 AM "@AnnCoulter: AMAZING press conference by @realDonaldTrump w/ parents of kids killed by illegals.
- Jul 15, 2015 09:50:16 AM .@BradSteinle Thank you for yr wonderful tweet of July 4. I wanted a little time to go by before calling. Your sister & family are amazing.
- Jul 15, 2015 10:01:37 AM Why do people listen to clown @KarlRove on @FoxNews? Spent $430M & lost all races—a Bushy!
- Jul 15, 2015 10:01:52 AM .@FoxNews should not put @KarlRove on—he has no credibility, a bush plant who called all races wrong.

- Jul 15, 2015 10:11:13 AM ".@PolitiTrends @realdonaldtrump is dominating the discussion on Twitter with 79352 mentions today (via http://t.co/nexlCVB8ml)"
- Jul 15, 2015 03:01:56 PM .@StephenBaldwin7 You were fabulous on CNN last night--I greatly appreciate your support. Best wishes.
- Jul 15, 2015 03:18:22 PM Thank you Piers. https://t.co/uH6h74qShv
- Jul 15, 2015 03:52:23 PM "@ReevesMH it's been a long time since I've been excited about a candidate. How refreshing to have a bold voice. Go Trump!"
- Jul 15, 2015 04:02:41 PM "@UncleLouie Clearly Trump gets social media. His tweets are everywhere & no sugar coating, he keeps it real. Wish all candidates did that"

- Jul 16, 2015 04:44:07 AM "@HoustonWelder: Donald Trump is one of the sexiest men on this planet. Every woman dreams of a good man who tells it like it is." So true!
- Jul 16, 2015 05:10:17 AM Irrelevant clown @KarlRove sweats and shakes nervously on @FoxNews as he talks "bull" about me. Has zero cred. Made fool of himself in '12.
- Jul 16, 2015 05:18:31 AM I hear @pennjillette show on Broadway is terrible. Not surprised, boring guy (Penn). Without The Apprentice, show would have died long ago.
- Jul 16, 2015 08:10:00 AM I loved firing goofball atheist Penn @pennjillette on The Apprentice. He never had a chance. Wrote letter to me begging for forgiveness.
- Jul 16, 2015 08:14:15 AM I hope the boycott of @Macys continues forever. So many people are cutting up their cards. Macy's stores suck and they are bad for U.S.A.
- Jul 16, 2015 08:33:03 AM "@joshdronzek @realDonaldTrump @Macys GO TRUMP"
- Jul 16, 2015 09:02:01 AM .@andydean2014 Thank you, you were great. You can defend me anytime. Amazing job.
- Jul 16, 2015 09:46:22 AM .@BradSteinle Great talking to you and your parents—fantastic people. Keep your sister's very important memory alive—big impact!
- Jul 16, 2015 10:02:03 AM .@FoxNews You shouldn't have @KarlRove on the air—he's a clown with zero credibility—a Bushy!

- Jul 16, 2015 10:02:34 AM .@KarlRove wasted $400 million + and didn't win one race—a total loser. @FoxNews
- Jul 16, 2015 10:20:44 AM "@MichaelPlu @realDonaldTrump @Macys we never shopped at Macy's anyway & will now encourage three daughters not to as well"
- Jul 16, 2015 12:30:32 PM "@RasmussenNews @weeklystandard Yea, but you know the only problem I see? The Donald is the ONLY one willing to tell it like it is!!"
- Jul 16, 2015 12:31:00 PM "@pbstwo @RasmussenNews @realDonaldTrump @weeklystandard. And the Donald owes NOTHING to lobbyists."
- Jul 16, 2015 12:33:54 PM "@ChanRogers I literally give a fist pump when I see @realDonaldTrump tell things the way they are & calling out those with no credibility"
- Jul 16, 2015 12:36:17 PM Thank you. https://t.co/iGNIDSqlfZ
- Jul 16, 2015 12:40:54 PM They are great people! https://t.co/7RTinwz1a8
- Jul 16, 2015 12:49:11 PM "@ChristianInst @MorenoDadKC @BarbaraGarro The Democratic party has never given latinos anything! Just manipulate them through Univision."
- Jul 16, 2015 12:52:21 PM "@danforc as a legal immigrant I'm so glad someone standing up for us, the millions who do things by the book to earn our place here" Thx
- Jul 16, 2015 01:35:32 PM Via @BreitbartNews by Steve Bannon: "'TIME TO GET TOUGH': TRUMP'S BLOCKBUSTER POLICY MANIFESTO" http://t.co/rrRd7AkFED
- Jul 16, 2015 01:37:18 PM Is this true about Univision and Fusion? Wow!?! http://t.co/y7nd9BziBP
- Jul 16, 2015 01:45:41 PM "30,000 MACY'S CUSTOMERS RETALIATE IN SUPPORT OF DONALD TRUMP" http://t.co/vL4ifAkxRt via @BreitbartNews by @ASwoyer
- Jul 16, 2015 01:51:22 PM Via @FSMtweet: "Trump is Right: Illegal Alien Crime is Staggering in Scope and Savagery" http://t.co/najLkku1zE
- Jul 16, 2015 01:53:43 PM Via @TIME by @ZekeJMiller: "Trump Talks Politics at His Virginia Winery" http://t.co/h3eIc4mgu3
- Jul 16, 2015 02:10:27 PM FLASHBACK – "Donald Trump Blasts Obama for Failing to Secure Christian Pastor's Freedom in Iran" http://t.co/AwCVNdzyry via @theblaze'

- Jul 16, 2015 02:20:45 PM No deal is better than a bad deal. America out negotiated again. #Iran
- Jul 16, 2015 02:49:24 PM Dopey @Lawrence O'Donnell, whose unwatchable show is dying in the ratings, said that my Apprentice $ numbers were wrong. He is a fool!
- Jul 16, 2015 02:54:31 PM The worst show in Las Vegas, in my opinion, is @pennjillette. Hokey garbage. New York show even worse!
- Jul 16, 2015 02:57:10 PM The Iran deal poses a direct national security threat. It must be stopped in Congress. Stand up Republicans!
- Jul 16, 2015 03:02:34 PM Leaving for New Hampshire now. Making a speech—packed house. Love it!
- Jul 16, 2015 03:03:29 PM We need leaders who can negotiate great deals for Americans. It is common sense. Let's Make America Great Again! https://t.co/u25yI5T7E8
- Jul 16, 2015 03:06:38 PM More Bush cronyism – "Jeb Bush and the Common Core Money Trail" http://t.co/SbeHmuQJak It's the Bush way!
- Jul 16, 2015 03:27:08 PM "No government ever voluntarily reduces itself in size. So governments' programs, once launched, never disappear." – Ronald Reagan
- Jul 16, 2015 03:28:53 PM CNN: "New GOP polls show Trump's favorability is up" http://t.co/lEBOJST9dA @MichaelCohen212
- Jul 16, 2015 03:38:16 PM The thousands of people that showed up for me in Phoenix were amazing Americans. @SenJohnMcCain called them "crazies"-- must apologize!
- Jul 16, 2015 03:39:56 PM .@SenJohnMcCain should be defeated in the primaries. Graduated last in his class at Annapolis--dummy!
- Jul 16, 2015 03:48:19 PM .@GovernorPerry just gave a pollster quote on me. He doesn't understand what the word demagoguery means.
- Jul 16, 2015 03:49:34 PM .@GovernorPerry failed on the border. He should be forced to take an IQ test before being allowed to enter the GOP debate.
- Jul 16, 2015 04:02:38 PM Thoughts and prayers to the families of the four great Marines killed today.

- Jul 17, 2015 04:44:29 AM Get rid of gun free zones. The four great marines who were just shot never had a chance. They were highly trained but helpless without guns.

- Jul 17, 2015 04:49:16 AM "@GotMade: @realDonaldTrump @JohnMcCain Trump speaks the truth about foolish leaders negotiating and you hate the truth McCain"
- Jul 17, 2015 04:51:28 AM "@TheRealCamSand: It would be to cool if @realDonaldTrump was the president." Thanks!
- Jul 17, 2015 04:52:15 AM "@Tamaralynn212: @RWSurferGirl @realDonaldTrump The whole Gov. needs to be remodeled, he's the man for the job. I'd love to see him Prez."
- Jul 17, 2015 11:36:57 AM I had thousands join me in New Hampshire last night! @HillaryClinton had 68. The #SilentMajority is fed up with what is going on in America!
- Jul 17, 2015 12:31:19 PM Looking forward to speaking at the @ARGOP Reagan-Rockefeller Dinner tonight! Record crowd. We are no longer silent! #MAKEAMERICAGREATAGAIN!
- Jul 17, 2015 12:31:57 PM MILITARY LIVES MATTER! END GUN FREE ZONES! OUR SOLDIERS MUST BE ABLE TO PROTECT THEMSELVES! THIS HAS TO STOP!
- Jul 17, 2015 12:32:26 PM We will no longer be silent. We can take our country back! Let's Make America Great Again! https://t.co/u25yI6aIvG
- Jul 17, 2015 01:09:47 PM Via @AP March,2013: Jeb said "he was open to…pathway for citizenship for illegal immigrants" http://t.co/zeEKCFXroE Lying on campaign trail!
- Jul 17, 2015 01:10:09 PM "Donald Trump was proven right on another one of his top issues Thursday: 'gun free zones' at military bases." http://t.co/x1swUrw8l1
- Jul 17, 2015 01:10:29 PM "God's word is the same, yesterday and today and a million years from now." - @Franklin_Graham
- Jul 17, 2015 02:03:35 PM Via @BreitbartNews- http://t.co/IKP5DSD5nY
- Jul 17, 2015 02:04:28 PM Via @WashTimes by @dsherfinski http://t.co/hVNrE2XVWw
- Jul 17, 2015 02:05:23 PM Via @TPInsidr http://t.co/8Habr989Yw
- Jul 17, 2015 04:46:36 PM Response to Huffington Post- http://t.co/WxwQWHlgOO
- Jul 17, 2015 09:20:31 PM .@genesimmons really great job handling the wise guys --- so easy for you--- such talent! I won't forget.

- Jul 17, 2015 09:25:06 PM .@genesimmons, Amazing! Thank you. http://t.co/kCP39adNvR
- Jul 17, 2015 10:49:47 PM "@nonstop85716: @realDonaldTrump.I am always on the road. I am gonna do the absentee ballot thing in the primary's and Mr Trump has my vote"
- Jul 17, 2015 10:49:56 PM "@JCippy: @realDonaldTrump for our next President !!"
- Jul 17, 2015 10:57:11 PM "@amandajoan40: This is the first time in my adult life that I have been excited about an election #Trump2016 #TrumpForPresident"
- Jul 17, 2015 10:58:44 PM "@JoeyCarna: @realDonaldTrump if you don't win I'm moving to Europe." We will all win together!
- Jul 17, 2015 11:00:34 PM "@BillyParker03: @realDonaldTrump The @BillAndMoShow has your back! TRUMP FOR PREZ!"
- Jul 17, 2015 11:01:02 PM "@SteveMullaney1: @realDonaldTrump has all of my support!!"
- Jul 17, 2015 11:02:33 PM "@jimlibertarian: @realDonaldTrump @nonstop85716 it doesn't matter how you vote for Donald, just remember to vote Donald Trump for POTUS
- Jul 17, 2015 11:03:02 PM "@rua1ri: @realDonaldTrump your what America needs Donald!" Thank you.

- Jul 18, 2015 08:20:27 AM "@koltonbittner: .@realDonaldTrump makes me proud to be an American" So nice, thank you!
- Jul 18, 2015 08:37:55 AM The liberal clown @ariannahuff told her minions at the money losing @HuffingtonPost to cover me as enterainment. I am #1 in Huff Post Poll.
- Jul 18, 2015 08:44:28 AM It's driving @ariannahuff & the money losing @HuffingtonPost post crazy that I am #1 in their poll and they only write bad stories about me!
- Jul 18, 2015 08:49:36 AM Made a speech in Arkansas last night before a record GOP crowd. Great spirit and amazing people. MAKE AMERICA GREAT AGAIN!
- Jul 18, 2015 08:57:21 AM Ratings starved @CNN and @CNNPolitics does not cover me accurately. Why can't they get it right - it's really not that hard!

- Jul 18, 2015 09:03:49 AM The $10 billion (net worth) is AFTER all debt and liabilities. So simple to understand but @CNN & @CNNPolitics is just plain dumb!
- Jul 18, 2015 09:09:25 AM I am now in Iowa getting ready to speak. People are always amazed to find out that I am Protestant (Presbyterian). GREAT.
- Jul 18, 2015 12:58:18 PM Statement on John McCain- http://t.co/Nh0rJPeUNl
- Jul 18, 2015 12:58:56 PM Just left Family Leadership Summit in Iowa, got a standing ovation from many wonderful people. I will be back soon.
- Jul 18, 2015 12:59:14 PM In addition to doing a lousy job in taking care of our Vets, John McCain let us down by losing to Barack Obama in his run for President!
- Jul 18, 2015 12:59:29 PM Captured or not, all our soldiers are heroes!
- Jul 18, 2015 01:15:12 PM The Veterans of our country have been treated like third class citizens for many years...
- Jul 18, 2015 01:15:19 PM ....John McCain has failed miserably to fix the situation and to make it possible for Veterans to successfully manage their lives.
- Jul 18, 2015 01:15:36 PM All he does is go on television is talk, talk, talk, but incapable of doing anything.
- Jul 18, 2015 01:15:49 PM I will make this right for our great Vets!
- Jul 18, 2015 01:16:26 PM It's a national embarrassment that an illegal immigrant can walk across the border and receive free health care and one of our Veterans.....
- Jul 18, 2015 01:16:32 PM ....that has served our country is put on a waiting list and gets no care.
- Jul 18, 2015 01:51:48 PM I have a proven track record supporting our Veterans. Veterans deserve universal access to care. VA scandal proves politicians are inept.
- Jul 18, 2015 03:18:21 PM Congrats to the new Gov. of Texas, @GregAbbott_TX, for taking a tough & bold stance at the border. Should have been done long ago by Perry.
- Jul 18, 2015 03:46:53 PM Why would anybody listen to @MittRomney? He lost an election that should have easily been won against Obama. By the way,so did John McCain!
- Jul 18, 2015 04:45:48 PM Via @fitsnews: "Donald Trump: John McCain Is 'A Loser'" http://t.co/sgiETvdUqi

- Jul 18, 2015 06:18:24 PM One of the reasons I am no fan of John McCain is that our Vets are being treated so badly by him and the politicians. I will fix VA quickly.
- Jul 18, 2015 11:19:30 PM Wow, @SharylAttkisson just wrote the definitive piece on what I said about John McCain https://t.co/P1dxTmeCmQ
- Jul 18, 2015 11:38:51 PM "@deannecox777: @SharylAttkisson Because she shoots straight like you do, Mr Trump. No bullsh!t. Just TRUTH! #FactCheck #QuitHatin'"
- Jul 18, 2015 11:38:59 PM "@sloopjohnb15: @realDonaldTrump @SharylAttkisson I'm on the #TrumpTrain2016"
- Jul 18, 2015 11:39:16 PM "@amsardina: @realDonaldTrump @SharylAttkisson kick there ass Trump"
- Jul 18, 2015 11:39:55 PM "@dunn_cheri: @SharylAttkisson Mr Trump the only one telling the truth. Liberals can't stand the fact that your are leading in the poll"
- Jul 18, 2015 11:42:01 PM "@mwood_79: @SharylAttkisson Why do they attack Mr Trump? Because he has something they dont. The ability of truth! Trump is here!"

- Jul 19, 2015 05:15:50 AM John McCain called thousands of people "crazies" when they came to seek help on illegal immigration last week in Phoenix. He owes apology!
- Jul 19, 2015 05:22:11 AM The Veterans Administration is in shambles and our veterans are suffering greatly. John McCain has done nothing to help them but talk.
- Jul 19, 2015 01:53:52 PM A true piece about the standing ovations I got yesterday http://t.co/EplLsBWgBE
- Jul 19, 2015 04:03:06 PM The Republican Party must get tougher and smarter, and fast, or it will go down to a very big defeat - just like the last two times!
- Jul 19, 2015 04:06:45 PM I will be making some very big campaign stops next week - big crowds and tremendous energy! MAKE AMERICA GREAT AGAIN
- Jul 19, 2015 07:02:34 PM My @USATOpinion piece: "Trump: I don't need to be lectured" http://t.co/luEYQhgrr9
- Jul 19, 2015 08:28:57 PM "@HL3tweets: McCain epitomizes the career politicians who have gotten us into our $19 TRILLION train-wreck, including the VA debacle."

- Jul 19, 2015 08:29:41 PM "@pg_rant: They can't handle you Donald so want you out the race, well good luck,because we know you won't walk away! Give it to them"
- Jul 19, 2015 08:30:36 PM "@2014_vince: The left wing politically correct cannot handle big don giving the truth....reality....keep saying it like it is !!!!"
- Jul 19, 2015 08:31:18 PM "@sjbatis: @realDonaldTrump Bravo for saying whats on most of Americans mind. Lets make America great, again!"
- Jul 19, 2015 08:31:31 PM "@GinaandersonRN: @realDonaldTrump ...RN for 27 yrs. Veterans have less benefits than medicaid recipients. Thnx for speaking#TRUTH"
- Jul 19, 2015 08:32:03 PM "@ebalky: @realDonaldTrump that's all the career politicians do is talk"
- Jul 19, 2015 08:36:40 PM "@kda20151223: @realDonaldTrump trump for president http://t.co/I9VxZ0MlNQ"
- Jul 19, 2015 09:07:30 PM "@MaxChupailo: @kuuleme69 @cspan @realDonaldTrump Gotta love the honesty"
- Jul 19, 2015 09:09:42 PM "@97Musick: @realDonaldTrump Voters LIKE "tough and smart"... that's why we are voting TRUMP 2016!!"
- Jul 19, 2015 09:11:14 PM "@restore_US_now: @JohnnyG__62 @realDonaldTrump @GinaandersonRN ...what do you say now??? http://t.co/RdMXfnuBMH"
- Jul 19, 2015 09:11:59 PM "@bdean1468: @realDonaldTrump @MaxChupailo @kuuleme69 @cspan WE LOVE YOU TRUMP!!! TRUMP FOR PRESIDENT! #MakeAmericaGreatAgain"
- Jul 19, 2015 09:12:24 PM "@janetaylorann: @realDonaldTrump Will make the best President ever"
- Jul 19, 2015 09:14:13 PM "@andres_3v: @realDonaldTrump you have the guts and backbone this country politics has needed for years. #Trump2016 #TrumpForAmerica"
- Jul 19, 2015 09:14:23 PM "@KathleenLove10: @realDonaldTrump @MaxChupailo @kuuleme69 @cspan The truth hurts sometimes, who cares...keep telling it like it is!!"
- Jul 19, 2015 09:16:31 PM "@vettesetter: RT @realDonaldTrump: My @USATOpinion piece: "Trump: I don't need to be lectured" http://t.co/ORa0H4A2xJ"

- Jul 19, 2015 09:17:26 PM "@Jenism101: @realDonaldTrump @97Musick Trump is the only person we believe will actually set things right."
- Jul 19, 2015 09:18:07 PM "@RW84JR: @realDonaldTrump Glad U R Man Enough 2 Speak the Truth in this Pathetic Politically Correct World!

- Jul 20, 2015 09:25:14 AM The ever dwindling @WSJ which is worth about 1/10 of what it was purchased for, is always hitting me politically. Who cares!
- Jul 20, 2015 09:25:52 AM We will soon be at a point with our incompetent politicians where we will be treating illegal immigrants better than our veterans.
- Jul 20, 2015 10:10:41 AM " @johnjcarp61 At least we're talking about the #VA! We weren't a month ago! @realDonaldTrump @JohnMcCain"
- Jul 20, 2015 10:22:17 AM "@VetApologist This is big criticism of the Republican field. Speak truth and stop being so PC. This is why @realDonaldTrump resonates!"
- Jul 20, 2015 10:24:52 AM "@DanScavino @realDonaldTrump hosts events around the #USA 4our #Veterans. Long before a presidential run. He loves our military."
- Jul 20, 2015 10:45:04 AM "@_EOD I believe we have passed that point. There are Homeless Veterans in USA & yet Illegal Aliens get Government Housing"
- Jul 20, 2015 10:51:51 AM "@RTMatador Trump says things that no one else would even consider saying, I agree with him on the immigration situation, i love honesty"
- Jul 20, 2015 10:53:31 AM "@MJJustus1 @AndrewStilesUSA @realDonaldTrump Trump already hosts vets at his resorts. What does Hillary do?"
- Jul 20, 2015 10:55:05 AM "@Valenti317 @realDonaldTrump the left is petrified of you! Why else would they be attacking you so vigorously?"
- Jul 20, 2015 11:16:48 AM "@LinFlies @GhostDancer_2 @contrarian11 @MichaelCohen212 @ChrisCuomo @DeptVetAffairs ...rest of GOP only cries but Trump gets stuff DONE"
- Jul 20, 2015 11:22:46 AM "@amit_ @realdonaldtrump I agree 100%. McCain is fighting for illegal immigrant but never did anything for our Vets."
- Jul 20, 2015 11:41:40 AM It was only after I informed NBC that I wouldn't do the Apprentice that they became upset w/ me. They couldn't care less about "inclusion"

- Jul 20, 2015 11:46:38 AM This story is no longer about John McCain, it's about our horribly treated vets. Illegals are treated better than our wonderful veterans.
- Jul 20, 2015 03:24:14 PM Look how small the pages have become @WSJ. Looks like a tabloid—saving money I assume!
- Jul 20, 2015 06:27:55 PM I will be interviewed on @oreillyfactor tonight at 8:00. Will be talking about the poor treatment of our veterans, illegal immigration, etc.
- Jul 20, 2015 07:31:00 PM "@mikeezepek: @DLoesch Great interview! Give Trump a hot mic and watch out! It is the rawness, the non-PC guy. #MakeAmericaGreatAgain"
- Jul 20, 2015 07:31:42 PM "@Malibu101834: @realDonaldTrump @oreillyfactor I'll watch anything that gives you a chance to share your views. Go donald."
- Jul 20, 2015 07:32:47 PM "@alyssathgreat: "SenJohnMcCain is always talking, talking but nothing gets done. These #veterans are living in hell." #OReillyFactor""
- Jul 20, 2015 07:35:34 PM "@kpmck63: I'm going to listen to @realDonaldTrump LONG before I listen to georgelopez #MakeAmericaGreatAgain"
- Jul 20, 2015 07:36:48 PM "@ShepherdGarrett: It doesn't matter what the media thinks--It matters what the American people think Keep It Up! #MakeAmericaGreatAgain"
- Jul 20, 2015 07:38:39 PM "@PJTV: ON TOP The GOP, Democrats and media have all hit @realDonaldTrump Here's the result: http://t.co/e6APNLGNGS http://t.co/OrEpbtXh3H"
- Jul 20, 2015 07:40:56 PM "@Dark_Red_Hair: .@realDonaldTRUMP - u hit a home run on THE FACTOR"
- Jul 20, 2015 07:44:25 PM "@djf123: @realDonaldTrump @PJTV #DonaldWillBeTheGOPNominee!
- Jul 20, 2015 07:44:49 PM "@Drake4444444: @realDonaldTrump You're killing Jeb in the polls! Keep it up!"
- Jul 20, 2015 08:21:22 PM "@BrianCstandsup: @realDonaldTrump I'm convinced. Let's go Trump. #Trump2016"

- Jul 20, 2015 08:38:10 PM "@2009softail: You nailed it on @oreillyfactor tonite. You say what most middle class folks YELL at their TV every night - you speak 4 us"
- Jul 20, 2015 08:40:32 PM "@TCastilonia: @realDonaldTrump @oreillyfactor Your the opening story on every political show,radio or tv.
- Jul 20, 2015 08:41:09 PM "@tonyparker1981: @Nate_Cohn @chrislhayes Not a huge surprise all day T.V. is all about @realDonaldTrump and nothing about BernieSanders
- Jul 20, 2015 08:43:17 PM "@MrsJRobbins: America needs @realDonaldTrump !!! #Trump2016"
- Jul 20, 2015 08:43:27 PM "@greengolf56: @realDonaldTrump Keep going Mr trump America needs you"
- Jul 20, 2015 08:48:22 PM "@BJSeastoneAMP: Proud of you @realDonaldTrump keep cutting through the #politicalcrap and tell it like it is"
- Jul 20, 2015 08:49:56 PM "@lizaperri: @realDonaldTrump The more the media attacks you, the more I know you are the right person for the job."
- Jul 20, 2015 08:50:25 PM "@schwartzb: @realDonaldTrump we need your help Donald! Make us great again!"
- Jul 20, 2015 08:51:52 PM "@JWCarrr: @AnnCoulter @SenTenCes Ben Carson has not criticized Trump! And there's no need to mention Dr. Carson's education!"
- Jul 20, 2015 08:52:32 PM "@bxldgxng: @realDonaldTrump i've never felt more strongly about anything in my life, you are the only person who can truly fix America"
- Jul 20, 2015 08:55:14 PM "@erintighe_: @realDonaldTrump your the only person who really wants to save America"

- Jul 21, 2015 12:22:59 AM "@kpdelbridge: FOX NEWS-Get your facts straight! Trump did not put down Vets-he put down a clown named McCain! @seanhannity
- Jul 21, 2015 12:30:52 AM Wow, new @ABCnews/@WashingtonPost @GOP preference poll has DonaldTrump 11 points up! Thank you.
- Jul 21, 2015 12:35:59 AM "@azuriterealtor: @realDonaldTrump @erintighe_ Keep going on, you can win!"

- Jul 21, 2015 12:38:01 AM "@AlbertoZambrano: @HeinzFGuderian Well get your facts straight. McCain was so bad he gave us Obama. He gave arms to Islamic terrorists"
- Jul 21, 2015 12:39:11 AM "@AlleyKat2: @realDonaldTrump doesn't need the influence peddlers money so he can be his own man" So true.
- Jul 21, 2015 12:40:17 AM "@MrdannyArthur: @Paul_Beiss @Lg4Lg @seanhannity @SenJohnMcCain Phoenix VA, led the league in scandals! McCain knew! Did nothing!"
- Jul 21, 2015 12:42:23 AM "@Tea_Party_Chris: @RepDavid @RepMattSalmon @RepTrentFranks @RealJamesWoods #Trump2016 #Trump #TrumpForPresident https://t.co/3EnJ5u4kzL"
- Jul 21, 2015 12:44:30 AM "@ultradave1951: @realDonaldTrump check out mccains record on blocking legislation - blocking Mia/pow records"
- Jul 21, 2015 12:46:21 AM "@SteveMarz1: @Felix_Clay @kpdelbridge @seanhannity but McCain is not a hero. McCain abandoned POW http://t.co/g6XlYt4Cod McCain lies."
- Jul 21, 2015 12:47:34 AM "@EdwardFrancisII: "Can't Be Bought" @realDonaldTrump - #2016election http://t.co/3JmAo2Y94S"
- Jul 21, 2015 12:50:01 AM "@AhmedBawazir: I'm very sure that @realDonaldTrump does things excellently http://t.co/dk28Bx89Et"
- Jul 21, 2015 12:50:37 AM "@Knight276: @realDonaldTrump @kpdelbridge @seanhannity I'm a veteran. I'm not offended by Trump"
- Jul 21, 2015 12:52:03 AM "@THENORAWILLIAMS: I'm #africanamerican & I KNOW without a doubt that DonaldTrump is THE ONLY ANSWER to get the #USA out of this mess!
- Jul 21, 2015 12:53:34 AM "@WesleyRuedy: Donald Trump is the man. And people don't appreciate his honesty. @realDonaldTrump" Thank you.
- Jul 21, 2015 12:53:52 AM "@ConnorBaldwin21: @realDonaldTrump has the balls to say what needs to be said and I love it"
- Jul 21, 2015 12:54:31 AM "@bigg_ritch: The reason Trump is the man... He wants Americans to work not illegal aliens. they live better than we do illegally.
- Jul 21, 2015 12:59:49 AM "@1Barbara1: @realDonaldTrump @SteveMarz1 @Felix_Clay @kpdelbridge @seanhannity Vietnam Veterans Against McCain- https://t.co/Ap8l0JHZML"

- Jul 21, 2015 01:00:16 AM "@ileadliberty: I truly love this Land of the Free and I know that DonaldTrump will cut through the confusion and Make America Great Again!"
- Jul 21, 2015 01:02:02 AM "@dancriscuolo: If Donald Trump isn't my president by 2017 I'm gettin' the h**k outta here! @realDonaldTrump #MakeAmericaGreatAgain"
- Jul 21, 2015 06:42:33 AM "@michaeljohns: #Trump support surges even higher after #McCain statement. Why? Trump is a fighter. #GOP https://t.co/YhEE7NSKp8"
- Jul 21, 2015 06:55:43 AM Just got great national poll numbers - double digit lead! Thank you, we will all MAKE AMERICA GREAT AGAIN!
- Jul 21, 2015 09:11:42 AM "@DillyDoesIt Trump has no problem telling it how it is, isn't that what everyone has been wanting from a President? #MakeAmericaGreatAgain"
- Jul 21, 2015 09:14:53 AM Good luck to my new friends on your testimony in DC. You are amazing people doing something so important--- stopping illegal immigration!
- Jul 21, 2015 09:30:52 AM Rick Perry did an absolutely horrible job of securing the border. He should be ashamed of himself. Gov. Abbott has since been terrific.
- Jul 21, 2015 09:47:56 AM .@BreitbartNews is much smarter than sleepy eyes @chucktodd @nbc http://t.co/Lb3PBlN3u0 Thanks to Steve Bannon & real reporters.
- Jul 21, 2015 10:00:13 AM .@ZachJohnsonPGA You're one of the truly great competitiors. I've said it for years. Great going winning @OpenChampionship - Not surprised!
- Jul 21, 2015 10:52:40 AM Via @AP by @kronayne & @colvinj: "Disavowed by GOP leaders, Trump has supporters cheering" http://t.co/xfgPmrEtKv
- Jul 21, 2015 11:21:24 AM Response to the Des Moines Register- http://t.co/krftGdPHN4
- Jul 21, 2015 11:45:40 AM Flags to be flown at Half-Staff at all Trump Properties in Honor of the Five Fallen Soldiers-http://t.co/bgKmJ8TU67
- Jul 21, 2015 01:32:28 PM "@Billd111 @seanhannity Any candidate that says Trump or anyone else should step down for speaking his mind should himself step down."
- Jul 21, 2015 01:33:33 PM I'm glad President Obama followed my lead and lowered the flags half-staff. It's about time!

- Jul 21, 2015 01:41:04 PM "@woofeous @realDonaldTrump GOP establishment forgets that Donald does not speak nor act like a 'retail politician'."
- Jul 21, 2015 02:59:49 PM "@jinx510 @realDonaldTrump don't get discouraged, keep telling the truth. Your detractors can't handle the truth."
- Jul 21, 2015 03:53:28 PM "@iAmerican All Talk No Walk. Old Politics. Let's Go @realDonaldTrump #MakeAmericaGreatAgain #GetItDone"
- Jul 21, 2015 04:44:40 PM My response to the failing Des Moines Register, the ultra liberal paper that has no power in Iowa https://t.co/4bEAW1sDzU
- Jul 21, 2015 05:51:44 PM Via @gatewaypundit: "Mother of Murdered Teen Thanks Donald Trump During Senate Hearing" http://t.co/uQrcCwmjhq
- Jul 21, 2015 07:27:40 PM Great day today in South Carolina. Fantastic capacity crowd, amazing people!
- Jul 21, 2015 07:29:08 PM "@insuradude: @foxandfriends @foxnation tell your owner Murdoch we are turning Fox off if he keeps belittling @realDonaldTrump. No Fox!
- Jul 21, 2015 07:53:41 PM I hear a failing New York newspaper is going to publish one of my old cell phone numbers. So original - just one of many!
- Jul 21, 2015 07:56:30 PM "@MeOnAJourney: @realDonaldTrump @Billd111 @seanhannity Trump is the Alpha of the #GOP candidates, the rest are betas! #Trump2016"
- Jul 21, 2015 07:57:50 PM "@PValk16: Many are missing the point, the US needs @realDonaldTrump to get things done. Instead they focus on sensation and media.
- Jul 21, 2015 08:54:34 PM "@jimlibertarian: @NBCNewYork In God we trust and in Donald we trust, Donald will make America second to none in every aspect known to man!
- Jul 21, 2015 08:55:52 PM "@PrestonsDayOff: @Montel_Williams @oreillyfactor Mr. Trump has the stones to tell the truth about this country! no more career politicians
- Jul 21, 2015 08:59:50 PM "@waite_lane:If you don't want Trump as president, then you don't want what your great grandfather fought so hard for #MakeAmericaGreatAgain
- Jul 21, 2015 08:59:59 PM "@Forrestben94: I don't care what people say, I love @realDonaldTrump confidence"

- Jul 21, 2015 09:00:36 PM "@drewcarter49: @realDonaldTrump @PrestonsDayOff @Montel_Williams @oreillyfactor Donald Trump is the new Ronald Reagan!" Thank you.
- Jul 21, 2015 09:16:17 PM "@Chr:DonaldTrump reminds me of Reagan his first time.Everyone was like "is he for real" Yup! Libs hate him and make fun of him. IM ON BOARD
- Jul 21, 2015 09:17:06 PM "@PJAliveguy: No matter what @realDonaldTrump says the media and the republican establishment will attack it. Time for something that works!
- Jul 21, 2015 09:26:27 PM "@HalangManok: Will be the the Leader that everyone wants! Cant be sold and speaks the truth! Everyone run! https://t.co/dcVP0kehG3"

- Jul 22, 2015 08:10:36 AM "@BAM4AU @CNN @realDonaldTrump @LindseyGrahamSC keep punching, Donald! Trump it!! Trump is telling the truth!"
- Jul 22, 2015 08:16:26 AM True, thanks. https://t.co/xqlRporCwT
- Jul 22, 2015 09:13:57 AM .@GovernorPerry in my office last cycle playing nice and begging for my support and money. Hypocrite! https://t.co/axPAVsLEqx
- Jul 22, 2015 09:31:54 AM I'm going to the BORDER tomorrow. Will be seeing some really brave people. Look forward to a big day!
- Jul 22, 2015 09:59:02 AM Thank you @chucktodd for your commentary last night on @NBCNightlyNews. Very fair -- we are making progress together!
- Jul 22, 2015 12:14:59 PM Via @ BreitbartNews by @BobPriceBBTX: "DONALD TRUMP HEADING TO TEXAS BORDER" http://t.co/xcxP1l8S5E
- Jul 22, 2015 12:20:56 PM "Donald Trump on VA woes: 'I'd fire everybody'; 'you fix it by getting Trump elected'" http://t.co/jpqYBBN6gx via @washtimes by @dsherfinski
- Jul 22, 2015 12:43:53 PM Obama still will keep all military recruitment centers & bases Gun Free Zones! It has to stop. MILITARY LIVES MATTER!
- Jul 22, 2015 12:56:26 PM Will be interviewed by @andersoncooper on @CNN tonight. Let's see if he treats me fairly—enjoy!
- Jul 22, 2015 01:39:45 PM Shouldn't George Will have to give a disclaimer every time he is on Fox that his wife works for Scott Walker?
- Jul 22, 2015 02:03:08 PM Let's Trump the Establishment! We are no longer silent. We will Make America Great Again! https://t.co/u25yI6aIvG

- Jul 22, 2015 02:34:19 PM It's going to take an outsider to clean up after Clinton, Bush and Obama. Let's Make America Great Again! https://t.co/u25yI5T7E8
- Jul 22, 2015 05:58:13 PM Via @CBNNews by @TheBrodyFile: "Brody File Exclusive: Donald Trump Comes Out In Support Of 20 Week Abortion Ban" http://t.co/xPHdH74OXf
- Jul 22, 2015 08:58:47 PM "@jimlibertarian: @realDonaldTrump is leaving Rick Perry in the dust,and everyone else for that matter, Donald will be our next POTUS
- Jul 22, 2015 08:59:19 PM "@CherokeeShaman2: Donald Trump was Right ! McCain amongst other RNC's voted to cut US Military Veterans Pensions. http://t.co/DFUFUTIbxY"
- Jul 22, 2015 09:14:12 PM .@FrankLuntz knows nothing about me or my religion. Came to my office looking for work. I had NO interest. I will save the vets!
- Jul 22, 2015 09:19:26 PM "@BB1959_: @FrankLuntz I am not impressed with Luntz. Never have been. What makes him an expert - he has a good racket going."
- Jul 22, 2015 09:20:23 PM "@bhill3333: We don't know Trump positions & he's dominating polls. @GOP should learn we don't want soft PC Focus Group driven speeches #GOP
- Jul 22, 2015 09:20:39 PM "@bitchpuuuhlease: @realDonaldTrump @FrankLuntz mr trump, thank you for getting the American people excited about politics again!!!"
- Jul 22, 2015 09:30:15 PM .@tedcruz you were terrific on @seanhannity tonight. I am going to the border tomorrow.
- Jul 22, 2015 09:37:53 PM "@tarabernie: Hey @realDonaldTrump check out Access Hollywood: http://t.co/p8WoUOmDqH" Thank you Dan Rather, we have just begun!
- Jul 22, 2015 09:39:12 PM "@gene70: @realDonaldTrump @macys America Hears You Donald!!! And The People You Are Running Against Will Hear All Of Us Soon! Donald Donald
- Jul 22, 2015 09:40:24 PM "@PATRIOT4657: @megynkelly The other candidates are scared. Trump tells it like it is. Maybe rich, but talks like he is an everyday Joe"

- Jul 22, 2015 09:41:48 PM "@RonNussbeck: @Maxinerunner I am a veteran from Arizona John McCain voted to give illegal Aliens benefits & take them from disabled Vets"
- Jul 22, 2015 09:47:26 PM .@AC360 Has the absolutely worst anti-Trump talking heads on his show. Dopey writer O'brian knows nothing about me or my wealth. A waste!
- Jul 22, 2015 09:54:31 PM "@woodardralph31: @gene70 @Macys We the people are so tired of all the guys talking the same old same Donald will back up his words!!!!"
- Jul 22, 2015 09:57:01 PM Boycott @Macys, no guts, no glory. Besides, there are far better stores!
- Jul 22, 2015 10:23:07 PM "@moekamerow: @AC360 Anderson Cooper only wants to hear his answers. Mr. Trump tells the truth and can't be bought Democrat for Trump"
- Jul 22, 2015 11:17:43 PM "@akawhit1: @Maxinerunner @RonNussbeck @realDonaldTrump MCCAIN WHO? #Vets Give Donald Trump Standing Ovation http://t.co/3z3IqhnfKM …"

- Jul 23, 2015 04:07:18 AM "@fedupwithgovern: Congress Can't Find Money for Veterans *Houses, Feeds, Educates, Provide Drs for illegals *Gives Iran over $200 Billion"
- Jul 23, 2015 04:29:03 AM "@3rdedit: Media attacking you early this morning. A GOOD SIGN!America is proud of you for ignoring the MEDIA & telling it like it is!"
- Jul 23, 2015 05:36:53 AM What a waste of time being interviewed by @andersoncooper when he puts on really stupid talking heads likeTim O'Brien- dumb guy with no clue!
- Jul 23, 2015 08:07:34 AM .@BillKristol Bill, your small and slightly failing magazine will be a giant success when you finally back Trump. Country will soar!
- Jul 23, 2015 08:22:55 AM Getting ready to lift off for Laredo. Will land at 1:OO P.M. Should be exciting and informative!
- Jul 23, 2015 08:33:43 AM "@rox473: @realDonaldTrump Keep telling it like it is. Refreshing no political BS"
- Jul 23, 2015 08:47:30 AM "@SanchezBrutus: Plz stay safe dear Sir, the World needs you.Your competition is no more presidential than an alley cat is a mountain lion."

- Jul 23, 2015 08:47:50 AM "@Kathe56Kat: @realDonaldTrump please be careful" Thank you!
- Jul 23, 2015 08:52:43 AM "@LAgirlrebelyell:Safe travels DonaldTrump Can't wait to hear the report later today! TY for all you are doing to take this Country back
- Jul 23, 2015 09:02:53 AM "@MichaelCohen212 Michael Cohen on Wolf Blitzer #CNN @wolfblitzer http://t.co/sWWWqAt8or …
- Jul 23, 2015 09:28:07 AM True! https://t.co/sEdzvjuHgY
- Jul 23, 2015 09:41:30 AM "@Jaybaby63 Mr. Trump thank you! For having a clue and not being afraid of what others think or say about you. I want my country back!"
- Jul 23, 2015 09:45:29 AM Thanks. https://t.co/CD3SYvgKfj
- Jul 23, 2015 09:53:10 AM "@themakaylamarie @realDonaldTrump is exactly what we need. He says what the others are too afraid to say! I'm for him 110%." Thanks.
- Jul 23, 2015 10:12:00 AM "@TheJordanHafizi @realDonaldTrump is the only candidate that isn't politically correct and that speaks the truth on what's on his mind!"
- Jul 23, 2015 12:18:23 PM Great! https://t.co/FFzhWLUfzF
- Jul 23, 2015 03:09:55 PM "@grant_hose I like @realDonaldTrump . He isn't fake. He tells you the truth not "what you wanna hear".
- Jul 23, 2015 03:29:45 PM "@tmautner1211 If all the Hispanics hate the @realDonaldTrump, why was he surrounded by so many Hispanics at the border?"
- Jul 23, 2015 03:57:35 PM "@RTylerR4 Don't let the press put words in your mouth! @realDonaldTrump Awesome job at the border! You're doing great!"
- Jul 23, 2015 05:04:31 PM .@bobbyjindal watched you on @TeamCavuto. Made some excellent points. Best Wishes.
- Jul 23, 2015 09:10:53 PM "@Woodsy_gal: Been a long time since I've cared abt politics since the GOP been a disaster. That's changed bc of YOU. Love U! #Trump2016"
- Jul 23, 2015 09:15:20 PM You're just not getting there @DanaPerino. Sometimes things just don't work out, but don't worry--- no problem!
- Jul 23, 2015 09:33:02 PM Thoughts & prayers with everyone in Lafayette, Louisiana this evening.

- Jul 23, 2015 09:39:00 PM "@facingeast52: @realDonaldTrump Please be careful there, the boarder is a dangerous place according to those who live near there."
- Jul 23, 2015 09:39:49 PM "@flanny1971: @realDonaldTrump clearly puts this country first! Security, vets, economy and won't bow down to other world leaders!

- Jul 24, 2015 07:38:07 AM True. https://t.co/kbdTazxEZG
- Jul 24, 2015 08:23:17 AM "@TitanicQueen @LadySandersfarm What frightens them abt Trump is his totally NON POLITICAL CORRECT nature~Donald is shaking up the house!"
- Jul 24, 2015 08:56:04 AM "@mitchellvii @thehill @slone Here's a crazy thought. Maybe Trump is gaining traction because HE'S RIGHT?"
- Jul 24, 2015 11:21:07 AM Great read: "How New York's Veterans Day Parade Became 'America's Parade'" http://t.co/PuYQl4CRg3
- Jul 24, 2015 11:35:30 AM .@williebosshog watched you on @foxandfriends. You were great and I appreciate the nice statements. I'm sending out for your new book now!
- Jul 24, 2015 11:43:23 AM When will anyone be held accountable for the VA scandal? The politicians are experts in never facing any consequence.
- Jul 24, 2015 11:48:52 AM DC has shrunk our military and exploded our country with debt. We can't send another politician to the White House https://t.co/u25yI6aIvG
- Jul 24, 2015 12:18:12 PM I love Bluffton, SC, what a great place -- what great people.
- Jul 24, 2015 12:46:34 PM Arriving to check out the border. https://t.co/nZMeKl3siW
- Jul 24, 2015 12:47:22 PM From an amazing day on the border in Laredo. https://t.co/vIcDmjUiJV
- Jul 24, 2015 12:56:44 PM Be sure to get a copy of @williebosshog's new book, American Hunter.
- Jul 24, 2015 01:18:28 PM It is time to send someone from the outside to fix DC from the inside. Let's Make America Great Again! https://t.co/u25yI5T7E8
- Jul 24, 2015 01:32:21 PM "@gpavlik7 1/2 of new California driver's licenses go to undocumented immigrants. Read the Sac' Bee, July 17th. Go get'em, Trump!"

- Jul 24, 2015 01:35:48 PM "@paulkellysr Mr Trump thanks for saying what millions are thinking. We need to turn America around if we want to save her."
- Jul 24, 2015 01:38:49 PM "@nozzero @realDonaldTrump Finally someone who is not sugar coating the mess in this country!!!"
- Jul 24, 2015 01:41:51 PM "@DanScavino: Via Economist/YouGov 7•24•2015 #MakeAmericaGreatAgain #Trump2016" http://t.co/GSXf8Tfzvn
- Jul 24, 2015 01:50:46 PM True, thanks. https://t.co/xD2hlCobgo
- Jul 24, 2015 02:01:26 PM True! https://t.co/zuI0QYYCaQ
- Jul 24, 2015 02:03:24 PM "@KimBredesen @realDonaldTrump I appreciate that you don't apologize when someone is "offended" by what you say. #MakeAmericaGreatAgain"
- Jul 24, 2015 02:46:11 PM .@marklevinshow has written a great book, Plunder and Deceit. He powerfully analyzes issues that are crucial to us today. Read it!
- Jul 24, 2015 03:29:19 PM Thank you @DennisRodman. It's time to #MakeAmericaGreatAgain! I hope you are doing well! https://t.co/H7d2ZLmod2
- Jul 24, 2015 03:46:59 PM Isn't it amazing that @Macys paid a massive fine for profiling African Americans--& then criticized me for discussing illegal immigration!
- Jul 24, 2015 04:54:19 PM Via @BreitbartNews by @NolteNC: "DONALD TRUMP SURGES TO COMMANDING LEAD IN POST-MCCAIN BACKLASH POLL" http://t.co/OvL90Hm1KN

- Jul 25, 2015 05:36:01 AM "@MYKALFURY: @seanhannity @realDonaldTrump I hear same doubters as I heard when Reagan ran against Carter. Press said he'd lose. Reagan WON.
- Jul 25, 2015 05:40:55 AM "@AndreaWeslien: #DEBATE @seanhannity @realDonaldTrump If not for Donald, who'd watch GOP upcoming debate? SOUR GRAPES
- Jul 25, 2015 06:03:04 AM "@lucascoon1: @realDonaldTrump Reaganomics created 16 million new jobs and Trumpenomics will create 16 million more"
- Jul 25, 2015 06:29:51 AM "@ConnieHegel: @realDonaldTrump if trump is not on that stage no one will watch" So true!
- Jul 25, 2015 06:34:00 AM "@hammetjohn: In my Lifetime I've Never Seen Americans Energized, Excited about Voting. @realDonaldTrump Woke up about 300 Million people

- Jul 25, 2015 06:35:37 AM "@Shella_Bella: @ConnieHegel MY GOD! WHY can't the GOP see that Trump is doing this solely 4 R country! He HAD a VERY comfortable life!"
- Jul 25, 2015 06:35:53 AM "@Operator1975: @realDonaldTrump Please Mr. Trump keep the pressure on and bring change to this country!!!!!"
- Jul 25, 2015 06:42:18 AM "@GarethBale22: @realDonaldTrump you're going to turn America around Donald I can feel it"
- Jul 25, 2015 06:43:41 AM "@sandrapatriot: @stephenfhayes WHAT U REALLY SHOULD B ANGRY ABT IS THE INVASION OF MILLIONS OF ILLEGALS TKING OVER AMERICA! NOT DonaldTrump
- Jul 25, 2015 06:57:50 AM Getting ready to go to Iowa today. Big crowd - will be a great day!
- Jul 25, 2015 07:09:05 AM Big poll just out by @TheEconomist has me in 1st. place by a lot. A great honor but we have a long way to go to MAKE AMERICA GREAT AGAIN!
- Jul 25, 2015 07:10:40 AM "@kerrygold1914: @realDonaldTrump @TheEconomist the Donald is crushing it"
- Jul 25, 2015 07:13:27 AM "@StoneZipper: @stephenfhayes Donald Trump if he stops running for president he's not what we the people think he is." Will never happen!
- Jul 25, 2015 07:14:27 AM "@energypryde: @realDonaldTrump @TheEconomist Trump in office restores US swagger."
- Jul 25, 2015 08:16:32 AM The ultra liberal and seriously failing Des Moines Register is BEGGING my team for press credentials to my event in Iowa today- but they lie!
- Jul 25, 2015 08:33:56 AM Isn't it funny that I am now #1 in the money losing @HuffingtonPost (poll), and by a big margin. Dummy @ariannahuff must be thrilled!
- Jul 25, 2015 10:52:24 AM .@Macy's is a big contributor to @PPFA . Anybody against Planned Parenthood should boycott racial profiling Macy's.
- Jul 25, 2015 11:14:59 AM .@ShawnJohnson Congratulations on your engagement --- he is a lucky guy. You are a true winner and will be an amazing couple.
- Jul 25, 2015 11:59:49 AM .@ScottWalker despite your coming to my office to give me an award, your very dumb fundraiser hit me very hard--- not smart!

- Jul 25, 2015 12:17:34 PM Supporters waiting to hear me speak in Oskaloosa, Iowa. #MakeAmericaGreatAgain https://t.co/qEUeu8cDwO
- Jul 25, 2015 12:32:10 PM Packed venue of people who want to #MakeAmericaGreatAgain https://t.co/wisZRVAmPR
- Jul 25, 2015 08:11:23 PM Great success in Iowa today. Fantastic sold out crowd. Will be back soon!
- Jul 25, 2015 08:30:55 PM Always great to speak with Veterans - our nation's heroes. We will Make America Great Again! http://t.co/P58AGMmBwY
- Jul 25, 2015 09:00:17 PM "@gqforbes: TRUMP ON JOBS. pls rt http://t.co/gupiYMQNA2 @realDonaldTrump http://t.co/e7CWiHj95r"
- Jul 25, 2015 09:00:36 PM "@RustyOsborne15: @realDonaldTrump you got my vote" Thanks.
- Jul 25, 2015 09:01:48 PM "@twendencyUSA: #Twendency Tweet of the Hour in USA politics #9pm by @realDonaldTrump https://t.co/7K0CIh2Zrj http://t.co/9aflKwjogc"
- Jul 25, 2015 09:02:36 PM "@CoachAbda: Please don't change a thing. Your attitude is exactly what this country needs.No tip-toeing, this man tells it how it is!"
- Jul 25, 2015 09:05:10 PM "@YossiGestetner: Whoa! @realDonaldTrump shoots up to 28% in YouGov from 15% two wks ago; outperforms McCain in favorables among Vets. Great
- Jul 25, 2015 09:05:19 PM "@dc1a7ce3d7f7402: @realDonaldTrump veterans for Trump 2016"
- Jul 25, 2015 09:06:26 PM "@TriciaNC1: @Centaur6D If I were Walker, I'd be afraid of Trump outing his 14 yr support of amnesty, benefits, pathway for illegals"
- Jul 25, 2015 09:08:21 PM "@g_pluth: @RedNationRising Hats off to @realDonaldTrump for sticking it to liberal msm. @DMRegister" A horrible newspaper, failing badly.
- Jul 25, 2015 09:09:38 PM "@Foshay504: @greta DonaldTrump-Love him! It's time to run America like a business. We've given all our wealth to China n Mexico!! No more!
- Jul 25, 2015 09:10:05 PM "@otto2468: @realDonaldTrump He built up his company to be prosperous and successful. Why can't he do the same with America? #Trump2016"

- Jul 25, 2015 09:10:59 PM "@HL3tweets: @CoachAbda Trump is the only candidate who doesn't test his statements before focus groups to be sure no one is offended. True
- Jul 25, 2015 09:12:01 PM "@ZacharySmitty: @realDonaldTrump I just listened to this speech and loved it!"
- Jul 25, 2015 09:12:09 PM "@RICHMCLOUGHLIN: @realDonaldTrump @YossiGestetner GIVE THEM HELL."
- Jul 25, 2015 09:12:44 PM "@KingSchnabel: @realDonaldTrump College students love trump. Never change." Great.
- Jul 25, 2015 09:12:53 PM "@guthrie_kelley: @realDonaldTrump AMEN. Thank you Trump"
- Jul 25, 2015 09:14:03 PM "@Hturne: @realDonaldTrump vets tired of McCain using them as talking points and photo ops, AND NOTHING BEING DONE."
- Jul 25, 2015 09:19:49 PM .@ScottWalker is a nice guy, but not presidential material. Wisconsin is in turmoil, borrowing to the hilt, and doing poorly in jobs etc.
- Jul 25, 2015 09:47:12 PM "@Faithful_USA: I'm a 10th generation American of Spanish descent I support DonaldTrump Hispanic DOESN'T mean ILLEGAL #MakeAmericaGreatAgain
- Jul 25, 2015 09:48:52 PM "@ModerateMic: .DonaldTrump: Ask @ScottWalker why he left 1,000+ WI jobs on the table due to a political deal with the @paysbig Potawatomi
- Jul 25, 2015 09:49:18 PM "@WalterWhfla: @realDonaldTrump unless u got cheese for brains you are not voting for walker ! NEXT"
- Jul 25, 2015 09:54:39 PM "@_John_Handel: @realDonaldTrump @ScottWalker and Walker is destroying once great Wisconsin universities.
- Jul 25, 2015 09:55:35 PM "@Brammz3: In full support of @realDonaldTrump for #POTUS! No reason he shouldn't win the @GOP nomination. #MakeAmericaGreatAgain #Trump2016

- Jul 26, 2015 06:37:01 AM "@bluestarwindow: @realDonaldTrump @bdean1468 Putin knows that Obama is a danger to the world. Putin will respect President Trump" True!
- Jul 26, 2015 06:37:58 AM "@EOetzel: @peddoc63 @realDonaldTrump JebBush I think we the people would prefer many other choices over jeb...."

- Jul 26, 2015 06:40:09 AM "@DavidKyleOnline: @realDonaldTrump attack Walker on Common Core. State grassroots not happy with him on CC inaction."
- Jul 26, 2015 06:40:45 AM "@about_life: @realDonaldTrump I Luv America 4 Trump 2016 - Let's Make America Great Again! - iluvamerica4trump2016@gmail.com"
- Jul 26, 2015 06:42:04 AM "@about_life: @realDonaldTrump Silent Warriors 4 Trump 2016 - Vets! Let's Take America Back! - silentwarriors4trump2016@gmail.com"
- Jul 26, 2015 06:45:12 AM "@Agent_54 @theblaze @pretrim10 MSM can't push DonaldTrump around. http://t.co/vCY91c05dm No More PC Political Hacks! http://t.co/6XsgLPKugY
- Jul 26, 2015 06:46:09 AM "@fubaglady: .@npomalley @YossiGestetner You understand McCain is a RINO Senator who voters can't stand & who's over stayed his welcome?"
- Jul 26, 2015 06:47:49 AM "@about_life: Politician Have Been Running(Ruining) America For Years; Lets Change That Now -Trump 2016 - iluvamerica4trump2016@gmail.com"
- Jul 26, 2015 06:48:01 AM "@billyjowiggins: @realDonaldTrump The lion does not concern himself with the opinion of sheep"
- Jul 26, 2015 06:48:25 AM "@PaulaDuvall2: Outsider Donald Trump assesses & addresses major American problems. What has Congress been doing for the past 7 years?"
- Jul 26, 2015 06:48:38 AM "@DDiTarant: America needs @realDonaldTrump ! #Trump2016 #BuildTheFence #MakeAmericaGreatAgain"
- Jul 26, 2015 06:49:22 AM "@Man_In_The_Hole: "Our leaders are dummies. They don't know what's going on. It's true, they're incompetent. #Trump #MakeAmericaGreatAgain"
- Jul 26, 2015 08:26:05 PM "@luismp77: @realDonaldTrump Team Trump all the way!"
- Jul 26, 2015 08:26:47 PM "@sorensen_ao: @HuffPostUKPol @realDonaldTrump #DonaldTrump will shake up politics like no other ever could or will. #InterestingTimesAhead"
- Jul 26, 2015 08:27:22 PM "@eddiebrognano: ScottWalker THANK YOU FOR SAYING WHAT THE MEDIA HASNT SAID ABOUT WALKER. Wisconsin is a hot mess and it's his fault."

- Jul 26, 2015 08:27:35 PM "@bluestarwindow: @bdean1468 @realDonaldTrump @twendencyUSA We SHALL make America great again."
- Jul 26, 2015 08:28:09 PM "@PaulaDuvall2: Washington politicians are either dishonest or incompetent. Must be, since 7 yrs of LAWLESSNESS in WH are ignored."
- Jul 26, 2015 08:28:27 PM "@Arful1dodger: @realDonaldTrump I know seniors that are in 70s and go to shooting ranges weekly to protect their family and self !"
- Jul 26, 2015 08:29:36 PM "@PaulaDuvall2: Before Mr. Trump's Presidential bid, I was leaning toward Walker! Glad I was saved from stepping in something TERRIBLE."
- Jul 26, 2015 08:30:06 PM "@SilverSharen: Obama is in Africa pledging 1billion dollars to help them. How about that money to help America. Trump for POTUS."
- Jul 26, 2015 08:32:48 PM "@bollweevil51: @realDonaldTrump Great speech in Iowa....Obama/Kerry throw Israel under the bus."
- Jul 26, 2015 08:33:28 PM "@BfgBobgrant: @realDonaldTrump @hammetjohn I've been awake, but now see a chance of real hope with Trump."
- Jul 26, 2015 08:33:39 PM "@BfgBobgrant: @realDonaldTrump @Operator1975 Agreed! We need you!"
- Jul 26, 2015 08:42:27 PM "@MitchPrefach: DonaldTrump Iowa speech excellent. Particularly the end about Israel and Iran. More foreign policy please. You have my vote.
- Jul 26, 2015 08:45:10 PM "@rp53pierce: @realDonaldTrump Mr Trump you're a breath of fresh air all these career politicians are not doing the business for the people"

- Jul 27, 2015 12:24:13 PM Thank you, Wayne Root -- we will #MakeAmericaGreatAgain!http://t.co/L3cKIEDZ2X
- Jul 27, 2015 12:28:59 PM Thank you, Greta. https://t.co/CWQZlIBV78
- Jul 27, 2015 12:30:39 PM "@AlexPagliano Caught @realDonaldTrump's speech from Iowa. Why is the media portraying him so poorly? Guy has passion, great ideas."
- Jul 27, 2015 12:35:14 PM Great news, I'm now leading in most polls w/ new CNN poll also having me #1. NBC, I am #1 in NH by a lot, #2 in Iowa, close & gaining.

- Jul 27, 2015 01:01:15 PM When people find out how bad a job Scott Walker has done in WI, they won't be voting for him. Massive deficit, bad jobs forecast, a mess.
- Jul 27, 2015 01:05:31 PM "@jimlibertarian @grantrobertb @MichaelCohen212 you're damn right we want the truth,we've been lied to 4 years and we've had it.#Trump2016"
- Jul 27, 2015 01:33:28 PM "@Cj112Connie I don't get the media??Trump is ahead in every poll, but won't give him credit, they say he won't make it?? 60% of us say yes"
- Jul 27, 2015 01:39:32 PM "@scorpio5053 @realDonaldTrump is the real deal. Hes not running for his health. Believes in the Red White & Blue.@UnitedCitizen01"
- Jul 27, 2015 01:40:24 PM "@MDTaylorJr Everyone else have fun being politically correct. Meanwhile, @realDonaldTrump is speaking the truth. #Trump2016"
- Jul 27, 2015 01:51:17 PM .@SteveRattner While I think you should have gone to prison for what you did, I guess Obama saved you. But watch – I will win!
- Jul 27, 2015 02:05:36 PM "@Read_my_note No wonder why @realDonaldTrump is ahead in the presidential polls.. People are tired of the same old crap from Washington!"
- Jul 27, 2015 02:10:32 PM Thanks. https://t.co/xU5h2BwojR
- Jul 27, 2015 02:11:36 PM "@TomMcPeek More people r gravitating to @realDonaldTrump because they're tired of all the usual BS"
- Jul 27, 2015 02:24:23 PM Via @nytpolitics by @AshleyRParker: "Strong Showings for Donald Trump in Iowa and New Hampshire Polls" http://t.co/UARuXLir8b
- Jul 27, 2015 02:25:03 PM "Iowans Drawn to Donald Trump Praise His Antiestablishment Bent" http://t.co/nyYk3DBXD5 via @WSJ by @heatherhaddon & @reidepstein
- Jul 27, 2015 02:44:23 PM We must build a wall to secure our border. It will save lives and help Make America Great Again! https://t.co/u25yI5T7E8
- Jul 27, 2015 02:50:26 PM Veterans, please call 855- VETS- 352 or email address veterans@donaldtrump.com to share your stories about the need to reform the VA.
- Jul 27, 2015 03:15:08 PM Thanks Lou. https://t.co/hDm7MrrwTD

- Jul 27, 2015 03:23:18 PM "@ScoodieGolden Twitter loves Trump. 1000's of retweets for Mr. Trump while @ScottWalker gets 5 to 10 #MakeAmericaGreatAgain!"
- Jul 27, 2015 04:01:07 PM .@GovernorSununu who couldn't get elected dog catcher in NH forgot to mention my phenomenal biz success rate: 99.2% https://t.co/WsA3Jnjhwa
- Jul 27, 2015 04:13:12 PM "@AmyMek The Media hates Trump b/c he's a Proud American Entrepreneur who loves his country, wants others 2 succeed & calls out their lies"
- Jul 27, 2015 04:42:52 PM I own Turnberry, in Scotland, one of great resorts in world. Women's British Open there this week. I'll go for two days & back on trail.
- Jul 27, 2015 04:47:35 PM Be in Turnberry on Thurs AM for start of Women's British Open, one of world's great golf tournaments. Back soon to #MakeAmericaGreatAgain!
- Jul 27, 2015 04:49:59 PM I'll be on @seanhannity tonight at 10 PM and look forward to it. Lots to discuss! Enjoy.
- Jul 27, 2015 06:32:49 PM "@moses11211: Donald Trump leads in new #GOP polls.. @foxandfriends @realDonaldTrump http://t.co/lVNSZmY9La"
- Jul 27, 2015 06:53:44 PM Boston's Mayor Walsh wasted a lot of time and money on going for the Olympics, and then he gave up. I don't want him negotiating for me!
- Jul 27, 2015 06:57:37 PM Will be interviewed tonight on @seanhannity at 10:00. There is so much to talk about!
- Jul 27, 2015 08:19:54 PM "@LifeZette:Jeb & Hillary could stand to learn a thing or two from @realDonaldTrump about making America great again http://t.co/JJw1blEjNy
- Jul 27, 2015 08:28:15 PM "@robertaritzen: @AnnCoulter @seanhannity We love him! I love his truth telling. That he's so real and calls it how he sees it. #Trump2016"
- Jul 27, 2015 10:15:10 PM Thank you @scottienhughes for the great job you did on @CNN. Great energy and smarts! I will not let you down.
- Jul 27, 2015 10:19:39 PM .@TheBrodyFile was fantastic tonight on @CNN. Thank you, we will MAKE AMERICA GREAT AGAIN!

- Jul 27, 2015 10:23:26 PM "@USARestoring: @HillaryClinton's toast. Dems had better get the"B Team" off the bench. @TGowdySC for Attorney General under President Trump
- Jul 27, 2015 10:24:34 PM "@Whitejl0111: @FoxNews @realDonaldTrump McCain hasn't done anything for the Vets; fact! He only talks about himself! "
- Jul 27, 2015 11:06:25 PM "@dc1a7ce3d7f7402: @michaeljohns @realDonaldTrump veterans for Trump 2016"

- Jul 28, 2015 09:32:34 AM "@thehill @realDonaldTrump The people of NH know what the American people know: Trump is the only one with any CLUE about how to fix things"
- Jul 28, 2015 10:38:07 AM After all is said and done, more is said than done. -- Aesop
- Jul 28, 2015 11:04:46 AM Thank you @mcuban for your nice words. I am rapidly becoming a @dallasmavs fan! https://t.co/sLXkCh9qfg
- Jul 28, 2015 11:23:09 AM We must protect our veterans. #MakeAmericaGreatAgain https://t.co/erwKxZVGpP
- Jul 28, 2015 11:33:50 AM My @FoxNews int. with @seanhannity on Obama being all talk & no action & making America Great Again! http://t.co/RqP6MNnR7h
- Jul 28, 2015 11:49:20 AM Via @politico by "Poll: Trump has twice the support of Bush in New Hampshire" http://t.co/aeHiTqEZlq
- Jul 28, 2015 12:17:26 PM .#IranDeal will go down as one of the dumbest & most dangerous misjudgments ever entered into in history of our country— incompetent leader!
- Jul 28, 2015 01:01:20 PM Via cnsnews by @SJonesCNS: "Trump Explains His Appeal: 'People Are Tired...Of These Incompetent Politicians'" http://t.co/Y36EQiGE5a
- Jul 28, 2015 01:11:39 PM "@marklevinshow: 'PLUNDER AND DECEIT'" http://t.co/dQ4OHpT227 via @AmSpec by @JeffJlpa1
- Jul 28, 2015 01:40:00 PM Via @limbaugh: "Trump Doubled Down -- and It Worked" http://t.co/91i6FWWxGf
- Jul 28, 2015 02:00:35 PM Obama's nuclear deal with the Iranians will lead to a nuclear arms race in the Middle East. It has to be stopped.
- Jul 28, 2015 02:25:57 PM We can make Washington work for us. It's time for real leadership. Let's #MakeAmericaGreatAgain! https://t.co/u25yI6aIvG

- Jul 28, 2015 02:46:49 PM "Government's first duty is to protect the people, not run their lives." – Ronald Reagan
- Jul 28, 2015 03:22:56 PM While I'm beating my opponents in the polls, I'm also beating lobbyists, special interests & donors that are supporting them with billions.
- Jul 28, 2015 04:20:58 PM A nation WITHOUT BORDERS is not a nation at all. We must have a wall. The rule of law matters. Jeb just doesn't get it.
- Jul 28, 2015 05:49:30 PM Via @BreitbartNews by @mboyle1: "TRUMP: OBAMA SHOULDN'T ATTACK AMERICANS OVERSEAS, HILLARY'S EMAIL WAS 'CRIMINAL" http://t.co/BWrHxT50sy
- Jul 28, 2015 11:57:35 PM "@AnnCoulter: .DonaldTrump leads w/ Hispanics. Christie, who supported in-state tuition 4 illegals -scrape bottom. http://t.co/CGqNnUtwQg"

- Jul 29, 2015 06:28:02 AM Public Policy Polling (PPP) has just come out with a major poll putting me #1 with Hispanics - leading all Republican candidates.Told you so
- Jul 29, 2015 06:31:33 AM "@jan102345678: @realDonaldTrump Mr.Trump,I am thrilled you are running for President of USA.You are the only man for the job!!!
- Jul 29, 2015 07:28:24 AM .@CNN & @CNNPolitics did not say that lawyer Beck lost the case and I got legal fees. Also, she wanted to breast pump in front of me at dep.
- Jul 29, 2015 07:32:53 AM Lawyer Elizabeth Beck was easy for me to beat. Ask her clients if they are happy with her results against me. Got total win and legal fees.
- Jul 29, 2015 07:40:14 AM .CNN & @CNNPolitics Lawyer Elizabeth Beck did a terrible job against me, she lost (I even got legal fees). I loved beating her,she was easy
- Jul 29, 2015 07:44:59 AM .@CNN Why is somebody (Beck) I beat so soundly all of a sudden an expert on Donald Trump (all over television). She knows nothing about me.
- Jul 29, 2015 07:56:35 AM So many people who know nothing about me are commenting all over T.V. and the media as though they have great D.J.T. insight. Know NOTHING!

- Jul 29, 2015 08:54:28 AM Thank you @Morning_Joe for throwing the pathetic reporter from the failing and money losing Daily Beast off the air. Really cool!
- Jul 29, 2015 08:58:36 AM I truly LOVE all of the millions of people who are sticking with me despite so many media lies. There is a great SILENT MAJORITY looming!
- Jul 29, 2015 09:17:47 AM "@TomNocera @DanScavino @dallasmavs @mcuban Trump's work ethic gives me hope - he's a tireless and smart worker: a winner not a whiner."
- Jul 29, 2015 01:04:53 PM This is an outrage! Bias-Free Language Guide claims the word 'American' is 'problematic' -- WHAT?! http://t.co/vKz8a0ICGs
- Jul 29, 2015 01:10:56 PM "@JereeGeeStavich @realDonaldTrump You are blowing everyone else away. Not just ahead, but doubling. Wow."
- Jul 29, 2015 02:21:01 PM Via @SaintPetersblog by @MitchEPerry: "Shock poll: Donald Trump leads Jeb Bush 26-20% … in Florida" http://t.co/49IAe1Nlm7
- Jul 29, 2015 03:54:45 PM Per @rushlimbaugh: Why does Hillary Clinton get the benefit of the doubt (after she DESTROYS her illegal email server) ...
- Jul 29, 2015 03:54:56 PM ... while Tom Brady is guilty because he REPLACED his LEGAL cellphone?
- Jul 29, 2015 04:15:54 PM Trump Will Make America GREAT!!!! #ChangeTheWorldIn5Words
- Jul 29, 2015 04:44:56 PM How can a dummy dope like Harry Hurt, who wrote a failed book about me but doesn't know me or anything about me, be on TV discussing Trump?
- Jul 29, 2015 04:45:13 PM People like lawyer Elizabeth Beck and failed writer Harry Hurt & others talk about me but know nothing about me—crazy!
- Jul 29, 2015 04:53:12 PM Thank you. https://t.co/oRATmdIzqE
- Jul 29, 2015 07:00:45 PM I really like the Koch Brothers (members of my P.B. Club), but I don't want their money or anything else from them. Cannot influence Trump!
- Jul 29, 2015 07:08:00 PM Getting ready to leave for my GREAT resort, Turnberry, in Scotland. Hosting The Women's British Open (biggest tournament). Will be back Sat.
- Jul 29, 2015 09:57:37 PM "@BillLester651: @DanScavino @realDonaldTrump Latinos for Trump believes in Trump"

- Jul 29, 2015 09:58:23 PM "@me_lisa_m: @DanScavino @realDonaldTrump Just updated voter registration in FL #VoteTrump"
- Jul 29, 2015 09:59:07 PM "@linablue: @realDonaldTrump I love the fact you can't be "bought"..."

- Jul 30, 2015 08:10:41 AM "@LinFlies @califortrump @realDonaldTrump we love #TrumpForPresident & thankful"
- Jul 30, 2015 11:08:09 AM "@Jennifer75AR @AmyMek He's not for sale like the politicians are! That's why he gives us truth! Trump for Prez! #Trump2016"
- Jul 30, 2015 02:10:28 PM "@lasannewton @realDonaldTrump The only candidate who will not owe favors to campaign contributors"
- Jul 30, 2015 02:12:28 PM "@bdean1468 The alpha male in the 2016 race: @realDonaldTrump He has real success stories, tons of money, confident, & he's his own backer"
- Jul 30, 2015 02:36:36 PM Carl Cameron @FoxNews is the only reporter I know who consistently fumbles & misrepresents poll results. He has been so wrong & he hates it!
- Jul 30, 2015 02:39:29 PM Just at a news conference from Trump Turnberry in Scotland. Everybody was there & will be all over television tonite. Back on trail Saturday
- Jul 30, 2015 02:46:37 PM I look forward to the debate on Thursday night & it is certainly my intention to be very nice & highly respectful of the other candidates.
- Jul 30, 2015 03:27:42 PM The polls have been consistently great. The silent majority is speaking. Politicians are failing. #MakeAmericaGreatAgain!
- Jul 30, 2015 06:58:59 PM Thank you. https://t.co/BbD9deWjbQ
- Jul 30, 2015 07:00:58 PM Thank you for your service! https://t.co/xBJ47fUXC0

- Jul 31, 2015 08:36:33 AM Should not raise taxes in Wisconsin, but massive budget deficit. Education, roads, etc suffering. @DanHenninger lies. @WSJ
- Jul 31, 2015 08:39:08 AM Will be leaving Trump Turnberry tomorrow--place & Women's British Open are great. Will be back hitting hard tomorrow. @Turnberrybuzz
- Jul 31, 2015 08:40:04 AM Wow, some new and even greater polls--thank you!

- Jul 31, 2015 08:54:06 AM If you think you can do a thing or think you can't do a thing, you're right. -- Henry Ford
- Jul 31, 2015 11:11:21 AM "@sjh2222 Difference Between Politicians and @realDonaldTrump = Pols Are Bought & Paid For. Trump Can't be Bought, Bullied or Bribed!"
- Jul 31, 2015 02:20:50 PM "@blindtothetruth Trump is polling well because he speaks his mind. Not like some of the career politicians he's running against. Cowards."
- Jul 31, 2015 03:37:12 PM "@ColinSWood @realDonaldTrump is worth more than ALL of the other Presidential candidates combined and plenty more."

August, 2015

- Aug 1, 2015 09:33:09 AM Watch my interview with @ericbolling on @FoxNews today at 11:30AM ET

- Aug 2, 2015 09:00:16 AM I wish good luck to all of the Republican candidates that traveled to California to beg for money etc. from the Koch Brothers. Puppets?
- Aug 2, 2015 06:08:32 PM "@Dark_Red_Hair2: .@realDonaldTRUMP will get things done for America https://t.co/BuRAg7G7NH"
- Aug 2, 2015 08:15:11 PM "@RoniSeale: @DanScavino @FoxNews @EricTrump @ericbolling #GoTrump #MakeAmericaGreatAgain #gop #Trump2016 http://t.co/WgVNBFK4ik"
- Aug 2, 2015 08:15:32 PM "@winkiechance: @VickyBrush @RWSurferGirl @realDonaldTrump He has MY vote too! #MakeAmericaGreatAgain"
- Aug 2, 2015 08:17:10 PM "@scorpio5053: @nowandthan @RealMarkCole @realDonaldTrump The GOP TREETED Reagan the same way. Until he beat em then turned into ass kissers

- Aug 2, 2015 08:48:51 PM "@gqforbes: DOMINATING SOCIAL MEDIA! @realDonaldTrump's twitter edge @DanScavino @FoxNews @EricTrump @ericbolling" http://t.co/r2FOMm5Tr0
- Aug 2, 2015 10:18:46 PM "@DavidBougs: @scorpio5053 @nowandthan @RealMarkCole Amen! GOP elite called Reagan a cowboy, B- movie actor, dangerous,unelectable.Trump!
- Aug 2, 2015 10:23:45 PM I will be interviewed on @foxandfriends tomorrow morning at 7:00. Enjoy!
- Aug 2, 2015 10:28:01 PM "@CoachZachCooper: Congratulations on leading the polls currently and for acquiring the Center Stage Position In The Upcoming Debates!"
- Aug 2, 2015 10:30:08 PM "@IvoryRymes: @realDonaldTrump Donald Trump summed up in one word.....TRAILBLAZER !!!" Thanks.
- Aug 2, 2015 10:31:04 PM "@TPFA_KathyA_1: We'll be watching. @realDonaldTrump 2016! Will #MakeAmericaGreatAgain @foxandfriends : http://t.co/5ED5TFC6xc"
- Aug 2, 2015 10:31:48 PM "@brady2edelman: @realDonaldTrump Mr. Trump you are the next President of the United States. And the next President Reagan.God Bless America
- Aug 2, 2015 10:33:12 PM "@RaxsonDFS: There is no way President Trump loses this election. He will win by historical landslide. Will be greatest #POTUS ever!" Thanks
- Aug 2, 2015 10:33:24 PM "@squirtlong: @realDonaldTrump @foxandfriends Trumps the Man of 2016!"
- Aug 2, 2015 10:34:47 PM "@AliasHere: RT @realDonaldTrump: I will be interviewed on @foxandfriends tomorrow morning at 7:00. Enjoy!"
- Aug 2, 2015 10:36:17 PM "@WreckThisPro: @realDonaldTrump @foxandfriends I'll be watching it. Can't wait until you become our president Trump."
- Aug 2, 2015 10:37:55 PM "@adair_ariel: @realDonaldTrump @foxandfriends looking forward to it!"
- Aug 2, 2015 10:38:03 PM "@TeamFalowwBack: @realDonaldTrump @foxandfriends - #Trump2016"
- Aug 2, 2015 10:45:42 PM "@bdean1468: @realDonaldTrump @CoachZachCooper AMERICA WANTS TRUMP"

- Aug 2, 2015 10:46:49 PM "@VickyBrush: @MANX38 @JEDTHEFISH7 Only those who aren't brain-dead. Time to take back our country & Mr. Trump is the ONLY man who can."
- Aug 2, 2015 10:49:44 PM "@BigBrett45: @realDonaldTrump @foxandfriends TRUMP 2016!! PERIOD....."

- Aug 3, 2015 03:10:17 AM "@FoxNews: .@ericbolling: "Polls show [@realDonaldTrump would] be the GOP nominee if the vote was held today." http://t.co/OOtx0Rqwjs"
- Aug 3, 2015 03:14:28 AM "@BDubLasVegas: @realDonaldTrump @foxandfriends Thats early here in Vegas, but I set my DVR!!! #MakeAmericaGreatAgain"
- Aug 3, 2015 03:19:52 AM "@tudybone4: @realDonaldTrump @foxandfriends got up extra early to watch Mr. Trump's interview #Trump2016 #MakeAmericaGreatAgain" Great.
- Aug 3, 2015 03:20:51 AM "@jesuspacheco58: @realDonaldTrump I've been supporting you since I was 12 can I get a fav or something #Trump2016"
- Aug 3, 2015 03:21:18 AM "@MalachiNorris: @realDonaldTrump will win every state in 2016. http://t.co/GTQtZ7yWTb"
- Aug 3, 2015 03:23:19 AM "@bdean1468: @realDonaldTrump @BDubLasVegas @foxandfriends WE LOVE U TRUMP"
- Aug 3, 2015 04:47:16 AM "@MalachiNo: How will anybody beat Isis besides Trump. They have never made a deal with another country, Trump beats everyone all the time."
- Aug 3, 2015 04:48:22 AM "@PizzaPartyBen: @realDonaldTrump huge supporter out here in Alaska! Let's make this country great again!"
- Aug 3, 2015 04:58:59 AM Bush is pretending that the "Trump surge" is great for him and the @nytimesworld is reporting Bush "delight" - con job, a Bush nightmare!
- Aug 3, 2015 05:00:31 AM "@jordanallen21: @realDonaldTrump you'll be the first person I ever vote for. #Trump2016"
- Aug 3, 2015 08:19:56 AM "@lynn_weiser: @realDonaldTrump @DanScavino @EricTrump @ericbolling It's a trailblazing campaign A campaign that connects to people!"
- Aug 3, 2015 08:21:51 AM "@raleynicole143: I can't wait to be able to tell my kids I voted for @realDonaldTrump #MakeAmericaGreatAgain"

- Aug 3, 2015 10:11:37 AM "@AndrewMillerKC We have to vote for @realDonaldTrump ! Our nation can't afford another #Bush! #MakeAmericaGreatAgain"
- Aug 3, 2015 10:33:34 AM Wow, did the @nytimes fall into the Bush trap where his people convinced them how happy he was that I was hurting other candidates & not him
- Aug 3, 2015 10:33:44 AM Despite the false @nytimes story about Jeb Bush being happy with the Trump surge, he fell more than anybody & is miserable.
- Aug 3, 2015 10:41:57 AM .@DottieandBogey Thanks for nice comments over weekend re Turnberry. You and your husband have fantastic taste! Also, great commentary.
- Aug 3, 2015 10:42:43 AM .@Jrprotalker Thanks Judy for the wonderful statements on @TrumpTurnberry. Great seeing you there & you did a fabulous job on commentary.
- Aug 3, 2015 10:50:33 AM It came out that Huma Abedin knows all about Hillary's private illegal emails. Huma's PR husband, Anthony Weiner, will tell the world.
- Aug 3, 2015 01:17:15 PM New Poll Shows Donald Trump Blowing Everyone Else Out of the Water. http://t.co/sAVTGaswcl
- Aug 3, 2015 03:31:13 PM We cannot solve our problems with the same thinking we used when we created them. -- Albert Einstein
- Aug 3, 2015 03:57:43 PM "@ValetaSue57 @greta @FoxNews Like Trump more & more everyday, he is saying what we all need to hear & understand, He loves USA"
- Aug 3, 2015 03:59:13 PM My #GOPDebate @facebook question for the other candidates- http://t.co/3aSLoZYDLx
- Aug 3, 2015 07:44:29 PM Thank you @krauthammer for your nice comments on @oreillyfactor. A lot of progress is being made!
- Aug 3, 2015 08:14:12 PM "@Dan__Crocker: @foxandfriends Trump opens his mouth, his numbers go up. When Hillary does it, hers go down. Must be something to it."
- Aug 3, 2015 08:15:08 PM "@RoniSeale: @foxandfriends Trump is surging, leading,& breaking EVERY poll because #TrumpIsRight #GoTrump #MakeAmericaGreatAgain #Trump2016

- Aug 3, 2015 08:17:45 PM "@_trump4potus: Trump continues to rise in the polls! The American People are speaking and speaking loudly. #2016election #Trump2016"

- Aug 3, 2015 09:43:48 PM "@bedard_nancy: @realDonaldTrump TRUMP STANDS FOR TRUTH"
- Aug 4, 2015 06:28:15 AM Will be interviewed on @Morning_Joe at 7:3O. Enjoy!
- Aug 4, 2015 09:24:00 AM "@jimlibertarian @jerome_corsi @MichaelCohen212 we the people are making it quite clear Donald is the People's choice, we want truthfulness"
- Aug 4, 2015 09:35:39 AM "@Daaahawks @jimlibertarian @jerome_corsi @MichaelCohen212 That is why I like Mr. Trump he speaks the truth and stands by it."
- Aug 4, 2015 09:38:50 AM Diligence is the mother of good luck. -- Benjamin Franklin
- Aug 4, 2015 10:38:25 AM Thank you @gawker! Call me on my cellphone 917.756.8000 and listen to my campaign message.
- Aug 4, 2015 01:44:43 PM "92-year-old registers to vote for first time, says will vote for Trump" http://t.co/ckTmTsaIY2
- Aug 4, 2015 04:19:56 PM I will be on @oreillyfactor tonight on @FoxNews at 8 PM and 11 PM.
- Aug 4, 2015 06:14:41 PM "@sr_stocks: @WSJ @realDonaldTrump winner Trump. get use to it.Trump2016"
- Aug 4, 2015 06:15:48 PM "@jimlibertarian: @Dan__Crocker @foxandfriends Donald Trump is full of honesty and sincerity#on the other hand Hillary is a total liar"
- Aug 4, 2015 06:17:29 PM "@RoniSeale: @realDonaldTrump @foxandfriends #GoTrump #GOP #VoteTrump #MakeAmericaGreatAgain #Trump2016"
- Aug 4, 2015 06:18:46 PM "@ctmommy: @megynkelly #KellyFile #WTF? You do realize @realDonaldTrump isn't the #GOP enemy - @HillaryClinton is."
- Aug 4, 2015 06:19:38 PM "@TrumpsGucciGirl: @realDonaldTrump: oh yeah @megynkelly you don't want it to be all about Trump- he's # 1 not #17
- Aug 4, 2015 06:19:57 PM "@TSettles14: I'd be proud to say the first President I voted for was @realDonaldTrump #MakeAmericaGreatAgain"

- Aug 4, 2015 06:21:00 PM "@Kathlee08380944: @WSJ @hookjan Trump is the only cand talking about building a wall on the border That's getting great attention Go Trump
- Aug 4, 2015 06:22:19 PM "@BADfundraisers: @realDonaldTrump All Donald Trump knows how to do is win! Go Trump 2016!" I do love winning!
- Aug 4, 2015 08:12:05 PM "@Mike_Beacham: Trump Leads, Jeb Slips, Rubio Crashes In WSJ/NBC News Poll http://t.co/ZR3PvOAARe #StraightTalk @SenTedCruz #ccot #tcot #2A"

- Aug 5, 2015 07:56:57 AM "@DBottenhagen: @realDonaldTrump the United states needs Donald Trump, go Don"
- Aug 5, 2015 08:00:29 AM "@SeaBeeVietN: Go Donald...Nowhere in the Constitution does it say that our President must be a lawyer/politician. Our founders weren't."
- Aug 5, 2015 08:01:35 AM "@LaneLynmil: @realDonaldTrump I have been hoping for a bigger than life candidate and I believe I finally have one. Go Donald." Thanks.
- Aug 5, 2015 08:03:04 AM "@Keeganbcall: @realDonaldTrump I support you because I know you are person who gets things done right. This nation needs someone like that.
- Aug 5, 2015 08:03:49 AM "@cookingdoll: @realDonaldTrump Yet another illegal arrested for bludgeoning a woman. Stop the invasion.
- Aug 5, 2015 09:37:04 AM Many of Hillary's donors are the same donors as Jeb Bush's—all rich, will have total control—know them well.
- Aug 5, 2015 09:37:31 AM Do you notice that Hillary spews out Jeb's name as often as possible in order to give him status? She knows Trump is her worst nightmare.
- Aug 5, 2015 10:19:01 AM "@InsureRetire @realDonaldTrump @Gawker best response ever! Give Trump lemons and he will sell them back to you for a steep profit."
- Aug 5, 2015 10:23:26 AM Thanks. https://t.co/6G7hVhrtiY
- Aug 5, 2015 10:25:14 AM "@breadman28 @realDonaldTrump make America great again. We're running out of time!"
- Aug 5, 2015 10:27:57 AM Thank you. https://t.co/uA1LZ0EoAo

- Aug 5, 2015 10:29:38 AM "@ToTheTanr @realDonaldTrump You are the closest thing to Teddy Roosevelt. Tough as hell, and speaks his damn mind. And NEVER BS's"
- Aug 5, 2015 10:34:14 AM "@iuhoops2015 @realDonaldTrump it should be an honor and a privilege to be in this country. Not a right. Make America great again! "
- Aug 5, 2015 10:38:35 AM "@tweet2u2 #Trump only attacks those that attack him first. He's not going to be abused by a #politician @marthamaccallum #tcot"
- Aug 5, 2015 11:06:51 AM "@JoeDurak If Jeb is the nominee Hillary is our next president."
- Aug 5, 2015 04:05:42 PM Poll: Trump Leads GOP Field Among Hispanics, Records 34% Favorability http://t.co/AANybghvCv
- Aug 5, 2015 04:07:43 PM Wow! Such a wonderful article from fantastic people--my great honor! https://t.co/LO14es9CLp
- Aug 5, 2015 04:16:41 PM "AmyMek Amen! @realDonaldTrump has drawn more attention to Veterans issues in 1 week than these politicians have in decades!"
- Aug 5, 2015 07:13:10 PM "@SemiNoland: @realDonaldTrump Hilary is trying to make Jeb the republican candidate b/c she is afraid of The Donald." True!
- Aug 5, 2015 07:15:21 PM "@real_one23: Sure they want Mr. Trump @realDonaldTrump out. He can't be bought. #notapuppet https://t.co/qz3ujpVUIv"
- Aug 5, 2015 07:16:57 PM "@FrankLuntz: Trump is leading with almost every major group of Republican primary voters. http://t.co/fwIZR6XhYP"
- Aug 5, 2015 07:17:44 PM "@Women4Trump: @realDonaldTrump @SemiNoland Yup. And Clinton's leaked meeting with The Donald because they are skeered of all his support."
- Aug 5, 2015 07:50:15 PM "@anotherTRUMPvot: The way DonaldTrump handled the release of his phone number compared to @LindseyGrahamSC tell you all you need to know.
- Aug 5, 2015 07:51:04 PM "@hbtc23: @realDonaldTrump backs down from nobody!! #MakeAmericaGreatAgain #Trump2016 @steveaustinBSR @WWE http://t.co/rD0ZYcHgmF"
- Aug 5, 2015 07:51:46 PM "@WillDangelo: Sunset reflects on @realDonaldTrump tower in Las Vegas. What a view! http://t.co/Zq2BAqqgl1"

- Aug 5, 2015 07:52:47 PM "@ChadSchiebler: I can't remember a candidate that I've been this excited about @realDonaldTrump don't let us down! We believe! #landslide"
- Aug 5, 2015 07:53:26 PM "@Women4Trump: @mauigirl56 @realDonaldTrump We shall see. All I know is The Donald is the only one who can #MakeAmericaGreatAgain!!!!!"
- Aug 5, 2015 07:54:28 PM "@suandres2013: My dad is a Korean and Vietnam vet. 51 years total with Govt. He's 81 and sharp as a tack. You got his vote. Go Donald"
- Aug 5, 2015 07:57:32 PM "@HowardJax50: @FrankLuntz NBC says Trump leads with HS grads or less...doesn't bother saying Trump leads with college grads, too"
- Aug 5, 2015 07:58:10 PM "@Shelia1965A: God Bless You Donald Trump. I am so glad you decided to run. The Democrats have run this Country into the ground."

- Aug 6, 2015 08:54:44 AM "@RKMCPHERSON2014: Tonights, The GOP aka @realDonaldTrump show. Projected to be the most watched GOP debate in history. Will u b watching??
- Aug 6, 2015 08:55:42 AM "@jessicarnewman: The only reason most viewers will be watching the #RepublicanDebate tonight... @realDonaldTrump http://t.co/XKdqVT82p5"
- Aug 6, 2015 09:12:44 AM "@lesleyclark "Anyone would be lying if they said they weren't tuning in to watch @realDonaldTrump," http://t.co/YR1YX5bLkw #FoxDebate"
- Aug 6, 2015 09:26:21 AM .@realbobmassi, who does a show called "Bob Massi Is The Property Man" on @FoxNews, really knows his stuff--a total pro!
- Aug 6, 2015 09:31:57 AM I look forward to tonight's "debate" -- but look far more forward to making America great again. It can happen!
- Aug 6, 2015 03:56:53 PM Just arrived for the #GOPdebate #MakeAmericaGreatAgain http://t.co/rQ8LZHgHyJ
- Aug 6, 2015 11:28:29 PM Wow! What a great honor from @DRUDGE_REPORT http://t.co/fokcASBVuN
- Aug 6, 2015 11:40:55 PM #MakeAmericaGreatAgain #GOPdebate http://t.co/SNrr9YZmou

- Aug 7, 2015 12:03:57 AM Thank you @TIME readers- a great honor! http://t.co/2KRx2TBETS
- Aug 7, 2015 12:12:03 AM "@FoxNews: @realDonaldTrump: "When you have $18-$19 trillion in debt, they need someone like me to straighten it out" http://t.co/hTUJ35ja0Q
- Aug 7, 2015 02:04:13 AM Wow! What a great honor from @DRUDGE_REPORT http://t.co/fokcASBVuN
- Aug 7, 2015 02:22:48 AM "@ept_rudyru: @DRUDGE_REPORT Excellent job! @realDonaldTrump You are real & everyone saw that 2nite! #MakeAmericaGreatAgain #SilentMajority
- Aug 7, 2015 02:23:31 AM "@RubenMMoreno: @realDonaldTrump The biggest loser in the debate was @megynkelly. You can't out trump Donald Trump. You will lose!
- Aug 7, 2015 02:24:12 AM "@timjcam: @megynkelly @FrankLuntz @realDonaldTrump Fox viewers give low marks to bimbo @MegynKelly will consider other programs!"
- Aug 7, 2015 02:28:40 AM .@FrankLuntz is a low class slob who came to my office looking for consulting work and I had zero interest. Now he picks anti-Trump panels!
- Aug 7, 2015 02:31:10 AM "@FrankLuntz: I'm getting a lot of @MegynKelly hatemail tonight. #GOPDebate" She is totally overrated and angry. She really bombed tonite
- Aug 7, 2015 02:37:32 AM .@FrankLuntz I won every poll of the debate tonight by massive margins @DRUDGE_REPORT & @TIME so where did you find that dumb panel.
- Aug 7, 2015 02:40:41 AM Wow, @megynkelly really bombed tonight. People are going wild on twitter! Funny to watch.
- Aug 7, 2015 02:45:18 AM .@FrankLuntz, your so-called "focus groups" are a total joke. Don't come to my office looking for business again. You are a clown!
- Aug 7, 2015 02:53:46 AM I really enjoyed the debate tonight even though the @FoxNews trio, especially @megynkelly, was not very good or professional!
- Aug 7, 2015 02:58:04 AM "@11phenomenon: Despite the hype, @realDonaldTrump wins the debate by a wide margin. http://t.co/2KRx2TBETS"
- Aug 7, 2015 02:58:13 AM "@Lking2fly: I gotta have @realDonaldTrump in the White House that'd be such a game changer"

- Aug 7, 2015 02:58:35 AM "@JetRanger69: @realDonaldTrump @FoxNews @megynkelly @BretBaier WAS A DISASTER ALSO."
- Aug 7, 2015 02:58:57 AM "@Resi_Diederich: @PlatinumRosie @realDonaldTrump @FoxNews @megynkelly is that all you've got??? Haha."
- Aug 7, 2015 02:59:59 AM "@Reid2962: @realDonaldTrump @FoxNews I expected better from @megynkelly, wondering what is her hidden agenda.
- Aug 7, 2015 03:02:50 AM "@Diplomtc_Immnty: @realDonaldTrump They tried to take you out & your poll numbers skyrocketed. Voters matter, not @FOXNews moderators.
- Aug 7, 2015 03:05:08 AM "@agcaddauan: @realDonaldTrump @DRUDGE_REPORT Megyn could have done a far better job*"
- Aug 7, 2015 03:06:16 AM "@BrianCraigShow: @realDonaldTrump your rocked & won BIG TIME!!!! Make America Great Again Mr. Trump"
- Aug 7, 2015 03:07:20 AM "@stinger_inc: @realDonaldTrump @megynkelly's behaviour at the #GOPDebate was astonishingly biased."
- Aug 7, 2015 03:09:01 AM "@Diplomt: @realDonaldTrump is in a greater position w/ 52% to 12% @Drudge_Report even after @MegynKelly & @BretBaier tried to take him out.
- Aug 7, 2015 03:10:53 AM "@Mannamalistic: I'm s lifelong liberal and have come to fucking love @realDonaldTrump. He speaks the truth!"
- Aug 7, 2015 03:11:16 AM "@678b4612a62641f: @realDonaldTrump @Reid2962 @FoxNews @megynkelly my vote remains for trump!"
- Aug 7, 2015 03:18:42 AM "@italy2320: @Reid2962 @FoxNews @megynkelly Tell me what I can do to help you. She really has made me want to never watch fox again"
- Aug 7, 2015 03:22:30 AM "@Sulli1963: @AnnCoulter final four-Trump, Cruz, Walker, Carson wild card Fiorina"
- Aug 7, 2015 03:59:57 AM "@Domenclature: TIME POLL: @RealDonaldTrump wins the first #Republicanpresidentialdebate by Wild Margin http://t.co/mzR62luvWq #Politics
- Aug 7, 2015 04:03:21 AM "@joshuapantoja: @megynkelly @FrankLuntz @realDonaldTrump you tried to attack Trump, he took it and smiled. Trump will be the next president
- Aug 7, 2015 04:04:36 AM "@Southern_Anon63: I am a stone cold down to the bone democrat. But I will be voting @realDonaldTrump on Election Day."

- Aug 7, 2015 04:05:29 AM "@StefanVersac: @megynkelly @ChrisStirewalt @ChrisChristie @realDonaldTrump Rosie O'Donnell was the best answer of that whole debate"
- Aug 7, 2015 04:07:16 AM "@CaptTimScrim: Dear @megynkelly , your attempted hatchet job on @realDonaldTrump was unbecoming & a total failure. @FoxNews
- Aug 7, 2015 04:15:53 AM @TIME poll: @realDonaldTrump winner of last night's debate by wide margin.. 45% v.12% @RealBenCarson, 10% @JohnKasich http://t.co/mzR62luvWq
- Aug 7, 2015 04:18:35 AM "@GotMade: @realDonaldTrump Great Job!!! Winning the debate last night will take over half the field out, @FoxNews was not fair to Trump"
- Aug 7, 2015 04:19:23 AM "@ElvisFever: @megynkelly @FoxNews Out to get you with baited questions. She was angry at you. Very hostile and unprofessional"
- Aug 7, 2015 08:47:05 AM "@TomNocera: @DanScavino @realDonaldTrump "TRUMP DOMINANT" screams headline in today's Tampa Bay Times. #Trump2016" http://t.co/A08sQFzBLR
- Aug 7, 2015 03:31:24 PM via Bloomberg: Fox News Couldn't Kill Trump's Momentum, Made Him Stronger @FoxNews @business http://t.co/rWPZTeoc6j
- Aug 7, 2015 03:35:08 PM .@FoxNews you should be ashamed of yourself. I got you the highest debate ratings in your history & you say nothing but bad...
- Aug 7, 2015 03:35:32 PM ....Dopey @krauthammer should be fired. @FoxNews
- Aug 7, 2015 03:36:56 PM The hatred that clown @krauthammer has for me is unbelievable – causes him to lie when many others say Trump easily won debate.
- Aug 7, 2015 09:14:21 PM "@John832TheTruth: @FrankLuntz your focus groups are rigged and your company ran out of $ in 2011. KEEP SPEAKING THE TRUTH! TRUMP 2016!"
- Aug 7, 2015 10:22:05 PM "@katygolf: @Maxinerunner: Newsmax poll http://t.co/eA3gvLBri8 @realDonaldTrump: 65% @marklevinshow @RWSurferGirl" Another debate win!
- Aug 7, 2015 10:33:14 PM "@katygolf: @Maxinerunner: Newsmax poll http://t.co/eA3gvLBri8 @realDonaldTrump: 65% @marklevinshow @RWSurferGirl" @krauthammer APOLOGIZE!

- Aug 7, 2015 10:46:43 PM "@DRUDGE_REPORT: ROBINSON: Establishment didn't get Trump fall they want.... http://t.co/VITAdGFAja" Thank you!

- Aug 8, 2015 07:29:09 AM So many "politically correct" fools in our country. We have to all get back to work and stop wasting time and energy on nonsense!
- Aug 8, 2015 07:46:18 AM Re Megyn Kelly quote: "you could see there was blood coming out of her eyes, blood coming out of her wherever" (NOSE). Just got on w/thought
- Aug 8, 2015 08:26:28 AM .@redstate I miss you all, and thanks for all of your support. Political correctness is killing our country. "weakness."
- Aug 8, 2015 02:38:59 PM Wow, CNN just said that Donald Trump won the DEBATE, connected best with audience. Also, Time, Drudge, Newsmax, N.Y.Times and more!
- Aug 8, 2015 03:40:17 PM Almost universal support that "Trump won the debate." Only @FoxNews is consistantly fighting the Trump win, and I got them the ratings!
- Aug 8, 2015 10:45:40 PM Small crowds at @RedState today in Atlanta. People were very angry at EWErickson, a major sleaze and buffoon who has saved me time and money

- Aug 9, 2015 02:48:50 AM "@sacquisto23: .@realDonaldTrump you are the best candidate this great country has seen in decades. #MakeAmericaGreatAgain"
- Aug 9, 2015 03:05:10 AM "@george_frye: @realDonaldTrump Finally a candidate that speaks on behalf of the people and not on behalf of the government. Go Donald!"
- Aug 9, 2015 03:20:11 AM "@granitttg: @realDonaldTrump it'll be my first year voting and guess who got my vote #DonaldTrump"
- Aug 9, 2015 03:21:46 AM "@CommissarOfGG: You are being attacked from all sides, yet you have the people's hearts. Just be calm and trust yourself. We love you."
- Aug 9, 2015 03:26:24 AM "@OUTOF_3_9_0: •• You got the the largest rating in HISTORY .. That should say all needed about you to @FoxNews! https://t.co/EQIvPHz7mQ"
- Aug 9, 2015 03:30:31 AM "@WWDBLane: @realDonaldTrump Nice try Jeb, my wife agrees with Trump over Megyn.

- Aug 9, 2015 03:32:31 AM "@jonnati77: @EWErickson : TWITTER...has allowed the silent majority to have a voice and we want TRUMP 2016!!! #MakeAmericaGreatAgain"
- Aug 9, 2015 03:37:39 AM "@strayamaaaate: DonaldTrump shaking things up in US elections. Jeb Bush is really weak. Carly Fiorina shud go back to HP
- Aug 9, 2015 02:06:21 PM I just realized that if you listen to Carly Fiorina for more than ten minutes straight, you develop a massive headache. She has zero chance!
- Aug 9, 2015 02:42:34 PM It amazes me that other networks seem to treat me so much better than @FoxNews. I brought them the biggest ratings in history, & I get zip!
- Aug 9, 2015 03:36:27 PM Wonderful Frank Gifford has just passed away at age 84. He was my friend and a truly great guy! Warmest condolences to family.
- Aug 9, 2015 07:41:06 PM "@Libsaredemfools: @realDonaldTrump: No one knows more about business and the economy than you. You are what's right for America!"

- Aug 10, 2015 04:20:55 AM I will be interviewed on @TODAY Show at 7:00 A.M. and on Morning Joe at 7:20.
- Aug 10, 2015 04:29:19 AM .@KathieLGifford, Melania and I send our deepest condolences. Frank was a special and amazing person. He will be missed by all!
- Aug 10, 2015 08:23:28 AM Oh really, check out innocent @megynkelly discussion on @HowardStern show 5 years ago--I am the innocent (pure) one!http://t.co/8Hg7f5Q2jE
- Aug 10, 2015 10:35:38 AM Roger Ailes just called. He is a great guy & assures me that "Trump" will be treated fairly on @FoxNews. His word is always good!
- Aug 10, 2015 11:40:15 AM Enough is Enough- no more Bushes! https://t.co/0k0Y0pgbhC
- Aug 10, 2015 12:39:15 PM Frank was a great guy married to an absolutely wonderful woman @KathieLGifford. What a couple! http://t.co/2mZlN3UO94
- Aug 10, 2015 01:25:27 PM .@OMAROSA You were fantastic on television this weekend. Thank you so much – you are a loyal friend!
- Aug 10, 2015 03:09:27 PM .@BrandenRoderick I was pleased to see the wonderful statements you made about me to the media.I'm not surprised, you're a special person

- Aug 10, 2015 03:09:57 PM .@KatrinaCampins Thank you so much for the wonderful statements you made about me on TV. Also, keep up the great work!
- Aug 10, 2015 07:29:16 PM Again, illegal immigrant is charged with the fatal bludgeoning of a wonderful and loved 64 year old woman. Get them out and build a WALL!
- Aug 10, 2015 07:41:58 PM Truly weird Senator Rand Paul of Kentucky reminds me of a spoiled brat without a properly functioning brain. He was terrible at DEBATE!
- Aug 10, 2015 07:43:31 PM "@Roy_Propsner: @realDonaldTrump ...Don't give up, don't surrender your 3rd party OPTION"
- Aug 10, 2015 07:45:50 PM "@officialjtw: @realDonaldTrump You're iconic! You are going down in the history books! #trump2016" So nice, thank you.
- Aug 10, 2015 07:58:57 PM We must stop the crime and killing machine that is illegal immigration. Rampant problems will only get worse. Take back our country!
- Aug 10, 2015 08:03:56 PM Why is @RandPaul allowed to take advantage of the people of Kentucky by running for Senator and Pres. Why should Kentucky be back up plan?
- Aug 10, 2015 08:18:23 PM .@ericbolling you can do much better than you did tonight on @oreillyfactor. Better luck tomorrow!
- Aug 10, 2015 09:36:26 PM .@SenTedCruz had a very good debate, far better than Rand Paul.

- Aug 11, 2015 08:10:29 AM "@johncook4189: @realDonaldTrump @ericbolling @oreillyfactor http://t.co/KhmPz1WpFq"
- Aug 11, 2015 08:10:40 AM "@pokeyisme1971: @realDonaldTrump @ericbolling @oreillyfactor why are people scared of someone who wants to fix a broken system trump 2016"
- Aug 11, 2015 11:17:02 AM Our online store is officially open! Visit http://t.co/3zYiIYWs87 to shop the latest #MakeAmericaGreatAgain merchandise.
- Aug 11, 2015 12:29:32 PM Will be interviewed by @seanhannity tonight for the full hour. Hope you enjoy it and, more importantly, hope you agree!
- Aug 11, 2015 01:24:52 PM "@mikerotondo86 Only Trump can bring us back from 20 Trillion in debt... He's the only one with the experience and skill set to do so."

- Aug 11, 2015 02:17:15 PM The #IranDeal is a catastrophe that must be stopped. Will lead to at least partial world destruction & make Iran a force like never before.
- Aug 11, 2015 02:46:40 PM My official #MakeAmericaGreatAgain hat is now available online. To shop please visit http://t.co/3zYiIYWs87 --- it is selling fast!

- Aug 12, 2015 08:47:06 AM Our online campaign store is officially open! Visit http://t.co/3zYiIYWs87 to shop the latest #MakeAmericaGreatAgain merchandise.
- Aug 12, 2015 12:22:54 PM "@DavidHerjavec @realDonaldTrump completely right on China...just watch the news #GoTrump"

- Aug 13, 2015 09:58:50 AM Not under my watch- https://t.co/cju8E0Y0xJ
- Aug 13, 2015 12:48:12 PM Our campaign store is officially open! Visit http://t.co/3zYiIYWs87 to shop the latest #MakeAmericaGreatAgain merchandise.
- Aug 13, 2015 03:15:19 PM People don't understand that I left The Apprentice to run for Pres—the Apprentice DID NOT leave me. Bob Greenblatt & folks @NBC were GREAT!
- Aug 13, 2015 03:55:01 PM .@AP and @HuffingtonPost should change their fraudulent story to say THAT I DROPPED @NBC & The Apprentice to run for President!

- Aug 14, 2015 04:02:23 PM Making speech tonight in New Hampshire - leaving now. Fantastic people, fantastic crowd!

- Aug 15, 2015 08:17:12 AM In the plane heading to Iowa State Fair. Will be great fun. Hopefully giving helicopter rides to some of the kids.
- Aug 15, 2015 10:38:43 AM LIVE on #Periscope: Good morning Iowa! Let's #MakeAmericaGreatAgain #Trump2016 https://t.co/zSLKMCk0tW
- Aug 15, 2015 05:09:24 PM Just got back from the Iowa State Fair. Record crowds, phenomenal people. Thank you IOWA, I will never let you down!
- Aug 15, 2015 05:12:58 PM "@javonniandjeno: @realDonaldTrump @AP @nbc Donald Trump is Clint Eastwood, the perfect hero not scared of American terrorists. Vote Trump!"

- Aug 15, 2015 05:15:15 PM "@WriteReadRock: @thehill DonaldTrump is EVERYWHERE! At this moment he is the most famous person on Earth. And for a GOOD reason! #TRUMP2016

- Aug 17, 2015 09:37:28 AM .@NicolleDWallace Your father is a brilliant man with wonderful sense -- therefore, you must be good!
- Aug 17, 2015 09:45:16 AM I really enjoyed being at the Iowa State Fair. The crowds, love and enthusiasm is something I will never forget.
- Aug 17, 2015 10:28:10 AM The polls have been really amazing--we are all tired of incompetent politicians and bad deals! http://t.co/wZiNNsvZx2
- Aug 17, 2015 11:48:15 AM "@KNDetweiler: @hrkbenowen @thetimes @realDonaldTrump just released immigration plan is superior to everyone else's. Including Cruz.
- Aug 17, 2015 11:49:31 AM "@Techn9cian1923: @ChrisCuomo It felt Like a moment of silence when U said @realDonaldTrump DOESN'T PLAY! Powerful Interview #Trump2016"
- Aug 17, 2015 12:31:41 PM "@1776Pirate: @LindseyGrahamSC @WashTimes @madisongesiotto agreed. We need @realDonaldTrump as president ASAP."
- Aug 17, 2015 12:37:51 PM "@PrimMrs: @Rockprincess818 The best Immigration Policy yet! Time for @realDonaldTrump to #MakeAmericaGreatAgain"
- Aug 17, 2015 12:38:44 PM "@paulfincher2: I truly believe @realDonaldTrump is America's best choice to get our economy back on course & create needed jobs.
- Aug 17, 2015 12:40:53 PM "@BannermanJack: Rush is on fire today!He really does have his finger on the pulse. The @realDonaldTrump shamers can't win against El Rushbo
- Aug 17, 2015 01:05:16 PM "@NobamaDotCom: An FYI to all the DonaldTrump haters: We've won. Most admit TRUMP CAN WIN. And @GeorgeWill & @krauthammer - watch and learn
- Aug 17, 2015 01:08:22 PM "@RuizSeferino: @paulfincher2 Please have mercy on all Veterans. All we wished to do is serve a county who serves us not. Trump for Pres!"
- Aug 17, 2015 01:13:11 PM Why does @FoxNews keep George Will as a talking head? Wrong on so many subjects!

- Aug 17, 2015 01:13:15 PM Listening to @rushlimbaugh on way back to Jury Duty. Fantastic show, terrific guy!
- Aug 17, 2015 04:03:13 PM My official #MakeAmericaGreatAgain hat is now available online. To shop please visit http://t.co/3KWOl2ibaW --- it is selling fast!

- Aug 18, 2015 10:14:36 AM It does matter! htttps://t.co/SDfmHgneAf
- Aug 18, 2015 12:42:13 PM I want talented people to come into this country—to work hard and to become citizens. Silicon Valley needs engineers, etc.
- Aug 18, 2015 12:42:49 PM When foreigners attend our great colleges & want to stay in the U.S., they should not be thrown out of our country.
- Aug 18, 2015 02:26:02 PM Our online campaign store is open! Visit http://t.co/3zYiIYWs87 for #MakeAmericaGreatAgain merchandise including my signature hat!
- Aug 18, 2015 03:17:56 PM .@jasondhorowitz I am very proud of my sister, your story was terrific. Thank you so much.
- Aug 18, 2015 03:28:30 PM "@JohnBerman Two explanations on @realDonaldTrump that seem no longer sufficient: 1) It's early. 2) It is all a media creation."
- Aug 18, 2015 03:39:18 PM If I am elected President I will immediately approve the Keystone XL pipeline. No impact on environment & lots of jobs for U.S.
- Aug 18, 2015 03:52:54 PM "@ktumulty Polls indicate that a Trump presidency is now inevitable. #August"
- Aug 18, 2015 03:55:45 PM "@JoeWeissnmb @realDonaldTrump @MichaelCohen212 Walker & Bush want to be like Trump. My Mom88 "They sound like boys compared to Trump."
- Aug 18, 2015 04:00:12 PM "@aduanebrown New CNN/ORC poll: @realdonaldtrump #1 w/ 24% -- favorability rating on the rise while Jeb's declines. 60% among women!!"
- Aug 18, 2015 04:26:20 PM My H-1B reform plan will transform program so it delivers for country, not lobbyists, & will have bipartisan support: http://t.co/xDay480qfv
- Aug 18, 2015 09:18:46 PM I am looking forward to being in New Hampshire tomorrow. The silent majority is taking our country back. We will MAKE AMERICA GREAT AGAIN!

- Aug 18, 2015 10:03:20 PM "@Maxinerunner: @MarkSteynOnline loved you on #Hannity speaking truth @realDonaldTrump has awakened Patriots all over this Great Country.
- Aug 18, 2015 10:25:10 PM .@MarkSteynOnline - Thank you and great job on @seanhannity tonight!

- Aug 19, 2015 10:38:32 AM My official #MakeAmericaGreatAgain hat is now available online. To shop please visit http://t.co/3zYiIYWs87 -- it is selling fast!
- Aug 19, 2015 01:33:18 PM Will be in New Hampshire and then on @CNN Special at 9 PM tonight.
- Aug 19, 2015 08:48:21 PM Just got back from New Hampshire. Amazing people, we all had a great time together!
- Aug 19, 2015 08:53:26 PM "@WendyJFluga28: DonaldTrump is an emblem of HOPE that the best is yet to come for America! The good Trump name will be proudly displayed
- Aug 19, 2015 08:54:44 PM "@LKDUSA: @LKDUSA Now you need not wonder why we are attracted to a strong leader like @realDonaldTrump. The rest don't cut it. ALL WIMPS!!"
- Aug 19, 2015 09:23:31 PM Another great poll result! Thank you! http://t.co/loMirPFLIZ
- Aug 19, 2015 09:34:45 PM Thank you New Hampshire! Together we will Make America Great Again! http://t.co/ovxQMw4kob

- Aug 20, 2015 09:57:58 AM On the cover of @TIME Magazine—a great honor! http://t.co/zlEHp49oPs
- Aug 20, 2015 10:06:21 AM Had a special visitor in my office yesterday for @TIME photo shoot. http://t.co/GoloYLeRZz
- Aug 20, 2015 10:29:19 AM Behind the scenes video with "Uncle Sam" (eagle's name) and me. https://t.co/pOXbchdHbd
- Aug 20, 2015 11:04:52 PM @ABCPolitics must apologize. My statement "we're going to get them out so fast, so quick" applied to hard core criminals & gang members. LIE
- Aug 20, 2015 11:38:51 PM .@TomLlamasABC cannot report the news truthfully. Why not apologize for your fraudulent story on World News Tonight.Gang members & criminals

- Aug 20, 2015 11:48:30 PM "@MattyJack33: @TomLlamasABC So refreshing to have someone call out these left wingers posing as journalists. Keep it up Trump!"
- Aug 20, 2015 11:49:55 PM "@2ndVoter: @SteveHuang68 agree. One of the things that is good abt @realDonaldTrump is he's forcing others out of status quo politicking."
- Aug 20, 2015 11:57:55 PM We are going to make our country so strong again, so great again. No more ripping off the United States. We will MAKE AMERICA GREAT AGAIN!

- Aug 21, 2015 12:03:29 AM Alabama will shine tomorrow. It will be a big and glorious day!
- Aug 21, 2015 08:49:56 AM Jeb Bush signed memo saying not to use the term "anchor babies" offensive. Now he wants to use it because I use it. Stay true to yourself!
- Aug 21, 2015 08:56:00 AM How crazy - 7.5% of all births in U.S. are to illegal immigrants, over 300,000 babies per year. This must stop. Unaffordable and not right!
- Aug 21, 2015 09:32:43 AM We are going to have a wild time in Alabama tonight! Finally, the silent majority is back! http://t.co/Vj8vho1ro7
- Aug 21, 2015 10:25:01 AM Great! https://t.co/oJ6sqHB3MA
- Aug 21, 2015 10:35:18 AM "@AmyMek Every Time I see @realDonaldTrump address a crowd I want to start chanting USA, USA, USA! #AmericanPride is Back #Trump2016"
- Aug 21, 2015 11:35:21 AM Boston incident is terrible. We need energy and passion, but we must treat each other with respect. I would never condone violence.
- Aug 21, 2015 03:01:32 PM Leaving for Mobile, Alabama, right now - can't be late!
- Aug 21, 2015 03:06:26 PM Dow dives more than 500 points - down 9% from high. Be careful!
- Aug 21, 2015 08:28:30 PM #MakeAmericaGreatAgain #TrumpRallyAL http://t.co/UokCEy7e4N
- Aug 21, 2015 11:06:55 PM .@jessebwatters, You did a great job hosting @oreillyfactor. Everybody loved it! Thank you for the nice words.

- Aug 22, 2015 06:58:08 AM Alabama was great last night, amazing people. 30,000 folks was largest crowd of political season. Nice!
- Aug 22, 2015 02:38:58 PM "@crstin0516: @DanScavino @keraladubai @realDonaldTrump That chant gave me sweet, sweet chills!! #USA #America"
- Aug 22, 2015 02:39:40 PM "@dojiedojie: @realDonaldTrump Keep talking Donald....The people want to hear it loud and clear!!!!!"
- Aug 22, 2015 02:44:38 PM .@politico covers me more inaccurately than any other media source, and that is saying something. They go out of their way to distort truth!
- Aug 22, 2015 03:13:21 PM I had 15,000 people in Phoenix but @politico said "the rooms capacity is just over 2000." But said Bernie Sanders had 11,000 in same room.
- Aug 22, 2015 03:18:59 PM Thank you to the @washingtonpost for the accurate and very discriptive story on my speech in Alabama last night. It was a great evening!
- Aug 22, 2015 03:23:47 PM How is Bernie Sanders going to defend our country if he can't even defend his own microphone? Very sad!
- Aug 22, 2015 03:28:50 PM It has just been confirmed by the City of Mobile, Alabama, that there were 30,000 people at last nights event, making it #1for pol season.
- Aug 22, 2015 04:22:03 PM Now that I started my war on illegal immigration and securing the border, most other candidates are finally speaking up. Just politicians!
- Aug 22, 2015 05:19:05 PM Jeb Bush is weak on illegal immigration, in favor of common core, bad on women's health issues and thinks the Iraq war was a good thing.
- Aug 22, 2015 05:27:37 PM Jeb Bush has a photoshopped photo for an ad which gives him a black left hand and much different looking body. Jeb just can't get it right!

- Aug 23, 2015 05:39:52 AM The last thing we need is another Bush in the White House. Would be the same old thing (remember "read my lips, no more taxes"). GREATNESS!

- Aug 23, 2015 06:01:19 AM New Reuters Poll just came out and has me at 32%, highest number yet.The silent majority is back and we will MAKE AMERICA GREAT AGAIN!

- Aug 24, 2015 08:30:48 AM As I have long stated, we are so tied in with China and Asia that their markets are now taking the U.S. market down. Get smart U.S.A.
- Aug 24, 2015 08:38:59 AM "@john_franco: When people start losing their savings & home value, they will be begging Trump to fix the economy #MakeAmericaGreatAgain"
- Aug 24, 2015 08:43:13 AM Markets are crashing - all caused by poor planning and allowing China and Asia to dictate the agenda. This could get very messy! Vote Trump.
- Aug 24, 2015 08:44:39 AM "@ZephyrusMatrix: Will you finally get respect for predicting U.S. concerns even weeks before disaster strikes.The country needs a visionary
- Aug 24, 2015 08:45:31 AM "@glendabelle_11 @FoxNewsInsider @foxandfriends @realDonaldTrump Trump supporters- volunteer ,contribute, assist campaign etc .We need Trump
- Aug 24, 2015 08:46:06 AM "@sweetspottrader: only @realDonaldTrump can save us form this turmoil #Trump2016" Perhaps so!
- Aug 24, 2015 10:04:00 AM Depression- be careful of China! https://t.co/6BGk0ZjKwT
- Aug 24, 2015 12:17:49 PM Even Barbara Bush agrees with me- https://t.co/y3SSyF7xxX
- Aug 24, 2015 01:17:58 PM Thank you Greta. https://t.co/dty0C6K6fz
- Aug 24, 2015 01:29:32 PM Via Int'l Business Times: Jeb Bush Got $1.3M Job at Lehman After Florida Shifted Pension Cash To Bank. http://t.co/UbprPUWHQ9
- Aug 24, 2015 01:57:07 PM Via The Brody File: "The Lesson Evangelicals Can Learn From Donald Trump" Thank you David & CBN News--so nice. http://t.co/XSbTUXxs7K
- Aug 24, 2015 08:31:18 PM "@JeriHyatt: @megynkelly @JebBush @realDonaldTrump Pfffffftttt we need to do something about illegals who get more than our vets!!!!!"

- Aug 24, 2015 08:42:42 PM .@megynkelly must have had a terrible vacation, she is really off her game. Was afraid to confront Dr. Cornel West. No clue on immigration!
- Aug 24, 2015 08:50:30 PM I liked The Kelly File much better without @megynkelly. Perhaps she could take another eleven day unscheduled vacation!
- Aug 24, 2015 08:55:15 PM "@ColeHudson68: @megynkelly @FoxNews @theBlaze @greta @OreillyFactor Megyn needs to go back on vacation. What a waste of an hour on Fox."
- Aug 24, 2015 08:56:01 PM "@bigpaulfla: @realDonaldTrump She has come back looking like Nancy Grace"
- Aug 24, 2015 08:57:53 PM "@swamp_bug: @seanhannity Cruz is my second/third choice. Carson is also a good man. I look at it as war, so my choice is TRUMP."
- Aug 24, 2015 08:59:24 PM "@MikeRaj7: @megynkelly Show has become a opinion show. Leading questions, Stirrwalt and Thiessen, used, Fair and balanced, NOT"
- Aug 24, 2015 09:02:46 PM "@mstanish53: @realDonaldTrump @megynkelly The bimbo back in town . I hope not for long ."
- Aug 24, 2015 09:05:07 PM "@YankeesJC1: DonaldTrump Thanks for the picture! You were Awesome in Alabama! "Roll Trump Roll #TrumpInAL #Trump2016 http://t.co/GUDBOAzp06
- Aug 24, 2015 09:07:02 PM "@toneantone96: @realDonaldTrump No man or women on this Planet can give us back America with the exception of @realDonaldTrump Leadership!
- Aug 24, 2015 09:08:33 PM "@jdwarren12: @realDonaldTrump Mr Trump I appreciate you and your honesty sir" Thank you.
- Aug 24, 2015 09:09:30 PM "@AdriannaMarie: @realDonaldTrump People always take cheap shots at you,they can't handle the truth.You tell it like it is.They're cowards.
- Aug 24, 2015 09:10:41 PM "@TheBrianMo: The Lesson Evangelicals Can Learn From @RealDonaldTrump http://t.co/e40rUzfTUE #DonaldTrumpForPresident"
- Aug 24, 2015 09:11:02 PM "@Barbavh: @realDonaldTrump @megynkelly Ordered my Trump banner today. Can't wait!"

- Aug 24, 2015 09:14:54 PM "@YoungYoung54: @JeriHyatt @megynkelly @JebBush So true. Jeb Bush is crazy, who cares that he speaks Mexican, this is America, English !!"
- Aug 24, 2015 09:15:44 PM "@PatrickStinard: @megynkelly Kelly File was much better without Megyn Kelly. Her replacement while she was out on vacation was much better!
- Aug 24, 2015 09:57:09 PM Jeb Bush never uses his last name on advertising, signage, materials etc. Is he ashamed of the name BUSH? A pretty sad situation. Go Jeb!

- Aug 25, 2015 05:49:06 AM In a clumsy move to get out of his "anchor babies" dilemma, where he signed that he would not use the term and now uses it, he blamed ASIANS
- Aug 25, 2015 05:52:28 AM Asians are very offended that JEB said that anchor babies applies to them as a way to be more politically correct to hispanics. A mess!
- Aug 25, 2015 07:39:01 AM Jeb Bush just talked about my border proposal to build a "fence." It's not a fence, Jeb, it's a WALL, and there's a BIG difference!
- Aug 25, 2015 07:49:42 AM .@GovernorPataki did a terrible job as Governor of New York. If he ran again, he would have lost in a landslide. He and Graham ZERO in polls
- Aug 25, 2015 07:53:57 AM "@ibemoshing: No hope for Jeb Bush anymore, @realDonaldTrump has been on fire! Really hope he can get the win and fix this country!
- Aug 25, 2015 07:54:31 AM "@Dlund22226523: Gov. Scott Walker has ran Wisconsin's economy into the ground. How dare he criticize you. You would fire him in a second."
- Aug 25, 2015 07:56:54 AM "@RageFelix: @GovernorPataki ... I LIVED IN NY WHEN "TACKY PATAKI" WAS GOV... HE WAS A TOTAL DISASTER FOR THE PEOPLE OF NEW YORK
- Aug 25, 2015 07:58:14 AM "@ASA_Patriot: @realDonaldTrump @PatrickStinard @megynkelly I could not agree more ! I now flip to other channels at 9:00pm"
- Aug 25, 2015 07:59:14 AM "@linda_lcarson: @realDonaldTrump Rubio and Bush cant say Wall. I guess it is not pc. Just like obama cant say islamic terrorists !!

- Aug 25, 2015 08:49:59 AM Congrats @LindseyGrahamSC. You just got 4 points in your home state of SC—far better than zero nationally. You're only 26 pts behind me.
- Aug 25, 2015 08:52:29 AM Another good poll result in the great state of SC. Trump at 30%. Carson at 15% and Bush at 9%. http://t.co/FjQfdCrfdT
- Aug 25, 2015 09:53:03 AM Thanks. https://t.co/qVDlJToLqz
- Aug 25, 2015 09:56:57 AM "@beck_coulter @realDonaldTrump Trump is the ONLY person capable of fixing this corrupt, bankrupt, divided country! #MakeAmericaGreatAgain"
- Aug 25, 2015 10:15:47 AM "@CodyShirk @genemarks @Entrepreneur @realDonaldTrump Because he speaks & acts like a real person; not like a slimy, calculated politician."
- Aug 25, 2015 10:50:39 AM "@ladycatherinecd @realDonaldTrump he has more smarts than any one of the politicians - he TRUMPED again ! #Trump #tcot #Election2016"
- Aug 25, 2015 11:09:57 AM True, thanks. https://t.co/HDZt12Oaid
- Aug 25, 2015 02:01:19 PM Great American heroes who averted an attack in France. THANK YOU! Spencer Stone, Anthony Sadler, & Alex Skarlatos. http://t.co/5P0tX9Mq8u
- Aug 25, 2015 02:47:52 PM Thank you @BillKristol. I am going to Make America Great Again!
- Aug 25, 2015 03:07:35 PM Heading to Iowa to a packed house. Just released polls, all first place, are amazing. Thank you!
- Aug 25, 2015 11:34:51 PM Just got back from Iowa. Fantastic evening with truly fabulous people. Will be back again soon. Thanks!
- Aug 25, 2015 11:38:46 PM Will be interviewed on the @TODAYshow this morning at 7:00. Talking about politics, polls and whatever. Enjoy!

- Aug 26, 2015 11:03:04 AM Thank you Christian Broadcasting Network @TheBrodyFile @CBNNews http://t.co/FWPGgISlu8
- Aug 26, 2015 01:08:06 PM .@DennisDMZ Thanks for the nice words. You are fantastic!
- Aug 26, 2015 02:58:48 PM .@KatrinaCampins You were absolutely great on @CNN! Thank you.
- Aug 26, 2015 10:22:31 PM Great job on @CNN tonight @heytana. We are all proud of you! Also, congrats on a great son - he is going places.

- Aug 27, 2015 09:06:26 AM The press has very inaccurately covered this event - see for yourself! https://t.co/z00nIlB7NI
- Aug 27, 2015 09:24:04 AM .@BenFergusonShow just watched you on @CNN. Thank you for your nice comments.
- Aug 27, 2015 05:27:58 PM Who wants the endorsement of a guy (@EricCantor) who lost in perhaps the greatest upset in the history of Congress?
- Aug 27, 2015 07:18:39 PM Will be interviewed on @Morning_Joe at 7:00 A.M. So much to talk about!
- Aug 27, 2015 07:20:28 PM "@FoxNews: .@Rub: @jorgeramosnews should've disclosed his daughter works for HillaryClinton & Univision is being sued by @realDonaldTrump."
- Aug 27, 2015 07:23:42 PM "@irisodle: Love you man! I'm one of the silent majority that's so excited to finally have us a spokesman! Behind you all the way!"
- Aug 27, 2015 07:28:16 PM "@LandmanMarius: @realDonaldTrump Trump for President of the USA"
- Aug 27, 2015 07:37:51 PM "@PeteNice1976: @realDonaldTrump @irisodle #ToughTimes NEED A #ToughPRESIDENT #SilentMajority is back & #Trump will handle #IranDeal & #ISIS
- Aug 27, 2015 08:45:48 PM "@therealbigdt: @FoxNews @krauthammer @realDonaldTrump #Trump is the Real Deal, Baby." Thank you.
- Aug 27, 2015 08:51:13 PM Great job tonight on @FoxNews Tony. I am with you all the way! Make America Great Again @tperkins
- Aug 27, 2015 08:52:08 PM "@kathystone1221: @realDonaldTrump @therealbigdt @FoxNews @krauthammer #MakeAmericaGreatAgain #TeamTrump#usa....Trump 2016 !!!"
- Aug 27, 2015 08:52:56 PM "@jp_sitles: @realDonaldTrump HillaryClinton: she compared republicans to terrorist but will not call terrorists , terrorists. #OhMe"
- Aug 27, 2015 08:53:45 PM "@TheLongShotzz: @realDonaldTrump @FoxNews @tperkins Trump wins"

- Aug 28, 2015 09:32:32 AM Via CNN: Trump now leads in odds to win GOP nomination http://t.co/6ExyTO6BpJ

- Aug 28, 2015 12:33:41 PM #MakeAmericaGreatAgain From my speech in South Carolina yesterday- http://t.co/pv8sIVxCzu
- Aug 28, 2015 12:39:14 PM A phony story that I am trying to buy a soccer team in Argentina is untrue. Never even heard of the team—no interest! http://t.co/YCQAQBarfj
- Aug 28, 2015 01:43:07 PM Thank you @AmSpec http://t.co/BpybnpXMc9
- Aug 28, 2015 04:50:23 PM "@NancyLLeonard: Love 'em or hate 'em @realDonaldTrump is changing the playing field, finally. Our country needed this wake-up call.
- Aug 28, 2015 04:58:16 PM "@TDarbyMitchell: I love you Donald Trump! I've never liked politics before u came on the scene but I finally feel like there's hope for USA
- Aug 28, 2015 05:59:26 PM Will be interviewed by @SarahPalinUSA tonight at 10:00 on OAN Network. Enjoy!

- Aug 29, 2015 07:11:47 AM "@joehos18: BOOM - Univision Reluctantly Reports Donald Trump Leading With Latino Republicans.... http://t.co/MmsebE0LPP via @thelastrefuge2
- Aug 29, 2015 07:40:29 AM Great rally last night in Massachusetts. 2000 people at a house - must be a record! Unbelievable spirit to MAKE AMERICA GREAT AGAIN.
- Aug 29, 2015 07:43:35 AM Leaving now for Tennessee. Big crowd!
- Aug 29, 2015 07:45:55 AM Wow, Jeb Bush just lost three of his top fundraisers - they quit!
- Aug 29, 2015 07:19:31 PM Via @BreitbartNews "TRUMP WINS NASHVILLE GRASSROOTS STRAW POLL WITH 52 PERCENT"- http://t.co/kmNU8IkI5Q
- Aug 29, 2015 10:30:08 PM "@teapartynews: Trump Wins Tea Party Group's 'Nashville Straw Poll' - Newsmax http://t.co/tGJEeapJga" GREAT, THANK YOU!
- Aug 29, 2015 10:34:04 PM "@Ricky_Vaughn99: Herschel Walker: Donald Trump is 'my frontrunner' for president http://t.co/242hWZ8C8k via @USATODAY"

- Aug 31, 2015 05:27:56 AM Loved being with my many friends in Tennessee. The crowd and enthusiasm was fantastic. I won the straw poll big!

- Aug 31, 2015 05:33:10 AM Leading in the Bloomberg Iowa poll. Also, my favorability numbers went up at a record, almost unheard of, clip. Thank you Iowa!
- Aug 31, 2015 06:04:21 AM "@nodramahea: @realDonaldTrump Gaining more supporters every day. People want change. Trump2016"
- Aug 31, 2015 06:52:44 AM Huma Abedin, the top aide to Hillary Clinton and the wife of perv sleazebag Anthony Wiener, was a major security risk as a collector of info
- Aug 31, 2015 10:05:50 AM For those that don't think a wall (fence) works, why don't they suggest taking down the fence around the White House? Foolish people!
- Aug 31, 2015 11:23:25 AM This is no "act of love" as Jeb Bush said… https://t.co/K4FKTKpaTI
- Aug 31, 2015 01:18:14 PM See, I told you so http://t.co/UOC8xu11z3
- Aug 31, 2015 02:54:47 PM Very proud of Trump Int'l Golf Links in Aberdeen, Scotland. Just got the five star award from @VisitScotNews https://t.co/VA4rHFO9Eh
- Aug 31, 2015 07:38:17 PM President Obama wants to change the name of Mt. McKinley to Denali after more than 100 years. Great insult to Ohio. I will change back!
- Aug 31, 2015 07:43:46 PM 150 Clinton E-mails still contain classified information. More sensitive when she was Sec.of State. This is a very big deal.
- Aug 31, 2015 09:05:32 PM Just out - new PPP NATIONAL POLL has me in first place by a wide margin at 29%. I wonder why only @FoxNews has not reported this? Too bad!

September, 2015

- Sep 1, 2015 03:57:20 AM "@socalmike_SD: #Trump2016 @realdonaldtrump unofficial fight song http://t.co/Qt9rEY4qoM via @youtube" Such hard work and imagination-thanks
- Sep 1, 2015 04:25:20 AM "@highwayhopper66: @ConnieMackIV @00patriot My wife and I are both voting for trump in florida over our previous governor PERIOD!" Thank you
- Sep 1, 2015 04:39:38 AM The just released Public Policy Polling (PPP - national result) is the best yet. MAKE AMERICA GREAT AGAIN!
- Sep 1, 2015 04:40:53 AM "@BelAirCA: Only Trump is capable of cleaning up the mess America is in, that's why he has my vote! #MakeAmericaGreatAgain #Trump So true!
- Sep 1, 2015 10:56:32 AM Yet another weak hit by a candidate with a failing campaign. Will Jeb sink as low in the polls as the others who have gone after me?
- Sep 1, 2015 10:56:44 AM Jeb is spending millions of dollars on "hit" ads funded by lobbyists & special interests. Bad system.

- Sep 1, 2015 10:57:20 AM While millions are being spent against me in attack ads, they are paid for by the "bosses" and "owners" of candidates. I am self funding.
- Sep 1, 2015 01:41:08 PM Congrats everyone--we topped 4 million today on Twitter--and heading up fast!
- Sep 1, 2015 02:26:30 PM No more Clintons or Bushes! https://t.co/bHz4Etnhw7
- Sep 1, 2015 03:05:31 PM Many Super Pacs, funded by groups that want total control over their candidate, are being formed to "attack" Trump. Remember when u see them
- Sep 1, 2015 03:07:25 PM I'm turning down millions of dollars of campaign contributions—feel totally stupid doing so, but hope it is appreciated by the voters.
- Sep 1, 2015 07:49:55 PM Why does @oreillyfactor and @FoxNews always have Karl Rove on. He spent $430 million and lost ALL races. A dope who said Romney won election
- Sep 1, 2015 08:35:02 PM Every Poll has me winning BIG.If you listen to dopey Karl Rove, a Trump hater, on @oreillyfactor, you would think I'm doing poorly. @FoxNews
- Sep 1, 2015 08:39:22 PM "@RoniSeale: BIG LEADS FOR THE PEOPLE'S POTUS #2016GOPNOMINATION #TRUMP2016 #MAKEAMERICAGREATAGAI http://t.co/it7papSmwv" Great!
- Sep 1, 2015 08:46:58 PM "@TheKrankyGirl: @realDonaldTrump Keep the momentum going! #Trump2016 #MakeAmericaGreatAgain"
- Sep 1, 2015 09:05:52 PM The president of the pathetic Club For Growth came to my office in N.Y.C. and asked for a ridiculous $1,000,000 contribution. I said no way!
- Sep 1, 2015 09:15:06 PM When I intelligently turned down The Club For Growth crazy request for $1,000,000, they got nasty.What a waste of money that would have been

- Sep 2, 2015 05:12:06 AM "@Patrick0215: @Thatsalrighty @oreillyfactor @FoxNews @KarlRove Rove is suffering from @JebBush defeatism. #MakeAmericaGreatAgain"
- Sep 2, 2015 05:13:57 AM "@gulfportedd: @realDonaldTrump Jeb bush couldn't shine MR trumps shoes...give me a break. Bushes are so over..."

- Sep 2, 2015 05:15:21 AM "@LBabcock2: @oreillyfactor @FoxNews I have always wondered why Fox kept Rove on after his disastrous election predictions." He is a joke!
- Sep 2, 2015 05:16:30 AM "@sparkey03: @realDonaldTrump Go #Trump2016"
- Sep 2, 2015 05:17:39 AM "@ywu510: #TrumpOnCNN revealed character and spirit. Even as @donlemon changed subjects abruptly, @realDonaldTrump spoke from heart.
- Sep 2, 2015 05:24:39 AM Will be interviewed on @GMA this morning at 7:00. Thanks for the GREAT poll results!
- Sep 2, 2015 05:35:06 AM "@DRUDGE_REPORT: MEGYN KELLY TOP OF CABLE NEWS... http://t.co/ExfY7Q6C73" Megyn, say "thank you Donald!" @FoxNews also should say "thanks!"
- Sep 2, 2015 01:17:38 PM A terrible deal with Iran! https://t.co/dHDFOG3tfp
- Sep 2, 2015 02:20:21 PM .@kevinolearytv Great job on @foxandfriends this morning. You tell it like it is! Also, thx for the nice mention. Your book sounds great!
- Sep 2, 2015 03:54:20 PM 2016 GOP Nomination Polls have me as #1 as seen on @SpecialReport with @BretBaier. http://t.co/iZZg1N8Mwu
- Sep 2, 2015 03:55:44 PM Tracking 149 polls from 29 pollsters nationwide/HuffPost Pollster #GOP http://t.co/slsvuxcEhF
- Sep 2, 2015 09:04:12 PM .@brithume, I am in first place by a lot in all polls, tied for first place with Ben Carson in one Iowa poll. I thought you knew this- thanks
- Sep 2, 2015 09:15:50 PM "@LettyNTX: Obama left our American hostages in Iran. #Trump2016 @realDonaldTrump" Sadly, so true!
- Sep 2, 2015 09:35:23 PM The deal with Iran will go down as one of the most incompetent ever made. The U.S. lost on virtually every point. We just don't win anymore!

- Sep 3, 2015 11:49:11 AM Congratulations to Tom Brady on yet another great victory- Tom is my friend and a total winner!
- Sep 3, 2015 01:06:58 PM LIVE on #Periscope: Watch major press conference live from @TrumpTowerNY now! #MakeAmericaGreatAgain https://t.co/wwdgQKEHD3

- Sep 3, 2015 02:15:57 PM The Pledge #MakeAmericaGreatAgain http://t.co/5OVWdxgLn9
- Sep 3, 2015 09:14:38 PM "@linnie13: @greta @realDonaldTrump @FoxNews I love Donald Trump. For ONCE I feel like someone out there running actually cares about us."
- Sep 3, 2015 09:14:59 PM "@LettyNTX: Obama left our American hostages in Iran. #Trump2016 @realDonaldTrump"
- Sep 3, 2015 09:15:13 PM "@bentomchik: @chucktodd: is there something to learn from @realDonaldTrump success? #Election2016"

- Sep 4, 2015 05:54:59 AM Will be on @Morning_Joe in 5 minutes - at 7:00. Enjoy!
- Sep 4, 2015 11:40:51 AM I'll be in Dallas at the American Airlines Center on Sept 14th at 6 PM. Will be great to be back in Texas. http://t.co/rC8JO7Fzqx
- Sep 4, 2015 11:50:05 AM Daily Caller: Trump Surpasses Field, Flirts With 40 Percent in Alabama Poll http://t.co/LzG5M8SmYC
- Sep 4, 2015 12:22:29 PM So nice, thank you Laura. https://t.co/F42OC3yFa9
- Sep 4, 2015 01:44:30 PM Terrific response to my previous tweet: "I'll be in Dallas at the American Airlines Center on Sept 14th at 6 PM." http://t.co/rC8JO7Fzqx …

- Sep 5, 2015 06:56:51 AM .@MeghanMcCain was terrible on @TheFive yesterday. Angry and obnoxious, she will never make it on T.V. @FoxNews can do so much better!
- Sep 5, 2015 07:05:31 AM The Dallas event in two weeks, at the American Airlines Center, is filling up fast. Get your tickets fast, before it is too late!
- Sep 5, 2015 07:14:11 AM Very low ratings radio host Hugh Hewitt asked me about Suleiman, Abu Bake al-Baghdad, Hassan Nasrallah and more - typical "gotcha" questions
- Sep 5, 2015 07:20:39 AM Why would a very low ratings radio talk show host like Hugh Hewitt be doing the next debate on @CNN. He is just a 3rd rate "gotcha" guy!
- Sep 5, 2015 07:28:21 AM Just announced that because of "Trump", advertising rates for debate on @CNN are going from $5000 to $200,000, a 4000% increase.PAY CHARITY?

- Sep 5, 2015 04:33:28 PM Saudi Arabia was "vehemently" against the Iran nuclear deal. Then today they embraced it. What happened? What did we give them to endorse?
- Sep 5, 2015 04:36:41 PM Hillary Clinton made a speech today using the biggest teleprompter I have ever seen. In fact, it wasn't even see through glass, it was black
- Sep 5, 2015 04:42:32 PM Hillary said such nasty things about me, read directly off her teleprompter...but there was no emotion, no truth. Just can't read speeches!
- Sep 5, 2015 04:46:47 PM Remember that I am self-funding my campaign. Hillary, Jeb and the rest are spending special interest and lobbyist money.100% CONTROLLED
- Sep 5, 2015 04:50:25 PM By self-funding my campaign, I am not controlled by my donors, special interests or lobbyists. I am only working for the people of the U.S.!
- Sep 5, 2015 04:54:41 PM The hedge fund guys (gals) have to pay higher taxes ASAP. They are paying practically nothing. We must reduce taxes for the middle class!

- Sep 6, 2015 06:23:44 AM If the presidential election were held today, according to this @surveyusa poll, Donald Trump would defeat any Dem: http://t.co/wmfHKnNSWm"
- Sep 6, 2015 06:28:48 AM "@PressTV: Poll: Trump beats Clinton head-to-head matchup http://t.co/ZRndXNN67K http://t.co/bkzQolegeo" Thank you!
- Sep 6, 2015 06:43:30 AM "@HardcoreRepub: @realDonaldTrump AMERICA will be working again. BUSINESSMAN > POLITICIAN. Private sector growth above all. #Trump2016"
- Sep 6, 2015 06:44:32 AM "@ryanamberwhite: Check it out, @realDonaldTrump, all the way from Wyoming! #MakeAmericaGreatAgain http://t.co/fevBToLwGV" Thank you.
- Sep 6, 2015 06:50:23 AM "@tropic20: @realDonaldTrump do you see what's in Tom Brady's Locker? http://t.co/KDybxqvCuf"
- Sep 6, 2015 03:11:43 PM The phony Club For Growth, which asked me in writing for $1,000,000 (I said no), is now wanting to do negative ads on me. Total hypocrites!
- Sep 6, 2015 03:24:00 PM Our country needs a president with great leadership skills and vision, not someone like Hillary or Barack, neither of which has a clue!

- Sep 6, 2015 03:28:01 PM The Dallas event on September 14 at 6:00 P.M. at the American Airlines Center looks like it will be a giant success. Tickets are going FAST!
- Sep 6, 2015 03:37:32 PM I will be in Washington D.C. on Wednesday,1 P.M.,in front of the Capitol, to protest the horrible and incompetent deal being made with Iran.
- Sep 6, 2015 07:11:53 PM "@SamSteel10: @shook_stephanie @slone as long as we can stay strong and give @realDonaldTrump our support. He's the leader."
- Sep 6, 2015 07:16:42 PM "@Michelleri: Trump Leads as Bush Crashes http://t.co/EnXVS8WaGi No #GOP establishment and/or pro-amnesty candidates #MakeAmericaGreatAgain"
- Sep 6, 2015 07:18:01 PM "@jasonusmc2017: @blayne_troy @realDonaldTrump: He was right when he called Obama the 5 for 1 president. 5 terrorist for one no good traitor
- Sep 6, 2015 07:28:21 PM .@club4growth should release the letter they sent me asking for $1,000,000. When I said no, they came out against me. A scam operation?
- Sep 6, 2015 07:35:00 PM "@cadigirl13: @realdonaldtrump You are our only hope ! Keep strong Mr.Trump" Thank you.
- Sep 6, 2015 07:36:42 PM "@SlwStdySqueeze: @realDonaldTrump is gonna do some great things! #MakeAmericaGreatAgain #Trump2016"
- Sep 6, 2015 07:40:53 PM "@DeanAllen12: @club4growth Club4Growth will do anything for a handout just like every other POLITICIAN running... Pay to Say organization"
- Sep 6, 2015 07:43:32 PM "@1ns1de_J9b: @realDonaldTrump @club4growth Borderline extortion scam. They would have used your $1M to extract "donations" from others"
- Sep 6, 2015 07:45:16 PM "@broewads: @realDonaldTrump @club4growth They are all just phony cronies. Keep up the Real Deal Mr. TRUMP YOU ARE THE MAN."
- Sep 6, 2015 07:46:26 PM "@Lo7us_: vote for Trump #Trump2016 @realDonaldTrump"
- Sep 6, 2015 07:47:06 PM "@jackson3pack: @realDonaldTrump @BOB_EWASHINGTON @club4growth Wow. So disengenuos in asking for a million dollars! Like its no big deal."

- Sep 6, 2015 07:47:51 PM "@SeanBolza: Sure hope you will do great things. You are giving us something to look forward to, and make America great again. Go Trump"
- Sep 6, 2015 07:49:00 PM "@TheUSDesigns: @seanhannity WOW! Here is letter that mafia organization of extortion, Club for Growth, sent http://t.co/23mmupZcLw"
- Sep 6, 2015 07:50:16 PM "@soz58: @realDonaldTrump @BOB_EWASHINGTON @club4growth it's good to show the public such things,a lot of nerve to ask for a million dollars
- Sep 6, 2015 07:50:55 PM "@jimlibertarian: @SlwStdySque Donald has already done many great things,he has woke America up and people are screaming Donald everywhere"
- Sep 6, 2015 07:52:14 PM "@rnull65: I am 72 year old female. You give me hope 1st time in years America can come back..stay the course we need you in 2016!"
- Sep 6, 2015 07:53:17 PM "@afievoli: @realDonaldTrump We need a strong leader to fix the mess our country in! Go Mr.Trump!!"
- Sep 6, 2015 07:54:30 PM "@kylesteckel: @club4growth @realDonaldTrump The letter is out, liars."
- Sep 6, 2015 09:46:32 PM "@MJosephSheppard: No other GOP candidate has potential to win Ohio & Pennsylvania-thus the presidency except "jobs" @realDonaldTrump.

- Sep 7, 2015 01:56:36 PM "@sunnykcollins: Jeb Bush, Family Ties and a Museum That Never Materialized http://t.co/RTANPzuwU2" Not good!
- Sep 7, 2015 02:04:56 PM Thank you @scottienhughes for your powerful words on @FoxNews. I am with the Evangelicals and Tea Party big time. We will all WIN together!
- Sep 7, 2015 02:07:41 PM "@MJosephSheppard: No other GOP candidate has potential to win Ohio & Pennsylvania-thus the presidency, except "jobs" pres @realDonaldTrump!
- Sep 7, 2015 02:09:44 PM "@saneplanet: @toddwmoore01 @realDonaldTrump I know. Gives in secret without even a writeoff. @greta spilled beans about 25k" Thank you!

- Sep 7, 2015 02:11:46 PM "@georgeokc: @realDonaldTrump @libertyladyusa For my mind, do whatever you think is right, you have nothing to prove, just save our nation."
- Sep 7, 2015 02:29:48 PM Remember, I'll see you in D.C. at the Capitol Building on Wednesday at 1:00 o'clock. Then Dallas on Sept.14 at 6:00 P.M. American Air Center
- Sep 7, 2015 02:35:32 PM Both Washington D.C. and DALLAS are turning out to be really big events. D.C. is protest of incompetent Iran deal and Dallas is big speech!
- Sep 7, 2015 03:25:19 PM Looking forward to being with @SenTedCruz at our big rally in D.C. on Wednesday (1:00 P.M. at the Capitol) to protest insane Iran nuke deal!

- Sep 8, 2015 10:22:51 AM Look forward to being in DC tomorrow—big crowd expected for our protest against the truly stupid nuclear deal we are making with Iran.
- Sep 8, 2015 10:24:48 AM Tomorrow in DC: 1 PM West Front Lawn of the Capitol. Not even believable that we would do this deal with Iran.
- Sep 8, 2015 10:49:11 AM Wow! Such nice words from Robert Redford on my running for President. Thank you, Robert. http://t.co/TpV3w18BW6
- Sep 8, 2015 12:43:32 PM Thank you @IngrahamAngle for your strength & wonderful words last night on @FoxNews, but @KarlRove is easy to beat!
- Sep 8, 2015 01:55:22 PM Wake up Jeb supporters! https://t.co/h51DpgM9JK
- Sep 8, 2015 02:41:18 PM I'm self funding my campaign but lobbyists & special interests for Jeb & others are starting to do big ads—desperate! Don't believe them.
- Sep 8, 2015 02:41:52 PM The lobbyists & special interests have just put out an ad for Jeb which hits me "just a little" but is very false!
- Sep 8, 2015 02:44:50 PM Jeb's policies in Florida helped lead to its almost total collapse. Right after he left he went to work for Lehman Brothers—wow!
- Sep 8, 2015 02:57:05 PM I'm on Bill @oreillyfactor tonight at 8 PM. It will be another lively interview about how to #MakeAmericaGreatAgain!
- Sep 8, 2015 04:20:40 PM A great honor to receive polling numbers like these. Record setting African American (25%) & Hispanic numbers (31%). http://t.co/p7d6RJeMTZ

- Sep 8, 2015 04:47:40 PM Will be on Bill O'Reilly @oreillyfactor tonight at 8 PM. Enjoy!
- Sep 8, 2015 06:27:47 PM Via @USATODAY- "Amateur hour with the Iran nuclear deal" http://t.co/vdLxPLPj7i
- Sep 8, 2015 10:17:18 PM "@Chris0u24: @realDonaldTrump I've just lost hope Mr Trump. Hope you put America back the way it was"
- Sep 8, 2015 10:17:35 PM "@christa_dorsett: @realDonaldTrump we want Trump! America needs him desperately!
- Sep 8, 2015 10:20:28 PM "@americanhowl: While @realDonaldTrump rallies #NoIranDeal tomorrow, @JebBush will call China to ask for donations http://t.co/dCoGJYF6fU"
- Sep 8, 2015 10:23:25 PM See you in D.C. tomorrow at 1:00 P.M. at the Capitol to protest the horribly negotiated deal with Iran. Really sad!

- Sep 9, 2015 09:32:14 AM A letter to @CNN President Jeff Zucker- http://t.co/HKUYv9tFRm
- Sep 9, 2015 12:33:24 PM I will be speaking at the #StopIranDeal rally shortly- watch live here- http://t.co/hSTaPf0QqO
- Sep 9, 2015 02:46:28 PM Man did JEB throw his brother under the bus last night on @colbertlateshow . Probably true, but not nice!
- Sep 9, 2015 07:29:20 PM I had a great day in D.C. even though the subject was an unpleasant one, the horrible Iran Nuke deal. Amazing crowd and enthusiasm!
- Sep 9, 2015 07:42:58 PM Wow, I am ahead of the field with Evangelicals (am so proud of this) and virtually every other group, and Ben Carson just took a swipe at me

- Sep 10, 2015 12:58:06 PM I'll be on @greta ON THE RECORD tonight at 7 PM
- Sep 10, 2015 03:15:19 PM "@Plruble58 @realDonaldTrump The numbers are amazing! #GoGoGo "
- Sep 10, 2015 04:11:06 PM Bobby Jindal did not make the debate stage and therefore I have never met him….
- Sep 10, 2015 04:11:26 PM .... I only respond to people that register more than 1% in the polls. I never thought he had a chance and I've been proven right.

- Sep 11, 2015 07:42:00 AM I will be on The Tonight Show with Jimmy Fallon tonight at 11:30. Should be fun! @jimmyfallon
- Sep 11, 2015 07:49:20 AM Very good news—the new Quinnipiac poll just came out—I am #1 in Iowa.
- Sep 11, 2015 07:49:53 AM Also, tomorrow night I will be going to Boone and Ames. Really look forward to seeing all of my friends in Iowa.
- Sep 11, 2015 08:12:09 AM Oh wow, lightweight Governor @BobbyJindal, who is registered at less than 1 percent in the polls, just mocked my hair. So original!
- Sep 11, 2015 10:19:03 AM Let's all take a moment to remember all of the heroes from a very tragic day that we cannot let happen again!
- Sep 11, 2015 10:31:05 AM Just purchased NBC's half of The Miss Universe Organization and settled all lawsuits against them. Now own 100% -- stay tuned!
- Sep 11, 2015 12:24:44 PM .@robertjeffress I greatly appreciate your kind words last night on @FoxNews. Have great love for the evangelicals -- great respect for you.
- Sep 11, 2015 02:01:58 PM Via The Hill "No Tickets Left for Trump's Dallas Rally" http://t.co/mc5bPDt6s8
- Sep 11, 2015 04:27:48 PM On @FallonTonight with @jimmyfallon at 11:30 PM. Enjoy!
- Sep 11, 2015 04:49:48 PM .@GovernorPerry is a terrific guy and I wish him well- I know he will have a great future!
- Sep 11, 2015 05:29:02 PM Amazing crowd outside @FallonTonight. Tune in tonight at 11:30. http://t.co/4dxoEV0wia
- Sep 11, 2015 05:58:27 PM The Tonight Show @nbc will be amazing - 11:30 P.M. ENJOY!
- Sep 11, 2015 10:57:47 PM Backstage with @jimmyfallon before opening skit- great fun! @fallontonight https://t.co/tOriFU4vr0
- Sep 11, 2015 11:37:43 PM "@GinHay: Trump's polls are going to skyrocket after appearance on @jimmyfallon tonight. The young people are going to love him!"
- Sep 11, 2015 11:37:57 PM "@jenilynn1001: @FallonTonight @realDonaldTrump #Trump2016 #MakeAmericaGreatAgain"

- Sep 12, 2015 05:50:33 AM "@DesignerDeb3: @realDonaldTrump is the only candidate against illegals. We will have America back - & jobs"

- Sep 12, 2015 05:54:43 AM "@Chrisofficer23: @realDonaldTrump @jenilynn1001 @FallonTonight loved the show....trump2016"
- Sep 12, 2015 05:55:30 AM "@debra0155: @realDonaldTrump @GinHay @jimmyfallon absolutely, he's just simply the best #realdonaldtrump"
- Sep 12, 2015 05:56:28 AM "@davist19: If I was 18 I'd vote for @realDonaldTrump" Thank you!
- Sep 12, 2015 05:57:03 AM "@unknown_resist: @realDonaldTrump @GinHay @jimmyfallon Trump will be our leader and we will be thankful!"
- Sep 12, 2015 05:57:29 AM "@lizaperri: @realDonaldTrump @GinHay @jimmyfallon You even made the show great again."
- Sep 12, 2015 05:58:47 AM "@KittenHoliday: At the neighborhood bar talking about @realDonaldTrump we need him" We will make America great again!
- Sep 12, 2015 05:59:37 AM "@5SOS_jrt1d: Mr. Trump, you weren't just HUGE on @FallonTonight - you were AWESOME. WISDOM and HUMOR ARE A POWERFUL COMBINATION!!!"
- Sep 12, 2015 06:01:19 AM "@iamapatsfan: What are your thoughts on your good friend Tom Brady's performance yesterday? He was fantastic, a total winner!
- Sep 12, 2015 06:02:18 AM "@pennybishop16: @realDonaldTrump @GinHay @jimmyfallon Great show! Trump you are Awesomeness! God Bless! #MakeAmericaGreatAgain
- Sep 12, 2015 06:02:47 AM "@JohnnnnyT: @realDonaldTrump blew it away on @FallonTonight. The ratings will be HUUUGE."
- Sep 12, 2015 06:06:22 AM "@TrumpDemocrats: Carson on @CNN now. He is worse than Jeb; like ambien for insomnia. We need energy in the White House. We need DonaldTrump
- Sep 12, 2015 06:07:38 AM "@HamishP95: @realDonaldTrump My Dad is thinking of voting for the first time ever for you. http://t.co/1u9qi8qUPc" Great.
- Sep 12, 2015 06:10:05 AM "@ravila30:Loved you on Jimmy lastnight & how you showed you like to have fun/are able to laugh at yourself! Do you ever sleep tho? Not much
- Sep 12, 2015 06:10:44 AM "@LukeDillon6: If @realDonaldTrump doesn't become the next president, then that just shows how dumb America really is. #trump" Nice, thanks!
- Sep 12, 2015 06:12:02 AM "@MlSSTHOT: @realDonaldTrump I want our president to be smart AND witty like you Mr Trump" Thanks.

- Sep 12, 2015 06:12:32 AM "@DanielleBoussel: "I fully believe in apologies but you have to be wrong"-@realDonaldTrump"
- Sep 12, 2015 06:13:40 AM "@Trump_in_2016: @realDonaldTrump does best imitation of himself - we got ourselves a winner ready to hang on for the long haul.
- Sep 12, 2015 06:15:09 AM "@ColinCavall: You were a great sport on the show and I have total confidence in you rebuilding this country and making America great again.
- Sep 12, 2015 06:17:50 AM "@joehos18: Trump 96% success rate in business, only 4 out of 100+ companies went south. Better than any other candidate. Better than all"
- Sep 12, 2015 06:19:28 AM "@MlSSTHOT: @realDonaldTrump: Ignore the losers and the haters, you are going to make this country great again"
- Sep 12, 2015 06:20:27 AM "@ArthurOHara: #Trump International Hotel & Golf Links. Luxury resort in #Doonbeg on Ireland's @wildatlanticway https://t.co/JYRWwMdSwG"
- Sep 12, 2015 06:21:10 AM "@BrandyDianeK2: @realDonaldTrump @davist19 That's awesome when younger people can see we need Trump!"
- Sep 12, 2015 06:25:58 AM Will be on @foxandfriends at 8:00. Enjoy!
- Sep 12, 2015 10:43:51 AM .@mercedesschlapp thank you so much for your kind words on television -- fantastic job and greatly appreciated!
- Sep 12, 2015 10:51:38 AM Trump's Campaign Hat Becomes an Ironic Summer Accessory - The New York Times. http://t.co/XLELUQfxof
- Sep 12, 2015 10:58:47 AM Donald Trump Sends @FallonTonight to Highest Friday Rating in 18 Months. @JimmyFallon, that is #HUGE! http://t.co/mRHdW7dOws
- Sep 12, 2015 02:55:54 PM Lightweight Senator @RandPaul should focus on trying to get elected in Kentucky--- a great state which is embarrassed by him.
- Sep 12, 2015 02:56:39 PM I truly understood the appeal of Ron Paul, but his son, @RandPaul, didn't get the right gene.
- Sep 12, 2015 03:01:55 PM Too many people on stage for debate. @RandPaul at 11th, with 2% in @RealClearNews, shouldn't be allowed to participate.
- Sep 12, 2015 03:51:32 PM I am having a great time in Iowa at Jack Trice Stadium! Unbelievable people.
- Sep 12, 2015 03:53:34 PM Had a record crowd in Boone, Iowa. A fantastic day--- we will #MakeAmericaGreatAgain https://t.co/octCvAYQOO

- Sep 12, 2015 06:13:01 PM "@BigBrotherKat: I hated to love it, but @realDonaldTrump was hilarious on @jimmyfallon last night! @nbc #thedonald"
- Sep 12, 2015 06:15:15 PM "@Edward1:Trump Knows how to get things done. He has guts to say what needs to be said. He'll deal with Putin more effectively than anyone."
- Sep 12, 2015 06:16:26 PM "@joeearle: @Pistol044 There's only one I'll never support: @realDonaldTrump
- Sep 12, 2015 06:17:31 PM "@DaveInKeno: Mr. Trump, Sir, this country is, and has been, on a path of self destruction and needs you to MAKE AMERICA GREAT AGAIN!"
- Sep 12, 2015 06:19:04 PM "@jeffraykovich: @realDonaldTrump Are you going to come to Wisconsin in the near future?#Trump2016 #MakeAmericaGreatAgain" Yes.
- Sep 12, 2015 06:21:01 PM "@whyWinblo: @realDonaldTrump please make this country great again & help secure our borders Mr. Trump, you're our last hope. #Trump2016"
- Sep 12, 2015 06:23:28 PM "@Mey: I don't know how any American can watch this video and not want to vote for @realDonaldTrump #TeamTrump https://t.co/387cDb55nH"
- Sep 12, 2015 06:24:32 PM "@Hashtag1USA: @realDonaldTrump Trump rocked Iowa today heard his message was positive and built much enthusiasm among the voters #Trump2016

- Sep 13, 2015 08:41:32 AM Why is someone like George Pataki, who did a terrible job as Governor of N.Y. and registers ZERO in the polls, allowed on the debate stage?

- Sep 14, 2015 10:20:03 AM "@Doctr__Wang @CNN Nice! I love how Trump has a way of putting people on the spot. I wonder what CNN will do. The Veterans appreciate it!"
- Sep 14, 2015 10:25:30 AM My honor, thank you. https://t.co/0wKLnSIss6
- Sep 14, 2015 11:39:14 AM Congrats to my friend @Schwarzenegger who is doing next season's Celebrity Apprentice. He'll be great & will raise lots of $ for charity.
- Sep 14, 2015 11:39:55 AM To all my fans, sorry I couldn't do The Apprentice any longer—but equal time (presidential run) prohibits me from doing so. Love!

- Sep 14, 2015 11:52:40 AM Thanks Mark, will be fun. https://t.co/hzlkPLebET
- Sep 14, 2015 01:23:39 PM My opponents big bosses--lobbyists and donors--are trying to do damage. They will fail! Money down the drain!
- Sep 14, 2015 02:46:27 PM Looking forward to joining @V4SA Tuesday 9/15 in L.A. aboard the @USSIowa - The Battleship of Presidents! Join us! http://t.co/oiPQsJt7fh
- Sep 14, 2015 02:47:46 PM The event with me and @V4SA in L.A on 9/15 is turning out to be huge. Get your tickets before they're gone http://t.co/oiPQsJt7fh
- Sep 14, 2015 03:36:00 PM Vets mistreated, NO border security? I'm with @V4SA this Tuesday 9/15 to #MakeAmericasMilitaryGreatAgain! Join us! http://t.co/oiPQsJt7fh
- Sep 14, 2015 09:03:30 PM Unbelievable crowd in Dallas! https://t.co/9HNgVyBJEz
- Sep 14, 2015 11:56:50 PM Speech in Dallas went really well. Big and wonderful crowd. Just arrived in L.A. Big day tomorrow!

- Sep 15, 2015 07:50:23 AM I will rebuild the military, take care of vets and make the world respect the US again! Join me today. Info: http://t.co/oiPQsJt7fh
- Sep 15, 2015 09:31:58 AM Loved Dallas and the tremendous crowd last night. Will be back!
- Sep 15, 2015 09:39:52 AM Our vets are treated like 3rd class citizens. Enough! Join me & @V4SA on @USSIOWA at LA Waterfront to hear my plan for vets & the military!
- Sep 15, 2015 09:59:33 AM Am now in L.A. Will be going to the U.S.S. IOWA at 5:30 P.M. to speak to our great VETERANS and other friends!
- Sep 15, 2015 10:15:27 AM Little respected Club For Growth asked me for $1,000,000 - I said "NO". Now they are spending lobbyist and special interest money on ads!
- Sep 15, 2015 12:46:43 PM My plan will lower taxes for our country, not raise them. Phony @club4growth says I will raise taxes—just another lie.
- Sep 15, 2015 12:47:53 PM .@club4growth asked me for $1 million. I said no. Now falsely advertising that I will raise taxes. I'll lower big league for middle class.
- Sep 15, 2015 12:53:03 PM Everyone is talking about the incredible event we had in Dallas last night. Spectacular crowd & arena! Thank you @mcuban.

- Sep 15, 2015 01:00:34 PM The polls are really looking good—#1 everywhere despite all lobbyist & special interest $ being spent against me. I'm turning down millions.
- Sep 15, 2015 01:39:28 PM .@rushlimbaugh Rush, I am in LA inspecting property (big job creator) & listening to you. You are truly fantastic--thanks!
- Sep 15, 2015 09:39:02 PM Just finished the wonderful event on the U.S.S. Iowa. VETERANS FOR A STRONG AMERICA endorsed me. Such a great honor, thank you!
- Sep 15, 2015 10:18:05 PM I hope Arnold S. does well with the Apprentice because he is a nice guy and also, because I get a big percentage of the profits!
- Sep 15, 2015 11:41:25 PM "@97Musick: @AC360 @CNN The "sold to lobbyists" candidates are wasting their money. ON the BORDER and IMMIGRATION, Trump WILL win."
- Sep 15, 2015 11:42:10 PM "@almy23841665: @DISCORD @realDonaldTrump More Veterans will vote for Trump than you can believe! I can't imagine they wouldn't!
- Sep 15, 2015 11:45:42 PM "@chriscoxb2b: @realDonaldTrump - Donald...keep pushing...the nation needs a real leader."
- Sep 15, 2015 11:47:02 PM "@PMgeezer: Only 15 percent of @GOP voters said they would not back @realDonaldTrump as the party's standard-bearer. http://t.co/hqt7WXTepm"
- Sep 15, 2015 11:49:32 PM "@skulls2001: We are a Cuban family from Miami Florida and would love very much to work on your political campaing here in Miami." Great.

- Sep 16, 2015 01:16:39 AM "@onesoldiersmom: @seanhannity @MarkSteynOnline No one can imitate Trump. He's one of a kind. I love him more each day. #Trump2016" Thanks
- Sep 16, 2015 03:03:56 PM Will be heading over to the debate soon. Can you believe @CNN is "milking" it for almost 3 hours? Too long, too many people on stage!
- Sep 16, 2015 03:10:05 PM A great honor from somebody that knows how to win! https://t.co/syJII9OT0zX
- Sep 16, 2015 03:32:19 PM Thank you to Tom Brady, Coach Ditka, Coach Bobby Knight and all of the many champions that have been so supportive!

- Sep 16, 2015 10:47:06 PM #CNNDebate Winning the @drudge_report poll- http://t.co/fokcASBVuN
- Sep 16, 2015 10:54:15 PM The #CNNDebate was amazing --- so much fun! http://t.co/tj3Cnqp3PU
- Sep 16, 2015 11:04:24 PM #CNNDebate http://t.co/X4m9WfewX2
- Sep 16, 2015 11:10:37 PM #CNNDebate http://t.co/0r8fc2zzvY

- Sep 17, 2015 12:17:03 PM Just announced that in the history of @CNN, last night's debate was its highest rated ever. Will they send me flowers & a thank you note?
- Sep 17, 2015 12:18:22 PM Every poll done on debate last night, from Drudge to Newsmax to Time Magazine, had me winning in a landslide. #MakeAmericaGreatAgain!
- Sep 17, 2015 12:28:58 PM Going to New Hampshire in a little while. Big crowds! #MakeAmericaGreatAgain!
- Sep 17, 2015 02:33:12 PM Will be interviewed tonight by @seanhannity on @FoxNews at 10 PM. Enjoy!
- Sep 17, 2015 02:40:49 PM Would be really bad if columnist Mike Lupica left the @NYDailyNews. A wonderful and talented guy!

- Sep 18, 2015 12:56:06 PM Wow, great post-debate poll: "Trump Increases Lead" via Breitbart http://t.co/B3yJk2lJ8I
- Sep 18, 2015 02:08:48 PM GIVE AMERICA BACK ITS DREAM! -- Donald J. Trump
- Sep 18, 2015 02:15:37 PM Thank you. https://t.co/G4CLmowE4U
- Sep 18, 2015 04:06:39 PM I've just released my position papers on The Second Amendment. https://t.co/ssFXVGWTIP
- Sep 18, 2015 04:11:32 PM Looking forward to meeting the students of Urbandale High School tomorrow- http://t.co/Urj3Tic2e3

- Sep 19, 2015 07:45:57 AM Am I morally obligated to defend the president every time somebody says something bad or controversial about him? I don't think so!
- Sep 19, 2015 07:52:27 AM This is the first time in my life that I have caused controversy by NOT saying something.

- Sep 19, 2015 07:58:08 AM If someone made a nasty or controversial statement about me to the president, do you really think he would come to my rescue? No chance!
- Sep 19, 2015 08:19:25 AM If I would have challenged the man, the media would have accused me of interfering with that man's right of free speech. A no win situation!
- Sep 19, 2015 08:37:14 AM Christians need support in our country (and around the world), their religious liberty is at stake! Obama has been horrible, I will be great
- Sep 19, 2015 02:15:11 PM On my way to Iowa. Will be landing in Des Moines in two hours. See ya!
- Sep 19, 2015 02:31:24 PM #MakeAmericaGreatAgain #Trump2016 http://t.co/O5v9oX3pyd
- Sep 19, 2015 07:49:15 PM A great night in Iowa! https://t.co/vfCRhwTkTU
- Sep 19, 2015 08:52:36 PM Thank you Faith and Freedom Forum & @UrbandaleSchool. I had a great time in Iowa today! http://t.co/PeEEHTVtC8

- Sep 20, 2015 04:07:35 AM "@MoeHoward86: THE best interview thus far...keep it up Trump! Donald Trump: "Enough With the Nice!" https://t.co/3sOY0pTCNB via @YouTube"
- Sep 20, 2015 04:27:54 AM "@LeghanLiptak712: CNN tried to destroy Donald Trump with vaccine autism question, but he gave this AMAZING response http://t.co/nQttFpyzaC"
- Sep 20, 2015 08:17:28 AM I will be on @meetthepress at 10:30. @nbc will be releasing their new poll numbers. Based on the debate results, I should do well- who knows?
- Sep 20, 2015 07:30:07 PM There is no way that Carly Fiorina can become the Republican Nominee or win against the Dems. Boxer killed her for Senate in California!
- Sep 20, 2015 07:51:49 PM I have been leading big in all polls, with two more today, @nbc and @CNN. The NBC poll is more than double next, at 29%. Fiorina has 11%.
- Sep 20, 2015 07:56:52 PM I am attracting the biggest crowds, by far, and the best poll numbers, also by far. Much of the media is totally dishonest. So sad!
- Sep 20, 2015 07:59:16 PM We are going to WIN and MAKE AMERICA GREAT AGAIN, maybe better than ever before!

- Sep 20, 2015 08:34:00 PM Carly Fiorina did such a horrible job at Lucent and HP, virtually destroying both companies, that she never got another CEO job offer! Pres.
- Sep 20, 2015 10:22:58 PM "@SaijoSaijo75: @realDonaldTrump thank you for your personal and financial sacrifices to make america great again!"

- Sep 21, 2015 06:32:57 AM Will be on @foxandfriends now. Enjoy!
- Sep 21, 2015 07:28:14 AM The @TODAYshow refused to use their just in poll numbers where I have a massive lead but instead used @CNN numbers where my lead is smaller.
- Sep 21, 2015 07:29:46 AM "@MNTwisterChaser: Thanks @SavannahGuthrie and @NBCNews for showing us how lopsided you are! Use your own poll! #trainwreck #Trump2016
- Sep 21, 2015 07:30:38 AM "@PaulkDebra: @TODAYshow @realDonaldTrump I totally support you! You have this Ga. Girl's vote!!!"
- Sep 21, 2015 07:32:07 AM "@TheBrodyFile: On the Muslim issue: It might help @BarackObama if he didn't take five years to visit Israel"
- Sep 21, 2015 07:32:47 AM "@TheBrodyFile: On the Muslim issue: It might help @BarackObama if he actually supported Christians religious liberty rights.
- Sep 21, 2015 07:33:43 AM "@nunyabus1: @realdonaldtrump @foxandfriends you go trumpy, don't back down" I won't.
- Sep 21, 2015 07:36:15 AM "@JohnSte38475254: @realDonaldTrump @FoxNews ...Why is Fox being so hard on u? I don't get it...are they idiots?"
- Sep 21, 2015 07:37:45 AM "@Dis_labeledVet: @realDonaldTrump here is a Clinton insider who admitted Hillary started the whole Obama's a Muslim https://t.co/UqkW16u3Kz
- Sep 21, 2015 07:38:16 AM "@talsept58: @realDonaldTrump @foxandfriends You are great!!"
- Sep 21, 2015 07:38:36 AM "@mickelsenkyle: @TODAYshow could you make your interview with @realDonaldTrump any more biased or... #TrumpForPresident"
- Sep 21, 2015 07:39:23 AM "@linley4067_jane: @realDonaldTrump @foxandfriends Fox is using you for ratings. They want u out of the race. Refuse."

- Sep 21, 2015 07:39:46 AM "@alivelutheran: @TODAYshow touts CNN polls instead of their own!! Of course, the NBC one shows him much higher. Trump corrects them!
- Sep 21, 2015 08:59:31 AM New Zogby poll— highly respected— but the media won't report it because it gives me an even bigger lead! http://t.co/YAZyKwVxNJ
- Sep 21, 2015 09:03:44 AM #AskTrump Send me your questions to answer live from @TwitterNYC later this afternoon.
- Sep 21, 2015 09:56:10 AM Carly Fiorina is terrible at business--the last thing our country needs! http://t.co/n7lO0llhK8
- Sep 21, 2015 10:26:53 AM Jeb has been confused for forty years- https://t.co/MoqjlnwryJ
- Sep 21, 2015 11:14:08 AM Has the media picked up the new Zogby poll that was just put out? I doubt it! http://t.co/YAZyKwVxNJ
- Sep 21, 2015 12:07:15 PM #AskTrump Getting ready to answer your questions. http://t.co/MiSqyasjhu
- Sep 21, 2015 12:10:15 PM .@dixierhilton #asktrump http://t.co/dbK8jckT5s
- Sep 21, 2015 12:12:18 PM .@MarketMavensInc #asktrump http://t.co/6uShpC3BM2
- Sep 21, 2015 12:20:01 PM .@EliseChristine #asktrump http://t.co/KV1NPNYJTC
- Sep 21, 2015 12:21:37 PM .@KyleStephens30 #asktrump http://t.co/gjudtw87K7
- Sep 21, 2015 12:22:49 PM .@HighSock_Sunday #asktrump http://t.co/qVakUzXZAb
- Sep 21, 2015 12:23:49 PM .@ARealSuperMan #asktrump http://t.co/x2j6yiaBzU
- Sep 21, 2015 12:25:46 PM .@Modern_Do_Good #asktrump http://t.co/I7AaH7AVRw
- Sep 21, 2015 12:26:45 PM .@joycefinance #asktrump http://t.co/P8CwErG0lt
- Sep 21, 2015 12:28:22 PM .@MarieLeff #asktrump http://t.co/ufCLFKeFrN
- Sep 21, 2015 12:29:20 PM .@_Just_Mads_ #asktrump http://t.co/zElKKmMjTU
- Sep 21, 2015 12:36:23 PM I just wrapped up a Q&A @TwitterNYC. Thanks for all your questions! #AskTrump http://t.co/zpbcRHfxy6

- Sep 21, 2015 12:38:49 PM I had a great time at @TwitterNYC #AskTrump http://t.co/RfWQdDPB33
- Sep 21, 2015 12:39:52 PM #AskTrump @TwitterNYC http://t.co/hJHO1Rk06y
- Sep 21, 2015 01:22:21 PM "@JudgeMoroz Zogby is respected in the business of polling ~ the media is attempting to silence the message @realDonaldTrump"
- Sep 21, 2015 04:11:42 PM Thank you Dan--I agree! Best wishes. https://t.co/DAEomTNoMq
- Sep 21, 2015 04:39:57 PM I got to know @ScottWalker well—he's a very nice person and has a great future.
- Sep 21, 2015 04:40:58 PM I will be interviewed tonight at 7pm ET by @greta #OnTheRecord
- Sep 21, 2015 04:44:16 PM Via HuffPost Pollster #1 http://t.co/IXCbCtDUIp
- Sep 21, 2015 07:24:32 PM "@alivelutheran: @TODAYshow touts CNN polls instead of their own!! Of course, the NBC one shows him much higher. Trump corrects them!
- Sep 21, 2015 07:49:48 PM .@oreillyfactor was very negative to me in refusing to to post the great polls that came out today including NBC. @FoxNews not good for me!
- Sep 21, 2015 07:55:55 PM .@oreillyfactor, why don't you have some knowledgeable talking heads on your show for a change instead of the same old Trump haters. Boring!
- Sep 21, 2015 07:57:26 PM "@RagingCynicism: @realDonaldTrump @oreillyfactor they're not Trump haters. They're spoon fed morons."
- Sep 21, 2015 07:58:18 PM "@Patrick92299179: @realDonaldTrump @oreillyfactor Couldn't agree more!"
- Sep 21, 2015 07:59:44 PM "@bewhatjesuswas: @oreillyfactor @FoxNews You dominate not because of them-but despite them;They need you more than you need them"
- Sep 21, 2015 08:01:26 PM "@coolgirl6978: @oreillyfactor @FoxNews this is bull fox. O'Reilly, I expect better from you. What is going on? Fair and balanced my ass"
- Sep 21, 2015 08:01:44 PM "@tammyhorne19: @realDonaldTrump @oreillyfactor love you trump"
- Sep 21, 2015 08:04:26 PM "@blewthebigone: @realDonaldTrump Can't even think what the race would be without you in it."

- Sep 21, 2015 08:04:53 PM "@Rbbrkhd: @realDonaldTrump @oreillyfactor @FoxNews The way you have treated @realDonaldTrump is totally unacceptable...CNN has been fair"
- Sep 21, 2015 08:44:01 PM "@diannrr: @megynkelly Do you dream about @realDonaldTrump? He's in your head. Let it go." She is the worst - all anti-Trump! Terrible show.
- Sep 21, 2015 08:44:53 PM "@john_dipaolo: @realDonaldTrump will get out disaffected Repub base voters as well as Democrats looking for a real choice on immigration.
- Sep 21, 2015 09:00:26 PM I am having a really hard time watching @FoxNews.
- Sep 21, 2015 09:22:27 PM .@RichLowry is truly one of the dumbest of the talking heads - he doesn't have a clue!
- Sep 21, 2015 09:24:01 PM "@ellenEspence: @marklevinshow Thank you for maintaining your integrity during this disgusting lynching of @realDonaldTrump" Thanks Mark!
- Sep 21, 2015 09:24:19 PM "@waynearmstron10: @realDonaldTrump you must be relentless and maintain energy, and respond as you have been. It's a marathon." True.
- Sep 21, 2015 09:26:39 PM "@PhyllisA: @Hopeisalive66 @jdanielmoore @theblaze @megynkelly @realDonaldTrump that's ok! The more they talk the better POTUS Trump looks!"
- Sep 21, 2015 09:27:43 PM "@joeoh89: @seanhannity @realDonaldTrump What happened to The Pledge? Walker quits and slams Trump. Losers proving Pledge was sham."
- Sep 21, 2015 09:28:52 PM "@TheMindWave: @FoxNews Im not sure why u r giving them this much importance, they had wanted to take u down in debate and they failed!!"
- Sep 21, 2015 09:30:02 PM "@seleti00: @realDonaldTrump @FoxNews They attack you more then CNN or MSNBC combined. Just a bunch of old Bush appointee Rhinos."
- Sep 21, 2015 09:30:50 PM "@madscape: @realDonaldTrump @FoxNews and millions will agree with you! Most of us on twitter now view OAN network"
- Sep 21, 2015 09:32:36 PM "@ethansimmons111: @AllRepublicans @Ecsullie @RagingCynicism @FoxNews @oreillyfactor @KarlRove Karl Rove is a JOKE OWNED BY the BUSH family"

- Sep 21, 2015 09:33:40 PM "@JodiL792: @FoxNews I have been since you started running & I noticed Meghan Kelly's attacks. Stopped watching. Only Hannity 4 sure." Yes!
- Sep 21, 2015 09:34:14 PM "@AngelaTribble: @realDonaldTrump WE LOVE YOU DONALD TRUMP BECAUSE WE KNOW YOU ARE THE ONLY ONE TO #MakeAmericaGreatAgain" Thanks.
- Sep 21, 2015 09:34:51 PM "@wallen_jeanine: @realDonaldTrump I can only watch Hannity. I think he is the only one in your corner"
- Sep 21, 2015 09:37:11 PM "@VickyBrush: Do what most of us are doing! Turn off @FoxNews! There is a major boycott going on with them, anyway. Problem solved!

- Sep 22, 2015 07:09:59 AM "@bobby990r_1: @MediaBiasAlert @megynkelly @realDonaldTrump is fighting for middle class and veterans! Discussing trade deals."
- Sep 22, 2015 07:11:09 AM "@EdwardChelednik: @realDonaldTrump @FoxNews Hey Donald your not alone. I can't watch it at all. Used to be all i watched.
- Sep 22, 2015 07:12:25 AM "@glendabelle_11: @FoxNews Fox has become a supporter of Liberals!They are Not supporting the GOP candidates-especially Trump! Quit watching
- Sep 22, 2015 07:12:50 AM "@JimClarkFarrier: @Rockprincess818 @LeahR77 @realDonaldTrump is the only one who can get us out of this mess!" True!
- Sep 22, 2015 07:14:01 AM "@MiriamRoseMc: #TRUMp2016 would be the best for the country, jobs, trade and taxes - all others are status quo #MakeAmericaGreatAgain"
- Sep 22, 2015 07:14:38 AM "@IgnatiusGReilly: @charlescwcooke @realDonaldTrump @FoxNews will you cry when Marco Amnesty loses nomination?"
- Sep 22, 2015 07:15:21 AM "@BradANGSA: Trump is the only candidate telling the truth... the GOP is planning to stab Trump in the back... https://t.co/xhqhUVXrsx"
- Sep 22, 2015 07:17:51 AM "@HuskerPower811: @celestefick @realDonaldTrump Have you listened to his plans for Vets when he takes office? They're Incredible!!"

- Sep 22, 2015 07:18:21 AM "@JimShellenback: @realDonaldTrump @EdwardChelednik @FoxNews I steer away from Fox now. Never thought that would happen."
- Sep 22, 2015 07:59:53 AM 2016 Republican Primary Morning Consult Poll was just released. TRUMP 32, CARSON 12, BUSH 11, FIORINA 6, RUBIO 5, CRUZ 5. Taken after debate
- Sep 22, 2015 08:58:42 AM Morning Consult poll: "Trump Leads" http://t.co/61LFN0pfSw
- Sep 22, 2015 03:48:55 PM Yom Kippur blessings to all of my friends in Israel and around the world. #YomKippur
- Sep 22, 2015 05:31:52 PM I will be on the @colbertlateshow tonight at 11:30 http://t.co/BnCG1XqvcW
- Sep 22, 2015 08:46:13 PM Senator Marco "amnesty" Rubio, who has worst voting record in Senate, just hit me on national security-but I said don't go into Iraq. VISION
- Sep 22, 2015 09:00:20 PM Do you ever notice that lightweight @megynkelly constantly goes after me but when I hit back it is totally sexist. She is highly overrated!
- Sep 22, 2015 09:07:58 PM I think @megynkelly should take another eleven day "unscheduled" vacation.
- Sep 22, 2015 09:16:44 PM Just remember, the birther movement was started by Hillary Clinton in 2008. She was all in!
- Sep 22, 2015 09:31:34 PM I will be the featured guest on the season opener of @60Minutes this Sunday. There certainly is plenty to talk about!
- Sep 22, 2015 09:32:35 PM I will be doing @colbertlateshow at 11:30 on CBS. Enjoy! http://t.co/VDzpYct3Aq
- Sep 22, 2015 09:42:59 PM "@Mark60644: @megynkelly still cannot figure out this massive base of support for Trump is because he is anti- politician. #Trump2016"

- Sep 23, 2015 08:53:54 AM .@JuliInkster Congratulations on your great win-- what a captain, what a champion!
- Sep 23, 2015 10:12:18 AM Headline reads" Rubio passes Bush in Florida poll" -- Unfair, because Trump destroys them both! Trump 31.5%, Rubio 19.2%, Bush 11.3%

- Sep 23, 2015 10:16:23 AM Yogi Berra was not only a great baseball player, he was a great guy. Yogi will be missed. https://t.co/bC9pIOnmEh
- Sep 23, 2015 11:02:53 AM .@FoxNews has been treating me very unfairly & I have therefore decided that I won't be doing any more Fox shows for the foreseeable future.
- Sep 23, 2015 11:22:55 AM Wow! What a great night. Thank you to all of the viewers and congratulations to @StephenAtHome http://t.co/5rq2iMpHx6 @colbertlateshow
- Sep 23, 2015 08:21:54 PM Incompetent @RichLowry lost it tonight on @FoxNews. He should not be allowed on TV and the FCC should fine him!
- Sep 23, 2015 08:22:59 PM .@FoxNews owes me an apology for allowing clueless pundit @RichLowry to use such foul language on TV. Unheard of!

- Sep 24, 2015 05:01:40 AM Will be on @CNN at 7:00 A.M.
- Sep 24, 2015 05:03:26 AM Will be on @Morning_Joe at 6:30 A.M.
- Sep 24, 2015 09:46:26 AM So happy about my daughter @IvankaTrump's announcement that she will be having a baby this spring. Congratulations!
- Sep 24, 2015 11:23:45 AM New Bloomberg Poll: Trump Leads Big http://t.co/Eu0rMDbUPW
- Sep 24, 2015 11:24:35 AM Despite the establishment and the media's best efforts, the people are speaking loudly and clearly. Thank you to my amazing supporters!
- Sep 24, 2015 11:33:21 AM Bloomberg: Trump leads GOP field https://t.co/kWqWeRzIkl
- Sep 24, 2015 11:55:20 AM Dishonest @nytimes reporter Jonathan Martin refused to acknowledge massive crowd surge forward… https://t.co/9Emtq4NdbZ
- Sep 24, 2015 04:41:27 PM .@politico, which is not read or respected by many, may be the most dishonest of the media outlets--- and that is saying something.
- Sep 24, 2015 04:42:25 PM The failing @politico news outlet, which I hear is losing lots of money, is really dishonest!
- Sep 24, 2015 04:51:29 PM Wow, a really nice lead in New Hampshire--- an increase since my last poll! http://t.co/Cr0OOd5Loi
- Sep 24, 2015 10:11:28 PM "@yayala19: @politico WHEN THE OTHER CANDIDATES ARE TALKING POLITICS TRUMP IS TALKING SOLUTIONS. HE IS THE MOST TALENTED CANDIDATE."

- Sep 24, 2015 10:23:51 PM Just watched @marcorubio on television. Just another all talk, no action, politician. Truly doesn't have a clue! Worst voting record in Sen.
- Sep 24, 2015 10:48:23 PM "@yayala19: @marcorubio WHAT THE LOBBYISTS, THE MEDIA AND CAREER POLITICIANS WILL DO NEXT TO TRY TO STOP TRUMP? SILENT MAJORITY IS BACK"
- Sep 24, 2015 10:48:57 PM "@JoeMarzocco: @realDonaldTrump They attack Trump for not giving policy http://t.co/oEnDff1jkD is the most important detail, he WINS."
- Sep 24, 2015 10:55:24 PM .@megynkelly, the @FoxNews poll said very plainly I came in second in the debate. All others, Time, Drudge, Slate etc. said I came in 1st.
- Sep 24, 2015 10:59:44 PM "@Rketeltas: @JoeMarzocco Waiting for the biased media to write about the 30,000 Carly fired as a failed CEO. America is for Trump!"

- Sep 25, 2015 12:06:06 PM Great reception in D.C. At the Values Voter Summit. Now checking on my job at the Old Post Office...
- Sep 25, 2015 12:06:46 PM .....Ahead of schedule and under budget! Will be in Oklahoma tonight!
- Sep 25, 2015 01:10:08 PM I am now inspecting the Old Post Office on Pennsylvania Avenue - will be a great hotel. Soon off to the Oklahoma State Fair!
- Sep 25, 2015 01:36:19 PM At the Old Post Office- http://t.co/8Rs1fbcAIz
- Sep 25, 2015 01:51:35 PM Dishonest @politico just called to say that none of the polls including Fox, NBC, CNN, Zogby, & Morning Consult matter. Serious haters.
- Sep 25, 2015 02:18:59 PM .@MarcoRubio is weak on illegal immigration and will allow anyone into the country.....
- Sep 25, 2015 02:19:29 PM .....Has worst attendance record in Senate- rarely there to vote on a bill! @marcorubio
- Sep 25, 2015 02:36:36 PM .@TheHill- Trump on Boehner resignation: 'It's a good thing' http://t.co/flB93n4FoK
- Sep 25, 2015 03:37:26 PM .@THR "The Donald Trump Ratings Bump: Who's Benefiting Most?" http://t.co/uNdO1kRfus
- Sep 25, 2015 05:40:35 PM I will be on @cbs @60minutes this Sunday. A great honor-- hope you enjoy it.

- Sep 25, 2015 07:47:36 PM Thank you @FrankLuntz https://t.co/gpJBNXKV3e
- Sep 25, 2015 07:47:58 PM Just left Oklahoma--- the most amazing crowd and people! What a night!
- Sep 25, 2015 09:09:42 PM An updated POLL tracker (with all polls thru the weekend) reveals I maintained a double digit lead at… https://t.co/FGxhzluIJA

- Sep 26, 2015 12:46:47 AM "@Vote_Trump: Think about it. When's the last time a Prez actually did what he said? TRUMP does what he says. Will Be Greatest Prez Ever"
- Sep 26, 2015 07:41:55 AM "@realDonaldTrump: I will be on @cbs @60minutes this Sunday. A great honor-- hope you enjoy it."
- Sep 26, 2015 08:03:36 AM Lightweight Senator Marco Rubio is VERY weak on immigration, knows nothing about finance and would be incapable of making great trade deals!
- Sep 26, 2015 08:06:38 AM "@taurus82409: @CBS @60Minutes Lok forward to it, Donald. You are doing Great! Please keep up the fight, many of us are behind you 100%!!
- Sep 26, 2015 08:07:22 AM "@Karentalk: @RogerJStoneJr @megynkelly Fiorina is not surging..she is begging for money..and she owns this. http://t.co/kOkyNtWkeE"
- Sep 26, 2015 08:12:32 AM Marco Rubio is a member of the Gang Of Eight or, very weak on stopping illegal immigration. Only changed when poll numbers crashed.
- Sep 26, 2015 06:14:53 PM "@TheIntellect111: @realDonaldTrump Mr Trump Please Do not give in.You are Changing History. We Need you as our Next Leader, Its Your Time"
- Sep 26, 2015 06:17:25 PM "@FreeStateYank: Ex-wife Ivana Trump says @realDonaldTrump can win, likely WILL win, and will be a great President. http://t.co/kI1xij3v6w"
- Sep 26, 2015 06:20:40 PM "@itsblakec: @realDonaldTrump we are tired of lies. Trump 2016"
- Sep 26, 2015 06:21:18 PM "@JokerzWild_: @realDonaldTrump @TheIntellect111 Trump will win, I know it."
- Sep 26, 2015 06:23:09 PM "@Incazzato2015: @realDonaldTrump Time for real change, TRUMP 16"

- Sep 26, 2015 06:25:43 PM Hope we all enjoy @60Minutes tomorrow night. I do believe they will treat me fairly!

- Sep 27, 2015 07:56:29 PM "@truthshallbe: @60Minutes @realDonaldTrump Been watching!!! Brilliant Mr. Trump, he is so Awesome!! And real."
- Sep 27, 2015 07:57:00 PM "@MeOnAJourney @realDonaldTrump Imagine that, an American president standing up for the American people! Go Trump Go! #Trump2016"
- Sep 27, 2015 09:26:41 PM "@midwestcaucus: @60Minutes Great interview,Trump ruled. Great response 2 Trade War claim. All anyone has 2 do is look at foreign tariffs
- Sep 27, 2015 09:27:56 PM "@Rketeltas: @realDonaldTrump While the former KGB Putin gets softballs, Trump gets the Matt Harvey fastball and hits it out of the park."
- Sep 27, 2015 09:29:16 PM "@greta: . @realDonaldTrump announces his tax plan tomorrow morning http://t.co/bQ0Xjs63XH"
- Sep 27, 2015 09:30:36 PM "@Apipwhisperer: @MarkPavelich @gentlemanirish @60Minutes EXCELLENT WATCHING PUTIN'S BRILLIANCE AND TRUMP'S. @CBS I LOVED THE INTERVIEWS."
- Sep 27, 2015 09:31:55 PM "@SkyeShepard: Trump went way up in my 'poll' when he said he'd take money from what US is giving 2 other countries 2 save social security"
- Sep 27, 2015 09:32:30 PM "@JennaLeeUSA: When asked why he has his own magazine covers on his walls - @realDonaldTrump replies: "It's cheaper than wall paper..." Ha!
- Sep 27, 2015 09:33:59 PM "@AdiosLiberty: @60Minutes @realDonaldTrump @ScottPelley Haven't seen that much hatred in an interviewer since the 1st debate. #trump2016"
- Sep 27, 2015 09:37:28 PM "@yang_karl: All Scott Pelley did by being disrespectful was make it easier to make up my mind who to vote for and that will be Trump."
- Sep 27, 2015 09:38:15 PM "@JodiL792: @DefendingtheUSA @america_trump @60Minutes Thats exactly what I thought. We haven't had great leader since Reagan&now Trump"
- Sep 27, 2015 09:38:46 PM "@fanodale: @60Minutes @realDonaldTrump watched 60 mins first time ever. Love Trump hate Scotty"

- Sep 27, 2015 09:40:18 PM "@ReversingASD: @60Minutes notice how your twits about @realDonaldTrump are the most RT! We the American ppl love and want #Trump2016 !"

- Sep 28, 2015 09:03:30 AM Looking forward to press conference on taxes at 11AM at @TrumpTowerNY.
- Sep 28, 2015 10:04:15 AM LIVE on #Periscope: Tax Plan Press Conference #Trump2016 https://t.co/DQQS5d9R3O
- Sep 28, 2015 10:41:22 AM I know you will enjoy reading my tax plan- http://t.co/FxtUQNXEFH #MakeAmericaGreatAgain
- Sep 28, 2015 01:27:08 PM "@SpurrellJulie First time in my life I wish I was an American citizen so I could vote for @realDonaldTrump !!"
- Sep 28, 2015 01:28:33 PM Thanks. http://t.co/SXUUL7l8vp https://t.co/FbNl1G5Awg
- Sep 28, 2015 02:01:00 PM Will be doing @OutFrontCNN with @ErinBurnett tonight at 7 pm re: tax reductions and various other topics.
- Sep 28, 2015 02:21:25 PM Conservative? Jeb Bush doubled Florida State debt!http://t.co/kDOyCqwuqI
- Sep 28, 2015 02:44:15 PM Zogby Poll: Trump Widens Lead After GOP Debate http://t.co/YAZyKwVxNJ
- Sep 28, 2015 03:06:11 PM "The GOP Debate Scorecard: Donald Trump and Energy" by Wayne Allyn Root. http://t.co/MmFJeGRNf8
- Sep 28, 2015 05:00:33 PM Wow, the ratings for @60Minutes last night were their biggest in a year--- very nice!
- Sep 28, 2015 06:53:17 PM Do you believe this - Iran wants to trade our 3 prisoners (not 4) for 19 prisoners held by the U.S. Should have been let go with last deal!
- Sep 28, 2015 10:51:52 PM "@polina6: @realDonaldTrump MAN WITH A PLAN-THE BEST TAX PLAN! GO TRUMP 2016!"

- Sep 29, 2015 10:04:21 AM Prediction: Rand Paul has been driven out of the race by my statements about him-- he will announce soon. 1%!
- Sep 29, 2015 10:04:30 AM I hope when Rand Paul gets out of the race—he is at 1%--his supporters come over to me. I will do a much better job for them.

- Sep 29, 2015 10:20:39 AM Definitely watch @Carl_C_Icahn 's 'Danger Ahead'. Very insightful, particularly on how corp inversions hurt America: http://t.co/PJN89SwvTF
- Sep 29, 2015 11:49:40 AM Carl Icahn said this about me: "I think at this moment in time, he's the only candidate that speaks out about the country's problems."
- Sep 29, 2015 03:31:23 PM Great! https://t.co/Je440dDZbs

- Sep 30, 2015 06:24:13 AM I watched lightweight Senator Marco Rubio, who is all talk and no action, defend his WEAK position on illegal immigration. Pathetic!
- Sep 30, 2015 06:51:35 AM Just read that "Trump" has the largest (and I add most enthusiastic) crowds. Tonight I will be in New Hampshire - the place will be packed!
- Sep 30, 2015 07:13:28 AM "@kissmeandrocco: @realDonaldTrump who ever thinks Donald trump is a bad person u just don't want a good country" Thank you.
- Sep 30, 2015 07:20:21 AM Rubio is totally owned by the lobbyists and special interests. A lightweight senator with the worst voting record in Senate. Lazy!
- Sep 30, 2015 09:52:33 AM Highly respected economist @Larry_Kudlow is a big fan of my tax plan—thank you Larry. http://t.co/VT8Y7c8PSn
- Sep 30, 2015 09:59:10 AM Anyone reading this profile of Marco Rubio would never vote for him. Never made ten cents & is totally controlled! http://t.co/KA0LvfFJfM
- Sep 30, 2015 11:43:53 AM Great news! Just out--the highly respected USA Today/Suffolk University Poll. Enjoy! https://t.co/11pDloDTHV
- Sep 30, 2015 12:22:57 PM Wow, so nice! Thank you Wayne Allyn Root. http://t.co/dZuLHDZSoI
- Sep 30, 2015 03:14:42 PM Interesting, polls on who won the GOP debate. http://t.co/iB6NGQsg5v
- Sep 30, 2015 03:53:06 PM I will be interviewed by @donlemon tonight on @CNN at 10PM.
- Sep 30, 2015 04:33:01 PM "Trump's Tax Plan: A Proposal Reagan Would Approve?" by Jeff Bell http://t.co/KmPeSwvslr
- Sep 30, 2015 09:53:56 PM "@Hashtag1USA: I just watched D Trumps interview on @CNN i get more impressed everytime i hear him speak! @realDonaldTrump #Trump2016-Thanks

- Sep 30, 2015 09:55:16 PM "@jaycatalyst1: @realDonaldTrump Univision execs are hypocrites.They dish out the most discrimination. You should highlight that point."
- Sep 30, 2015 09:55:46 PM "@AnnieClarkCole: How can anyone vote for Hillary when she careless with emails that jeopardize our security. She is not to be trusted."
- Sep 30, 2015 09:57:35 PM "@angeloftruth11: @realDonaldTrump great interview with @donlemon. Thank you.
- Sep 30, 2015 09:58:48 PM "@CFT1: .@realDonaldTrump Great interview on @CNN @donlemon @CNNTonight #MakeAmericaGreatAgain #Trump2016 #TRUMP"
- Sep 30, 2015 09:59:51 PM "@TIMENOUT: @CNN @donlemon congratulations Don that was a great interview @realDonaldTrump"
- Sep 30, 2015 10:02:54 PM "@sternbutgreg: @realDonaldTrump is pulling away from the pack. I live in Iowa. It's real." Thank you!
- Sep 30, 2015 10:06:21 PM Just got back from New Hampshire. Great crowd, great people! Will be back soon!

October, 2015

- Oct 1, 2015 07:12:38 AM "@WMikeW: It's hard to get through corrupt media filter but Trump is doing it. Check out 9/30/15 @donlemon int'view https://t.co/MR6U8qtrbk"
- Oct 1, 2015 07:13:11 AM "@Margaretweber48: @realDonaldTrump Rand Paul put the nail in his coffin when he bashed Ted Cruz. Bye, bye Rand!"
- Oct 1, 2015 07:19:16 AM "@JoyCardinShow: Latest @MULawPoll finds @ScottWalker at 37 percent approval, @realDonaldTrump leading GOP in #Wisconsin.
- Oct 1, 2015 07:21:42 AM "@JayRHaw: @realDonaldTrump was right. @RandPaul wont last. Even Paul knew it. Thats why he's still running for his Senate seat #Trump2016"
- Oct 1, 2015 01:45:04 PM Thanks. https://t.co/OJ0mbxv1uc
- Oct 1, 2015 02:15:57 PM .@MittRomney is trying to hit back at me because I'm saying that he let the Repub Party down w/ his loss to Obama. Should've won—he choked!

- Oct 1, 2015 05:52:34 PM "@barreto_eugenio: @MittRomney it's sad, but GOP does not want you as their candidate. But we the people do. Latinos for Trump."
- Oct 1, 2015 05:57:45 PM "@msann43: How can Illinois keep @realDonaldTrump off the ballot? Illinois citizens should protest. Just another phony Politico story. Easy!
- Oct 1, 2015 06:02:32 PM "@EthaBrooke: @MittRomney Like always you are telling the truth.I liked Romney and voted for him but he didn't fight hard enough." True!
- Oct 1, 2015 06:19:08 PM "@EthaBrooke: @cs1racefan @realDonaldTrump @MittRomney The truth about Romney...he didn't want the presidency bad enough!" He choked!
- Oct 1, 2015 06:36:48 PM "@Def: CNBC's John Harwood Today "We don't have Superman presidents" "No" DonaldTrump replied .."But we WILL if you have Trump!" #Trump2016
- Oct 1, 2015 06:38:26 PM "@gedion_t: @realDonaldTrump @EthaBrooke @MittRomney No body knows foreign policy any better than Trump. Vote "T"
- Oct 1, 2015 06:52:07 PM I will be interviewed on @seanhannity tonight at 10:00. Many things, mostly bad, to talk about!
- Oct 1, 2015 06:53:50 PM "@JYakburger: @EthaBrooke IF @MittRomney ran more like @realDonaldTrump and less like McCain, he would've won. Failed campaign tactics.
- Oct 1, 2015 07:41:22 PM My warmest condolences to the families of the horrible Roseburg, Oregon, shootings.
- Oct 1, 2015 07:54:30 PM "@WETHEPEOPLE65: @realDonaldTrump @BigStick2013 @TIMENOUT @CNN @donlemon GO TRUMP, OUR GUY"
- Oct 1, 2015 07:56:53 PM "@TheBrodyFile: The HUGE @TheBrodyFile DonaldTrump faith-based story runs tomorrow (Friday) on @700club. @ABCFamily channel at 10am ET."
- Oct 1, 2015 08:06:28 PM "@RLHoldenSr: @realDonaldTrump Mr Trump we are praying that you win the 2016 election! Obama is destroying the US!"
- Oct 1, 2015 08:06:45 PM "@Renhowe: I enjoyed @donlemon's interview with @realDonaldTrump on @CNN Need more interviews like that." Thanks.
- Oct 1, 2015 08:08:34 PM "@VoteDonaldTrump: @realDonaldTrump @Renhowe @donlemon @CNN we love trump"

- Oct 2, 2015 08:18:57 AM I was so looking forward to being in Virginia Beach, Virginia, today. The demand for tickets was amazing. Good luck with storm, back soon!
- Oct 2, 2015 08:22:40 AM Will be in Nashville, Tennessee, tomorrow (Saturday) at 2:30 P.M. So much to talk about - see you there!
- Oct 2, 2015 08:24:11 AM "@DoDFiredawg78: @realDonaldTrump Virginians stand with you sir! #MakeAmericaGreatAgain #Trump2016 #TrumpForPresident"
- Oct 2, 2015 08:29:10 AM "@billsupdates: Why Buffalo Bills could be responsible for Donald Trump becoming president https://t.co/JxF7kjfaZR" Team has a great owner!
- Oct 2, 2015 08:50:56 AM "@Tea4Freedom: Pastor Robert Jeffres accurately gushes about Donald Trump http://t.co/iRcAPKF7yZ" Pastor Jeffres is a great guy!
- Oct 2, 2015 05:15:55 PM Congratulations to my brother Robert & Ann Marie on the success of @MontesKitchen in Dutchess County, New York (Amenia.) Great food!
- Oct 2, 2015 05:32:16 PM Pictures of my beautiful mother, amazing father, and family hanging @MontesKitchen in upstate, New York. http://t.co/lvx5SEhQVv
- Oct 2, 2015 07:34:34 PM "@swterry91: Donald Trump Leads by 9 Points in Pew Poll – Jeb Bush in Free Fall #tcot http://t.co/uyxre0ei92"
- Oct 2, 2015 07:52:08 PM "@thehill: P. Diddy is a fan of Donald Trump: http://t.co/VQv3ivgrwq http://t.co/Z66TTG3DpJ"
- Oct 2, 2015 08:49:11 PM "@MNManstein2: Polling Convergence - OAN/GRAVIS and Reuters Show Donald Trump Surging With 34 - 35% Support... http://t.co/ckXH2JfBNt
- Oct 2, 2015 08:56:23 PM "@KenPettigrew: Don't slow down the Trump storm... American needs leadership not a Paper President like Obama. Don't leave us with Jeb!"
- Oct 2, 2015 08:57:42 PM "@TheNewsClub_US: RT "@MNMans: Polling Convergence - OAN/GRAVIS and Reuters… http://t.co/3NXztsLOhx #RT #CNN #HBO http://t.co/zzKm8wUYqY"
- Oct 2, 2015 08:58:42 PM "@KelliHeathman1: Megan Kelly admitted Trump was leading by a lot!! That talk with Ailes must have worked... Time to get tough. TRUMP 2016"

- Oct 2, 2015 08:59:37 PM "@apolloNC1: @realDonaldTrump @MNManstein2 You will be the next president of the USA!! Thank you Mr Trump. Sincerely the middle class!!"
- Oct 2, 2015 09:01:23 PM "@valerieannt: @DRUDGE_REPORT @JebBush Jeb you are falling in polls because conservatives feel that you cannot #MakeAmericaGreatAgain"
- Oct 2, 2015 09:17:18 PM "@HowardKurtz: Trump's big lead in a new poll and whether Jeb's "stuff happens" was taken out of context with @megynkelly tonight" Thanks H!
- Oct 2, 2015 09:18:32 PM "@HowardKurtz: @JoeNBC It'd be humorous to cull tweets from "experts" over past few mos who have predicted Trump's immediate collapse"
- Oct 2, 2015 09:19:10 PM "@misskellyaudrey: @FoxNews @HowardKurtz @MELANIATRUMP Melania is a beautiful woman who conducts her self with Class and Dignity #Trump2016"
- Oct 2, 2015 09:20:30 PM "@carrillo_pete: @realDonaldTrump great numbers #MakeAmericaGreatAgain" Thanks.
- Oct 2, 2015 09:21:43 PM "@tvegan: DonaldTrump your kicking everyone's ASS! always believed in this Country ! your going to make America Great Again ! Mr President!
- Oct 2, 2015 09:21:56 PM "@mormontim: Going to see @realDonaldTrump tomorrow in franklin TN #MakeAmericaGreatAgain"
- Oct 2, 2015 09:25:10 PM "@gse_says: Overwhelming wins by @realDonaldTrump in primaries will prove what will happen (landslide) in the general election.
- Oct 2, 2015 09:51:08 PM Thank you @megynkelly for the nice things you said about Melania. You will like her, great heart and smart - always wanting to help people!

- Oct 3, 2015 04:36:43 AM "@collegestump: Can't wait for @realDonaldTrump to be the next pres. @CNN @FoxNews @DRUDGE_REPORT @blackrepublican http://t.co/F9pM0gE2yz"
- Oct 3, 2015 04:46:12 AM "@elkay14: @jordanfax I like gutsy brave guys like #Trump #Reagan , I hate all those bloody hypocrites @realDonaldTrump" Thank you.

- Oct 3, 2015 06:16:43 AM Bush and Rubio are finally attacking each other, as I knew they would, in order to be the last "establishment" man standing against me.Great
- Oct 3, 2015 06:21:38 AM Rubio was very disloyal to Bush, his mentor, when he decided to run against him. Both said they "love" each other.They don't - word is hate!
- Oct 3, 2015 05:10:09 PM Just leaving Nashville, Tennessee. Had a great time with a fabulous crowd of people! Love Nashville -- back soon! http://t.co/CS8DOd8wfm
- Oct 3, 2015 05:12:18 PM I will be on @MeetThePress with @ChuckTodd tomorrow morning at 10:30am ET on @NBC. Enjoy!
- Oct 3, 2015 05:12:51 PM Tune in to see me on @ThisWeekABC with @GStephanopoulos at 10am ET. Enjoy!
- Oct 3, 2015 11:06:13 PM "@JWbananastand: @nbcsnl I think I just heard @realDonaldTrump's ratings go up another 5% #Trump #SNL"
- Oct 3, 2015 11:06:32 PM "@RealReagan0503: It's funny how they say @realDonaldTrump doesn't give specifics but he's the only one who put out more than 2 policies.
- Oct 3, 2015 11:06:46 PM "@leftfootjustice: If @realDonaldTrump becomes @POTUS we will finally have a @WWE Hall of Famer as President."
- Oct 3, 2015 11:08:06 PM "@scottferson: .@TaranKillam plays a way better fake @realDonaldTrump than a real @HillaryClinton plays herself @nbcsnl"
- Oct 3, 2015 11:09:46 PM "@SolFusionGreg: @Mediaite The more the Progressives & RINO's poke at the DonaldTrump the stronger he gets and more REAL PEOPLE like him!"
- Oct 3, 2015 11:35:19 PM "@piercingshawn: @realDonaldTrump Please don't roll over . You are this country's last hope and our kids need you. Don't lose this deal !"
- Oct 3, 2015 11:38:33 PM "@sfurnbac: Thank you @realDonaldTrump for the great #SNL this week!!!"
- Oct 3, 2015 11:39:07 PM "@topcota1SG: @PhxKen I am Hispanic and will vote for @realDonaldTrump"
- Oct 3, 2015 11:41:21 PM "@NeilForell: Watched the roast of @realDonaldTrump You took those jokes like a champ, what a good sport! Im voting for you now" Great.

- Oct 3, 2015 11:45:31 PM "@BillPwr1: @collegestump @CNN @FoxNews @DRUDGE_REPORT @blackrepublican FYI @batchelorshow @larry_kudlow #Trump2016 appeal grows!"

- Oct 4, 2015 06:45:44 AM "@misterdish69: @IAmFreedomMan @seanhannity @rushlimbaugh @realDonaldTrump @CNN http://t.co/f9UAbiFaab"
- Oct 4, 2015 06:46:08 AM "@lindaleereyes: @realDonaldTrump Great Job Donald!!! Can't waite for you to be President and neither can America!!"
- Oct 4, 2015 06:46:56 AM "@polemicism: Okay okay @realDonaldTrump was right: LaGuardia Airport is a total dump. Like really, really bad."
- Oct 4, 2015 06:49:04 AM "@joetoohey: This morning on @meetthepress - @chucktodd's sit down with @realDonaldTrump in his NYC Campaign HQ #MTP http://t.co/9Oqz7aWhaS
- Oct 4, 2015 06:49:50 AM "@laurencristmann: @realDonaldTrump @topcota1SG @PhxKen i can't wait to cast my vote for Donald J TRUMP in MAY and NOVEMBER" Thanks.
- Oct 4, 2015 06:54:43 AM "@DeborahCroce5: @realDonaldTrump ends speech in Franklin, Tennessee w/ Thank You I Love You All!! We love you 2 #MakeAmericaGreatAgain
- Oct 4, 2015 06:58:11 AM "@TheNewsClub_US: RT @realDonaldTrump Will be interviewed on @foxandfriends at 8:30. #RT #CNN #HBO"
- Oct 4, 2015 06:59:08 AM "@TheNewsClub_US: RT @realDonaldTrump "@laurencristmann: @topcota1SG @PhxKen i can't wait to cast my vote for Donald J TRUMP... #RT #CNN #HBO"
- Oct 4, 2015 07:01:14 AM The people of Tennessee yesterday were amazing. Thank you!
- Oct 4, 2015 07:05:23 AM "@TrumpNewMedia: @carrillo_pete ILLEGAL ALIENS FOUND GUILTY OF MURDERING BORDER PATROL AGENT http://t.co/jEgkaegj8T http://t.co/lR8u7mBzAb
- Oct 4, 2015 08:23:59 AM Will be interviewed by @GStephanopoulos on @ABC at 10:00 A.M.
- Oct 4, 2015 08:26:07 AM Will be interviewed by @chucktodd on @meetthepress at 10:30 A.M.
- Oct 4, 2015 09:49:27 AM "@nathanpaul1975: @realDonaldTrump Hollywood doesn't get to pick our presidents we the people do!! GO TRUMP!"

- Oct 4, 2015 03:45:57 PM "@Margee11: WATCH @realDonaldTrump Fires Up the Crowd in Franklin, Tennessee http://t.co/6aWwyanQ4w via @trumpstump2016"
- Oct 4, 2015 03:46:41 PM "@keksec_org: @realDonaldTrump You said it best! #MakeAmericaGreatAgain"
- Oct 4, 2015 03:49:29 PM "@DGrant39107133: @nathanpaul1975 Clinton may go to jail but is still running for president? 99% of people would be in jail for what she did
- Oct 4, 2015 03:51:06 PM "@AndreaTantaros: DonaldTrump is right. And sadly Christians were treated better under Hussein & Gaddafi than ISIS. https://t.co/AZdLqydRM1
- Oct 4, 2015 04:29:11 PM "@MichellePippin: @realDonaldTrump When are you coming to #virginiabeach?" Very soon!
- Oct 4, 2015 04:35:18 PM I'm leading by big margins in every poll but the press keeps asking, would you ever get out? They are just troublemakers, I'm going to win!
- Oct 4, 2015 06:34:49 PM "@PaulRSidneyUK: I cannot believe the increase in illegals here in San Antonio Texas. We are the minority constantly discriminated against
- Oct 4, 2015 11:29:56 PM For all of my fantastic supporters, and for the U.S.A., we are going to win and MAKE AMERICA GREAT AGAIN, maybe greater than ever before!

- Oct 5, 2015 03:46:08 PM The incompetence of our current administration is beyond comprehension. TPP is a terrible deal.
- Oct 5, 2015 04:12:45 PM Thoughts and prayers for those in the floods affecting the great people of South Carolina.
- Oct 5, 2015 06:40:16 PM Political strategist Stuart Stevens,who led Romney down the tubes in what should have been an easy victory,has terrible political instincts!
- Oct 5, 2015 06:48:57 PM "@marklevinshow: Donald Trump will be on my show tonight at 8:30 PM eastern time." Will be my great honor, so much to talk about!
- Oct 5, 2015 06:56:21 PM "@WayneDupreeShow: HEADLINES: Donald Trump maintains huge lead on opponents as polls go #KeepingItReal http://t.co/AsRJp5AcmZ"

- Oct 5, 2015 06:57:09 PM "@TODAYshow: "We're pleased to announce that Donald Trump has just accepted our invitation for a town hall." - @SavannahGuthrie" So true!
- Oct 5, 2015 06:59:43 PM "@Forbes: "If Donald Trump puts his name on X, it will sell for 3.7 times more than it would otherwise." Nice!
- Oct 5, 2015 07:06:16 PM So, so, so important - MAKE AMERICA GREAT AGAIN!
- Oct 5, 2015 07:57:11 PM "@KingVantes: @AnnCoulter @RedState TRUTH .Just like Perry, Walker, Bush .. all y'all who go after @realDonaldTrump WILL FAIL #Trump2016"
- Oct 5, 2015 07:58:39 PM "@TheWTFTahoe: @realDonaldTrump will #MakeAmericaGreatAgain"
- Oct 5, 2015 08:00:44 PM "@Raddmom: @realDonaldTrump - don't let the media & the @GOP elites push you out- Americans are with you!" Thanks, I won't!
- Oct 5, 2015 08:02:19 PM "@4udirtyrat: @realDonaldTrump 9 million MORE out of work because of this BAD DEAL.Will have over 100 MILLION out of work. Nice going Obama"
- Oct 5, 2015 08:02:39 PM "@Knight276: @Writeonright @Real_Carl_Icahn @DanScavino @realDonaldTrump media is confused they bash trump he rises in polls!"
- Oct 5, 2015 08:07:54 PM "@Q1776: Love fest for DonaldTrump on @marklevinshow just now. Top 5 talk radio audience in country. Great being on the show with Mark!
- Oct 5, 2015 08:08:17 PM "@jaxx613: @realDonaldTrump @Renhowe @donlemon @CNN . Mark Levin interview was great"
- Oct 5, 2015 08:57:19 PM Don't ever forget, we will, together, MAKE AMERICA GREAT AGAIN!
- Oct 5, 2015 11:00:53 PM "@CASuperrunner: @cu_mr2ducks @FoxNews @foxnewspolitics Trump talked about this weeks ago as a possibility .... this is not Rubio's idea"

- Oct 6, 2015 06:31:41 AM "@LarrySchweikart: @peddoc63 @RickCanton @realDonaldTrump @marcorubio Funny. The Donald living rent-free in lil Marco's head"

- Oct 6, 2015 06:31:48 AM "@Karentalk: @CNNPolitics @realDonaldTrump Stop interrupting Trump..Please..He is CORRECT ON EVERYTHING.."
- Oct 6, 2015 06:32:06 AM "@LindaRicker6: My choice @realDonaldTrump just finished a great interview on CNN. Pathetic questions from Cuomo but Trump cleared the air."
- Oct 6, 2015 06:32:56 AM "@AngelaDale143: @realDonaldTrump @CNN wow, did Trump kick ass with Cuomo! You are the man, Mr. Trump; certainly not the lamb chop, Rubio."
- Oct 6, 2015 06:33:14 AM "@realbigstriper: @ChrisCuomo Pew poll: @realDonaldTrump holds commanding lead @CNNPolitics http://t.co/iw2vk9Wx9L"
- Oct 6, 2015 06:34:01 AM "@Lisa_Steen: seriously Cuomo hates DonaldTrump he was a pathetic interviewer AS USUAL! Please don't go anywhere Mr Trump AMERICA NEEDS YOU"
- Oct 6, 2015 06:34:26 AM "@Tea4Freedom: @realDonaldTrump @CNN That was awesome, boss! #trump2016"
- Oct 6, 2015 06:35:14 AM "@Nay_2xTimes: Great interview on #NewDay @realDonaldTrump #MakeAmericaGreatAgain"
- Oct 6, 2015 06:36:17 AM "@AJ_Nix: @realDonaldTrump @CNN Great job Mr Trump,,,Kept em on topic,, Got your message though."
- Oct 6, 2015 06:37:40 AM "@jpm05880: @realDonaldTrump @CNN TRUMP EVEN SHARPER THAN LAST WEEK!!YOU ARE BEAUTIFUL..."
- Oct 6, 2015 06:38:36 AM "@WMikeWood: @cnn Trump Shuts down Cuomo. "I am not getting out." I am going to win. Cuomo tries sleazy tricks . Epic Fail. Unprofessional."
- Oct 6, 2015 06:39:13 AM "@CPO_Mark_2010: @realDonaldTrump is fired up on @cnn!!! So are your supporters!! #Trump2016"
- Oct 6, 2015 06:39:39 AM "@SteveBrainard1: @realDonaldTrump @CNN great interview Trump!"
- Oct 6, 2015 06:39:47 AM "@kitkat123frank: @realDonaldTrump @CNN @SpecialKMB1969. You have my vote"
- Oct 6, 2015 10:03:07 AM .@WayneNewtonMrLV Wayne, such a pleasant surprise--so nice. Thank you very much.
- Oct 6, 2015 10:16:47 AM Crooked @club4growth has given up advertising in Iowa on me—remember they wanted my million dollars—I said no—total frauds!

- Oct 6, 2015 02:29:42 PM "Labor Unions Giving Serious Thought to Endorsing Trump" via Washington Examiner http://t.co/XrEpSyuDsj
- Oct 6, 2015 02:42:37 PM I will be on @SpecialReport with @BretBaier tonight at 6PM. http://t.co/iEh3RHp98S
- Oct 6, 2015 04:04:51 PM True! https://t.co/v3Y6exaQGY
- Oct 6, 2015 06:14:46 PM "@4mostcoach: I enjoy every @realDonaldTrump speech IN ITS ENTIRETY NOBODY's going 2 tell me what our NEXT PRESIDENT says but HIM.
- Oct 6, 2015 06:15:12 PM "@Jrdavisii: @realDonaldTrump was great! @stephenfhayes is jealous that Trump didn't mention him. It's because SH is so wrong!
- Oct 6, 2015 06:16:43 PM "@TN_RiverFolk: My 2016 Vote will B based on #MakeAmericaGreatAgain NOT Eminent Domain●Americans need 2Prioritize http://t.co/hPPy3gw3Ld"
- Oct 6, 2015 06:16:55 PM "@rogerhartford8: @realDonaldTrump hope you win it all . Time for a change !!"
- Oct 6, 2015 06:17:25 PM "@TheConnieMoore: @realDonaldTrump see u Sat in GA !!" Great!
- Oct 6, 2015 06:18:51 PM "@ChadR73: Guess Barry Diller is afraid @realDonaldTrump is about to upset the crony applecart. #Trump2016 @Carl_C_Icahn" An angry fool!
- Oct 6, 2015 06:19:07 PM "@lewgeraldine: @FoxNews @realDonaldTrump TRUMP FOR "PRESIDENT" YOU HAVE MY VOTE." GREAT.
- Oct 6, 2015 06:19:32 PM "@pnicastro1: @WayneNewtonMrLV He did give tremendous praise for you this morning on @foxandfriends. Keep it up!Make America Great Again!"
- Oct 6, 2015 06:20:56 PM "@bluegirlvi: @BretBaier @FoxNews DonaldTrump GOD voters are NOT getting tired of Trump! He's winning over others too #MakeAmericaGreatAgain
- Oct 6, 2015 06:53:54 PM "@For2016: pundits love to take a snippet, out of context, from something DonaldTrump says, and then weave a blanket of bullshit around it
- Oct 6, 2015 06:59:04 PM "@GardiBates: @ananavarro @cnn @realDonaldTrump Why are you even on tv? U sound like nails on a chalkboard. Biased against Trump. So true!

- Oct 6, 2015 07:01:21 PM "@nedbello: @realDonaldTrump Your Doing GREAT!" Thanks.
- Oct 6, 2015 07:02:36 PM "@darcy027027: @GardiBates @ananavarro @CNN Just In! 10/6/15 Morning Poll Trump +18% Trump 31 Carson 13 Rubio 10 Bush 7 Fiorina 6"
- Oct 6, 2015 07:04:23 PM "@ManahawkinMikey: @realDonaldTrump @GardiBates @ananavarro @CNN At least @megynkelly came to her senses #asksean http://t.co/5tR7cq76mC"
- Oct 6, 2015 07:06:32 PM "@sempek1: @BretBaier @realDonaldTrump Trump is talking about highways, huge building projects - not as Steve Hayes said - small fry."
- Oct 6, 2015 07:06:53 PM "@Foosball38: @realDonaldTrump we need a Real LEADER to LEAD. Let's make America great again! VOTE TRUMP 2016"
- Oct 6, 2015 10:06:59 PM "@sharonDay5: The ONLY hope for America to break from the single Party Establishment is to Vote for @realDonaldTrump #Trump2016"
- Oct 6, 2015 10:12:38 PM "@trumpgasm: NEW- 10/6/15 REUTERS IPSOS POLL DONALD TRUMP CONTINUES TO DOMINATE! OVER 37%!! http://t.co/qBsldeV4je http://t.co/GCtpS1WfeQ"
- Oct 6, 2015 10:13:54 PM "@darcy027027: @realclearspam @ElliekeMary @AnnCoulter @GardiBates @ananavarro @CNN Don't worry. Trump will put it back when he is Pres !"

- Oct 7, 2015 06:51:38 AM Ben Carson was speaking in general terms as to what he would do if confronted with a gunman, and was not criticizing the victims. Not fair!
- Oct 7, 2015 09:34:04 AM If Stuart Stevens' book is as bad as his horrible political advice to Mitt Romney, don't waste your money. Arrogant guy but a zero!
- Oct 7, 2015 09:39:29 AM Heading to a packed house in Waterloo, Iowa! Will celebrate today's great poll numbers together. See you soon!
- Oct 7, 2015 10:46:52 AM I wonder why somebody doesn't do something about the clowns @politico and their totally dishonest reporting.
- Oct 7, 2015 10:47:34 AM .@politico has no power, but so dishonest!

- Oct 7, 2015 02:29:59 PM Just found out I won the Rockingham County Republican Booth Straw Poll at the Deerfield Fair in New Hampshire this past weekend. 39% ---Wow!
- Oct 7, 2015 06:05:05 PM .@stuartpstevens made some of the dumbest political decisions of all time in helping Romney to get destroyed by Obama. Should have won!
- Oct 7, 2015 06:17:34 PM Iowa was amazing today. Great crowd, great people. Thanks, will be back soon!
- Oct 7, 2015 06:19:52 PM "@sugarofsaturn: @realDonaldTrump @stuartpstevens On the bright side Romney's loss gave us Donald Trump!" So true!
- Oct 7, 2015 06:21:16 PM "@3462727: @BretBaier @Norsu2 @realDonaldTrump tired of FOX bashing Trump & pushing GOP establish / Christie/Rubio/Bush"
- Oct 7, 2015 06:46:39 PM "@DarrenJJordan: @realDonaldTrump @stuartpstevens And he's still a consultant? For what?" Only a fool would pay Stuart for his advice.
- Oct 7, 2015 06:51:36 PM Just arrived in Las Vegas for a packed house speech tomorrow. Big poll results today, Leading big everywhere. MAKE AMERICA GREAT AGAIN!
- Oct 7, 2015 06:54:29 PM "@metskins10: @realDonaldTrump @DarrenJJordan @stuartpstevens Pay him, just do the opposite and you will win in a landslide."
- Oct 7, 2015 06:55:42 PM "@Sandikay60: @realDonaldTrump @DarrenJJordan @stuartpstevens Donald Trump, our next president of the United States! #trump2016" Thank you.
- Oct 7, 2015 06:57:40 PM "@keksec_org: @realDonaldTrump I truly believe you are the best #MakeAmericaGreatAgain" Thank you so much!
- Oct 7, 2015 08:13:34 PM "@GraggQuinton: This is the size crowd you get when people care what you say -Trump in Oklahoma . Got even bigger http://t.co/PnRXfvEgxL"
- Oct 7, 2015 08:14:01 PM "@PjwJ316: @realDonaldTrump YES!!!!!!!!!! AMERICA NEEDS @realDonaldTrump FOR PRESIDENT!!! CAN'T WAIT FOR AMERICA TO BE GREAT AGAIN!!!!"

- Oct 8, 2015 10:44:04 AM Wacky @glennbeck who always seems to be crying (worse than Boehner) speaks badly of me only because I refuse to do his show--a real nut job!
- Oct 8, 2015 10:45:06 AM I hear @glennbeck is in big trouble. Unlike me, his viewers & ratings are way down & he has become irrelevant—glad I didn't do his show.
- Oct 8, 2015 10:57:09 AM Wow, great news! I hear @EWErickson of Red State was fired like a dog. If you read his tweets, you'll understand why. Just doesn't have IT!
- Oct 8, 2015 11:01:02 AM What a time we all had in Iowa yesterday, massive overflow crowd. Love them!
- Oct 8, 2015 11:12:07 AM I'm at Trump Int'l Hotel in Las Vegas, tallest/most beautiful building in town. Speaking to another great crowd at Treasure Island (12 noon)
- Oct 8, 2015 11:31:33 AM Great, Kevin McCarthy drops out of SPEAKER race. We need a really smart and really tough person to take over this very important job!
- Oct 8, 2015 11:38:57 AM "@Moonwkr: @realDonaldTrump I would like to nominate @IvankaTrump for Speaker of the House" What a great idea, she is a total winner! (Nice)
- Oct 8, 2015 11:46:37 AM Washington (D.C.) is such a mess - nothing works! I will MAKE AMERICA GREAT AGAIN! It's not going to happen with anyone else.
- Oct 8, 2015 11:47:59 AM "@MidOhioMilitia: I haven't missed a speech or interview. Love hearing you speak for ME! #Trump2016 #MakeAmericaGreatAgain #IBelieve"
- Oct 8, 2015 11:51:30 AM "@GaryGaryt52: @DanScavino @JudiLoera @realDonaldTrump WHEN IS TRUMP COMING TO FLORIDA? CAN'T WAIT.GO TRUMP! . FL FOR TRUMP
- Oct 8, 2015 11:52:13 AM "@SKennedy1979: No one else brings the passion, conviction, experience that you have. Your message is resonating w America! I'm excited."
- Oct 8, 2015 11:54:11 AM "@PennySingletary: @realDonaldTrump we know this and that's why you will be our next President" Thank you.
- Oct 8, 2015 12:22:17 PM "@DesignerDeb3 Wow 5000+ in Line in Las Vegas For our Next President of these United States Mr @realDonaldTrump !"

- Oct 8, 2015 01:31:51 PM "This Man Is the Most Dangerous Political Operative in America" via Bloomberg Politics http://t.co/5htys6nqtR
- Oct 8, 2015 02:07:22 PM 'The goal is to be the winner': Donald Trump's campaign is for real. Via The Guardian http://t.co/7yP6iW2srp
- Oct 8, 2015 03:00:22 PM Website Exposing Marco 'Amnesty' Rubio Goes Live: A 'Donor Class Puppet'? - Breitbart http://t.co/GArR1v5736
- Oct 8, 2015 03:24:01 PM Thanks. https://t.co/FgcU1Ih3ew
- Oct 8, 2015 03:32:05 PM "@Momfullofhope @BorderWall @realDonaldTrump rocks it everywhere he goes" Thanks.
- Oct 8, 2015 03:57:50 PM Thank you! https://t.co/bFSu7j5mCq
- Oct 8, 2015 04:04:46 PM Just leaving Las Vegas. Unbelievable crowd! Many Hispanics who love me and I love them! https://t.co/t7hzDV9wEr
- Oct 8, 2015 04:08:33 PM A great event in Las Vegas, Nevada! http://t.co/LI75orkoqT
- Oct 8, 2015 04:59:35 PM .@EWErickson is a total low life--- read his past tweets. A dummy with no "it" factor. Will fade fast.
- Oct 8, 2015 05:00:07 PM .@EWErickson ran @RedState into the ground. A change was necessary. Congratulations to @RedState and good luck in the future!
- Oct 8, 2015 06:49:43 PM I was so happy when I heard that @Politico, one of the most dishonest political outlets, is losing a fortune. Pure scum!

- Oct 9, 2015 05:52:55 AM Will be interviewed on @Morning_Joe at 7:20. Great crowd in Las Vegas yesterday!
- Oct 9, 2015 09:53:10 AM "@AlisaApps @realDonaldTrump you were fantastic yesterday in Las Vegas - a great event. Passionate people. Keep it up! #AlisaReal" Thx
- Oct 9, 2015 11:24:19 AM "@DavidFoody @realDonaldTrump Thank you for taking on the Establishment.They don't know what to do, do they?"
- Oct 9, 2015 11:24:48 AM "@LauraRosenCohen @MarkSteynOnline on @realDonaldTrump "There is nothing Trump does that doesn't work for him."
- Oct 9, 2015 11:26:54 AM Good luck! Enjoy. https://t.co/ddfPtVYpXv
- Oct 9, 2015 12:19:51 PM Thanks Larry. Best wishes. https://t.co/AZwPbSjj7T
- Oct 9, 2015 12:43:01 PM "@BarbMuenchen @grindingdude the book to read is Time to get Tough making America great again." Thanks.
- Oct 9, 2015 12:44:21 PM I will be interviewed on @FacetheNation Sunday 10AM on CBS. @johndickerson is a true pro!

- Oct 9, 2015 12:50:05 PM I will be going to Atlanta, Georgia tomorrow—here's the info: http://t.co/Ty3VYUMphm. Hope to see you there! #MakeAmericaGreatAgain!
- Oct 9, 2015 02:28:14 PM "@JayMichaelsProd Trump won the crowd yesterday curious to see how many are changing their registrations from Democrat to Republican??"
- Oct 9, 2015 02:29:26 PM Thanks. https://t.co/aZXLgvWeGm
- Oct 9, 2015 02:30:47 PM True. Thanks. https://t.co/BjNeF2YFvq
- Oct 9, 2015 02:32:26 PM "@JBOD2001 @realDonaldTrump yeah, you're really wearing out your welcome. Who's dominating the polls? YOU!!! Go Trump!"
- Oct 9, 2015 02:35:21 PM "@ept_rudyru @AnnCoulter I'm Hispanic & @realDonaldTrump has my vote! And a lot of other Hispanics here in the Borderland! "
- Oct 9, 2015 02:38:37 PM "@Women4Trump MSM cut off intro of Trump in LV where we were told he just gave $20 million to St. Jude's Charity http://t.co/WNfBUWk17w …
- Oct 9, 2015 02:40:12 PM Thank you. https://t.co/VSsa4N3OL7
- Oct 9, 2015 02:42:29 PM "@michaeljohns With this month's 224-page @simonschuster book Crippled America, Trump has most specific policy agenda of any candidate.."
- Oct 9, 2015 02:46:40 PM "@paulfincher2 Keep the faith. Elect @realDonaldTrump and there will be no more sanctuary cities. and very few illegals."
- Oct 9, 2015 02:50:47 PM Crowd gathers to hear Trump speech in Las Vegas http://t.co/ox6YyCV5s4
- Oct 9, 2015 03:35:12 PM New Gravis Poll in NH just out: Trump 32%, Carson 13% http://t.co/mJcWOEijkv
- Oct 9, 2015 03:39:43 PM Good luck to the US Men's National Team in tomorrow's CONCACAF Cup vs. Mexico! It should be a great game! https://t.co/nH31afzjNz
- Oct 9, 2015 05:22:14 PM Mark--They could use you. https://t.co/tOJ3ecOjNZ
- Oct 9, 2015 05:43:35 PM Great Gravis Poll on the great state of NH. Also, watch @FaceTheNation on CBS & @HowardKurtz #mediabuzz -- both on Sunday.

- Oct 9, 2015 09:13:13 PM Will be interviewed on "Media Buzz" with Howie Kurtz on Fox, Sunday at 11:00 A.M.
- Oct 9, 2015 09:17:46 PM Heading for Atlanta tomorrow morning for noon speech at North Atlanta Trade Center. Big crowds, great people!
- Oct 9, 2015 09:18:29 PM "@bdean1468: @realDonaldTrump ATL LOVES TRUMP!!!" Thanks!
- Oct 9, 2015 09:19:04 PM "@Jamgrigs: @realDonaldTrump Trump keep fighting the fight for America, we got your back. The future is looking bright. THE TRUMP REVOLUTION
- Oct 9, 2015 09:19:59 PM "@TheWTFTahoe: Please don't ever give up. This country is in such a mess and needs a non-politician to fix it. #MakeAmericaGreatAgain"
- Oct 9, 2015 09:20:44 PM "@AliceEngle3: @trumpiowa @TRUMPVICTORY16 @realDonaldTrump The next generation will be better off because Trump was in the Oval Office!"
- Oct 9, 2015 09:21:17 PM "@w_gorham: @realDonaldTrump Go President Trump! Many Canadians up here are behind you... totally! https://t.co/sS0njTyZnj"
- Oct 9, 2015 10:50:16 PM "@thehill: .@realDonaldTrump's biggest Hispanic fan: "He's my perfect man" http://t.co/bP8KJ1P9SK http://t.co/GiqUAJzYcX" A great woman!
- Oct 9, 2015 10:55:33 PM "@MyPresidentme: @realDonaldTrump @thehill She represents how thousands of us feel. You have the BEST supporters BAR NONE! #Trump2016

- Oct 10, 2015 07:12:02 AM "@nypost: People are writing tribute songs for Donald Trump http://t.co/YEPsqFmBGY" Thanks to all of these great songwriters. Get rich!
- Oct 10, 2015 08:31:55 AM Paul Ryan is far from my first choice, but a very nice guy. The Republicans should go for tough and (very) smart this time - no games!
- Oct 10, 2015 08:47:54 AM I'm leading big in every poll and we are going to WIN! Remember, Trump NEVER gives up!
- Oct 10, 2015 01:46:34 PM .@ChuckTodd just informed us that my interview last week on @MeetthePress was their highest rated show in 4 years. Congrats!

- Oct 10, 2015 01:51:54 PM Thank you Georgia! I had a great afternoon with all of you! I will be back soon. #MakeAmerciaGreatAgain http://t.co/gkFoShg2xh
- Oct 10, 2015 02:10:40 PM .@ThisWeekABC with @GStephanopoulos had fantastic numbers last Sunday --- Trump interview. Nice!
- Oct 10, 2015 02:11:14 PM My interview with @HowardKurtz on #MediaBuzz will air tomorrow on @Fox at 11am and 5pm. Great job Howie, very insightful.
- Oct 10, 2015 02:11:50 PM Will be interviewed on @FaceTheNation with @JDickerson tomorrow at 10:30am EST. Enjoy!
- Oct 10, 2015 02:14:21 PM With the fantastic ratings last weekend, @meetthepress & @ThisWeekABC, I think it's only fair that I go on @FoxNewsSunday w/ Chris Wallace.
- Oct 10, 2015 02:18:17 PM Via Breitbart - "Riding High in Polls Donald Trump Storms the American South to Overflow Crowds in Georgia" http://t.co/iLcaMZxc82
- Oct 10, 2015 04:36:52 PM Little Barry Diller, who lost a fortune on Newsweek and Daily Beast, only writes badly about me. He is a sad and pathetic figure. Lives lie!
- Oct 10, 2015 04:41:55 PM Just got back from Georgia. The crowds and love for U.S. was so amazing! We all had a great day together - will be back soon!
- Oct 10, 2015 04:49:22 PM "@Clint_Goodrich: They used to call Barry Diller the father of "e-commerce"-what a joke that was - and that he is. 100%clueless on Internet"

- Oct 11, 2015 07:09:52 AM I will be on Face The Nation (CBS) today at 10:30 A.M. and Media Buzz (Fox News) at 11:00 A.M. Enjoy!
- Oct 11, 2015 07:02:36 PM "@TheFix: Tuesday's Democratic debate is missing just one thing: Donald Trump." True, can you think of anyone who wants to watch?
- Oct 11, 2015 07:06:52 PM "@kausmickey: .@realDonaldTrump was calling out Paul Ryan for his entitlement plans back in 2011 http://t.co/nVgWXaYhUN" So true!
- Oct 11, 2015 07:09:47 PM "@CNNPolitics: .@clayaiken praises "good guy" Trump and his "upstanding" and "grounded" kids http://t.co/sewrn2VkJ8 http://t.co/oRIPL1xDBG

- Oct 11, 2015 08:43:08 PM President Obama was terrible on @60Minutes tonight. He said CLIMATE CHANGE is the most important thing, not all of the current disasters!
- Oct 11, 2015 08:52:15 PM Great, everyone is saying I did much better on @60Minutes last week than President Obama did tonight. I agree!

- Oct 12, 2015 11:25:38 AM Leaving soon after a great time in New Hampshire, a truly special place!
- Oct 12, 2015 12:13:19 PM "@CFT1 @realDonaldTrump doing a great job in New Hampshire today ! #MakeAmericaGreatAgain"
- Oct 12, 2015 12:45:47 PM Via RealClear Politics http://t.co/U7JPpgszvn
- Oct 12, 2015 03:50:13 PM Thank you. https://t.co/hFDFvwMY7Q
- Oct 12, 2015 04:44:13 PM Will be interviewed by @SeanHannity on @foxnews at 10PM tonight. Enjoy!
- Oct 12, 2015 06:05:57 PM "@connie_lee1: @realDonaldTrump @seanhannity @FoxNews Looking forward to a great interview with a great interviewee and a great interviewer!
- Oct 12, 2015 06:07:29 PM "@VickyBrush: That young girl asking if she'll have control over her own body looked like she was planted there! @HorseShort
- Oct 12, 2015 10:26:40 PM "@GregWescott: @realDonaldTrump @seanhannity @FoxNews Another great interview. You were point on .... As good as it gets!" Thanks!
- Oct 12, 2015 10:27:26 PM "@heavenlyitalian: @seanhannity @FoxNews time we had a businessman in the WH,who can bring back jobs to America and restore the middle class
- Oct 12, 2015 10:29:56 PM "@kyredblood: @realDonaldTrump Great Fox interview" @seanhannity
- Oct 12, 2015 10:30:39 PM "@mimi_saulino: @seanhannity @FoxNews Syrian Muslims escorted into U.S. through Mexico. Now arriving to Oklahoma and Kansas! Congress?"
- Oct 12, 2015 10:32:23 PM "@BackOnTrackUSA: @seanhannity You are looking & sounding more Presidential everyday. The country is ready for you to #MakeAmericaGreatAgain

- Oct 13, 2015 03:53:53 AM "@codyave: @drudgereport @BreitbartNews @Writeintrump "You Can't Stump the Trump" https://t.co/0xITB7XeJV http://t.co/iF6S05se2w"
- Oct 13, 2015 04:03:52 AM "@TopherCarlton: .@JebBush Sickening attempt. I hope .@realDonaldTrump jumps another 10 points. #WakeUpAmerica https://t.co/GT86RlB0t3"
- Oct 13, 2015 04:05:33 AM "@Parker_Votes: California Gov. Jerry Brown signs bill allowing illegals right to VOTE using drivers lic.ID. @realDonaldTrump
- Oct 13, 2015 04:24:29 AM "@deqwik2: @SaraMurray @realDonaldTrump Sorry link above not working. Here's good link http://t.co/0DoJeMrzC9" @CNN and Jeb - apologize!
- Oct 13, 2015 04:43:56 AM At the request of many, and even though I expect it to be a very boring two hours, I will be covering the Democrat Debate live on twitter!
- Oct 13, 2015 04:49:36 AM Someone should inform @CNN that, despite spending millions of $'s on graphics, it is not the Democratic Debate, rather the Democrat (s) D!
- Oct 13, 2015 04:56:09 AM "@farrightgregy: Dan Rather: Donald Trump Could Be Our Next President http://t.co/0OyeDcOfSE" I agree - thanks Dan!
- Oct 13, 2015 04:59:53 AM "@ryan_padraic: Get the popcorn, Donald Trump plans to live-tweet the #CNNDebate. #DemDebate https://t.co/RNNqqdyXDP"
- Oct 13, 2015 05:02:03 AM "@Politics_Reddit: That feminist who called out Trump last night? She's a Jeb intern. http://t.co/aRroatryt6" Jeb always gets caught, sad!
- Oct 13, 2015 05:40:19 AM "@jonygitar: #morningjoe @morningmika @Morning_Joe @JoeNBC Surely you read reports that woman at no labels event was a pol. operative?"
- Oct 13, 2015 05:46:46 AM Sheldon Adelson is looking to give big dollars to Rubio because he feels he can mold him into his perfect little puppet. I agree!
- Oct 13, 2015 06:39:52 AM The arrogant young woman who questioned me in such a nasty fashion at No Labels yesterday was a Jeb staffer! HOW CAN HE BEAT RUSSIA & CHINA?
- Oct 13, 2015 06:42:01 AM "@ElviNichols: Will @CNN be tough as they were with @realDonaldTrump ? Not sure..https://t.co/NNnFMXrXMj" No way, they will be very gentle!

- Oct 13, 2015 06:43:09 AM "@007lLisav: @CNN @realDonaldTrump @CNNPolitics can't wait for his insightful & intelligent tweets." Will be so much better than CNN!
- Oct 13, 2015 08:29:43 AM "@Ma1973sk I can't wait for @realDonaldTrump live tweets during Dem debate tonight. Won't watch debate but will watch Trump's Twitter"
- Oct 13, 2015 08:35:29 AM Very honored: "Trump Is Tops As Clinton Drops In Connecticut Primaries, Quinnipiac University Poll Finds" http://t.co/6d8WiLa8fB
- Oct 13, 2015 10:09:24 AM Everybody's talking about my doing twitter during the likely very boring debate tonight. @realDonaldTrump #DemDebate
- Oct 13, 2015 10:37:43 AM So nice, thank you very much. https://t.co/OmbuWUHA0m
- Oct 13, 2015 10:52:02 AM How can Jeb Bush expect to deal with China, Russia + Iran if he gets caught doing a "plant" during my speech yesterday in NH?
- Oct 13, 2015 11:21:20 AM "Exclusive--Davi: Trump, The Lion We Need" http://t.co/OYnWVnfsge
- Oct 13, 2015 12:34:01 PM It was just announced that I will be hosting Saturday Night Live on Nov. 7th -- look forward to it! http://t.co/D74EQyvR0P
- Oct 13, 2015 02:18:03 PM Live from New York- November 7th! @nbcsnl http://t.co/rfEE86Mbbp
- Oct 13, 2015 03:56:03 PM "@seancduarte @TeamCavuto #Yourworld If @realDonaldTrump wins Barry Diller will move out of country. Sounds like a win, win."
- Oct 13, 2015 06:58:03 PM "@007lLisav: @CNN @realDonaldTrump @CNNPolitics can't wait for his insightful & intelligent tweets." You sound like a very smart person!
- Oct 13, 2015 06:59:01 PM "@CNN: .@realDonaldTrump will be live-tweeting the #DemDebate http://t.co/5OQYwGQHzu via @CNNPolitics http://t.co/7qmu8kM1u7"
- Oct 13, 2015 07:00:08 PM "@ElviNichols: Will @CNN be tough as they were with @realDonaldTrump ? No way, they will want to be soooo nice!
- Oct 13, 2015 07:08:14 PM Should be interesting but too bad the three guys at 《 1% will be taking up so much time - but who knows, maybe a star will be born (unlikely)

- Oct 13, 2015 07:08:54 PM "@xai7126: @greta I'd rather see @realDonaldTrump be the debate moderator!"
- Oct 13, 2015 07:10:47 PM "@StreckerJosh: The Hillary love fest on CNN is ridiculous. I feel bad for the other candidates...especially the non-criminal ones."
- Oct 13, 2015 07:12:54 PM "@hapearce1: @realDonaldTrump they need to take the debate slow, a lot of low energy on the stage tonight." I hope not!
- Oct 13, 2015 07:13:44 PM "@moshe_mkmdca: @realDonaldTrump @007lLisav @CNN @CNNPolitics following Donald is beautiful. If it's not beautiful it's not Donald" So nice!
- Oct 13, 2015 07:14:21 PM "@MintzShire: @realDonaldTrump @007lLisav @CNN @CNNPolitics We need Trump Now!!!" Make America Great Again!
- Oct 13, 2015 07:20:39 PM We will all have fun and hopefully learn something tonight. I will shoot straight and call it as I see it, both the good and the bad. Enjoy!
- Oct 13, 2015 07:27:08 PM "@JoethomasSmith: #DemDebate The @IvankaTrump interview tomorrow on @CNN will have better ratings than the #democraticdebate #Trump2016
- Oct 13, 2015 07:29:41 PM "@sassylassee: My tv is off, twitter is up, waiting for the real show, starring @realDonaldTrump #CNNSocialistDebate" #DemDebate
- Oct 13, 2015 07:36:06 PM "@valmouw: @realDonaldTrump where are you? I'm already getting bored and it hasn't even started #DemDebate"
- Oct 13, 2015 07:37:58 PM "@HL3tweets: @TDsVoice @CNN @CNNPolitics I'm watching now and will watch the entire debate while reading Trump's Tweets. Grab the popcorn"
- Oct 13, 2015 07:45:08 PM Putin is not feeling too nervous or scared. #DemDebate
- Oct 13, 2015 07:46:52 PM Get rid of all of these commercials. #DemDebate
- Oct 13, 2015 07:54:03 PM "@adamscottnow: @realDonaldTrump,If I have the #DemDebate on CNN, but pay attention more to my phone, does it still count as me watching it?
- Oct 13, 2015 07:56:48 PM "@0Nonsense: @realDonaldTrump Good luck commenting on this snooze fest, I'm out."
- Oct 13, 2015 07:58:53 PM "@wayway71: @realDonaldTrump Webb is OUT!!" Bad opening! #DemDebate

- Oct 13, 2015 08:00:06 PM "@MichaelTribunel: @realDonaldTrump imagine Chafey standing up to Putin"
- Oct 13, 2015 08:03:37 PM The trade deal is a disaster, she was always for it! #DemDebate
- Oct 13, 2015 08:05:37 PM "@amd9890: .@realDonaldTrump was right...#DemDebate is boring these ppl are so scripted" So far!
- Oct 13, 2015 08:06:07 PM "@tr3s3can: @realDonaldTrump @realDonaldTrump Make America Great Again!! Would not even watch Dem debate except Donald is tweeting about it!
- Oct 13, 2015 08:08:59 PM Can anyone imagine Chafee as president? No way.
- Oct 13, 2015 08:11:14 PM O'Malley, as former Mayor of Baltimore, has very little chance.
- Oct 13, 2015 08:11:55 PM "@Jeff_Gabe: I miss @realDonaldTrump #CNNDebate"
- Oct 13, 2015 08:12:27 PM "@maxxgadog: @LindaSuhler @realDonaldTrump if you got rid of commercials you would have nothing worth watching"
- Oct 13, 2015 08:16:34 PM "@princeolivier13: Why do we have to be tortured by watching these clowns! Have the election tomorrow! #trump2016 #DemDebate"
- Oct 13, 2015 08:17:43 PM "@rjdicksii: @realDonaldTrump. These cats are like bad used car salesmen."
- Oct 13, 2015 08:19:12 PM "@KOsbornSullivan: On our 25th anniversary my husband and I are happily staying in to watch #DemDebate and read @realDonaldTrump comments.
- Oct 13, 2015 08:20:01 PM "@LaurenDa123: @realDonaldTrump I think @JebBush and @marcorubio are supposed to be on this stage"
- Oct 13, 2015 08:20:39 PM "@JuliaTock: @realDonaldTrump Sure you are laughing listening to these 5 try and explain how business and the economy works. Scary!
- Oct 13, 2015 08:21:32 PM "@Roolaloo: Joined twitter tonight JUST to follow along with @realDonaldTrump and #DemDebate. Lets make America great again! #trump2016"
- Oct 13, 2015 08:21:59 PM "@jennasnowy69: @realDonaldTrump why is Webb there??"
- Oct 13, 2015 08:23:49 PM "@theericker: @realDonaldTrump not watching debate....just your tweets" Nice!

- Oct 13, 2015 08:28:19 PM "@FEDEnergy: @NRA @nranews Support the NRA more then ever, @nationalrifle needs to back @realDonaldTrump who wants to protect 2nd amendment!
- Oct 13, 2015 08:28:38 PM "@prissyalways: @realDonaldTrump I cannot stop yawning...Twitter is more interesting. #DemDebate"
- Oct 13, 2015 08:30:59 PM "@Pandorasandy1: @realDonaldTrump we need Donald Trump to make America great again !!!" Thanks!
- Oct 13, 2015 08:33:46 PM Who is winning the debate so far (just last name)? #DemDebate
- Oct 13, 2015 08:37:34 PM "@NexiaVauxhall: @realDonaldTrump I love that NO group can buy @realDonaldTrump"
- Oct 13, 2015 08:38:13 PM "@DNorrell: This is one of the most dysfunctional debates I've seen in my lifetime. @realDonaldTrump"
- Oct 13, 2015 08:39:31 PM "@Iamnewhere: Webb is trying to be @realDonaldTrump and its not working." He is not doing well!
- Oct 13, 2015 08:40:18 PM "@mikerichterp: @realDonaldTrump I joined Twitter tonight just to hear Mr.Trump tweet about this silly debate.
- Oct 13, 2015 08:40:52 PM "@XGDesignsNYC: Yada yada...It's a bore fest... Best part of this is Trumps tweets! @realDonaldTrump #DemDebate" Thanks.
- Oct 13, 2015 08:42:18 PM "@Achilarre: I couldn't even imagine the bloodbath that would ensue if the @realDonaldTrump debated any one of these five jabronis"
- Oct 13, 2015 08:48:30 PM All are very scripted and rehearsed, two (at least) should not be on the stage.
- Oct 13, 2015 08:54:05 PM The hardest thing Clinton has to do is defend her bad decision making including Iraq vote, e-mails etc.
- Oct 13, 2015 08:55:31 PM Good move by Bernie S.
- Oct 13, 2015 09:02:02 PM Sorry, there is no STAR on the stage tonight!
- Oct 13, 2015 09:04:05 PM "@julieruot: I want a president who believes all lives matter and that is why we need @realDonaldTrump."
- Oct 13, 2015 09:05:07 PM "@RealNinjetta: @realDonaldTrump @IngrahamAngle Why did Hillary get to skate past the "Do Black Lives Matter" Anderson let her off hook!
- Oct 13, 2015 09:06:28 PM "@TimCooperTweets: How amazing is it that the #1 trending topic is @realDonaldTrump talking about the #DemDebate-more than the debate itself

- Oct 13, 2015 09:07:39 PM "@TS01171980: @FoxNews @realDonaldTrump isn't on the stage, turning this garbage off
- Oct 13, 2015 09:09:47 PM "@keksec_org: The only winner of the #DemDebate is @realDonaldTrump." This is not a great debate - a little sad!
- Oct 13, 2015 09:12:00 PM "@i_am__tyler: I can't wait for @realDonaldTrump to debate one of these clowns! All are so weak!
- Oct 13, 2015 09:15:50 PM Sanders said only black lives matter - wow! Hillary did not answer question!
- Oct 13, 2015 09:33:13 PM Notice that illegal immigrants will be given ObamaCare and free college tuition but nothing has been mentioned about our VETERANS #DemDebate
- Oct 13, 2015 09:35:51 PM "@ObamaTax: After @hillaryclinton poor performance, waffling in debates, @Teamsters14 should support @realDonaldTrump"
- Oct 13, 2015 09:37:41 PM "@Jtrink97: @Hell0ThereLydia @realDonaldTrump his commentary is making an otherwise shitty night outstanding" Thanks.
- Oct 13, 2015 09:38:16 PM "@Jamesppierce: These 5 make @realDonaldTrump look like Winston Churchill #DemDebate" Cute!
- Oct 13, 2015 09:39:52 PM "@mcowgerFL: @realDonaldTrump Thank you for ALWAYS REMEMBERING America's veterans!"
- Oct 13, 2015 09:43:03 PM "@Cola0531: @realDonaldTrump watching OAN great speech calling out super pacs and media in Norcross, GA"
- Oct 13, 2015 09:46:37 PM "@FrankGuaragna: @realDonaldTrump OMalley destroyed Maryland.. True, he was a disaster.
- Oct 13, 2015 09:48:09 PM "@suzyserb: @realDonaldTrump 100,000 people watching tonight for real change. THAT WOULD BE TRUMP 2016. Checking out the clown competition
- Oct 13, 2015 09:56:33 PM Check out OAN and compare to what you are watching now!
- Oct 13, 2015 09:59:40 PM "@magnifier661: @realDonaldTrump they make Jeb Bush look like the energizer bunny #DemDebate #USADJT2016"
- Oct 13, 2015 10:09:32 PM "@debateless: @realDonaldTrump I cannot wait to see you debate these clowns #CNNDebate #CNN #Debate #DNC"
- Oct 13, 2015 10:09:44 PM "@Angie58493041: @sadmexi @realDonaldTrump sucess of Mr Trump is another success of america 2015"

- Oct 13, 2015 10:09:56 PM "@PauperInAPinch: @realDonaldTrump Thank goodness #DemDebate is over. Not impressed... TRUMP2016!!! #MakeAmericaGreatAgain"
- Oct 13, 2015 10:10:38 PM "@releafpen: Dem debate message summary = More free handouts. They will be voting in droves. We need to get out and vote Trump BIG TIME!"

- Oct 14, 2015 09:55:03 AM The latest book on Hillary—Wow, a really tough one! http://t.co/ZCoUAutdI8 @RogerJStoneJr
- Oct 14, 2015 09:55:58 AM Like her or not, Hillary did what she had to do in the debate last night—get through it. Her opponents were very gentle and soft!
- Oct 14, 2015 09:57:25 AM #DemDebate was really boring but had a lot of fun live tweeting and picked up by far the most followers.
- Oct 14, 2015 10:33:57 AM We need a strong leader- and fast! https://t.co/UVhbC0JNxD
- Oct 14, 2015 11:31:34 AM The debate last night proved that Hillary is running against the "B" team. She won't be so lucky when it comes to me!
- Oct 14, 2015 12:27:50 PM Will be going to Richmond, Virginia today. Big crowd! See you there.
- Oct 14, 2015 01:18:07 PM Even though I have the legal right to use Steven Tyler's song, he asked me not to. Have better one to take its place!
- Oct 14, 2015 01:18:18 PM Steven Tyler got more publicity on his song request than he's gotten in ten years. Good for him!
- Oct 14, 2015 01:23:55 PM CNN/ORC Poll results just out for Nevada—WOW! Trump 38, Carson 22, Fiorina 8, Bush 6, Cruz 4 http://t.co/X2Kv6qzPia
- Oct 14, 2015 01:47:23 PM .@andersoncooper did an excellent job of hosting the #DemDebate last night. Tough, firm, but fair.
- Oct 14, 2015 01:48:50 PM CNN Poll just out on South Carolina – great #'s http://t.co/E6do3oi10Z
- Oct 14, 2015 07:31:24 PM "@JeremyHL: RT @FoxNews: .@realDonaldTrump: I have thousands of Hispanics working for me & they like me very much. http://t.co/A7RaXDC4gH"
- Oct 14, 2015 07:32:52 PM "@TrumpFix: I swear, Donald is getting better, bolder, brasher, and more kick ass with every event/intvw he does! HE WILL WIN!

- Oct 14, 2015 07:33:14 PM "@CHM1321: @realDonaldTrump is "in it to win it"."
- Oct 14, 2015 07:33:27 PM Just did @OReillyFactor. Will be back on at 11pm on @FoxNews.
- Oct 14, 2015 07:36:11 PM "@FoxGotTrumped: @realDonaldTrump with another great speech today with another huge crowd!!!!! We love you Trump!!!! #Trump2016
- Oct 14, 2015 07:36:57 PM Incredible crowd in Richmond, Virginia tonight! So much spirit and energy! #makeamericagreatagain https://t.co/B0PfF9AdZf

- Oct 15, 2015 10:18:58 AM I'm very proud of my daughter Ivanka. Great interview. http://t.co/aNL95tOVrO
- Oct 15, 2015 12:13:20 PM Signing my tax return.... http://t.co/XJfXeaORbU
- Oct 15, 2015 12:31:49 PM A great day in New Jersey for Trump! http://t.co/IdaYonGiL4 & http://t.co/YsqPfea6KE
- Oct 15, 2015 01:33:07 PM .@KevinHart4real joined @woodmank104 @katek104 @K1047 & was asked about his thoughts on @realDonaldTrump #Trump2016 Thanks Kevin--so nice!
- Oct 15, 2015 01:44:04 PM The @GOP should not agree to the ridiculous debate terms that @CNBC is asking unless there is a major benefit to the party.
- Oct 15, 2015 01:44:47 PM .@CNBC is pushing the @GOP around by asking for extra time (and no criteria) in order to sell more commercials.
- Oct 15, 2015 01:45:35 PM Why is the @GOP being asked to do a debate that is so much longer than the just-aired and very boring #DemDebate?
- Oct 15, 2015 02:56:30 PM Will be on @bloombergtv tomorrow with @sruhle. Enjoy!
- Oct 15, 2015 08:43:27 PM "@davidaxelrod: .Met @IvankaTrump a few years back. DonaldTrump is wise to enlist his daughter's help. She's a throughly impressive person."
- Oct 15, 2015 08:44:33 PM "@IsupportTrump16: @realDonaldTrump Has lived the American dream and has inspired MILLIONS! He will #MakeAmericaGreatAgain for ALL of us.
- Oct 15, 2015 08:47:01 PM "@bigmikeobrien: @EricTrump @skyjones55 @greta @FoxNews @oreillyfactor @CarlRove is in the tank for Bush we are tired of the establishment"

- Oct 15, 2015 08:48:31 PM "@RedScareBot: @brandongordy1: @realDonaldTrump is what we millennials need. I used to support that socialist from VT, what a mistake."
- Oct 15, 2015 09:00:12 PM Megyn Kelly has two really dumb puppets, Chris Stirewalt & Marc Threaten (a Bushy) who do exactly what she says. All polls say I won debates
- Oct 15, 2015 09:12:26 PM .@marcthiessen is a failed Bush speechwriter whose work was so bad that he has never been able to make a comeback. A third rate talent!
- Oct 15, 2015 09:22:29 PM Every poll, Time, Drudge, Slate and others, said I won both debates - but heard Megyn Kelly had her two puppets say bad stuff. I don't watch
- Oct 15, 2015 09:29:27 PM "@RickStans1: Donald, Megyn Kelly seeks ratings, not truth Not much of a journalist. Stay focused & make your own narrative. It's working"
- Oct 15, 2015 09:43:08 PM "@Hohummm: Did you also hear Megyn say "Carson is the front-runner ...according so some polls ..tied in other polls" OUTRIGHT LIE!" Hatred!
- Oct 15, 2015 09:58:41 PM "@lance_combrink: @realDonaldTrump Karl Rove still thinks Romney won. Why is he still on TV?"

- Oct 16, 2015 05:22:34 AM .@CNBC has just agreed that the debate will be TWO HOURS. Fantastic news for all, especially the millions of people who will be watching!
- Oct 16, 2015 06:46:23 AM .@EricTrump was FANTASTIC on @foxandfriends this morning. He may be my son but he is a special guy!
- Oct 16, 2015 06:50:32 AM "@JoeyL3rd: @foxandfriends @EricTrump Grt interview, I'm telling ya, @realDonaldTrump children r going 2 b a HUGE asset 2 him & his campaign
- Oct 16, 2015 06:53:53 AM "@SHLOMO_ABADDON: @TODAYshow @MLauer @realDonaldTrump Matt will vote for Trump i just know he will !"
- Oct 16, 2015 06:54:00 AM "@Pjdahling: @mitchellvii the truth prevails when it is so obvious. @realDonaldTrump is a force that is unstoppable"
- Oct 16, 2015 06:56:11 AM "@JohnNew2015: @lance_combrink Well, @KarlRove is an establishment hack big government RINO whose only hope is @JebBush - That's sad, eh!?"

- Oct 16, 2015 06:58:13 AM "@jimmy_jkmorgan: @JoeyL3rd @foxandfriends @EricTrump Totally agree! Great Father with a great family - winning combination at life."Thanks
- Oct 16, 2015 07:53:06 AM "@jamesdschulzejr: @FoxNews http://t.co/TveCbOaQDM You GOPe supporters wrong again on Trump, give it up. Get on the Trump train. GREAT NEWS
- Oct 16, 2015 07:54:23 AM "@samijs1: Hahahahahahaha...love it! #MakeAmericaGreatAgain #Trump2015 #TrumpTrain Choo choo...all aboard! :) http://t.co/HNp2DfdgpS"
- Oct 16, 2015 07:57:25 AM .@scottienhughes Keep up the great work Scottie. Polls are best ever!
- Oct 16, 2015 03:14:15 PM Nice story from @businessinsider http://t.co/O0snYivV0M
- Oct 16, 2015 04:28:18 PM A great new poll-33%! http://t.co/3EheiVyD5A
- Oct 16, 2015 04:33:41 PM Rumor has it that the grubby head of failing @VanityFair Magazine, "Sloppy" Graydon Carter, is going to be fired or replaced very soon?
- Oct 16, 2015 04:54:28 PM Heading to Boston to see another huge crowd! My friend Tom Brady is a great competitor and golf partner. https://t.co/lWpbffq5bp
- Oct 16, 2015 06:17:20 PM In Massachusetts --- the place is packed! #MakeAmericaGreatAgain
- Oct 16, 2015 08:07:32 PM .@JebBush, At the debate you said your brother kept us safe- I wanted to be nice & did not mention the WTC came down during his watch, 9/11.
- Oct 16, 2015 08:29:28 PM "@TRUMPHIANT2016: I've never seen a candidate as dominant in early states as @realDonaldTrump http://t.co/5aeyPlLFzp #TrumpTrain #VOTETRUMP
- Oct 16, 2015 08:29:35 PM No @JebBush, you're pathetic for saying nothing happened during your brother's term when the World Trade Center was attacked and came down.
- Oct 16, 2015 08:31:09 PM .@JebBush, like it or not, our country needs more energy and spirit than you can provide! #MakeAmericaGreatAgain
- Oct 16, 2015 09:15:15 PM "@myhealthcoach1: @NoahGrayCNN Thank You Police Force for your efforts of Protecting Donald Trump We Love You For This, God Bless You!!!"

- Oct 16, 2015 10:49:19 PM .@KatrinaPierson, you did a fantastic job tonight on @FoxNews. Thank you for your very tough and very smart representation!

- Oct 17, 2015 09:42:55 AM Thank you @thefix for your very honest commentary. One thing, we do have great teams in IA, NH, SC and beyond. https://t.co/ZVQiw6CpCO
- Oct 17, 2015 09:47:38 AM .@HillaryClinton is on the front page of the @nytimes waving to 200 people in New Hampshire. My crowd next door was 5,000 people – no pic!
- Oct 17, 2015 11:01:35 AM Via CNET: Donald Trump Bests Jeb Bush in Website Performance, Experts Say- http://t.co/ioHAZOT8lK
- Oct 17, 2015 11:01:57 AM Via Business Insider: Donald Trump's Poll Dominance in 2 Key States is Mind-Blowing- http://t.co/FqIApU6gVC
- Oct 17, 2015 04:54:45 PM Russia and the world has already started to respect us again! http://t.co/3hdsUtMHim
- Oct 17, 2015 04:55:16 PM A great story in the New York Post ---really well written! http://t.co/ZXFte8aqYf
- Oct 17, 2015 05:46:14 PM "@aspiesmom: NYPost "gets it", you talk like a New Yorker. My Dad is a Democrat Long-Islander, he "gets it" too, and you've got his vote"
- Oct 17, 2015 06:43:04 PM I will be interviewed on Fox News Sunday With Chris Wallace at 9:00 A.M. or 10:00 A.M. (depending on location). Will be tough but good!
- Oct 17, 2015 06:44:50 PM "@mimi_saulino: @mariclaire81 @realDonaldTrump Jeb supports open borders-common core- Visa H-IB Visa's for illegals. Super PAC Saudis.
- Oct 17, 2015 06:50:02 PM Good news for those that want to Make America Great Again - I am winning every poll in every STATE and NATIONAL - and by big numbers! Thanks
- Oct 17, 2015 07:36:34 PM "@vlynpowell: @realDonaldTrump At happy hour tonight in Charleston, SC, everyone at the bar said they were supporting Donald Trump. Thanks!
- Oct 17, 2015 07:38:01 PM "@HL3tweets: Jeb and Marco OWE IT to their contributors to admit they have NO CHANCE of winning, and figure out how to PAY BACK everyone"

- Oct 17, 2015 07:39:01 PM "@bk2seattle: @realDonaldTrump I was with you in Tyngsboro, Ma. last night! You WILL be our next President!!!" What a fantastic evening!
- Oct 17, 2015 07:43:00 PM "@mklloydva: Some of you already know. I have made the Jump to Trump. Donald Trump is the man that will win the GOP.http://t.co/bMMrb2XZsn"
- Oct 17, 2015 10:02:10 PM Amazing! Thank you! #MakeAmericaGreatAgain #Trump2016 http://t.co/fnRIXJWCVf

- Oct 18, 2015 07:38:08 AM "@ClaytonMorris: Donald Trump is so far ahead in two key state polls. http://t.co/AtdlgoZXzB http://t.co/b8SWhe6HTB" Thanks Clayton
- Oct 18, 2015 07:59:20 AM On at 9:00A.M. or 10:00 A.M. (depending on your location) on Fox is a tough but really good interview with Chris Wallace. Enjoy!
- Oct 18, 2015 08:04:36 AM Jeb Bush should stop trying to defend his brother and focus on his own shortcomings and how to fix them. Also, Rubio is hitting him hard!
- Oct 18, 2015 08:09:48 AM This morning Chris Wallace has the best political show on television - but that's only because I'm on it (kidding)! Have fun.
- Oct 18, 2015 08:29:03 AM Jeb, why did your brother attack and destabalize the Middle East by attacking Iraq when there were no weapons of mass destruction? Bad info?
- Oct 18, 2015 08:53:48 AM .@FoxNewsSunday
- Oct 18, 2015 10:01:04 AM "@blondesforjesus: @FoxNewsSunday Loving @realDonaldTrump interview. #TrumpSwagger #ChrisWallace" Thank you.
- Oct 18, 2015 10:06:21 AM .@MittRomney can only speak negatively about my presidential chances because I have been openly hard on his terrible "choke" loss to Obama!
- Oct 18, 2015 10:14:11 AM .@MittRomney and his campaign manager should not be critical of candidates after they blew an election that should never have been lost!
- Oct 18, 2015 10:20:12 AM Does everyone remember @MittRomney and his famous remarks about "self-deportation" and "47%". He was done. I don't need his angry advice!

- Oct 18, 2015 10:25:21 AM "@girl_iowagirl20: #STOPTHEPRESSES @britthume just admitted DonaldTrump will probably be the Republican nominee! #HellJustFrozeOver @FoxNews
- Oct 18, 2015 10:26:12 AM "@Glitter_alex: @realDonaldTrump is what we need to fix this mess! #MakeAmericaGreatAgain Im only 11 but my parents are voting for Trump!"
- Oct 18, 2015 10:27:02 AM "@97Musick: @FoxNewsSunday @skyjones55 @realDonaldTrump Of course they're going up! Trump is going to WIN this!! #Trump2016" Thanks.
- Oct 18, 2015 10:28:09 AM "@WalterEKurtzJr: @realDonaldTrump Chris Wallace: "After my interview and listening to his answers, I think Donald Trump could be President
- Oct 18, 2015 10:29:39 AM "@BBCARKING: @JoeTrippi @realDonaldTrump @scottienhughes Joe have U resigned to the inevitable? Take UR seat on the http://t.co/SIppNYk834
- Oct 18, 2015 10:31:14 AM "@smr111382: @realDonaldTrump One of the best interviews I have seen!" @FoxNews
- Oct 18, 2015 10:32:52 AM "@AdamBlickstein:I never thought I'd say this but @realDonaldTrump sparking a critical conversation on reality that Bush didn't keep US safe
- Oct 18, 2015 10:41:51 AM I should release the sad and totally apologetic letter that Penn @pennjillette hand delivered to me. Minds would be changed very fast!
- Oct 18, 2015 10:45:11 AM "@danlifting: @realDonaldTrump Get a life George Will. USA doesn't make anything anymore. TRUMP will bring manufacturing Back to USA!"
- Oct 18, 2015 10:48:55 AM "@d_seaman: @realDonaldTrump Trump wins, hands down: https://t.co/HX87yTSqXs Jeb is weak, Rubio is broke."
- Oct 18, 2015 10:50:04 AM "@mesiaindo: @chazermann26 I don't think @NBC will cave. They've seen ratings soar with @realDonaldTrump and Money matters!"
- Oct 18, 2015 11:15:19 AM Replay of Fox News Sunday With Chris Wallace at 2:00 P.M. on @FoxNews. Big statement made by Chris!
- Oct 18, 2015 01:00:53 PM I will be interviewed by Chris Wallace at 2:00 P.M. on @FoxNews - Turn off the football for 15 minutes, Make America Great Again!

- Oct 18, 2015 01:09:28 PM "@DefendingtheUSA: @realDonaldTrump @FoxNews LOVED the brutal zinger against the Wall Street journal!!!"
- Oct 18, 2015 01:12:22 PM "@DefendingtheUSA: @realDonaldTrump @FoxNews LOVED the brutal zinger against the Wall Street Journal!!!"
- Oct 18, 2015 01:15:24 PM It's amazing that some of the dumbest people on television work for the Wall Street Journal, in particular a real dope named Charles Lane!
- Oct 18, 2015 02:12:23 PM Just reported by CNN that "the Trump halo effect" caused a record-shattering Democratic Debate rating of 15.3 million viewers. So true!
- Oct 18, 2015 02:38:09 PM "@AnnCoulter:He's right. Trump on 9/11 happening on Bush's watch: With my immigration policy, I doubt those ppl wld have been in the country
- Oct 18, 2015 02:40:35 PM "@AnnCoulter: Read this DJT full-p ad from 1989 and tell me DonaldTrump is a Johnny-Come-Lately "fake" conservative: http://t.co/DBNIc3MIOl
- Oct 18, 2015 03:00:54 PM "@HardcoreRepub: @kencampbell66 Dude, @realDonaldTrump 's tactics are just on a level we've never seen before. http://t.co/jXTWQLpRdM"
- Oct 18, 2015 03:01:28 PM "@UndEngel: @realDonaldTrump @AnnCoulter Couldn't have said it, better... Nothing "fake" about you, sir."
- Oct 18, 2015 03:05:03 PM "@Pappenjazz: An Incredibly Strong Interview Of @realDonaldTrump @FoxNewsSunday, Good Response IC Those @FoxNews NaySayers dissapating!"
- Oct 18, 2015 04:09:59 PM "@American1st: @ofccadjust @AnnCoulter GW Bush was open borders like @JebBush. TERRORISTS CAN COME ACROSS MEXICAN BORDER AT WILL!"
- Oct 18, 2015 04:10:37 PM "@muhfuck: @BernieSanders Donald Trump is the only candidate for middle class America @realDonaldTrump #Trump2016 #MakeAmericaGreatAgain"
- Oct 18, 2015 04:11:08 PM "@Tuvarkz: @realDonaldTrump Can't Stump the Trump"
- Oct 18, 2015 04:12:55 PM "@RD_2008: @JebBush Quit Jeb Quit. Your poll is even lower than your apprentice Rubio. @realDonaldTrump"
- Oct 18, 2015 04:17:10 PM "@Kellmat2: @realDonaldTrump @RD_2008 @JebBush Jeb is no conservative in my book. Common core is a disaster."

- Oct 18, 2015 04:19:01 PM "@tweet4upatriots: I believe @realDonaldTrump can make AMERICA GREAT again #C2GTHR http://t.co/vt0nIgBBmJ" Thank you!
- Oct 18, 2015 04:27:58 PM Fox News Sunday With Chris Wallace will be re-broadcast on @FoxNews at 6:00 P.M.
- Oct 18, 2015 05:17:14 PM "@paulferguson17: @FoxNewsSunday @realDonaldTrump @JebBush @FoxNews. Chris this is awesome what an interview. Go donald"
- Oct 18, 2015 05:18:33 PM "@howddyd: @FoxNewsSunday @realDonaldTrump is correct u can't allow 1 woman 2 fain luv of house 2 get more $$$ holding up huge #'s of jobs."
- Oct 18, 2015 05:20:34 PM "@clar: @GeorgeWill @brithume The TV's made in SC are Element Electronics Come on guys. @realDonaldTrump is right @BretBaier #WakeUpAmerica"
- Oct 18, 2015 05:21:11 PM "@rdpaga: @JebBush we were attacked on ur brothers watch. That's not safe. I have respect 4 GW but truth is no WMD in Iraq & 911
- Oct 18, 2015 05:21:32 PM "@Karen05866992: @realDonaldTrump @FoxNews So far this is one of the BEST interviews with Trump.!!" Thank you.
- Oct 18, 2015 05:22:26 PM "@SongBird1154: Again SNL (10/17) exposes CarlyFiorina as failed CEO, an unwanted Senatorial candidate, & GOD forbid next Prez #NTXForum"
- Oct 18, 2015 05:23:37 PM "@RebelCapsGal: @realDonaldTrump THANK YOU for speaking out against Common Core and how horrible it is for kids!"
- Oct 18, 2015 05:25:29 PM "@BentleyforTrump: @FoxNewsDear Sir. Chris Wallace believes that you can be elected president.Great Great news for America! #Trump2016"
- Oct 18, 2015 05:25:56 PM "@rfscottga: @realDonaldTrump @FoxNews It was Excellent interview sir. May watch it again. Trump 2016"
- Oct 18, 2015 05:26:36 PM "@traceclmbs82: @FoxNews Pampered @GeorgeWill who never had a real job has no problem w/USA losin jobs 2 foreign countries @FoxNewsSunday"
- Oct 18, 2015 05:27:19 PM "@kathystone1221: @realDonaldTrump @FoxNews A must see. Trump is brilliant. as usual !!!! #MakeAmericaGreatAgain #TeamTrump #Trumptrain"

- Oct 18, 2015 05:28:05 PM "@PattiPav1: @realDonaldTrump Great interview!" Thanks
- Oct 18, 2015 05:29:20 PM "@PattyDs50: @FoxNews We want Donald !! Yah next president! #TrumpTrain #TrumpForPresident" We will all MAKE AMERICA GREAT AGAIN!
- Oct 18, 2015 05:30:02 PM "@Svingali: @realDonaldTrump @FoxNews Can't wait for @megynkelly to jump on the TRUMP Train as Chris Wallace just did!" Won't happen!
- Oct 18, 2015 05:30:49 PM "@Justice41ca: @realDonaldTrump @FoxNews I'm watching it again right now in California"
- Oct 18, 2015 05:30:57 PM "@Karen05866992: @realDonaldTrump @FoxNews So far this is one of the BEST interviews with Trump.!!"
- Oct 18, 2015 05:50:10 PM Best thing my supporters can do if you don't like the way @megynkelly and her puppets unfairly treat "us" is don't watch her show!
- Oct 18, 2015 06:57:37 PM "@ConserveCast: The Definition of a Pretentious Establishment Henchman is @GeorgeWill . He is such a sourpuss, HATES @realDonaldTrump
- Oct 18, 2015 06:59:01 PM "@ChefMama32: @realDonaldTrump Good interview with Chris! Chris even gave you a thumbs up for POTUS"
- Oct 18, 2015 07:01:23 PM "@rikemohome: @GeorgeWill @FoxNewsSunday George is full of Crap SC Element TV's Are CHINESE MADE. http://t.co/V48wKD9Tot WHAT A LIAR!!"
- Oct 18, 2015 07:02:17 PM "@Crowebar_67: @megynkelly Been boycotting her since 1st debate Mr. Trump and so have plenty of other decent people. Ratings R going down
- Oct 18, 2015 07:30:04 PM "@vbonina: @ConserveCast @GeorgeWill why does Fox even talk to Will? He is clueless and doesn't represent what our party is about."
- Oct 18, 2015 07:31:23 PM "@Weaverinc31: The problem is @MittRomney was a weak establishment candidate who couldn't even turn out the base. Weak at best!"
- Oct 18, 2015 07:36:27 PM "@lwentzel1: Link of the day! Most popular link among people I follow is http://t.co/IuMDrygxbO by @realDonaldTrump"
- Oct 18, 2015 07:37:36 PM "@theratzpack: @Svingali @FoxNews @megynkelly i don't care if she jumps on the train .be gr8 if she were just FAIR and BALANCED"

- Oct 18, 2015 07:38:12 PM "@JulesSiscoe: We finally have a voice with @realDonaldTrump! #VoteTrump #CoalitionForTrump #CitizensForTrump"
- Oct 18, 2015 07:43:18 PM "@SweetFreedom29: Hey @realDonaldTrump --> FLASHBACK: Jeb Bush Admitted 'Leaky' Immigration Led to 9/11 http://t.co/Jmm7wd32UD #tcot" WOW!
- Oct 18, 2015 07:43:40 PM "@TMoody: @realDonaldTrump @megynkelly why would I watch ANYONE who trusted THIS GUY with nuclear codes? @JebBush http://t.co/FsHOXrj6cV"
- Oct 18, 2015 07:50:23 PM "@aldeguer_elsa: @American1st @ofccadjust @AnnCoulter @JebBush HISPANICS UNITED TO MAKE AMERICA GREAT AGAIN #Trump http://t.co/P5Oh6fhMIa"
- Oct 18, 2015 07:53:05 PM "@joshdill64: Our passion for @realDonaldTrump is amazing! https://t.co/mOoXkbhaVC"

- Oct 19, 2015 08:30:30 AM It's really cold outside, they are calling it a major freeze, weeks ahead of normal. Man, we could use a big fat dose of global warming!
- Oct 19, 2015 08:36:31 AM Jeb is fighting to defend a catastrophic event. I am fighting to make sure it doesn't happen again.Jeb is too soft-we need tougher & sharper
- Oct 19, 2015 11:26:25 AM Bruce Willis wearing my hat on @FallonTonight last Friday- http://t.co/d2PlEBk3m2
- Oct 19, 2015 12:42:17 PM NEW POLL: Trump Blue Collar Support highest since FDR in 1930s--WOW! http://t.co/fnRIXJWCVf
- Oct 19, 2015 12:53:43 PM Interesting reading re September 11th http://t.co/eFgd00dZQO
- Oct 19, 2015 02:21:07 PM Via @IBTimes: "Under Fire From Donald Trump, Jeb Bush Focuses On 9/11 Even Though Hijackers Got Florida Licenses" https://t.co/a9s6mHsk07
- Oct 19, 2015 03:31:38 PM See, the attack very possibly could have been stopped. We need real leadership and vision. https://t.co/JA1Fo5H6FP
- Oct 19, 2015 07:00:38 PM Tonight's official count--7,943. An all time record for the Anderson Civic Center in SC! Thanks! #Trump2016 https://t.co/bMJcymz1Qp

- Oct 19, 2015 09:53:22 PM "@cb_beach_bum: Great job @seanhannity you slayed Mr. Sanchez with the #truth thx 4 defending @realDonaldTrump https://t.co/TcNTiAuvrK"
- Oct 19, 2015 09:53:48 PM "@marcoinjersey: I think America had enough of the faking and is ready for someone REAL just look at @realdonaldtrump.
- Oct 19, 2015 09:55:40 PM "@Trump4potusplz: Had to join Twitter for the first time just to support Donald @realDonaldTrump . TRUMP 2016" Great!
- Oct 19, 2015 09:56:26 PM "@nickmichaels12: Since late July 2015, DJT consistently been the front-runner in public opinion polls for the Republican Party nomination.
- Oct 19, 2015 09:57:40 PM "@Mike350Zdriver: Many Hispanics agree with @realDonaldTrump on enforcing the border Trump for President https://t.co/iTWCCQfJzP"

- Oct 20, 2015 01:58:31 PM Bill Clinton wants to #MakeAmericaGreatAgain https://t.co/rVOZHzrlEB
- Oct 20, 2015 02:27:29 PM I will be on @seanhannity tonight at 10 PM @FoxNews. #Hannity
- Oct 20, 2015 02:33:05 PM Lots of great new polls--big leads! https://t.co/Og4SN4eXbO https://t.co/xJaAWC9RgO https://t.co/8FyxYEna0h
- Oct 20, 2015 02:42:19 PM "Donald Trump tops Franklin-Pierce/Herald poll at 28 percent in N.H." https://t.co/gXXJ4YhKIW
- Oct 20, 2015 02:49:43 PM Both Aberdeen and Turnberry in Scotland, and the soon to open Doonbeg in Ireland, blow Bandon Dunes away. Bandon is a toy by comparison!
- Oct 20, 2015 06:58:03 PM "@Trekwolf164: @wbtonyturner @RadioFreeTom @realDonaldTrump no magic just cut off USA aid money to Mex until cost is recovered.Simple really
- Oct 20, 2015 07:05:13 PM I will be interviewed on @seanhannity tonight at 10:00. You will find it very interesting (I hope). Enjoy!
- Oct 20, 2015 07:21:43 PM .@KarlRove Had my best day ever in the polls, one had me at 41% - Morning Consult. Boston Globe, Monmouth, NBC and CNN all great. More!
- Oct 20, 2015 07:23:31 PM "@PatriotByGod: @GSamUSA1 @Carolde @realDonaldTrump Trumps new VA plan will solidify Vets. Support of Trump" I love the VETS.

- Oct 20, 2015 07:25:53 PM "@Portosj81J: @realDonaldTrump #Trump2016 #Trump hits his highest poll number yet; #Carson, #Rubio make small gains https://t.co/1f8dmS2Uza
- Oct 20, 2015 07:40:18 PM "@GirlDayTrader: Our new President will provide something we've never had before. #TRUTH even if it hurts. #Trump https://t.co/lZFolvR38a"
- Oct 20, 2015 07:58:34 PM .@seanhannity at 10:00.
- Oct 20, 2015 08:11:02 PM "@btodd539: @seanhannity Now they are All saying Donald really Could Be President! I Knew This from Start! We ALL must work together!"
- Oct 20, 2015 08:11:27 PM "@AshlieJuliard: @KarlRove @realDonaldTrump Trump is the only candidate that I've ever been excited about #SomethingSpecialIsHappening"
- Oct 20, 2015 09:46:47 PM I will be interviewed on @GMA Good Morning America tomorrow at 7:00 A.M. Big new ABC poll coming out - I hope I do well!
- Oct 20, 2015 09:49:08 PM .@MonicaCrowley you were GREAT on @seanhannity tonight. Thank you for the nice words!
- Oct 20, 2015 10:12:30 PM "@ansun_sayavong: Your opponents have no idea what they're dealing with. Sun Tzu would be very proud. You are a tactical genius. #artofwar"
- Oct 20, 2015 10:15:21 PM "@saadvisory: @realDonaldTrump Donald keep fighting - you are the only hope for America!
- Oct 20, 2015 10:20:37 PM "@blewthebigone: The establishment can try all they want to keep @realDonaldTrump from winning. They are not stronger than we the people!!"
- Oct 20, 2015 10:22:42 PM "@OUSoonerManiac: We are looking forward to meeting you at your rally in Burlington, Iowa tomorrow! #MakeAmericaGreatAgain" See you there!
- Oct 20, 2015 10:23:10 PM "@aaron_athman: @realDonaldTrump first time I can ever vote and you've got mine! I want to make America great again!!!" FANTASTIC!
- Oct 20, 2015 10:24:37 PM "@EricSjursen: @FoxNews @SheriffClarke @MonicaCrowley There you go! Everyone loves Donald Trump bcuz he's the real thing, not a politician"

- Oct 20, 2015 10:25:01 PM "@ccorreia401: @realDonaldTrump @blewthebigone well said. We the people want the truth. We the people want to make America great again."
- Oct 20, 2015 10:25:40 PM "@Chocolate3Way: I have never loved a candidate as much as I love @realDonaldTrump, I can't wait for him to make America great again!" Nice!
- Oct 20, 2015 10:26:12 PM "@AliceCarozza: @realDonaldTrump You were so much better than Jeb on Hannity. So Great and presidential. I'm happy this was discussed."
- Oct 20, 2015 10:47:04 PM "@piersmorgan: Donald Trump still dominating all polls, debate, cable news, gossip...everything. The GOP nomination is his, he rarely loses!
- Oct 20, 2015 10:57:43 PM "@printingsharon: @realDonaldTrump Never been so excited about voting for a candidate since I voted for Reagan"
- Oct 20, 2015 10:58:46 PM .@GMA at 7:00 A.M.

- Oct 21, 2015 05:36:45 AM Just out: Boston Herald/Franklin Pierce Poll N.H. TRUMP 28 (up 10) CARSON 16 BUSH 9 RUBIO 6 CRUZ 5 Press will say they are surging!
- Oct 21, 2015 05:41:40 AM I will be interviewed on @GMA Good Morning America at 7:00 A.M. @ABC will be announcing new poll numbers. MAKE AMERICA GREAT AGAIN!
- Oct 21, 2015 06:13:23 AM "@dcexaminer: Rasmussen: @realDonaldTrump now beats @HillaryClinton 38%-36% nationally https://t.co/NuNulI0Voi https://t.co/1BAPAKad62"
- Oct 21, 2015 06:33:11 AM New poll by ABC News/Washington Post TRUMP 32 CARSON 22 RUBIO 10 BUSH 7 Wow, how will the media put a negative spin on this one?
- Oct 21, 2015 09:04:52 AM .@TrumpToronto was just voted the #1 hotel in Canada in Conde Nast Traveler's prestigious Reader's Choice Awards https://t.co/Uc9Txu7O8g
- Oct 21, 2015 11:21:41 AM The great workers who just completed the skylight at Trump International Hotel, D.C. (Old Post Office) https://t.co/wEj6IjyBDK
- Oct 21, 2015 12:24:35 PM I think Joe Biden made correct decision for him & his family. Personally, I would rather run against Hillary because her record is so bad.

- Oct 21, 2015 02:26:23 PM "@i_am_tyler @MichaelCohen212 I can promise you the only reason I watched the democrat's debate is because of @realDonaldTrump"
- Oct 21, 2015 03:58:35 PM Can u believe that Jeb Bush's campaign manager is in Berlin, Germany looking for money? What's he giving to Germany? https://t.co/HDdWRBteNe
- Oct 21, 2015 10:38:04 PM "@USATrustTrump: WOW! The More Opponents Push The Higher The #Trump2016 Reach! Keep Pushing DEMS And Jealous GOPs! https://t.co/RaS4FJAsls"
- Oct 21, 2015 10:43:49 PM "@carrillo_pete: @realDonaldTrump people are for you #Trump2016 keep up the good work and we will win this and #MakeAmericaGreatAgain"

- Oct 22, 2015 11:15:51 AM "Trump Nears 100 days on Top" via The Hill https://t.co/MDzpY89TRE
- Oct 22, 2015 11:25:53 AM #ChrisWallace, who interviewed me on Sunday, had his highest ratings since Feb of '09. Congratulations! https://t.co/o49V73AZZB
- Oct 22, 2015 11:43:27 AM "@toddinwichita @realDonaldTrump Hillary is doing a HORRIBLE job at #BenghaziHearings reading from the script. #pathetic . She is no leader"
- Oct 22, 2015 11:54:01 AM Joe, thanks for not running! https://t.co/yYAMVXWc7t
- Oct 22, 2015 01:59:31 PM The young intern who accidentally did a Retweet apologizes.
- Oct 22, 2015 03:53:58 PM "@dpdax @realDonaldTrump Thanks for standing for Vets Take care of those that give so much"
- Oct 22, 2015 06:43:37 PM "@MiamiHerald: For Donald Trump, South Florida makes it rain — dollars, that is https://t.co/E1zMC3kism https://t.co/nz5QTpsktk" Very nice
- Oct 22, 2015 06:47:26 PM "@ThomaOlivia: Donald Trump Hands 'Fox News Sunday' Its Biggest #Crowd In 6 Years https://t.co/rp0ffSCHMu https://t.co/oEh5cVJCFa" Great!
- Oct 22, 2015 07:19:00 PM "@autumnandews08: @KatrinaPierson @AnnCoulter @MichaelCohen212 Trump blows them all away! He's our next president! #Trump2016"

- Oct 23, 2015 12:02:32 AM "@Ir0nSpirit: Can't wait for you to take the White House. Our country will once again be strong! Sorry JebBush, but you got no chance!"
- Oct 23, 2015 12:08:46 PM Remember, official campaign merchandise (hats, apparel etc.) can only be bought at https://t.co/SXUUL7l8vp. Be careful, don't get ripped-off
- Oct 23, 2015 06:17:14 PM So nice of @Cher--- greatly appreciated! https://t.co/11hmnFEP1S
- Oct 23, 2015 10:33:32 PM Crowd was amazing tonight at Trump National Doral in Miami. Love and excitement in the ballroom. Tomorrow at noon in Jacksonville!

- Oct 24, 2015 05:46:50 AM "@cher: Never thought I'd Say…Donald Trump is a Giant Among Gop front runners!! cruz=devil rubio=RAGE AGAINST WOMEN carson=JUST TELL ME WHY
- Oct 24, 2015 05:54:01 AM "@Tony_Leers: Hillary Clinton is a deceitful career politician, Donald Trump is a no-nonsense billionaire businesses man...pick one.."
- Oct 24, 2015 05:54:14 AM "@oshack: A surprising number of Republicans think Donald Trump is their best hope in 2016 https://t.co/Rq1s5tqBDA"
- Oct 24, 2015 05:58:11 AM "@santiagos58: YouGov National Poll Donald Trump Continues To Dominate Field With All Demographics. The Last Refuge https://t.co/HrMActE2e6
- Oct 24, 2015 05:59:47 AM "@HuffPostEnt: Donald Trump to host "Saturday Night Live" https://t.co/tzHHk7XIYq https://t.co/MBTRL47Nko"
- Oct 24, 2015 06:40:06 AM Massive crowds already forming in Jacksonville - will be and incredible day - 12 noon! MAKE AMERICA GREAT AGAIN!
- Oct 24, 2015 08:46:17 AM Leaving for Jacksonville now. See you there! Miami was great.
- Oct 24, 2015 11:26:09 AM Saying goodbye to some of my great workers at @TrumpDoral in Miami. https://t.co/C8AG3eGSus
- Oct 24, 2015 01:22:39 PM Just finished speaking in Jacksonville, Florida. Incredible crowd, fantastic people. Thank you!
- Oct 24, 2015 02:40:08 PM Will be doing a sit down interview with @JakeTapper @CNN on Sunday morning at 9:00. Tough questions and hopefully very good answers!

- Oct 24, 2015 02:40:39 PM I will be doing the @TodayShow live from New Hampshire at 7am on Monday morning. #TrumpToday
- Oct 24, 2015 02:41:08 PM Expecting a great crowd of amazing people. Questions will be live! #TrumpToday
- Oct 24, 2015 03:42:41 PM .@JebBush is totally lost -- he spends too much time managing the bloated staff of his campaign & not enough talking about America's future.
- Oct 24, 2015 03:43:25 PM .@JebBush had a tiny 300 person crowd at Senator Tim Scott's forum. I had thousands, and they had real passion! https://t.co/osBW3TM4UO
- Oct 24, 2015 03:44:18 PM .@JebBush is slashing campaign salaries, people making millions. If he can't manage his campaign, how can he manage our countries finances?
- Oct 24, 2015 06:29:13 PM "@BeverlySimcic: TRUMP: JEB BUSH HAS NO MONEY, HE'S MEETING WITH MOMMY AND DADDY- CAN'T RUN HIS OWN CAMPAIGN https://t.co/2znAQAm7Ry"
- Oct 24, 2015 06:35:19 PM "@HankCampbell: Democrats seem to be more interested in Donald Trump than Hillary Clinton.
- Oct 24, 2015 09:37:18 PM "@bravehart60: 20 Reasons Why It Should Be Donald Trump in 2016 https://t.co/2JsHqNRHUu via @BreitbartNewsl" A.J., thank you, soooo nice!
- Oct 24, 2015 10:24:42 PM While Jeb Bush is cutting staff and salaries, after having paid ridiculous amounts of money, why did he pay so much in the first place?
- Oct 24, 2015 10:25:34 PM "@politicalwire:"Bush has no money, he's meeting today with mommy and daddy, and they're working on his campaign." https://t.co/QTi3NXtSfc"
- Oct 24, 2015 10:32:03 PM "@christotepis: Donald Trump Leads in Expectations, Shows Strength on Attributes (POLL) - ABC News - https://t.co/5YvRmCqL6B via @ABC"
- Oct 24, 2015 10:34:46 PM "@Bane1349: They ALL Want Jobs and a Bright Future. They KNOW Donald Trump is the one and only choice to make that A REALITY!
- Oct 24, 2015 10:43:37 PM "@JaredChristophr: Donald Trump is the only person that can make this country great again @realDonaldTrump" I fully agree!

- Oct 24, 2015 10:47:03 PM "@aviv1818: Trumpachusetts: Donald Trump Tops Poll of Bay State Voters: https://t.co/VC6mogbdMt @foxnewspolitics AC360" Thanks, great news
- Oct 24, 2015 11:06:16 PM "@voxdotcom: Trump has figured out Jeb Bush's greatest weakness as a candidate, and it's not his energy level https://t.co/l4V3EoxXlv"

- Oct 25, 2015 05:14:13 AM "@agreatimage: @realDonaldTrump Can ANY Democrat or Republican fix this country except Trump? NOT A CHANCE!! #Trump2016 #ElectTrump"
- Oct 25, 2015 05:28:32 AM I will be doing a major sit down interview on State of the Union With Jake Tapper at 9:00 A.M. on @CNN. Enjoy!
- Oct 25, 2015 05:31:23 AM "@EasyEarl: Doug Ross @ Journal: AWESOME: Donald Trump Blessed by Black, White Pastors and Rabbis https://t.co/JDEw856k6h via @directorblue
- Oct 25, 2015 05:36:39 AM This is just not the right time for Jeb Bush. His campaign is in total disarray, too much staff being paid way too much money = U.S. GOVT.
- Oct 25, 2015 05:43:24 AM "@katiesinex: 20 Reasons Why It Should Be Donald Trump in 2016 https://t.co/2JsHqNRHUu" Wow, so nice!
- Oct 25, 2015 05:44:21 AM "@LandmanMarius: @realDonaldTrump AUSTRALIA SUPPORTS DONALD TRUMP. Please immigrate to Australia and make Aussie great as well." Cute!
- Oct 25, 2015 06:18:17 AM A big POLL will be announced this morning on @CBSNews Face The Nation. I wonder if I do well if the press will report the results? Doubt it
- Oct 25, 2015 06:34:59 AM I spell out some of the differences between Ben Carson and myself at 9:00 A.M. on @CNN @jaketapper. Ben is very weak on illegal immigration.
- Oct 25, 2015 06:41:08 AM Ben Carson has never created a job in his life (well, maybe a nurse). I have created tens of thousands of jobs, it's what I do.
- Oct 25, 2015 08:13:03 AM Watch @CNN at 9:00 A.M. @jaketapper. Then interviewed on @ABC @GStephanopoulos at 10:00 A.M. and then, at 10:30 A.M., watch Face The Nation.
- Oct 25, 2015 08:40:57 AM Big poll comes out today on Face The Nation at 10:30 on @CBSNews.

- Oct 25, 2015 08:46:08 AM "@msbul: Your a gentlemen Ben but not our next President, @realDonaldTrump https://t.co/R6SUEwhP3g"
- Oct 25, 2015 08:48:35 AM "@russia890: @CNNPolitics @realDonaldTrump Trump is the smartest of all. My comment is non partisan. I heard everybody n im on Trump side."
- Oct 25, 2015 08:55:58 AM "@ron_fournier: .@realDonaldTrump rightly denounces Super PAC-driven campaign $ system. Another example of how DC deserves this guy" Great!
- Oct 25, 2015 09:22:31 AM "@MachadoKirk: @StrengthenTheUS @realDonaldTrump Carson is not a nice guy. He knows his SuperPAC throws Mud on Trump 24/7 #ActingMeek"
- Oct 25, 2015 09:29:51 AM Watch my interview on @CBSNews Face The Nation now and, also, the new CBS POLLS which, if good for me, the media won't report!
- Oct 25, 2015 11:11:58 AM .@CBSNews Poll - WOW! New Hampshire TRUMP 38% CARSON 12% BUSH 8% South Carolina TRUMP 40% CARSON 23% CRUZ 8% Iowa TRUMP 27% CARSON 27%
- Oct 25, 2015 12:53:31 PM Do you believe that @FoxNews is still playing up the old Iowa poll numbers and no mention of the ABCWashington Post or just out CBS results?
- Oct 25, 2015 01:36:34 PM .@ByronYork Great numbers from @CBSNews Poll. Also from ABC-Washington Post Poll. Thank you! @CNN
- Oct 25, 2015 01:46:26 PM "@thatgirlflorida: @realDonaldTrump @ByronYork @CBSNews @CNN Florida Loves Trump !!! We had a ball in Jacksonville Saturday!"
- Oct 25, 2015 01:54:50 PM "@concerningtimes: @JebBush needs to drop out your, hurting the republican cause . @realDonaldTrump is our choice"
- Oct 25, 2015 01:55:36 PM "@Tirolian2: @realDonaldTrump @ByronYork @CBSNews @CNN # TRUMP is Unstoppable US US US" Thank you.
- Oct 25, 2015 01:56:40 PM "@josemen31: @realDonaldTrump this Mexican here loves you man!! Keep doing your thing #mexicolovestrump" Great!
- Oct 25, 2015 01:59:33 PM "@TheCRwire: Mitt Romney finally takes the credit he deserves… for #Obamacare https://t.co/17XKfwxJ7O . https://t.co/HNBjSX4yGw"

- Oct 25, 2015 02:05:04 PM "@nepafortrump: @ByronYork @CBSNews @CNN We R here FIGHTING for you DJT! You are the only person who can #MakeAmericaGreatAgain #TeamTrump"
- Oct 25, 2015 02:07:04 PM "@kathystone1221: @ByronYork @CBSNews @CNN OMG! Carson is more LOW KEY than Jeb!! Tried to watch him, but fell asleep! #NOISYMAJORITY!"
- Oct 25, 2015 02:20:11 PM "@cospy8: @realDonaldTrump @ByronYork @CBSNews @CNN WAY ahead in all the polls that matter. TRUMP FOR PRESIDENT"
- Oct 25, 2015 02:20:34 PM "@Thuglife602: @realDonaldTrump Bad position for Jeb, if his Mommy, Daddy and brother get involved the skeletons come back out of the closet
- Oct 25, 2015 02:21:35 PM "@curtismuddog: @ByronYork Latest Poll shows Donald Trump winning 70% of Electoral Vote Against Hillary Clinton! https://t.co/OT98Y8f0GE"
- Oct 25, 2015 03:31:15 PM "@ObfuscateClear: Wow, imagine what he'll do as President. Thanks @realDonaldTrump https://t.co/mZzQhDjoIO" FORD LISTENED TO ME, GREAT!
- Oct 25, 2015 03:36:19 PM Word is that Ford Motor, because of my constant badgering at packed events, is going to cancel their deal to go to Mexico and stay in U.S.
- Oct 25, 2015 03:39:07 PM Do you think I will get credit for keeping Ford in U.S. Who cares, my supporters know the truth. Think what can be done as president!
- Oct 25, 2015 03:41:30 PM "@jfgrcar: @realDonaldTrump Gentle Ben is no match for Putin or if the truth be told even for Hilary. USA needs a winner."
- Oct 25, 2015 03:42:19 PM "@Desheay: TO ALL MY CALIFORNIA TRUMP SUPPORTERS! Lets join up and work together on Twitter! Lets do this!!! @realDonaldTrump #Trump2016 !"
- Oct 25, 2015 03:44:47 PM "@mmolina44: @realDonaldTrump @ByronYork @CBSNews @CNN Donald Trump will be our next President of the United States."
- Oct 25, 2015 03:46:26 PM "@jpm05880: @Carolde @JebBush @realDonaldTrump @NancyRomano17 #JEBbush CAPTIVATES CROWDS WITH STIRRING SPEECH https://t.co/s3pprv6T8J" Wow

- Oct 25, 2015 03:46:50 PM "@Rketeltas: @realDonaldTrump Bush appears to be low on cash may need to do drop out or perhaps get a loan from Hillary.
- Oct 25, 2015 03:49:16 PM Remember that Carson, Bush and Rubio are VERY weak on illegal immigration. They will do NOTHING to stop it. Our country will be overrun!
- Oct 25, 2015 06:31:42 PM An aerial shot of Jacksonville crowd yesterday! I may as well show you because the media won't. #Trump2016 https://t.co/iJf87UVMEt
- Oct 25, 2015 07:06:43 PM Leaving for New Hampshire now. Will be doing the @TODAYshow there, live at 7:00 A.M. New @CBSNews Poll of New Hampshire: Trump 38 Carson 12!
- Oct 25, 2015 07:08:37 PM "@radioworldsv:Tomorrow on TODAY @MLauer moderates @realDonaldTrump town hall, live from New Hampshire. #TrumpTODAY https://t.co/SqzsV2K2zh
- Oct 25, 2015 07:20:48 PM Ben Carson wants to abolish Medicare - I want to save it and Social Security.
- Oct 25, 2015 07:51:54 PM "@DanSaltsman: @realDonaldTrump @Ford @crainsdetroit @detnews @CNBC https://t.co/k2JFVTDDbW Do you think Hillary, Ben or Jeb could do this?
- Oct 25, 2015 09:26:23 PM "@maria_heck: @RobertsLiardon @realDonaldTrump. The more I hear Trump the more I like him!"
- Oct 25, 2015 09:39:46 PM "@hoosierclinger: Good job @realDonaldTrump for badgering Ford. Why didnt POTUS or Hillary care about those UAW jobs in Ohio?"
- Oct 25, 2015 09:41:20 PM "@CindyBl: I voted 4 Reagan to make America Great. I will vote 4 @realDonaldTrump to #MakeAmericaGreatAgain #TRUMP https://t.co/BAPJGbR4ho"

- Oct 26, 2015 09:35:13 AM This whole Super PAC scam is very unfair to a person like me who has disavowed all PAC's & is self-funding.
- Oct 26, 2015 09:35:28 AM Re Super PAC scam: What the other candidates are doing is a disgrace.
- Oct 26, 2015 09:36:14 AM All Presidential candidates should immediately disavow their Super PAC's. They're not only breaking the spirit of the law but the law itself

- Oct 26, 2015 11:57:19 AM #TrumpTODAY Watch my appearance on the @TODAYshow from this morning https://t.co/9NbOEguzU1
- Oct 26, 2015 05:19:56 PM Dopey @BillKristol, who has lost all credibility with so many dumb statements and picks, said last week on @Morning_Joe that Biden was in.
- Oct 26, 2015 08:55:26 PM "@coloradojoe2001: How is any one taking Carson seriously when he "suspends" his presidential campaign for a book signing tour?"
- Oct 26, 2015 09:23:23 PM "@BobD746847: There shouldn't be a problem with this election. "WE THE PEOPLE" finally have someone that speaks on OUR behalf. TRUMP-2016"
- Oct 26, 2015 09:24:41 PM "@TheWhiteHatter: Thanks to @TODAYshow for giving great attention to the Town of Atkinson at #TrumpTODAY w/ https://t.co/kJF8SB2CXh"
- Oct 26, 2015 09:25:32 PM "@TheJusticeEngle: @realDonaldTrump I'm 18 years old from Florida, and just registered to vote. You got my vote in the primaries!" THANKS.
- Oct 26, 2015 09:26:51 PM "@AlbertoMarsano: @realDonaldTrump Looking forward to seeing you in Reno Nevada this Thursday! Nevada stands with you!!!!!!!!!!!!!!!" Nice.
- Oct 26, 2015 10:32:40 PM "@julian771177: Mike Tyson endorses @realDonaldTrump https://t.co/rKMkXAFeop #MakeAmericaGreatAgain" Thanks Iron Mike, greatly appreciated!

- Oct 27, 2015 06:59:35 AM "@JordanDworaczyk: @DrHawk12 @elvisknievil I'm voting for @realDonaldTrump too." Thanks.
- Oct 27, 2015 07:01:35 AM "@bawl: I agree @BillKristol hasn't be right about anything in a very long time. Shocking that @Morning_Joe gives him a platform."
- Oct 27, 2015 07:02:51 AM "@RhatPatriot: @FoxBusiness @realDonaldTrump Why not post the other polls where Trump has 40 percent and Carson is in the teens? Strange?"
- Oct 27, 2015 09:43:37 AM New Gravis national poll just out --- 36%! Very nice! #MakeAmericaGreatAgain
- Oct 27, 2015 09:46:25 AM Thank you @SahilKapur for the wonderful story. https://t.co/3ipTylrLzz

- Oct 27, 2015 11:14:20 AM "Trump's National Lead Increases to 35.6% Going into the Third GOP Debate it's Trump, Carson and Rubio" https://t.co/8SJazkQ3I1
- Oct 27, 2015 01:25:57 PM National GOP Presidential Poll via @OANN @realDonaldTrump 35.6% #Trump2016 https://t.co/Mvcj1ZH3Ql
- Oct 27, 2015 01:52:20 PM I am leaving for Sioux City, Iowa - great event (rally).
- Oct 27, 2015 01:59:41 PM "@faagifts: @OANN WTG, GREAT JOB. U R THE BEST PICK OUT OF ALL OF THE CANDIDATES & OHIO KNOWS THIS 2.THAT IS WHY U R LEADING THERE TOO"
- Oct 27, 2015 02:01:52 PM "@Indies4Trump: @HuffPostPol composite national poll #MakeAmericaGreatAgain #Trump2016 #TrumpTrain... https://t.co/VKDiYgpCEI"
- Oct 27, 2015 02:02:25 PM "@Rketeltas: @realDonaldTrump At least the real frontrunner is actually campaigning in Iowa and not on book tours. TRUMP 2016!"
- Oct 27, 2015 04:46:46 PM Just out, wonderful poll in North Carolina. #Trump2016 #MakeAmericaGreatAgain https://t.co/xdZGkdtNev
- Oct 27, 2015 09:46:36 PM Via the Washington Post: Inside the World of Donald Trump's Super Fans: https://t.co/QL6VhkZ8pm
- Oct 27, 2015 10:02:25 PM "@fairy_tabibi: Loved seeing @realDonaldTrump speak to the wounded warrior & his family.He has a caring heart and will take care of our vets
- Oct 27, 2015 10:03:35 PM Thank you Iowa! Great night---see you soon! #Trump2016 https://t.co/aCHH90cNRg
- Oct 27, 2015 10:05:55 PM "@RickSt. How many MSM outlets will carry a clip of @realDonaldTrump leaving the podium to enter a crowd & listen to the concerns of a VET?
- Oct 27, 2015 10:08:10 PM "@laura_damron: @FoxNews @realDonaldTrump This Hispanic woman believes Trump has the brains & energy to "Make America Great Again"."
- Oct 27, 2015 10:18:32 PM "@2bigj: @realDonaldTrump A lot of people I know are voting Trump in NC none have been polled your lead is bigger than anyone can imagine."
- Oct 27, 2015 11:47:45 PM "@BarbaraJensen1: @realDonaldTrump @OANN @GravisMarketing https://t.co/evyzpgIJ1V"

- Oct 27, 2015 11:50:36 PM "@Polling: DonaldTrump's and BenCarson's support up since Sept as they head into tomorrow's @CNBC #RepublicanDebate https://t.co/Wx3TY29i3p

- Oct 28, 2015 07:25:00 AM "@HMaewest: Via the Washington Post: Inside the World of Donald Trump's Super Fans: https://t.co/QL6VhkZ8pm https://t.co/wfbcBcsCov"
- Oct 28, 2015 07:28:46 AM "@JayknightJay: @RealBenCarson good morning. Easy on each other & finish off the establishment guys. They hope you 2 will fight it out."True
- Oct 28, 2015 07:46:44 AM "@MarieLeff: Debate night! #TeamTrump16 is behind you 5000% National Lead TRUMP 35.6% CARSON 21.7% https://t.co/KVgRDHlJH1"
- Oct 28, 2015 09:53:25 AM After a great evening and packed auditorium in Iowa, I am now in Colorado looking forward to what I am sure will be a very unfair debate!
- Oct 28, 2015 10:01:42 AM .@CNBC continues to report fictious poll numbers. Number one, based on every statistic, is Trump (by a wide margin). They just can't say it!
- Oct 28, 2015 10:18:45 AM .@Morning_Joe can you believe Kasie Hunt's poor and purposely inaccurate reporting on my great night and crowd in Iowa. @politico is a scam!
- Oct 28, 2015 10:21:06 AM "@1Barbara1: @realDonaldTrump @Morning_Joe @politico I watched the entire rally and Trump was very well received the place was packed."
- Oct 28, 2015 10:32:17 AM Does anybody think that @CNBC will get their fictitious polling numbers corrected sometime prior to the start of the debate. Sad!
- Oct 28, 2015 10:45:58 AM "@mozarttaig1: @CNBC is trying to drive down poll numbers to install Carson - who the Establishment GOP will promptly roll. Win Don Win!"
- Oct 28, 2015 10:47:14 AM "@cmrose111: @realDonaldTrump @CNBC get your polls straight. Trump is going to win. He is the only one tough enough to run this country."
- Oct 28, 2015 10:47:57 AM "@Vaporcon2015: @realDonaldTrump The Liberals are terrified that you'll be the one to go against Hillary.

- Oct 28, 2015 10:50:20 AM "@buckleybro40: @realDonaldTrump @CNBC why only Donald Trump can beat Hillary. https://t.co/lQtpC2rD6I #YUGE #Trump2016 #TeamTrump #"
- Oct 28, 2015 12:51:07 PM I'm sure the media will not report the highly respected new national poll that just came out via The Economist. 32%! https://t.co/aalSqnGHa3
- Oct 28, 2015 01:22:36 PM .@TheEconomist Poll, one of the most highly respected, was just released. Wow, wait until the media digests these numbers - won't be happy!
- Oct 28, 2015 03:10:46 PM @CNBC POLL TOTAL: TRUMP 25.22 CARSON 19.78 RUBIO 9.67....
- Oct 28, 2015 03:13:43 PM "@jaxsiete: @realDonaldTrump Love your sense of humor...LOL Your rallies are amazing. We're standing behind you 1000%:)" @FoxNews
- Oct 28, 2015 06:26:15 PM Via @MailOnline "Trump still in the lead by a whopping 14 points after fluke survey had put Carson on top"- https://t.co/tfaOARLoZb
- Oct 28, 2015 10:20:13 PM Thanks everyone, they all said I won the debate. Even won the @CNBC Poll!
- Oct 28, 2015 10:25:07 PM Thank you! #GOPDebate MakeAmericaGreatAgain https://t.co/u6bJBPu30T https://t.co/UB8XqapdzZ
- Oct 28, 2015 10:27:43 PM The #CNBCGOPDebate poll closed with #Trump2016 declared the official winner. Thank you! https://t.co/3mFHLcSbwD https://t.co/ZPiXAR5rFC
- Oct 28, 2015 10:32:59 PM Thanks, @PiersMorgan. You're great!
- Oct 28, 2015 10:48:02 PM "@hyatt1942: @realDonaldTrump @piersmorgan WE ALL VOTED FOR YOU TONIGHT AS WINNER OF THE DEBATE..
- Oct 28, 2015 10:48:49 PM "@BarbaraDeStasio: @realDonaldTrump GREAT debate, way to go!!"
- Oct 28, 2015 10:49:29 PM "@rfscottga: @realDonaldTrump Congrats Mr. Trump. You did great tonight. You made us ALL proud :) YES! SAYING IT AGAIN....Trump #1"
- Oct 28, 2015 10:55:38 PM Thank you, Jonathan. Greatly appreciated! https://t.co/eW0qDCax8P

- Oct 29, 2015 12:53:20 AM Thank you Colorado! An honor to win @NBC @9News #GOPDebate Poll. https://t.co/rvnUQemej0
- Oct 29, 2015 12:58:00 AM Drudge Poll on who won the 3rd #GOPDebate. Thank you! https://t.co/lCdolIJMsL
- Oct 29, 2015 01:16:58 AM "@coolgirl6978: You were very poised and professional at the debate. You looked Presidential tonight. Hit a homerun #MakeAmericaGreatAgain"
- Oct 29, 2015 01:19:36 AM "@ngb6060: @realDonaldTrump showing why he should be our next President. Tremendous Debate. Winning all the post Debate polls.
- Oct 29, 2015 01:20:28 AM "@currentlyFeed: The #CNBCGOPDebate poll closed with #Trump2016 declared the official winner.
- Oct 29, 2015 01:24:55 AM "@Sisters4everT: Good Night all supporters. Great night Mr @realDonaldTrump, You ROCKED the Rocky Mountains & the Nation tonight!!!"
- Oct 29, 2015 01:25:21 AM "@4mostcoach: 100% @realDonaldTrump SUPPORTERS ARE TRUE BLUE and we are MOTIVATED! https://t.co/piVuC981j7"
- Oct 29, 2015 02:22:01 AM "@TaylorWrightAU: #Trump came out as a clear winner in the polls yet again! Next #GOPDebate we need max 5 candidates, too many on the stage!
- Oct 29, 2015 05:47:56 AM The money losing @politico is considered by many in the world of politics to be the dumbest and most slanted of the political sites. Losers!
- Oct 29, 2015 05:49:47 AM "@GravisMarketing: @OANN Gravis Marketing Poll @realDonaldTrump leading. https://t.co/5bPZOBhz4h" Great!
- Oct 29, 2015 05:51:04 AM "@iStandWithUSA: 62% said that @realDonaldTrump won #GOP Debate Vote your stand: https://t.co/l3XVkWXIEP #USA #Election2016
- Oct 29, 2015 07:48:32 AM Thank you @morningmika and @JoeNBC for all of your nice words and comments on the debate!
- Oct 29, 2015 07:49:33 AM "@HorseShort: @jstaggs362 @sburton305 @Vermont5girl @realDonaldTrump #TRUMP IS TRUTH! We want #Trump! "

- Oct 29, 2015 08:00:08 AM "@truthinvest: @ChrisChristie @HillaryClinton good job for Christie last night.Maybe he will face her 8 yrs from now after @realDonaldTrump"
- Oct 29, 2015 08:13:50 AM "@BornToBeGOP: @realDonaldTrump you have inspired us to #MakeAmerciaGreatAgain"
- Oct 29, 2015 08:14:11 AM "@jakistheman: @realDonaldTrump keep you're momentum until you win over the White House"
- Oct 29, 2015 08:15:53 AM "@eVDefuse: @realDonaldTrump they should just let you be president already, you're already leading in the polls."
- Oct 29, 2015 08:16:16 AM "@AtheistWWonka: @realDonaldTrump @jakistheman by the time you're done everyone will be wearing a Trump tie"
- Oct 29, 2015 08:17:40 AM "@8723g: One thing I learned from @realDonaldTrump : "Sometimes the best deals are the deals you never make" We will have strong deal makers
- Oct 29, 2015 08:25:15 AM Thank you to everybody for your wonderful comments on my debate performance - it was a lot of fun! Today I will be speaking in Reno, Nevada.
- Oct 29, 2015 08:56:53 AM "@misterdish69: @cathyspartanj @realDonaldTrump @AshleyEdam @GravisMarketing @OANN https://t.co/W0dgkioGMy" Great, thank you!
- Oct 29, 2015 08:58:42 AM "@derekcarlson: DonaldTrump turned a $1 Million loan into $10 Billion. That's like you turning a $1,000 loan into $10 Million. CouldYouDoIt?
- Oct 29, 2015 09:03:21 AM "@SteveBashino: Trump good for legal immigration, economy, defense, taxes, Social Security, Medicare, 2nd Amendment, and ALL Americans."
- Oct 29, 2015 09:04:15 AM "@lvphillies08: Once again haters gonna hate...hands down #winner will always be @realDonaldTrump #Trump #Trump2016
- Oct 29, 2015 09:36:58 AM "@agentvf: @realDonaldTrump Stay strong and get ready for next debate. Great job last night."
- Oct 29, 2015 09:42:01 AM "@DRUDGE_REPORT: TRUMP WINS CNBC INSTANT POLL; RUBIO SECOND... DEVELOPING... https://t.co/6fnTksKipQ"
- Oct 29, 2015 09:47:29 AM "@Dad_Trump: @realDonaldTrump @DRUDGE_REPORT YES!"

- Oct 29, 2015 09:48:18 AM "@MikeandDawnNY: @seanmdav Dipshit @JohnJHarwood lied debate always being set for 2 hours If not 4 @realDonaldTrump calling @cnbc out.
- Oct 29, 2015 09:49:27 AM Thank you! https://t.co/MEIiUqKeS9
- Oct 29, 2015 10:21:06 AM CNBC poll: Trump won #GOPDebate #MakeAmericaGreatAgain #Trump2016 https://t.co/JEyniIGJPJ https://t.co/wEdauo3Drm
- Oct 29, 2015 10:28:51 AM Via @Slate: Who won the #GOPDebate? https://t.co/YHsCQpG63v
- Oct 29, 2015 10:30:58 AM "@T_Johnson_TJ: @realDonaldTrump you have my vote in my first election great debate last night keep up the good work! #Trump2016" Thanks.
- Oct 29, 2015 10:42:23 AM Failing host @glennbeck, a mental basketcase, loves SUPERPACS - in other words, he wants your politicians totally controlled by lobbyists!
- Oct 29, 2015 10:45:45 AM "@robertaritzen: @realDonaldTrump We Support You! And Believe that your America's Hope" Thanks.
- Oct 29, 2015 10:50:24 AM .@SpeakerRyan Congratulations and good luck - you will do a GREAT job for our wonderful U.S.A.!
- Oct 29, 2015 10:52:15 AM "@ApolloBohono69: @realDonaldTrump This country needs an unscripted hero like The Donald... #MakeAmericaGreatAgain" Thank you.
- Oct 29, 2015 10:52:29 AM "@BentleyforTrump: @realDonaldTrump @DRUDGE_REPORT We need a wall not a Rubio"
- Oct 29, 2015 10:53:37 AM "@derekcarlson: People need to wake up Mr. Trump. You are the most qualified person to ever run for President Of The United States. #Truth"
- Oct 29, 2015 10:54:20 AM "@skillethead58: @realDonaldTrump hell of a job"
- Oct 29, 2015 10:57:05 AM "@xXFlameriumXx: @MikeandDawnNY Good job Mr. Trump. The way you respond shows that you truly are ready to be the next US president! #Trump"
- Oct 29, 2015 10:57:44 AM "@neraex: I'm not even american and I want to see @realDonaldTrump win! A person like him is going to set a new standard for world leaders!"
- Oct 29, 2015 10:58:19 AM "@Kotcha301: @realDonaldTrump I sleep better at night knowing u will soon be POTUS! https://t.co/5gIjiPufMx" Thank you.

- Oct 29, 2015 10:58:51 AM "@victoryorbust: The One, The Only, Donald Trump, will and can Make America Great Again ! @Reince @blewthebigone https://t.co/5kAtLBBFJA"
- Oct 29, 2015 11:01:58 AM "@ZankMatt: Another WIN! @realDonaldTrump https://t.co/yvW3WFA1mP"
- Oct 29, 2015 12:57:55 PM Join me Tuesday, Nov. 3rd at 12pm in Trump Tower NYC. I'll be signing copies of my new book CRIPPLED AMERICA. Don't miss it!
- Oct 29, 2015 03:20:58 PM I was #1 on Twitter -- and so positive. Thank you! https://t.co/7JBjeWt6XK
- Oct 29, 2015 03:23:32 PM Post-Debate via @OANN. Thank you! #Trump2016 #MakeAmericaGreatAgain https://t.co/VHyPDZFKPZ
- Oct 29, 2015 08:59:22 PM My interview on @ThisWeekABC with @GStephanopoulos had a 40%+ ratings increase over same Sunday last year. 20% over last week.
- Oct 29, 2015 09:06:03 PM Wow, just heard really bad stuff about the failing @politico. How much longer will they be around? Some very untalented reporters.
- Oct 29, 2015 09:26:03 PM Loved doing the debate last night on @CNBC. Check out all of the polls! Everyone agrees that Harwood bombed!
- Oct 29, 2015 10:01:38 PM Thank you @CharlesHurt for the nice words on @seanhannity. I will win and Make America Great Again!
- Oct 29, 2015 10:05:45 PM "@FreeStateYank: "The only way anybody's gonna beat Trump is being better than he is."~@rushlimbaugh on @realDonaldTrump."

- Oct 30, 2015 09:38:19 AM "@giatny: Rubio an orator/liar like Obama but totally unqualified. Rubio visa bill did NOT protect American workers. See Disney."
- Oct 30, 2015 11:49:38 AM Thank you @Morning_Joe for explaining to @CNN and @andersoncooper and so many others that I am leading in almost all national & state polls.
- Oct 30, 2015 01:08:16 PM Happy Birthday to my wonderful daughter, @IvankaTrump.
- Oct 30, 2015 01:36:13 PM Thank you @rushlimbaugh for your wonderful words. We will #MakeAmericaGreatAgain

- Oct 30, 2015 01:57:39 PM Super PACs should be disavowed by anyone running for President. They are a total scam on our system and country! I am self-funding.
- Oct 30, 2015 02:30:28 PM Donald Trump Leads Polls in Florida https://t.co/EhSFxH8N8U
- Oct 30, 2015 02:58:07 PM Via The Political Insider: "Donald Trump Just Received The Best News Possible!" https://t.co/kFa5wxUXqE
- Oct 30, 2015 04:05:44 PM Happy Birthday to my friend @garyplayer...https://t.co/WuN4AV9IMT
- Oct 30, 2015 07:57:03 PM "@teed_chris: DonaldTrump,NAME ONE CANDIDATE WHO CAN MAKE DEALS WITH CHINA ! IF WE DONT BRING JOBS BACK! WERE DEAD https://t.co/u4qcXps6QB"
- Oct 30, 2015 08:14:20 PM "@Parker_Votes: Everyone under 10% in polls should DROP OUT and support TRUMP @realDonaldTrump https://t.co/zu1QL95XqQ" Great idea!
- Oct 30, 2015 08:23:07 PM "@UnitedCitizen01: @DanScavino @realDonaldTrump Would be AWESOME moderators for next debate #RushLimbaugh #SeanHannity #MarkLevin"
- Oct 30, 2015 08:46:49 PM .@GovMikeHuckabee Great job on @FoxNews tonight. Thanks for your nice words about my children. Class!
- Oct 30, 2015 08:57:09 PM "@smithsj1: @realDonaldTrump Mr. Trump do you swear to provide for, protect and care for our soldiers, including Vets?" YES, YES, YES!
- Oct 30, 2015 08:58:47 PM "@Roadstarr1: @realDonaldTrump @GovMikeHuckabee @FoxNews Mike Huckabee is a very nice gentleman and yes Donald you raised wonderful children
- Oct 30, 2015 10:23:14 PM "@dblack15nc: @realDonaldTrump https://t.co/7IfJNe4XHn Republican is 28%; support for Carson is 23%." Poll used by @megynkelly last month
- Oct 30, 2015 10:24:45 PM "@jimmcvey1: @eddiern @DeusVultUSMC @deadeyemadoc @smithsj1 Trump is the closest thing to Gen.Patton that we will ever see again." Cool!
- Oct 30, 2015 10:26:03 PM "@BornToBeGOP: @realDonaldTrump you are always many steps ahead of the game!" Thank you.

- Oct 30, 2015 10:30:00 PM "@eonline: Who had the best Donald Trump Halloween costume--Kelly Ripa, Lara Spencer or Mario Batali? https://t.co/YPMtXgKzrD"
- Oct 30, 2015 10:42:38 PM "@billboard: .@RodStewart on his (naked) "young and carefree" days and pal Donald Trump https://t.co/47RflaEHXG" Rod, album is great!
- Oct 30, 2015 10:47:32 PM "@SandraOpines: @realDonaldTrump I LOVE watching Donald Trump in action. Free education. Just watch and learn. LOVE IT. #TrumpTrain" Nice.
- Oct 30, 2015 10:52:11 PM "@JackDix03868724: Arizona polls for Democrats only say they would prefer Donald Trump over Hillary Clinton 60%"
- Oct 30, 2015 11:12:38 PM "@Biracial_Chick: Trump Rights Ship on Immigration: Demands Disney Rehire Workers Replaced by Cheap Foreign Labor. https://t.co/P69gvPCaR1"
- Oct 30, 2015 11:14:19 PM "@AnonymouSyndica: Donald Trump: I Think Obama 'Hates Israel' https://t.co/ICVK3981Sm"
- Oct 30, 2015 11:20:52 PM When candidate John Kasich, on the @oreillyfactor, talked about dismantling Medicare and Medicaid, he was referring to Ben Carson.
- Oct 30, 2015 11:30:23 PM I am going to save Medicare and Medicaid, Carson wants to abolish, and failing candidate Gov. John Kasich doesn't have a clue - weak!

- Oct 31, 2015 06:18:04 AM "@Hopeisalive66: We need a REAL change. @realDonaldTrump you are the only1who can stand up& #MakeAmericaGreatAgain.
- Oct 31, 2015 06:20:11 AM "@dalva1616: So true! Vote @realDonaldTrump and have America greatness back to where it belongs : The United States of America.
- Oct 31, 2015 06:27:02 AM Black Lives Matter protesters totally disrupt Hillary Clinton event. She looked lost. This is not what we need with ISIS, CHINA, RUSSIA etc.
- Oct 31, 2015 07:18:35 AM The new NBC POLL has me in first place but said I was third in the debate - I demand a recount (just kidding!). EVERY other poll had me #1.

- Oct 31, 2015 07:23:15 AM I see Marco Rubio just landed another billionaire to give big money to his Superpac, which are total scams. Marco must address him as "SIR"!
- Oct 31, 2015 07:28:51 AM I am leaving for Norfolk, Virginia - the great battleship U.S.S. Wisconsin - for a big rally and really big crowd. See you soon!
- Oct 31, 2015 08:48:06 AM I told you so-@politico just lost it's top person. Poor results and no money to pay him. If they were legit, they would be doing far better!
- Oct 31, 2015 09:10:51 AM Lifting off right now for U.S.S. Wisconsin in Norfolk. See ya'
- Oct 31, 2015 09:18:46 AM The @WSJ Wall Street Journal loves to write badly about me. They better be careful or I will unleash big time on them. Look forward to it!
- Oct 31, 2015 09:21:12 AM "@WavRidr101: @realDonaldTrump DO A FLYOVER @NauticusNorfolk USS WISCONSIN!" Cool idea, we will try!
- Oct 31, 2015 09:22:40 AM "@MarshallFSmith: @LexingtonBobby @realDonaldTrump And its a Glorious Fall Day in Norfolk!! Knock'em dead Donald!" Thanks!
- Oct 31, 2015 09:25:26 AM "@Maxinerunner: @realDonaldTrump surges in Post-debate Poll! Trump puts US 1st and foremost @BraveLad @TIMENOUT https://t.co/bTKoYjdPD0"
- Oct 31, 2015 09:32:13 AM "@michael_favreau: @WSJ Evangelicals don't like lairs. This Carson Mannatech video and story show be shown in Iowa https://t.co/G5sl0dgH0q"
- Oct 31, 2015 02:09:34 PM .@ColinCowherd said such nice things about me during the debate that I thought I'd do his show, @TheHerd, on Monday (2:30pm EST).
- Oct 31, 2015 02:11:53 PM Just left Virginia where I unveiled my healthcare and other plans for our great Veterans! They will be very happy! https://t.co/rhdiCocPyv
- Oct 31, 2015 02:17:45 PM Support Coach Kennedy and his right, together with his young players, to pray on the football field. Liberty Institute just suspended him!
- Oct 31, 2015 02:24:09 PM #MakeAmericaGreatAgain https://t.co/UWyANGV8IR

- Oct 31, 2015 05:24:19 PM Thank you James Freeman of the @WSJ for the very nice words. All polls said I won the debate except NBC (3rd). Explain to Daniel Henninger!
- Oct 31, 2015 05:31:29 PM No complaints but how many people would be watching these really dumb but record setting debates if I wasn't in them? Interesting question!
- Oct 31, 2015 05:34:30 PM "@hillx123: @realDonaldTrump #MakeAmericaGreatAgain https://t.co/NbiUrwMY37" Leading big Nationwide in Reuters poll - great!
- Oct 31, 2015 05:35:13 PM "@danlifting: @realDonaldTrump I wouldn't watch it at all if Mr. trump was not on it. See u on your book signing on 11/3. Trump all the way.
- Oct 31, 2015 05:36:11 PM "@shawnslawns4u: @terrykimk93 @WSJ this coming election is THE MOST IMPORTANT PRESIDENTIAL ELECTION in my lifetime VOTE FOR TRUMP"
- Oct 31, 2015 05:36:56 PM "@Rketeltas: @realDonaldTrump has won all three debates and all that matters is that Trump supporters know that & will vote Trump!" THANKS!
- Oct 31, 2015 05:37:46 PM "@realOllieTaylor: @realDonaldTrump no one would have watched the debates if Trump had not been in them"
- Oct 31, 2015 05:50:13 PM "@antSTACKSgrieco: @realDonaldTrump you were great in it!!" Thanks!
- Oct 31, 2015 05:50:24 PM "@JodiL792: @realDonaldTrump I wouldn't be watching at all!!! Honestly!"
- Oct 31, 2015 05:52:07 PM "@SallyAvicii2014: @realOllieTaylor Agree This is The Only Time #Americans have been More involved in President Elections since Kennedy!!!"
- Oct 31, 2015 05:53:06 PM "@twillnurse: @realDonaldTrump saw this and had to share! He wants to be you! Love it!!!! U r his HERO! https://t.co/dL22Vuon6q" So cute!
- Oct 31, 2015 05:53:44 PM "@sean_in_NH: @realDonaldTrump @realOllieTaylor so true. In all previous debates, no one watched and they were cancelled"
- Oct 31, 2015 05:54:58 PM "@BorderWall: Floridian here I quit watching debates years ago & most TV except GATOR football until you decided to run for President"

- Oct 31, 2015 05:56:54 PM "@DanielGenseric: Another STRONG pro-American position with Dept of Veterans Affairs reform policy. #Trump2016 https://t.co/rhdiCocPyv"
- Oct 31, 2015 06:13:46 PM Few people know that @FortuneMagazine is still in business. Tell your writer Alisa Soloman that I left The Apprentice to run for president
- Oct 31, 2015 06:21:44 PM .@thehill John Oliver had his people call to ask me to be on his very boring and low rated show. I said "NO THANKS" Waste of time & energy!
- Oct 31, 2015 06:33:08 PM "@KatyTurNBC: This is the most focused Trump stump I've heard - really drilling down on vets issues here in Virginia."
- Oct 31, 2015 06:33:20 PM "@costareports: The Post's latest on Trump: https://t.co/vqs4gN4sQU From Trump's rally today in Virginia: https://t.co/yg6z0SGPVM"
- Oct 31, 2015 06:34:15 PM "@thehill: WATCH LIVE: Trump talks about treatment of veterans in Norfolk, Va. https://t.co/zPBVBhtH3V https://t.co/KVC8UbktDa"
- Oct 31, 2015 06:35:19 PM "@WayneDupreeShow: Trump:Our educational sys is ranked #28 in the world-Get rid of #CommonCore Watch LIVE and CHAT: https://t.co/tNBiaAXkry
- Oct 31, 2015 06:36:45 PM "@CBSNews: WATCH: Donald Trump holds rally at USS Wisconsin in Virginia https://t.co/sjfTOxp4Kg https://t.co/8FIDOPO37H" A great day.
- Oct 31, 2015 06:39:24 PM "@TheMsDlr: Donald Trump Releases Plan to Reform Veterans Affairs - ABC News - https://t.co/MDArX5HKNk via @ABC"
- Oct 31, 2015 06:40:39 PM "@SueSabo: MEDIA WANTS A PUPPET.WE WANT DONALD TRUMP TO MAKE AMERICA GREAT AGAIN, LAST CHANCE TO MAKE AMERICA GREAT https://t.co/frUmviBPhR
- Oct 31, 2015 09:31:01 PM Gov. John Kasich has really failed on the campaign trail. I thought he would have been far more talented. He is just wasting time & money!
- Oct 31, 2015 09:32:07 PM "@PamelaJaneVP: Watch "FULL Speech: Donald Trump MASSIVE Rally in Norfolk, VA (10-31-15)" on YouTube - https://t.co/B4LkayZayE"
- Oct 31, 2015 09:48:52 PM "@PaulaPedene: Trump Leads GOP, Carson Stays Strong, Rubio 3rd: Poll https://t.co/7dfIDd0Edn"

November, 2015

- Nov 1, 2015 12:15:59 AM "@N_R_Mandela: @realDonaldTrump And you're still a negative loser and Trump is still a positive winner. I'm Black and proudly voting TRUMP!"
- Nov 1, 2015 07:17:51 AM "@Michael_0000: [First Vote News Video | Mike Tyson Endorses Donald Trump for President] - https://t.co/7c0VeVj5ko" Thanks Mike!
- Nov 1, 2015 07:19:08 AM "@BellicWolf: @and_is_w Anyway, for me the most original costume was Donald Trump like President!!!!"
- Nov 1, 2015 07:29:58 AM Further proof that Gang of Eight member Marco Rubio is weak on illegal immigration is Paul Singer's, Mr. Amnesty, endorsement.Rubs can't win
- Nov 1, 2015 07:40:44 AM Anybody that believes in strong borders and stopping illegal immigration cannot vote for Marco Rubio READ THIS: https://t.co/Tj85IsBPG8"

- Nov 1, 2015 08:48:26 AM Jeb's new slogan - "Jeb can fix it". I never thought of Jeb as a crook! Stupid message, the word "fix" is not a good one to use in politics!
- Nov 1, 2015 08:52:09 AM I told you in speeches months ago that Jeb and Marco do not like each other. Marco is too ambitious and very disloyal to Jeb as his mentor!
- Nov 1, 2015 08:58:31 AM Marco Rubio will not win. Weak on illegal immigration, strong on amnesty and has the appearance to killers of the world as a "lightweight".
- Nov 1, 2015 09:03:53 AM If Jeb Bush were more competent he could not have lost the skirmish with Marco in the debate. BAD facts for Marco if properly delivered!
- Nov 1, 2015 01:38:00 PM Join me Tuesday Nov. 3rd at 12 PM in #TrumpTower in NYC. I'll be signing copies of my book CRIPPLED AMERICA. Don't miss it!
- Nov 1, 2015 07:00:40 PM While in politics it is often smart to send out false messages, one thing is clear: That Hillary does not want to run against TRUMP.
- Nov 1, 2015 08:54:57 PM Thank you @JoeTrippi for the nice, and true, words on #Media Buzz with terrific Howie Kurtz. Leading New Hampshire 30 to 12. @FoxNews
- Nov 1, 2015 09:09:55 PM "@BornToBeGOP: @realDonaldTrump 9 years from now we will thank President Trump for making us great again!" Thank you!
- Nov 1, 2015 09:17:37 PM Now that Iran ripped us off by making one of the best deals of any kind in history, they have just moved to block any imports from the U.S. .
- Nov 1, 2015 09:19:03 PM "@robmont777: @StrengthenTheUS @GOP @realDonaldTrump. We The People want Mr Trump to be our President!!! https://t.co/rkppbgre0n" Great pic
- Nov 1, 2015 09:24:09 PM "@TheNewsClub_US: RT "@robmo: @StrengthenTheUS @GOP @realDonaldTrump. We The People want Mr Trump… #RT #CNN #HBO https://t.co/afbwQCvUDs"
- Nov 1, 2015 09:26:52 PM "@HenryTheZebra: @realDonaldTrump America needs you to start your 8-year shift a bit early to start fixing this disaster."
- Nov 1, 2015 09:27:31 PM "@Tar_Heel_73: @realDonaldTrump We shouldn't be surprised.No leadership in the White House.Glad @realDonaldTrump will #MakeAmericaGreatAgain

- Nov 1, 2015 09:28:14 PM "@Truth_or_Rumor: @realDonaldTrump It's not so much that Iran made a good deal, it's that Kerry and Obama gave away the store." O.K.!
- Nov 1, 2015 09:28:50 PM "@DAMRON88: @realDonaldTrump @BornToBeGOP I sure in the hell hope so. Trump please make this country great again."
- Nov 1, 2015 09:29:46 PM "@LandmanMarius: @realDonaldTrump @robmont777 @StrengthenTheUS @GOP WE ACCEPT THE BEST. We want Trump!"

- Nov 2, 2015 06:42:56 AM Sirius National News at 7:30 A.M. Steve Bannon. @BreitbartNews
- Nov 2, 2015 07:24:05 AM .@Morning_Joe: Marco only won the debate in the minds of desperate people. I won every on-line poll, even crazy @CNBC. Marco good looking?
- Nov 2, 2015 07:26:04 AM "@taurus82409: @Morning_Joe DONALD TRUMP is the absolute WINNER!! You "heads" try to talk around him, WHY, WHY??? Go TRUMP!"
- Nov 2, 2015 07:26:50 AM "@Morning_Joe: Online poll: @realDonaldTrump 'best to handle economy' by far https://t.co/SZvSzNzoIk" Very true, thanks!
- Nov 2, 2015 08:18:45 AM "@trump_world: "The MAN with a PLAN! Go Trump! We got your back! https://t.co/zXl6SyiWdm" DonaldTrump #MakeAmericaGreatAgain #Trump2016"
- Nov 2, 2015 08:31:58 AM Thank you Carl Higbie (former Navy Seal) for you support of my plan to straighten out the Veterans Administration-a mess!Great job @kilmeade
- Nov 2, 2015 11:07:01 AM Meet me at @TrumpTowerNY and get your copy of my new book CRIPPLED AMERICA signed on 11/3 at 12pm! https://t.co/9M0C0vc2fv
- Nov 2, 2015 01:21:51 PM .@CharlesMBlow Why don't you use new polls instead of the single ancient national poll that was a tiny bit negative. Dishonest reporting!
- Nov 2, 2015 01:31:09 PM .@megynkelly used this poll (nobody else did) when I was down—wonder if she'll use it now that I'm up? https://t.co/wEhqux6Ss8
- Nov 2, 2015 04:42:01 PM My interview with @jheil & @MarkHalperin at @WollmanRink airing at 5PM on @bpolitics. https://t.co/qErQu7CeEH

- Nov 2, 2015 05:12:04 PM Join me tomorrow, Nov. 3rd, at 12pm in #TrumpTowerNY. I'll be signing copies of my new book CRIPPLED AMERICA. Don't miss it!
- Nov 2, 2015 08:31:55 PM "@DDietlin3: @ColinCowherd fantastic job with your interview with @realDonaldTrump today!"
- Nov 2, 2015 08:33:08 PM "@TrumpFix: @meganena13 @robertew2945 agreed Luisa. @realDonaldTrump WILL WIN! This is what he does!"
- Nov 2, 2015 08:35:24 PM "@shelbycockaxe: @realDonaldTrump Trump is our last chance to turn this country around #Trump2016"
- Nov 2, 2015 08:35:39 PM "@theBrandonMcKee: Read all about the Wollman deal and many other successful deals in "The Art of the Deal" by @realDonaldTrump"
- Nov 2, 2015 08:36:16 PM "@kemper34: @TheHerd @ColinCowherd @realDonaldTrump @FS1 Great interview. Ranks just above the @JimHarbaugh49 interview."
- Nov 2, 2015 08:36:52 PM "@TdavisTonya: @brucedhendrix @Poetry4Bitcoin Nope. Trump isn't taking 2 weeks off to promote his book. Trump is donating all to charity"
- Nov 2, 2015 08:38:57 PM "@kingster73: @realDonaldTrump Rubio is irresponsible on finances and doesn't show up for work! Who would hire him? Not the American People!
- Nov 2, 2015 08:39:09 PM "@HarpAmyStabler: @FS1 @realDonaldTrump @ColinCowherd this interview is great."

- Nov 3, 2015 06:06:27 AM I will be interviewed on @GMA at 7:00 A.M. and @foxandfriends at 7:50. Talking about my new book, out today, Crippled America.
- Nov 3, 2015 08:40:32 AM "@NickEgoroff: BREAKING: Latest poll of Florida voters shows enormous lead for Trump! He'd beat Hillary! https://t.co/TvLEH4NcXt #tcot"
- Nov 3, 2015 08:52:30 AM Join me today, Nov 3rd, in #TrumpTowerNYC at noon. I'll be signing copies of my new book CRIPPLED AMERICA. Don't miss it!
- Nov 3, 2015 09:34:12 AM "@DianeHauschildt: @FoxNews @freelancer1787 @realDonaldTrump @RealBenCarson https://t.co/0EVXJ7WW6C"

- Nov 3, 2015 09:36:39 AM "@freebird_Pepper: @realDonaldTrump is the only candidate speaking on the horrible treatment our vets are getting and he has solutions!
- Nov 3, 2015 09:36:58 AM "@TIMENOUT: @realDonaldTrump Book in hand waiting for The Next President https://t.co/83tJMZUUIa"
- Nov 3, 2015 09:37:21 AM "@JayJohnsonLikes: @realDonaldTrump been here in line for two hours already. reading book while waiting. I'll see you at noon!"
- Nov 3, 2015 09:44:06 AM "@Freedomrings22: @realDonaldTrump I Trust @OANN 's polls They are actually really Fair and really balanced on all their news" Iowa lead!
- Nov 3, 2015 09:49:14 AM .@CharlesGKoch is looking for a new puppet after Governor Walker and Jeb Bush cratered. He now likes Rubio--next fail.
- Nov 3, 2015 09:49:48 AM "@keksec_org: @realDonaldTrump Your performances in every state have been amazing! #MakeAmericaGreatAgain
- Nov 3, 2015 09:50:12 AM "@realOllieTaylor: @realDonaldTrump @Freedomr@OANN Trump is the only one who can make America great again. Carson's sleepy, Jeb low energy."
- Nov 3, 2015 09:51:44 AM "@LookerCherry: @realDonaldTrump The polls are for the news cycle. Trump is miles ahead and leaving all others in the dust, "don't doubt me"
- Nov 3, 2015 10:47:01 AM Marco Rubio would keep Barack Obama's executive order on amnesty intact. See article. Cannot be President. https://t.co/JW5f8OouyA
- Nov 3, 2015 04:54:54 PM I will be on @SeanHannity tonight at 10pmE talking about my new book #CrippledAmerica and much more! #MakeAmericaGreatAgain #Trump2016
- Nov 3, 2015 11:17:54 PM "@ethansimmons111: @DanScavino @realDonaldTrump https://t.co/d9QlsddCRy"
- Nov 3, 2015 11:18:23 PM "@DJTrump2016: DONALD TRUMP FULL INTERVIEW: Fox and Friends (11-03-15) https://t.co/hvEavMtbac #MakeAmericaGreatAgain #Trump2016"
- Nov 3, 2015 11:20:05 PM "@norge1956: @realDonaldTrump https://t.co/uV345JyDdF" Rubio wants Common Core for education.
- Nov 3, 2015 11:22:38 PM "@TwallMa: @realDonaldTrump. He is a common sense powerhouse that gets things done! Excellent book! https://t.co/sMoLTsiSAk"

- Nov 3, 2015 11:23:23 PM "@misstozak: @realDonaldTrump @seanhannity @OANN This says it ALL. TRUMP 2016. https://t.co/gsXFtFNuix"
- Nov 3, 2015 11:23:52 PM "@David360NC: @adenunzio We finally have a voice with @realDonaldTrump , Let's do our part & VOTE IN THE PRIMARY 4 #Trump2016 #TrumpArmy"
- Nov 3, 2015 11:24:06 PM "@JulesSiscoe: The Complete @realDonaldTrump Interview: Getting Things Done https://t.co/OTLC2XpFRv via @bpolitics"
- Nov 3, 2015 11:24:36 PM "@Mr_Holtzworth: @realDonaldTrump Sarah Palin Defends Donald Trump's Immigration Plan On Fox News https://t.co/IhaCiY07US via @YouTube"
- Nov 3, 2015 11:26:00 PM "@nbcsnl: Shooting promos for #TrumpOnSNL with Cecily and @realDonaldTrump. https://t.co/K1JKOgHrhY"
- Nov 3, 2015 11:27:34 PM "@DougDWiley: @realDonaldTrump I can't wait to read your new book! We are supporting you here in Boise Idaho!"

- Nov 4, 2015 12:51:46 AM "@seanhannity: @realDonaldTrump on sending 50 Special Ops Forces troops to Syria: This country needs to be less predictable."
- Nov 4, 2015 12:53:03 AM "@SJavner: Reading Crippled America ....feeling love for our country first, in it's pages. That's why I stand with TRUMP"
- Nov 4, 2015 12:54:19 AM "@JudgeMoroz: Republicans in Congress can learn a lot from @realDonaldTrump on dealing with Obama! They should read #CrippledAmerica!"
- Nov 4, 2015 01:01:55 AM "@svn2hd: @realDonaldTrump Crippled AMERICA is a must read. So right. Great job on another best seller."
- Nov 4, 2015 01:03:16 AM "@LeStudio1: DONALD TRUMP-CRIPPLED AMERICA The new book by @realDonaldTrump is best seller in the making."
- Nov 4, 2015 01:07:53 AM "@peter_smells: @realDonaldTrump Just read #CrippledAmerica! Great book! I haven't felt this enthusiastic about #America since #Reagan"
- Nov 4, 2015 01:13:47 AM "@JoshuaEnglishh: @realDonaldTrump every single real American needs to read #CrippledAmerica ! Beyond awesome I couldn't be more thrilled"
- Nov 4, 2015 01:26:38 AM #MakeAmericaGreatAgain #Trump2016 https://t.co/f9ujgy3NSk
- Nov 4, 2015 08:28:10 AM Isn't it terrible that @megynkelly used a poll not used before (I.B.D.) when I was down, but refuses to use it now when I am up?

- Nov 4, 2015 09:58:00 AM Just landed in New Hampshire - a very exciting morning planned!
- Nov 4, 2015 06:18:58 PM Wow! @FoxNews poll just came out. #1 with 26%! Almost as importantly, I am the strongest on economic issues by far! #Trump2016
- Nov 4, 2015 06:18:58 PM Wow! @FoxNews poll just came out. #1 with 26%! Almost as importantly, I am the strongest on economic issues by far! #Trump2016
- Nov 4, 2015 06:24:55 PM Also, tune in to the @TodayShow at 7:00am. I will be on to discuss the campaign, my new ads and #CrippledAmerica.

- Nov 5, 2015 04:00:46 AM Jeb Bush just said about Marco Rubio, "he's my friend!" Pure political speak. Why can't he be truthful and say "disloyal guy, no friend!"
- Nov 5, 2015 04:06:09 AM "@spiritofshiloh: Carson has the WORST health plan EVER re: Soc Sec and Medicare. @realDonaldTrump He wants to abolish Medicare - no way!
- Nov 5, 2015 04:07:48 AM "@Destiny: Why didn't @seanhannity correct Jeb when he said @realDonaldTrump has run 4 president 2X B4~Jeb needs 2B corrected b/c he lied."
- Nov 5, 2015 04:08:48 AM "@lizzym420: @amrightnow @realDonaldTrump What other candidate begins to rival Trump in his knowledge, breadth of issues, stamina?" Thanks!
- Nov 5, 2015 04:09:49 AM "@Hanan_Khan2: @realDonaldTrump I am a lifelong democrat. And I will be voting trump!!!! #democratsfortrump" Great!
- Nov 5, 2015 04:17:13 AM .@seanhannity should have corrected Jeb Bush when he said that I "ran for president twice." Never ran, merely considered running!
- Nov 5, 2015 04:19:41 AM "@curtismuddog: @destiny @seanhannity JEB'S! Whole campaign is fueled by lies. Just like his brother lied about Iraq. BUSH DYNASTY=LIES"
- Nov 5, 2015 04:21:41 AM "@NottaLiberal: @realDonaldTrump @destiny @seanhannity No need, Everyone knows Jeb is full of blank.
- Nov 5, 2015 04:22:38 AM "@TeamSpringsteen: @realDonaldTrump I just finished reading Crippled America. It's a detailed blueprint to get America back on track."

- Nov 5, 2015 04:23:48 AM "@marklindsay78: @Hanan_Khan2 @realDonaldTrump poll numbers are higher then most think, no one is asking Democrats if they are voting Trump"
- Nov 5, 2015 06:30:32 PM Rubio lied about my meeting w/ Hispanic activists. I didn't change my opinion but treated them w/ respect. Shame! https://t.co/O9Kgfi5xcH
- Nov 5, 2015 09:12:19 PM "@Reagan_Girl: MSM are LYING to you about Hispanics hating Trump. Here's the real deal! #HispanicsForTrump https://t.co/zGXIwsKnlC"
- Nov 5, 2015 09:32:14 PM The Carson story is either a total fabrication or, if true, even worse-trying to hit mother over the head with a hammer or stabbing friend!
- Nov 5, 2015 10:16:42 PM "@SandraJenners: I love to see the respect you have shown to your parents, siblings and children. Proven Respect and Class needed in USA!"
- Nov 5, 2015 10:22:28 PM "@chriskyleband: TRUMP Supporters aren't Angry We're Smart ! We're Men / Women / Millennials / Politically Saavy https://t.co/2uokmrkRWd"

- Nov 6, 2015 04:18:53 AM "@keksec_org: @realDonaldTrump Ivanka said it and you said it too, you'll be great for women. #MakeAmericaGreatAgain"
- Nov 6, 2015 04:21:38 AM "@SoCal4Trump: Wow @megynkelly. You openly LIE about who's ahead in the GOP race. Trump is LEADING in 99% of polls. Shameful... #StopTheLies
- Nov 6, 2015 04:28:18 AM A great honor to easily finish FIRST in the @FoxNews poll tabulation even though some of my best polls were not used in determining winner!
- Nov 6, 2015 04:33:36 AM "@DeeMcNa: @FoxNews Silent majority did not try to kill their mothers, like Ben Carson, but wants America rebuilt by only one capable:TRUMP"
- Nov 6, 2015 04:37:59 AM "@Rick_Sa: @greta Interesting presidential race; Carson tries to beat his mom with a hammer, and @realDonaldTrump beats Carson in the polls!
- Nov 6, 2015 04:51:08 AM "@reganharycki: @realDonaldTrump it's about time we find a republican that can take on the democrats! https://t.co/lfI1rUjWRV"

- Nov 6, 2015 04:54:28 AM "@GrundleMan27: Marco Rubio can't even handle his own credit card how is he going to be able to handle the U.S. finances #trump"
- Nov 6, 2015 04:58:05 AM "@AliceEngle3: @realDonaldTrump-huge lead in Reuters National poll https://t.co/afdvXHzvIx"
- Nov 6, 2015 04:59:21 AM "@rhinostate: .@realDonaldTrump @GrundleMan27 Rubio is a Manchurian Candidate. People will own him if he ever became president."
- Nov 6, 2015 06:58:25 AM Florida Ethics Commission Advocate comes down hard on Rubio. So do two people who worked with him. Said he used the wrong credit card! Sure.
- Nov 6, 2015 07:16:29 AM Such bad reporting: A puff piece on Ben Carson in the @nytimes states that Carson "is trying to solidify his lead." But I am #1, easily! Sad
- Nov 6, 2015 09:08:17 AM With Ben Carson wanting to hit his mother on head with a hammer, stab a friend and Pyramids built for grain storage - don't people get it?
- Nov 6, 2015 09:08:41 AM Carson now admits his friend named "Bob," who he tried to stab (Bob was saved by his belt buckle!), no longer exists as Bob. Wrong name!
- Nov 6, 2015 09:48:35 AM I think it would be a good idea—and fair—to include @GovChristie & @MikeHuckabeeGOP in the debate. Both solid & good guys. @FoxBusiness
- Nov 6, 2015 10:06:20 AM .@AJDelgado13 Thank you so much for the nice words and support--really enjoy listening to your ideas and thoughts.
- Nov 6, 2015 11:41:32 AM "@JimmyForTrump: @insighter007 @OAmericanGirl All Rep should stand with #Trump2016 Forget Bush, Rubio and knife attackers! #Trump2016"
- Nov 6, 2015 11:46:22 AM "@Robostop10: @realDonaldTrump This is not good. https://t.co/lvv0MRfgtH" WOW, one of many lies by Ben Carson! Big story.
- Nov 6, 2015 12:24:48 PM Getting ready for @nbcsnl commercial. https://t.co/asHECYFBRv
- Nov 6, 2015 12:51:35 PM "@CaptainMark_: @Robostop10 KEEP IT COMMING TRUMP!!!! People need to be warned about that Carson figure who is not who they think!"

- Nov 6, 2015 12:51:58 PM "@BornToBeGOP: @realDonaldTrump @Robostop10 @politico How anyone could see him as president baffles me. Lies and insane theories.
- Nov 6, 2015 12:52:18 PM "@TrumpsMyHomeboy: @realDonaldTrump @Robostop10 @politico The #MSM straw man candidate is falling apart!"
- Nov 6, 2015 12:56:42 PM "@bigsampolkcoga: @GovChristie @MikeHuckabeeGOP @FoxBusiness and they kept Rand Paul on the main stage. Let's get Huck and Christie back."
- Nov 6, 2015 01:02:10 PM "@eric_wagaman94: Super excited to watch @realDonaldTrump tomorrow night on @nbcsnl #MakeAmericaGreatAgain"
- Nov 6, 2015 01:05:06 PM "@DefendingtheUSA: GREAT Video. Which of these 4 Polls is Suspect? Kudos to @OANN https://t.co/kKlRLIDrLC #Trump https://t.co/BiEUTt2k6Z"
- Nov 6, 2015 01:07:00 PM "@pjs307: @WalshFreedom Will be highest rated show ever, @realDonaldTrump is a marketing genius #SNL" Hope it does well!
- Nov 6, 2015 01:09:41 PM "@bob_forbes2: DonaldTrump has built a lifetime reputation of doing what he says he will do. He keeps his promises. https://t.co/VBFuJOWIMa
- Nov 6, 2015 01:10:45 PM "@swargcoming: @AnnCoulter @rushlimbaugh @greta @OANN @FoxNews IS CARSON HALLUCINATING? NOW LIES ABOUT WESTPOINT? https://t.co/lvv0MRfgtH"
- Nov 6, 2015 02:33:30 PM Happy Birthday to the great @BillyGraham. He's done so many wonderful things, not the least of which is his fantastic family. I love Billy!
- Nov 6, 2015 02:47:32 PM So sad that Obama rejected Keystone Pipeline. Thousands of jobs, good for the environment, no downside!
- Nov 6, 2015 03:00:13 PM Will be on @oreillyfactor tonight. Signing a copy of Crippled America for Bill! https://t.co/AgYUvlCU1u
- Nov 6, 2015 06:38:38 PM "@PhinsDiehard: @CNN Only Donald Trump can #MakeAmericaGreatAgain" Thank you!
- Nov 6, 2015 06:41:59 PM "@FBeadon: @realDonaldTrump don't let the Keystone Pipeline die. The US needs to be good neighbors with Canada, and energy independent."
- Nov 6, 2015 06:54:36 PM @BillKristol has become a sad case. His magazine is failing badly, probably doesn't have long to go, and his predictions are always wrong!

- Nov 6, 2015 07:07:28 PM Would be nice if @jmartNYT learned how to read the polls before writing his next story. Probably done on purpose, but not good reporting!
- Nov 6, 2015 07:08:54 PM "@nbcsnl: One more day! Donald Trump hosts #SNL with @Sia tomorrow. https://t.co/MMRYVpPpKu https://t.co/ENx4acClxg" Will be a wild night!
- Nov 6, 2015 10:23:44 PM "@Bubbachitchat1: THIS IS WHY THE POLLS ARE WRONG! @Hanan_Khan2: I am a lifelong democrat. And I will be voting trump! #democratsfortrump""

- Nov 7, 2015 12:20:25 AM One of the dumbest political pundits on television is Chris Stirewalt of @FoxNews. Wrong facts - check Fox debate rankings, Trump #1. Dope!
- Nov 7, 2015 12:23:18 AM "@essygalloway: @realDonaldTrump @nbcsnl @Sia I can't wait to watch snl tomorrow." A really big show!
- Nov 7, 2015 12:29:11 PM .@RobertGBeckel Please thank your brother for his nice words on television. Seems like a great guy and character! @CNN
- Nov 7, 2015 12:34:50 PM Saturday Night Live has some incredible things in store tonight. The great thing about playing myself is that it will be authentic! Enjoy
- Nov 7, 2015 12:36:11 PM "@SocialInNewYork: We unearthed Donald Trump's Vine account from 2013 and it's incredible https://t.co/UVMusN4Bmv" Thank you.
- Nov 7, 2015 12:39:36 PM "@Live5News: Live from New York, Donald Trump will soon be hosting 'SNL': https://t.co/LAIUCTCxGb" Frazier, enjoy the show and best wishes!
- Nov 7, 2015 12:40:37 PM "@HouseCracka: Donald Trump is going to win the Presidency. Get on board the #TrumpTrain its going to be #YUGE" Thanks.
- Nov 7, 2015 12:47:55 PM They are saying that tickets to tonight's Saturday Night Live are the hardest to get in the history of this great show! Off to a good start!
- Nov 7, 2015 12:50:08 PM "@keksec_org: @realDonaldTrump I haven't seen anyone carry themselves so Presidential since Reagan. #MakeAmericaGreatAgain" Great!
- Nov 7, 2015 12:52:04 PM "@tazz53098: @realDonaldTrump can't wait to watch. #trump for president #saturday night live"

- Nov 7, 2015 01:26:55 PM "@nbcsnl: We're live from Studio 8H tonight. #SNL https://t.co/Uiq9llzwEC"
- Nov 7, 2015 01:27:51 PM "@nbcsnl: See you at Rockefeller Center. #SNL https://t.co/C4Kx5qId6M"
- Nov 7, 2015 01:28:46 PM "@nbcsnl: Cecily also has a Trump impression. https://t.co/rlMwEqXFG3 #SNL https://t.co/Kk1JFO7RDC"
- Nov 7, 2015 01:28:55 PM "@nbcsnl: Everyone loves @Sia's new look. #SNL https://t.co/oqsASGtwpb"
- Nov 7, 2015 01:29:16 PM "@nbcsnl: Backstage with Trump. #SNL https://t.co/8CTmfAnyro"
- Nov 7, 2015 01:30:00 PM "@nbcsnl: From the last time Donald Trump hosted #SNL — The Boardroom Band. https://t.co/dL7y4dCWhL https://t.co/apGm3gKNdD"
- Nov 7, 2015 02:25:19 PM "@Albusinvogue: @Sia is performing, DonaldTrump is hosting. Tonight's #saturdaynightlive is going to be legendary. https://t.co/hMB6OreNh9"
- Nov 7, 2015 02:26:20 PM "@RealCinders2: @realDonaldTrump use SNL to tell Hispanics you are for them , you want them to have jobs and be here legally" Great idea!
- Nov 7, 2015 02:29:05 PM "@BMW_e38forever: @realDonaldTrump so let it be written, so lets get him elected in a landslide victory in 2016! https://t.co/V6fXXEFSvD"
- Nov 7, 2015 02:32:28 PM "@AmesMoreno: @DesignerDeb3 @garyinlv01 @sueinwny @megynkelly @realDonaldTrump https://t.co/mGgGuxnYiG" Wow Marco, is this true?
- Nov 7, 2015 02:41:05 PM "@BornToBeGOP: @realDonaldTrump You want them here legally and they want to be here legally!"
- Nov 7, 2015 02:41:37 PM "@Waxking911: @CBSNews @realDonaldTrump https://t.co/3r0jabQKzi"
- Nov 7, 2015 02:42:05 PM "@jak00seven: If you like how @HillaryClinton handled #Benghazi, then you'll just [heart] her as Commander-in-Chief #MakeAmericaGreatAgain"
- Nov 7, 2015 02:44:59 PM "@sherrysue66: I am working a #12HR #AMERICAN SHIFT BUT WILL STAY UP 2 WATCH! I COULD USE A SATURDAY NIGHT LIVE LAUGH! #WE [heart] U. Nice.

- Nov 7, 2015 07:17:09 PM I am at the Saturday Night Live Studio - electricity all over the place. We will be doing a "tweeting" skit, so stay tuned!

- Nov 8, 2015 07:15:18 AM Amazing evening at Saturday Night Live!
- Nov 8, 2015 07:16:42 AM Will be on @foxandfriends at 8:00 A.M.
- Nov 8, 2015 07:17:00 AM "@PearlsPolkaDots: @realDonaldTrump Loved the show! Best #SNL in years! #TrumpTrainSNL"
- Nov 8, 2015 07:17:13 AM "@b_ranzetta: The books great @realDonaldTrump #CrippledAmerica https://t.co/SIQSKhZa9s"
- Nov 8, 2015 07:17:25 AM "@martydrinksbeer: @realDonaldTrump It was FANTASTIC!!"
- Nov 8, 2015 07:18:11 AM "@David360NC: We finally have a voice with Let's do our part & VOTE IN THE R PRIMARY 4 #Trump2016 #TrumpArmy https://t.co/ri0ORHBefU"
- Nov 8, 2015 07:18:31 AM "@redletter99: @realDonaldTrump thanks donald great show,when r u coming back to massachusetts?" Very soon!
- Nov 8, 2015 07:18:54 AM "@ChristineMMoran: @realDonaldTrump great show !!! https://t.co/gcvaTeo4lk"
- Nov 8, 2015 07:19:44 AM "@wakeupfla: Please stand up for American Hispanic families and fight illegal immigration it is destroying USA! https://t.co/AKZO4lTnLj"
- Nov 8, 2015 07:19:53 AM "@jackmarchione: @realDonaldTrump Loved the show!"
- Nov 8, 2015 07:20:05 AM "@PizzaPartyBen: @realDonaldTrump we need you elected tomorrow!"
- Nov 8, 2015 07:20:31 AM "@ccakul: @realDonaldTrump it was a great show!"
- Nov 8, 2015 07:21:34 AM "@EEGRC98: @realDonaldTrump I am Hispanic - I am with you"
- Nov 8, 2015 07:23:39 AM "@mcjeff42: @realDonaldTrump you made SNL great again"
- Nov 8, 2015 07:24:09 AM "@nbcsnl: What a show. Thanks for watching, everyone! #SNL https://t.co/10fmssLyDE"
- Nov 8, 2015 08:19:08 AM .@nbcsnl - So much fun last night!
- Nov 8, 2015 08:36:41 AM "@justintupper: @realDonaldTrump You are a machine. Success leaves clues. #MakeAmericaGreatAgain"

- Nov 8, 2015 08:38:22 AM "@HillsGypsydad05: @foxandfriends Awesome time on Saturday Night Live Mr. Trump! Thanks for being YOU! #MakeAmericaGreatAgain" Thank you!
- Nov 8, 2015 08:40:35 AM .@CNN Will be interviewed by Jake Tapper at 9:00 A.M. Enjoy.
- Nov 8, 2015 09:17:18 AM I will be interviewed by @GStephanopoulos on @ABC at 10:00 A.M.
- Nov 8, 2015 09:24:17 AM At 10:30 I will be interviewed on both @meetthepress by @chucktodd and @CBSNews Face The Nation by John Dickerson. This after long evening!
- Nov 8, 2015 09:25:45 AM "@CleopattraUSA: @realDonaldTrump @nbcsnl You've got it going on!!! Nothing is boring or low energy about you. #EverybodyRockW/TrumpNow #SNL
- Nov 8, 2015 10:57:36 AM Television ratings for @nbcsnl Saturday Night Live just came out and they were great - the best since 2011. Very few protesters!
- Nov 8, 2015 05:17:36 PM .@EricShawnonFox Highest rated Saturday Night Live in four years. 47% higher than their opening night with Hillary & Miley Cyrus. Nice words
- Nov 8, 2015 05:24:20 PM "@coltsfan322: @realDonaldTrump @EricShawnonFox https://t.co/bO63wm27qE"
- Nov 8, 2015 05:24:50 PM "@EmitteLucemTuam: @realDonaldTrump @EricShawnonFox Great job Donald! Good luck from Canada!"
- Nov 8, 2015 05:24:55 PM "@tegodreaux: @realDonaldTrump @EricShawnonFox HUUUUUGE"
- Nov 8, 2015 05:25:34 PM "@MyPresidentme: @EricShawnonFox That's because people are interested in you, & you've got a great sense of humor, unlike Hillary #Trump2016
- Nov 8, 2015 05:26:38 PM "@SpecialKMB1969: @nbcsnl @realDonaldTrump was hilarious ty we so enjoyed it! #TrumpTrainSNL #TrumpOnSNL #MakeAmericaGreatAgain"
- Nov 8, 2015 05:27:13 PM "@mcjeff42: @realDonaldTrump you made SNL great again" @nbcsnl
- Nov 8, 2015 05:40:56 PM "@WineChics: Trump Winery: https://t.co/JBFhqq2OGt via @WineChics Always an amazing experience at Trump Winery Beautiful fall foliage

- Nov 8, 2015 05:46:12 PM "@salyboy3: @realDonaldTrump great job on SNL mr trump, funny funny." Thanks.
- Nov 8, 2015 05:48:31 PM "@Watchman4the1: Chuck Schumer: Sen Marco Rubio Is "Totally Committed To Obama's Immigration Agenda" https://t.co/yieqFMRxwH DonaldTrump
- Nov 8, 2015 06:26:18 PM "@Variety: Ratings: DonaldTrump lifted #SNL to a near four-year high. https://t.co/DDhsj9SZ03 https://t.co/jFYaKx2WYW" TRUMP RATINGS GOLD!
- Nov 8, 2015 06:31:27 PM "@TradingStreetCo:Donald Trump Is Ratings 'Gold' For SNL: Donald Trump Is Ratings 'Gold' For SNL... https://t.co/leEPs9OoAe @FoxNews @CNN
- Nov 8, 2015 07:47:41 PM Thank you to all of those who gave me such wonderful reviews for my performance on @nbcsnl Saturday Night Live. Best ratings in 4 years!
- Nov 8, 2015 07:55:18 PM "@dlustv: Trump SNL Episode Generates Highest Ratings Since 2012: At the very least, Donald Trump is making Sat... https://t.co/sNQZv8YPaO"

- Nov 9, 2015 01:04:08 PM .@Betsy_McCaughey Thanks so much. Really appreciate your comments. I will help the veterans like no one else. https://t.co/2iK0mWpuJx
- Nov 9, 2015 03:03:30 PM .@CNN should listen. Ana Navarro has no talent, no TV persona, and works for Bush—a total conflict of interest. https://t.co/mynTMrdTE9
- Nov 9, 2015 03:43:36 PM Thanks Piers. Greatly appreciated. @piersmorgan https://t.co/2mIMzNRMOc
- Nov 9, 2015 07:27:15 PM Great job on @Greta @DonaldJTrumpJr. Nobody could have done it better!
- Nov 9, 2015 10:21:35 PM A great evening in Springfield, Illinois. Thank you for all of the support! #Trump2016 https://t.co/mqOfuI08PX
- Nov 9, 2015 10:35:35 PM Marco Rubio is a total lightweight who I wouldn't hire to run one of my smaller companies - a highly overrated politician!
- Nov 9, 2015 10:37:37 PM Marco Rubio couldn't even respond properly to President Obama's State of the Union Speech without pouring sweat & chugging water. He choked!

- Nov 9, 2015 10:39:14 PM Marco Rubio is totally weak on illegal immigration & in favor of easy amnesty. A lightweight choker - bad for #USA!
- Nov 9, 2015 11:03:39 PM Thank you to @NYPost's Robert Rorke for the really nice review of #SNL. So many enjoyed it - very gratifying! https://t.co/TT29WgelUT
- Nov 9, 2015 11:42:27 PM #MakeAmericaGreatAgain #Trump2016 https://t.co/arJERjlYCO

- Nov 10, 2015 12:54:44 AM "@KazmierskiR: @realDonaldTrump @DonaldJTrumpJr OuTsTaNdInG!!! Is obvious that Jr. has much of his father's 'charisma' and intelligence!"
- Nov 10, 2015 12:58:02 AM "@teed_chris: @Loyal2Trump2016 @TrumpAlabama @FoxNews Look when you try to kill Your mom,that's it for me ,no walking on water"
- Nov 10, 2015 01:00:01 AM "@freedoms411: @wakeuppeopleSOS @mitchellvii @CNN @ABC @CBS It shouldn't be ignored, and I doubt it will be, Carson will drop in polls."
- Nov 10, 2015 01:00:53 AM "@kniala: @realDonaldTrump Exactly. Marco has no accomplishments."
- Nov 10, 2015 01:01:50 AM "@burgettn: @AB1132 @realDonaldTrump it's the only way we can make America great again."
- Nov 10, 2015 01:03:51 AM "@JimmyGould07: Only one man has the appeal, nerve, commitment, ideas, & motivation. He's the icon, business tycoon, and lovable DonaldTrump
- Nov 10, 2015 03:12:10 AM "@BreitbartNews: Ratings were HUGE for @realDonaldTrump's appearance on Saturday Night Live -> https://t.co/wdQXRq36yF"
- Nov 10, 2015 03:13:14 AM "@Fox411: DonaldTrump 'Saturday Night Live' episode garners highest viewership since 2012 https://t.co/AFMcaRWGm2 https://t.co/n5Zw20H9zp"
- Nov 10, 2015 03:17:56 AM "@foxandfriends: Trump helps 'SNL' blow roof off the ratings, most viewers since 2012 https://t.co/Z0pCZYXxcp https://t.co/a28U65mge6"
- Nov 10, 2015 03:22:14 AM "@USATODAY: Donald Trump lifted #SNL to its best ratings since 2012. https://t.co/h2jQI9PpvP (Photo: NBC) https://t.co/YLlXQO9mtf"

- Nov 10, 2015 03:40:38 AM "@piersmorgan: Why @realdonaldtrump nailed SNL. My new column. https://t.co/2mIMzNRMOc"
- Nov 10, 2015 03:40:49 AM "@foxnation: #DonaldTrump Gives SNL Its Biggest Ratings In Years https://t.co/zMnZoMamu9"
- Nov 10, 2015 06:51:15 AM I will be interviewed by @GStephanopoulos on @GMA at 7:00 A.M. There is much to talk about!
- Nov 10, 2015 09:28:15 AM "@JezzaK: If the Trump Hotel Honolulu is any reflection how you would be as President then I think the U.S will be in good hands" Thank you!
- Nov 10, 2015 09:29:45 AM "@curtismuddog: @limbaugh @seanhannity @realDonaldTrump is Hillary's worst nightmare! Just take a look at Illinois rally last night."
- Nov 10, 2015 10:32:12 AM "@jspence80: @jspence80: Like him or hate him @realDonaldTrump runs a brilliant campaign for #POTUS2016 !" Thank you!
- Nov 10, 2015 10:37:35 AM "@ray_aub: Funny all the real polls have @realDonaldTrump way ahead.
- Nov 10, 2015 11:54:23 AM Go out and buy CRIPPLED AMERICA: How to Make America Great Again. Doing really well. Great Thanksgiving or Christmas present!
- Nov 10, 2015 12:42:27 PM Thank you New Jersey! #Trump2016 https://t.co/YUIBEP7JcZ
- Nov 10, 2015 01:01:25 PM Thank you South Carolina! #Trump2016 https://t.co/DDK89IcmxX
- Nov 10, 2015 01:32:40 PM People Magazine: "Donald Trump Was Right: He Gave SNL Its Best Ratings in Nearly 4 Years--Plus, What You Didn't See" https://t.co/Bh7K8l0bIO

- Nov 11, 2015 01:57:08 AM I will be on @Morning_Joe live from New Hampshire tomorrow at 7am. #Trump2016 #MakeAmericaGreatAgain
- Nov 11, 2015 05:37:44 AM "@Rmac747: Keep up the good work, Donald! Hello from Vancouver where the new & amazing Trump Tower and Hotel almost complete!
- Nov 11, 2015 05:46:49 AM Will be on @Morning_Joe live from New Hampshire - 7:00 A.M. Talking about the debate and more!
- Nov 11, 2015 05:50:13 AM Loved doing the debate...won Drudge and all on-line polls! Amazing evening, moderators did an outstanding job.

- Nov 11, 2015 10:48:52 AM Thank you @Morning_Joe & @morningmika -- a great show! #Trump2016 #MakeAmericaGreatAgain https://t.co/teauhiQd3i
- Nov 11, 2015 11:34:53 AM Happy Veterans Day. To those who have served, thank you for your special work.
- Nov 11, 2015 11:36:36 AM Just returned home from the great state of New Hampshire. Have made so many friends there--special place!
- Nov 11, 2015 05:59:49 PM I never said that China was in the bad TPP trade deal but that China would come in the back door at a later date. @CNN @FoxBusiness
- Nov 11, 2015 06:02:31 PM .@gerardtbaker Gerard—wonderful job last night as moderator of the debate. I told many, "really smart and elegant."
- Nov 11, 2015 06:03:41 PM I will be on @marklevinshow at 8PM tonight. Tune in!
- Nov 11, 2015 06:12:07 PM Will be interviewed by @oreillyfactor tonight at 8 PM.
- Nov 11, 2015 07:19:07 PM "@Christianlord12: RUBIO sat back during debate on Immigration hoping no 1 would ask him about Gang of 8. https://t.co/sevUe7bikR"
- Nov 11, 2015 09:07:56 PM "@frankieguy85: This 92-Year-Old Woman Registered to Vote Just to Cast a Ballot for Trump https://t.co/6REhiGankb"
- Nov 11, 2015 09:13:17 PM "@BornToBeGOP: @realDonaldTrump You will bring out more voters to vote for you than we've seen in any election!" Great.
- Nov 11, 2015 09:18:51 PM "@ellenEspence: I'm not convinced that any candidate other than @realDonaldTrump is committed to securing our borders. #VoteTrump2016"

- Nov 12, 2015 06:16:31 AM All seven on-line polls, including Drudge and Time, with thousands of respondents, said I won the debate. @krauthammer said I was "so, so."
- Nov 12, 2015 06:24:16 AM I will be interviewed on @MariaBartiromo @FoxBusiness at 7:30
- Nov 12, 2015 06:36:40 AM Today's @WSJ Editorial is WRONG again. I know that China is not in the new T.P.P. trade deal but would come in latter through a back door.

- Nov 12, 2015 06:41:07 AM .@WSJ Editorial Board should review my debate statement re China and T.P.P. and apologize. China not part but will get their way in later.
- Nov 12, 2015 06:45:47 AM The @WSJ Editorial Board is so wrong, so often. They got info from an incorrect story in another pub. Why not watch and listen to debate.
- Nov 12, 2015 06:51:38 AM When and how are the dummies at the @WSJ going to apologize to me for their totally incorrect Editorial on me. I want "smart" trade deals.
- Nov 12, 2015 07:23:14 AM Why wouldn't the @WSJ call for comment or clarification before writing an editorial which is so totally wrong. No wonder it is doing poorly!
- Nov 12, 2015 07:50:11 AM We, as a country, either have borders or we don't. IF WE DON'T HAVE BORDERS, WE DON'T HAVE A COUNTRY!
- Nov 12, 2015 10:00:34 AM .@KarlRove is a biased dope who wrote falsely about me re China and TPP. This moron wasted $430 million on political campaigns and lost 100%
- Nov 12, 2015 10:08:08 AM Why does the failing @WSJ write a false editorial about me and let dummy @KarlRove make the same mistake in the same edition of the paper?
- Nov 12, 2015 12:03:14 PM .@WSJ and dopey Karl Rove made a mistake and purposely mischaracterized my statement on the terrible TPP deal. https://t.co/t9JZGIUAYl
- Nov 12, 2015 02:10:05 PM Total fool @KarlRove is part of the Republican Establishment problem. An all talk, no action dummy! https://t.co/CxLHA87hS1
- Nov 12, 2015 02:21:39 PM Wow, pres. candidate Ben Carson, who is very weak on illegal Immigration, just said he likes amnesty and a pathway to citizenship.
- Nov 12, 2015 03:38:00 PM From 2% to 27% in Texas - quite a jump into first place!
- Nov 12, 2015 03:43:04 PM Thank you @Forbes for showing the @WSJ was wrong. So dishonest! https://t.co/wOjEXdEkNg
- Nov 12, 2015 04:05:28 PM Macy's was very disloyal to me bc of my strong stance on illegal immigration. Their stock has crashed! #BoycottMacys https://t.co/WsvZtwZbBf

- Nov 12, 2015 04:49:09 PM I will be on with @BretBaier tonight at 6PM. #Trump2016
- Nov 12, 2015 04:49:33 PM I will be on @OutFrontCNN with @ErinBurnett at 7PM. Tune in! #Trump2016
- Nov 12, 2015 06:35:52 PM First candidate in Virginia with over 16,000 validated signatures for the ballot. An honor - thank you! #Trump2016 #MakeAmericaGreatAgain
- Nov 12, 2015 10:06:34 PM Thank you Iowa! I appreciate all of your support @IowaCentral & @ethanolbyPOET this evening! #Trump2016 #IACaucus https://t.co/mJzLcXjtpf

- Nov 13, 2015 11:07:07 AM Happy Friday the 13th https://t.co/Br6AUzgGoi
- Nov 13, 2015 02:42:05 PM "@DRUDGE_REPORT: REUTERS 5-DAY ROLLING POLL: TRUMP 34%, CARSON 19.6%, RUBIO 9.7%, CRUZ 7.7%..." Thank you - a great honor!
- Nov 13, 2015 03:16:02 PM .@CarlyFiorina Carly, not just you, I also told Gov. Kasich to "let Jeb talk, give him a chance" because Kasich was constantly cutting in.
- Nov 13, 2015 03:16:21 PM .@CarlyFiorina Carly—I did graduate from Wharton and did very well. Who is your fact checker? Will you apologize?
- Nov 13, 2015 03:17:53 PM .@CarlyFiorina Ben Carson said in his own book that he has a pathological temper & pathological disease. I didn't say it, he did. Apology?
- Nov 13, 2015 03:18:12 PM .@CarlyFiorina I only said I was on @60Minutes four weeks ago with Putin—never said I was in Green Room. Separate pieces— great ratings!
- Nov 13, 2015 03:55:51 PM .@CarlyFiorina had to inject herself into my factual statements concerning Ben Carson in order to breathe life into her failing campaign!
- Nov 13, 2015 04:04:01 PM .@seanhannity Carly, whose campaign is dead, is making false statements about me in order to salvage hope! Sad.
- Nov 13, 2015 04:11:05 PM Great honor to be inducted into the NJ Boxing Hall of Fame last night. Thank you! Timing could not have been better! https://t.co/IU6peXoVL2

- Nov 13, 2015 04:35:45 PM Thank you @JakeTapper for giving me credit for my vision on bombing the oil fields. Should have been done long ago. #Trump2016
- Nov 13, 2015 04:36:29 PM They laughed at me when I said to bomb the ISIS controlled oil fields. Now they are not laughing and doing what I said. #Trump2016
- Nov 13, 2015 04:54:18 PM Boy is this guy @ShepNewsTeam tough on me. So totally biased. As a reporter, he should be ashamed of himself! #Trump2016
- Nov 13, 2015 06:52:06 PM My prayers are with the victims and hostages in the horrible Paris attacks. May God be with you all.

- Nov 14, 2015 08:39:56 AM President Obama said "ISIL continues to shrink" in an interview just hours before the horrible attack in Paris. He is just so bad! CHANGE.
- Nov 14, 2015 08:42:27 AM We need much tougher, much smarter leadership - and we need it NOW!
- Nov 14, 2015 01:07:37 PM "@Mario_Posillico: @realDonaldTrump you need to win for not just America, but for humanity."
- Nov 14, 2015 01:10:42 PM "@ABCinSC: @realDonaldTrump - a tough man for a tough job in tough times. Gloves off, game on! https://t.co/l2ea1ZJ5Ps"
- Nov 14, 2015 01:11:07 PM "@dlt912: @realDonaldTrump you definitely have my vote!"
- Nov 14, 2015 01:15:07 PM "@jrpantiques: @realDonaldTrump @ABCinSC @KatrinaPierson THE WORLD IS PLAYING EVERYTHING RIGHT FOR TRUMP! EVERY DAY HIS POINTS ARE PROVEN"
- Nov 14, 2015 06:27:20 PM "@HaloOneForTrump: @realDonaldTrump has what MONEY CAN'T BUY: VISION & LOYAL & MOTIVATED SUPPORT! #veterans #military @foxnews @cnn @GOP"
- Nov 14, 2015 06:30:52 PM "@shawnlivinlife: I still haven't heard the WH say the words islamic terrorist. Call it what it is. #Trump2016 can't happen fast enough.
- Nov 14, 2015 06:31:33 PM "@Gman0623: @realDonaldTrump @HaloOneForTrump @FoxNews @CNN @GOP I love you Trump! MAKE AMERICA GREAT AGAIN!"
- Nov 14, 2015 06:32:18 PM "@MikeOG_: @realDonaldTrump was right! close the borders! #Trump2016"

- Nov 14, 2015 10:21:10 PM Great news out of New Hampshire! DonaldTrump is pulling away from the pack w/ 2nd is 17% behind him! #Trump2016 https://t.co/hASWradHMe"
- Nov 14, 2015 10:23:23 PM "@jcooper75: #DemDebate this debate stinks. CBS News, major fail. @realDonaldTrump"
- Nov 14, 2015 10:23:35 PM "@jaslohr_: @realDonaldTrump are you watching this circus?!? #DemDebate what a joke! #Trump2016"
- Nov 14, 2015 10:25:38 PM "@TomRichey: Enough of these party debates. What I wanna see is a @SenSanders vs @realDonaldTrump one on one debate!" That would be easy!
- Nov 14, 2015 10:25:53 PM "@redletter99: @realDonaldTrump I absolutely love this, can't wait till u debate Clinton"
- Nov 14, 2015 10:26:26 PM "@Oliviaand24: @realDonaldTrump TrumpOn America needs you in office Now! #MakeAmericaGreatAgain #Trump2016"
- Nov 14, 2015 10:30:52 PM Why won't President Obama use the term Islamic Terrorism? Isn't it now, after all of this time and so much death, about time!
- Nov 14, 2015 10:40:02 PM Hillary and Sanders are not doing well, but what is the failed former Mayor of Baltimore doing on that stage? O'Malley is a clown.
- Nov 14, 2015 10:52:24 PM Wow, Bernie Sanders just admitted that the real unemployment rate is 10% (it is actually over 20%) and for African American youth - 51%.
- Nov 14, 2015 10:57:36 PM I think everyone will like my new and very successful book, Crippled America. Go get it and let me know what you think!
- Nov 14, 2015 11:00:48 PM "@tasteofaz: Poll: Trump Surges to 42% Nationally; 'Bad News for Marco Rubio' https://t.co/9IrLrlpjfM @realdonaldtrump" Great news!

- Nov 15, 2015 01:17:34 AM "@TejadaDennes: @realDonaldTrump Crippled America is an incredible book! People need to read truth. #HispanicsForTrump #DemocratsForTrump"
- Nov 15, 2015 01:20:19 AM "@mnrosrnr: @realDonaldTrump the best book I've read in years, Trump is right on every issue and has the best ideas, a true economic genius"
- Nov 15, 2015 09:18:42 AM When will President Obama issue the words RADICAL ISLAMIC TERRORISM? He can't say it, and unless he will, the problem will not be solved!

- Nov 15, 2015 03:33:46 PM .@realDonaldTrump on ISIS&OIL FIELDS! Saying it for years! @AndersonCooper, you should acknowledge this! #Trump2016 https://t.co/ocoB9WlP7R
- Nov 15, 2015 03:46:01 PM I had a great time in Texas yesterday. A tremendous crowd of wonderful and enthusiastic people. Will be back soon!
- Nov 15, 2015 03:48:09 PM We need strong, tough and brilliant leadership now more than ever! MAKE AMERICA GREAT AGAIN!
- Nov 15, 2015 05:33:07 PM "@thewatcher23579: One of Paris terrorist came as Syrian refugee. Donald Trump is right again. BOMB THEIR OIL - TAKE AWAY THEIR FUNDING"
- Nov 15, 2015 05:38:21 PM "@mholsbunes: Donald Trump says tough gun control laws in Paris contributed to tragedy: https://t.co/ifVJmLw2Sx Presidential candidate??"
- Nov 15, 2015 05:54:31 PM "@USATrumpDiva: Donald Trump surges in poll among likely Republican voters https://t.co/uZ5nZUuqKq"
- Nov 15, 2015 06:39:05 PM .@VanityFair Magazine is doing really poorly. It has gotten worse and worse over the years, and has lost almost all of it's former allure!
- Nov 15, 2015 06:47:06 PM I have watched sloppy Graydon Carter fail and close Spy Magazine and now am watching him fail at @VanityFair Magazine. He is a total loser!
- Nov 15, 2015 07:10:29 PM Glad to see that @RondaRousey lost her championship fight last night. Was soundly beaten - not a nice person!
- Nov 15, 2015 07:13:07 PM "@Hturne: @VanityFair You're spot on! He tries 2b an intellectual elitist.The truth: he has a low IQ, no imagination, no creativity"
- Nov 15, 2015 07:23:22 PM "@RealReagan0503: If you missed it, here is the most popular link among people I follow https://t.co/lOppBvYMRy by @realDonaldTrump"
- Nov 15, 2015 07:25:54 PM "@davenorthYV: Does anybody ever realize that HillaryClinton doesn't make eye contact with anyone, even the camera. That's a sign of lying"
- Nov 15, 2015 07:27:49 PM "@syoka68: Reading the comments of the leftists on here makes me nauseated. We SO NEED YOU, MR. TRUMP! Make America Great Again"

- Nov 15, 2015 07:29:23 PM "@Parker_Votes: We finally have a voice with Let's do our part & VOTE IN THE R PRIMARY, 4 #Trump2016 #TrumpArmy https://t.co/fIl3hXOERS"
- Nov 15, 2015 07:30:46 PM "@760_831: @DanSaltsman @realDonaldTrump @MichaelCohen212 @IvankaTrump i have faith he will win and save America"
- Nov 15, 2015 07:31:44 PM "@760_831: @DanSaltsman @realDonaldTrump @MichaelCohen212 @IvankaTrump I have faith he will win and save America"
- Nov 15, 2015 07:37:03 PM "@peg4cats: @TerryLambert201 @realDonaldTrump you are so right. I only trust Trump to be tough on immigration"
- Nov 15, 2015 07:57:48 PM .@JohnLegere @TMobile John, focus on running your company, I think the service is terrible! Try hiring some good managers.
- Nov 15, 2015 08:03:21 PM President Obama just told President Putin how important the Russian air strikes against ISIS have been. I TOLD YOU SO!
- Nov 15, 2015 08:09:01 PM Tom Brady just did it again. He is not only a great guy, he is, without question, the BEST quarterback!
- Nov 15, 2015 08:10:58 PM "@StreetR77: @JohnLegere @TMobile didn't know he was CEO of tmobile, I have T-Mobile, it's pathetic, dropped calls, no service."
- Nov 15, 2015 09:26:16 PM "@SarahPalinUSA: From St. Patrick's Cathedral, NYC: blessings, prayers and heartfelt concern for those in Paris.

- Nov 16, 2015 07:43:30 AM Remember, I was the one who said attack the oil (ISIS source of wealth) a long time ago. Everyone scoffed, now they're attacking the oil.
- Nov 16, 2015 01:41:09 PM Interesting article from highly respected Wayne Allyn Root https://t.co/1esS0QV46V
- Nov 16, 2015 01:47:19 PM Wow, @Macys shares are down more than 40% this year. I never knew my ties & shirts not being sold there would have such a big impact!
- Nov 16, 2015 03:23:43 PM Republicans must stop listening to dopes like @KarlRove who still insists Mitt Romney won the last election. Think big & think strong!
- Nov 16, 2015 04:47:19 PM Will be landing in Knoxville, Tennessee shortly - tremendous crowd expected. It's all very simple, we want to #MakeAmericaGreatAgain!

- Nov 16, 2015 05:47:20 PM Discussing #SyrianRefugees with @EricBolling on @FoxNews back on 10/3/2015. #ISIS https://t.co/rUX57o2BzM
- Nov 16, 2015 05:52:02 PM I agree! The headline says it all. #Trump2016 #MakeAmericaGreatAgain https://t.co/TWslpJPQG0
- Nov 16, 2015 06:09:23 PM Just landing in Knoxville, Tennessee! Massive crowd expected! Will all have a great time, despite serious subject matter.
- Nov 16, 2015 08:44:32 PM Just leaving Knoxville, TN --- what a crowd, what amazing people! #Trump2016 #MakeAmericaGreatAgain https://t.co/5qr5deOlEl
- Nov 16, 2015 09:16:36 PM Great poll numbers out of @UMassAmherst. Thank you! #Trump2016 #MakeAmericaGreatAgain https://t.co/ePlQRgjMYw
- Nov 16, 2015 09:53:37 PM Just received a copy of @SarahPalinUSA new book -- a great read! Sarah is a terrific person.
- Nov 16, 2015 10:33:43 PM Thank you Tennessee! #Trump2016 https://t.co/RNZ3hvbVvM

- Nov 17, 2015 08:14:52 AM So many great polls like Reuters - big leads everywhere. New Hampshire really special! We will win big and MAKE AMERICA GREAT AGAIN!
- Nov 17, 2015 08:19:03 AM I, along with almost everyone else, have so little confidence in President Obama. He has a horrible attitude-a man who is resigned to defeat
- Nov 17, 2015 08:54:30 AM Refugees from Syria are now pouring into our great country. Who knows who they are - some could be ISIS. Is our president insane?
- Nov 17, 2015 10:01:26 AM "GOP Voters Trust Donald Trump to Keep Our Country Safe" https://t.co/TWslpJPQG0
- Nov 17, 2015 10:35:11 AM What is our President doing? https://t.co/8p0A80kaaX
- Nov 17, 2015 03:48:34 PM One of the saddest things in journalism is what happened to the formerly great @AP. They have lost their way and are no longer credible.
- Nov 17, 2015 03:48:53 PM .@AP is doing very badly. I can say from experience their reporting is terrible & highly inaccurate. Sadly, they are now irrelevant!

- Nov 17, 2015 04:16:55 PM Melania and I just had interview with the legendary @BarbaraJWalters. Watch #abc2020 this Friday. Tonight we talk ISIS @WNTonight
- Nov 17, 2015 05:39:17 PM I will be interviewed by @seanhannity tonight at 10:00 on @FoxNews . Much, much, much to talk about!
- Nov 17, 2015 05:58:11 PM "@Ashevillelaura: @realDonaldTrump @seanhannity @FoxNews Obama has no credibility on terrorist threats & ISIS. Trump best to protect us"
- Nov 17, 2015 06:01:43 PM The great Barbara Walters interviews Melania Trump and me on a Special Friday night at 10:00 on ABC.... https://t.co/28q3QgfIbM
- Nov 17, 2015 10:08:33 PM Thank you for all of your support! Let's #MakeAmericaGreatAgain! #Trump2016 https://t.co/G7o6b0cfZz

- Nov 18, 2015 05:27:57 AM "@KatrinaPierson: #MakeAmericaGreatAgain #Trump2016 https://t.co/Aja00L81uf" Katrina, great job on @FoxNews last night!
- Nov 18, 2015 10:34:18 AM How does Ben Carson survive this problem – really big. Similar story on front page of New York Times. https://t.co/y9fqUUYRnD
- Nov 18, 2015 11:57:58 AM Great New Poll https://t.co/178k1ERFqT
- Nov 18, 2015 02:04:58 PM Very nice article from Daily Mail https://t.co/SIxmYzPXv1
- Nov 18, 2015 02:23:18 PM Via Politico: "Trump Extends Lead in New Hampshire Poll" https://t.co/PaJOAi3rGa
- Nov 18, 2015 06:53:43 PM "@FoxNews New Hampshire Poll: @realDonaldTrump 'Rules GOP Race in New Hampshire.' Trump 27, Rubio 13, Cruz 11, Bush 9, Carson 9, & Kasich 7"

- Nov 19, 2015 08:11:49 AM Eight Syrians were just caught on the southern border trying to get into the U.S. ISIS maybe? I told you so. WE NEED A BIG & BEAUTIFUL WALL!
- Nov 19, 2015 11:30:16 AM Everyone is now saying how right I was with illegal immigration & the wall. After Paris, they're all on the bandwagon.
- Nov 19, 2015 01:11:58 PM The POLICE in Paris did a fantastic job. Very brave - not easy!

- Nov 19, 2015 01:32:38 PM Thank you for your support! Together we can #MakeAmericaGreatAgain! #Trump2016 https://t.co/qni36GI6fV
- Nov 19, 2015 03:03:43 PM I told you! Premiums are soaring! #RepealObamacare #Trump2016 https://t.co/Ey50582uND
- Nov 19, 2015 03:32:46 PM Just the beginning & it is going to get worse. Rates & deductibles are so high nobody is going to be able to use it. https://t.co/iwqLODke50
- Nov 19, 2015 04:28:44 PM Thank you Worcester, Massachusetts!#MakeAmericaGreatAgain #Trump2016 https://t.co/D6QinyBLW6 https://t.co/sZDJr3Tkd8
- Nov 19, 2015 04:34:39 PM The legendary Barbara Walters interviews Melania Trump and me on a special this Friday night at 10:00 on ABC. Don't miss it!
- Nov 19, 2015 08:04:55 PM Governor Kasich, whose failed campaign & debating skills have brought him way down in the polls, is going to spend $2.5 million against me.
- Nov 19, 2015 08:05:16 PM John Kasich should focus his special interest money on building up his failed image, not negative ads on me.
- Nov 19, 2015 08:05:35 PM John Kasich, despite being Governor of Ohio, is losing to me in the Ohio polls. Pathetic!
- Nov 19, 2015 08:05:54 PM I want to do negative ads on John Kasich, but he is so irrelevant to the race that I don't want to waste my money.
- Nov 19, 2015 08:06:04 PM Watch Kasich squirm --- if he is not truthful in his negative ads I will sue him just for fun!
- Nov 19, 2015 08:06:15 PM Kasich has already spent $6 million on ads in New Hampshire and his numbers have gone down. People from NH are smart!
- Nov 19, 2015 08:06:28 PM I loved beating John Kasich in the debates, but it was easy—he came in dead last!
- Nov 19, 2015 08:06:49 PM Doesn't help Kasich to do negative ads on me because he still has to go through everyone else - he's almost last.
- Nov 19, 2015 08:06:59 PM John Kasich fell right into President Obama's trap on ObamaCare, and the people of Ohio are suffering for it. Shame!
- Nov 19, 2015 08:47:31 PM Once John Kasich announced he was running for president, and opened his mouth, people realized he was a complete & total dud!
- Nov 19, 2015 08:55:47 PM John Kasich was managing director of Lehman Brothers when it crashed, bringing down the world and ruining people's lives. A total failure!

- Nov 19, 2015 09:28:38 PM A great evening in Iowa! Thank you Des Moines Area Community College for a great forum! #Trump2016 #IAForums https://t.co/092t2VrMEw
- Nov 19, 2015 09:54:44 PM A wonderful afternoon in Iowa! Great people! Heading now to Florida - tomorrow, South Carolina! #MakeAmericaGreatAgain #Trump2016

- Nov 20, 2015 07:50:14 AM The media must immediately stop calling ISIS leaders "MASTERMINDS." Call them instead thugs and losers. Young people must not go into ISIS!
- Nov 20, 2015 08:00:30 AM The media must denigrate ISIS at all levels or youth will continue to be drawn to it. These are low level degenerates, NOT masterminds!
- Nov 20, 2015 09:30:27 AM Going to South Carolina now, great place, SRO crowd. Iowa was amazing yesterday!
- Nov 20, 2015 10:03:04 AM .@mkhammer, a Fox contributor, isn't smart enough to know what is going on at the border. @TheJuanWilliams made the point far better!
- Nov 20, 2015 10:24:21 AM My family has the honor of being interviewed for a full hour by the legendary @BarbaraJWalters tonight @ABC - 10pmE. https://t.co/cm4fv1Ye9L
- Nov 20, 2015 11:08:18 AM Under our President, ISIS is gaining great strength- https://t.co/28VsmV8xng
- Nov 20, 2015 01:51:41 PM I didn't suggest a database-a reporter did. We must defeat Islamic terrorism & have surveillance, including a watch list, to protect America
- Nov 20, 2015 02:37:40 PM Thank you for a great afternoon, South Carolina! See you next Tuesday! #MakeAmericaGreatAgain #Trump2016 https://t.co/kWWMlmy7gQ
- Nov 20, 2015 03:13:29 PM Can you believe the worst Mayor in the U.S., & probably the worst Mayor in the history of #NYC, @BilldeBlasio, just called me a blow hard!
- Nov 20, 2015 03:14:33 PM .@BilldeBlasio should focus on running #NYC & all of the problems that he has caused with his ineptitude, & not be so focused on me!

- Nov 20, 2015 04:17:31 PM The legendary @BarbaraJWalters interviews my family and me tonight at 10:00 on @ABC2020 . Don't miss it! https://t.co/JHTF7f9aTo
- Nov 20, 2015 04:38:57 PM .@HillaryClinton is weak on illegal immigration & totally incompetent as a manager and leader - no strength or stamina to be #POTUS!
- Nov 20, 2015 05:51:24 PM Just got back from South Carolina. Going to Alabama tomorrow!
- Nov 20, 2015 06:57:39 PM .@Gracematters Thank you, a very wise bet! Best wishes.
- Nov 20, 2015 07:01:02 PM "@GeraldSoelz: Awesome news. Keep your focus on the issues. You just might get more blue collar Democrats to vote for you than Reagan."
- Nov 20, 2015 07:01:46 PM "@Unicurls: @realDonaldTrump I'll be in attendance. #YUGE #MakeAmericaGreatAgain #bamaforTrump" Nice!
- Nov 20, 2015 07:02:47 PM "@meganweaver321: @realDonaldTrump Alabama loves you" Great!
- Nov 20, 2015 07:03:34 PM "@samsellars: @realDonaldTrump North Carolina. Come on down." Will be there very soon!
- Nov 20, 2015 07:03:59 PM "@The2ndguardsUS: @realDonaldTrump ROLL TIDE"
- Nov 20, 2015 07:07:10 PM .@washingtonpost @BretBaier Please thank Charles Lane for his new found confidence. He has made a very good bet!
- Nov 20, 2015 07:07:49 PM Tune into the legendary @BarbaraJWalters at 10pmE on @ABC2020 tonight. #MeetTheTrumps for a full hour @ABC #ABC2020! https://t.co/exF5aUhrEW
- Nov 20, 2015 07:09:51 PM "@smith_jere: @realDonaldTrump You are amazing Mr. Trump! Thank you!!!" So nice.
- Nov 20, 2015 07:29:19 PM Looking forward to watching the legendary @BarbaraJWalters interview my family (and me) tonight on @ABC at 10:00. Many things to talk about!
- Nov 20, 2015 07:39:17 PM "@mia_liner: @GSRPygmies @realDonaldTrump Trump supporters are a very loyal breed! We see the truth, only Trump can fix this mess we are in
- Nov 20, 2015 07:41:14 PM "@JamesPWilson1: @realDonaldTrump When you become president, we will avenge all of the innocents who isis killed"

- Nov 20, 2015 07:42:27 PM "@2timeslucky: No one can take @realDonaldTrump down because it is the WILL of the people for him to win!
- Nov 20, 2015 08:56:33 PM #ICYMI: I joined #OnTheRecord with @kimguilfoyle on @FoxNews this evening. #Trump2016 #MakeAmericaGreatAgain https://t.co/FlJutjpR35
- Nov 20, 2015 09:52:18 PM Join us at 10pmE on @ABC2020 @ABC with @BarbaraJWalters! #MeetTheTrumps #ABC2020 https://t.co/vMeLS00GnJ

- Nov 21, 2015 12:06:32 AM "@VincentKunicki: @realDonaldTrump @kimguilfoyle @FoxNews Long live Donald Trump our next Ronald Reagan!!! God bless you we need you" Nice!
- Nov 21, 2015 12:06:39 AM "@hotroddergirl: @realDonaldTrump trump 20/20 shows just what hard work and good family can do. Blue collar with you."
- Nov 21, 2015 12:07:04 AM "@Greg39529063: @ABC2020 @ABC @BarbaraJWalters Watching now! Great! Always true to his word and the USA! A real leader! So nice to hear!!!"
- Nov 21, 2015 12:08:17 AM "@ClassySnobbb: @realDonaldTrump AMAZING interview. You and your family will be great role models for America!!! #MakeAmericaGreatAgain"
- Nov 21, 2015 12:09:19 AM "@realkingrobbo: @realDonaldTrump @Greg39529063 @ABC2020 @ABC @BarbaraJWalters the best man for the job!" Thanks!
- Nov 21, 2015 12:11:46 AM "@TCash78: @realDonaldTrump @VincentKunicki @kimguilfoyle @FoxNews he will make America great again
- Nov 21, 2015 12:13:55 AM "@hiddenspeed42: @AY4WEB No pay or compensation to make our beautiful country again!! That's his promise to us!! We love u trump"
- Nov 21, 2015 12:17:01 AM "@BornToBeGOP: @realDonaldTrump Your family is a better watch than the Kardashians by a mile!" Cute!
- Nov 21, 2015 12:18:58 AM "@realkingrobbo: @hotroddergirl You're the hero America needs! #Trump2016" Thank you, I only want to make America great again!
- Nov 21, 2015 12:20:13 AM "@michaelglassner: A GREAT DAY in South Carolina for DonaldTrump & #TeamTrump! #Trump2016 #MakeAmericaGreatAgain https://t.co/Re655JmhqJ"

- Nov 21, 2015 12:23:04 AM "@RenaSummersLtd: Watched @ABCNetwork special tonight! You have such amazing children. Lots to be proud of! Love your wife! Class Act!"
- Nov 21, 2015 12:23:38 AM "@TLCastle: @realDonaldTrump Do you plan on making any campaign stops in West Virginia?" YES, soon.
- Nov 21, 2015 12:24:25 AM "@RustyBlissUSA: @realDonaldTrump we're ready to thwart the establishment attempts in the Buckeye State. #Trump2016 #TeamTrump"
- Nov 21, 2015 12:25:49 AM "@thetylerjames9: @realDonaldTrump cannot be bought! Therefore he cannot be silenced!"
- Nov 21, 2015 08:09:09 AM "@jaazee1: @CNN anchor's shocked that DonaldTrump's comments resonate with GOP base will go apoplectic that he does with democrats too.
- Nov 21, 2015 08:09:31 AM "@tas0727: @realDonaldTrump Make America Great again vote Donald Trump"
- Nov 21, 2015 08:13:13 AM People are really liking my new book, "Crippled America." Check it out!
- Nov 21, 2015 09:29:03 AM We're stuck with the worst mayor in the United States. Too bad, but New York City will survive!
- Nov 21, 2015 09:35:20 AM To show you how politicians act, Bobby Jindal spent $1,000 to register in New Hampshire & dropped out the next day. Such a waste!
- Nov 21, 2015 09:36:20 AM Heading to Birmingham, Alabama, and a massive crowd of incredible people! 12 noon - will be wild.
- Nov 21, 2015 10:23:06 AM A woman who got fired after two days of working with Scott Walker - a wacko - now trying to raise funds to fight me.
- Nov 21, 2015 10:26:48 AM So nice when media properly polices media. Thank you @BreitbartNews. https://t.co/IGUh57zOJz
- Nov 21, 2015 10:35:30 AM Rumor has it - Pataki, Kasich, & Senator Lindsey Graham are dropping out of the race very soon. Hope it's not true, they're so easy to beat!
- Nov 21, 2015 10:44:38 AM Thank you John Nolte for wonderful analysis & reporting.
- Nov 21, 2015 03:13:03 PM It's too bad so few people showed up to @bobvanderplaats Family Leader dinner. Next year I'll try & be there- and they'll have a huge crowd!

- Nov 21, 2015 03:40:38 PM Thank you for a great afternoon Birmingham, Alabama! #Trump2016 #MakeAmericaGreatAgain https://t.co/FrOkqCzBoD
- Nov 21, 2015 03:41:20 PM Thank you to all law enforcement agencies for a fabulous job! #LEO #LESM #Trump2016 https://t.co/SuH1jfOQR4
- Nov 21, 2015 04:49:04 PM .@heytana, great job - we are all proud of you!
- Nov 21, 2015 06:01:58 PM "@THR: Trump's Wife, Children Open Up About GOP Candidate: "There's No One Else Like Him" https://t.co/wOn9AwEyNk https://t.co/WXsq41nK17"
- Nov 21, 2015 06:02:13 PM "@GStephanopoulos: I'll talk to Donald Trump about his comments on Syrian refugees, and much more, Sunday on @ThisWeekABC."
- Nov 21, 2015 06:11:00 PM "@politico: Palin on 2016: "I think it would come down to Cruz and Trump! https://t.co/jSNS5Yv7Pt | Getty https://t.co/y5wN0AhK0E"
- Nov 21, 2015 06:12:14 PM "@foxnation: Report: #DonaldTrump Heckler Convicted Of Attempting To Blow Up Marine Recruitment Center https://t.co/8p4yBnbEL5"
- Nov 21, 2015 06:16:15 PM "@FortuneMagazine: Do successful CEOs sleep less than everyone else? https://t.co/SBkP1QZKEh https://t.co/15ZgyzSr1J"
- Nov 21, 2015 06:17:50 PM "@WayneDupreeShow: "It's clear that Donald Trump was NOT even talking about a Muslim Database!" https://t.co/3tLDZj2WGV"
- Nov 21, 2015 06:27:21 PM "@marklevinshow: Well said https://t.co/Is4xshwUpg"
- Nov 21, 2015 06:30:09 PM "@Ma1973sk: Great family. Great interview @realDonaldTrump ! https://t.co/IFcjTwd5ey"
- Nov 21, 2015 06:40:44 PM "@boreed615: Donald Trump retakes lead in GOP race; Ted Cruz makes gains: poll: https://t.co/G8z5ek7emn # via AOL"
- Nov 21, 2015 07:48:16 PM "@TomLydon: What Financial Pros Can Learn from Donald Trump's Communication Style https://t.co/D5fG5cY25U @DanSondhelm" Very nice, thanks!
- Nov 21, 2015 07:50:30 PM "@2timeslucky: @steph93065 @FoxNews Kimberly G. hosted Greta last nights& told the TRUTH about Trump! https://t.co/wwmKjAbIlR"

- Nov 21, 2015 07:52:25 PM "@iliveamongyou: URGENT "@GOP…in an effort to destroy their own front runner." #MakeAmericaGreatAgain https://t.co/HWABcAeu8z" I HIT BACK!
- Nov 21, 2015 09:31:58 PM .ccolvinj @AP is one of the truly bad reporters---working for an organization that has totally lost its way. Stories are fictional garbage.
- Nov 21, 2015 09:32:37 PM I find that @Reuters is a far more professional operation than @AP.

- Nov 22, 2015 07:16:40 AM Will be interviewed on @foxandfriends at 8:00 A.M.
- Nov 22, 2015 07:26:36 AM .@GStephanopoulos just announced that I am leading BIG in the new @ABC Poll which will be shown on This Week at 9:00 A.M. I will be on show
- Nov 22, 2015 07:33:23 AM Big new @ABC Poll to be announced at 9:00 A.M. on This Week with @GStephanopoulos. I will be interviewed on show!
- Nov 22, 2015 09:50:56 AM Great poll numbers all over and beating Hillary Clinton one on one. Thank you!
- Nov 22, 2015 10:53:38 AM 13 Syrian refugees were caught trying to get into the U.S. through the Southern Border. How many made it? WE NEED THE WALL!
- Nov 22, 2015 10:59:40 AM We better get tough with RADICAL ISLAMIC TERRORISTS, and get tough now, or the life and safety of our wonderful country will be in jeopardy!
- Nov 22, 2015 01:26:13 PM Great poll numbers! Thank you! #MakeAmericaGreatAgain #Trump2016 https://t.co/51CRR6m5Eg
- Nov 22, 2015 02:59:17 PM "@heiressarts: @realDonaldTrump By going after you, Jindal also lost the LA governor race! Politicians Beware.
- Nov 22, 2015 03:05:09 PM "@SeanSean252: @WayneDupreeShow @Rockprincess818 @CheriJacobus https://t.co/5GUwhhtvyN"
- Nov 22, 2015 03:06:04 PM "@jakub_lisa: @HillaryClinton A Clinton Cannot be trusted!How many x's do we allow them to disgrace this country? #NoClintonInWHEverAgain"
- Nov 22, 2015 03:07:10 PM "@drewtheg: Trump is the epitome of integrity, good spirit, forthright honesty... you pull no punches and call a spade a spade. diggin it!"

- Nov 22, 2015 05:26:06 PM "@TheFix: The Paris attacks have only made Donald Trump stronger https://t.co/F8vgxYNa5t https://t.co/Y3SevhrRp1" Very interesting!
- Nov 22, 2015 05:32:09 PM "@MJP1370: @realDonaldTrump @TheFix @pbump We need Trump now! Obama isn't protecting Americans !!"
- Nov 22, 2015 05:32:42 PM "@bloggerjulie: @FoxNews The reporter is the one who mentioned the national database FIRST and not DonaldTrump. Y not report HONEST NEWS?"
- Nov 22, 2015 05:33:42 PM "@jrpantiques: @realDonaldTrump @TheFix @pbump THE SCRIPT FOR A GREAT WORLD CHANGING LEADER TO ARISE HAS BEEN WRITTEN & IT WAS FOR MR. TRUMP
- Nov 22, 2015 05:42:34 PM "@ktd101551: @CNNPolitics Trump gave a great speech in Ala. What's more important a protester? I wouldn't give these folks 1 sec of attn"
- Nov 22, 2015 05:46:17 PM "@ny_conservative: @BarbMuenchen #CrippledAmerica is an excellent resource for the 2016 race #TeamTrump #Trump2016 #MakeAmericaGreatAgain"
- Nov 22, 2015 05:56:56 PM Hillary Clinton is weak on illegal immigration, among many other things. She is strong on corruption - corruption is what she's best at!
- Nov 22, 2015 07:58:05 PM .@MatthewJDowd thank you for the nice comments recently, especially on @BarbaraJWalters. My family & I greatly appreciate your kind words.

- Nov 23, 2015 11:22:42 AM .@AP continues to do extremely dishonest reporting. Always looking for a hit to bring them back into relevancy—ain't working!
- Nov 23, 2015 11:23:10 AM .@AP has one of the worst reporters in the business -- @JeffHorwitz wouldn't know the truth if it hit him in the face.
- Nov 23, 2015 11:26:10 AM Going to Columbus, Ohio today for a tremendous rally of thousands. The silent majority is no longer silent!
- Nov 23, 2015 11:49:46 AM Hillary, there is nothing to laugh about- https://t.co/bkmWFZ9JI9
- Nov 23, 2015 01:45:58 PM When you do your Christmas shopping remember how disloyal @Macys was to the subject of illegal immigration. #BoycottMacys #DumpMacys

- Nov 23, 2015 02:02:36 PM Via @washingtonpost 9/18/01. I want an apology! Many people have tweeted that I am right! https://t.co/CpsMxs54qv https://t.co/wrDEhXJlvR
- Nov 23, 2015 02:36:34 PM .@WSJ reports that @GOP getting ready to treat me unfairly—big spending planned against me. That wasn't the deal!
- Nov 23, 2015 05:11:48 PM Going to Ohio, home of one of the worst presidential candidates in history--Kasich. Can't debate, loves #ObamaCare--dummy!
- Nov 23, 2015 05:18:34 PM Heading for Ohio - really big crowd of amazing people! Much to talk about!
- Nov 23, 2015 05:25:20 PM "@DonnySmith557: @realDonaldTrump Everything Mr. Trump touches turns to gold, what a great negotiator! !!!!!" Thanks.
- Nov 23, 2015 05:26:18 PM "@iliveamongyou: @BostonGlobe: Ben Carson advisers say he struggles with foreign policy https://t.co/phTAgT5qP6 https://t.co/044xgNYLth"
- Nov 23, 2015 09:08:23 PM Just left Columbus rally of 14,000 people --- a far bigger crowd than even I expected! Unbelievable evening, incredible spirit in the arena!
- Nov 23, 2015 10:28:24 PM "@beingmesuzieeJ: @realDonaldTrump... You ROCKED IT AGAIN IN OHIO!!!! Come to Nebraska.. Please!! Trump 2016!!" Thanks and I will!
- Nov 23, 2015 10:29:44 PM "@David360NC: We have a voice with DonaldTrump, Let's do our part & VOTE IN THE R PRIMARY 4 #Trump2016 #TeamTrump https://t.co/2xHujNNNFT"
- Nov 23, 2015 10:30:55 PM "@JeffPage5: @realDonaldTrump @WSJ @GOP they're finally gettin the message, we're fed up & we're not going establishment.
- Nov 23, 2015 10:31:38 PM "@Port3Star: @JDiamond1 @CNNPolitics You know he has great vision. The very best. Many people have told him so. Thousands of people!"
- Nov 23, 2015 10:42:22 PM "@Sandikay60: @realDonaldTrump it was awesome! #Trumponly. Great crowd! Wonderful"
- Nov 23, 2015 10:44:24 PM "@Good2bqueen67: .@realDonaldTrump @Sandikay60 I enjoyed the speech so much tonight, you were on point Sir!" Thanks.

- Nov 24, 2015 03:02:19 PM Republicans must stop relying on losers like @KarlRove if they want to start winning presidential elections. Be tough and get smart!
- Nov 24, 2015 03:54:08 PM Heading to Myrtle Beach, South Carolina. Really big crowd—so much to talk about!
- Nov 24, 2015 04:08:29 PM Will be doing @seanhannity at 10 PM on @FoxNews. As always with Sean, will be interesting!
- Nov 24, 2015 04:13:27 PM "@AnnCoulter: If you run anyone but Trump, Hillary wins. So Rubio, Christie, Jeb! & Kasich must hate the country. https://t.co/lExEBrwDT3"
- Nov 24, 2015 04:16:40 PM "@Nick95B: @realDonaldTrump I'll only vote for TRUMP! If eGOP screw things up I won't vote for ANY republicans; ANY https://t.co/mHyCIL9VpD
- Nov 24, 2015 04:20:00 PM "@Maryland4T: @SmallBiz4Trump Keep up the good work! Americans of ALL kinds are rallying behind jlDonaldTrump to help #MakeAmericaGreatAgain
- Nov 24, 2015 04:22:36 PM "@cecki: Leave our candidate @realDonaldTrump alone! Do not embarrass yourselves further.
- Nov 24, 2015 04:55:45 PM .@BradPaisley came up to see me. A really nice and talented guy. https://t.co/duJ7vXLGZw
- Nov 24, 2015 05:03:45 PM What is Frank VanderSloot getting for agreeing to back Marco Rubio? Last victim was Mitt Romney - see how that turned out.
- Nov 24, 2015 05:12:44 PM Thank you for your nice words @MikeNeedham @Heritage for the nice words on @FoxNewsSunday with Chris Wallace. #FNS #Trump2016
- Nov 24, 2015 05:57:14 PM New @OANN national poll released. Thank you America! #Trump2016 https://t.co/yopcngFzFv
- Nov 24, 2015 10:57:21 PM "@PatSheldon10913: @realDonaldTrump had a great time in Myrtle Beach tonight."
- Nov 24, 2015 11:36:24 PM A wonderful evening in South Carolina - big crowd, amazing energy!
- Nov 24, 2015 11:50:13 PM Myrtle Beach, South Carolina #MakeAmericaGreatAgain #Trump2016 https://t.co/JlY5sbumpY
- Nov 24, 2015 11:53:15 PM "@MichaelCohen212: .@realDonaldTrump @OANN no one is even close to #Trump"

- Nov 24, 2015 11:53:29 PM "@GlendaAhrens: @realDonaldTrump @OANN Fantastic winning all the way to WH #Trump2016"
- Nov 24, 2015 11:53:51 PM "@idawhannadoyou: @realDonaldTrump @OANN Love it. Wish I could get @OANN I hear good things about them such as objective unbiased reporting.

- Nov 25, 2015 07:51:37 AM Why would @greta use @KarlRove as an election analyst when he has made so many mistakes. He still thinks Romney won. An establishment dope!
- Nov 25, 2015 08:23:15 AM South Carolina was so great last night. Will be back soon!
- Nov 25, 2015 08:24:30 AM "@DonnySmith557: @karl @Morning_Joe @FoxNews Karl is a total joke!!!! If he didn't have the Bush family and Fox he wouldn't have anything! !
- Nov 25, 2015 08:25:16 AM "@patty_laughlin: DonaldTrump @karl @Morning_Joe @FoxNews Never thought much of Carl.. Make America Great Again Trump for President 2016"
- Nov 25, 2015 08:30:14 AM "@raider8381: @Morning_Joe @FoxNews America wants DONALD TRUMP! "TV Heads" still refuse to embrace that reality! Media are LIARS."
- Nov 25, 2015 08:31:18 AM "@jbclemson: @realDonaldTrump @karl @Morning_Joe @FoxNews Bombed is an understatement. Pathetic attempt by #GOP. Rove embarrassed himself"
- Nov 25, 2015 08:32:30 AM "@FranMFarber: @Morning_Joe @FoxNews @morningmika did not say very nice things about you this morning on her show. Typical liberal!" True!
- Nov 25, 2015 08:40:35 AM @KarlRove just totally bombed on @Morning_Joe. @FoxNews has him on even though he has lost all credibility - a loser! Fox should dump Rove.
- Nov 25, 2015 02:36:14 PM Thank you for your continued support! #MakeAmericaGreatAgain #Trump2016 https://t.co/SLo49cY9KB
- Nov 25, 2015 06:05:37 PM "@realdctaylor: The Establishment is afraid of @realDonaldTrump. Once we try a business man we may never want a politician again! #TeamTrump

- Nov 25, 2015 07:22:00 PM I LIVE IN NEW JERSEY & @realDonaldTrump IS RIGHT: MUSLIMS DID CELEBRATE ON 9/11 HERE! WE SAW IT! https://t.co/1SksZU9qlj
- Nov 25, 2015 07:55:48 PM #MakeAmericaGreatAgain #Trump2016 https://t.co/r9ARuMdyMn
- Nov 25, 2015 08:03:10 PM Credible Source on 9-11 Muslim Celebrations: FBI https://t.co/UICDNcftJS via @WKRG
- Nov 25, 2015 08:12:05 PM "@Keeping__Real: So good to see the @realDonaldTrump family out with him on the campaign trail! It really shows the family man that he is!"
- Nov 25, 2015 08:21:54 PM The failing @nytimes should be focused on good reporting and the papers financial survival and not with constant hits on Donald Trump!
- Nov 25, 2015 08:24:35 PM "@RioSunny3: @realDonaldTrump @WKRG I lived in New Jersey at that time and witnessed all that as well.
- Nov 25, 2015 08:29:29 PM The @nytimes is so poorly run and managed that other family members are looking to take over control. With unfunded liabilities-big trouble!
- Nov 25, 2015 08:35:50 PM The dopes at the @nytimes bought the Boston Globe for $1.3 billion and sold it for $1.00. Their great old headquarters-gave it away! So dumb
- Nov 25, 2015 08:41:15 PM So, since the people at the @nytimes have made all bad decisions over the last decade, why do people care what they write. Incompetent!
- Nov 25, 2015 08:51:00 PM The numbers at the @nytimes are so dismal, especially advertising revenue, that big help will be needed fast. A once great institution-SAD!

- Nov 26, 2015 07:52:15 AM Happy Thanksgiving to all. Have a great day and look forward to the future. We will MAKE AMERICA GREAT AGAIN!
- Nov 26, 2015 03:44:48 PM https://t.co/T5JBFXOz3F
- Nov 26, 2015 03:51:01 PM "@PrisonPlanet: .@realDonaldTrump gets it. Never apologize for fake controversies whipped up by the perpetually offended media."
- Nov 26, 2015 04:34:25 PM Great new poll numbers! Thank you for your support! #Trump2016 https://t.co/vmrsOnsMRo

- Nov 26, 2015 04:40:30 PM I do not know the reporter for the @nytimes, or what he looks like. I was showing a person groveling to take back a statement made long ago!
- Nov 26, 2015 04:46:31 PM The failing @nytimes should focus on fair and balanced reporting rather than constant hit jobs on me. Yesterday 3 boring articles, today2!
- Nov 26, 2015 09:50:56 PM "@BeezakaMrB: @realDonaldTrump Shopping @Macys is NO LONGER a family CHRISTMAS TIME tradition in my house." Great, a very disloyal chain!
- Nov 26, 2015 09:57:21 PM "@pthebnyc: @realDonaldTrump @Sari_Swensen @nytimes no need to explain, Sir. We've got your back." Thanks!
- Nov 26, 2015 09:57:48 PM "@Rketeltas: @realDonaldTrump If you combine the business models for both Macy's & the NY Times, both are on a rapid decline, such a pity."

- Nov 27, 2015 03:10:59 AM "@MarkSimoneNY: Great twitter quote about Donald Trump: "Never apologize for fake controversies whipped up by the perpetually offended media
- Nov 27, 2015 03:33:21 AM "@VaughnVhalen: Donald Trump Rises to 38% Nationally; Ted Cruz Edges into 2nd at 12%
- Nov 27, 2015 01:35:04 PM "@DeusVultGeorgia: @MingBlueTeaCup @RickCanton @_Holly_Renee @realDonaldTrump should the reporter's dishonesty be shielded from ridicule?"
- Nov 27, 2015 04:40:25 PM "@MargaretCrowth1: @realDonaldTrump So like the media to make something out of nothing. Don't let them sidetrack from the message."
- Nov 27, 2015 04:41:17 PM "@reallyo1: @realDonaldTrump @MarkSimoneNY Don't let the jackals in the media trip u up. Their getting desperate"
- Nov 27, 2015 04:44:08 PM "@MargaretCrowth1: @realDonaldTrump Incompetence now the norm. NYTimes is an example. Need competent leader as role model. Trump2016"
- Nov 27, 2015 06:21:02 PM Pollster Trend National GOP Average 223 national polls & 33 pollsters. #MakeAmericaGreatAgain #Trump2016 https://t.co/mILAGwjvS2

- Nov 27, 2015 09:38:55 PM "@tweetybird2009: @GulfWarVet123 That's why @realDonaldTrump's THE MAN. CANNOT BE BOUGHT BY #Establishment #Media #PUNDITS. #TheyRMad

- Nov 28, 2015 05:49:35 AM "@Trump2016online: Live Stream: Donald Trump Rally in Sarasota, FL Nov 28 - 12:00 PM (EST) https://t.co/OSkVKDRhrr #Trump2016 #RobartsArena
- Nov 28, 2015 06:12:02 AM I will be going to Sarasota, Florida, today for a big rally with amazing people! I have one goal on mind: MAKE AMERICA GREAT AGAIN!
- Nov 28, 2015 09:32:29 AM The reporter who pulled-back from his 14 year old never retracted story is having fun. I don't know what he looks like and don't know him!
- Nov 28, 2015 09:38:18 AM Virtually no-one has spent more money in helping the American people with disabilities than me. Will discuss today at my speech in Sarasota
- Nov 28, 2015 09:38:52 AM "@munciewolves: @realDonaldTrump America backs you. Your our next President!!!!" Thank you!
- Nov 28, 2015 11:46:49 AM We boarded the helicopter for Sarasota earlier & will be landing soon! See you there. #Trump2016 https://t.co/x4RbbKXHCu
- Nov 28, 2015 02:46:10 PM Sarasota was an unbelievable success. We expected 5,000, a record, but 12,000 showed up! Great love in the air! https://t.co/utmlCpGNGu
- Nov 28, 2015 06:06:19 PM "@Jameslauer6: @David360NC @azblonde2015 NOW'S THE TIME 4 CHRISTIANS TO GET OUT THE VOTE BIG TIME TO SAVE CHRISTIANITY ONCE & 4 ALL. TRUMP"
- Nov 28, 2015 06:10:54 PM "@nobaddog: @RepBJNikkel @CindyBlackwel12 JohnKasich All you career Politicians are shaking in your shoes for fear Trump gets elected"
- Nov 28, 2015 06:14:59 PM "@buckleybro40: @RichLowry @maggieNYT @TheFix @pbump @realDonaldTrump so great in Sarasota, FL! #TurntTrump We're following T all the way!"
- Nov 28, 2015 07:03:13 PM .@CNN Kayleigh McEnany was great on you network today. You should have her on more often! Thank you Kayleigh for your nice words.

- Nov 28, 2015 07:22:18 PM The Sarasota, Florida, rally today was amazing. 12,000 people chanting their love for our country. It's going to happen, this is a MOVEMENT!
- Nov 28, 2015 10:47:46 PM "@JacoH: @CNN @realDonaldTrump I can't believe how low CNN can go. Obviously a bunch of Killary fans." @CNN only says negative-bad reporters
- Nov 28, 2015 10:49:03 PM "@ArtPar17: @CNN Your story is a total fraud" I agree!
- Nov 28, 2015 10:51:27 PM I will be on @meetthepress in an interview with @chucktodd on Sunday morning. So much to talk about!
- Nov 28, 2015 10:57:19 PM "@Pablo44x: @CNN @realDonaldTrump Another hit piece by CNN. "What? We're not biased!""
- Nov 28, 2015 11:03:24 PM .@CNN has to do better reporting if it wants to keep up with the crowd.So totally one-sided and biased against me that it is becoming boring
- Nov 28, 2015 11:05:17 PM "@Allibiis: @realDonaldTrump @ArtPar17 @CNN story is bogus. Donald Trump has the most diverse group of voters/supporters in the GOP field."

- Nov 29, 2015 04:38:37 AM "@DailyCaller: How High Corporate Taxes Lost America The World's Next Biggest Drug Company https://t.co/tsrFghb7l2 https://t.co/12vwdc0cPs
- Nov 29, 2015 04:40:13 AM "@Asmurfinmypants: I can't wait to vote for @realDonaldTrump #MakeAmericaGreatAgain"
- Nov 29, 2015 04:40:42 AM "@thatx209xguy: @realDonaldTrump @DailyCaller Trump is our last hope to make America great again. #Trump2016" So true!
- Nov 29, 2015 04:31:35 PM Just watched Cookie Roberts on @ABC. Her predictions have been so wrong for so long that she has lost all credibility. Just another sad case
- Nov 29, 2015 04:37:33 PM Will be meeting on Monday at Trump Tower with a large group of African American Pastors. Many I know-wonderful people! Not a press event.
- Nov 29, 2015 04:41:43 PM After my meeting with the pastors, it's off to Georgia for a big rally - many thousands of great people will be there, a beautiful movement!

- Nov 29, 2015 04:44:13 PM "@boogiefinger: @realDonaldTrump @meetthepress @chucktodd Chuck doesn't know that 100,000 x 2 = 200,000 https://t.co/WZI8EbqZTi"
- Nov 29, 2015 08:25:19 PM Great job @MariaTCardona on @ThisWeekABC. You made kooky Cokie Roberts and @BillKristol look even dumber than they are. You will be right!
- Nov 29, 2015 08:28:48 PM "@johnwilson12511: @realDonaldTrump is Up! Up! Up! No other candidate is even close!! #Trump2016 #POTUS https://t.co/6c1KuhCY6W"
- Nov 29, 2015 08:29:31 PM "@Antonio92692: @CNNPolitics @realDonaldTrump TRUMP IS THE SMARTEST AND BEST MAN TO SAVE AMERICA. https://t.co/6pf1a0yDRa" Thank you!
- Nov 29, 2015 08:33:23 PM "@Rketeltas: Every time Trump is gracious enough to do a MSM interview he gets ambushed with nonsensical questions, why is that."
- Nov 29, 2015 08:34:17 PM "@Born2RunJosh: @realDonaldTrump @Antonio92692 @CNNPolitics Trump for president! #TRUMP2016 #MakeAmericaGreatAgain"
- Nov 29, 2015 08:35:28 PM "@Dmsrcmc12Bob: @realDonaldTrump They should all get on the Trump train!" So true!
- Nov 29, 2015 08:36:31 PM "@lee_richter: TRUMP will make America SAFE again...He will make America LEGAL again...He will make America GREAT again! #Trump2016 USA"
- Nov 29, 2015 09:51:02 PM "@ThisWeekABC: Maria, why do you work with such dummies as Cokie Roberts, @BillKristol, @mattbai? You can do much better! @MariaTCardona.
- Nov 29, 2015 09:57:50 PM "@Barber2012Jeff: @realDonaldTrump John Kasich-it didn't work I'm still voting for #Trump" John has done so poorly in the debates he's done!
- Nov 29, 2015 10:01:14 PM "@BeckyOmz: @JuvenIle @thehill We could use a new era of greatness! America needs to return to its place in the world--leading!"

- Nov 30, 2015 07:44:45 AM When will @CNN get some real political talent rather than political commentators like Errol Louis, who doesn't have a clue! Others bad also.

- Nov 30, 2015 08:13:42 AM "@wompol: @realDonaldTrump @CNN we also saw numerous (since scrubbed) videos of celebrations on 9/11"
- Nov 30, 2015 08:14:18 AM "@wzpd8z: Mr. Trump, Chuck Todd is a moron, all kinds of youtube videos showing muslims celebrating 911. I would show it on your ads."
- Nov 30, 2015 08:16:50 AM "@charlottepturn: @Morning_Joe THERE WERE NO VIDEO CELL PHONES!IS AreUall looking4bonus?Near StJoes Hosp Paterson NJ Arab area outside celeb
- Nov 30, 2015 09:08:01 AM Wow, the MSM is really going after me. 12,000 in Sarasota, a love fest, hardly a mention. Only one negativity - they only want negatives!
- Nov 30, 2015 09:09:34 AM How is Chris Christie running the state of NJ, which is deeply troubled, when he is spending all of his time in NH? New Jerseyans not happy!
- Nov 30, 2015 10:23:33 AM The Republican establishment, out of self preservation, is concerned w/ my high poll #'s. More concerned are Dems—I beat Hillary heads up!
- Nov 30, 2015 10:40:26 AM We better be vigilant, careful, and strong. https://t.co/ADb1Tss9Jg
- Nov 30, 2015 01:26:43 PM We need a great leader- now! https://t.co/TSuU2Xe7EM
- Nov 30, 2015 04:17:23 PM Meeting with African American Pastors at Trump Tower was amazing. Wonderful news conference followed. Now off to Georgia for big speech!
- Nov 30, 2015 05:41:13 PM Order signed copy of CRIPPLED AMERICA & have opportunity to submit question for my live streaming book signing 12/3 https://t.co/TICkBt5xnH
- Nov 30, 2015 10:55:21 PM A great night in Macon, Georgia! Thank you for all of the support. Together, we will #MakeAmericaGreatAgain! https://t.co/NnyonhWcye

December, 2015

- Dec 1, 2015 09:32:54 AM A signed copy of CRIPPLED AMERICA makes a great gift. Order & join my live streaming book signing event on 12/3 https://t.co/TICkBt5xnH
- Dec 1, 2015 10:06:41 AM I want to thank all my friends in Macon for the special evening and great reception. What a crowd of incredible people!
- Dec 1, 2015 10:16:07 AM Jamiel Shaw was incredible on @foxandfriends this morning. His son, who was viciously killed by an illegal immigrant, is so proud of pop!
- Dec 1, 2015 10:20:40 AM Look at the editorial I was just sent from the NY Post on 9/14/01 - 3 days after collapse of WTC. Any apologies? https://t.co/b6DKEOk8Px
- Dec 1, 2015 10:45:38 AM Curtis Sliwa - doing tv commentary on 9/13/2001. Good job Curtis. Please send your apologies to @realDonaldTrump. https://t.co/g07VZmNmAW
- Dec 1, 2015 11:12:11 AM What is Obama thinking? https://t.co/YWINe9t8w3

- Dec 1, 2015 01:22:57 PM Order a signed copy of CRIPPLED AMERICA & submit a question for my live streaming book signing on 12/3 at 7:30 pm https://t.co/TICkBt5xnH
- Dec 1, 2015 03:46:51 PM Highly untalented Wash Post blogger, Jennifer Rubin, a real dummy, never writes fairly about me. Why does Wash Post have low IQ people?
- Dec 1, 2015 03:47:17 PM You would think a paper like the Washington Post would be fair and objective. For the record, almost all polls showed I won all debates.
- Dec 1, 2015 04:46:36 PM Just arrived in New Hampshire. Another packed venue! Will be fun.
- Dec 1, 2015 04:49:34 PM "@KathyPica1: @DanScavino @CarmineZozzora @realDonaldTrump YES HE IS & SHOULD APOLOGIZE All people trying 2 take Trump down, not a chance"
- Dec 1, 2015 04:50:35 PM "@joyciej2: @realDonaldTrump Have a great rally !!!#Trump2016"
- Dec 1, 2015 04:53:02 PM "@HyperbolicX: @realDonaldTrump I just signed up in support of your campaign on your website https://t.co/mq1It15s5b."
- Dec 1, 2015 04:53:42 PM "@iluvbks1: @realDonaldTrump I live in NJ & you've got that right! NJ wants ChrisChristie OUT of NJ! #tellingitlikeitis"
- Dec 1, 2015 05:59:01 PM "@Dollfinish: @AgsEliza @Citizens4Trump @realDonaldTrump ***Howard Stern Caller day after 9/11 https://t.co/1d9ySVrvty … …"
- Dec 1, 2015 06:01:13 PM "@TrussElise: #Trump I will NOT vote for Cruz or #GOP. My vote is pledged to @realDonaldTrump &my grandchildren. Pray for the USA.
- Dec 1, 2015 06:05:48 PM "@Christo20722105: @TrussElise Conservatives, Dems, independents alike all want trump. There is no one else. #MakeAmericaGreatAgain"
- Dec 1, 2015 06:34:22 PM "@fooschamp95: @business @nytimes Any GOP candidate will lose except for @realDonaldTrump" I agree!
- Dec 1, 2015 09:18:35 PM "@ReversingASD: @CNN @CNNOpinion @realDonaldTrump Stupid "opinion"! #Trump is Winning! why will he leave? dummy! https://t.co/2gmWapqqOE"

- Dec 1, 2015 09:20:51 PM The truth continues to come out after 14 years. A truth that many in the media did not want to tell. #Trump2016 https://t.co/AtuacgxOW1

- Dec 2, 2015 07:25:09 AM I WILL BE ON @foxandfriends AT 7:30 -NOW!
- Dec 2, 2015 08:39:09 AM Order signed copy of CRIPPLED AMERICA & submit a question for my live streaming book signing on 12/3 at 7:30 pm. https://t.co/TICkBt5xnH
- Dec 2, 2015 09:41:10 AM Illegal immigrant children, non-Mexicans surge across border at record rate https://t.co/V6TP55dRAC
- Dec 2, 2015 01:34:45 PM Join me at 2:00pmEST today - live from Trump Tower - via Facebook & Periscope! https://t.co/FQHNiJet2v
- Dec 2, 2015 02:15:19 PM LIVE on #Periscope: Live with the Donald https://t.co/AKgvYBZHEE
- Dec 2, 2015 03:19:22 PM I beat Hillary in the new @FoxNews Poll head to head. SHE HAS NO STRENGTH OR STAMINA, both of which are needed to MAKE AMERICA GREAT AGAIN!
- Dec 2, 2015 03:26:52 PM Thank you CBS & Breitbart-total vindication! Will the mainstream media apologize? Many, many witnesses. #Trump2016 https://t.co/AsxnfFWipJ
- Dec 2, 2015 03:38:08 PM California shooting looks very bad. Good luck to law enforcement and God bless. This is when our police are so appreciated!
- Dec 2, 2015 04:57:06 PM A signed copy of CRIPPLED AMERICA is the ultimate gift. Order now & join my live streaming book signing on 12/3 https://t.co/TICkBtn8ff
- Dec 2, 2015 05:35:09 PM "@MichaelCohen212: @BreitbartNews @NewDay @CNN @ABC @NBCNews yet, ChrisChristie claims absolutely did not happen in #NewJersey. #wrong!"
- Dec 2, 2015 05:36:13 PM "@thumpmomma: I likewise saw militant Muslims burning our flag and burning George Bush photos and figures, right after 9/11! Not#here!"
- Dec 2, 2015 05:37:11 PM "@iceblink62: @realDonaldTrump Mr. Trump, the Establishment both sides are out to stop your presidency, and the American people!" True!

- Dec 2, 2015 06:38:03 PM "@DrRPSmall: Amen, Mr. Trump! The liberal media morons do indeed owe you an apology! Bravo,sir! Your friend and supporter #DocinMich.
- Dec 2, 2015 06:42:00 PM "@DanScavino: Bruce LeVell, former GOP Chairman of Gwinnett County (GA) endorsed @realDonaldTrump today. #TeamTrump https://t.co/OY4Uo3tcJu
- Dec 2, 2015 06:46:39 PM "@TRUMPHIANT2016: This country is being frayed by the inept politicians in DC. We need to vote smarter and be more informed. #TeamTrump"
- Dec 2, 2015 06:47:44 PM "@BOSSYtxmar55: #Trump WILL WIN! He's counting on ALL supporters TO VOTE Then "WE" CELEBRATE WITH TAILGATE STYLE PARTIES! #TeamTrump
- Dec 2, 2015 06:48:21 PM "@Blacks4Trump16: Legal & illegal immigration drive down American wages. Only DonaldTrump can fix this. @AnnCoulter #Trump2016 #TeamTrump"
- Dec 2, 2015 06:48:55 PM "@SaraGreenwell: @realDonaldTrump #VoteTrump2016 Chris Christie needs to #apologize 2 along with everyone else who doubted u. #TeamTrump"
- Dec 2, 2015 06:53:00 PM #TeamTrump. Police and law enforcement seem to have killed one of the California shooters and are in a shootout with the others. Go police
- Dec 2, 2015 06:58:22 PM Heading to Manassas, Virginia, for a rally. Will have a moment of silence for the victims of the California shootings. So sad!

- Dec 3, 2015 06:40:07 AM "@theratzpack: @PattonDivision if only we had a leader like this. We will soon. DonaldTrump will look out for the interests of Americans.
- Dec 3, 2015 06:41:06 AM "@Mike05999224: @FoxNews @HowardKurtz @MediaBuzzFNC start backing @realDonaldTrump real change is coming !"
- Dec 3, 2015 06:41:44 AM "@DLake66675: @ChateauEmissary @trumpettes16 @realDonaldTrump his poll numbers jump every time instances like this occur.
- Dec 3, 2015 06:52:53 AM Congratulations on the GREAT job done by POLICE and law enforcement on the California shootings. Give credit where credit is due.

- Dec 3, 2015 06:58:37 AM "@iliveamongyou: @chucktodd APOLOGIZE HYPOCRITE Jersey City 9/11 Celebration Report #MakeAmericaGreatAgain https://t.co/nUsAbueyaL …"
- Dec 3, 2015 07:01:17 AM "@Co: CBS reports "swarms" of celebrators were on roofs in Jersey on 9/11/2001!!!! VIDEO: https://t.co/1KBPRCSXEt https://t.co/C6nKmbQK8a"
- Dec 3, 2015 07:19:11 AM I consider my health, stamina and strength one of my greatest assets.The world has watched me for many years and can so testify-great genes!
- Dec 3, 2015 07:23:01 AM "@politico: Trump: Mideast peace 'something I'd really like to do' https://t.co/9K9rN5KIHP | AP Photo https://t.co/TbtmIuziUp"
- Dec 3, 2015 08:08:23 AM As a presidential candidate, I have instructed my long-time doctor to issue, within two weeks, a full medical report-it will show perfection
- Dec 3, 2015 08:11:33 AM "@PatrickAnna: @realDonaldTrump You can definitely thank God for you health, stamina, strength, and all the good things in your life!" True!
- Dec 3, 2015 08:12:41 AM "@derektheeight: Will be interesting to see how many times Jersey rooftop will be brought up now that video has miraculously been found..."
- Dec 3, 2015 08:13:14 AM "@2timeslucky: @DLake66675 @ChateauEmissary @trumpettes16 The more frightening the world is , the more safe we feel with President Trump"
- Dec 3, 2015 08:15:01 AM "@robstanley79: @realDonaldTrump Your the man Don. You make me smile every day. Look forward to your inauguration." Nice!
- Dec 3, 2015 09:22:08 AM CRIPPLED AMERICA is perfect gift for friends & family. Order signed copy & join me tonite live streaming 7:30 https://t.co/TICkBt5xnH
- Dec 3, 2015 11:48:16 AM Loved being in Manassas, VA last night. Such incredible spirit! Now in DC for a speech, will then visit Old Post Office under construction.
- Dec 3, 2015 11:49:45 AM Why can't @Politico get better reporters than Ben Schreckenger? Guy is a major lightweight with no credibility. So dishonest!
- Dec 3, 2015 01:53:08 PM CRIPPLED AMERICA is the perfect gift for friends & family. Order signed copy & join me at 7:30pm, live streaming! https://t.co/TICkBt5xnH

- Dec 3, 2015 01:56:23 PM Thank you! #Trump2016 https://t.co/tcyun7Mffy
- Dec 3, 2015 02:06:53 PM Thank you! Vote in 2016! #MakeAmericaGreatAgain https://t.co/XFD3h2N50J
- Dec 3, 2015 02:28:05 PM Thank you so much for the wonderful article, Robert Davi. https://t.co/vwht7S0QC3
- Dec 3, 2015 02:31:13 PM It was recently reported that 3rd rate $ losing @Politico is a foil for the Clintons. Questions given to Clinton in advance. No credibility.
- Dec 3, 2015 02:55:32 PM Great to see the construction of the Old Post Office on Penn Ave. Going fast - under budget, ahead of schedule!
- Dec 3, 2015 03:00:40 PM Via @DrudgeReport: https://t.co/tGu2vCGNYq
- Dec 3, 2015 03:01:20 PM Thank you, New Hampshire! Great people -- see you next week! https://t.co/R83Xq8kXp5
- Dec 3, 2015 03:17:28 PM Thank you!! #Trump2016 https://t.co/EjZTiQyQCW
- Dec 3, 2015 03:21:57 PM Purchase your copy of CRIPPLED AMERICA now & be on potential call list for my live streaming signing event tonite. https://t.co/TICkBt5xnH
- Dec 3, 2015 05:29:32 PM I invite you to join my campaign to Make America Great Again! Sign up to Volunteer! https://t.co/2XBs5SSRC3
- Dec 3, 2015 07:25:03 PM Watch my live book signing now! https://t.co/1xnEdQyIhh
- Dec 3, 2015 10:59:07 PM "@GaryT212: @realDonaldTrump America needs a real leader, America needs Donald Trump for President!"
- Dec 3, 2015 11:55:07 PM "@Kacee50: @realDonaldTrump We can't take 8 years of Hilary or 8 years of establishment GOP!!! We need Trump!!"
- Dec 3, 2015 11:57:06 PM "@MarkStahlbaum: Great job on O'Reilly @realDonaldTrump Stay who you are, it's refreshing. #StayStrong"

- Dec 4, 2015 12:00:49 AM "@Jessi_Libertad: Show 'em how it's done in Raleigh tomorrow, President Trump! @realDonaldTrump" I will!
- Dec 4, 2015 12:04:39 AM "@Hot_Steam_: As a professional handicapper @realDonaldTrump is a 3/5 favorite for presidency. #hotsteam #unload"
- Dec 4, 2015 12:01:41 AM "@TomNocera: @realDonaldTrump Your hand must be tired from all the Crippled America books you autographed tonight-one is mine." Great!

- Dec 4, 2015 05:18:32 AM .@MarkHalperin I totaly won the RJC meeting yesterday. Know many members who said "not even close." Only FULL standing O. But don't want $'s
- Dec 4, 2015 05:40:56 AM "@aews: Another clip that seems to vindicate The Donald... https://t.co/ffXmpjxUrV"
- Dec 4, 2015 05:51:17 AM "@RussOnPolitics: The GOP establishment: Republican voters think Donald Trump would be most electable nominee. https://t.co/zhnWklsseS"
- Dec 4, 2015 08:24:20 AM .@CNN Poll just came out, amazing numbers for those who want to MAKE AMERICA GREAT AGAIN! TRUMP 36%, a 20 point lead over 2nd place. Thanks.
- Dec 4, 2015 09:41:38 AM .@CNN & @CNNPolitics Please thank Alisyn Camerota, David Chalian and John King for the very professional reporting of the new CNN Poll.
- Dec 4, 2015 10:00:45 AM The virtually incompetent Republican Strategist who has had a failed career, Cheri Jacobus, is incoherent with anger that her puppets died!
- Dec 4, 2015 11:22:32 AM Great Live Signing last nite! Over 25k views. I am signing books for next two weeks. Order yours for holiday gifts: https://t.co/jg50w3rcnn
- Dec 4, 2015 12:14:50 PM .@marthamaccallum Martha, great interview with my son @EricTrump -- smart, tough & professional. Thank you! @FoxNews
- Dec 4, 2015 03:35:17 PM The horrible shooting that took place in San Bernardino was an absolute act of terror that many people knew about. Why didn't they report?
- Dec 4, 2015 03:37:37 PM .@JRubinBlogger one of the dumber bloggers @washingtonpost only writes purposely inaccurate pieces on me. She is in love with Marco Rubio?
- Dec 4, 2015 04:43:23 PM https://t.co/ZbyQQkfwAh #MakeAmericaGreatAgain #Trump2016 https://t.co/y2XPvEoy7B
- Dec 4, 2015 05:56:23 PM A total refutation of the disgraceful David Brooks column in the failing @NYTimes by the @WashingtonPost: https://t.co/WbToL9lqD3
- Dec 4, 2015 06:01:04 PM Congratulations, Chuck. Must be wonderful to have Donald Trump as your guest --- #BeCool! #Trump2016 https://t.co/9BxQGTb5m2

- Dec 4, 2015 06:52:37 PM Good news, disloyal @Macys stock is in a total free fall. Don't shop there for Christmas! https://t.co/wpDDCWcLFD https://t.co/vT3uGjiZ9B
- Dec 4, 2015 07:33:22 PM Great Live Signing last nite! Over 25k views. I am signing books for next two weeks. Order yours for holiday gifts. https://t.co/jg50w3rcnn
- Dec 4, 2015 08:59:25 PM A great night in Raleigh, North Carolina! THANK YOU! #Trump2016 https://t.co/oouSXAe267
- Dec 4, 2015 10:22:38 PM "@bjmgraphics: @MarkHalperin Trump understands freedom needs defending with full heart and diligence. He will fight for America!
- Dec 4, 2015 10:24:04 PM "@DanScavino: .@realDonaldTrump #Raleigh, #NorthCarolina! #Trump2016 https://t.co/dMsHEBVqQC"
- Dec 4, 2015 10:31:46 PM "@CwiseCwise1: @iliveamongyou @pennybishop16 @realDonaldTrump @GOP we are with you Mr Trump. We back you 100 percent."
- Dec 4, 2015 10:33:45 PM "@curtiscraven76: @CNN @realDonaldTrump keep up your good work Mr trump cause u have my vote"
- Dec 4, 2015 10:36:08 PM "@nepafortrump: @CwiseCwise1 @iliveamongyou @pennybishop16 @GOP #TeamTrumpPA WILL TURN PA from Clinton Blue to TRUMP RED! Team WONT STOP
- Dec 4, 2015 10:36:46 PM "@ben_techpro: Donald Trump opens up 'massive' lead in national poll https://t.co/yBfezuPX9a #makeamericagreatagain #wakeupamerica @GOP"
- Dec 4, 2015 10:38:13 PM "@PattyDs50: @CwiseCwise1 @iliveamongyou @pennybishop16 @GOP Yes! We love you Donald!! We are behind you all the way to Whitehouse!!"
- Dec 4, 2015 10:39:30 PM "@jasthompcountry: @realDonaldTrump @DanScavino Thanks for coming to Raleigh Mr. Trump. I enjoyed every minute of your epic speech!" Thanks
- Dec 4, 2015 10:42:48 PM "@AmericanAsPie: @DiamondandSilk you were awesome at the @realDonaldTrump rally. It was exciting to see you."

- Dec 5, 2015 06:17:49 AM "@AmericanAsPie: @DiamondandSilk you were awesome at the @realDonaldTrump rally. It was exciting to see you." Two truly fantastic women!

- Dec 5, 2015 07:35:37 AM Raleigh, North Carolina, was fantastic last night. Such incredible spirit. We all want to, and will, MAKE AMERICA GREAT AGAIN!
- Dec 5, 2015 10:30:00 AM Done by a real fan! #TRUMP https://t.co/R7fzPgcwmx
- Dec 5, 2015 02:17:30 PM Re CRIPPLED AMERICA -- I am signing books for the next two weeks. Order yours for holiday gifts! https://t.co/jg50w3rcnn
- Dec 5, 2015 06:13:48 PM A great day in both Spencer & Davenport, Iowa! THANK YOU for the support! #Trump2016 #FITN #IAPolitics https://t.co/QsyNbM7ssg
- Dec 5, 2015 07:36:03 PM .@KatyTurNBC, 3rd rate reporter & @SopanDeb @ CBS lied. Finished in normal manner&signed autos for 20min. Dishonest! https://t.co/sCglbQjB3o
- Dec 5, 2015 07:39:04 PM @Maddow, you copied incompetent @KatyTurNBC incorrect story. I'm sure you would like to apologize to me on show. Thank you for the courtesy.
- Dec 5, 2015 07:39:42 PM "@Pimpburgh2015: @KatyTurNBC @realDonaldTrump just tweeted that you are a third rate reporter." That's only because I'm being nice!
- Dec 5, 2015 07:40:17 PM .@KatyTurNBC & @DebSopan should be fired for dishonest reporting. Thank you @GatewayPundit for reporting the truth. #Trump2016
- Dec 5, 2015 07:42:36 PM Wonder if Obama will ever say RADICAL ISLAMIC TERRORIST?

- Dec 6, 2015 09:32:50 AM Was going to do a phoner this morning with @jaketapper on @CNN but they could not get their phone equipment to hook in. Will do next week.
- Dec 6, 2015 09:39:17 AM I will be interviewed on Face The Nation @CBSNews at 10:30 A.M. Should be interesting - ENJOY!
- Dec 6, 2015 09:52:55 AM "@dr_tweedy: @CNN @JohnKasich Kasick message is as muddled and stagnant as his political career. Lied about Trump crowd." Media-he LIED!
- Dec 6, 2015 09:55:01 AM "@JSears68: Poll numbers will go up even more for @realDonaldTrump after Obama's 'address'

- Dec 6, 2015 10:19:51 AM "@CindyBlackwel12: @dr_tweedy @CNN @JohnKasich AMERICA WANTS #TRUMP https://t.co/ZH11ytGroV" @jaketapper Politicians are so dishonest!
- Dec 6, 2015 10:25:04 AM Hillary just said that she will not use the term "radical Islamic" - but was incapable of saying why. She is afraid of Obama & the e-mails!
- Dec 6, 2015 10:32:22 AM Watch Face The Nation - will be on now!
- Dec 6, 2015 11:30:34 AM So, how did I do on Face The Nation?
- Dec 6, 2015 12:49:35 PM "@BrianBl43802294 @JohnKasich Trump is not controlled by donors,special interests,Lobbyists like U.Ur a total puppet.Trump is working 4 U.S.
- Dec 6, 2015 12:58:33 PM .@BrookslawBrooks Thank you so much for your nice words. I will make you look very smart!
- Dec 6, 2015 01:00:35 PM "@ShellyLeigh123: Awesome interview. You are always honest with the American people Thank you Mr. Trump!! https://t.co/4FVZR7nbgr"
- Dec 6, 2015 01:01:00 PM "@revdojoe: We will elect @realDonaldTrump for President! We must! https://t.co/Ivgy8VqLku"
- Dec 6, 2015 01:08:54 PM "@mollymaguires61: @politichick_ @nytpolitics @FoxNews @rupertmurdoch @GOP in bed together & hate Trump. Win it for the USA & the 21st Cent
- Dec 6, 2015 01:09:26 PM "@Trumpismyhero: @realDonaldTrump only President Donald J Trump can #MakeAmericaGreatAgain"
- Dec 6, 2015 02:24:21 PM I will be live-tweeting President Obama's prime-time speech tonight starting at 7:50 P.M. (Eastern).Will he finally state the real problems?
- Dec 6, 2015 02:39:58 PM Wow, @GeorgeWill said some very nice things about me today on @FoxNewsSunday with Chris Wallace. I am making progress, thanks George!
- Dec 6, 2015 03:52:43 PM Thank you America! Together, we will all #MakeAmericaGreatAgain! #Trump2016 https://t.co/DQiox2k2DV
- Dec 6, 2015 03:53:48 PM "@FieldRoamer: America's most reliable bellwether county has fallen for @realDonaldTrump https://t.co/KkNnQDiLfb" Great story, thanks!

- Dec 6, 2015 04:43:16 PM Order my book CRIPPLED AMERICA for your holiday gifts. I will be signing books for the next two weeks! https://t.co/jg50w3rcnn
- Dec 6, 2015 05:36:05 PM I have been saying it for sometime now! #MakeAmericaGreatAgain #Trump2016 https://t.co/QFCHFo88rN
- Dec 6, 2015 06:11:58 PM May the Festival of Lights bring our Jewish friends from around the world, health & happiness! Happy Hanukkah! https://t.co/03UZBGCswB
- Dec 6, 2015 07:09:07 PM Gee, @meetthepress with @chucktodd was getting terrible ratings then, with me, he set records - I saved his job, but Chuck still not nice!
- Dec 6, 2015 07:27:17 PM BIG NIGHT ON TWITTER TONIGHT. I WILL BE LIVE TWEETING PRESIDENT OBAMA'S SPEECH AT 7:50 P.M. (EASTERN). MUST TALK RADICAL ISLAMIC TERRORISM!
- Dec 6, 2015 07:51:24 PM I will be re-tweeting some of your better, most imaginative and hopefully insightful tweets. Make them good (great)! Important stuff.
- Dec 6, 2015 07:55:56 PM Hillary won't call out radical Islam! She will be soundly defeated.
- Dec 6, 2015 07:58:30 PM The podium in the Oval Office looks odd! Not good, but the words will be the key.
- Dec 6, 2015 08:01:53 PM Hope he won't spend too much time ripping apart the 2nd. Amendment!
- Dec 6, 2015 08:05:10 PM "@dboiarsky: @realDonaldTrump MAKE AMERICA GREAT AGAIN, DT!"
- Dec 6, 2015 08:06:52 PM "@10inchpolitics: @realDonaldTrump air strikes? Who's air strikes??"
- Dec 6, 2015 08:08:53 PM "@LivNow: THIS IS WHO WE R REGISTER AS REP ONLINE 2VOTE TRUMP IN PRIMARY : https://t.co/1xS5L6UbkY #MAKEAMERICAGREATAGAIN @Carolde"
- Dec 6, 2015 08:09:56 PM "@JFK4701: @realDonaldTrump he is reading off the TelePrompTer." But that is O.K. in this case.
- Dec 6, 2015 08:10:57 PM "@homefreeee: @realDonaldTrump He needs to stop all Visas not look at them!"
- Dec 6, 2015 08:16:34 PM Is that all there is? We need a new President - FAST!

- Dec 6, 2015 08:27:05 PM Wish Obama would say ISIS, like almost everyone else, rather than ISIL.
- Dec 6, 2015 08:28:13 PM Should have gone after the oil years ago (like I have been saying).
- Dec 6, 2015 08:45:34 PM Well, Obama refused to say (he just can't say it), that we are at WAR with RADICAL ISLAMIC TERRORISTS.
- Dec 6, 2015 08:57:02 PM "@WiggintonRandy: @realDonaldTrump He will never say it, therefore he will never have a solution!"

- Dec 7, 2015 12:32:32 AM Thank you Graham Ledger of the Daily Ledger @OANN for your really fair coverage and your great interview with Peter Roff of U.S. NEWS & W.R.
- Dec 7, 2015 12:50:31 AM Obama said in his speech that Muslims are our sports heroes. What sport is he talking about, and who? Is Obama profiling?
- Dec 7, 2015 08:44:45 AM I spoke with other candidates to a Jewish group, many friends, in D.C. I said "I'm a negotiator like you" Got standing O-rated best of day!
- Dec 7, 2015 09:04:23 AM N.Y.C. has the worst Mayor in the United States. I hate watching what is happening with the dirty streets, the homeless and crime! Disgrace
- Dec 7, 2015 10:08:20 AM The @washingtonpost, which loses a fortune, is owned by @JeffBezos for purposes of keeping taxes down at his no profit company, @amazon.
- Dec 7, 2015 10:18:25 AM The @washingtonpost loses money (a deduction) and gives owner @JeffBezos power to screw public on low taxation of @Amazon! Big tax shelter
- Dec 7, 2015 10:22:48 AM If @amazon ever had to pay fair taxes, its stock would crash and it would crumble like a paper bag. The @washingtonpost scam is saving it!
- Dec 7, 2015 11:29:26 AM I am signing copies of my book CRIPPLED AMERICA. Order yours now--makes a great holiday gift! https://t.co/jg50w3rcnn
- Dec 7, 2015 11:43:48 AM "Credible Source on 9-11 Muslim Celebrations: FBI" https://t.co/UICDNcftJS
- Dec 7, 2015 12:29:20 PM Poor @JohnKasich doesn't have what it takes- https://t.co/ijaxXpe6xT

- Dec 7, 2015 12:29:43 PM Today we honor the fallen at #PearlHarbor, 74 years ago today. If you see a vet today, thank them! #RememberOurVets https://t.co/HVrucgzWfs
- Dec 7, 2015 02:40:46 PM "@BornToBeGOP @DanScavino Trump will only increase his lead after the terror attacks. America believes Trump will get rid of ISIS!"
- Dec 7, 2015 03:26:53 PM .@washingtonpost is going out of its way to tell failing candidates how to beat Donald Trump.The Post doesn't get that I'm good at winning!
- Dec 7, 2015 04:42:05 PM I am greatly honored by the results of the CNN poll in Iowa. In the end, I believe the final results will be even better than that!
- Dec 7, 2015 04:42:24 PM I am especially grateful for the tremendous support I have received from the Evangelicals in the just out Iowa CNN poll. Thank you!
- Dec 7, 2015 04:43:36 PM Thank you Iowa! #Trump2016 #MakeAmericaGreatAgain #FITN https://t.co/uymSlYv7Jq
- Dec 7, 2015 04:47:39 PM Just put out a very important policy statement on the extraordinary influx of hatred & danger coming into our country. We must be vigilant!
- Dec 7, 2015 05:32:07 PM Statement on Preventing Muslim Immigration: https://t.co/HCWU16z6SR https://t.co/d1dhaIs0S7
- Dec 7, 2015 05:45:51 PM On my way to Charleston/Mount Pleasant, South Carolina. Big crowd. Look forward to it! #USSYorktown https://t.co/1Z9Z4uDWaf
- Dec 7, 2015 06:39:56 PM The main stream media wants to surrender constitutional rights -- I believe #ISIS needs to surrender!
- Dec 7, 2015 10:22:27 PM Just released @CNN Poll gives me a big 13 point lead in Iowa. Change your false story failing @nytimes. Thank you Iowa!
- Dec 7, 2015 10:23:02 PM Great video of tonights crowd reacting to my latest proposal in SC. #Trump2016 https://t.co/CBxrWeRZhP https://t.co/Ko0rypNsx8
- Dec 7, 2015 10:24:36 PM "@back2reason: @realDonaldTrump Can't wait for President Trump to put things in order in US. We desperately need patriot with,finally,brains
- Dec 7, 2015 10:25:59 PM "@Truth_or_Rumor: @realArthurSpina @realDonaldTrump Hey Hillary, America will feel much safer once you've failed to get into office."

- Dec 7, 2015 10:27:56 PM "@LexingtonBobby: @CLewandowski_ Today, "New Iowa poll finds Trump in the lead by double digits" https://t.co/00phDHSb37 #Trump16"
- Dec 7, 2015 10:31:04 PM "@ShellyPayne4328: @WayneRoot @realDonaldTrump Amen! Looking forward to a happy new year. It's been too long! #voteTrump2016"
- Dec 7, 2015 10:32:38 PM "@CharlesMarino8: @3DOT DonaldTrump preach it brother! First election I've been excited about in many many years. Since Reagan to be exact"
- Dec 7, 2015 10:37:21 PM "@GeneMcGee6: @realDonaldTrump @seanhannity is so great towards you. Just doesn't like people on his show to bad mouth you. He is great ."
- Dec 7, 2015 10:41:28 PM "@CRinQC: RT @thehill: New Iowa poll finds .@realDonaldTrump in the lead by double digits. https://t.co/00phDHSb37 https://t.co/t6DSOopCXd
- Dec 7, 2015 10:43:26 PM "@XGNRaging: @realDonaldTrump I hope you become president!
- Dec 7, 2015 11:38:38 PM Thank you for the support, South Carolina! #USSYorktown #MakeAmericaGreatAgain #Trump2016 https://t.co/n0Ph35qsKV

- Dec 8, 2015 09:25:21 AM Just won IOWA @CNN Poll BIG: Trump 33% Cruz 20% Rubio 11%, but @WSJ reported "Cruz momentum" but nothing about the fact that I easily won!
- Dec 8, 2015 09:30:04 AM I wish the @WSJ Wall Street Journal had reported the just out @CNN Iowa Poll correctly. I lead by a wide margin,13 points, going up big!
- Dec 8, 2015 09:55:30 AM I am signing copies of my book CRIPPLED AMERICA. Order yours now--makes a great holiday gift! https://t.co/jg50w3rcnn …
- Dec 8, 2015 02:58:54 PM A new poll indicates that 68% of my supporters would vote for me if I departed the GOP & ran as an independent. https://t.co/ztP5d2ctZl
- Dec 8, 2015 03:50:50 PM A very big poll is coming out at 6 PM in New Hampshire. Will be very interested in the results.

- Dec 8, 2015 04:21:48 PM The legendary @BarbaraJWalters will be asking me questions about the Presidential campaign on @WNTonight at 6:30 PM.
- Dec 8, 2015 06:14:19 PM Will be on @ABC News tonight at 6:30. Interviewed by the legendary @BarbaraJWalters! Enjoy
- Dec 8, 2015 06:30:17 PM Great new poll from NH. Thank you! We need to keep this country safe! #Trump2016 https://t.co/r5K58xu8Mp https://t.co/EAqHZ5ttmp
- Dec 8, 2015 07:13:15 PM Prior to the end of the year, I will be traveling to Israel. I am very much looking forward to it.
- Dec 8, 2015 07:16:23 PM Despite my great respect for King Abdullah II, I will not be visiting Jordan at this time. This is in response to the false @AP report.
- Dec 8, 2015 09:56:41 PM Our country is facing a major threat from radical Islamic terrorism. We better get very smart, and very tough, FAST, before it is too late!
- Dec 8, 2015 11:15:51 PM Wow, what a day. So many foolish people that refuse to acknowledge the tremendous danger and uncertainty of certain people coming into U.S.
- Dec 8, 2015 11:21:15 PM Great poll numbers just coming out of New Hampshire. BIG lead for "Trump" according to @CNN!
- Dec 8, 2015 11:32:02 PM "@YitzySchwartz: @CNN anyone who hates on Trump hates on America. We are a proud nation lacking a leader. Choose Trump to bring us"
- Dec 8, 2015 11:33:00 PM "@USAforDJTRUMP: @realDonaldTrump @CNN Mr. Trump, you need to get some rest. We need you to stay healthy so that you can be our President!"

- Dec 9, 2015 07:06:06 AM The failing @nytimes does not mention the new @CNN Poll that has me leading Iowa by a massive 13 points - I am at 33%. Maggie Haberman, sad!
- Dec 9, 2015 08:14:17 AM The last person corrupt Hillary Clinton wants to run against is Donald J. Trump. I'll end up beating her in every state. New Fox Poll- Trump!
- Dec 9, 2015 08:17:21 AM Hillary Clinton does not have the STRENGTH or STAMINA to be President. We need strong and super smart for our next leader - or trouble!

- Dec 9, 2015 08:18:15 AM "@ray_aub: @nytimes @CNN People forget the policies of leaders like @JebBush allowed 9/11 killers to immigrate, drive, & pilot planes"
- Dec 9, 2015 08:18:44 AM "@ssheaver: @realDonaldTrump @nytimes @CNN https://t.co/QrsEZy8U3e" Wow!
- Dec 9, 2015 08:20:01 AM "@mysteriousLoser: @realDonaldTrump did you hear the mayor nutter of philadelphias comments towards you? Ignorance" Yes, he is a crude dope!
- Dec 9, 2015 08:53:59 AM I told you @TIME Magazine would never pick me as person of the year despite being the big favorite They picked person who is ruining Germany
- Dec 9, 2015 10:22:34 AM "Rupert Murdoch Defends Trump: 'Complete Refugee Pause' Makes Sense' " https://t.co/HWOLO4RVAC
- Dec 9, 2015 10:53:06 AM I am signing copies of my book CRIPPLED AMERICA. Makes a great holiday gift. Order yours now! https://t.co/jg50w3rcnn … …
- Dec 9, 2015 11:01:25 AM .@Mayor_Nutter of Philadelphia, who is doing a terrible job, should be ashamed for using such a disgusting word in referring to me.Low life!
- Dec 9, 2015 11:13:22 AM Thank you, Piers, they don't know what they're getting into. https://t.co/UvKt1Go6nT
- Dec 9, 2015 01:46:12 PM Thank you @JebBush- you finally get it! https://t.co/QXqHpAH4jo
- Dec 9, 2015 02:21:31 PM The police in London say I'm right. Major article in Daily Mail. "We can't wear uniform in our own cars." https://t.co/xok4UTsXaN
- Dec 9, 2015 03:33:53 PM " Haim Saban: Hillary Clinton's Top Hollywood Donor Demands Racial Profiling of Muslims" https://t.co/d99X4O9ysG
- Dec 9, 2015 03:41:17 PM "Carter Banned Iranians From Coming To U.S. During Hostage Crisis" https://t.co/Kok27117dl
- Dec 9, 2015 06:47:29 PM I am interviewed on the @oreillyfactor tonight at 8:00. Then at 10:00, I am interviewed by @donlemon on @CNN. Enjoy!
- Dec 9, 2015 06:48:46 PM Thank you for all of your support, South Carolina! #Trump2016 https://t.co/JWFE5tDg50
- Dec 9, 2015 09:08:42 PM .@donlemon on @CNN at 10:00 P.M.

- Dec 9, 2015 09:15:31 PM .@secupp, who can't believe that her candidate has bombed so badly, is one of the dumber pundits on T.V. Hard to watch, zero talent! @CNN
- Dec 9, 2015 09:25:58 PM Why does @CNN bore their audience with people like @secupp, a totally biased loser who doesn't have a clue. I hear she will soon be gone!
- Dec 9, 2015 10:08:28 PM Great leaders listen to and support law enforcement officials. Police discuss no-go areas: https://t.co/hEM6UGuiTs https://t.co/VmkTnHcwto
- Dec 9, 2015 10:16:44 PM Thank you @oreillyfactor for your wonderful editorial as to why I should have been @TIME Magazine's Person of the Year. You should run Time!
- Dec 9, 2015 10:26:34 PM "@michaelUrso2: Mr Trump did you deny Megyn Kelly. What is her issue! I used to like her. Can't stand her now. Very little talent! @FoxNews
- Dec 9, 2015 10:38:56 PM "@Ajdx4Sdesq: @CNN @donlemon @realDonaldTrump this is the best interview so far. Honest, well reasoned and without all the name calling.
- Dec 9, 2015 11:12:00 PM "@MisterGoldiloxx: @michaelUrso2 @FoxNews Megyn clearly was out to make a bigger name for herself and struck first blow. #ItIsntAboutHer"
- Dec 9, 2015 11:12:22 PM "@TheCarCzarsPage: @TeaPartyCat You're a funny guy! Vote: @realDonaldTrump https://t.co/RltPmxcifL"
- Dec 9, 2015 11:15:56 PM Great interview tonight @donlemon - very professionally done. @CNN
- Dec 9, 2015 11:17:26 PM "@QuinnLisaq: @CNN @donlemon . The people do not care what politician said about Trump . We still support him all the way"
- Dec 9, 2015 11:24:40 PM Weak and totally conflicted people like @TheRickWilson shouldn't be allowed on television unless given an I.Q. test. Dumb as a rock! @CNN
- Dec 9, 2015 11:26:00 PM "@jimparkey: @realDonaldTrump @donlemon @CNN great interview! Speaking calmly but carrying a heavy stick!" Thank you!
- Dec 9, 2015 11:48:19 PM .@Megynkelly spent a big part of her show talking about other shows spending so much time on me. Really weird, she's being driven crazy!

- Dec 10, 2015 06:44:11 AM Wow, my poll numbers have just been announced and have gone through the roof!
- Dec 10, 2015 06:50:45 AM I will be interviewed on @foxandfriends this morning at 7:30. So much to talk about!
- Dec 10, 2015 07:00:15 AM Our VISA system is broken, like so much else in our country. We better get it fixed really fast. MAKE AMERICA GREAT AGAIN!
- Dec 10, 2015 07:12:04 AM I have decided to postpone my trip to Israel and to schedule my meeting with @Netanyahu at a later date after I become President of the U.S.
- Dec 10, 2015 07:49:41 AM The United Kingdom is trying hard to disguise their massive Muslim problem. Everybody is wise to what is happening, very sad! Be honest.
- Dec 10, 2015 08:00:55 AM Thank you to respected columnist Katie Hopkins of Daily https://t.co/LgtY0qdv9U for her powerful writing on the U.K.'s Muslim problems.
- Dec 10, 2015 08:06:16 AM The politicians of the U.K. should watch Katie Hopkins of Daily https://t.co/LgtY0qdv9U on @FoxNews. Many people in the U.K. agree with me!
- Dec 10, 2015 10:46:04 AM I am signing copies of my book CRIPPLED AMERICA. Order yours now--makes a great holiday gift! https://t.co/jg50w3rcnn … …
- Dec 10, 2015 12:39:14 PM Thank you for your support! Being #PoliticallyCorrect will NOT #MakeAmericaGreatAgain! https://t.co/lC9l8PnRZX https://t.co/yOJTHcSPJo
- Dec 10, 2015 12:53:38 PM Dummy @KarlRove continues to make and write false statements. He still thinks Romney won--he should get a life!
- Dec 10, 2015 12:56:19 PM Establishment flunky @KarlRove is going crazy with the just released CBS poll that has me way ahead. New Fox poll has me beating Hillary.
- Dec 10, 2015 02:27:16 PM "Why Franklin Graham says Donald Trump is right about stopping Muslim immigration" https://t.co/iVPJcDQLeO
- Dec 10, 2015 08:10:37 PM An honor to be endorsed by the New England Police Benevolent Association. Thank you! https://t.co/zj47db1Yj1 https://t.co/JrjHyLRkD6

- Dec 10, 2015 08:11:45 PM Thank you to @Franklin_Graham. I have always appreciated your courage, but now more so than ever!
- Dec 10, 2015 08:21:27 PM In Britain, more Muslims join ISIS than join the British army. https://t.co/LQVNz7b2Eb
- Dec 10, 2015 08:30:15 PM Respected Morning Consult poll just out. I lead all Republicans and beat Hillary head to head by a wide margin- 45 to 40!
- Dec 10, 2015 10:58:56 PM "@edwards_cristy: @realDonaldTrump I hope that you will be the next POTUS."
- Dec 10, 2015 11:38:23 PM "@FoxNews: @FrankLuntz: Time for the Republican establishment to accept the fact that Trump is not only a viable candidate, but lead is real
- Dec 10, 2015 11:39:23 PM "@FoxNewsInsider: .@FrankLuntz Explains Why @realDonaldTrump Has Plenty of Staying Power @seanhannity #Hannity
- Dec 10, 2015 11:44:00 PM .@BernardGoldberg was not good tonight on @oreillyfactor. He just doesn't know about winning! But he is a nice guy.

- Dec 11, 2015 06:34:50 AM Great evening last night in New Hampshire. Got the endorsement from the New England Police Union - big territory, great people! Thank you.
- Dec 11, 2015 07:45:08 AM .@Morning_Joe is so off on Iowa, which I am leading big in new @CNN poll. I will win Iowa. Also, I beat Hillary easily!
- Dec 11, 2015 07:49:46 AM Looks like @tedcruz is getting ready to attack. I am leading by so much he must. I hope so, he will fall like all others. Will be easy!
- Dec 11, 2015 07:53:34 AM .@tedcruz should not make statements behind closed doors to his bosses, he should bring them out into the open - more fun that way!
- Dec 11, 2015 07:59:25 AM .@Morning_Joe just went off the rails. I will beat Hillary easily - she does not want to run against me. I am tuning them out, waste of time
- Dec 11, 2015 08:04:16 AM .@chucktodd is a nice guy , but just hopeless. He knows so little about politics and, in particular, winning! I fixed his rating problem.
- Dec 11, 2015 02:54:18 PM Our spectacular ballroom under construction at the great Turnberry resort in Scotland. https://t.co/QmXD8kHFhS

- Dec 11, 2015 03:50:09 PM Great news in Georgia! The just out Landmark poll shows me in first with 43%! Wow. https://t.co/mG6uZQxBWG https://t.co/UZ03GJDvOV
- Dec 11, 2015 03:56:40 PM Never get good #'s from failing Des Moines Register/Bloomberg. I think something's going on w/them. Up 13 in IA according to respected CNN.
- Dec 11, 2015 04:37:58 PM Tom Ridge should be focused on trying to bring the party together rather than ripping it apart w/ your faulty thought process. I will win!
- Dec 11, 2015 04:49:27 PM Tom Ridge is a failed 'Bushy' & PA Governor. Him & his friend @KarlRove shouldn't be allowed to do their bias commentary-nobody listens!
- Dec 11, 2015 05:23:48 PM I will not let you down! #Trump2016 #MakeAmericaGreatAgain https://t.co/3bbHsaGSUm https://t.co/IKXGxoi0lA
- Dec 11, 2015 06:50:02 PM Thank you! We are at 35% in new Reuters poll with #2 coming in at 12%. Time to #MakeAmericaGreatAgain!#Trump2016 https://t.co/0l00OVCo5b
- Dec 11, 2015 10:26:56 PM Thank you @SeanHannity & @BoDiet! #MakeAmericaGreatAgain
- Dec 11, 2015 10:53:02 PM Dopey Prince @Alwaleed_Talal wants to control our U.S. politicians with daddy's money. Can't do it when I get elected. #Trump2016
- Dec 11, 2015 11:07:43 PM .@MonicaCrowley you were great with @SeanHannity on @FoxNews tonight. Thank you for your kind words. We will keep Americans safe.
- Dec 11, 2015 11:22:21 PM I had a great time in Des Moines, Iowa tonight! Thank you for all of the support. #Trump2016 https://t.co/2Xzs2aSqII https://t.co/2HdnA6snnz
- Dec 11, 2015 11:55:41 PM Just got back from Iowa, great people!

- Dec 12, 2015 01:41:20 AM "@ComatoseJeb: I will follow @realDonaldTrump all the way to #victory #MakeAmericaGreatAgain https://t.co/qBQMdLAozQ"
- Dec 12, 2015 06:09:32 AM "@theblaze: Donald Trump unleashes verbal assault on "nice guy" Ted Cruz: https://t.co/yBfCR4jXzX https://t.co/tQOgTwrEbL"

- Dec 12, 2015 06:11:01 AM "@Keeblerqueen: @realDonaldTrump Good Lord ... Donald.. Your following went up so much lately ... Crazy love for you and what you stand for!
- Dec 12, 2015 06:24:16 AM "@JenniferJJacobs: Trump says he was establishment. "I backed McCain he lost. I backed Romney he lost. This time I'm doing it myself.
- Dec 12, 2015 06:25:29 AM "@JenniferJJacobs: Iowa's RNC committeewoman Tamara Scott praises Trump and asks why the RNC would not be thrilled with his candidacy.
- Dec 12, 2015 06:28:02 AM "@JenniferJJacobs: Trump: "Protect the 2nd amendment...And by the way we're going to be saying Merry Christmas again." Iowa crowd LOVES it."
- Dec 12, 2015 06:47:08 AM .@loudobbsnews did a fantastic interview with syndicated columnist Michelle Malkin. Congrats to both!
- Dec 12, 2015 06:48:30 AM I will be interviewed on @foxandfriends at 8:00 A.M. So much to talk about!
- Dec 12, 2015 09:54:01 AM Thank you! #Trump2016 https://t.co/0DA5isXMRz https://t.co/ENjJkTEQIJ
- Dec 12, 2015 09:59:37 AM .@Franklin_Graham, so many people have tweeted about your amazing words to me, thank you! Heading to big crowd in South Carolina!
- Dec 12, 2015 10:01:48 AM Getting the support of @DanaWhite of UFC means a lot. A total winner, who has done an amazing job. Just ordered his fight to watch tonight!
- Dec 12, 2015 02:13:26 PM John Podesta says nominee will be Cruz b/c last person Hillary wants to face is Trump! Use your head folks! 46-41! https://t.co/K2XzwZygYk
- Dec 12, 2015 02:16:36 PM Reports say #ISIS now has a passport machine to have its believers infiltrate our country. I told you so. https://t.co/LRPDW10zwl
- Dec 12, 2015 02:21:15 PM A great afternoon. Thank you South Carolina! #MakeAmericaGreatAgain #Trump2016 https://t.co/iOnhK3l3xU https://t.co/EtpzrfChMZ
- Dec 12, 2015 04:51:14 PM Thank you General. #Trump2016 https://t.co/FCrYNoqYTb

- Dec 12, 2015 05:56:36 PM New CNN Iowa poll --- Trump 33, Cruz 20. Everyone else way down! Don't trust Des Moines Register poll- biased towards Trump!
- Dec 12, 2015 06:59:58 PM I will be on CNN's - State of the Union tomorrow morning at 9amE. https://t.co/VgxjEVFGJK https://t.co/svQQhAHBow
- Dec 12, 2015 11:57:25 PM I will be interviewed on @jaketapper @CNN at 9:00 A.M. and Fox News Sunday with Chris Wallace at 10:O0 A.M. CNN Iowa Poll -13 point lead!

- Dec 13, 2015 12:02:16 AM "@ofccadjust: @realDonaldTrump @jaketapper @CNN DVR SET!"
- Dec 13, 2015 12:03:17 AM "@Latinos4Trump16: @realDonaldTrump @jaketapper @CNN I'll be watching"
- Dec 13, 2015 12:03:49 AM "@EveWicked: @realDonaldTrump @jaketapper @CNN love you Trump! Please #MakeAmericaGreatAgain"
- Dec 13, 2015 12:17:11 AM "@LoriPatriot: https://t.co/ZXUrHTdtqQ Son Don Jr. on Fox says Sr. more concerned about the 'safety of Americans' than 'offending people'"
- Dec 13, 2015 12:28:50 AM Something must be done with dopey @KarlRove - he is pushing Republicans down the same old path of defeat. Don't fall for it, Karl is a loser
- Dec 13, 2015 01:57:35 AM "@Michael2014abc: @Alwaleed_Talal @realDonaldTrump Has your country, Saudi Arabia, taken ANY of the Syrian refugees? If not, why not?"
- Dec 13, 2015 07:38:55 AM .@Peggynoonannyc Interesting article, but I will beat Hillary easily. People that have given up on the system will come out to vote for me!
- Dec 13, 2015 07:44:07 AM .@Peggynoonannyc An election between Hillary and myself will be the biggest voter turnout in U.S. history. Just like the debates 24 M vs 2M.
- Dec 13, 2015 07:48:10 AM .@CNN @jaketapper at 9:00 A.M.
- Dec 13, 2015 08:03:59 AM #MakeAmericaGreatAgain #Trump2016 https://t.co/UB7Fx7A835 https://t.co/iWcW5kfI9i
- Dec 13, 2015 08:19:04 AM Chris Wallace @fox at 10:00 A.M.

- Dec 13, 2015 08:19:45 AM "@mikepetrella17: @Peggynoonannyc I agree with Trump. Record turnouts . There's a lot of potential voters that Trump is tapping into.
- Dec 13, 2015 08:20:31 AM "@khoges34: #MakeAmericaGreatAgain #Trump2016 @realDonaldTrump"
- Dec 13, 2015 08:21:00 AM "@StraightHand: @realDonaldTrump I'd pay to watch that - The Donald vs Hillary" Get ready!
- Dec 13, 2015 08:22:26 AM "@rosemarylowe105: @ShahKourosh @SpacemanChris @realDonaldTrump That is why we don't need a politician to be the next president."
- Dec 13, 2015 08:23:48 AM "@JPMORGAN2016: @realDonaldTrump @Peggynoonannyc TRUMP IS WINNING BY SO MUCH MORE, IT'S NEAR 60% NATIONALLY. THEY ARE ALL BIASED POLLS!!!!"
- Dec 13, 2015 08:26:58 AM "@Yoel_NY: @realDonaldTrump @Peggynoonannyc As a democrat I have to say, since Hillary is the front-runner, I will choose Trump."
- Dec 13, 2015 08:27:43 AM "@dragonian3333: @DanScavino @seanhannity CRUZ doesn't do anything about ILLEGALS and "REFUGEES" invading Texas. https://t.co/usJvsZlb3Y"
- Dec 13, 2015 11:31:15 AM People that have read it tell me that @KarlRove book is terrible (and boring). Save your money! @FoxNews should can him, no credibility!
- Dec 13, 2015 12:20:49 PM .@danawhite Great job last night - very exciting! You have come a long way from those difficult early days, I am proud of you.
- Dec 13, 2015 12:31:35 PM "@BernieSanders: ABC News spent 81 minutes on Donald Trump and only 20 seconds on our campaign. That's because @ABC is smart!
- Dec 13, 2015 12:37:25 PM A very good NBC/Wall Street Journal Poll was just released wherein I went up from last month and am in the lead. Nice!
- Dec 13, 2015 04:47:29 PM Many think that the Championship Course at Turnberry, home of The Duel In The Sun, will be the worlds best after the renovation.
- Dec 13, 2015 05:00:46 PM "@VYlvisaker: @AnnCoulter TRUMP HAS STAMINA, HE IS WORKING HARDER THAN ANY OTHER CANDIDATE. He REALLY loves AMERICA . He deserves to win."

- Dec 13, 2015 05:14:57 PM "@schnoepoe: @foxnews I find myself more and more drawn to CNN for fairness regarding @realDonaldTrump" The Fox News Sunday pundits a joke!
- Dec 13, 2015 05:18:01 PM "@TheProdigy3D: Everyone vote for @realDonaldTrump and no he did not pay me for this endorsement."
- Dec 13, 2015 05:23:19 PM I did interview with Chris Wallace of @FoxNews in order to be fair. He then puts on Rove, Lane and Will, three Trump bashers, to discuss.
- Dec 13, 2015 05:31:01 PM I was disappointed that Ted Cruz would speak behind my back, get caught, and then deny it. Well, welcome to the wonderful world of politics!
- Dec 13, 2015 05:32:00 PM "@energy43: @schnoepoe @FoxNews Not so much fairness as it is about ratings . Megan Kellys hate nightly of Trump is turn-off for FOX"
- Dec 13, 2015 05:35:24 PM "@1rdgreenberg: @FoxNews That's why, after your interview, I couldn't watch the panel discussion, which is usually my favorite segment."
- Dec 13, 2015 05:52:12 PM "@JPMORGAN2016: TRUMP NEEDS HIS OWN POLL A REAL POLL, IN EVERY STATE. THESE POLLS ARE SO RIDICULOUS.THE MEDIA WILL ONLY GET WORSE FROM HERE"
- Dec 13, 2015 05:53:45 PM "@trumpisawinner: .You're the real deal. For my money, tedcruz just doesn't cut the mustard. Go Trump! #DonaldTrump #THEDonald"
- Dec 13, 2015 05:55:00 PM "@LesgartCPA: @jaketapper @realDonaldTrump Problem is I never watched you until Trump started giving you interviews and ratings on CNN."
- Dec 13, 2015 05:58:33 PM "@ajodom60: @FoxNews and as far as that low-info voter base goes, I have an IQ of 132. So much for that theory. #MakeAmericaGreatAgain"
- Dec 13, 2015 07:33:04 PM People have got to stop working to be so politically correct and focus all of their energy on finding solutions to very complex problems!
- Dec 13, 2015 09:53:27 PM "@Barbara_NC: Trump did not need 2acquire wealth & power, owes nothing to anyone. Candidates owe their backers https://t.co/B1x6ImsWzU"

- Dec 13, 2015 09:57:34 PM "@suzost: UFC President Dana White Endorses Donald Trump [VIDEO] https://t.co/MwQtFzuDpY via @dailycaller" Love this from a real winner!

- Dec 14, 2015 12:55:40 AM Why doesn't @FoxNews quote the new Iowa @CNN Poll where I have a 33% to 20% lead over Ted Cruz and all others. Think about it!
- Dec 14, 2015 10:40:55 AM EXCLUSIVE: Newt Gingrich: 'The Country Is in Rebellion,' Trump Can 'Kick Down the Doors' https://t.co/UwTKKhhO3C
- Dec 14, 2015 01:23:50 PM #MakeAmericaGreatAgain #Trump2016 https://t.co/vqrkZwc2ae https://t.co/vz73TaAjjc
- Dec 14, 2015 03:09:15 PM Record of Health: https://t.co/ZDDDawwYVl #MakeAmericaGreatAgain #Trump2016
- Dec 14, 2015 04:11:12 PM Another great accolade for @TrumpGolf. Highly respected Golf Odyssey- awarded @TrumpDoral Blue Monster with best redesign. Thank you!
- Dec 14, 2015 04:19:40 PM Thank you @WayneAllynRoot. Very nice! #Trump2016 https://t.co/cgdLz26mdA
- Dec 14, 2015 04:25:50 PM .@PatrickBuchanan was great on @TeamCavuto @FoxNews. Thank you Pat! #Tump2016
- Dec 14, 2015 05:25:35 PM .@scottienhughes - you were fantastic on CNN. Thank you for the nice words. See you at the #GOPDebate.
- Dec 14, 2015 06:15:07 PM Can't believe Major League Baseball just rejected @PeteRose_14 for the Hall of Fame. He's paid the price. So ridiculous - let him in!
- Dec 14, 2015 06:36:03 PM #MakeAmericaGreatAgain #Trump2016 https://t.co/yjAIiFuVWm https://t.co/dfH0ABwZk0
- Dec 14, 2015 07:20:55 PM Thank you @hardball_chris for your nice words. They are very much appreciated. I fully understand that you really get it.
- Dec 14, 2015 07:27:28 PM Thank you @CarlHigbie. Great work on @CNN. #Trump2016
- Dec 14, 2015 08:16:53 PM Why doesn't @CNN use the #CNN Iowa poll? @andersoncooper @andydean2014
- Dec 14, 2015 08:51:46 PM @oreillyfactor, horrible defense of me against highly overrated @krauthammer. I will bring more people into the party & easily beat Hillary!

- Dec 15, 2015 12:06:49 AM What an evening in Las Vegas, Nevada! THANK YOU for your continued support. #Trump2016 https://t.co/uUwRk7RuGK https://t.co/J0qJaIg35u
- Dec 15, 2015 01:53:53 AM "@Carolin42539648: @realDonaldTrump oh my word what a crowd.. just breathtaking. #Trump2016 #MakeAmericaGreatAgain #DonaldTrumpForPresident
- Dec 15, 2015 01:54:56 AM "@LadyKellLiberty: @AnnCoulter I'm in PA near PBurgh. Dad will register to vote first time for Trump. Mom is changing from D to R!"
- Dec 15, 2015 02:00:21 AM "@piersmorgan: Donald Trump vs Hillary Clinton would be the greatest presidential battle in history."
- Dec 15, 2015 08:58:12 AM Thank you for your support! #MakeAmericaGreatAgain #Trump2016 https://t.co/yohiKUsL3V
- Dec 15, 2015 09:29:02 AM Wow, I just had two very good Iowa polls and a phenomenal just out National Poll from @ABC @washingtonpost - 38%. MAKE AMERICA GREAT AGAIN!
- Dec 15, 2015 09:47:56 AM Isn't it amazing that @CNN paid a fortune for an Iowa Poll, which shows me in first place over Cruz by 13%, 33% to 20% - then doesn't use it
- Dec 15, 2015 09:54:17 AM Why isn't anyone using the @CNN Iowa Poll with me having a big lead. They only want to use the one negative poll (2nd place).Dishonest press
- Dec 15, 2015 10:30:25 AM .@megynkelly, the most overrated anchor at @FoxNews, worked hard to explain away the new Monmouth poll 41 to 14 or 27 pt lead. She said 15!
- Dec 15, 2015 10:34:25 AM .@megynkelly is very bad at math. She was totally unable to figure out the difference between me and Cruz in the new Monmouth Poll 41to14.
- Dec 15, 2015 10:40:47 AM I wonder if @megynkelly and her flunkies have written their scripts yet about my debate performance tonight. No matter how well I do - bad!
- Dec 15, 2015 10:47:29 AM I am in Trump International Hotel, Las Vegas, getting ready and waiting for the debate tonight. Look forward - hope I get treated fairly!

- Dec 15, 2015 12:12:39 PM Between Iraq war monger @krauthammer, dummy @KarlRove, deadpan @GeorgezWill, highly overrated @megynkelly, among others, @FoxNews not fair!
- Dec 15, 2015 12:23:03 PM I won every debate so far according to all debate polls including @DRUDGE_REPORT, @TIME @Slate and more. Too bad dopey @megynkelly lies!
- Dec 15, 2015 12:38:52 PM . #JoeTheismann was great as a political analyst on @FoxNews. He knows far more than football. Thanks for the nice words Joe!
- Dec 15, 2015 01:34:04 PM #TheRemembranceProject https://t.co/zMW0mkkFEg https://t.co/XHIweo9LWG
- Dec 15, 2015 04:30:13 PM .@ConradMBlack, what an honor to read your piece. As one of the truly great intellects & my friend, I won't forget! https://t.co/3FGB0NyfaO
- Dec 15, 2015 04:43:24 PM New PPP poll just released in Iowa- up 6 points from last poll. Leading w/ 28%! Don't worry - media won't report it! https://t.co/yjWiLBGUpm
- Dec 15, 2015 06:12:52 PM Highly respected PUBLIC POLICY POLLING (PPP) just announced that I am number one in IOWA. Thank you!
- Dec 15, 2015 06:56:49 PM "@SurfPHX: Geez Mr. Trump, they are coming for you even before the REAL debate. @wolfblitzer asks all negative Trump questions! #Trump"
- Dec 15, 2015 06:57:56 PM "@BillDaley1: @CNN @LindseyGrahamSC @realDonaldTrump Sour grapes graham. Dont blame Trump because you cant interest voters."
- Dec 15, 2015 06:59:44 PM "@MrDeuce25: @CNN @LindseyGrahamSC DonaldTrump Good were glad he doesn't represent what you stand for Lindsey. You are weak and have no clue
- Dec 15, 2015 07:01:32 PM "@twlhb: @realDonaldTrump @GovernorPataki just called you "this PRESIDENT" !!! https://t.co/z5pRWZgS08" But I don't want his endorsement!
- Dec 15, 2015 07:03:05 PM "@RobertH25937464: @CNN @LindseyGrahamSC @realDonaldTrump Lindsey still doesn't hear Americans! Still at Zero! It's like Monty Python.
- Dec 15, 2015 07:04:25 PM "@JaniBetancoirt: @CNN @LindseyGrahamSC @realDonaldTrump Pataki needs a brain surgeon!"

- Dec 15, 2015 07:06:47 PM "@DonaldTrumpFink: .@GovMikeHuckabee: If Donald becomes president, he will do a whole lot more to protect us than Hillary will." #GOPDebate
- Dec 15, 2015 07:11:11 PM "@ConradMBlack: Many thanks Donald, and all good wishes in helping to clean up the American government. Honored to be your friend. C."
- Dec 15, 2015 08:21:17 PM Departing for #GOPDebate. Let's #MakeAmericaGreatAgain! https://t.co/nMNilyuL2F https://t.co/Bwyu1U3rHU
- Dec 15, 2015 09:05:49 PM #GOPDebate #Trump2016 https://t.co/czHzN0QkQN
- Dec 15, 2015 09:12:32 PM We're not talking about religion; we're talking about security. #GOPDebate https://t.co/OhI1qXEOzC
- Dec 15, 2015 11:21:22 PM Thank you, @FrankLuntz - for saying I was a winner tonight. It is my great honor. #Trump2016

- Dec 16, 2015 08:14:50 AM "@insuradude: The fix is in Donald did his best performance and @MarkHalperin @Morning_Joe has Jeb scoring higher? Jeb looked in pain" Joke
- Dec 16, 2015 08:29:47 AM Thank you, so many people have given me credit for winning the debate last night. All polls agree. It was fun and interesting!
- Dec 16, 2015 08:40:25 AM Thank you @davidaxelrod for your nice words this morning on @CNN. It was a good night!
- Dec 16, 2015 08:46:22 AM .@MarkHalperin works so hard but just doesn't have a natural instinct for politics. Others do, and those are the people you want to follow!
- Dec 16, 2015 08:49:35 AM Bill O'Reilly calls Trump and campaign brilliant. In first place by 27 points.
- Dec 16, 2015 09:53:20 AM Will be interviewed on the @oreillyfactor tonight at 8:00 P.M. Will be talking about the debate, and more!
- Dec 16, 2015 09:58:14 AM Thank you for the nice words @ktmcfarland. The debate was interesting, and fun. Keep up the great work!
- Dec 16, 2015 10:20:57 AM Jeb Bush had a tough night at the debate. Now he'll probably take some of his special interest money, he is their puppet, and buy ad's.
- Dec 16, 2015 10:25:21 AM "@BornToBeGOP: @realDonaldTrump @oreillyfactor The only person in politics who shouldn't have term limits is President Trump!" Cute!

- Dec 16, 2015 10:25:43 AM "@2timeslucky: @realDonaldTrump @oreillyfactor You were amazing !"
- Dec 16, 2015 10:25:52 AM "@SteelerDan619: @realDonaldTrump @oreillyfactor Your the man!!"
- Dec 16, 2015 10:26:02 AM "@chained111: @realDonaldTrump @oreillyfactor yes sir"
- Dec 16, 2015 10:26:19 AM "@EndlessMike03: @realDonaldTrump @oreillyfactor OMG awesome! What time zone!?"
- Dec 16, 2015 10:29:30 AM Hillary Clinton is weak and ineffective - no strength, no stamina.
- Dec 16, 2015 02:20:48 PM Clear winner of the #GOPDebate. Thank you for your support! #MakeAmericaGreatAgain #Trump2016 https://t.co/dl6IuSHwtK
- Dec 16, 2015 07:43:57 PM Will be on @jimmykimmel tonight at 11:35pmE on @ABC. #Kimmel #Trump2016 #MakeAmericaGreatAgain
- Dec 16, 2015 07:57:20 PM I will be doing @oreillyfactor tonight at 8:00pmE from Mesa, Arizona - will be talking about the #GOPDebate & more. https://t.co/Z3fVfHCKIo
- Dec 16, 2015 11:09:39 PM .@GlennBeck got fired like a dog by #Fox. The Blaze is failing and he wanted to have me on his show. I said no - because he is irrelevant.
- Dec 16, 2015 11:12:37 PM Will be on @jimmykimmel in 20 minutes on @ABC. #Kimmel #Trump2016 #MakeAmericaGreatAgain

- Dec 17, 2015 03:37:12 AM Thank you! #MakeAmericaGreatAgain https://t.co/xkki2M6ht1
- Dec 17, 2015 04:11:19 AM #MakeAmericaGreatAgain #Trump2016 https://t.co/uJu4zrzXL8
- Dec 17, 2015 01:05:34 PM #MakeAmericaGreatAgain I will be in Cedar Rapids,IA this Saturday. Get your tickets-https://t.co/QcqOsG3jqo
- Dec 17, 2015 08:17:53 PM There is no question who will handle the threat of terrorism best as #POTUS. #Trump2016 https://t.co/frS7alctbB https://t.co/0P4qSnAltb
- Dec 17, 2015 11:09:33 PM #ISIS is making $400M/year on oil. I have been saying it for years. We need to bomb the oil! https://t.co/vObIAhilWs https://t.co/teKBaKdXzK

- Dec 18, 2015 12:09:16 AM New Reuters poll - thank you! #MakeAmericaGreatAgain #Trump2016 https://t.co/zOe0gDe0AJ
- Dec 18, 2015 11:45:10 AM As I have been saying. Only the beginning: "ISIS Suspects Arrested in Turkey, 150 European Passports Seized." https://t.co/55NWoy7OHG
- Dec 18, 2015 01:02:12 PM .@MelindaDC Don't misrepresent in order to make a point. I was always tough on ISIS--as you'll find out after I get elected.
- Dec 18, 2015 01:25:35 PM I have an idea for @JebBush whose campaign is a disaster. Try using your last name & don't be ashamed of it!
- Dec 18, 2015 02:50:19 PM Weak & ineffective @JebBush is doing ads where he shows his statement in the debate but not my response. False advertising!
- Dec 18, 2015 03:24:37 PM #MakeAmericaGreatAgain #Trump2016 https://t.co/PUGaxGCASM https://t.co/1O67oFDofU
- Dec 18, 2015 03:43:44 PM .@JebBush has embarrassed himself & his family with his incompetent campaign for President. He should remain true to himself.
- Dec 18, 2015 03:59:05 PM The last thing our country needs is another BUSH! Dumb as a rock!
- Dec 18, 2015 06:14:08 PM Thank you for all of your support! Most importantly - we need to get everyone out to VOTE! #VoteTrump2016 https://t.co/ezCsk3cWaJ
- Dec 18, 2015 07:15:22 PM Another new post-debate poll. THANK YOU! #VoteTrump2016 #MakeAmericaGreatAgain https://t.co/Pa9PCuPbyr
- Dec 18, 2015 07:36:31 PM "@thehill: NEW POLL: Trump's massive lead grows in post-debate poll https://t.co/jNDY8kgIgl https://t.co/bPlj1VPz8T"
- Dec 18, 2015 07:41:01 PM "@nepafortrump: We now LIVE in a #CrippledAmerica but @realDonaldTrump WILL make the USA STRONGER than EVER b4 https://t.co/FsGNXnVljs"
- Dec 18, 2015 07:41:16 PM "@WilliamESammon1: #HillaryForPrison2016 https://t.co/RUEU1ctbz8"

- Dec 19, 2015 10:56:51 AM See, Sanders backed Hillary on E-mails at the debate, hurting himself, and then she threw him under the bus (but failed). Disloyal person!
- Dec 19, 2015 02:25:05 PM President Obama spends so much time speaking of the so-called Carbon footprint, and yet he flies all the way to Hawaii on a massive old 747.

- Dec 19, 2015 05:28:10 PM Thank you Cedar Rapids, Iowa! #MakeAmericaGreatAgain https://t.co/0llSs8U77Q https://t.co/dlpd0EkR45
- Dec 19, 2015 06:23:32 PM Thank you America! @FoxNews post-debate poll with +/- from previous poll. #VoteTrump2016 #MakeAmericaGreatAgain https://t.co/KorKlSr01P
- Dec 19, 2015 06:46:38 PM #MakeAmericaGreatAgain #Trump2016 https://t.co/7FkgBAqF4A
- Dec 19, 2015 10:44:41 PM .@GStephanopoulos stupidly believes that Hillary wants to run against me because she said so. She says that so people believe it - opposite!
- Dec 19, 2015 11:00:21 PM "@ofccadjust: @kellyz713 @tedb75 @TeresaC85469500 @MichaelCohen212 Right, same old political bullshit year after year, #WhyISupportTrump"
- Dec 19, 2015 11:00:56 PM "@twister2445: @realDonaldTrump all I heard from the debate is a pathway to citizenship for all and taking our guns away. #tryme!!"

- Dec 20, 2015 12:05:20 AM "@TheRealRyder: You are a blessing to America, Mr. Trump. Thank you for all you are doing! #VoteTrump2016 #MakeAmericaGreatAgain"
- Dec 20, 2015 12:11:04 AM "@DomineekSmith: @realDonaldTrump is the best Republican presidential candidate of all time." Thank you.
- Dec 20, 2015 12:25:13 AM "@autumnandews08: @realDonaldTrump @jonkarl Hillary is so worried because she knows you will take her out! #TrumpRocksAmerica"
- Dec 20, 2015 03:21:23 AM "@constant4change: Trump tops Dem candidates on Google before Dem debate https://t.co/vLi1g2Ry7z"
- Dec 20, 2015 03:30:11 AM "@AniesiODaniels: #DemDebate Q: Who are you voting for in 2016. A: #Trump! Donald Trump! Donald Trump!. #Trump2016 https://t.co/wv37BOoArX"
- Dec 20, 2015 04:05:41 AM Hillary Clinton lied when she said that "ISIS is using video of Donald Trump as a recruiting tool." This was fact checked by @FoxNews: FALSE
- Dec 20, 2015 08:27:23 AM "@blueeyd2020: @JebBush reminds me now of @BobbyJindal but no one cares Jeb! You lost your chance. #Trump2016 @realDonaldTrump"

- Dec 20, 2015 04:21:55 PM We need a #POTUS with great strength & stamina. Hillary does not have that. #Trump2016 https://t.co/n2C6bAdYNa https://t.co/cUy3VaDAGo
- Dec 20, 2015 06:13:09 PM .@JebBush was terrible on Face The Nation today. Being at 2% and falling seems to have totally affected his confidence. A basket case!
- Dec 20, 2015 06:37:15 PM Hillary Clinton spokesperson admitted that their was no ISIS video of me. Therefore, Hillary LIED at the debate last night. SAD!
- Dec 20, 2015 06:44:10 PM It was really strange when Hillary was missing from the podium last night. Not very presidential!
- Dec 20, 2015 07:45:26 PM My friend, @AriEmanuel of @IMG, bought the Miss Universe pageants from me and they are on tonight on #Fox! Tune in!
- Dec 20, 2015 09:49:09 PM .@MissUniverse final 3 on now. Great people, great new owner @IMG. WATCH.
- Dec 20, 2015 10:16:37 PM "@Themyamccurry: Where's @realDonaldTrump when you need em? #MissUniverse2015"
- Dec 20, 2015 11:17:30 PM Great poll out of Illinois! Thank you! #MakeAmericaGreatAgain #Trump2016 https://t.co/Fd48umfyCw
- Dec 20, 2015 11:42:21 PM .@JebBush today said he didn't want to be the front-runner, he would rather be where he is now, 2%. That is the talk of a loser, can't win!

- Dec 21, 2015 12:31:07 AM "@drdoucette: #MissUniverse DonaldTrump must be overjoyed that as soon as he sells the pageant it goes off the rails. We need you Mr Trump
- Dec 21, 2015 06:34:54 AM "@msully65: Tell this knitwit @SpeakerRyan, the ppl want @realDonaldTrump, not him or his choice for President! Thts why Trump has 40%"
- Dec 21, 2015 06:41:30 AM Very sad what happened last night at the Miss Universe Pageant. I sold it 6 months ago for a record price. This would never have happened!
- Dec 21, 2015 06:47:58 AM Hillary said at debate ISIS is "going to people showing videos in order to recruit more radical jihadistst." She made up story- want apology!

- Dec 21, 2015 06:51:04 AM I demand an apology from Hillary Clinton for the disgusting story she made up about me for purposes of the debate. There never was a video.
- Dec 21, 2015 07:34:40 AM Hillary said with respect to ISIS, "we are finally where we need to be." Do we want 4 more years of incompetent leadership? MAGA!
- Dec 21, 2015 07:52:56 AM Just out: TRUMP GOP DEBATE - 18,000,000. CLINTON DEMOCRAT DEBATE - 6,700,000. And they were on major network vs. cable!
- Dec 21, 2015 10:20:43 AM Getting ready to go to the great State of Michigan. Big crowd tonight. Make America Great Again!
- Dec 21, 2015 11:56:21 AM Phyllis Schlafly: Trump is 'last hope for America' https://t.co/jCxqfVCGB6 https://t.co/sk713ir5NQ
- Dec 21, 2015 12:38:03 PM It's the Democrats' total weakness & incompetence that gave rise to ISIS -- not a tape of Donald Trump that was an admitted Hillary lie!
- Dec 21, 2015 12:42:48 PM "@DRUDGE_REPORT: UPDATE: ISIS jihadists stole 'tens of thousands' of blank passports... https://t.co/qg3uo1hm1J" Here we go!
- Dec 21, 2015 01:08:46 PM A suicide bomber has just killed U.S. troops in Afghanistan. When will our leaders get tough and smart. We are being led to slaughter!
- Dec 21, 2015 01:14:38 PM Thanks @AndreaTantaros for all of your kind words and thoughts. Big progress is being made. Keep up the great work!
- Dec 21, 2015 01:51:21 PM Do you think that Hillary Clinton will apologize to me for the lie she told about "the video" of me being used by ISIS. There is no video.
- Dec 21, 2015 03:08:37 PM Getting ready to leave for Michigan - will be an amazing evening! See you there.
- Dec 21, 2015 05:21:47 PM @HerschelWalker, thanks for your support- it is very much appreciated!
- Dec 21, 2015 09:27:59 PM THANK YOU Grand Rapids, Michigan! Time to end political correctness & secure our homeland! https://t.co/cyRCfwxJg3 https://t.co/PPrriLTFgA

- Dec 22, 2015 09:57:32 AM Thank you - New Hampshire! #MakeAmericaGreatAgain #Trump2016 https://t.co/VlGF418r2x https://t.co/zZleg3vnJN
- Dec 22, 2015 12:07:13 PM Thank you - Michigan! #MakeAmericaGreatAgain #Trump2016 https://t.co/5GilNQKyzJ
- Dec 22, 2015 02:06:04 PM THANK YOU America! #MakeAmericaGreatAgain #Trump2016 https://t.co/x0QaqjjMj0
- Dec 22, 2015 02:32:02 PM Video from Michigan last night. After asking for months, the media panned their cameras! https://t.co/jXwS0y08L7 https://t.co/ikjkpmOAeu
- Dec 22, 2015 04:11:05 PM "@TrumpUSA16: Trump is the only leader with plan expertise passion to bring back jobs/companies to USA #Trump2016 https://t.co/LLgJnmGcXv"
- Dec 22, 2015 04:13:37 PM "@janienorris22: @realDonaldTrump Got my autographed book yesterday can't wait to read it. You got them scared to death! Love it.". Great!
- Dec 22, 2015 04:14:33 PM "@daveandlouanns: THANK YOU SIR FOR CARING FOR THE PEOPLE OF AMERICA. I WAS IN NEWMARKET NH. OFFICE. https://t.co/VRBYXBC6I4"
- Dec 22, 2015 04:15:17 PM "@philmonaco67: @realDonaldTrump 100% Donald Trump Supporter Go Trump Make AMERICA GREAT AGAIN"
- Dec 22, 2015 04:17:23 PM "@realNevaDie: This suggests that online polls are more reliable so Trump is crushing both parties. @realDonaldTrump
- Dec 22, 2015 04:17:58 PM "@_MSFL_: @realDonaldTrump @TrumpUSA16 A GREAT PATRIOT"
- Dec 22, 2015 04:19:16 PM Weak and low energy @JebBush, whose campaign is a disaster, is now doing ads against me where he tries to look like a tough guy.
- Dec 22, 2015 04:20:33 PM .@JebBush just took millions of $'s in special interest money to look like a tough guy. Will never work!
- Dec 22, 2015 04:22:50 PM Will @JebBush, in his phony advertising campaign, show himself asking me to apologize to his wife in the debate?
- Dec 22, 2015 04:23:57 PM Why doesn't @JebBush, in his ads, show my answer to his statement in the debate?
- Dec 22, 2015 04:25:08 PM .@JebBush's opening and closing in the debate were said by all to be terrible--fumbled around, incoherent.

- Dec 22, 2015 04:40:45 PM "@qbeacademy: Well I'm at 42% and your at 3% .You know Jeb you started over here you keep on moving further and further off stage. Classic"
- Dec 22, 2015 05:10:52 PM "@schoremis1: @JebBush The Donald should've been named Man of the Year. He dominates the polls, news, talk shows & social media. MAGA!"
- Dec 22, 2015 05:13:13 PM Women defy media narrative, love Trump at packed Michigan rally. VIDEO: https://t.co/yreUny7shA https://t.co/dE9odwIRQi
- Dec 22, 2015 05:39:11 PM Watching @CNN and consider @secupp to be one of the least talented people on television. Boring and biased!
- Dec 22, 2015 05:50:23 PM Jeb's big ad buy against me, paid for by lobbyists, shows my face but doesn't have me answering Jeb's statements. He is really pathetic!
- Dec 22, 2015 07:47:59 PM Once again, #MSM is dishonest. "Schlonged" is not vulgar. When I said Hillary got "schlonged" that meant beaten badly.
- Dec 22, 2015 07:48:24 PM NPR's @NealConan said "schlonged" to WaPo re: 1984 Mondale/Ferraro campaign: "That ticket went on to get schlonged at the polls." #Hypocrisy
- Dec 22, 2015 07:52:12 PM For those on TV defending my use of the word "schlonged," bc #MSM is giving it false meaning-tell them it means beaten badly. Dishonest #MSM
- Dec 22, 2015 09:59:33 PM Wow, new Reuters Poll just out. Big lead if you want to MAKE AMERICA GREAT AGAIN! TRUMP 37 CRUZ 11 This is at the top of Drudge!
- Dec 22, 2015 10:10:19 PM #MakeAmericaGreatAgain #Trump2016 https://t.co/TUDwrg6RsD
- Dec 22, 2015 10:37:51 PM When I said that Hillary Clinton got schlonged by Obama, it meant got beaten badly. The media knows this. Often used word in politics!

- Dec 23, 2015 12:48:08 AM It is a shame that the biased media is able to so incorrectly define a word for the public when they know that the definition is wrong. Sad!
- Dec 23, 2015 01:02:10 AM We need a PRESIDENT with strength, stamina, heart and incredible deal making skill if our country is ever going to be able to prosper again!

- Dec 23, 2015 07:02:24 AM Big news just out - NEW @CNN POLL TRUMP 39 and leads in every major category. Likeability way up. CRUZ 18 CARSON 10 RUBIO 10
- Dec 23, 2015 07:42:25 AM Thank you America! Together- we will #MakeAmericaGreatAgain! https://t.co/MWMFn4asWH
- Dec 23, 2015 07:43:45 AM #MakeAmericaGreatAgain #Trump2016 https://t.co/e9dEs4HuwQ
- Dec 23, 2015 09:20:57 AM The Hillary Clinton staged event yesterday was pathetic. Be careful Hillary as you play the war on women or women being degraded card.
- Dec 23, 2015 09:40:52 AM The silent majority- is silent no more! Remember the importance of VOTING! #MakeAmericaGreatAgain #Trump2016 https://t.co/wBdSg5ab25
- Dec 23, 2015 09:55:24 AM The @washingtonpost, which is the lobbyist (power) for not imposing taxes on #Amazon, today did a nasty cartoon attacking @tedcruz kids. Bad
- Dec 23, 2015 10:49:01 AM .@FoxNews treats me so badly. Using old Quinnipiac Poll where I have a much smaller lead than the just out @CNN Poll. All negative!
- Dec 23, 2015 10:55:23 AM Why does @FoxNews give @KarlRove so much airtime. He (and other Fox pundits) is so biased. Still thinks Romney won. Unfair coverage of Trump
- Dec 23, 2015 12:20:55 PM It is hard to believe I am winning by so much when I am treated so badly by the media. New @CNN Poll amazing in ALL categories. 21 pt. Lead
- Dec 23, 2015 06:17:09 PM Hillary, when you complain about "a penchant for sexism," who are you referring to. I have great respect for women. BE CAREFUL!
- Dec 23, 2015 08:57:28 PM Merry Christmas & Happy Holidays! #MakeAmericaGreatAgain #Trump2016 https://t.co/XIVw5LdTqv https://t.co/Sqim2YyoCH
- Dec 23, 2015 10:22:59 PM Hillary said "I really deplore the tone and inflammatory rhetoric of his campaign." I deplore the death and destruction she caused-stupidity
- Dec 23, 2015 10:25:20 PM "@ihatematt: @realDonaldTrump why is Hillary even allowed to run... She's a criminal." Good question!

- Dec 24, 2015 09:53:19 AM "@ihatematt: @realDonaldTrump why is Hillary even allowed to run... She's a criminal."
- Dec 24, 2015 02:45:35 PM A great Christmas movie & perfect #TBT! #MakeAmericaGreatAgain Story: https://t.co/qUpZphfhV3 https://t.co/PSeVbWUJIV
- Dec 24, 2015 03:02:02 PM "@classyexplorer: @gatewaypundit Jim you fail to mention in your CNN POLL that in the GOP RACE...Trump is leading Cruz 39 to 18...Big Detail
- Dec 24, 2015 03:10:14 PM Poor @JebBush spent $50 million on his campaign, I spent almost nothing. He's bottom (and gone), I'm top (by a lot). That's what U.S. needs!
- Dec 24, 2015 05:14:10 PM In the ridiculous @JebBush ad about me, Jeb is speaking to me during the debate, but doesn't allow my answer, which destroys him - SO SAD!
- Dec 24, 2015 05:20:24 PM Wow, even lowly Rand Paul has just past @JebBush in the new @CNN Poll. Jeb is at 3%, I'm at 39%. Stop throwing your money down the drain!
- Dec 24, 2015 05:31:41 PM Third rate reporters Amy Chozick and Maggie Haberman of the failing @nytimes are totally in the Hillary circle of bias. Think about Bill!
- Dec 24, 2015 05:35:38 PM Next year will be an interesting one. I look forward to running against Hillary Clinton, a totally flawed candidate, and beating her soundly
- Dec 24, 2015 05:42:10 PM Wow, because of the pressure put on by me, ICE TO LAUNCH LARGE SCALE DEPORTATION RAIDS. It's about time!
- Dec 24, 2015 05:56:55 PM Why isn't @chucktodd using the much newer @CNN Poll when discussing how well I am doing instead of the older Q Poll? CNN even better!
- Dec 24, 2015 06:04:08 PM .@meetthepress and @chucktodd very dishonest in not showing the new @CNN Poll where I am at 39%, 21points higher than Cruz. Be honest Chuck!
- Dec 24, 2015 06:28:54 PM I am now in Palm Beach, Florida, and will be going to church tonight. MAKE AMERICA GREAT AGAIN!

- Dec 24, 2015 08:50:38 PM "@YesMrGilbert: @NBCNightlyNews @HallieJackson should have talked to Megyn Kelly about this story" True, a total distortion of the facts!
- Dec 24, 2015 08:56:08 PM .@HallieJackson Why didn't you report Hillary lying about the ISIS video. Bad reporting. Perhaps @NBC will do better next year-but doubt it!
- Dec 24, 2015 09:22:42 PM .@danielhalper Great job on @CNN today. Very wise indeed!
- Dec 24, 2015 09:55:58 PM Merry Christmas to all. Have a great day and have a really amazing year. Together, we will MAKE AMERICA GREAT AGAIN! It will be done!

- Dec 25, 2015 02:38:17 PM .@deedeesorvino was GREAT today on @FoxNews She gets what is going on in politics, and sees it very clearly. Have her on more!
- Dec 25, 2015 03:11:18 PM Does everyone see that the Democrats and President Obama are now, because of me, starting to deport people who are here illegally. Politics!
- Dec 25, 2015 03:15:25 PM We have many problems in our house (country!), and we need to fix them before we let visitors come over and stay. MAKE AMERICA GREAT AGAIN!
- Dec 25, 2015 03:24:41 PM Remember when failed candidate @JebBush said that illegals came across the border as AN ACT OF LOVE? He's spent $59 million and is at 3%.
- Dec 25, 2015 03:31:40 PM Our great VETERANS are being treated very badly because of corruption and incompetence at the V.A. That will stop, I will fix this quickly!
- Dec 25, 2015 03:45:06 PM When will the Democrats, and Hillary in particular, say "we must build a wall, a great wall, and Mexico is going to pay for it?" Never!
- Dec 25, 2015 03:49:55 PM "@ClassySnobbb: @realDonaldTrump @FoxNews I'm reading #CrippledAmerica! Best book ever. Thank you!
- Dec 25, 2015 03:51:33 PM "@Jacobsac2015: @FoxNews Thank you for your tweet today on Christmas. Can't wait to see you as President, Mr. Trump. You are awesome."

- Dec 25, 2015 03:52:03 PM "@JodiL792: You know what's making my Christmas Great, Family/food/friends&YOU! I HAVE MY TRUMP SHIRT ON W/HOPE IN MY HEART for America"
- Dec 25, 2015 03:55:35 PM "@deedeegop: Thank u Mr. Trump, I look forward to when u are elected next President of the United States #MakeAmericaGreatAgain. So nice!
- Dec 25, 2015 04:11:23 PM @CNN just announced that TRUMP was #1 story of 2015. Totally meaningless, however, if we don't WIN IT ALL and Make America Great Again!
- Dec 25, 2015 04:42:39 PM .@chucktodd is so dishonest in his reporting...and to think he was going off the air until I came along-no ratings. I will beat Hillary!
- Dec 25, 2015 04:49:30 PM The same people that said I wouldn't run, or that I wouldn't lead or do well (1st place and leading by 21%), now say I won't beat Hillary.

- Dec 26, 2015 08:00:26 AM The Phoenix V.A., it has just been reported, is in worse shape than ever before. The wait is horrendous, and people are dying. I will fix it
- Dec 26, 2015 09:11:40 AM Criminal deportations in the U.S. are the lowest number in many years. We are letting criminals knowingly stay in our country. MUST CHANGE!
- Dec 26, 2015 12:47:03 PM #MakeAmericaGreatAgain #Trump2016 Story: https://t.co/PBOKbGIaVB https://t.co/wm9Y7E9RzB
- Dec 26, 2015 05:27:17 PM A new terror warning was issued for European cties. At what point do we say we have had enough and get really tough and smart. Weak leaders!
- Dec 26, 2015 06:47:29 PM "@greta: If the insurance companies are making lots of money and the # of uninsured is still large,Obamacare is a failure since so expensive
- Dec 26, 2015 07:31:07 PM Hillary Clinton has announced that she is letting her husband out to campaign but HE'S DEMONSTRATED A PENCHANT FOR SEXISM, so inappropriate!
- Dec 26, 2015 09:05:01 PM Thank you! #Trump2016 https://t.co/CE9f0mukFm https://t.co/XNV9Bg2ccY

- Dec 26, 2015 10:05:19 PM I will do far more for women than Hillary, and I will keep our country safe, something which she will not be able to do-no strength/stamina!

- Dec 27, 2015 07:37:24 AM "@Sir_Max: andreajmarkley: Rubio finally gets an endorsement – from #Benghazi loser Gowdy #Tcot #pjnet https://t.co/lJcHG0IHaM via dailyne
- Dec 27, 2015 07:45:25 AM "@mitchellvii: Face it, Trey Gowdy failed miserably on Benghazi. He allowed it to drag out and in the end, let Hillary get away with murder.
- Dec 27, 2015 07:45:41 AM "@mitchellvii: My prediction on the Trey Gowdy endorsement of Rubio is that it will do nothing for Rubio and finish Gowdy."
- Dec 27, 2015 07:46:42 AM "@CAC8438: He supports amnesty and now they are so desperate that Trey Gowdy is going to campaign with him.
- Dec 27, 2015 11:04:38 AM It begins, Republican Party of Virginia, controlled by the RNC, is working hard to disallow independent, unaffiliated and new voters. BAD!
- Dec 27, 2015 11:19:51 AM R.P.Virginia has lost statewide 7 times in a row. Will now not allow desperately needed new voters. Suicidal mistake. RNC MUST ACT NOW!
- Dec 27, 2015 11:25:35 AM The voters the Republican Party of Virginia are excluding will doom any chance of victory. The Dems LOVE IT! Be smart and win for a change!
- Dec 27, 2015 11:49:55 AM .@BernieSanders-who blew his campaign when he gave Hillary a pass on her e-mail crime, said that I feel wages in America are too high. Lie!
- Dec 27, 2015 11:59:15 AM Straighten out The Republican Party of Virginia before it is too late. Stupid! RNC
- Dec 27, 2015 10:03:29 PM Hopefully the Republican National Committee can straighten out the total mess that is taking place in Virginia's Republican Party. FAST!
- Dec 27, 2015 10:05:04 PM "@BornToBeGOP: @realDonaldTrump We need a real President to get things done, and that's why we want you!" Thank you.

- Dec 28, 2015 07:12:10 AM If Hillary thinks she can unleash her husband, with his terrible record of women abuse, while playing the women's card on me, she's wrong!
- Dec 28, 2015 07:30:43 AM The middle-class has worked so hard, are not getting the kind of jobs that they have long dreamed of - and no effective raise in years. BAD
- Dec 28, 2015 07:42:06 AM Many of the great jobs that the people of our country want are long gone, shipped to other countries. We now are part time, sad! I WILL FIX!
- Dec 28, 2015 07:50:23 AM Wages in are country are too low, good jobs are too few, and people have lost faith in our leaders.We need smart and strong leadership now!
- Dec 28, 2015 08:34:30 AM Strange, but I see wacko Bernie Sanders allies coming over to me because I'm lowering taxes, while he will double & triple them, a disaster!
- Dec 28, 2015 05:45:19 PM Thank you to a #Trump2016 supporter for this video of my campaign- over the past 6 months. Video: https://t.co/yawywElMwa
- Dec 28, 2015 05:51:33 PM Thank you! #Trump2016 https://t.co/dTL7uybyeH https://t.co/yhQUQiuswl
- Dec 28, 2015 10:28:54 PM Thank you- Nashua, New Hampshire! #MakeAmericaGreatAgain #Trump2016 #NHPolitics #FITN https://t.co/QPj5gb3wib https://t.co/I1lMmcYk3l
- Dec 28, 2015 10:40:41 PM "@slone: FLASHBACK1986: @realDonaldTrump Saved a Georgia Farm https://t.co/EoKDLePxUR https://t.co/MaEHiEQoMI" Thank you, nice memories!
- Dec 28, 2015 10:45:21 PM "@sunquist007: @JebBush Why do u keep trying to attack Trump? Really dumb strategy! U lose, he wins! #lets make America great again!!!!!"
- Dec 28, 2015 10:45:58 PM "@IJNIPGM: No casualties. Just victory, victory, and more victory as you proclaim the truth that is in your heart. We love God and USA"
- Dec 28, 2015 10:46:24 PM "@umakemeill: @FoxNews @JebBush @HillaryClinton @realDonaldTrump https://t.co/uI6tmYH5ka"
- Dec 28, 2015 10:52:26 PM "@LeeMiracle3: @FoxNews @CharlesHurt @realDonaldTrump Trump listening to voters, unlike GOP"

- Dec 28, 2015 11:31:18 PM Remember that Bill Clinton was brought in to help Hillary against Obama in 2008. He was terrible, failed badly, and was called a racist!
- Dec 28, 2015 11:39:36 PM .@jessebwatters is terrific at hosting on @FoxNews - he really gets it!

- Dec 29, 2015 07:38:02 AM "Minorities line up behind.....Donald Trump" #Trump2016 #MakeAmericaGreatAgain https://t.co/cEMKihLZbK https://t.co/SxuutW2onm
- Dec 29, 2015 09:33:51 AM My campaign for president is $35,000,000 under budget, I have spent very little (and am in 1st place).Now I will spend big in Iowa/N.H./S.C.
- Dec 29, 2015 09:39:30 AM So, I have spent almost nothing on my run for president and am in 1st place. Jeb Bush has spent $59 million & done. Run country my way!
- Dec 29, 2015 01:50:05 PM Looking forward to being in Council Bluffs, Iowa, later today. Despite weather, rally is on -- will be fantastic! #MakeAmericaGreatAgain!
- Dec 29, 2015 02:20:15 PM We need a real President! https://t.co/nw7BIAW7HV
- Dec 29, 2015 03:36:35 PM I hope @TGowdySC does better for Rubio than he did at the #Benghazi hearings, which were a total disaster for Republicans & America!
- Dec 29, 2015 07:36:45 PM Shows how dumb Joe McQuaid (@deucecrew) of the dying Union Leader is to put out the letter I wrote saying why I didn't do his failed debate!
- Dec 29, 2015 07:37:11 PM The great people of New Hampshire, who I love, are not properly served by the dying Union Leader newspaper.
- Dec 29, 2015 07:37:25 PM Joe McQuaid (@deucecrew) of the dying Union Leader wanted ads, lunches, donations, speeches from me, and tweets---very unethical.
- Dec 29, 2015 11:02:06 PM THANK YOU Council Bluffs, Iowa! The silent majority, is silent no more! #Trump2016 #FITN https://t.co/VTAe68eQ1k https://t.co/IPsJPVH5JP

- Dec 30, 2015 07:31:59 AM .@CharlesHurt You were great on @seanhannity last night. Thanks for the nice words. MAKE AMERICA GREAT AGAIN!
- Dec 30, 2015 08:08:07 AM Iowa was fantastic last night, amazing crowd and people. I'm now in Florida, getting ready to go to South Carolina. Big crowd, very exciting
- Dec 30, 2015 08:12:03 AM "@Hashtag1USA: @realDonaldTrump what do you think of Jeb cancelling his Iowa rally last night ? https://t.co/1oe798AAEU" I went, he didn't!
- Dec 30, 2015 08:12:53 AM "@videosigninc: @realDonaldTrump Keep the momentum going Mr. Trump. All the best to you for the New Year. Make America Great Again !" Thanks
- Dec 30, 2015 08:15:03 AM "@hammetjohn: DonaldTrump - How do u do it Donald. No one could keep up with u at your pace. Shows how hard u will work for us as President"
- Dec 30, 2015 08:16:08 AM "@bfb123456: @trumpiowa @PlaysTrumpCard @realDonaldTrump WOW! FANTASTIC!. WHO KNEW AMERICANS WERE SO SMART? GREAT TO KNOW WE'RE so smart"
- Dec 30, 2015 08:16:31 AM "@TruthisAll1: @realDonaldTrump @CharlesHurt @seanhannity Good morning, Mr. Trump. You're so AWESOME. #Trump2016 https://t.co/LljQbi4fdP"
- Dec 30, 2015 09:06:34 AM The dying @UnionLeader newspaper in NH is in turmoil over my comments about them- like a bully that got knocked out!
- Dec 30, 2015 10:22:44 AM Joe McQuaid (@deucecrew) is desperately trying to sell the @UnionLeader. It's a loser, and my comments haven't helped him much.
- Dec 30, 2015 10:52:41 AM I never thought I'd be saying this but I've really enjoyed @RichLowry on television lately, and he was terrific hosting @seanhannity
- Dec 30, 2015 01:28:44 PM Thank you Hilton Head, South Carolina! @SCTeamTrump #Trump2016 https://t.co/RLCz17tIas https://t.co/L5IAlbsdkw
- Dec 30, 2015 03:04:39 PM Thank you Hilton Head, South Carolina! #MakeAmericaGreatAgain #Trump2016 https://t.co/TBAD5MeYCE
- Dec 30, 2015 03:28:58 PM I'm going to be live with @ericbolling and @kimguilfoyle to ring in the New Year 2016. Everybody should tune in to @foxnews tomorrow night!

- Dec 30, 2015 04:22:22 PM Great poll- thank you Nevada! #MakeAmericaGreatAgain #Trump2016 https://t.co/9Lr1v6vjJb
- Dec 30, 2015 04:57:02 PM A lovely letter from the daughter of the late great John Wayne. Our country could use a John Wayne right now. https://t.co/RhN5gVNBqM
- Dec 30, 2015 11:11:37 PM I predict that dying @UnionLeader newspaper, which has been run into the ground by publisher "Stinky" Joe McQuaid, will be dead in 2 years!
- Dec 30, 2015 11:15:32 PM A GREAT day in South Carolina. Record crowd and fantastic enthusiasm. This is now a movement to MAKE AMERICA GREAT AGAIN!

- Dec 31, 2015 12:01:23 AM "@BentleyforTrump: @realDonaldTrump ALL OF AMERICA LOVES TRUMP! #TrumpOrNobody2016 #MakeAmericaGreatAgain" Thank you.
- Dec 31, 2015 12:10:16 AM .@JebBush has spent $63,000,000 and is at the bottom of the polls. I have spent almost nothing and am at the top. WIN! @hughhewitt
- Dec 31, 2015 04:52:39 AM "@Trump2016Donald: @realDonaldTrump @JebBush @hughhewitt Patriots for trump! https://t.co/0oBFd9pILR"
- Dec 31, 2015 04:53:33 AM "@Luciano031982: @realDonaldTrump Veterans Love Trump" But I love the VETS even more!
- Dec 31, 2015 04:56:51 AM "@nikkisue69: @realDonaldTrump @JebBush @hughhewitt Jeb is such a lightweight"
- Dec 31, 2015 04:58:17 AM "@ddpick18: @realDonaldTrump @JebBush @hughhewitt I get pissed off every time I see his ads on Fox. Waste of money! Go Trump!" Many do!
- Dec 31, 2015 05:04:36 AM People ask, "why do you tweet and re-tweet to millions about @JebBush when he is so low in the polls?" Because of his big $ hit ads on me!
- Dec 31, 2015 05:10:39 AM "@InsideGym: The Most Influential U.S. Gymnasts Of All Time: https://t.co/DIGT1wLIx4 @NastiaLiukin @ShawnJohnson @ASAQ_3" Fantastic Shawn
- Dec 31, 2015 05:15:22 AM "@BretBaier: .@realDonaldTrump's reaction that @LindseyGrahamSC is dropping out of the 2016 race. Your thoughts? https://t.co/6VItF0928E"

- Dec 31, 2015 05:28:33 AM "@SenSanders: I have a message for Donald Trump: No, we're not going to hate Latinos, we're not going to hate Muslims." I fully agree!
- Dec 31, 2015 05:42:47 AM "@stylin1188: Donald Trump is running the most cost-effective presidential campaign in modern history https://t.co/iGyTDDEpbv" Thank you!
- Dec 31, 2015 05:46:30 AM "@wmsolomon: 'On Point' with Gov. Sarah Palin & Donald Trump https://t.co/wPeScKLDs7"
- Dec 31, 2015 05:53:15 AM "@deggow: Just heard a 25 year old man say "I would rather work for Donald Trump than Bernie Sanders"it's time for me to leave this party."
- Dec 31, 2015 06:01:18 AM "@whispers34: Nevada Poll: Donald Trump 33%, Ted Cruz 20%, Marco Rubio 11%... https://t.co/Hniy4iAqNG via @thelastrefuge2" Great news!
- Dec 31, 2015 07:51:35 AM #MakeAmericaGreatAgain #Trump2016 https://t.co/IEIXos0wh9
- Dec 31, 2015 10:07:18 AM I would feel sorry for @JebBush and how badly he is doing with his campaign other than for the fact he took millions of $'s of hit ads on me
- Dec 31, 2015 11:52:38 AM HAPPY BIRTHDAY to my son, @DonaldJTrumpJr! Very proud of you! #TBT https://t.co/ULerCEOCGX https://t.co/nbxPVdarJM
- Dec 31, 2015 01:51:12 PM THANK YOU ILLINOIS! Let's not forget to get family & friends- out to VOTE IN 2016! https://t.co/lg5kMbNLYK https://t.co/dtMAsIq4cf
- Dec 31, 2015 06:11:35 PM Do you believe that The State Department, on NEW YEAR'S EVE, just released more of Hillary's e-mails. They just want it all to end. BAD!
- Dec 31, 2015 06:21:49 PM I would like to wish everyone A HAPPY AND HEALTHY NEW YEAR. WE MUST ALL WORK TOGETHER TO, FINALLY, MAKE AMERICA SAFE AGAIN AND GREAT AGAIN!
- Dec 31, 2015 07:44:14 PM I will be on @FoxNews live, with members of my family, at 11:50 P.M. We will ring in the New Year together! MAKE AMERICA GREAT AGAIN!
- Dec 31, 2015 10:25:27 PM HAPPY NEW YEAR & THANK YOU! https://t.co/YO1Yi8QbZy https://t.co/uxUXWJ1Rbv

January, 2016

- Jan 1, 2016 12:18:23 AM #HappyNewYearAmerica! https://t.co/EeQb8PDrUe
- Jan 1, 2016 01:07:28 AM Happy New Year from #MarALago! Thank you to my great family for all of their support. https://t.co/6UsqSiaaj7
- Jan 1, 2016 01:08:06 AM "@jallenaip: Hillary said she was in a "Fog of War" as explanation for the lies about Benghazi. No fog allowed in WH. Vote Trump POTUS!"
- Jan 1, 2016 04:29:56 PM "@sprinklermanus: @CNN @realDonaldTrump they're spending millions but you're still going to win - go Donald Trump"
- Jan 1, 2016 06:00:09 PM Well, the year has officially begun. I have many stops planned and will be working very hard to win so that we can turn our country around!
- Jan 1, 2016 06:02:05 PM "@marie7777777777: @realDonaldTrump we love u to Trump Family. God bless you."
- Jan 1, 2016 06:06:09 PM "@JodiL792: We are Standing with you! Spreading the Word...Trump for President 2016!! I wake & sleep praying for you & the USA!+Israel2"

- Jan 1, 2016 06:08:18 PM "@MEMEoryHead: I'm one of your biggest fans Mr Trump and I can't wait for you to Make America Great ifAgain! Never forget you have support!"
- Jan 1, 2016 06:10:25 PM "@CASuperrunner: @georgehenryw Huckabee is a good man...but he needs to get behind @realDonaldTrump" I agree!
- Jan 1, 2016 06:24:13 PM I will be going to Mississippi tomorrow night - hear the crowds are going to be massive! Look forward to it.
- Jan 1, 2016 06:25:54 PM "@codyraymille: I have never been interested in politics but because of you I want to get my political science degree. #trump2016" Great!
- Jan 1, 2016 06:40:51 PM The person that Hillary Clinton least wants to run against is, by far, me. It will be the largest voter turnout ever - she will be swamped!
- Jan 1, 2016 10:26:54 PM Thank you so much to https://t.co/8OMryrUVET for naming me the 2015 Man of the Year. This is indeed a great honor for me!
- Jan 1, 2016 10:32:13 PM #VoteTrump2016 & together we will #MakeAmericaGreatAgain! THANK YOU for your support! https://t.co/bziqUSHnbi
- Jan 1, 2016 11:17:23 PM Massive crowds expected in Mississippi tomorrow night. Look forward to it! 2015 IN PHOTOS: https://t.co/29z0XuXVf0 https://t.co/utrl0UnQau

- Jan 2, 2016 07:10:21 AM .@JebBush is a sad case. A total embarrassment to both himself and his family, he just announced he will continue to spend on Trump hit ads!
- Jan 2, 2016 07:17:12 AM .@JebBush is a low energy "stiff" who should focus his special interest money on the many people ahead of him in the polls. Has no chance!
- Jan 2, 2016 08:23:00 AM Hillary Clinton said that it is O.K. to ban Muslims from Israel by building a WALL, but not O.K. to do so in the U.S. We must be vigilant!
- Jan 2, 2016 03:00:17 PM Hillary Clinton doesn't have the strength or stamina to be president. Jeb Bush is a low energy individual, but Hillary is not much better!
- Jan 2, 2016 03:04:58 PM I hope Bill Clinton starts talking about women's issues so that voters can see what a hypocrite he is and how Hillary abused those women!

- Jan 2, 2016 04:01:10 PM When I look at all of the money the special interests and lobbyists are giving to candidates, beware - the candidates are mere puppets $$$$!
- Jan 2, 2016 04:07:34 PM Remember, I am self-funding my campaign, the only one in either party. I'm not controlled by lobbyists or special interests-only the U.S.A.!
- Jan 2, 2016 05:42:16 PM Heading to Biloxi, Mississippi. Massive crowds expected. Thank you for your support! #VoteTrump2016 https://t.co/1VMngEMLzT
- Jan 2, 2016 07:24:45 PM Just arrived in Mississippi for the rally. Word is that the crowd is overflowing and massive. Will be an amazing evening!
- Jan 2, 2016 11:06:35 PM RT @EricTrump: So proud to be out on the campaign trail with @realDonaldTrump - thanks for an amazing night #Biloxi #Trump2016 https://t.co…
- Jan 2, 2016 11:45:45 PM "@Granite_Hope: @brandonstinney How can you deny this fact.HillaryClinton and BarackObama are the two people who made #ISIS a big problem"
- Jan 2, 2016 11:53:31 PM Thank you #Biloxi, #Mississippi! Remember this night & spread the word to get out & #VoteTrump2016! https://t.co/hfYdkY5DKq

- Jan 3, 2016 12:33:09 AM "@namusca: @realDonaldTrump @EricTrump @DiamondandSilk #Trump is much better than any rock concert! He knows how to fill a stadium."
- Jan 3, 2016 12:33:49 AM "@MMMDigits: Well done #Biloxi....great display of Southern pride and hospitality at @realDonaldTrump event. Fired up and ready to go!!"
- Jan 3, 2016 12:36:40 AM Just returned from Mississippi - a great evening.
- Jan 3, 2016 08:59:20 AM Hillary Clinton lied last week when she said ISIS made a D.T. video. The video that ISIS made was about her husband being a degenerate.
- Jan 3, 2016 09:12:02 AM Al-Shabbab, not ISIS, just made a video on me - they all will as front-runner & if I speak out against them, which I must. Hillary lied!
- Jan 3, 2016 09:27:19 AM Hillary said that guns don't keep you safe. If she really believes that she should demand that her heavily armed bodyguards quickly disarm!

- Jan 3, 2016 11:45:35 AM Thank you for your support in Biloxi, MS! Let's ALL get out & VOTE in 2016, so we can #MakeAmericaGreatAgain! https://t.co/RSZF12Kyhn
- Jan 3, 2016 12:55:26 PM Does anybody remember when Bill Clinton, in 2008, worked long and hard for Hillary? She LOST! Now Bill is at it again. Just watch.
- Jan 3, 2016 01:13:29 PM .@chucktodd said today on @meetthepress that "attacking Bill to get to Hillary has never worked before." Wrong - attacked him in '08 & won!
- Jan 3, 2016 02:03:56 PM .@RuthMarcus of the @washingtonpost was terrible today on Face The Nation.No focus, poor level of concentration-but correct on Hillary lying
- Jan 3, 2016 02:49:18 PM "@TINAHILLSTROM1: @FoxNews @KatrinaPierson I love @piersmorgan & @realDonaldTrump REAL MEN w/ an opinion Exciting interesting controversial
- Jan 3, 2016 02:54:24 PM "@barbaraslavin1: @RuthMarcus @washingtonpost bashing distinguished women journalists won't win you votes" She is 3rd rate, a total dummy!
- Jan 3, 2016 03:00:58 PM Iran, with all of the money and all else given to them by Obama, has wanted a way to take over Saudi Arabia & their oil. THEY JUST FOUND IT!
- Jan 3, 2016 06:18:47 PM The worst thing Hillary could do is have her husband campaign for her. Just watch.
- Jan 3, 2016 06:19:45 PM By the way, Hillary & the MSM forgot to mention that Hillary is in the Al-Shabaab terror video. https://t.co/gRannsRXJr
- Jan 3, 2016 07:26:23 PM "@icareeguns: This #Iowan is voting for @RealDonaldTrump #IACaucus. Thank you for supporting IOWA! https://t.co/w0zb668avg" My great honor

- Jan 4, 2016 06:42:55 AM "@RhettRiley1234: Trump only wins with our votes. we must grow Trump nation and do our part. vote. This is our time.
- Jan 4, 2016 12:31:48 PM I look forward to being in Lowell, Massachusetts, today. I hear a very big crowd is expected--we will have lots of fun!
- Jan 4, 2016 03:00:04 PM Woody Johnson, owner of the NYJets, is @JebBush's finance chairman. If Woody would've been w/me, he would've been in the playoffs, at least!

- Jan 4, 2016 09:20:58 PM The rally in Lowell, Massachusetts, was amazing. 10,000 people going wild. MAKE AMERICA GREAT AGAIN!
- Jan 4, 2016 09:22:57 PM "@troyconway: Now 2-more IT Firms going over seas? There is a huge difference between a global economy and GREED! #MakeAmericaGreatAgain
- Jan 4, 2016 09:28:32 PM "@thecybermenace: @realDonaldTrump Donald Trump hit one out of the ballpark in Lowell, MA tonight"
- Jan 4, 2016 10:33:17 PM "@samuelghaddad: Wow! Let's hear it for the Factor. Let the truth be known. More are beginning to realize @realDonaldTrump is the real deal!
- Jan 4, 2016 10:35:38 PM "@Mark98z: @realDonaldTrump Mr. TRUMP this was your best, most energized one to date. (and i have watched most of them)... WELL DONE
- Jan 4, 2016 10:36:36 PM "@djw11223: @realDonaldTrump The crowd was HUGE #MakeAmericaGreatAgain https://t.co/xKq957P6yr"
- Jan 4, 2016 10:36:53 PM "@SalRiccobono: @realDonaldTrump @troyconway Donald get big business back and# MAKE AMERICA GREAT AGAIN FOR 2016"
- Jan 4, 2016 10:39:11 PM "@iLoveiDevices: @EdwinRo47796972 @happyjack225 @FoxNews @krauthammer Minimizing dependency on China is crucial.Only Trump talks about that
- Jan 4, 2016 10:42:10 PM "@ghosthunter_lol: Iowa key endorsement for @realDonaldTrump Can't wait for the Iowa caucus in 4 weeks! #Trump2016 https://t.co/JBfyFrZfFb"
- Jan 4, 2016 10:44:17 PM "@marybnall01: @realDonaldTrump watched lowell mass speech. Awesome. Great crowd. Make America Great Again!!!!!!"
- Jan 4, 2016 10:47:14 PM "@lilredfrmkokomo: @realDonaldTrump My Facebook Groups are all voting TRUMP /4000 people! !!" Great!

- Jan 5, 2016 11:53:31 AM Wow @UnionLeader circulation in NH has dropped from 75,000 to around 10—bad management. No wonder they begged me for ads.
- Jan 5, 2016 12:42:47 PM I don't know @SamuelLJackson, to best of my knowledge haven't played golf w/him & think he does too many TV commercials—boring. Not a fan.
- Jan 5, 2016 12:53:33 PM "@Lucky5713 @NewDay What's wrong with showing Morocco? Nothing! It illustrates a Point! Duh! Love the video!"

- Jan 5, 2016 01:05:19 PM "@longtalltexan20 @realDonaldTrump I love it when TRUMP calls out MSM for what they really are! Cams starting to show crowds at rallies!"
- Jan 5, 2016 07:28:31 PM I am in New Hampshire. Just received great news from Reuters poll. Thank you for your support! https://t.co/yzp9dGfbce
- Jan 5, 2016 09:31:17 PM "@pearl_brendan: @dphilbs if @realDonaldTrump doesn't win, I'm leaving this country #Trump4President"
- Jan 5, 2016 09:33:40 PM "@trumpy17: @realDonaldTrump gave an AWESOME speech in Claremont tonight!!
- Jan 5, 2016 09:37:30 PM "@RubinsteinNel: @realDonaldTrump @pearl_brendan @dphilbs If Trump doesn't win, we may not be able to recuperate America."
- Jan 5, 2016 10:43:50 PM "@Boazziz: . @DanScavino Somewhere in that crowd am I. The Gymnasium was electric, the crowd unstoppable & @realDonaldTrump Kingly."
- Jan 5, 2016 10:45:56 PM "@dantegtmeyer: # ISIS Reportedly Murders Spies Calls #DavidCameron 'Slave of the #WH' Video https://t.co/b57TS93Jj8 ARE YOU WELCOME NOW"
- Jan 5, 2016 10:46:34 PM "@kristopheryan11: @realDonaldTrump mr trump you were excellent on @seanhannity tonight" Thank you!
- Jan 5, 2016 10:49:12 PM "@Kacee50: @realDonaldTrump Women make up the fastest growing market in gun sales. And Hillary wants to take those rights away from women!"
- Jan 5, 2016 10:50:46 PM "@CompresPhyllis: @seanhannity @FoxNews I am so glad u are for Trump your program is my favorite. The Don is by far the best"
- Jan 5, 2016 10:55:38 PM "@ArkaysDesign: @slone @realDonaldTrump Have to get people of all ages out to vote for Donald Trump!"
- Jan 5, 2016 10:59:46 PM "@becker_berta: @longtalltexan20 Trump single handedly did what no other politician ever dared to do, attacked the media for all their lies"

- Jan 6, 2016 09:25:28 AM Germany is going through massive attacks to its people by the migrants allowed to enter the country. New Years Eve was a disaster. THINK!
- Jan 6, 2016 10:01:58 AM HAPPY BIRTHDAY to my son, @EricTrump! Very proud of you! https://t.co/ZHMKIqnUwL https://t.co/IJzW2NDJyA

- Jan 6, 2016 02:22:16 PM I don't cheat at golf but @SamuelLJackson cheats—with his game he has no choice—and stop doing commercials!
- Jan 6, 2016 02:22:27 PM Don't like @SamuelLJackson's golf swing. Not athletic. I've won many club championships. Play him for charity!
- Jan 6, 2016 03:22:41 PM Huge crowd expected tomorrow night! VT Police say first come, first serve. Arrive early!
- Jan 6, 2016 04:09:42 PM I will be on @wolfblitzer for a @CNNSitRoom interview today. Please join us 5PM ET.
- Jan 6, 2016 06:15:24 PM Do you believe that @UnionLeader in NH was demanding ads? Look at enclosed letter from them, just received: https://t.co/NucdHBZAH9

- Jan 7, 2016 06:06:43 AM The failing @UnionLeader newspaper in N.H. just sent The Trump Organization a letter asking that we take ads. How stupid, how desperate!
- Jan 7, 2016 06:15:54 AM .@Macys was one of the worst performing stocks on the S&P last year, plunging 46%. Very disloyal company. Another win for Trump! Boycott.
- Jan 7, 2016 06:28:51 AM It was a very wise move that Ted Cruz renounced his Canadian citizenship 18 months ago. Senator John McCain is certainly no friend of Ted!
- Jan 7, 2016 08:17:40 AM I will be in beautiful Burlington, Vermont, tonight for a rally. Will be great fun. MAKE AMERICA GREAT AGAIN!
- Jan 7, 2016 08:24:31 AM Man shot inside Paris police station. Just announced that terror threat is at highest level. Germany is a total mess-big crime. GET SMART!
- Jan 7, 2016 11:05:15 AM Massive crowd in VT tonight. Venue not big enough. Officials say NO to outside event and sound system. Arrive early!
- Jan 7, 2016 11:14:38 AM .@SenTedCruz Ted--free legal advice on how to pre-empt the Dems on citizen issue. Go to court now & seek Declaratory Judgment--you will win!
- Jan 7, 2016 11:26:14 AM I have an idea for @JebBush whose campaign is a disaster. Try using your last name and don't be ashamed of it!
- Jan 7, 2016 11:30:06 AM Weak & ineffective @JebBush is doing ads where he shows his statement in the debate but not my response. False advertising!
- Jan 7, 2016 12:24:09 PM Hillary and her friends! https://t.co/q45tTapqMI

- Jan 7, 2016 01:08:59 PM RT @JoeNBC: Explosive Trump attack on HRC, Bill, Monica, Cosby, and Weiner. Trump camp just upped the ante on "women's rights" https://t.co...
- Jan 7, 2016 04:06:00 PM The @TheView @ABC, once great when headed by @BarbaraJWalters, is now in total freefall. Whoopi Goldberg is terrible. Very sad!
- Jan 7, 2016 04:06:19 PM Joy Behar, who was fired from her last show for lack of ratings, is even worse on @TheView. We love Barbara!
- Jan 7, 2016 04:11:05 PM I'm leaving now for Burlington, Vermont. It will be wild!
- Jan 7, 2016 09:23:07 PM We could only get a small fraction of this 25k crowd in. The movement to Make America Great Again is unbelievable! https://t.co/NHPdGm57YJ
- Jan 7, 2016 10:08:14 PM Great time in Burlington, Vermont. Crowd was amazing.
- Jan 7, 2016 10:12:06 PM "@hofmannken: DonaldTrump, wish I could attend one of your rallies, none are close enough. Make America Great Again for my Kids.Thank you
- Jan 7, 2016 10:29:38 PM "@LiberatedCit: @JebBush Key State Florida Poll: Trump 32% Beats #Rubio-#Bush Combined https://t.co/MKHc5nB27i https://t.co/ubJvEeCsom"
- Jan 7, 2016 10:30:54 PM "@pink_sprnva: @pastormike7 @thehill I agree with you on this. @realDonaldTrump won't be good. He will be great!"
- Jan 7, 2016 10:32:10 PM "@rlbenney: @realDonaldTrump You did great and showed courage going to Burlington. No other GOP candidate would do what you did tonight!"

- Jan 8, 2016 10:57:17 AM Hank Greenberg, formerly of AIG, gave $10 million to the @JebBush campaign 3 months ago. He is not happy, a total waste of money!
- Jan 8, 2016 01:47:39 PM Not good news for Jeb Bush https://t.co/5CrP5zdXsz
- Jan 8, 2016 04:20:02 PM On my way to South Carolina. Big Crowd--- look forward to it!
- Jan 8, 2016 05:03:35 PM I hope all workers demand that their @Teamsters reps endorse Donald J. Trump. Nobody knows jobs like I do! Don't let them sell you out!

- Jan 8, 2016 05:09:20 PM Love seeing union & non-union members alike are defecting to Trump. I will create jobs like no one else. Their #Dem leaders can't compete!
- Jan 8, 2016 05:36:09 PM #MakeAmericaGreatAgain #Trump2016 https://t.co/3HmclWL9GT
- Jan 8, 2016 06:12:35 PM #FoxNews Poll - THANK YOU! #MakeAmericaGreatAgain #Trump2016 https://t.co/dKuyzLRTZ3
- Jan 8, 2016 06:39:37 PM Will be at venue, in wonderful South Carolina, very soon. Big traffic back-up, tremendous crowd! Will be wild.
- Jan 8, 2016 09:08:42 PM Great even in SC tonight! Fire Marshall would not let everyone in-- 5,000 turned away. Thank you for coming!

- Jan 9, 2016 09:22:36 AM Pat Buchanan gave a fantastic interview this morning on @CNN - way to go Pat, way ahead of your time!
- Jan 9, 2016 09:26:28 AM South Carolina rally last night was so unbelievably exciting (and fun). I am now off to Iowa for two big rallies - packed houses. Love it!
- Jan 9, 2016 10:41:44 AM Constitutional law expert #Laurence Tribe of Harvard says "wrong to say it (natural born citizen) is a settled matter-it isn't settled).
- Jan 9, 2016 11:05:17 AM Thank you, @TheFix- Chris Cillizza. It is a true person of character that can change his opinion & do what is right. https://t.co/0VxlT9iEbr
- Jan 9, 2016 11:06:56 AM .@JonahNRO, watched on @seanhannity and appreciate your statements --- I have been waiting for them for a long time. Thank you.
- Jan 9, 2016 12:19:54 PM Thank you so much. Earnest must have been a great person. https://t.co/2DZp7YOadj https://t.co/2YtLlEwceB
- Jan 9, 2016 12:56:06 PM (1/2) Time Magazine has me on the cover this week. David Von Drehle has written one of the best stories I have ever had.
- Jan 9, 2016 12:56:10 PM (2/2) David brilliantly tells it like it is -- the real deal! Read it! https://t.co/9n5CCrefKn
- Jan 9, 2016 01:01:00 PM I'm protesting the @UnionLeader from having anything to do w/ ABC debate. Their unethical record doesn't give them the right to be involved!

- Jan 9, 2016 07:12:20 PM I will be interviewed by Chris Wallace on Fox tomorrow morning. Tune in!
- Jan 9, 2016 07:12:43 PM Will be on Meet the Press with @ChuckTodd tomorrow morning. Enjoy!
- Jan 9, 2016 07:13:03 PM I want to thank the people of Iowa for an unbelievable day. The crowds were amazing. Will be back Tuesday!

- Jan 10, 2016 08:49:06 AM "@redletter99: Trump pummels his opponents - and the press | SunHerald @realDonaldTrump https://t.co/9MQhOSpiWa" Thank you!
- Jan 10, 2016 01:23:57 PM Yesterday in Iowa was amazing - two speeches in front of two great sold out crowds. They love that I am the only candidate self-funding!
- Jan 10, 2016 01:28:54 PM In the just out @FoxNews Poll, I easily beat Hillary Clinton - and I havn't even focused on her yet. On our way: MAKE AMERICA GREAT AGAIN!
- Jan 10, 2016 01:31:47 PM Heading now for Reno, Nevada, for a big rally. Good poll numberd all over!
- Jan 10, 2016 03:15:30 PM Remember, get TIME magazine! I am on the cover. Take it out in 4 years and read it again! Just watch...
- Jan 10, 2016 04:05:29 PM I am pleased to announce that I had the Union Leader removed from the upcoming debate. https://t.co/DL8hDPzHoi
- Jan 10, 2016 04:06:07 PM If their highly unethical behavior, including begging me for ads, isn't questionable enough, they have endorsed a candidate who can't win.
- Jan 10, 2016 04:06:26 PM This is really unfair and a conflict for all the other candidates. I said it should not be allowed and ABC agreed.
- Jan 10, 2016 04:06:48 PM UL has lost all credibility under Joe McQuaid w circulation dropping to record lows. They aren't worthy of representing the great people NH.
- Jan 10, 2016 06:23:07 PM Union Leader refuses to comment as to why they were kicked out of the ABC News debate like a dog. For starters, try getting a new publisher!
- Jan 10, 2016 07:02:59 PM Thank you to our law enforcement officers! #LESM #Trump2016 https://t.co/sfuuVrx33E

- Jan 11, 2016 09:16:36 AM Why does @ThisWeekABC w/ @GStephanopoulos allow a hater & racist like @tavissmiley to waste good airtime? @ABC can do much better than him!
- Jan 11, 2016 09:18:34 AM Congratulations to my friend @TheSlyStallone on winning a #GoldenGlobe. A wonderful guy- who has created something special- well deserved!
- Jan 11, 2016 09:41:52 AM Great job on Fox this morning @KatiePavlich. I am sending out for your book immediately. Thank you very much!
- Jan 11, 2016 10:09:17 AM So professional of @ABC news to throw out the failing @UnionLeader newspaper from their debate. Paper won't survive, highly unethical!
- Jan 11, 2016 10:40:48 AM Just arrived in New Hampshire. Thank you to all of my supporters! #MakeAmericaGreatAgain #Trump2016 https://t.co/KSguIhkIwa
- Jan 11, 2016 02:10:00 PM Congratulations to @jdickerson of Face the Nation on his highest ratings in 15 years. 4.6 million people watched my interview! Thank you!
- Jan 11, 2016 02:10:53 PM .@RinglingBros is retiring their elephants-- the circus will never be the same.
- Jan 11, 2016 02:43:29 PM New Iowa poll. Thank you! #MakeAmericaGreatAgain #Trump2016 https://t.co/19sshZ8dSu
- Jan 11, 2016 03:20:54 PM .@megynkelly recently said that she can't be wooed by Trump. She is so average in every way, who the hell wants to woo her!
- Jan 11, 2016 05:55:17 PM Will be on @FallonTonight with @JimmyFallon on @NBC at 11:35pmE. Enjoy! #Trump2016 https://t.co/Z9zbKfXJqb
- Jan 11, 2016 08:46:13 PM Thank you Michael Harrison @Talkersmagazine for your kind words - greatly appreciated!
- Jan 11, 2016 08:49:59 PM .@MajorCBS Major Garrett of @CBSNews covers me very inaccurately. Total agenda, bad reporter!
- Jan 11, 2016 09:42:49 PM Face The Nation's interview of me was the highest rated show that they have had in 15 years. Congratulations and WOW! @CBSNews @jdickerson
- Jan 11, 2016 09:49:57 PM Don't forget to watch The Tonight Show with the wonderful @jimmyfallon at 11:30 P.M. You will not be disappointed! @NBC
- Jan 11, 2016 10:34:17 PM Fantastic job on @CNN tonight. @kayleighmcenany is a winner! @donlemon

- Jan 11, 2016 10:42:01 PM "@CLewandowski_: .@stuartpstevens --failed "strategist" who can't find clients criticizes winning #TeamTrump. Stop complaining & try winning
- Jan 11, 2016 11:19:17 PM .@stuartpstevens horrible advise to Mitt Romney made victory an impossibility. Don't blame Mitt! Now Stevens can't get a job!
- Jan 11, 2016 11:22:59 PM The Tonight Show begins in 5 minutes. Enjoy!

- Jan 12, 2016 10:06:58 AM THANK YOU! #Trump2016 https://t.co/QmDcCKppEu
- Jan 12, 2016 02:40:28 PM On my way to Cedar Falls, Iowa, now. Will be great--I love the people of Iowa!
- Jan 12, 2016 03:28:37 PM Such a serious problem for Ted & the GOP. Great doubt, Dems will sue! Let's all work together to solve this problem. https://t.co/cNl6dmFb6q
- Jan 12, 2016 04:44:22 PM Another new Iowa poll just released. Thank you! #IACaucus #FITN https://t.co/RGkrruqpM7
- Jan 12, 2016 09:56:14 PM New CBS poll. #Trump2016 https://t.co/sFPRHHeLbd
- Jan 12, 2016 09:59:41 PM The Iran deal is terrible. Why didn't we get the uranium stockpile - it was sent to Russia. #SOTU
- Jan 12, 2016 10:05:10 PM The #SOTU speech is really boring, slow, lethargic - very hard to watch!
- Jan 12, 2016 11:25:04 PM Just found out that @tedcruz is spending a fortune on Iowa push polls negative to me. Not nice, but OK! New polls are great.
- Jan 12, 2016 11:32:24 PM The State Of The Union speech was one of the most boring, rambling and non-substantive I have heard in a long time. New leadership fast!

- Jan 13, 2016 12:46:27 AM Numerous polls have me beating Hillary Clinton. In a race with her, voter turnout will be the highest in U.S. history-I get most new voters!
- Jan 13, 2016 07:09:54 AM Iran toys with U.S. days before we pay them, ridiculously, billions of dollars. Don't release money. We want our hostages back NOW!

- Jan 13, 2016 08:54:28 AM Thank you for your support last night, Iowa! #VoteTrump #Trump2016 #IACaucus #FITN #IAPolitics https://t.co/xRvznATrU7
- Jan 13, 2016 09:10:57 AM "@johnkurkosky: @Carolde @The_Lady_Colors @DRJAMESCABOT @TamiDurling @AceofSpadesHQ THIS ELECTION IS ABOUT AMERICAS FUTURE, VOTE TRUMP"
- Jan 13, 2016 09:26:25 AM Sadly, there is no way that Ted Cruz can continue running in the Republican Primary unless he can erase doubt on eligibility. Dems will sue!
- Jan 13, 2016 01:20:47 PM My nomination would increase voter turnout. #VoteTrump #MakeAmericaGreatAgain #Trump2016 https://t.co/6kjCaStCjG
- Jan 13, 2016 01:22:20 PM Thank you! #VoteTrump https://t.co/g7eeySMUdl
- Jan 13, 2016 01:23:32 PM RT @DRUDGE_REPORT: REUTERS ROLLING: TRUMP 39%, CRUZ 14.5%, BUSH 10.6%, CARSON 9.6%, RUBIO 6.7%... MORE... https://t.co/nRhtbzcqP9
- Jan 13, 2016 02:20:30 PM THANK YOU, IOWA! Highly respected @OANN @GravisMarketing poll just released. #VoteTrump #IowaCaucus https://t.co/Ecs9XYXaXL
- Jan 13, 2016 02:49:43 PM THANK YOU! #VoteTrump https://t.co/y7pnMqCs7j
- Jan 13, 2016 07:49:44 PM .@EricTrump- unbelievable job on #FoxNews with @greta. That was better than I could do! #Trump2016
- Jan 13, 2016 11:25:19 PM Why does @CNN & @andersoncooper waste airtime by putting failed campaign strategist, Stuart Stevens - who lost BIG for Romney - on the show?

- Jan 14, 2016 12:45:41 AM Iran humiliated the United States with the capture of our 10 sailors. Horrible pictures & images. We are weak. I will NOT forget!
- Jan 14, 2016 12:45:41 AM Stuart Stevens is a dumb guy who fails @ virtually everything he touches. Romney campaign,his book,etc. Why does @andersoncooper put him on?
- Jan 14, 2016 12:46:18 AM United States looks more and more like a paper tiger. Won't be that way if I win!
- Jan 14, 2016 01:42:53 PM .@TheBrodyFile: "Trump's appeal to evangelicals is real" #Trump2016 https://t.co/Xb04Quqj1M https://t.co/3xdEXZV5Ge

- Jan 14, 2016 02:20:56 PM "@melindaross123: @FoxNews @realDonaldTrump There isn't anything Donald Trump says that I don't agree with. Go Trump!"
- Jan 14, 2016 02:21:11 PM "@Bonfiredesigns: Standing with @realDonaldTrump as he defends our sailors and military and Americans in the USA https://t.co/YKvKNsZmih"
- Jan 14, 2016 02:25:16 PM Do you think Iran would have acted so tough if they were Russian sailors? Our country was humiliated.
- Jan 14, 2016 03:03:10 PM "@wpjenna: Thousands packed into the Pensacola Bay Center to see Donald Trump tonight... https://t.co/K5lIT2p7fL" A fantastic evening!
- Jan 14, 2016 03:03:48 PM "@CLewandowski_: Massive crowd in Pensacola, Florida! Unbelievable! THANK YOU! #VoteTrump https://t.co/9D2tsQaysd"
- Jan 14, 2016 03:07:25 PM "@ameriflames: @realDonaldTrump @CLewandowski_ no one wants a Bush or a Clinton, they want a straight shooter like TRUMP!"
- Jan 14, 2016 03:11:53 PM "@_BScarb: Enjoyed watching @realDonaldTrump at his rally yesterday! I've never seen the Bay Center that packed! https://t.co/ZXDKA5TYBo"
- Jan 14, 2016 06:35:00 PM WSJ/NBC Poll: Donald Trump Widens His Lead in Republican Presidential Race. #Trump2016 https://t.co/r2i8FHPjB4

- Jan 15, 2016 10:17:09 AM Jeb Bush, who did poorly last night in the debate and whose chances of winning are zero, just got Graham endorsement. Graham quit at O.
- Jan 15, 2016 10:30:38 AM Sen. Lindsey Graham embarrassed himself with his failed run for President and now further embarrasses himself with endorsement of Bush.
- Jan 15, 2016 02:45:40 PM Top searched candidate by state, as seen in the #GOPDebate media filing center. WE WILL MAKE AMERICA GREAT AGAIN! https://t.co/nwKPRmWFNr
- Jan 15, 2016 03:28:53 PM RT @JaniceTaylor912: @DonaldJTrumpJr @Reryan08 @IvankaTrump @EricTrump obvious to all that he raised some GREAT, responsible, patriotic kid…
- Jan 15, 2016 04:06:40 PM Jusr watched #HarveyPitt on @TeamCavuto - he was great!

- Jan 15, 2016 08:23:55 PM "@GeraldoRivera @SenTedCruz got ass kicked by @realDonaldTrump last night-He offended every New Yorker & has no answer to Natural Born issue
- Jan 15, 2016 08:41:10 PM .@GeraldoRivera Thank you Geraldo for your nice words on @oreillyfactor tonight. You are a true champion! Thank @ericbolling - great guy!
- Jan 15, 2016 08:45:55 PM Just got back from Iowa - had a great time with amazing people. Will be back soon!
- Jan 15, 2016 09:02:12 PM .@oreillyfactor please explain to the very dumb and failing @glennbeck that I supported John McCain big league in 2008, not Obama!
- Jan 15, 2016 09:18:52 PM .@FrankLuntz is a total clown. Has zero credibility! @FoxNews @megynkelly
- Jan 15, 2016 09:47:22 PM More radical Islam attacks today - it never ends! Strengthen the borders, we must be vigilant and smart. No more being politically correct.
- Jan 16, 2016 06:40:13 AM Ted Cruz was born in Canada and was a Canadian citizen until 15 months ago. Lawsuits have just been filed with more to follow. I told you so
- Jan 16, 2016 06:49:02 AM Ted Cruz said he "didn't know" that he was a Canadian Citizen. He also FORGOT to file his Goldman Sachs Million $ loan papers.Not believable
- Jan 16, 2016 06:52:46 AM Was there another loan that Ted Cruz FORGOT to file. Goldman Sachs owns him, he will do anything they demand. Not much of a reformer!
- Jan 16, 2016 07:12:45 AM The Ted Cruz wiseguy apology to the people of New York is a disgrace. Remember, his wife's employer, and his lender, is located there!
- Jan 16, 2016 07:17:32 AM Oh no, just reported that Ted Cruz didn't report another loan, this one from Citi. Wow, no wonder banks do so well in the U.S. Senate.
- Jan 16, 2016 07:23:00 AM Based on the fact that Ted Cruz was born in Canada and is therefore a "natural born Canadian," did he borrow unreported loans from C banks?
- Jan 16, 2016 08:31:10 AM Ted Cruz purposely, and illegally, did not list on his personal disclosure form personally guaranteed loans from banks. They own him!

- Jan 16, 2016 08:42:54 AM Great new numbers. Thank you! #MakeAmericaGreatAgain #Trump2016 https://t.co/Z1lQdxQvRL https://t.co/GFYNUWWCYn
- Jan 16, 2016 11:11:28 AM Ted is the ultimate hypocrite. Says one thing for money, does another for votes. https://t.co/hxdfy0mjVw
- Jan 16, 2016 01:21:03 PM If Ted Cruz is so opposed to gay marriage, why did he accept money from people who espouse gay marriage?
- Jan 16, 2016 01:22:40 PM Everybody that loves the people of New York, and all they have been thru, should get hypocrites like Ted Cruz out of politics!
- Jan 16, 2016 01:23:26 PM When will @TedCruz give all the New York based campaign contributions back to the special interests that control him.
- Jan 16, 2016 01:26:54 PM Greatly dishonest of @TedCruz to file a financial disclosure form & not list his lending banks- then pretend he is going to clean up Wall St
- Jan 16, 2016 01:31:39 PM Departing NH now- great morning with record crowd in Portsmouth- in a snow storm! Thank you! https://t.co/m98wooUwsG https://t.co/izBMhEZolh
- Jan 16, 2016 02:32:40 PM Wow! Ted Cruz received $487K in campaign contributions, $11M from a NY hedge fund mogul, & $1M low int. loan from Goldman Sachs. Hypocrite
- Jan 16, 2016 02:39:31 PM Is this the New York that Ted Cruz is talking about & demeaning? https://t.co/rYGX9vazku
- Jan 16, 2016 07:25:49 PM Interesting read from Peggy Noonan. https://t.co/jAxIy8xseM

- Jan 17, 2016 08:51:56 AM In Iran deal we get 4 prisoners. They get $150 billion, 7 most wanted and many off watch list. This will create great incentive for others!
- Jan 17, 2016 10:21:46 AM Iran is going to buy 114 jetliners with a small part of the $150 billion we are giving them...but they won't buy from U.S., rather Airbus!
- Jan 17, 2016 12:46:32 PM Big announcement in Ames, Iowa on Tuesday! You will not want to miss this rally! #Trump2016 https://t.co/J2wyAfXdlz https://t.co/lErVfowpMX

- Jan 17, 2016 03:57:35 PM Far more killed than anticipated in radical Islamic terror attack yesterday. Get tough and smart U.S., or we won't have a country anymore!
- Jan 17, 2016 04:05:47 PM I am self-funding my campaign - putting up my own money, not controlled. Cruz is spending $millions on ads paid for by his N.Y. bosses.
- Jan 17, 2016 10:33:18 PM "@pbralick: @BenKissel great on @greggutfeld @GregGutfeldShow @JoNosuchinsky too" Thank you Ben for your nice comments on debate!

- Jan 18, 2016 09:48:02 AM Thank you @IvankaTrump for the kind words. I am very proud of the role model you are for so many. NH & IA radio ad: https://t.co/NqJJVdapnG
- Jan 18, 2016 09:50:43 AM Just a reminder that Ted Cruz supported liberal Justice John Roberts who gave us #Obamacare. https://t.co/gBnsNgomom
- Jan 18, 2016 09:50:59 AM Leaving for Liberty University. I'll be speaking today in front of a record crowd. #Trump2016
- Jan 18, 2016 12:48:53 PM A great morning with everyone @LibertyU! Thank you! Off to New Hampshire now. #Trump2016 https://t.co/XUWGANbq8k https://t.co/aEMUMqSoWm
- Jan 18, 2016 02:50:56 PM We launched a new series of #Trump2016 videos via Facebook. A new topic everyday! Watch: https://t.co/NXWNOcWZgc https://t.co/52E3LU3W77
- Jan 18, 2016 06:45:23 PM I loved being at Liberty University today! Record setting crowd, unbelievable people! Thank you Jerry and Becki! https://t.co/YrLGb7wXyh
- Jan 18, 2016 08:50:57 PM Ted Cruz is falling in the polls. He is nervous. People are worried about his place of birth and his failure to report his loans from banks!
- Jan 18, 2016 08:57:26 PM I don't think Ted Cruz can even run for President until he can assure Republican voters that being born in Canada is not a problem. Doubt!
- Jan 18, 2016 09:36:29 PM ".@TheBrodyFile Exclusive: @realDonaldTrump Says He Will Protect Evangelicals Better Than @tedcruz https://t.co/BLdnkYzMBE… #CBNNews #2016"

- Jan 18, 2016 10:44:15 PM .@TheBrodyFile great job on @AC360. Thank you for the very smart and kind words!

- Jan 19, 2016 07:50:01 AM Wow, new polls just out have Trump up and Cruz down - he is a nervous wreck!
- Jan 19, 2016 09:18:57 AM .@tedcruz Conflicting Stances on Birthright Citizenship [14th Amendment] Gives #TeamTrump credit. https://t.co/0x2qed7174
- Jan 19, 2016 09:44:25 AM Dope Frank Bruni said I called many people, including Karl Rove, losers-true! I never called my friend @HowardStern a loser-he's a winner!
- Jan 19, 2016 09:44:43 AM Really disgusting that the failing New York Times allows dishonest writers to totally fabricate stories.
- Jan 19, 2016 10:04:29 AM On my way to Iowa- just received new national poll numbers. Thank you! #MakeAmericaGreatAgain #Trump2016 https://t.co/sQ9UEVW4Vp
- Jan 19, 2016 10:17:09 AM .@FreeJesseJames- Just read your complete statement. You are an amazing guy & I really appreciate your words & support. I will see you soon!
- Jan 19, 2016 10:22:12 AM Thank you Georgia! I appreciate all of your support. #Trump2016 https://t.co/oNbgRpjKDl
- Jan 19, 2016 10:47:20 AM Thank you for your strong testimony when welcoming me to Liberty University, yesterday- @JerryJrFalwell. https://t.co/VJgj7AC5tE
- Jan 19, 2016 11:19:49 AM In the just released SC poll I increased my lead by 4 points since last poll by same firm. Up by 14! Cruz dropped 3. https://t.co/qM4JUsyaqH
- Jan 19, 2016 01:11:19 PM A true honor to receive the endorsement of John Wayne's daughter....read: https://t.co/X6jR0WVBvd https://t.co/1e6gk0PsQH
- Jan 19, 2016 01:47:51 PM Wow, the highly respected Governor of Iowa just stated that "Ted Cruz must be defeated." Big shoker! People do not like Ted.
- Jan 19, 2016 05:25:59 PM RT @EricTrump: I look forward to being on @CNN with @ErinBurnett at 7:40pmET. @realDonaldTrump
- Jan 19, 2016 05:35:08 PM "Palin's brand among evangelicals is as gold as the faucets in Trump tower," said Ralph Reed, the chairman of the Faith & Freedom Coalition.

- Jan 19, 2016 08:48:36 PM #Trump2016 #MakeAmericaGreatAgain #ECONOMY - VIDEO: https://t.co/KrCUSYFPLb https://t.co/KsVYviVdc2
- Jan 19, 2016 08:49:58 PM Judge Jeanine Slams GOP Establishment: https://t.co/gEhfZ3NAhi
- Jan 19, 2016 11:05:45 PM I am greatly honored to receive Sarah Palin's endorsement tonight. Video: https://t.co/4P7AMKI4iq https://t.co/bjTPvwM4nW

- Jan 20, 2016 06:14:50 AM "@ron_fournier: President Donald Trump (just getting used to it)" Wow, very nice!
- Jan 20, 2016 06:16:00 AM "@nytimes: Breaking News: Sarah Palin has endorsed Donald Trump in the GOP primary - appeal to Tea Party loyalists https://t.co/9aKuuuD1wE"
- Jan 20, 2016 08:40:29 AM #MakeAmericaGreatAgain #Trump2016 LIFE CHANGING EXPERIENCE Video: https://t.co/8kAswDS0bc https://t.co/0bSTLvq7V9
- Jan 20, 2016 10:53:12 AM Great rally in Iowa! Such wonderful people. Traveling now with @SarahPalinUSA to Tulsa- massive crowd expected! https://t.co/gaK4KEbHOh
- Jan 20, 2016 01:02:58 PM RT @SarahPalinUSA: Trading in the beautiful snow of Iowa for the red dirt of Oklahoma as planned, despite what the media is try's no... htt…
- Jan 20, 2016 03:52:01 PM 15K in OK! Had to turn away 5k, but we are coming back soon to take care of them! So much love in the crowd! Thanks! https://t.co/XsOeREiYuA
- Jan 20, 2016 05:43:06 PM Thank you, Florida! #Trump2016 https://t.co/npcw1AN2ht
- Jan 20, 2016 05:44:55 PM Thank you, New Hampshire! #FITN #Trump2016 #NHPolitics https://t.co/3FkMZpaEdR
- Jan 20, 2016 06:40:20 PM Bob Dole Warns of 'Cataclysmic' Losses With Ted Cruz, and Says Donald Trump Would Do Better via New York Times: https://t.co/txEaLrZ4uY
- Jan 20, 2016 06:42:28 PM New CNN/WMUR New Hampshire poll just released. Thank you! #FITN #Trump2016 https://t.co/sZr9taU20G

- Jan 21, 2016 08:27:37 AM "@AnnCoulter: Trump destroyed Hillary & Sanders moved in. But he didn't destroy her, Trump did. https://t.co/WAuaujsP1o" So true!
- Jan 21, 2016 08:42:48 AM Wacko @glennbeck is a sad answer to the @SarahPalinUSA endorsement that Cruz so desperately wanted. Glenn is a failing, crying, lost soul!
- Jan 21, 2016 08:51:37 AM "@NeilTurner_: https://t.co/uvn95NB6M0 You're the only candidate we can trust, other candidates are controlled by their donors! #VoteTrump"
- Jan 21, 2016 08:52:42 AM #MakeAmericaGreatAgain #Trump2016 UNIFYING THE NATION Video: https://t.co/1ZWE5R183k https://t.co/Md10pL1wn8
- Jan 21, 2016 08:56:11 AM "@bigop1: @realDonaldTrump @SarahPalinUSA https://t.co/3kYQGqeVyD"
- Jan 21, 2016 08:57:39 AM "@AmericanAsPie: @glennbeck @SarahPalinUSA Remember when Glenn gave out gifts to ILLEGAL ALIENS at crossing the border? Me too!"
- Jan 21, 2016 09:04:54 AM So sad that @CNN and many others refused to show the massive crowd at the arena yesterday in Oklahoma. Dishonest reporting!
- Jan 21, 2016 09:19:26 AM Sad sack @JebBush has just done another ad on me, with special interest money, saying I won't beat Hillary - I WILL. But he can't beat me.
- Jan 21, 2016 09:32:57 AM Low energy candidate @JebBush has wasted $80 million on his failed presidential campaign. Millions spent on me. He should go home and relax!
- Jan 21, 2016 03:36:09 PM New Day on CNN treats me very badly. @AlisynCamerota is a disaster. Not going to watch anymore.
- Jan 21, 2016 03:40:07 PM Happy birthday to my friend, the great @jacknicklaus - a totally special guy!
- Jan 21, 2016 06:21:42 PM Thank you, Iowa! #Trump2016 https://t.co/ryhEheTLqN
- Jan 21, 2016 06:29:04 PM Thank you! #Trump2016 https://t.co/pcdmyIO1Zt
- Jan 21, 2016 06:29:43 PM Thank you, New Hampshire! #Trump2016 https://t.co/TG9oZKly4l
- Jan 21, 2016 06:30:55 PM #Trump2016 #MakeAmericaGreatAgain https://t.co/vfUwGIGjN4

- Jan 21, 2016 07:54:16 PM Why does @Greta have a fired Bushy like dummy, John Sununu on- spewing false info? I will beat Hillary by a lot, she wants no part of Trump.
- Jan 21, 2016 07:57:10 PM Thank you, Iowa! #FITN #IACaucus #MakeAmericaGreatAgain #Trump2016 https://t.co/wVJldvTSag
- Jan 21, 2016 10:56:44 PM National Review is a failing publication that has lost it's way. It's circulation is way down w its influence being at an all time low. Sad!
- Jan 21, 2016 10:56:57 PM Very few people read the National Review because it only knows how to criticize, but not how to lead.
- Jan 21, 2016 10:57:22 PM The late, great, William F. Buckley would be ashamed of what had happened to his prize, the dying National Review!

- Jan 22, 2016 12:23:08 AM RT @williebosshog: Make America Great Again! #Trump2016 https://t.co/1h5j4DZDgy
- Jan 22, 2016 08:34:54 AM Ted Cruz complains about my views on eminent domain, but without it we wouldn't have roads, highways, airports, schools or even pipelines.
- Jan 22, 2016 08:36:16 AM "@realOllieTaylor: Isn't it time we had a president? Let goofy Glen keep Canada Cruz who can't win. The American people have Trump!"
- Jan 22, 2016 08:36:44 AM "@BornToBeGOP: @realDonaldTrump No sleep for the #TrumpTrain!"
- Jan 22, 2016 08:39:06 AM "@NeilTurner_: @realDonaldTrump https://t.co/uvn95NB6M0 With your help we can #MakeAmericaGreatAgain! #VoteTrump"
- Jan 22, 2016 08:41:22 AM #TedCruz eligibility to be President not settled law, says Cruz' Constitutional Law Professor, #LaurenceTribe https://t.co/GWKoJsBINZ"
- Jan 22, 2016 08:43:15 AM "@TruBluMajority: #laurencetribe calls Cruz "constitutional hypocrite" on @WBUR https://t.co/qRFINtcJlX @pbsgwen @charlierose @jaketapper
- Jan 22, 2016 08:54:21 AM Highly respected Constitutional law professor Mary Brigid McManamon has just stated, "Ted Cruz is not eligible to be President." Big problem

- Jan 22, 2016 08:59:21 AM "@D: #MaryBrigidMcManamon, Washington Post: Constitutionally speaking, #Cruz simply isn't eligible to be president https://t.co/DBtTgsC1il"
- Jan 22, 2016 09:00:47 AM "@CyberCiety: #MaryBrigidMcManamon clarified how #CommonLaw is used to interpret meaning of #NaturalBorn #TedCruz https://t.co/5y6SZrTdGr"
- Jan 22, 2016 09:10:54 AM "@MiamiNewTimes: Poll: Trump has more support in Florida than Rubio and Bush combined. https://t.co/uvH2BKQRHf https://t.co/2tvIaa2aFr"
- Jan 22, 2016 09:24:15 AM The failing @NRO National Review Magazine has just been informed by the Republican National Committee that they cannot participate in debate
- Jan 22, 2016 10:42:18 AM After spending $89 million, @JebBush is at the bottom of the barrel in polls. He is ashamed to use the name "Bush" in ads. Low energy guy!
- Jan 22, 2016 10:45:33 AM "@Lisa_Milicaj: Truth be told, I never heard of The National Review until they "tried" to declare war on you. No worries, you got my vote!"
- Jan 22, 2016 10:51:48 AM "@WhiteGenocideTM: @realDonaldTrump Poor Jeb. I could've sworn I saw him outside Trump Tower the other day! https://t.co/e5uLRubqla"
- Jan 22, 2016 12:24:37 PM Wow! This might be my highest # yet! Thank you to my opposition- you are totally ineffective & have been for years! https://t.co/o1l1XNZvhU
- Jan 22, 2016 03:47:34 PM The dying @NRO National Review has totally given up the fight against Barrack Obama. They have been losing for years. I will beat Hillary!
- Jan 22, 2016 04:06:37 PM New Reuters poll! Thank you! #MakeAmericaGreatAgain #Trump2016 https://t.co/KDVZoUia4I
- Jan 22, 2016 04:39:15 PM "National Black Republican Association Endorses Donald J. Trump" #Trump2016 #MakeAmericaGreatAgain https://t.co/9IPw30G5OG
- Jan 22, 2016 05:05:15 PM New National GOP Zogby Poll #MakeAmericaGreatAgain #Trump2016 https://t.co/Ma6OABMYpF https://t.co/evqFrWKBD1

- Jan 22, 2016 05:56:54 PM Leaving Nevada now for Iowa. Things are looking good - great new polls!
- Jan 22, 2016 06:08:31 PM Wow! New National Zogby Poll just out:.TRUMP 45. CRUZ 13. RUBIO 8. Big numbers.
- Jan 22, 2016 06:40:41 PM Just received the new Fox poll. Thank you, America! #Trump2016 https://t.co/QKNineuS8H
- Jan 22, 2016 06:48:22 PM The tax scam Washington Post does among the most inaccurate stories of all. Really dishonest reporting.
- Jan 22, 2016 06:49:42 PM Rush Limbaugh is great, tells it as he sees it---really honorable guy! Thanks Rush! #Trump2016
- Jan 22, 2016 06:58:14 PM Ted Cruz went down big in just released Reuters poll - what's going on? Is it Goldman Sachs/Citi loans or Canada?
- Jan 22, 2016 08:02:38 PM Just watched Jeb's ad where he desperately needed mommy to help him. Jeb --- mom can't help you with ISIS, the Chinese or with Putin.
- Jan 22, 2016 08:32:32 PM .@BrentBozell, one of the National Review lightweights, came to my office begging for money like a dog. Why doesn't he say that?
- Jan 22, 2016 08:33:17 PM The only reason irrelevant @GlennBeck doesn't like me is I refused to do his failing show - asked many times. Very few listeners - sad!
- Jan 22, 2016 08:34:26 PM Cruz says I supported TARP, which gave $25 million to Goldman Sachs, the bank which loaned him the money he didn't disclose. Puppet!
- Jan 22, 2016 09:04:23 PM Cruz did not renounce his Canadian citizenship as a US Senator- only when he started to run for #POTUS. He could be Canadian Prime Minister.
- Jan 22, 2016 09:08:41 PM Is Cruz honest? He is in bed w/ Wall St. & is funded by Goldman Sachs/Citi, low interest loans. No legal disclosure & never sold off assets.
- Jan 22, 2016 10:08:21 PM A wonderful article by a writer who truly gets it. I am for the people and the people are for me. #Trump2016 https://t.co/6rh849dlYZ

- Jan 23, 2016 08:12:22 AM "@TheSouthwasRite: @NRO cancelling my subscription- you people are idiots. @realDonaldTrump WILL be our next President. #Trump2016 #RNC"

- Jan 23, 2016 08:29:33 AM I am in Iowa. Will be making two speeches today. Good luck to all of the great folks on the East coast. Enjoy the beauty of the storm!
- Jan 23, 2016 08:32:58 AM "@LukeBrinker: One year from today. https://t.co/TcN6Z3XwyU"
- Jan 23, 2016 08:35:35 AM "@noamscheiber: Dow down almost 2000 pts since start of year, but still outperforming Wall Street's investment in Jeb. JEB wants Common Core
- Jan 23, 2016 08:57:53 AM I will be the greatest job-producing president in American history. #Trump2016 #VoteTrump https://t.co/tykxcT5ZtG https://t.co/oc480lwVQg
- Jan 23, 2016 09:45:31 AM .@AnnCoulter has been amazing. We will win and establish strong borders, we will build a WALL and Mexico will pay. We will be great again!
- Jan 23, 2016 10:01:34 AM I am in Iowa watching all of these phony T.V. ads by the other candidates. All bull, politicians are all talk and no action-it won't happen!
- Jan 23, 2016 10:07:04 AM Ted Cruz poll numbers are down big. Because he was born in Canada and was, until recently, a Canadian citizen, many believe he cannot run!
- Jan 23, 2016 11:50:22 AM Heading to Sioux County, Iowa, where the crowd is amazing. Dr. Robert Jeffress will make the introduction. Make America Great Again!
- Jan 23, 2016 11:52:17 AM Based on @MegynKelly's conflict of interest and bias she should not be allowed to be a moderator of the next debate.
- Jan 23, 2016 11:54:37 AM Failing @GlennBeck lost all credibility. Not only was he fired @ FOX, he would have voted for Clinton over McCain. https://t.co/dfCOkb7Ex8
- Jan 23, 2016 12:23:12 PM A wonderful story on Iowa voters by @arappeport of the @NYTimes. https://t.co/fGVQsMbRKj
- Jan 23, 2016 03:14:05 PM Just left Sioux Center, Iowa. My speech was very well received. Truly great people! Packed house- overflow!
- Jan 23, 2016 03:15:36 PM For the great people of Iowa, find your #IACaucus location at https://t.co/3KWOl20zMm. So important to vote! #MakeAmericaGreatAgain

- Jan 23, 2016 03:15:59 PM Heading now to Pella, Iowa. Big crowd! Remember, Trump is a big buyer of Pella windows. See you soon!
- Jan 23, 2016 03:28:22 PM .@williebosshog such an honor to get your endorsement. You are a fantastic guy! It will not be forgotten. Don and Eric say hello!
- Jan 23, 2016 04:42:55 PM I will be on FOX with the great @JudgeJeanine tonight at 9pm EST! Enjoy! #Trump2016
- Jan 23, 2016 06:36:30 PM Just left a great event in Pella. Going to church tomorrow in Muscatine, Iowa.
- Jan 23, 2016 08:20:49 PM Serious doubt in Illinois as to whether or not Cruz can run for President. First of many challenges. https://t.co/j9pngqvo5X
- Jan 23, 2016 08:21:16 PM Word is that crying @GlennBeck left the GOP and doesn't have the right to vote in the Republican primary. Dumb as a rock.
- Jan 23, 2016 08:39:28 PM Love making correct predictions. National Review is over. https://t.co/tEHJTl6tNA review-doomed

- Jan 24, 2016 03:47:50 AM "@snoozinglion1: Full Speech: Donald Trump Campaign Rally in Pella IA (1-23-16) https://t.co/dUWQyP00kN via @YouTube One of his best ever"
- Jan 24, 2016 03:48:39 AM "@CarolBurnett3: @AnnCoulter I just love the way Ann Coulter remembers your acts of kindness Donald Trump....GO Trump we love you"
- Jan 24, 2016 04:09:52 AM "@snoozinglion1: .@realDonaldTrump Great comment after last rally @rightside on @YouTube "Triumph with Trump or lose with Cruz." #Excellent"
- Jan 24, 2016 04:19:43 AM "@noamscheiber: Dow down almost 2000 pts since start of year, but still outperforming Wall Street's investment in Jeb.
- Jan 24, 2016 04:24:44 AM "@deacon6375: @realDonaldTrump i honestly believe you are the only one who can make #AmericaGreatAgain.
- Jan 24, 2016 09:06:08 AM I will be on @meetthepress this morning at various times across the U.S. @NBCNews Enjoy!
- Jan 24, 2016 09:13:08 AM I will be on Face The Nation this morning at various times across the U.S. @CBSNews Enjoy!
- Jan 24, 2016 10:08:34 AM I will make our Military so big, powerful & strong that no one will mess with us. #Trump2016 https://t.co/fxgCl9J1Wf https://t.co/PJECpbmkSE

- Jan 24, 2016 10:51:44 AM New Fox News Poll Thank you, Iowa! #Trump2016 #IACaucus https://t.co/aCj0Hq20hV
- Jan 24, 2016 04:06:22 PM Fox News Poll Thank you, New Hampshire! #FITN #Trump2016 https://t.co/jC1qisBbit
- Jan 24, 2016 05:06:08 PM "@keksec__org: @realDonaldTrump You said it best! #MakeAmericaGreatAgain https://t.co/z6R6r2gpyK"
- Jan 24, 2016 05:10:56 PM "@NeilTurner_: @realDonaldTrump https://t.co/uvn95NSIaA It's time we take America back! No more puppet presidents! #VoteTrump" So true!
- Jan 24, 2016 05:12:59 PM "@M0ther0f2kids: @meetthepress @NBCNews @clewandowski Everyone B smart! U know deep down Trump is the ONLY 1 able to best LEAD"
- Jan 24, 2016 05:14:34 PM "@MaryAnn1942: @realDonaldTrump @CBSNews ... You are like Superman, everywhere! But I'm keeping up. Great!
- Jan 24, 2016 05:14:41 PM RT @JoeNBC: Trump +15 on Cruz in 2 weeks. Cruz may look back and ask why he ever attacked Trump. DT has killed him ever since. https://t.c…
- Jan 24, 2016 05:20:44 PM "@JoeNBC: From Canada to Goldman Sachs to the kitchen sink, Trump has picked Cruz apart for 2 weeks. https://t.co/hkhTx4r6SC"
- Jan 24, 2016 11:01:47 PM "@Tuggers56: @PMgeezer Hillary is so afraid of him. The GOP is afraid of him. The American people embrace him! Let's elect him, DonaldTrump
- Jan 24, 2016 11:04:21 PM "@Knight276: @C4Constitution trump right again #With_Cruz_you_lose! Nobody supports Canuck Cruz #MakeAmericaGreatAgain #trump2016
- Jan 24, 2016 11:05:49 PM "@MrJuuon: #WeAreBernie will be overtaken by #WeWantTrump. We are superior and have more supporters. #makeamericagreatagain #trump."
- Jan 24, 2016 11:07:08 PM "@red77angelluis: @realDonaldTrump @NeilTurner_ @YouTube LET'S GET TRUMP!! GO TRUMP!! USA!USA!"
- Jan 24, 2016 11:08:41 PM "@Rketeltas: Rubio isn't experienced enough to be Commander in Chief. Rubio is a carbon copy of Obama. We need a true leader Vote Trump"

- Jan 25, 2016 08:26:21 AM It's time for Ted Cruz to either settle his problem with the FACT that he was born in Canada and was a citizen of Canada, or get out of race
- Jan 25, 2016 08:32:20 AM IPSOS/REUTERS POLL Thank you! #Trump2016 #MakeAmericaGreatAgain https://t.co/sbzp75EPSq
- Jan 25, 2016 08:46:48 AM I want to win for the people of this great country. The only people I will owe are the voters. #Trump2016 Video: https://t.co/rx7aOQqN7y
- Jan 25, 2016 11:51:55 AM I will be on The Situation Room with @wolfblitzer from 5-7pm est on CNN
- Jan 25, 2016 01:14:36 PM Join us in Iowa, tomorrow! #IACaucus #Trump2016 #MakeAmericaGreatAgain 3:00pm: https://t.co/cWQKRAgqfX 7:30pm: https://t.co/v2Ejh0TweS
- Jan 25, 2016 01:16:52 PM RT @GeraldoRivera: #NewYork tromps #Jonas. Day after storm of the century the big city is up and running unlike others in the northeast. Mu…
- Jan 25, 2016 01:17:28 PM RT @AnnCoulter: RUMSFELD: Trump "has a touched a nerve in our country...in a way that most politicians have not been able to do." - https:/…
- Jan 25, 2016 01:19:13 PM Obama's deal vs. Trump's deals- https://t.co/UpQ3LkUUpm
- Jan 25, 2016 02:51:25 PM Find out where to #VoteTrump on caucus night in Iowa on 2/1/16! #IACaucus #FITN #Trump2016 https://t.co/xd9iG0uh4l https://t.co/ocIpo2DInT
- Jan 25, 2016 04:02:18 PM I will be on Morning's with Maria on the Fox Business Network tomorrow during the 7am and 8am ET hours.
- Jan 25, 2016 04:47:42 PM I will be on @CNNSitRoom with @wolfblitzer from 5-7pm est. on @CNN.
- Jan 25, 2016 05:00:38 PM Ted Cruz is a nervous wreck. He is making reckless charges not caring for the truth! His poll #'s are way down!
- Jan 25, 2016 05:02:50 PM Cruz going down fast in recent polls- dropping like a rock. Lies never work!
- Jan 25, 2016 05:04:40 PM Cruz lies are almost as bad as Jeb's. These politicians will do anything to stay at the trough!
- Jan 25, 2016 05:13:44 PM Leaving now for New Hampshire. Big crowd- looking forward to it! #FITN

- Jan 25, 2016 06:32:30 PM Phyllis Schlafly's Eagle Forum: 'National Review Will Be Defunct In The Next Year' https://t.co/S7QmDkv2sg
- Jan 25, 2016 06:50:44 PM "@realDonaldTrump & @HillaryClinton leading POLLS w/ one week until #IowaCaucus ...MORE on the 2016 elections TONIGHT on @FoxBusiness 7PM"
- Jan 25, 2016 06:50:56 PM Just landed in New Hampshire. Will be at the venue shortly. #FITN
- Jan 25, 2016 09:28:36 PM Thank you - Farmington, New Hampshire! #FITN #Trump2016 https://t.co/bJ9Z3qZBQu
- Jan 25, 2016 11:15:12 PM "@jdenino1: @DavidWohl @realDonaldTrump https://t.co/RqMSSbfB0J BECK wanted to commit suicide after @ss surgery, clearly is unbalanced!"
- Jan 25, 2016 11:21:53 PM "@KurtSchlichter: My pal @DavidWohl was just on Megan Kelly's show! He digs Trump. Thank you David, you were great!
- Jan 25, 2016 11:25:18 PM "@Belizediver88: @CNNSitRoom @CNN @megynkelly It will never happen. Fox will drop Kelly if it means no Trump. Nobody will watch w/o Trump."
- Jan 25, 2016 11:27:32 PM "@JackBurtonReflx: @jdenino1 @DavidWohl @ss I listen to Glenn Beck and literally nothing he says makes any sense. Same with The View."
- Jan 25, 2016 11:56:32 PM "@Crusade4Honesty: @BornToBeGOP @megynkelly Megan can not contain her bias, it's in every show, Fox owners Saudi Prince agnstT"
- Jan 25, 2016 11:59:00 PM "@DittoPost: @realDonaldTrump @Crusade4Honesty @BornToBeGOP @megynkelly I believe in Trump!!!"

- Jan 26, 2016 12:00:05 AM "@WhiteJacketPink: @MyPresidentme @realDonaldTrump just google glenn beck bio. U can tell no education, very poorly written.
- Jan 26, 2016 12:09:33 AM "@Sharp_Trident: A huge disappointment to see @megynkelly constantly attack DonaldTrump. It has become almost unbearable to watch her show."
- Jan 26, 2016 05:43:04 AM I will be doing @GMA @GStephanopoulos this morning at around 7:00. Likewise, I will be doing @Morning_Joe at around 7:00. Figure it out!

- Jan 26, 2016 06:14:43 AM "@laurencristmann: @Sharp_Trident @megynkelly it makes me not wanna watch debate because I know they are going to treat Trump unfair"
- Jan 26, 2016 06:17:29 AM I will be interviewed by @MariaBartiromo on @MorningsMaria @FoxBusiness at 7:30 A.M. Enjoy.
- Jan 26, 2016 07:47:17 AM RT @Morning_Joe: VIDEO: @realDonaldTrump announces 'a very powerful endorsement' will be coming today. https://t.co/cJsMBcVcdY
- Jan 26, 2016 07:51:20 AM "Donald Trump retains national lead in new ABC News/WaPo poll with 37%: https://t.co/xPjA3TBbTa" https://t.co/6Uaecpwqwm
- Jan 26, 2016 07:53:34 AM "@realDonaldTrump hits new heights in national poll at 41%" https://t.co/1Tzszrkh4j
- Jan 26, 2016 09:33:43 AM "@xXFlame: .@bobvanderplaats Idiot Bob Plaats on CNN is DELUDED! Cruz's favorability ratings are 0%, NO ONE LIKES HIM. VOTE TRUMP INSTEAD!"
- Jan 26, 2016 09:33:56 AM "@AynsFriend: @bobvanderplaats CRUZ IS DONE @CNN @ChrisCuomo"
- Jan 26, 2016 09:35:17 AM "@puttster71: @bobvanderplaats The next president isn't on ur stage. @realDonaldTrump is the next president."
- Jan 26, 2016 10:04:19 AM I will end common core. It's a disaster. https://t.co/d83XYrqZ3m #MakeAmericaGreatAgain #Trump2016 https://t.co/r0Sc6zm80I
- Jan 26, 2016 10:55:01 AM Why doesn't phony @bobvanderplaats tell his followers all the times he asked for him and his family to stay at my hotels-didn't like paying
- Jan 26, 2016 11:16:23 AM For the great people of Iowa, find your #IACaucus location at https://t.co/ANvTcZqfOq - so important to vote! #MakeAmericaGreatAgain
- Jan 26, 2016 11:44:32 AM #MakeAmericaGreatAgain #Trump2016 https://t.co/oJyGTj5QX8
- Jan 26, 2016 11:55:37 AM Great honor- Rev. Jerry Falwell Jr. of Liberty University, one of the most respected religious leaders in our nation, has just endorsed me!
- Jan 26, 2016 01:03:07 PM .@bobvanderplaats begged me to do an event while asking organizers for $100,000 for himself—a bad guy!

- Jan 26, 2016 01:05:21 PM Should I do the #GOPdebate?
https://t.co/cjTywwIl85
- Jan 26, 2016 01:40:09 PM Do you think @SenTedCruz knows about
@bobvanderplaats dealings? Actually, I doubt it!
- Jan 26, 2016 02:51:42 PM THANK YOU! #Trump2016 #IACaucus finder:
https://t.co/ANvTcZqfOq https://t.co/CxqTh61ssz
- Jan 26, 2016 04:14:15 PM "Minorities Line Up Behind Donald Trump"
#Trump2016 https://t.co/ClcvOgWOMy
- Jan 26, 2016 04:17:15 PM "Trump shows complete domination of Facebook
conversation" https://t.co/tPiIyk4Dyc
- Jan 26, 2016 04:55:14 PM Thank you, America! #MakeAmericaGreatAgain
#Trump2016 https://t.co/7xxWD0au9H
- Jan 26, 2016 05:43:27 PM Pathetic attempt by @foxnews to try and build up
ratings for the #GOPDebate. Without me they'd have no ratings!
https://t.co/2bx54VKpQh
- Jan 26, 2016 09:26:18 PM https://t.co/SmTkLPiBYD
- Jan 26, 2016 11:40:29 PM CBS's FACE THE NATION - Posts Largest
Audience Since 2001 #Trump2016 #MakeAmericaGreatAgain
https://t.co/TzZx97FU1n

- Jan 27, 2016 06:44:04 AM I refuse to call Megyn Kelly a bimbo, because that
would not be politically correct. Instead I will only call her a lightweight reporter!
- Jan 27, 2016 08:02:52 AM The statement put out yesterday by @FoxNews was
a disgrace to good broadcasting and journalism. Who would ever say something
so nasty & dumb
- Jan 27, 2016 02:01:01 PM Just got to listen to Rush Limbaugh - the guy is
fantastic!
- Jan 27, 2016 02:33:57 PM Even though I beat him in the first six debates,
especially the last one, Ted Cruz wants to debate me again. Can we do it in
Canada?
- Jan 27, 2016 04:05:45 PM RT @DRUDGE_REPORT: LIMBAUGH: By not
showing, he's owning entire event... https://t.co/fdizXOkBFc
- Jan 27, 2016 04:21:04 PM I am self funding my campaign so I do not owe
anything to lobbyists & special interests. https://t.co/QYcedgsoV3
https://t.co/5f7zFDiVsN

- Jan 27, 2016 05:00:07 PM I will be interviewed on @oreillyfactor tonight at 8:00 P.M. (Eastern). Enjoy!
- Jan 27, 2016 05:49:44 PM It was the childishly written & taunting PR statement by Fox that made me not do the debate, more so than lightweight reporter, @megynkelly.
- Jan 27, 2016 10:00:36 PM Thank you- Lexington, South Carolina! #Trump2016 #MakeAmericaGreatAgain https://t.co/jaiRNIyYGL https://t.co/upAo2eDDVB
- Jan 27, 2016 10:34:44 PM FOX debate advertising rates falling like a rock! Tune into my special event for the Veterans at 9pm EST!
- Jan 27, 2016 10:41:21 PM On Greta, 87% of the people said they would not watch the debate if I'm not in it. Wow- what an honor!
- Jan 27, 2016 11:04:23 PM #Trump2016 #IACaucus Finder: https://t.co/ANvTcZqfOq https://t.co/thNiQh0nY6
- Jan 27, 2016 11:26:38 PM "@creta_r: @realDonaldTrump Looking forward to watching Donald Trump rally Thursday night on CNN!!"

- Jan 28, 2016 06:34:55 AM "@splashpoint50: @realDonaldTrump Our ReTrumplican Trump support group of 9500 members say 97% will not watch the debate tonight!"
- Jan 28, 2016 06:36:35 AM "@gene70: @FireFlyFury @megynkelly @realDonaldTrump And this is the bimbo that's asking presidential questions? https://t.co/oU1uUGnuWb"
- Jan 28, 2016 06:37:26 AM "@HenryOray: @CNNPolitics @tedcruz @realDonaldTrump is fighting corruption. Big donors took over Cruz. No to Donors"
- Jan 28, 2016 06:38:02 AM "@Davejager1: @creta_r 9 pm channel 70 CNN I will be watching Trump tonight. Want to have a person in the White House that takes no BS."
- Jan 28, 2016 06:39:14 AM "@HaloOneForTrump: @foxnews takes #YUGE hit on advertising revenues by screwing with @realDonaldTrump ROFL! https://t.co/ndyHNiUdks"
- Jan 28, 2016 06:39:48 AM "@CJCboi: @DRJAMESCABOT @realDonaldTrump @DanScavino @Carolde @PlaysTrumpCard Checked YOUR wallet lately, Mr Ailes?"

- Jan 28, 2016 06:41:04 AM "@dukeofbc: @megynkelly debate Cruz one on one. I would just tell him that you were to busy running for the President of USA, not Canada"
- Jan 28, 2016 06:42:52 AM "@_HankRearden: I respected Cruz ppl until this lie. We're just tired of it from your side. 1949z @steph93065 https://t.co/4K3u8JURiH" NO!
- Jan 28, 2016 06:43:55 AM "@Plazzmatic: @realDonaldTrump @danpgabriel Sounds like the advertisers want Trump, he knows what he is doing.
- Jan 28, 2016 06:44:38 AM "@Rick_Gobbi: @realDonaldTrump ...Hold up a mirror so the network cameras show how big the crowd is." GREAT IDEA!
- Jan 28, 2016 06:46:26 AM "@michaelG4NY: new @nbcnews WSJ poll shows @realDonaldTrump pulling ahead of @tedcruz in #Iowa. https://t.co/18ktk7IZUd" Great!
- Jan 28, 2016 06:56:16 AM Wow, two candidates called last night and said they want to go to my event tonight at Drake University.
- Jan 28, 2016 07:10:00 AM "@hollywoodJV: @realDonaldTrump Mr. Trump, why does Cruz hate Canada so much. He should embrace his roots, it's a great country" So true!
- Jan 28, 2016 08:07:55 AM "@laurencristmann: @realDonaldTrump why do they have so many debates this year?? Also, why is Cruz still allowed to run, he's not eligible"
- Jan 28, 2016 08:20:01 AM The "debate" tonight will be a total disaster - low ratings with advertisers and advertising rates dropping like a rock. I hate to see this.
- Jan 28, 2016 08:27:17 AM "@chgardens1: @mitchellvii Pathetic attempt to bribe @realDonaldTrump He can't be bought"
- Jan 28, 2016 08:29:56 AM "@BradCross4: @Drudge_Report_ @realDonaldTrump https://t.co/Ur1qgG291Z"
- Jan 28, 2016 08:30:27 AM "@rkirchmeyer: So @megynkelly brings in #MichaelMoore to add credibility in her fight with @realDonaldTrump? #FoxNews #ROGERAILES"
- Jan 28, 2016 09:00:16 AM "@GmoneyRainmaker: I hope @CNN has enough bandwidth tonight because not many will be watching @FoxNews. Watching Trump tonight #GOPDebate"

- Jan 28, 2016 10:03:28 AM "What America Needs: The Case for Trump" Great new book by the esteemed Jeffrey Lord @JeffJlpa1 Available now. https://t.co/xeHKbIDApr
- Jan 28, 2016 10:44:32 AM Being politically correct takes too much time. We have too much to get done! #Trump2016 https://t.co/8icSqEombg https://t.co/fkgkcVxVo7
- Jan 28, 2016 10:50:02 AM #Trump2016 #IACaucus Finder: https://t.co/ANvTcZqfOq https://t.co/1vjCHYYlzU
- Jan 28, 2016 12:32:06 PM It is my great honor to support our Veterans with you! You can join me now. Thank you! #Trump4Vets https://t.co/UVn3kUd2DV
- Jan 28, 2016 12:51:03 PM Tennessee GOP Poll https://t.co/hfSxKaXC42 Trump 32.7% Cruz 16.5% Carson 6.6% Rubio 5.3% Christie 2.4% Jeb 1.6%
- Jan 28, 2016 02:39:27 PM 20 Most Anticipated Hotel Openings of 2016: Trump International Hotel, Washington D.C. https://t.co/jd3H0LQcas
- Jan 28, 2016 02:52:03 PM I hear that @SenTedCruz's $$ man, Robert Mercer, a good man, is very angry because Cruz lied to him about liquidating his (Ted's) holdings.?
- Jan 28, 2016 05:45:25 PM #Trump2016 #IACaucus Finder: https://t.co/ANvTcZ8EpQ https://t.co/gicaoEOFCC
- Jan 28, 2016 05:58:41 PM "Donald Trump Hands Bill O'Reilly Cable TV Viewership Win"- @deadline-https://t.co/Ytid4IrW4y
- Jan 28, 2016 07:18:44 PM Watching biased Charles @krauthammer, a @FoxNews flunky who didn't know that I won every debate, in particular- the last one. Check polls!
- Jan 28, 2016 10:54:32 PM An unbelievable night in Iowa with our great Veterans! We raised $6,000,000.00 while the politicians talked! #GOPDebate

- Jan 29, 2016 12:17:17 AM I will take care of the Veterans who have served this country so bravely. #ThankAVet Video: https://t.co/WH9GSeSH29 https://t.co/WMR7jnmsyz
- Jan 29, 2016 12:29:31 AM Thank you for the kind words tonight, @OMAROSA. You were great! See you soon!
- Jan 29, 2016 12:40:07 AM #IACaucus • 2/1/2016 • 6:30pm #MakeAmericaGreatAgain! Iowa caucus finder: https://t.co/ANvTcZqfOq #GOPDebate https://t.co/HLuyCcuLcp
- Jan 29, 2016 01:10:12 AM Thank you, America! https://t.co/YJ0KIYpTaV

- Jan 29, 2016 01:19:59 AM Thank you for your support! https://t.co/Mjr8D4dDrK
- Jan 29, 2016 07:55:34 AM Good morning America! Thank you for all of your support in the latest Drudge poll! https://t.co/XDnixWnqwb https://t.co/yUTtLnALxy
- Jan 29, 2016 08:00:06 AM Thank you for your interest & support during last nights #GOPDebate! #IACaucus finder: https://t.co/ANvTcZqfOq https://t.co/yadQiPC49g
- Jan 29, 2016 08:42:58 AM Iowa was amazing last night. The event could not have worked out better. We raised $6,000,000 for our great vets. They were so happy & proud
- Jan 29, 2016 08:45:39 AM Getting ready to take off for Nashua, New Hampshire. Big crowd, will be there soon. Fun!
- Jan 29, 2016 09:43:21 AM Great Twitter poll- and I wasn't even there. Thank you! #GOPDebate https://t.co/yLJGkoOeBg
- Jan 29, 2016 12:02:06 PM Thank you! Mitchell FOX2 Michigan Poll finds Trump holds 3-1 lead over closest GOP opponents. Trump 47% Clinton 43% https://t.co/xpaeV0YzGV
- Jan 29, 2016 12:23:06 PM "Every American needs to say 2 simple words to every Vet they meet: THANK YOU!" John Wayne Walding https://t.co/wG8EzPHZt1
- Jan 29, 2016 01:27:38 PM Thank you- Nashua, New Hampshire! #MakeAmericaGreatAgain #Trump2016 https://t.co/NpJGvQwYU5 https://t.co/9h8CgrCXGB
- Jan 29, 2016 01:33:16 PM Join me tomorrow in Dubuque, Iowa! #IACaucus #Trump2016 https://t.co/rWbHdaYgBl
- Jan 29, 2016 01:53:07 PM Thank you, America! #Trump2016 Via @DRUDGE_REPORT https://t.co/hVa0gJiBNz
- Jan 29, 2016 03:40:16 PM They say that if I participated in last night's Fox debate, they would have had 12 million more & would have broken the all time record.
- Jan 29, 2016 04:26:32 PM Thank you for all of your support Iowa! #MakeAmericaGreatAgain #Trump2016 #IACaucus finder: https://t.co/ANvTcZqfOq https://t.co/fQAxuMe01b

- Jan 29, 2016 06:51:34 PM The new e-mail release is a disaster for Hillary Clinton. At a minimum, how can someone with such bad judgement be our next president?
- Jan 29, 2016 08:10:56 PM The great State of Nebraska can do much better than @BenSasse as your Senator. Saw him on @greta - totally ineffective. Wants paid for pols.
- Jan 29, 2016 08:15:43 PM .@BenSasse looks more like a gym rat than a U.S. Senator. How the hell did he ever get elected? @greta
- Jan 29, 2016 08:25:17 PM Amazing that Ted Cruz can't even get a Senator like @BenSasse, who is easy, to endorse him. Not one Senator is endorsing Canada Ted!
- Jan 29, 2016 08:31:51 PM .@FoxNews is the only network that does not even mention my very successful event last night. $6,000,000 raised in one hour for our VETS.
- Jan 29, 2016 08:41:51 PM .@oreillyfactor The people of Iowa love the fact that I stuck up for my rights, as I will do for the U.S. Also got $6,000,000 for our VETS!
- Jan 29, 2016 08:54:16 PM Looking forward to a great weekend in Iowa! #IACaucus #CaucusForTrump Tickets: https://t.co/nU39QHzxxX https://t.co/xZlwspf6xe
- Jan 29, 2016 08:57:10 PM "@classyexplorer: @oreillyfactor @DRUDGE So Bill if America was SO LONGING to learn more about candidates why the 50 percent audience loss?"
- Jan 29, 2016 09:00:03 PM "@gigglemitz: @GeraldoRivera @FoxNews damn fox is really acting like a baby today. I guess Trump got under their skin - pretty biased!
- Jan 29, 2016 09:43:18 PM THANK YOU to all of the incredible volunteers, behind the scenes in Iowa! #CaucusForTrump https://t.co/osvIsBwAgX https://t.co/EY0wNYv9XD
- Jan 29, 2016 10:52:49 PM Hillary Clinton is a major national security risk. Not presidential material!

- Jan 30, 2016 07:38:44 AM I will be in Iowa all day and until Tuesday morning. Finally, after all these years of watching stupidity, we will MAKE AMERICA GREAT AGAIN!

- Jan 30, 2016 09:05:31 AM I want to thank evangelical Christians for the warm embrace I've received on the campaign trail. Video: https://t.co/u6oOcWGePe
- Jan 30, 2016 10:31:51 AM #IACaucus #CaucusForTrump #iCaucused #iVoted https://t.co/jSYl2IYjPO
- Jan 30, 2016 11:29:53 AM MAKE AMERICA GREAT AGAIN! #IACaucus #CaucusForTrump https://t.co/nU39QHzxxX https://t.co/IrrzLCa2ev

- Jan 31, 2016 07:22:48 AM The Cruz campaign issued a dishonest and deceptive get out the vote ad calling voters "in violation." They are now under investigation. Bad!
- Jan 31, 2016 07:31:03 AM .@bobvanderplaats is a total phony and dishonest guy. Asked me for expensive hotel rooms, free (and more). I said pay and he endorsed Cruz!
- Jan 31, 2016 07:36:39 AM .@bobvanderplaats asked me to do an event. The people holding the event called me to say he wanted $100,000 for himself.Phony @foxandfriends
- Jan 31, 2016 07:42:28 AM .@bobvanderplaats is a total phony and con man. When I wouldn't give him free hotel rooms and much more, he endorsed Cruz. @foxandfriends
- Jan 31, 2016 07:49:34 AM I will be going to church in Iowa this morning with my wife, Melania. After church I will be making two speeches and touring the State!
- Jan 31, 2016 08:06:25 AM Ted Cruz is totally unelectable, if he even gets to run (born in Canada). Will loose big to Hillary. Polls show I beat Hillary easily! WIN!
- Jan 31, 2016 08:16:37 AM Ted Cruz is in trouble for not reporting his bank borrowing in his very important Financial Disclosure Form. Very low interest loans, scam!
- Jan 31, 2016 09:22:35 AM Wow, just saw an ad - Cruz is lying on so many levels. There is nobody more against ObamaCare than me, will repeal & replace. He lies!
- Jan 31, 2016 09:32:03 AM By not doing the failed, poorly rated debate, I was able to make the point of not allowing "unfairness" - while raising $6,000,000 for VETS.
- Jan 31, 2016 09:40:25 AM If I would have done the last debate, a record would have been set (instead of the poor ratings recieved). Also, VETS got $6,000,000.

- Jan 31, 2016 09:44:00 AM I am in Iowa. Will be interviewed on This Week With @GStephanopoulos this morning. ENJOY!
- Jan 31, 2016 09:47:07 AM I will be interviewed on Face The Nation with @jdickerson this morning. Enjoy!
- Jan 31, 2016 11:26:39 AM It is time to take back our country- and MAKE AMERICA GREAT AGAIN! #CaucusForTrump Video: https://t.co/y9Fa8Ut6IP https://t.co/bJ6a0t9Pv2
- Jan 31, 2016 11:47:44 AM So nice to get an endorsement from the founder and owner of Pizza Ranch in Iowa! A great guy and great places! #CaucusForTrump
- Jan 31, 2016 11:53:28 AM RT @CLewandowski_: Trump winning over Latino Republicans, poll says | New York Post https://t.co/yiC3zavrmi
- Jan 31, 2016 01:40:42 PM Watch @IvankaTrump show you how easy it is to #CaucusForTrump in Iowa! #IACaucus Video: https://t.co/Bf4J2OBtUU https://t.co/4Ma5JSkFu7
- Jan 31, 2016 04:03:18 PM .@DonaldJTrumpJr & his wife @MrsVanessaTrump attended the #SnowflakeGardenBrunch- here w/ Governor @TerryBranstad. https://t.co/mgLh9Im9QI
- Jan 31, 2016 09:51:22 PM Join us! #CaucusForTrump 11am WATERLOO: https://t.co/DGw5Yk2iSi 1:30pm CEDER RAPIDS: https://t.co/6WZTqOy4TW https://t.co/yyjQ1iFT2x

February, 2016

- Feb 1, 2016 08:25:20 AM It all begins today - WE WILL FINALLY TAKE OUR COUNTRY BACK AND MAKE AMERICA GREAT AGAIN!
- Feb 1, 2016 03:35:46 PM RT @ErinBurnett: Sat down w/ @EricTrump @DonaldJTrumpJr here in Iowa. Talked God, @realDonaldTrump late night tweets https://t.co/zLFMx4r5…
- Feb 1, 2016 03:53:10 PM RT @kevcirilli: CEDAR RAPIDS -- TRUMP'S DAUGHT IVANKA: "I can just say without equivocation, my father will make America great again."

- Feb 2, 2016 11:03:21 AM My experience in Iowa was a great one. I started out with all of the experts saying I couldn't do well there and ended up in 2nd place. Nice
- Feb 2, 2016 11:14:24 AM Because I was told I could not do well in Iowa, I spent very little there - a fraction of Cruz & Rubio. Came in a strong second. Great honor

- Feb 2, 2016 11:29:05 AM The media has not covered my long-shot great finish in Iowa fairly. Brought in record voters and got second highest vote total in history!
- Feb 2, 2016 11:34:02 AM I will be talking about my wonderful experience in Iowa and the simultaneous unfair treatment by the media-later in New Hampshire. Big crowd
- Feb 2, 2016 11:39:05 AM I don't believe I have been given any credit by the voters for self-funding my campaign, the only one. I will keep doing, but not worth it!
- Feb 2, 2016 01:55:03 PM RT @IngrahamAngle: The #CruzCrew prevailed! Smart for @MarcoRubio to keep his speech short & sweet. Ditto for @realDonaldTrump who was brie…
- Feb 2, 2016 02:15:55 PM .@Morning_Joe @mikebarnicle on @realDonaldTrump: He finished 2nd but he made the turn successfully like a pro"
- Feb 2, 2016 02:21:24 PM "@LoreWestphal @realDonaldTrump You MUST win the Presidency in 2016 !!!"
- Feb 2, 2016 02:22:35 PM RT @JoeNBC: Remarkable how cost-effective Post says Trump campaign was per vote and stunning how much Jeb spent per vote. https://t.co/A28…
- Feb 2, 2016 02:25:49 PM "@93101Dianne @realDonaldTrump if you can do that well in Iowa then I see you acing it in all other significant states. Momentum is growing"
- Feb 2, 2016 02:30:44 PM "@ellenEspence @realDonaldTrump Amazing job in Iowa! Cruz just barely won."
- Feb 2, 2016 02:33:38 PM RT @namusca: #VoteTrump2016 a real leader that truly cares about America & our values. He wants to bring prosperity back 2 USA https://t.co…
- Feb 2, 2016 02:41:15 PM "@restorereality Iowa is meaningless...keep pushing forward, run the table in NH SC NV and Super Tuesday. America needs you! #TrumpTrain"
- Feb 2, 2016 02:44:56 PM "@stephbewitching @realDonaldTrump All you haters need to realize Trump got the second highest vote in history. And he's never held office!"

- Feb 2, 2016 03:02:48 PM Anybody who watched all of Ted Cruz's far too long, rambling, overly flamboyant speech last nite would say that was his Howard Dean moment!
- Feb 2, 2016 05:23:53 PM On my way to New Hampshire- expecting a big and spirited crowd! #FITN #Trump2016 https://t.co/oUg1ErD0j7 https://t.co/9Hb7JO3wrZ

- Feb 3, 2016 12:12:23 AM Great job on @donlemon tonight @kayleighmcenany @cherijacobus begged us for a job. We said no and she went hostile. A real dummy! @CNN
- Feb 3, 2016 08:47:33 AM Ted Cruz didn't win Iowa, he stole it. That is why all of the polls were so wrong and why he got far more votes than anticipated. Bad!
- Feb 3, 2016 08:56:48 AM During primetime of the Iowa Caucus, Cruz put out a release that @RealBenCarson was quitting the race, and to caucus (or vote) for Cruz.
- Feb 3, 2016 09:07:25 AM Many people voted for Cruz over Carson because of this Cruz fraud. Also, Cruz sent out a VOTER VIOLATION certificate to thousands of voters.
- Feb 3, 2016 09:10:53 AM The Voter Violation certificate gave poor marks to the unsuspecting voter(grade of F) and told them to clear it up by voting for Cruz. Fraud
- Feb 3, 2016 09:21:03 AM And finally, Cruz strongly told thousands of caucusgoers (voters) that Trump was strongly in favor of ObamaCare and "choice" - a total lie!
- Feb 3, 2016 09:28:59 AM Based on the fraud committed by Senator Ted Cruz during the Iowa Caucus, either a new election should take place or Cruz results nullified.
- Feb 3, 2016 02:09:38 PM I will be interviewed on @greta at 7:00 P.M. Enjoy! @FoxNews
- Feb 3, 2016 02:20:55 PM This was sent out from Ted Cruz- as Iowans arrived at their caucus sites to vote. #CruzFraud https://t.co/tRM7KUCrSU
- Feb 3, 2016 02:25:08 PM The State of Iowa should disqualify Ted Cruz from the most recent election on the basis that he cheated- a total fraud!
- Feb 3, 2016 03:22:46 PM Cruz just lied again- I am, and have been totally against #ObamaCare- repeal and replace!

- Feb 3, 2016 03:44:28 PM Dr. Ben Carson blasted Ted Cruz for "deceit and dirty tricks and lies."
- Feb 3, 2016 03:44:37 PM Thank you New Hampshire! #MakeAmericaGreatAgain #FITN https://t.co/4EFJbQxJGW
- Feb 3, 2016 04:29:03 PM Stop the assault on American values. Stand w/ Trump to #MakeAmericaGreatAgain! #VotersSpeak: https://t.co/XRRJ0fMkNV https://t.co/c7EHokbLD1
- Feb 3, 2016 05:22:52 PM RT @DarrenJJordan: CONSTRUCTIVE WINS! @realDonaldTrump @CLewandowski_ @DanScavino @MichaelCohen212 @KatrinaPierson @DefendingtheUSA http…
- Feb 3, 2016 09:31:48 PM THANK YOU to everyone in Little Rock, Arkansas tonight! A record crowd of 12K. #Trump2016 https://t.co/MjtIq2ii0Q https://t.co/I9WkPN3pWm
- Feb 3, 2016 10:11:26 PM Sanders says he wants to run against me because he doesn't want to run against me. He would be so easy to beat!

- Feb 4, 2016 01:33:27 AM Thank you @billoreilly & @KarlRove. Ted Cruz should be immediately disqualified in Iowa, with each candidate moving up one notch.
- Feb 4, 2016 01:35:50 AM #ICYMI: @KarlRove & @oreillyfactor discuss what Ted Cruz did to the great people of Iowa- as they went to vote. https://t.co/Tv0FNezxse
- Feb 4, 2016 01:36:44 AM .@oreillyfactor @KarlRove- as per the show, an even more serious Cruz charge is the fraudulent voter violation certificate sent to everyone.
- Feb 4, 2016 01:38:05 AM This is the Cruz voter violation certificate sent to everyone, a misdemeanor at minimum. https://t.co/tMav17UGkf
- Feb 4, 2016 09:26:49 AM Politicians are trying to chip away at the 2nd Amendment. I won't let them take away our guns! #Trump2016 Watch: https://t.co/zl4sMjmOUc
- Feb 4, 2016 11:12:24 AM Taking a helicopter to New Hampshire, boarding now. Amazing activity planned. New UMASS poll, very nice! https://t.co/xFvGE0dRlA
- Feb 4, 2016 05:28:58 PM I will be interviewed by Anderson Cooper at 8pm on @CNN from New Hampshire. Should be very interesting!
- Feb 4, 2016 08:03:23 PM Watch @AC360 on NOW! @CNN

- Feb 4, 2016 08:54:50 PM "@rkswaney7: @CNN @realDonaldTrump I agree. Great businessman. I like your tone tonight! Keep it up & you'll have this Democrats vote."

- Feb 5, 2016 11:32:30 AM Join us Monday, February 8th @ the Verizon Wireless Arena in Manchester, New Hampshire! #FITN #NHPolitics #Trump2016 https://t.co/HVfhtJ6O6Z
- Feb 5, 2016 11:50:49 AM Big storm in New Hampshire. Moved my event to Monday. Will be there next four days.
- Feb 5, 2016 12:46:58 PM Live Free or Die: A motto for the whole country to follow. #NewHampshire #FITN #VoteTrumpNH https://t.co/W04ezOy28v
- Feb 5, 2016 03:29:19 PM I very much look forward to tomorrow's debate in New Hampshire—so many things to say, so much at stake. It will be an incredible evening!
- Feb 5, 2016 03:36:19 PM Such great support in New Hampshire. So many people are working so hard to #MakeAmericaGreatAgain!
- Feb 5, 2016 04:12:15 PM Heading to South Carolina, really big crowd! Will be back in New Hampshire tomorrow. #MakeAmericaGreatAgain
- Feb 5, 2016 05:53:20 PM Join me at Clemson University on Wednesday, February 10th! #MakeAmericaGreatAgain https://t.co/X6tp1bpIhi
- Feb 5, 2016 06:13:07 PM "@MaryAnn1942: @realDonaldTrump why vote for Trump? Unlike politicians all talk, Trump's talk materializes! He will make America great again
- Feb 5, 2016 06:13:50 PM RT @seanhannity: Watch: Donald Trump OWNS A Heckler Who Said Illegal Immigrants Are The Backbone Of America https://t.co/cRAOzIP0pH
- Feb 5, 2016 06:14:41 PM "@DharmaBum77: Donald Trump loves America! He loves Americans! He loves our Vets! #TrumpSupporters @realDonaldTrump https://t.co/NgcoHRLj2M
- Feb 5, 2016 09:01:35 PM Really dumb @CheriJacobus. Begged my people for a job. Turned her down twice and she went hostile. Major loser, zero credibility!
- Feb 5, 2016 09:08:16 PM 10,000 people in South Carolina, unbelievable evening! Will be in New Hampshire tomorrow- love it. https://t.co/tF033Yjhu3
- Feb 5, 2016 09:42:58 PM I told you so. Our country totally lost control of illegal immigration, even with criminals. https://t.co/IZgZqr6BgB
- Feb 5, 2016 09:51:26 PM It never ends! https://t.co/vdErsfh5H6

- Feb 5, 2016 10:10:23 PM I said this was happening long ago- I will stop this immediately! https://t.co/IWXGbBVwvT
- Feb 5, 2016 10:20:34 PM Border agent: "We might as well abolish our immigration laws altogether" https://t.co/LsrIXzCyJr
- Feb 5, 2016 10:26:13 PM "@ericnlin: @AC360 DonaldTrump: no raise in 8 years, home not worth what I paid for it, healthcare is a joke Obama is a liar. TRUMP 2016"
- Feb 5, 2016 10:26:39 PM "@autumnandews08: @realDonaldTrump Trump Will WIN the Debate like he has WON ALL the others! He is heads above the rest! #VoteTrump" Thanks!
- Feb 5, 2016 10:51:33 PM "@ukcatwoman52: @ericnlin @AC360 all candidates liars. Trump is the only one that speak the truth people need to hear what Trump is saying."
- Feb 5, 2016 11:03:54 PM "@billrey16929057: @seanhannity #Hannity @realDonaldTrump is the only hope to #MAKEAMERICAGREATAGAIN"

- Feb 6, 2016 09:37:35 AM Wow, Jeb Bush, whose campaign is a total disaster, had to bring in mommy to take a slap at me. Not nice!
- Feb 6, 2016 09:44:08 AM "@lisabrossman: @ukcatwoman52 @ericnlin @AC360 He is for America! Security for America! Jobs for America! There is no other leader!"
- Feb 6, 2016 10:18:18 AM The New Hampshire drug epidemic must stop. If elected POTUS- I will create borders & the drugs will stop pouring in. https://t.co/YdEnhqdTbS
- Feb 6, 2016 12:37:49 PM Join me tomorrow in Plymouth, New Hampshire! #FITN #NHPrimary https://t.co/zQscD1mCwM
- Feb 6, 2016 12:57:43 PM "@Enlighten2881: @ukcatwoman52 @ericnlin @AC360 How come Rubio&Cruz are going to turn America around but did nothing in the Senate for USA?"
- Feb 6, 2016 02:10:45 PM "@big_carsonrocks: AMERICA...Stop being duped...WAKE UP Cruz & Rubio establishment phonies. DonaldTrump only truthful & not owned candidate"
- Feb 6, 2016 02:41:46 PM "@paintonmyjeans: If I owned a big company that was failing, I'd hire DonaldTrump to make it great again-Rubio/Cruz wouldnt be considered"

- Feb 6, 2016 03:04:09 PM "@realOllieTaylor: @paintonmy: IA caucus hasn't picked nominee in 16 years! Cruz dirty tricks stole it. Trump way ahead in primary states.
- Feb 6, 2016 04:40:04 PM I love New Hampshire - will be an exciting evening!
- Feb 6, 2016 06:00:50 PM RT @EricTrump: Debate ready!!! @realDonaldTrump #MakeAmericaGreatAgain #TrumpTrain https://t.co/qE6suiO315
- Feb 6, 2016 07:14:01 PM Come join us at the Verizon Wireless Center-Manchester, New Hampshire on 2/8! Register now: https://t.co/xK5HYX226k https://t.co/zjRpnoV2ih

- Feb 7, 2016 01:24:11 AM "@ABCPolitics: .@realDonaldTrump led in @twitter conversation during the #GOPDebate. https://t.co/ZuMwroT8dl"
- Feb 7, 2016 01:26:17 AM "@ABCPolitics: .@realDonaldTrump dominating @Google searches throughout #GPLFers. https://t.co/IF35C2jcon"
- Feb 7, 2016 01:27:24 AM "@ABC:DonaldTrump: "The police in this country have done an unbelievable job of keeping law and order." #GOPDebate https://t.co/t2ocHFI6H3"
- Feb 7, 2016 05:20:40 AM "@JoeNBC: Cruz really seems out of his element in New Hampshire. It is such a different battlefield then Iowa and the South."
- Feb 7, 2016 05:24:33 AM "@MarkHalperin: My debate report card: Christie A-, Trump A-, Bush B+, Kasich B+, Cruz B, Carson C, Rubio D. Full report cards here.
- Feb 7, 2016 05:26:39 AM "@GOP_Left_Me: @JoeNBC Donald Trump won that debate hands down, Christi beat up Rubio.
- Feb 7, 2016 05:27:04 AM "@JoeNBC: Cokie Roberts says Donald Trump had a really good night."
- Feb 7, 2016 05:35:28 AM "@JoeNBC: Latest UMass Tracking Poll. NH GOP Trump 35 (+1) Rubio 14 (-1) Cruz 13 (-1) Jeb 10 (+2) Kasich 10 (+2)"
- Feb 7, 2016 05:37:08 AM "@JoeNBC: Trump, Kasich, Jeb and Christie all had good nights."
- Feb 7, 2016 05:44:53 AM "@newtgingrich: Trump hits it out of the park in describing effective deal making"
- Feb 7, 2016 05:46:39 AM "@newtgingrich: Trump shows courage in defending eminent domain as a necessity for construction of infrastructure"

- Feb 7, 2016 05:50:05 AM "@piersmorgan: Jeb Bush was as ineffectual as ever. As always, @David_Gergen calls it right: Trump held them off. #GOPDebate"
- Feb 7, 2016 05:51:04 AM "@piersmorgan: Trump won that debate. People can huff & puff all they like but he was the best candidate on the night. #GOPDebate
- Feb 7, 2016 05:52:45 AM "@JoeNBC: Trump just talked on MSNBC like a man who knows he had a very good night."
- Feb 7, 2016 05:53:35 AM "@JoeNBC: @jonkarl: "This has been a great debate for Donald Trump.""
- Feb 7, 2016 08:19:33 AM I will be on State of the Union @CNN with @jaketapper at 9am. Enjoy!
- Feb 7, 2016 08:43:47 AM I am on @foxandfriends now! Tune in!
- Feb 7, 2016 08:46:44 AM I will be on Meet the Press with Chuck Todd on NBC this morning. Enjoy! https://t.co/EIYyfFtnPs
- Feb 7, 2016 09:54:35 AM .@ABCPolitics #GOPDebate #MakeAmericaGreatAgain #FITN https://t.co/jM6wrUGQox
- Feb 7, 2016 11:29:09 AM Great to meet everyone while having breakfast @ChezVachon this morning! #FITN #VoteTrumpNH https://t.co/25UwkinUOd https://t.co/bmZvSmWe7Y
- Feb 7, 2016 03:05:00 PM We are going to have a big event at the Verizon Wireless Arena in Manchester, New Hampshire! 5K+! Join us tomorrow: https://t.co/HVfhtIPcIp
- Feb 7, 2016 03:20:56 PM Thank you Newt! https://t.co/6FkwdpI0Oj
- Feb 7, 2016 04:35:50 PM Thank you- Plymouth, New Hampshire! #FITN #NHPrimary https://t.co/1hzn6iZIEw
- Feb 7, 2016 05:40:07 PM I am in New Hampshire having a great time! Loved the #GOPDebate last night! Everybody enjoy the Super Bowl. #SuperBowlSunday #SB50
- Feb 7, 2016 09:03:31 PM So far the Super Bowl is very boring - not nearly as exciting as politics - MAKE AMERICA GREAT AGAIN!

- Feb 8, 2016 07:01:01 AM My two wonderful sons, Don and Eric, will be on @foxandfriends at 7:02 - now! Enjoy.
- Feb 8, 2016 07:20:11 AM Jeb Bush has zero communication skills so he spent a fortune of special interest money on a Super Bowl ad. He is a weak candidate!
- Feb 8, 2016 11:29:53 AM Thank you for your support at this mornings Town Hall- in Salem, New Hampshire. #FITN #NHPrimary https://t.co/4m6dabtxCV

- Feb 8, 2016 11:33:15 AM Jeb Bush is desperate - strongly in favor of #CommonCore and very weak on illegal immigration.
- Feb 8, 2016 11:38:00 AM Everybody is laughing at Jeb Bush-spent $100 million and is at bottom of pack. A pathetic figure!
- Feb 8, 2016 01:30:59 PM America needs strong leadership. Politicians can talk but they don't get things done. Video: https://t.co/YwZdQdzKcz https://t.co/lBXXyuZAcO
- Feb 8, 2016 01:34:28 PM RT @foxandfriends: .@DonaldJTrumpJr: Trump has had a lot more responsibility to deal with than any of the other GOP candidates https://t.co…
- Feb 8, 2016 01:35:02 PM RT @foxandfriends: "Jeb is a weak guy." @EricTrump https://t.co/w8YuC5bApY
- Feb 8, 2016 02:43:20 PM Today's third stop- Londonderry, New Hampshire! Thank you! #FITN #VoteTrumpNH https://t.co/pRpcxaZ7ov
- Feb 8, 2016 02:47:18 PM Now that Bush has wasted $120 million of special interest money on his failed campaign, he says he would end super PACs. Sad!
- Feb 8, 2016 05:21:41 PM #VoteTrumpNH #NHPrimary #FITN https://t.co/p4XCxNkXQO
- Feb 8, 2016 09:20:29 PM Thank you, New Hampshire! #FITN #NHPrimary #VoteTrumpNH Voting questions? https://t.co/BmZyKQOZJJ https://t.co/1tZfqVETrX
- Feb 8, 2016 11:06:58 PM Thank you, New Hampshire! #FITN https://t.co/uZItWkqQZa

- Feb 9, 2016 07:00:30 AM Remember @JebBush wants COMMON CORE (education from D.C.) and is very weak on ILLEGAL IMMIGRATION ("come as act of love"). Not a leader!
- Feb 9, 2016 07:08:19 AM I know the "Governors" and Jeb Bush, who has gone nasty with lies, is by far the weakest of the lot. His family used private eminent domain!
- Feb 9, 2016 07:16:37 AM No-one has done more for people with disabilities than me. I have spent many millions of dollars to help out-and am happy to have done so!
- Feb 9, 2016 07:23:37 AM The polls are now showing that I am the best to win the GENERAL ELECTION. States that are never in play for Repubs will be won by me. Great!

- Feb 9, 2016 08:32:26 AM I will be interviewed on @foxandfriends at 8:40. A.M. Enjoy!
- Feb 9, 2016 08:37:11 AM MAKE AMERICA GREAT AGAIN!
- Feb 9, 2016 09:21:19 AM Thank you for a great night at the Verizon Wireless Arena- New Hampshire! #VoteTrumpNH #MakeAmericaGreatAgain #FITN https://t.co/pbt7gDaw7y
- Feb 9, 2016 09:32:14 AM A message to the great people of New Hampshire on this important day! #VoteTrumpNH Video: https://t.co/7S2f2GSMB8 https://t.co/9WwRWnvqiv
- Feb 9, 2016 10:20:59 AM You can find your polling locations at: https://t.co/BmZyKQOZJJ #FITN #NHPrimary #VoteTrumpNH https://t.co/8lREIqhIuN
- Feb 9, 2016 11:46:17 AM New Hampshire vote today - MAKE AMERICA GREAT AGAIN!
- Feb 9, 2016 04:40:19 PM ISIS is making big threats today - no respect for U.S.A. or our "leader" - If I win it will be a very different story,with very fast results
- Feb 9, 2016 05:15:34 PM We will immediately repeal and replace ObamaCare - and nobody can do that like me. We will save $'s and have much better healthcare!
- Feb 9, 2016 05:19:31 PM We will stop heroin and other drugs from coming into New Hampshire from our open southern border. We will build a WALL and have security.
- Feb 9, 2016 10:38:08 PM Thank you, New Hampshire! Departing with my amazing family now! #FITN #NHPrimary https://t.co/rbFfcq8gQq https://t.co/73aoZk8uMG
- Feb 9, 2016 10:38:27 PM Thank you to the people of New Hampshire, I love you! Now, off to South Carolina.

- Feb 10, 2016 12:11:43 AM "@MarkHalperin: My report card grades for the 2 New Hampshire winners: DonaldTrump A: v strong energy/close. BernieSanders B+: went too long
- Feb 10, 2016 07:58:39 AM Dopey Mort Zuckerman, owner of the worthless @NYDailyNews, has a major inferiority complex. Paper will close soon!
- Feb 10, 2016 07:59:43 AM Worthless @NYDailyNews, which dopey Mort Zuckerman, is desperately trying to sell, has no buyer! Liabilities are massive!

- Feb 10, 2016 08:00:20 AM Like the worthless @NYDailyNews, looks like @politico will be going out of business. Bad reporting- no money, no cred!
- Feb 10, 2016 08:37:25 AM Such a great experience in New Hampshire - amazing people! Will be leaving for a big event in South Carolina today.
- Feb 10, 2016 10:22:51 AM So funny, Jeb Bush called me a "highly gifted politician and a great entertainer" - I assume that is a compliment!
- Feb 10, 2016 06:49:21 PM Big speech tonight in South Carolina - 7:00 P.M. Tremendous crowd!
- Feb 10, 2016 08:34:25 PM I was referring to the fact that Jeb Bush wants to keep common core.
- Feb 10, 2016 08:37:51 PM "@HARyder: Which is it @realDonaldTrump ?Are you planning on getting rid of Common Core or keeping it? Get rid of it fast.
- Feb 10, 2016 09:12:19 PM THANK YOU- Clemson, South Carolina! #MakeAmericaGreatAgain #SCPrimary https://t.co/FgACmaFxxc
- Feb 10, 2016 09:51:40 PM I have been consistent in my opposition to Common Core. Get rid of Common Core--- keep education local!

- Feb 11, 2016 09:13:09 AM There are no buyers for the worthless @NYDailyNews but little Mort Zuckerman is frantically looking. It is bleeding red ink - a total loser!
- Feb 11, 2016 10:11:56 AM Jeb Bush spent more than $40,000,000 in New Hampshire to come in 4 or 5, I spent $3,000,000 to come in 1st. Big difference in capability!
- Feb 11, 2016 10:40:04 AM .@MarkHalperin showed a focus group on @Morning_Joe me using a very bad word. I never said the word, left an open blank. Please apologize!
- Feb 11, 2016 11:14:10 AM Remember, it was the Republican Party, with the help of Conservatives, that made so many promises to their base, BUT DIDN'T KEEP THEM! Hi DT
- Feb 11, 2016 11:51:04 AM He (or she) who hesitates is lost: MAKE AMERICA GREAT AGAIN!
- Feb 11, 2016 02:45:59 PM Jeb failed as Jeb! He gave up and enlisted Mommy and his brother (who got us into the quicksand of Iraq). Spent $120 million.Weak- no chance!

- Feb 11, 2016 03:39:33 PM We are getting reports from many voters that the Cruz people are back to doing very sleazy and dishonest "pushpolls" on me. We are watching!
- Feb 11, 2016 06:03:54 PM Heading to Baton Rouge, Louisiana for a speech. Expecting a very large crowd! See you soon. #Trump2016 #MakeAmericaGreatAgain
- Feb 11, 2016 06:19:33 PM "@truthinvest: @CNN @tedcruz @realDonaldTrump Ted Cruz is the definition of sleaze. Just ask @RealBenCarson"
- Feb 11, 2016 07:44:06 PM Cruz caught cold in lie after denial of push polls like lies w/ @RealBenCarson. How can he preach Christian values? https://t.co/p3yGL02ABA
- Feb 11, 2016 08:06:30 PM Just landed in Baton Rouge, Louisiana. Reports are out that lines are three quarters of a mile to get in. Wow! #MakeAmericaGreatAgain
- Feb 11, 2016 10:28:28 PM THANK YOU- Baton Rouge, Louisiana! WE will #MakeAmericaGreatAgain! #Trump2016 https://t.co/XV7EIe7A2l
- Feb 11, 2016 11:10:52 PM Weak JEB getting thrown out by management during speech. Do you think he will be this tough on Putin & others? https://t.co/Tqej1euLVL
- Feb 11, 2016 11:20:33 PM Lying Cruz put out a statement, "Trump & Rubio are w/Obama on gay marriage." Cruz is the worst liar, crazy or very dishonest. Perhaps all 3?

- Feb 12, 2016 07:03:41 AM How can Ted Cruz be an Evangelical Christian when he lies so much and is so dishonest?
- Feb 12, 2016 09:48:17 AM NEVADA! Tomorrow is the deadline to register Republican. Visit: https://t.co/bHZ4JVckOp Message from @IvankaTrump: https://t.co/SZTq1QOXEg
- Feb 12, 2016 11:19:14 AM The failing @NYDailyNews, destroyed by little Morty Zuckerman, is preparing to close and save face by going online. It's dead!
- Feb 12, 2016 01:02:22 PM You must be registered Republican by February 16th to vote TRUMP in the Florida primary. https://t.co/xZzUkjV3lL https://t.co/lPuprzJBQ5

- Feb 12, 2016 01:22:06 PM Nothing conservative about the Club for Growth coming into my office and demanding a $1M contribution, which naturally, they did not get.
- Feb 12, 2016 01:22:20 PM After hearing the news that they would not be able to extort $1M from me, they went hostile w/ a series of incorrect & ill-informed ads.
- Feb 12, 2016 01:59:38 PM Lightweight @JebBush is spending a fortune of special interest against me in SC. False advertising- desperate and sad!
- Feb 12, 2016 02:45:53 PM If @TedCruz doesn't clean up his act, stop cheating, & doing negative ads, I have standing to sue him for not being a natural born citizen.
- Feb 12, 2016 03:30:07 PM Last time lightweight @JebBush tried to knock off @marcorubio he made a total fool of himself. If he doesn't do better this time, he is out!
- Feb 12, 2016 04:15:29 PM "@hillx123: @tedcruz you have just been put on notice @realDonaldTrump We Stand with you... #MakeAmericaGreatAgain" Thankyou.
- Feb 12, 2016 04:37:19 PM "@by @tedcruz good I want to see the court decide what I was always told "natural born" means - born on American soil"
- Feb 12, 2016 04:54:11 PM Millions of $'s of false ads, paid for by lobbyists-special interests of cheater @SenTedCruz and sleepy @JebBush, are now running in S.C.
- Feb 12, 2016 06:12:19 PM #MakeAmericaGreatAgain! https://t.co/7zuMD4oxUq
- Feb 12, 2016 07:31:58 PM I will end illegal immigration and protect our borders! We need to MAKE AMERICA SAFE & GREAT AGAIN! #Trump2016 https://t.co/wd3LlMz01I
- Feb 12, 2016 09:34:19 PM 11,000 inside venue tonight in Tampa! Broke record set by Elton John in 1988 w/out musical instruments! Another 5,000 outside. Will be back!
- Feb 12, 2016 09:44:07 PM When little Morty Zuckerman closes his failing @NYDailyNews will I at least be given some credit? Will happen soon.
- Feb 12, 2016 09:50:03 PM Word is that little Morty Zuckerman's @NYDailyNews loses more than $50 million per year---can that be possible?

- Feb 12, 2016 11:57:25 PM Just got back from Tampa. It was an amazing evening with an even more amazing crowd - fantastic people! Will be in South Carolina tomorrow.

- Feb 13, 2016 10:01:40 AM I am the only one who can fix this. Very sad. Will not happen under my watch! #MakeAmericaGreatAgain https://t.co/8MQ4imuTTi
- Feb 13, 2016 10:04:10 AM "@jd4160: Nice column by Bill Donahue, head of Catholic League. He's a blue collar New Yorker and gets it https://t.co/cbUPNuGnUB"
- Feb 13, 2016 10:16:43 AM Now an additional 600-700 jobs in America (2,000) being eliminated for move to Mexico- via Hartford Courant. https://t.co/bOIYQLqGRG
- Feb 13, 2016 11:37:07 AM The RNC, which is probably not on my side, just illegally put out a fundraising notice saying Trump wants you to contribute to the RNC.
- Feb 13, 2016 11:38:14 AM Totally unauthorized, do not pay. I am self funding my campaign! Notice has just been withdrawn. #Trump2016 #MakeAmericaGreatAgain
- Feb 13, 2016 11:43:32 AM A very big thank you to Bill Donohue, head of The Catholic League, for the wonderful interview on @CNN and article in Newsmax! Great insight
- Feb 13, 2016 11:48:50 AM "@Bonfiredesigns: @StellaDean Let's Get United In America With @realDonaldTrump https://t.co/a04Hne16Gp"
- Feb 13, 2016 11:49:18 AM "@nellalda: @DonaldJTrump45 @realDonaldTrump @Reince They are all going crazy! We the people do not care at all! We are with Trump!!"
- Feb 13, 2016 11:50:46 AM "@dj4k4000: @realDonaldTrump @CNN Trump will be our next POTUS..every American will benefit positivey from this."
- Feb 13, 2016 11:58:55 AM "@Elvisfan1976: @NRSC stop sending me emails asking me to donate and get a free DonaldTrump sticker. I support him and he's self funding!
- Feb 13, 2016 12:01:59 PM "@grammies28: @realDonaldTrump was right! Vote trump! Bring our jobs back. https://t.co/eUcpgNWqnr" I told you so, only going to get worse

- Feb 13, 2016 12:21:17 PM "Get on Trump's List" email from the RNC was not authorized. I am self funding my campaign! Do not pay. Email: https://t.co/6hKW7Ssxz4
- Feb 13, 2016 12:21:45 PM Thank you, South Carolina! We will MAKE AMERICA SAFE & GREAT AGAIN! https://t.co/8pfvTZngrZ https://t.co/QiO0nwcFSA
- Feb 13, 2016 12:21:59 PM RT @EricTrump: Nevada: Reminder that today is the LAST day to register to vote in the February 23rd caucus!https://t.co/SDQGGhkyjI https://…
- Feb 13, 2016 12:52:33 PM "@wino911: #Trump2016 We know better than to trust the RNC https://t.co/EMcgtK25fE" So cute!
- Feb 13, 2016 12:54:02 PM "@BrandonSawyer84: @realDonaldTrump will rule #SouthCarolinaPrimary! https://t.co/y0YNO1eyft"
- Feb 13, 2016 02:22:39 PM "@ThtsWhtKelSaid: I'm fed up w/ DC playing 3 card Monty w/ our tax $'s. It's time we the people play the Trump card, & take back our country
- Feb 13, 2016 02:24:26 PM "@AmFree: #Trump On #Ford, #Carrier, Shipping #Jobs To #Mexico: 'I'm The Only One Who Understands What's Going On' https://t.co/JsuiHpQpXX"
- Feb 13, 2016 05:27:19 PM Love the people of South Carolina - look very much forward to the debate tonight.
- Feb 13, 2016 05:34:25 PM The totally unexpected loss of Supreme Court Justice Antonin Scalia is a massive setback for the Conservative movement and our COUNTRY!
- Feb 13, 2016 07:00:49 PM Wow! Honored to be chosen by the highly respected + accurate Washington & Lee Mock Convention. I hope you are right - I will make you proud!
- Feb 13, 2016 07:11:36 PM Nasty Ted Cruz is at it again- same dirty tricks he used w/ @RealBenCarson- saying I may not be on ballot & I hold liberal positions. LIES!
- Feb 13, 2016 07:13:10 PM Ted Cruz is a cheater! He holds the Bible high and then lies and misrepresents the facts!
- Feb 13, 2016 08:17:51 PM On the way to the #GOPDebate with my wonderful wife @MelaniaTrump. https://t.co/SnOnu6IHTC https://t.co/f0C429tvHO

- Feb 14, 2016 12:24:32 AM Lightweight @JebBush said tonight he didn't know his family used private eminent domain in Texas- Lie! #GOPDebate
- Feb 14, 2016 12:27:38 AM Thank you! I miss my father. https://t.co/1IPVwX0avU
- Feb 14, 2016 12:37:59 AM How can @JebBush beat Hillary Clinton- if he can't beat anyone else on the #GOPDebate stage with $150M? I am the only one who can!
- Feb 14, 2016 01:12:28 AM All polls have me winning debate big- Drudge, TIME, etc. Dopey Charles Krauthammer still nasty. He has zero cred- totally dishonest!
- Feb 14, 2016 01:17:30 AM #MakeAmericaGreatAgain! https://t.co/Cwp6Ub5GqJ
- Feb 14, 2016 01:26:22 AM Hey @glennbeck- see how I beat your boy Ted- in your own Blaze poll? Your endorsement means nothing! #GOPDebate
- Feb 14, 2016 01:39:46 AM #GOPDebate #GoogleTrends https://t.co/yVxFubckNs
- Feb 14, 2016 06:52:54 AM "@jeffpaine: @realDonaldTrump you crushed the debate! Thank you!
- Feb 14, 2016 07:56:20 AM Even though every poll, Time, Drudge etc., has me winning the debate by a lot, @FoxNews only puts negative people on. Biased - a total joke!
- Feb 14, 2016 07:59:23 AM "@autumnandews08: @realDonaldTrump @JebBush Jeb is incompetent and will lose, don't waste your energy on that cry baby!"
- Feb 14, 2016 09:50:39 AM This shows what a complete & total liar Ted Cruz is- he said he wouldn't have nominated John Roberts. Really? https://t.co/gBnsNgomom
- Feb 14, 2016 09:51:02 AM I will be on Face the Nation with John Dickerson on CBS this morning. Enjoy!
- Feb 14, 2016 12:27:48 PM Thank you for your support! TOGETHER we will MAKE AMERICA GREAT AGAIN! https://t.co/fFN9pisyQ4 https://t.co/VxyuDwZmC9
- Feb 14, 2016 03:55:59 PM Loved the debate last night, and almost everyone said I won, but the RNC did a terrible job of ticket distrbution. All donors & special ints

- Feb 14, 2016 04:07:04 PM Tickets for future debates should be put out to the general public instead of being given to the lobbyists & special interests - the bosses!
- Feb 14, 2016 04:10:20 PM Wow, in the new CBS Poll I went way up into the forties! Thank you!
- Feb 14, 2016 05:02:19 PM Ted Cruz, along with Jeb Bush, pushed Justice John Roberts onto the Supreme Court. Roberts could have killed ObamaCare twice, but didn't!

- Feb 15, 2016 06:05:15 AM Funny that Jeb(!) didn't want help from his family in his failed campaign and didn't even want to use his last name.Then mommy, now brother!
- Feb 15, 2016 07:24:00 AM Jeb Bush and Ted Cruz are not electable presidential candidates, Hillary would destroy them. Ted may not be eligible to run - born in Canada
- Feb 15, 2016 08:55:08 AM I will be in South Carolina all week. Saturday is BIG, BIG, BIG! Get out and vote - MAKE AMERICA GREAT AGAIN
- Feb 15, 2016 09:04:31 AM Now that George Bush is campaigning for Jeb(!), is he fair game for questions about World Trade Center, Iraq War and eco collapse? Careful!
- Feb 15, 2016 12:24:42 PM I'd like to call JEB a liar, but the truth is he has no clue & never revealed that he used Eminent Domain- when criticizing me! (1/2)
- Feb 15, 2016 12:24:53 PM Jeb used Eminent Domain & took advantage of a disabled vet in the process. (2/2) https://t.co/eiBCld77tV
- Feb 15, 2016 12:29:40 PM JEB is a hypocrite! Used massive private "Eminent Domain" --- Just another clueless politician! https://t.co/yZT3lSutt9
- Feb 15, 2016 03:23:12 PM RESPONSE TO THE LIES OF SENATOR CRUZ: https://t.co/9PGo56YTqt #Trump2016 #VoteTrumpSC
- Feb 15, 2016 04:16:00 PM Thank you for your continued support! #MakeAmericaGreatAgain https://t.co/cykncrrSRE
- Feb 15, 2016 10:53:29 PM What a night! 10,000 amazing supporters in Greenville, South Carolina! THANK YOU! VOTE on Saturday! #VoteTrumpSC https://t.co/jXYLRDayB7
- Feb 15, 2016 11:18:28 PM New South Carolina poll from PPP. Thank you! #VoteTrumpSC https://t.co/6618Oi6vle

- Feb 16, 2016 05:52:09 AM Spent the full day at meetings and a major rally yesterday in South Carolina. Great people and spirit. Today will be more of the same.
- Feb 16, 2016 06:22:02 AM New PPP Poll just out - Trump up big, Cruz, Rubio and Bush down. The debate results, even with a stacked RNC audience, were wonderful!
- Feb 16, 2016 07:37:08 AM Thank you! #MakeAmericaGreatAgain https://t.co/tIBB3BMUvp
- Feb 16, 2016 12:59:42 PM Just sat down for a great interview with @PHussionWYFF in Greenville today. Watch at 5pm. An amazing day in South Carolina! #VoteTrumpSC
- Feb 16, 2016 01:21:12 PM #TeamTrump is thinking of Captain Andrew Maitner. A true American hero. #MaitnerStrong https://t.co/v96l7tUFWy https://t.co/uLuDOHEIB2
- Feb 16, 2016 04:09:52 PM Thank you to the 2,500+ in North Augusta, South Carolina. Lines down the block! Don't forget to VOTE on Saturday! https://t.co/KayUN9rfIV
- Feb 16, 2016 05:54:29 PM Thank you, South Carolina! #MakeAmericaGreatAgain #Trump2016 https://t.co/pIDqnY4IL3
- Feb 16, 2016 06:15:53 PM Will be interviewed by @StephenAtHome tonight by phone- a late show first @CBS @colbertlateshow. Enjoy! #Colbert #LSSC
- Feb 16, 2016 10:04:22 PM Explain to @brithume and @megynkelly, who know nothing, that I will beat Hillary and win states (and dem-indie votes) that no other R can!
- Feb 16, 2016 10:12:52 PM .@brithume thinks that when Republicans drop out of the race, someone will pick up ALL of that vote. The fact is I will get much of it!
- Feb 16, 2016 10:17:32 PM "@Good2bqueen67: @brithume @megynkelly They're too lame to get it, Sir. When you win the election they'll get it."
- Feb 16, 2016 10:44:39 PM Thank you @kayleighmcenany for your nice words - great knowledge and style! We are doing really well in South Carolina. @CNN @donlemon
- Feb 16, 2016 10:48:19 PM "@debdew2: @brithume @megynkelly @DiamondandSilk FOX: TRUMP HATERS R SCARED BECAUSE THEY LOSE - TRUMP IS WINNING https://t.co/6umGLYjWhT"

- Feb 16, 2016 10:58:40 PM Why does @megynkelly devote so much time on her shows to me, almost always negative? Without me her ratings would tank. Get a life Megyn!

- Feb 17, 2016 05:23:46 AM "@babo_sirin: BUSTED AGAIN: @TedCruz in Hot Water Over Possibly Illegal Fundraising #SCPrimary https://t.co/aaTtAbfOXx" The guy is bad news
- Feb 17, 2016 05:53:55 AM "@ChJLuc91: @YomasterJon @RichardTBurnett Scary how smoothly Cruz looks into the camera and lies about Trump, CANT be #POTUS! #Trump2016"
- Feb 17, 2016 06:08:15 AM Interesting how President Obama so haltingly said I "would never be president" - This from perhaps the worst president in U.S. history!
- Feb 17, 2016 09:39:52 AM .@lindseygraham, who had zero in his presidential run before dropping out in disgrace- saying the most horrible things about me on @FoxNews.
- Feb 17, 2016 09:40:24 AM I will beat Hillary easily, but Lindsey Graham says I won't, and yet he got zero against me- no cred! Why does FOX put him on?
- Feb 17, 2016 09:49:02 AM .@FoxNews is so biased it is disgusting. They do not want Trump to win. All negative!
- Feb 17, 2016 11:10:30 AM Just out Nevada poll shows Jeb Bush at 1%, he should take his dumb mouthpiece, @LindseyGrahamSC, and just go home.
- Feb 17, 2016 11:11:24 AM Jeb Bush just got contact lenses and got rid of the glasses. He wants to look cool, but it's far too late. 1% in Nevada!
- Feb 17, 2016 11:22:35 AM #MakeAmericaGreatAgain #Trump2016 https://t.co/uMLm0Gd3lX
- Feb 17, 2016 11:31:34 AM Thank you Nevada! #MakeAmericaGreatAgain #Trump2016 https://t.co/n6hGfdCWuv
- Feb 17, 2016 11:34:55 AM THANK YOU AMERICA! #MakeAmericaGreatAgain #Trump2016 https://t.co/TRrdR0nlpM
- Feb 17, 2016 06:17:33 PM Join us tomorrow in Kiawah, South Carolina! #SCPrimary #VoteTrumpSC #Trump2016 https://t.co/pG868uImBb

- Feb 18, 2016 05:44:28 AM Amazing that while I lead by big numbers in the new Q and and USA Today polls, the the press only wants to report on the phony WSJ/NBC poll.

- Feb 18, 2016 05:53:34 AM The just out USA Today National Poll, where I lead by big numbers, shows that in a head to head matchup, I beat both Hillary and Bernie.
- Feb 18, 2016 06:25:40 AM I love being in South Carolina. We are leading big in all of the State polls - Saturday is a BIG day. MAKE AMERICA GREAT AGAIN!
- Feb 18, 2016 07:26:46 AM New CBS National Poll just out - massive lead for Trump. The Wall Street Journal/NBC Poll is a total joke. No wonder WSJ is doing so badly!
- Feb 18, 2016 08:11:02 AM Thank you America! #Trump2016 https://t.co/U9L0ja3frk https://t.co/oqv2dSa1ET
- Feb 18, 2016 08:27:55 AM #MakeAmericaGreatAgain #Trump2016 https://t.co/nrcrU08sQ6
- Feb 18, 2016 08:30:38 AM Thank you South Carolina! Together, WE WILL MAKE AMERICA GREAT AGAIN! #VoteTrumpSC https://t.co/ZkXPm9lPL1
- Feb 18, 2016 09:05:38 AM .@FoxNews is changing their theme from "fair and balanced" to "unfair and unbalanced." But dying @WSJ is worse.Their phony poll is a joke!
- Feb 18, 2016 09:11:18 AM I agree with Marco Rubio that Ted Cruz is a liar!
- Feb 18, 2016 01:07:32 PM Response to the Pope: https://t.co/iWDjTIQyhE
- Feb 18, 2016 02:42:00 PM RT @TomOdell: .@FoxNews - Pope who lives in a Vatican city fortified with huge walls thinks it's wrong to build walls? Really? https://t.co…
- Feb 18, 2016 02:42:39 PM RT @benshapiro: Pope on Trump: "A person who thinks only about building walls...is not Christian." This is Vatican City. https://t.co/ehmsL…
- Feb 18, 2016 03:14:22 PM Join us tomorrow night in Charleston, South Carolina! #SCPrimary #Trump2016 https://t.co/VauoRmgcVz
- Feb 18, 2016 03:16:04 PM Join us Saturday night- for the South Carolina Primary Watch Party! #SCPrimary #Trump2016 https://t.co/AqRhLydI0u
- Feb 18, 2016 07:05:58 PM RT @JoeNBC: "Pope Francis, tear down that wall!" #vaticanwalls https://t.co/mDGANFtApb
- Feb 18, 2016 07:08:24 PM We will MAKE AMERICA SAFE & GREAT AGAIN! #Trump2016 #VoteTrumpSC https://t.co/wG4RgO0pNm https://t.co/3XpJvBZuk5

- Feb 18, 2016 07:11:57 PM Tonight I will be on @FoxNews with @SeanHannity at 10pm and @CNN w/ @AndersonCooper at 10:10pm. Enjoy! #VoteTrumpSC #Trump2016

- Feb 19, 2016 01:09:32 AM "@KathyTravels777: Í @andersoncooper Tonight on CNN @realDonaldTrump was GREAT. Loved the intimacy of conversation w the people"
- Feb 19, 2016 01:52:38 PM Thank you South Carolina! Everyone get out and vote tomorrow! We will #MakeAmericaGreatAgain! https://t.co/Q2qxHINAHo
- Feb 19, 2016 01:56:48 PM A message from @IvankaTrump! #SCPrimary #VoteTrumpSC #MakeAmericaGreatAgain Video: https://t.co/5NZw5Bs6NR https://t.co/KEx85mQxEv
- Feb 19, 2016 03:28:32 PM I was asked about healthcare by Anderson Cooper & have been consistent- I will repeal all of #ObamaCare, including the mandate, period.
- Feb 19, 2016 03:29:01 PM I was referring to a backstop for pre-existing conditions. I will eliminate the law, in its entirety, & replace it w/ something much better.
- Feb 19, 2016 03:29:22 PM I will replace it with private plans, health savings accounts, & allow purchasing across state lines. Maximum choice & freedom for consumer.
- Feb 19, 2016 03:29:43 PM I'm self-funding and I am going to take care of the people – not the special interests and insurance companies like the other candidates.
- Feb 19, 2016 03:30:24 PM Remember, Cruz and Bush gave us Roberts who upheld #ObamaCare twice! I am the only one who will #MAKEAMERICAGREATAGAIN!
- Feb 19, 2016 03:49:02 PM #MakeAmericaGreatAgain #Trump2016 https://t.co/zIn9Zl4Ukx
- Feb 19, 2016 03:49:57 PM #MakeAmericaGreatAgain #Trump2016 https://t.co/6hP6PzPkY5
- Feb 19, 2016 04:00:59 PM I have built so many great & complicated projects– creating tens of thousands of jobs-video: https://t.co/9cqt78cGiT https://t.co/4Q7oJHKoqV
- Feb 19, 2016 04:32:43 PM I use both iPhone & Samsung. If Apple doesn't give info to authorities on the terrorists I'll only be using Samsung until they give info.

- Feb 19, 2016 04:33:04 PM Hopefully others will follow suit. Our country needs & should demand security. It is time to get tough & be smart!
- Feb 19, 2016 04:38:07 PM Boycott all Apple products until such time as Apple gives cellphone info to authorities regarding radical Islamic terrorist couple from Cal
- Feb 19, 2016 04:49:15 PM Just finished two major speeches in South Carolina. Big crowds, great people. Going for a third now!
- Feb 19, 2016 04:51:51 PM MAKE AMERICA GREAT AGAIN!

- Feb 20, 2016 08:18:11 AM "@dnmiller2000: @realDonaldTrump I'm a Regan Dem and believe in your message! God bless you and your campaign!"
- Feb 20, 2016 08:18:54 AM "@rwalkerTennesse: #SouthCarolina If you want a job next January @Vote_For_Trump today. @realDonaldTrump will work for the people."
- Feb 20, 2016 08:59:13 AM Lying #Ted Cruz just (on election day) came out with a sneak and sleazy Robocall. He holds up the Bible but in fact is a true lowlife pol!
- Feb 20, 2016 09:02:25 AM "@Metazip: @AnnCoulter @DavidJMadeira TheTrump phenomenon summed up: "Leadership, Fighter and Winner." Not a Liar https://t.co/rz8BC4n8B5"
- Feb 20, 2016 09:02:59 AM "@TrumpNewMedia: Get out & #VoteTrump if you don't #VoteTrump NOTHING will change it's that simple! #VoteTrump https://t.co/0QUSXERSql"
- Feb 20, 2016 09:04:56 AM "@FamilyRedsFans: @FoxNews is really starting to campaign hard for marcorubio. #fairandbalancedmyass" He is weak on illegal immigration!
- Feb 20, 2016 09:07:42 AM "@ResisTyr: Mr.Trump...BOTH Cruz AND Rubio are ineligible to be POTUS! It's a SLAM DUNK CASE!! Check it! https://t.co/NjqWP0pP6X"
- Feb 20, 2016 10:15:03 AM "@TrumpNewMedia: WHY DOES TED CRUZ LIE SO MUCH? LET'S FACE IT TED NEVER CREATED EVEN 1 JOB HIS ENTIRE LIFE! #WATCH: https://t.co/modgRNn1DJ
- Feb 20, 2016 10:17:17 AM "@Blackan: #SCPrimary @realDonaldTrump is the only one who will protect American interests. #MakeAmericaGreatAgain https://t.co/Hbqjg1fb1t"

- Feb 20, 2016 10:18:07 AM "@BirgitOlsen1: @realDonaldTrump @Justice41ca @Vote_For_Trump EVERYBODY ON TWITTER GET OUT TO VOTE FOR TRUMP TODAY IN SOUTH CAROLINA"
- Feb 20, 2016 10:20:27 AM "@micah_micahk: @realDonaldTrump @blackan @DanScavino this veteran voted for Trump in TX early voting! https://t.co/DTtUvc59NJ"
- Feb 20, 2016 10:31:23 AM I am the only candidate (in many years) who is self-funding his campaign. Lobbyists and $ interests totally control all other candidates!
- Feb 20, 2016 11:19:21 AM "@JoeNBC: Trump expressed concerns months after the Iraq War began, while 60% of Americans still supported the war. https://t.co/YmJBSgPRa7"
- Feb 20, 2016 11:34:53 AM "@Carolyn82471448: @WayneDupreeShow @realDonaldTrump All aboard the Trump Train!"
- Feb 20, 2016 11:42:11 AM I wonder if President Obama would have attended the funeral of Justice Scalia if it were held in a Mosque? Very sad that he did not go!
- Feb 20, 2016 12:02:44 PM Remember that Marco Rubio is very weak on illegal immigration. South Carolina needs strength as illegals and Syrians pour in. Don't allow it
- Feb 20, 2016 12:39:24 PM South Carolina voters have the future of our country in their hands. Vote now (today), and MAKE AMERICA GREAT AGAIN!
- Feb 20, 2016 04:51:11 PM "@CarrollKuykend2: This veteran just voted @realDonaldTrump in the SC primary, let's make America great again!"
- Feb 20, 2016 07:05:57 PM People (pundits) gave me no chance in South Carolina. Now it looks like a possible win. I would be happy with a one vote victory! (HOPE)
- Feb 20, 2016 10:01:10 PM What a great night. Thank you South Carolina, a special place with truly amazing people! LOVE
- Feb 20, 2016 11:57:42 PM "@mikeliberation: This is the best reaction shot I've ever seen lol #Trump2016" https://t.co/jqxI7QoxEY

- Feb 21, 2016 06:09:50 AM Thank you @SarahPalinUSA for your amazing help and support. Big win, leaving now for Atlanta and Nevada.The people of South Carolina got it!

- Feb 21, 2016 06:36:28 AM I will be live on all of the major morning talk shows. Enjoy!
- Feb 21, 2016 06:52:51 AM The failing @WSJ Wall Street Journal should fire both its pollster and its Editorial Board. Seldom has a paper been so wrong.Totally biased!
- Feb 21, 2016 10:57:11 AM A quote was read from a parody account last night on MSNBC re: Jeb. https://t.co/4twxJ4blje
- Feb 21, 2016 11:04:46 AM Thank you South Carolina! https://t.co/U1HoDmuuH3
- Feb 21, 2016 01:55:03 PM RT @BretEastonEllis: Just back from a dinner in West Hollywood: shocked the majority of the table was voting for Trump but they would never…
- Feb 21, 2016 06:58:17 PM RT @EricTrump: Nevada we are on our way! #VoteTrumpNV #Trump2016 Caucus locator: https://t.co/r8ijPnCsmO https://t.co/kNhQcETaTV
- Feb 21, 2016 07:07:49 PM THANK YOU Atlanta, Georgia! Leaving for Nevada now. Lets MAKE AMERICA SAFE AND GREAT AGAIN! https://t.co/wHfraU67yX https://t.co/WqvxMwJk2S

- Feb 22, 2016 07:22:38 AM A number of months ago, I was not expected to win South Carolina,Ted Cruz was, and yet I won in a landslide - every group and category. WIN!
- Feb 22, 2016 07:31:15 AM "@EricTrump: Nevada we are on our way! #VoteTrumpNV #Trump2016 Caucus locator: https://t.co/aUSzSnOzlm https://t.co/bCRelzywxk"
- Feb 22, 2016 07:48:30 AM I am in Las Vegas, at the best hotel (by far), Trump International. I will be working with my wonderful teams and volunteers to WIN Nevada!
- Feb 22, 2016 08:36:39 AM The reason that Ted Cruz lost the Evangelicals in S.C. is because he is a world class LIAR, and Evangelicals do not like liars!
- Feb 22, 2016 08:41:13 AM "@gregusp61: You really rocked them hard in S.C. Rubio and Cruz were pummeled. So glad Jeb is gone! Next no liar!"
- Feb 22, 2016 08:42:06 AM "@1sonny12: @KSmith233035 @mitchellvii FLORIDIANS ARE UPSET BECAUSE RUBIO DID NOT DO WHAT HE PROMISED ONCE HE WAS ELECTED! VOTE TRUMP"

- Feb 22, 2016 09:42:50 AM I hear the Rickets family, who own the Chicago Cubs, are secretly spending $'s against me. They better be careful, they have a lot to hide!
- Feb 22, 2016 09:49:44 AM "@ScotMReed: No matter what liar sleazeball @rickwtyler says about @tedcruz in Tennessee. We have early voting and @realDonaldTrump has won.
- Feb 22, 2016 09:52:16 AM "@SandraR677582: @FLTrumpTeam Florida starts early voting on March 5 extending to March 15. Absentee ballots have been sent out! #Trump2016"
- Feb 22, 2016 11:12:21 AM Many people are now saying I won South Carolina because of the last debate. I showed anger and the people of our country are very angry!
- Feb 22, 2016 01:54:29 PM Thank you for your endorsement @paulteutulsr! #BikersForTrump #VoteTrumpNV Video: https://t.co/1JEdwPPCux https://t.co/56gkQTM7oc
- Feb 22, 2016 03:37:55 PM It is so important to audit The Federal Reserve, and yet Ted Cruz missed the vote on the bill that would allow this to be done.
- Feb 22, 2016 03:44:02 PM Wow, Ted Cruz falsely suggested Marco Rubio mocked the Bible and was just forced to fire his Communications Director. More dirty tricks!
- Feb 22, 2016 03:50:18 PM Ted Cruz has been playing an ad about me that is so ridiculously false - no basis in fact. Take ad down Ted. Biggest liar in politics!
- Feb 22, 2016 03:55:16 PM Ted Cruz has now apologized to Marco Rubio and Ben Carson for fraud and dirty tricks. No wonder he has lost Evangelical support!
- Feb 22, 2016 04:06:25 PM Just saw the phony ad by Cruz - totally false, more dirty tricks. He got caught in so many lies - is this man crazy?
- Feb 22, 2016 04:11:17 PM Ted Cruz should be disqualified from his fraudulent win in Iowa. Weak RNC and Republican leadership probably won't let this happen! Sad.
- Feb 22, 2016 07:19:37 PM I will be on @seanhannity tonight- from Las Vegas, Nevada at 10pmE. Enjoy! #Hannity #Trump2016 https://t.co/mx5rxf4oHl
- Feb 22, 2016 07:41:28 PM RT @DonaldJTrumpJr: Thank you Elko County, Nevada. So much amazing feedback from my forum today I really appreciate it #trump2016 #ICYMI ht…

- Feb 22, 2016 08:24:27 PM Thank you Illinois! Great news! #VoteTrumpIL on 3/15! Trump 28% Cruz 15% Rubio 14% Kasich 13% Bush 8% Carson 6% Simon Poll/SIU
- Feb 22, 2016 08:29:02 PM Just watched the very incompetent Mitt Romney Campaign Strategist, Stuart Stevens. Now I know why Mitt lost so badly. Stevens is a clown!
- Feb 22, 2016 08:29:26 PM WOW! Thank you Massachusetts! See you soon. #VoteTrumpMA https://t.co/mNbDUPrEeh
- Feb 22, 2016 08:34:44 PM Great poll! Thank you North Carolina! #VoteTrumpNC on 3/15! Trump 36% Cruz 18% Rubio 18% Carson 10% Kasich 7% Via @SurveyUSA
- Feb 22, 2016 08:37:52 PM Thank you Michigan! #VoteTrumpMI Trump 35% Kasich 17% Cruz 12% Rubio 12% Carson 9% Via: ARG
- Feb 22, 2016 08:44:02 PM Thank you Vermont! #VoteTrumpVT https://t.co/8KGOpqDb9t
- Feb 22, 2016 09:19:01 PM Great Town Hall tonight at 10:00 P.M. (Eastern) conducted by @seanhannity on @FoxNews
- Feb 22, 2016 09:27:20 PM A big fat hit job on @oreillyfactor tonight. A total waste of time to watch, boring and biased. @brithume said I would never run, a dope!
- Feb 22, 2016 09:31:20 PM Ted Cruz said on @oreillyfactor that illegals sent out of country by my administration would come right back as citizens. Another lie-crazy!
- Feb 22, 2016 10:12:41 PM RT @DonaldJTrumpJr: Nevada: Here is a quick video @IvankaTrump created on "How to Caucus" - very quick and simple! https://t.co/W8ohs9gDvY …
- Feb 22, 2016 10:51:04 PM Join me live- now in Las Vegas, Nevada! We will MAKE AMERICA SAFE & GREAT AGAIN! #VoteTrumpNV #NevadaCaucus https://t.co/IW9s9noxDT

- Feb 23, 2016 12:19:29 AM THANK YOU LAS VEGAS, NEVADA! #NevadaCaucus #VoteTrumpNV https://t.co/cZlNRrFtW3 https://t.co/scdxT24Dye
- Feb 23, 2016 09:37:10 AM Ted Cruz only talks tough on immigration now because he did so badly in S.C. He is in favor of amnesty and weak on illegal immigration.

- Feb 23, 2016 09:40:53 AM Wow was Ted Cruz disloyal to his very capable director of communication. He used him as a scape goat-fired like a dog! Ted panicked.
- Feb 23, 2016 10:07:26 AM Ted Cruz does not have the right "temperment" to be President. Look at the way he totally panicked in firing his director of comm. BAD!
- Feb 23, 2016 10:15:55 AM Ted Cruz lifts the Bible high into the air and then lies like a dog-over and over again! The Evangelicals in S.C. figured him out & said no!
- Feb 23, 2016 10:36:47 AM "@Vogelsong1: @EdRollins gets it. Was just on @FoxNews explaining how Trump wins the general election." Thank you Ed!
- Feb 23, 2016 10:38:24 AM "@jojo2foxy: TRUMP IS UNSTOPPABLE....HE IS WHAT COMMON SENSE AMERICANS WANT WHETHER REPUBLICAN, INDEPENDENT OR A REAGAN DEMOCRAT.
- Feb 23, 2016 10:47:08 AM I am growing the Republican Party tremendously - just look at the numbers, way up! Democrats numbers are significantly down from years past.
- Feb 23, 2016 10:50:00 AM "@StevenMeyers11: @Vogelsong1 @EdRollins @FoxNews Ed Rollins is the only one of those people that understands process & gets it right"
- Feb 23, 2016 11:46:06 AM Join us in Sparks, Nevada today! #NevadaCaucus #VoteTrumpNV https://t.co/5DyhPftng9
- Feb 23, 2016 11:47:13 AM RT @EricTrump: Nevada remember you can "Vote and Go" - walk in vote and walk out! Caucus locator: https://t.co/r8ijPnCsmO #TrumpLV https:/…
- Feb 23, 2016 12:11:30 PM Unlike the other Republican candidates, I will be in Nevada all day and night - I won't be fleeing, in and out. I love & invest in Nevada!
- Feb 23, 2016 12:16:42 PM Wow, great Ohio poll. Shows me leading by 5 points, beating K!
- Feb 23, 2016 01:12:51 PM Great. Just reported on @FoxNews that many people who supported @JebBush are now supporting me. I knew that would happen, pundits didn't!
- Feb 23, 2016 06:08:48 PM Club for Growth is the group that came to my office seeking $1 million dollars. I told them no and now they are doing negative ads.

- Feb 23, 2016 06:14:16 PM Thank you Sparks, Nevada! #VoteTrumpNV #NevadaCaucus Finder: https://t.co/Ryp3DwNe0u https://t.co/n74lmDoRQO https://t.co/sO5h9LmIMg
- Feb 23, 2016 08:45:21 PM My wife Melania will be on @Morning_Joe tomorrow morning at 8:00. Interviewed by @morningmika - Enjoy!
- Feb 23, 2016 08:52:12 PM RT @EricTrump: Very proud of what my father has accomplished in the past 7 months -Wishing him amazing luck and success tonight! #NVcaucus …
- Feb 23, 2016 08:52:32 PM GO VOTE FROM NOW TO 8:30 P.M. NEVADA. I WILL BE AT VARIOUS CAUCUS SITES. MAKE AMERICA GREAT AGAIN!
- Feb 23, 2016 08:56:15 PM Exclusive interview w/ my wife @MELANIATRUMP- tomorrow morning @ 8amE on @Morning_Joe w/ @morningmika @MSNBC. Enjoy! https://t.co/FQSEKWxnwj
- Feb 23, 2016 08:59:59 PM RT @TrumpNV: #NVcaucus locator -> https://t.co/WIzgQcbvOB
- Feb 23, 2016 09:00:18 PM Make sure you get on the Trump line and are not mislead by the Cruz people. They are bad! BE CAREFUL.

- Feb 24, 2016 12:41:02 AM THANK YOU NEVADA! WE WILL MAKE AMERICA SAFE & GREAT AGAIN! https://t.co/ClAnLIg0AD https://t.co/zVvyVCIaD4
- Feb 24, 2016 01:25:53 AM THANK YOU NEVADA! #Trump2016 #MakeAmericaGreatAgain @Snapchat! Username: realdonaldtrump https://t.co/e0HX1zekX8 https://t.co/uVBGpXzICo
- Feb 24, 2016 08:24:58 AM Melania will be interviewed by @morningmika on @Morning_Joe now (8:30 A.M.). ENJOY!
- Feb 24, 2016 10:43:13 AM @MELANIATRUMP did great on television this morning. Poised, smart and strong, with a big heart - so much to offer. We are all proud of you!
- Feb 24, 2016 11:09:46 AM Big defeat last night in Nevada for Ted Cruz and Marco Rubio. @KarlRove on @FoxNews is working hard to belittle my victory. Rove is sick!
- Feb 24, 2016 11:12:50 AM .@USATODAY Poll and @QuinnipiacPoll say that I beat both Hillary and Bernie, and I havn't even started on them yet!

- Feb 24, 2016 12:03:43 PM I am self funding my campaign & don't owe anybody anything! I only owe it to the American people! #Trump2016 Watch: https://t.co/fUzX92RYIm
- Feb 24, 2016 12:14:20 PM I am in Virginia @RegentU Presidential forum with Dr. Pat Robertson- beginning now! Watch here: https://t.co/LgucYLxFgG
- Feb 24, 2016 01:27:44 PM In all of television- the only one who said anything bad about last nights landslide victory-- was dopey @KarlRove. He should be fired!
- Feb 24, 2016 01:31:36 PM MAKE AMERICA GREAT AGAIN! https://t.co/IVSR0hmh5g
- Feb 24, 2016 04:36:35 PM The polls show that I picked up many Jeb Bush supporters. That is how I got to 46%. When others drop out, I will pick up more. Sad but true
- Feb 24, 2016 06:13:15 PM Mitt Romney,who totally blew an election that should have been won and whose tax returns made him look like a fool, is now playing tough guy
- Feb 24, 2016 06:14:39 PM "@Ward_II: Oh great @MittRomney is doing a @SenatorReid on @realDonaldTrump like losing the presidency wasn't enough #Trump2016" He's a fool
- Feb 24, 2016 06:26:19 PM When Mitt Romney asked me for my endorsement last time around, he was so awkward and goofy that we all should have known he could not win!
- Feb 24, 2016 06:45:06 PM Why would Texans vote for "liar" Ted Cruz when he was born in Canada, lived there for 4 years-and remained a Canadian citizen until recently
- Feb 24, 2016 06:49:15 PM When Ted Cruz quits the race and the field begins to clear, I will get most of his votes - no problem!
- Feb 24, 2016 08:08:05 PM .@RepChrisCollins Chris, thank you so much for your wonderful endorsement. I will not let you down! @CNN
- Feb 24, 2016 08:11:02 PM "@ddpick18: @realDonaldTrump This Texan will be voting Trump March 1st. Cruz is a fake Texan!"
- Feb 24, 2016 08:36:01 PM "@GriceCindy: That's why we are angry. The Republican Establishment will not support you. You are who the American people want!"

- Feb 24, 2016 08:47:30 PM Texas, Georgia & many more VOTE EARLY! This is a movement! #Trump2016 VOTE VIDEO: https://t.co/LWeckhLWNv https://t.co/o93j0A0BIR
- Feb 24, 2016 09:20:19 PM Ted Cruz is lying again. Polls are showing that I do beat Hillary Clinton head to head. Check out https://t.co/45g7qpxq7T Poll snd Q Poll.
- Feb 24, 2016 09:21:38 PM "@ahernandez85a: @realdonaldtrump Mr Tough Guy Romney should be backing Trump like Trump backed him last time #NoLoyalty"
- Feb 24, 2016 09:22:54 PM "@HosierN: @foxnewspolitics A vote for @tedcruz or @marcorubio is a vote for corruption, special interests and lobbyists. Trump for POTUS!
- Feb 24, 2016 09:24:34 PM "@Ausbiz: @realDonaldTrump Trump is so impressive and no other politician has his passion & energy to #MakeAmericaGreatAgain
- Feb 24, 2016 09:25:50 PM "@Stevekwebb: @realDonaldTrump Love it! @tedcruz is done. We need someone who is proven. @realDonaldTrump will make America Great Again"
- Feb 24, 2016 09:43:42 PM "@conservativevin: @ahernandez85a Romney should have been a tough guy with Obama. He cowered and lost. BADLY! He's not relevant!"
- Feb 24, 2016 09:51:16 PM "@classyexplorer: @ahernandez85a Romney is a pawn of the Establishment and has no individual thought process. He is jealous of Trump!"
- Feb 24, 2016 10:34:39 PM "@ChatteringTeef: @BornToBeGOP @realDonaldTrump @MittRomney hates to see Trump's success when he was so pathetic
- Feb 24, 2016 11:07:19 PM Great new poll. Thank you Texas! #VoteTrump #MakeAmericaGreatAgain https://t.co/VHqAvsIyuW

- Feb 25, 2016 07:34:11 AM Mitt Romney, who was one of the dumbest and worst candidates in the history of Republican politics, is now pushing me on tax returns. Dope!
- Feb 25, 2016 11:05:01 AM Why doesn't @MittRomney just endorse @marcorubio already. Should have done it before NH or Nevada where he had a little sway. Too late now!

- Feb 25, 2016 11:22:44 AM Just for your info, tax returns have 0 to do w/ someone's net worth. I have already filed my financial statements w/ FEC. They are great!
- Feb 25, 2016 11:35:12 AM Signing a recent tax return- isn't this ridiculous? https://t.co/UdwqF4iZIZ
- Feb 25, 2016 11:41:37 AM LETS MAKE AMERICA GREAT AGAIN! Schedule & tickets: https://t.co/nU39QHzxxX https://t.co/GUQo1TMsMo
- Feb 25, 2016 11:44:52 AM I'm going to do what @MittRomney was totally unable to do- WIN!
- Feb 25, 2016 12:41:26 PM Join me in Oklahoma tomorrow night! #MakeYoutubeGreatAgain #Trump2016 https://t.co/sUTcDoip3C
- Feb 25, 2016 12:49:48 PM Thank you Illinois! #Trump2016 https://t.co/Ol0u2Krkwc
- Feb 25, 2016 01:58:03 PM Early on Ted Cruz said that if he didn't win South Carolina, it's over. He didn't win- and lost to me in a landslide!
- Feb 25, 2016 03:27:15 PM FMR PRES of Mexico, Vicente Fox horribly used the F word when discussing the wall. He must apologize! If I did that there would be a uproar!
- Feb 25, 2016 05:16:26 PM THANK YOU! #MakeAmericaGreatAgain #Trump2016 https://t.co/nvgOPoo5qf https://t.co/0JCjfbcpJZ

- Feb 26, 2016 12:40:07 AM Failed presidential candidate @MittRomney was made to look like a fool by Senator Harry Reid & didn't release his tax returns until 9/21/12.
- Feb 26, 2016 12:53:13 AM Thank you! WE WILL MAKE AMERICA GREAT AGAIN! #Trump2016 https://t.co/aht7wYVIUg
- Feb 26, 2016 01:08:56 AM #MakeAmericaGreatAgain! https://t.co/in4raBhwqa
- Feb 26, 2016 01:49:51 AM Thank you! #GOPDebate Polls #MakeAmericaGreatAgain https://t.co/At5vOiLCSy
- Feb 26, 2016 01:52:24 AM #MakeAmericaGreatAgain #Trump2016 https://t.co/FvIUXMkrjj
- Feb 26, 2016 01:54:44 AM All the online polls have me winning the debate. I really enjoyed the evening. Not easy, but good. https://t.co/sLTmwVVM5I

- Feb 26, 2016 01:55:35 AM Big day in Texas tomorrow! Having a rally in Fort Worth. Tremendous crowd. Will be exciting! #Trump2016 https://t.co/JGUopujRIk
- Feb 26, 2016 02:33:59 AM "@morg25016893: @eventbrite Also, all the things Rubio&Cruz were using for hits, just petty. Trump, clearly the only one w/all the skills."
- Feb 26, 2016 02:34:58 AM "@Indies4Trump: Vote Early in the #LoneStarState #SuperTuesday @realDonaldTrump will #MakeAmericaGreatAgain https://t.co/GC8kmWFxoM"
- Feb 26, 2016 02:38:29 AM "@Slytle24: @davidaxelrod @realDonaldTrump @CNN he won almost all polls and Mark Halperin gave him an A-
- Feb 26, 2016 07:25:39 AM "@restorereality: Tonight you proved to America you are the real deal. You took fire from all sides, stayed composed, returned fire and WON!
- Feb 26, 2016 07:27:33 AM "@SkylerDeckard: @realDonaldTrump "that's because you've never hired anyone to do work before" favorite line from tonights debate."
- Feb 26, 2016 07:28:58 AM "@tdltdltdltdl: Marco Cruz and Ted Rubio (easy to get the two politicians confused) looked like desperate, panicked DC insiders tonight"
- Feb 26, 2016 07:29:42 AM "@donell27743094: @realDonaldTrump trump won the debate. Disgusting Rubio said "peed" - is he still in junior high school."
- Feb 26, 2016 07:29:59 AM "@MJP1370: @realDonaldTrump Cruz talks about Hillary all the time because he knows he can't beat you ! Trump will win Texas !"
- Feb 26, 2016 07:30:24 AM "@WaltSeher: @realDonaldTrump @morg25016893 @eventbrite yup 200 Polish immigrants were hired by his contractor not Trump"
- Feb 26, 2016 08:56:30 AM I will be making a speech at 12:00 in Fort Worth, Texas. Really big crowd expected. Will be talking about the debate last night- plus, plus!
- Feb 26, 2016 09:02:29 AM Have a good chance to win Texas on Tuesday. Cruz is a nasty guy, not one Senate endorsement and, despite talk, gets nothing done. Loser!
- Feb 26, 2016 09:49:40 AM Why would the people of Florida vote for Marco Rubio when he defrauded them by agreeing to represent them as their Senator and then quit!

- Feb 26, 2016 11:07:56 AM Will be at Fort Worth (Texas) Convention Center at 11:30 A.M. Big crowd - get there early! Big announcement to be made!
- Feb 26, 2016 11:15:06 AM Lying Ted Cruz and lightweight choker Marco Rubio teamed up last night in a last ditch effort to stop our great movement. They failed!
- Feb 26, 2016 11:16:14 AM Lightweight choker Marco Rubio looks like a little boy on stage. Not presidential material!
- Feb 26, 2016 11:17:29 AM Wow, every poll said I won the debate last night. Great honor!
- Feb 26, 2016 11:38:36 AM Lightweight Marco Rubio was working hard last night. The problem is, he is a choker, and once a choker, always a choker! Mr. Meltdown.
- Feb 26, 2016 03:52:02 PM They don't like Rubio in Florida- he left them high & dry. Doesn't even show up for votes!
- Feb 26, 2016 04:07:16 PM Thank you for your support & friendship- Governor @ChrisChristie! #MakeAmericaGreatAgain #Trump2016 https://t.co/jVI6Q6JH18
- Feb 26, 2016 04:11:30 PM Never let them see you sweat! https://t.co/qygVFf6JFF
- Feb 26, 2016 04:34:21 PM Thank you Texas! 10,000 amazing supporters! #Trump2016 #MakeAmericaGreatAgain https://t.co/T2cBdktPbp
- Feb 26, 2016 09:08:18 PM What I would do on my first day in office. #MakeAmericaGreatAgain Watch: https://t.co/DhANDG8uBd https://t.co/SzdZzYOnDG
- Feb 26, 2016 10:08:53 PM "@donnieboysmith: @realDonaldTrump in contrast to Rubio and Cruz you look like a giant. They look terribly weak" Thank you!
- Feb 26, 2016 11:53:34 PM "@itsblakec: @realDonaldTrump Trump is a genius. Rubio and Cruz are not. I want a brilliant mind to run this country."
- Feb 26, 2016 11:58:32 PM "@JerryJrFalwell: A majority of evangelicals believe @realDonaldTrump is best equipped to save the country. #Greta"

- Feb 27, 2016 12:06:27 AM Thank you Pastor Robert Jeffress! #MakeAmericaGreatAgain #Trump2016 https://t.co/ndKu8m8RY2
- Feb 27, 2016 07:47:25 AM "@SassyPantsjj: Michigan GOP poll 2/24/2016 Trump 35.5 Rubio 15.0 Cruz 14.3 Kasich 12.8 Carson 8.3 @realDonaldTrump" Wow!

- Feb 27, 2016 08:08:21 AM I will be on @foxandfriends at 8:30 A.M. Will be talking about lightweight Marco Rubio and lying Ted Cruz!
- Feb 27, 2016 09:30:42 AM RT @EricTrump: Friends: If you live in AL, AK, AR, CO, GA, MA, MN, OK, TN, TX, VT or VA, get out and VOTE on Tuesday! #Trump2016 https://t.…
- Feb 27, 2016 10:05:16 AM "@NeilTurner_: @realDonaldTrump There's only one real candidate, and it's you! Donors control the other candidates! #VoteTrump" Thank you.
- Feb 27, 2016 10:12:47 AM I unfairly get audited by the I.R.S. almost every single year. I have rich friends who never get audited. I wonder why?
- Feb 27, 2016 10:20:33 AM Tax experts throughout the media agree that no sane person would give their tax returns during an audit. After the audit, no problem!
- Feb 27, 2016 10:25:07 AM I am self-funding my campaign and am therefore not controlled by the lobbyists and special interests like lightweight Rubio or Ted Cruz!
- Feb 27, 2016 10:49:52 AM Fun to watch the Democrats working so hard to win the great State of South Carolina when I just won the Republican version - amazing people!
- Feb 27, 2016 11:04:35 AM I only wish my wonderful father, Fred, gave me $200 million to start my business like lightweight Rubio says. He didn't - total fabrication!
- Feb 27, 2016 11:08:40 AM I started my business with very little and built it into a great company, with some of the best real estate assets in the World. Amazing!
- Feb 27, 2016 12:11:35 PM .#RogerStone was just banned by @CNN - their loss! Tough, loyal guy.
- Feb 27, 2016 04:20:48 PM Just watched lightweight Marco Rubio lying to a small crowd about my past record. He is not as smart as Cruz, and may be an even bigger liar
- Feb 27, 2016 05:40:07 PM It was an honor to be the Grand Marshall- in the Salute to Israel Parade back in 2004. https://t.co/G7G6HFP0Dh
- Feb 27, 2016 05:57:20 PM Incredibly proud of my son @EricTrump & his efforts on behalf of @StJude in Memphis, TN. https://t.co/FUWhYKhhNK https://t.co/ZgxukBnQ3k

- Feb 27, 2016 09:13:27 PM THANK YOU Arkansas! Get out & #VoteTrump on Tuesday. We will MAKE AMERICA SAFE & GREAT AGAIN! https://t.co/evoiSpn8PX
- Feb 27, 2016 10:02:08 PM We need to fix our broken education system! #StopCommonCore #MakeAmericaGreatAgain Video: https://t.co/xZ1eCJPo8T https://t.co/S8gQ6cibhC

- Feb 28, 2016 05:23:47 AM "@RonnieMemo: DonaldTrump is a leader. He is a successful person that, like me, isn't afraid to tell it like it is." Governor @ChrisChristie
- Feb 28, 2016 05:49:02 AM "@tiarardis: @FoxNews @realDonaldTrump @JudgeJeanine GO TRUMP"
- Feb 28, 2016 05:54:11 AM "@sprivitor @realDonaldTrump Marco 'Amnesty' Rubio is the front man of Amnesty. https://t.co/D4zXazzbq8 #AlwaysTrump #Trump2016 #TrumpTrain
- Feb 28, 2016 05:55:43 AM "@fairess369: It is a sad commentary little boy Marco Rubio can't win in his home state. Floridians despise him as a opportunist phony."
- Feb 28, 2016 05:56:19 AM "@JimmyTheSaint09: @realDonaldTrump @RonnieMemo @ChrisChristie anything is better than @marcorubio"
- Feb 28, 2016 06:13:09 AM "@ilduce2016: "It is better to live one day as a lion than 100 years as a sheep." – @realDonaldTrump #MakeAmericaGreatAgain"
- Feb 28, 2016 06:15:10 AM "@CharlesHodgson1: A lot more water after this bombshell, Rubio. You are an enemy of America. @realDonaldTrump https://t.co/TnEnxt5NTDG"
- Feb 28, 2016 06:28:47 AM While I hear the Koch brothers are in big financial trouble (oil), word is they have chosen little Marco Rubio, the lightweight from Florida
- Feb 28, 2016 07:10:36 AM The Republican Establishment has been pushing for lightweight Senator Marco Rubio to say anything to "hit" Trump.I signed the pledge-careful
- Feb 28, 2016 07:20:19 AM While Hillary and I both won South Carolina by big margins, Repubs got far more votes with a massive increase from past cycles.GROWING PARTY

- Feb 28, 2016 07:43:28 AM I am the only Republican who will get large numbers of Dems and Indies (crossover). I will also get states that no other Republican can get.
- Feb 28, 2016 07:58:01 AM Making a big speech in Alabama today. So many people we had to move to a football stadium! Come and join us!
- Feb 28, 2016 11:07:48 AM Little Marco Rubio, the lightweight no show Senator from Florida, is set to be the "puppet" of the special interest Koch brothers. WATCH!
- Feb 28, 2016 11:12:36 AM #MakeAmericaGreatAgain #Trump2016 https://t.co/yFhZd55GD9
- Feb 28, 2016 11:47:13 AM Why would the people of Texas support Ted Cruz when he has accomplished absolutely nothing for them. He is another all talk, no action pol!
- Feb 28, 2016 12:35:29 PM As I stated at the press conference on Friday regarding David Duke- I disavow. https://t.co/OIXFKPUlz2
- Feb 28, 2016 12:47:56 PM Mitt Romney didn't show his tax return until SEPTEMBER 21, 2012, and then only after being humiliated by Harry R! A bad messenger for estab!
- Feb 28, 2016 12:50:23 PM Little Marco Rubio, the lightweight no show Senator from Florida is just another Washington politician. https://t.co/NsLrHrqjdx
- Feb 28, 2016 12:53:29 PM Lightweight Senator Marco Rubio is polling very poorly in Florida. The people can't stand him for missing so many votes - poor work ethic!
- Feb 28, 2016 12:57:36 PM "@EmaGabi23: Rubio was kicking back on his $80k boat he bought with lobbyist money and claimed it was from book sale profit lol"
- Feb 28, 2016 01:45:35 PM Little Marco Rubio is just another Washington D.C. politician that is all talk and no action. #RobotRubio https://t.co/HJWJeoZn4o
- Feb 28, 2016 02:06:17 PM Little Marco Rubio gave amnesty to criminal aliens guilty of "sex offenses." DISGRACE! https://t.co/mZwpynzsLb
- Feb 28, 2016 02:19:11 PM Little Marco Rubio treated America's ICE officers "like absolute trash" in order to pass Obama's amnesty. https://t.co/gm2wurLjFz
- Feb 28, 2016 02:32:27 PM Phylis Schlafly: 'Marco Rubio Betrayed Us All' https://t.co/nmXmLDQuaa

- Feb 28, 2016 04:56:49 PM I will be making a big surprise announcement to the massive crowd assembled in Huntsville/Madison Alabama! Landing now! #Trump2016
- Feb 28, 2016 05:02:55 PM Our law enforcement officers deserve our appreciation for the incredible job they do. Video: https://t.co/c4WjtoGpKT https://t.co/Z0XnapOu84
- Feb 28, 2016 07:25:14 PM THANK YOU ALABAMA! 32,000 supporters tonight. Get out & VOTE on Tuesday! WE WILL MAKE AMERICA GREAT AGAIN! https://t.co/rOkldN7dat
- Feb 28, 2016 08:09:46 PM Thank you @SenatorSessions! #MakeAmericaGreatAgain #Trump2016 https://t.co/Szs0QF88HR https://t.co/UL6t60TTjP

- Feb 29, 2016 07:36:08 AM My sons, Don and Eric, are on @foxandfriends now 7:35. Great kids, enjoy!
- Feb 29, 2016 07:43:13 AM Thank you America! Get out & VOTE tomorrow! #Trump2016 #MakeAmericaGreatAgain https://t.co/ypLELkprpu https://t.co/XKU8R5b8Lo
- Feb 29, 2016 09:28:43 AM Join me in Columbus, Ohio tomorrow! #MakeAmericaGreatAgain #Trump2016 https://t.co/yFhZd55GD9
- Feb 29, 2016 10:17:37 AM "Hillary could lose to Trump in Democratic New York" #MakeAmericaGreatAgain #Trump2016 https://t.co/fQR48CVIbt
- Feb 29, 2016 10:49:03 AM I am self funding my campaign and only work for YOU, the American people! #Trump2016 Video: https://t.co/8hDC0YUobe https://t.co/o0EB479uEF
- Feb 29, 2016 11:16:27 AM #Trump2016 #TrumpInstagram: https://t.co/tzHtny48nQ https://t.co/BpKZcISeKi
- Feb 29, 2016 11:29:11 AM Governor Alejandro García Padilla said presidential hopeful Sen. Marco Rubio "is no friend of Puerto Rico." https://t.co/I6mhYnAcZ3
- Feb 29, 2016 01:57:13 PM My wife @MELANIATRUMP will be joining @andersoncooper @AC360 tonight at 8pmE on @CNN. Enjoy! https://t.co/aTIXHgK32N
- Feb 29, 2016 02:46:58 PM Thank you Virginia! 15,000 amazing supporters! Everyone get out and #VoteTrump tomorrow! https://t.co/Zg0OhOdtkV
- Feb 29, 2016 05:48:15 PM Trump University has a 98% approval rating. I could have settled but won't out of principle!

- Feb 29, 2016 05:59:29 PM Phony Rubio commercial. I could have settled, but won't out of principle! See student surveys. https://t.co/KKHiBH554d
- Feb 29, 2016 07:39:29 PM Thank you Brian France, Bill Elliott, @chaseelliott, @DavidRagan, & @RyanJNewman! #NASCAR #Trump2016 #VoteTrump https://t.co/6UDcvm1GB2
- Feb 29, 2016 08:40:13 PM Great news- Former Mayor of Dallas, Tom Leppert, has just endorsed me! Thank you! Tomorrow is a big day- VOTE! #VoteTrump #SuperTuesday
- Feb 29, 2016 08:43:56 PM Thank you Georgia! 15,000 amazing supporters tonight! Everyone get out & #VoteTrump tomorrow! #SuperTuesday https://t.co/jNA5YON6hA

March, 2016

- Mar 1, 2016 06:15:32 AM Got the endorsement of Brian France and @NASCAR yesterday in Georgia. Also, many of the sports great drivers. Thank you Nascar and Georgia!
- Mar 1, 2016 02:14:43 PM RT @DanScavino: .@NikkiHaley in 2012 w/ Romney on tax returns (political ploy.) Fast forward..2016 w/ Robot Rubio #FAIL#Politician https:…
- Mar 1, 2016 02:14:57 PM RT @CLewandowski_: Gov Nikki Haley just became a liability for Rubio after this was published to social media! https://t.co/NBvl6bs223
- Mar 1, 2016 02:33:20 PM The people of South Carolina are embarrassed by Nikki Haley!
- Mar 1, 2016 02:34:01 PM Thank you Columbus, Ohio! https://t.co/D0tok8j6jj
- Mar 1, 2016 02:51:50 PM RT @EricTrump: Who has voted today??? Feedback from the polls? I'm like a kid on Christmas! #SuperTuesday #MakeAmericaGreatAgain https://t.…

- Mar 1, 2016 02:52:30 PM MAKE AMERICA GREAT AGAIN!
- Mar 1, 2016 03:43:24 PM Lets go America! Get out & #VoteTrump! #Trump2016 #MakeAmericaGreatAgain! #SuperTuesday https://t.co/w0eAglHeh8 https://t.co/rGanPzZHmS
- Mar 1, 2016 05:18:29 PM Wow! Thank you Louisville, Kentucky! #VoteTrump on 3/5/2016! Lets #MakeAmericaGreatAgain! https://t.co/frO6s3NKpp https://t.co/xFwWRrro3l
- Mar 1, 2016 07:01:21 PM Thank you Georgia! #SuperTuesday #Trump2016
- Mar 1, 2016 08:01:49 PM Thank you Massachusetts! #Trump2016 #SuperTuesday
- Mar 1, 2016 08:02:09 PM Thank you Tennessee! #Trump2016 #SuperTuesday
- Mar 1, 2016 08:02:19 PM Thank you Alabama! #Trump2016 #SuperTuesday
- Mar 1, 2016 08:49:51 PM Thank you Virginia! #Trump2016 #SuperTuesday
- Mar 1, 2016 11:05:52 PM Thank you Arkansas! #Trump2016 #SuperTuesday

- Mar 2, 2016 12:06:00 AM Thank you Vermont! #Trump2016 #SuperTuesday
- Mar 2, 2016 07:16:08 AM "@danpfeiffer: For the record, most Democrats would much rather face Cruz than Trump" So true!
- Mar 2, 2016 07:22:39 AM "@mikiebarb: "A nearly impossible path to the GOP nomination" for Rubio, says @apalmerdc: https://t.co/zCTpSAjPvc …"
- Mar 2, 2016 07:23:02 AM "@NorahODonnell: Looks like Rubio won't get any delegates from TX or AL because he didn't meet 20% threshold."
- Mar 2, 2016 07:23:13 AM "@JoeNBC: Marco Rubio just criticized Ted Cruz for underperforming tonight. Wow. #SuperTuesday"
- Mar 2, 2016 07:25:10 AM "@JoeNBC: FOX calls Virginia for Trump. If it holds, it's a big win for Trump and a big setback for Rubio, who needed to win the state.
- Mar 2, 2016 12:53:38 PM The special interests and people who control our politicians (puppets) are spending $25 million on misleading and fraudulent T.V. ads on me.
- Mar 2, 2016 01:11:23 PM Why would anyone in Florida vote for lightweight Senator Marco Rubio. Check out his credit card scam, his house sale & his no show voting!
- Mar 2, 2016 01:18:37 PM Marco Rubio lost big last night. I even beat him in Virginia, where he spent so much time and money. Now his bosses are desperate and angry!

- Mar 2, 2016 01:48:33 PM "@KinnardJan: @Itsjoeco @realDonaldTrump I took Trump University class and saved my home!"
- Mar 2, 2016 02:54:30 PM My wife @MELANIATRUMP will be #OnTheRecord w/ @greta tonight at 7pmE on @FoxNews. Enjoy! https://t.co/yxrRkJJSGG https://t.co/Trv1hj9hRI
- Mar 2, 2016 04:50:30 PM Why can't the leaders of the Republican Party see that I am bringing in new voters by the millions-we are creating a larger, stronger party!
- Mar 2, 2016 04:56:53 PM "@HavBat22: @TeamCavuto #KenLangone is 100% correct #NeilCavuto. And u and the rest of u #Fox muppets refuse to HEAR HIM." So true!
- Mar 2, 2016 06:18:54 PM .@CNN poll just hit 49% for Trump. Interesting how my numbers have gone so far up since lightweight Marco Rubio has turned nasty. Love it!
- Mar 2, 2016 06:29:28 PM I am going to repeal and replace ObamaCare! Read more about my positions on healthcare reform here: https://t.co/WwIVhIud06
- Mar 2, 2016 06:34:04 PM Failed Presidential Candidate Mitt Romney is having a news conference tomorrow to criticize me. (1/2)
- Mar 2, 2016 06:34:13 PM Just another desperate move by the man who should have easily beaten Barrack Obama. (2/2)
- Mar 2, 2016 06:54:31 PM I would love to see the Republican party and everyone get together- and unify. Video: https://t.co/RWEnPUJO23 https://t.co/RT8Gmf6WHL
- Mar 2, 2016 09:08:02 PM #MakeAmericaGreatAgain #Trump2016 Video: https://t.co/IbcE5tsRf7 https://t.co/bHqg1rkFy3
- Mar 2, 2016 10:05:35 PM Because of me, the Republican Party has taken in millions of new voters, a record. If they are not careful, they will all leave. Sad!
- Mar 2, 2016 10:11:35 PM "@Johnsmi01433966: The establishment doesn't like you because they can't control you and get you to lie to us and keep ripping us off."
- Mar 2, 2016 10:18:30 PM Millions of dollars being spent on false TV ads by special interest groups who own Rubio & Cruz.When you see them think of your puppet POLS
- Mar 2, 2016 10:33:07 PM Looks like two-time failed candidate Mitt Romney is going to be telling Republicans how to get elected. Not a good messenger!

- Mar 2, 2016 10:38:29 PM "@malski1954: I changed parties to vote for you, no one else measures up to you, The GOPe needs a reality check. Our country is at stake"

- Mar 3, 2016 06:22:32 AM Failed candidate Mitt Romney,who ran one of the worst races in presidential history,is working with the establishment to bury a big "R" win!
- Mar 3, 2016 06:30:35 AM I have brought millions of people into the Republican Party, while the Dems are going down. Establishment wants to kill this movement!
- Mar 3, 2016 06:40:17 AM Why would the great people of Florida vote for a guy who, as a Senator, never even shows up to vote - worst record. Marco Rubio is a joke!
- Mar 3, 2016 06:47:21 AM I am the only one who can beat Hillary Clinton. I am not a Mitt Romney, who doesn't know how to win. Hillary wants no part of "Trump"
- Mar 3, 2016 06:59:47 AM Why did Mitt Romney BEG me for my endorsement four years ago?
- Mar 3, 2016 09:17:45 AM RT @rupertmurdoch: As predicted, Trump reaching out to make peace with Republican "establishment". If he becomes inevitable party would be…
- Mar 3, 2016 09:21:14 AM The phony lawsuit against Trump U could have been easily settled by me but I want to go to court. 98% approval rating by students. Easy win
- Mar 3, 2016 09:26:15 AM "@CreativeXwalk: @realDonaldTrump teaching the GOP how to lose four years ago was not enough. Now Romney wants to do it again."
- Mar 3, 2016 09:27:12 AM "@blt21muttrades: People are just mad that you're doing so good so they are gonna do they're best to stop you. Not gonna happen #MAGA"
- Mar 3, 2016 10:23:09 AM Go to Trump Doral in Miami and watch the World Golf Championship! On NOW!
- Mar 3, 2016 10:51:29 AM Will miss @RealBenCarson tonight at the #GOPDebate. I hope all of Ben's followers will join the #TrumpTrain. We will never forget.

- Mar 3, 2016 11:09:34 AM On my way to see the great people of Maine. Will be landing in Portland in 2 hours. Look forward to it! #Trump2016
- Mar 3, 2016 03:14:34 PM THANK YOU PORTLAND, Maine! #MakeAmericaGreatAgain #Trump2016 https://t.co/6lMFR6z8xO https://t.co/eKGxNbG6wD
- Mar 3, 2016 08:20:00 PM Senator Sessions will serve as the Chairman of my National Security Advisory Committee. https://t.co/jQed1P6SD9 https://t.co/n83Cbs4jtA
- Mar 3, 2016 08:29:17 PM Rubio puts out ad that my pilot was a drug dealer- not true, not my pilot! Guy owned helicopter company- don't think I ever even used.
- Mar 3, 2016 11:30:45 PM The Better Business Bureau report, with an A rating for Trump University. #GOPDebate https://t.co/ldJ5EFp3HM https://t.co/1K9u09CFQQ

- Mar 4, 2016 12:24:18 AM MY POSITION ON VISAS #MakeAmericaGreatAgain #Trump2016 https://t.co/JGmOd5gr5z https://t.co/OLg6N3Ug9U
- Mar 4, 2016 07:13:00 AM Thank you America! #Trump2016 https://t.co/fNMPlXpkFf https://t.co/W1biUNTvFk
- Mar 4, 2016 07:27:21 AM "@AngieSteinberg: GET THAT POS WSJ LIAR FANTASY PUNDIT @marykissel OFF THE AIR. Blah blah. A real dummy! @Morning_Joe @realDonaldTrump
- Mar 4, 2016 07:29:12 AM "@SirHatchporch: Mary Kissel is an SNL character, right? She's not a real person, right? #MorningJoe" She is a major loser - no clue!
- Mar 4, 2016 11:35:25 AM Thank you Macomb County, Michigan! #MakeAmericaGreatAgain #Trump2016 https://t.co/9TBvy6obcE
- Mar 4, 2016 12:36:03 PM U.S. Senator Bob Corker (R-Tenn.) issued the following statement today regarding the 2016 presidential election: https://t.co/79y1KgC7S4
- Mar 4, 2016 01:24:25 PM #VoteTrumpKS #Trump2016 March 5, 2016 | Wichita, Kansas: https://t.co/BkvBzvsJ12 https://t.co/Q8eZU9yi6W
- Mar 4, 2016 04:03:34 PM Thank you Cadillac, Michigan! #VoteTrumpMI on 3/8/2016. We will MAKE AMERICA GREAT AGAIN! https://t.co/8RDmQCbHce https://t.co/94mFPx0EgH

- Mar 4, 2016 04:54:49 PM Join me in Wichita, Kansas tomorrow morning! Looking forward to it! #MakeAmericaGreatAgain #Trump2016 https://t.co/HtVKgLvlAZ
- Mar 4, 2016 06:51:37 PM RT @EricTrump: Friends: Remember to VOTE tomorrow if you live in Louisiana, Maine, Kentucky or Kansas! USUS #MakeAmericaGreatAgain https://…
- Mar 4, 2016 09:41:15 PM Thank you New Orleans, Louisiana! #MakeAmericaGreatAgain #VoteTrump https://t.co/tI1h9xT9GX https://t.co/0bf7BOlWEj
- Mar 4, 2016 10:49:17 PM Join me in Wichita, Kansas tomorrow morning! Looking forward to it! #MakeAmericaGreatAgain #Trump2016 https://t.co/HtVKgLdKcp

- Mar 5, 2016 08:11:17 AM I am in Kansas. Will be an exciting day. Big speech this morning in Wichita, and then go to caucus. Sorry CPAC (the format was fine!).
- Mar 5, 2016 08:14:05 AM Great time last night in Louisiana. Big and energetic crowd. Go out and vote now, polls open. MAKE AMERICA GREAT AGAIN!
- Mar 5, 2016 08:22:18 AM For all of today's voters please remember that I am the only candidate that is self funding my campaign, I am not bought and paid for!
- Mar 5, 2016 09:09:05 AM Wow, big lines in Kansas.
- Mar 5, 2016 09:39:43 AM Will be in Orlando, Florida, this afternoon. 25,000 people expected. This is a movement like our GREAT COUNTRY has never seen before!
- Mar 5, 2016 11:10:05 AM Why would anyone in Kentucky listen to failed presidential candidate Rand Paul re: caucus. Made a fool of himself (1%.) KY his 2nd choice!
- Mar 5, 2016 11:12:43 AM To the people of Kentucky, Rand Paul didn't want you. Now he runs back due to his presidential failure. #VoteTrump #MakeAmericaGreatAgain
- Mar 5, 2016 11:19:30 AM Thank you Kansas! Thousands of people inside- and thousands outside who couldn't get into the hall. Really amazing! #CaucusForTrump
- Mar 5, 2016 11:20:26 AM Getting ready to make my speech at #KansasCaucus. A great honor! #MakeAmericaGreatAgain #Trump2016

- Mar 5, 2016 11:23:27 AM #CaucusForTrump #Trump2016 https://t.co/pTUlDXgPkP
- Mar 5, 2016 12:23:14 PM Thank you, Kansas! The line going into the Orlando event is over a mile long. Massive crowd expected. Leaving Kansas now, be there soon!
- Mar 5, 2016 12:57:30 PM .@MittRomney was a disaster candidate who had no guts and choked! Romney is a total joke, and everyone knows it!
- Mar 5, 2016 01:08:11 PM Romney's failed advisors, like campaign mgr Stuart Stevens are all over TV telling people how to win. But they lost- don't know how to win!
- Mar 5, 2016 01:09:50 PM I am watching two clown announcers on @FoxNews as they try to build up failed presidential candidate #LittleMarco. Fox News is in the bag!
- Mar 5, 2016 01:30:10 PM I would love to be at the Cadillac World Golf Championship @TrumpDoral in Miami- but even more so in Orlando with the #TrumpTrain!
- Mar 5, 2016 01:33:04 PM Thank you Willie Robertson! #VoteTrump #MakeAmericaGreatAgain https://t.co/0TUpaNfUmR
- Mar 5, 2016 01:44:45 PM I will be at the Cadillac World Golf Championship @TrumpDoral in Miami tomorrow! Rory, Phil, Bubba, Adam, and Dustin all at the top!
- Mar 5, 2016 02:59:10 PM RT @DonaldJTrumpJr: If you live in Louisiana, Maine, Kentucky or Kansas remember to vote today! Together let's #MakeAmericaGreatAgain US htt…
- Mar 5, 2016 09:53:00 PM Thank you Louisiana! #Trump2016 #SuperSaturday
- Mar 5, 2016 10:48:02 PM Thank you Kentucky! #Trump2016 #SuperSaturday

- Mar 6, 2016 12:40:37 AM .@FoxNews is devastated that lightweight Senator Marco Rubio got trounced tonight and is the big loser. I won the two big states, great!
- Mar 6, 2016 08:12:39 AM I will be interviewed on @FaceTheNation this morning. Enjoy! @jdickerson
- Mar 6, 2016 10:43:39 AM FLORIDA: Do not miss this opportunity to #MakeAmericaGreatAgain! Thank you @IvankaTrump: https://t.co/LHRNDKsoKh https://t.co/7cnWT9RGSr

- Mar 6, 2016 12:24:46 PM Thank you Michigan! #Trump2016 https://t.co/ttwwvrTjwE
- Mar 6, 2016 12:25:25 PM David Brooks, of the New York Times, is closing in on being the dumbest of them all. He doesn't have a clue.
- Mar 6, 2016 12:26:01 PM Nancy Reagan, the wife of a truly great President, was an amazing woman. She will be missed!
- Mar 6, 2016 12:27:21 PM The primary plaintiff in the phony Trump University suit wants to abandon the case. Disgraceful!
- Mar 6, 2016 12:32:42 PM Fraud lightweight Marco made a TV ad on TrumpU featuring 2 people who signed these letters: https://t.co/tSpFBn6Rux https://t.co/KFmotmqfnN
- Mar 6, 2016 01:03:00 PM Thank you to @jdickerson and @FaceTheNation for a very fair and professional interview this morning. No wonder you are #1 in the ratings!
- Mar 6, 2016 01:15:29 PM I am at Trump National Doral-best resort in U.S. Rory and Adam Scott are doing great! Watch on NBC at 3:00 P.M. MAKE AMERICA GREAT AGAIN!
- Mar 6, 2016 01:19:13 PM .@meetthepress and @chucktodd did a 1 hour hit job on me today – totally biased and mostly false. Dishonest media!
- Mar 6, 2016 06:54:40 PM "@ChadRowland3: @jdickerson @FaceTheNation A solid interview and a fair one. Great job Mr. Trump. Keep up the good work. #TrumpTrain"
- Mar 6, 2016 06:57:24 PM "@Janetlarose1: @realDonaldTrump @FaceTheNation @jdickerson WASHINGTON VERSUS TRUMP &TRUMPS SUPPORTERS ... #TRUMPDOG"
- Mar 6, 2016 09:54:29 PM All of the phony T.V. commercials against me are bought and payed for by SPECIAL INTEREST GROUPS, the bandits that tell your pols what to do
- Mar 6, 2016 09:58:38 PM How do you fight millions of dollars of fraudulent commercials pushing for crooked politicians? I will be using Facebook & Twitter. Watch!

- Mar 7, 2016 06:48:39 AM Failed presidential candidate Lindsey Graham should respect me. I destroyed his run, brought him from 7% to 0% when he got out. Now nasty!

- Mar 7, 2016 07:03:59 AM Lindsey Graham is all over T.V., much like failed 47% candidate Mitt Romney. These nasty, angry, jealous failures have ZERO credibility!
- Mar 7, 2016 08:03:16 AM We cannot let the failing REPUBLICAN ESTABLISHMENT, who could not stop Obama (twice), ruin the MOVEMENT with millions of $'s in false ads!
- Mar 7, 2016 08:10:22 AM I will be using Facebook and Twitter to expose dishonest lightweight Senator Marco Rubio. A record no-show in Senate, he is scamming Florida
- Mar 7, 2016 08:55:14 AM Congratulation to Adam Scott and all of the folks at Trump National Doral on producing a really great WGC Tournament. Amazing finish!
- Mar 7, 2016 10:23:00 AM Leaving for North Carolina. Big crowd, will be fun!
- Mar 7, 2016 11:50:14 AM Don't believe the millions of dollars of phony television ads by lightweight Rubio and the R establishment. Dishonest people!
- Mar 7, 2016 04:23:58 PM It was great being in Michigan. Remember, I am the only presidential candidate who will bring jobs back to the U.S.and protect car industry!
- Mar 7, 2016 04:56:06 PM "@justin_sellers: Setup is underway @realDonaldTrump rally in Madison. #MSPrimary https://t.co/1HLgixbqia" Thank you!
- Mar 7, 2016 05:34:53 PM Lightweight Senator Marco Rubio features Trump Univ. students in FL. attack ads- who submitted "excellent" reviews. https://t.co/JGTD590pKE
- Mar 7, 2016 05:48:21 PM Thank you Idaho! I love your potatoes- nobody grows them better. As President, I will protect your market. https://t.co/kqx8un1jnw
- Mar 7, 2016 06:48:33 PM New ad concerning lightweight Senator Marco Rubio: https://t.co/cNe0skpB5i
- Mar 7, 2016 07:47:23 PM I will be interviewed by @SeanHannity tonight at 10pm EST on @FoxNews! Enjoy!
- Mar 7, 2016 08:49:39 PM Cruz came to Mississippi, there was nobody there, he left the state. I had a rally in Madison, MS with 10,000! Thank you!
- Mar 7, 2016 09:25:08 PM I employ many people in Hawaii at my great hotel in Honolulu. I'll be there very soon. Vote for me, Hawaii!

- Mar 7, 2016 09:47:19 PM Ted Cruz Was For Welcoming Syrian Refugees Before He Was Against It https://t.co/zw4o1DJgfB
- Mar 7, 2016 09:54:34 PM People forget, it was Club for Growth that asked me for $1 million. I said no & they went negative. Extortion! https://t.co/oq8jmoep7i
- Mar 7, 2016 09:55:32 PM The Club for Growth is a very dishonest group. They represent conservative values terribly & are bad for America. https://t.co/rnGoaprYuA

- Mar 8, 2016 09:17:43 AM Michigan, Mississippi, Idaho & Hawaii: Get out to VOTE and join the movement today! Video: https://t.co/fJw8Ax7E8P https://t.co/ZDbarevYAc
- Mar 8, 2016 10:23:17 AM Thank you @EricTrump! https://t.co/U1iTLmcbAc
- Mar 8, 2016 10:23:49 AM MAKE AMERICA GREAT AGAIN!
- Mar 8, 2016 10:26:54 AM "@EricTrump: Wishing our father tremendous luck in Michigan, Mississippi, Idaho & Hawaii today! Amazing father! https://t.co/cYpx4eC9W @Q"
- Mar 8, 2016 11:12:12 AM Sun Sentinel says: Rubio lacks the experience, work ethic and gravitas needed to be president. HE HAS NOT EARNED YOUR VOTE!
- Mar 8, 2016 11:21:11 AM Remember, I am the only one who is self-funding my campaign. All of the other candidates are bought and paid for by special interests!
- Mar 8, 2016 12:36:00 PM Mitt Romney had his chance and blew it. Lindsey Graham ran for president, got ZERO, and quit! Why are they now spokesmen against me? Sad!
- Mar 8, 2016 12:39:43 PM #VoteTrumpMS! #Trump2016 https://t.co/KaHD0uENla
- Mar 8, 2016 12:40:53 PM #VoteTrumpMI! #Trump2016 https://t.co/IWMxISjH6L
- Mar 8, 2016 12:44:37 PM #VoteTrumpHI! #Trump2016 https://t.co/cCCLxnisSO
- Mar 8, 2016 12:46:01 PM #VoteTrumpID! #Trump2016 https://t.co/c6NHn6d6jX
- Mar 8, 2016 12:52:32 PM Hawaii: https://t.co/MnIlk2l9hP Idaho: https://t.co/7y5RxLpZRQ Mississippi: https://t.co/n43cPeJIqa Michigan: https://t.co/GL5JiZbqIc

- Mar 8, 2016 03:57:48 PM The negative television commercials about me, paid for by the politicians bosses, are a total #Mediafraud. When you watch, remember!
- Mar 8, 2016 06:47:11 PM RT @EricTrump: Aloha Hawaii: We would be honored to have your vote! Find your caucus https://t.co/iNgQS80mxX #TrumpWaikiki #Mahalo https://...
- Mar 8, 2016 06:53:48 PM I hear @NBCNews / @WSJ came out with another one of their phony polls. While I am leading, they are totally discredited after last S.C. poll
- Mar 8, 2016 06:58:02 PM Word is I am doing very well in Michigan and Mississippi! Wow, and with all that money spent against me! Will be going to Trump Jupiter now!
- Mar 8, 2016 08:12:46 PM Thank you America! #Trump2016 https://t.co/jOD54EGGmG
- Mar 8, 2016 08:14:50 PM Thank you! #Trump2016 https://t.co/WvTkL8mMHY
- Mar 8, 2016 08:28:43 PM Thank you Mississippi! #Trump2016
- Mar 8, 2016 09:02:25 PM Thank you Michigan! #Trump2016
- Mar 8, 2016 09:10:20 PM RT @RSBNetwork: LIVE Stream now: Donald Trump press conference #TrumpTrain #Trump2016 https://t.co/s7WgNXR27A
- Mar 8, 2016 10:58:28 PM This was a great evening- I would like to thank everyone for their wonderful support.

- Mar 9, 2016 02:36:16 AM Thank you Hawaii! #Trump2016
- Mar 9, 2016 04:46:12 PM Phony Club For Growth tried to shake me down for one million dollars, & is now putting out nasty negative ads on me. They are total losers!
- Mar 9, 2016 05:39:30 PM Keep lightweight Marco and his friends out of the White House. #MakeAmericaGreatAgain #Trump2016 https://t.co/hNkkRx66Hc
- Mar 9, 2016 06:00:30 PM Another Dishonest Politician #LightweightSenatorMarcoRubio https://t.co/w7G5vJ511O

- Mar 10, 2016 04:41:18 PM Wow, you are all correct about @FoxNews - totally biased and disgusting reporting.

- Mar 11, 2016 12:12:02 AM "@adriparsonss: @The_Trump_Train @realDonaldTrump #Donald Trump is your man America. He is the best!! Vote for him!" Thank you!
- Mar 11, 2016 12:12:17 AM Thank you Mark. #GOPDebate https://t.co/jeaiAvgEEC
- Mar 11, 2016 12:56:24 AM Thank you America! #Trump2016 #MakeAmericaGreatAgain https://t.co/8B0J8Xt3dh
- Mar 11, 2016 01:05:13 AM "@JaredWyand: Let's be clear.. #NeverTrump is about "Never someone we don't own" You either play into it & let them win or vote Trump.
- Mar 11, 2016 01:49:58 AM Thank you! #GOPDebate https://t.co/BuJ1YFkjvm
- Mar 11, 2016 10:49:49 AM RT @CLewandowski_: The Scrum: Video Emerges to Suggest WaPo Reporter Ben Terris Misidentifies Lewandowski in Fields Incident Breitbart htt…
- Mar 11, 2016 10:51:38 AM RT @RealBenCarson: Many people fight for change in DC. @realDonaldTrump is a leader with an outsider's perspective & the vision, guts & ene…
- Mar 11, 2016 10:51:41 AM RT @RealBenCarson: I endorse @realDonaldTrump. It's time to unite behind the candidate who will beat Hillary Clinton and return government …
- Mar 11, 2016 10:55:54 AM RT @RealBenCarson: Please read my full endorsement of @realDonaldTrump for President of the United States: https://t.co/aSx9u3Ayz1.
- Mar 11, 2016 10:57:04 AM RT @greta: Prob w/ all pundits saying last fall @realDonaldTrump had no chance is that shows media so out of touch w/ Americans
- Mar 11, 2016 11:44:32 AM Dr. Ben Carson- I concur. "I believe in God who can change people- he can make any of us better." @RealBenCarson
- Mar 11, 2016 12:58:24 PM https://t.co/ZQ0osiFEJQ
- Mar 11, 2016 03:33:56 PM Rumor has it that @politico is going out of business. Losing too much money. Great news! Likewise, dopey Mort Zuckerman's @NYDailyNews
- Mar 11, 2016 04:25:40 PM Thank you St. Louis, Missouri! #MakeAmericaGreatAgain #Trump2016 https://t.co/qM1Mwq05j2 https://t.co/MxVFHvHfS3

- Mar 11, 2016 05:40:31 PM It means so much to me- receiving an endorsement from Phyllis Schlafly. A truly great woman & conservative. https://t.co/11rEMu99qc
- Mar 11, 2016 06:03:01 PM Great news! Thank you Governor Ralph DLG Torres! #Trump2016 https://t.co/hXwAK3iyPk
- Mar 11, 2016 09:00:38 PM I just got off the phone with the great people of Guam! Thank you for your support! #VoteTrump today! #Trump2016

- Mar 12, 2016 06:44:54 AM The organized group of people, many of them thugs, who shut down our First Amendment rights in Chicago, have totally energized America!
- Mar 12, 2016 08:35:19 AM Absentee Governor Kasich voted for NAFTA and NAFTA devastated Ohio - a disaster from which it never recovered. Kasich is good for Mexico!
- Mar 12, 2016 09:17:41 AM Ohio had the biggest budget increase in the U.S. If it were not for striking oil, they would be bust! Governor Kasich in favor of TPP fraud!
- Mar 12, 2016 09:35:09 AM The rally in Cincinnati is ON. Media put out false reports that it was cancelled. Will be great - love you Ohio!
- Mar 12, 2016 09:54:27 AM On my way to Dayton, Ohio. Will be there soon!
- Mar 12, 2016 09:55:15 AM MAKE AMERICA GREAT AGAIN!
- Mar 12, 2016 01:02:39 PM Thank you Dayton, Ohio! 20,000 supporters-largest in airport history! #MakeAmericaGreatAgain #Trump2016 https://t.co/ry2p5qGcFt
- Mar 12, 2016 01:02:41 PM The rally in Cincinnati is ON. Media put out false reports that it was cancelled! #MakeAmericaGreatAgain #Trump2016
- Mar 12, 2016 01:06:24 PM Word is-early voting in FL is very dishonest. Little Marco, his State Chairman, & their minions are working overtime-trying to rig the vote.
- Mar 12, 2016 01:07:04 PM We are asking law enforcement to check for dishonest early voting in Florida- on behalf of little Marco Rubio. No way to run a country!
- Mar 12, 2016 01:24:56 PM The last person that Hillary or Bernie want to run against is Donald Trump --- and that is fact!
- Mar 12, 2016 01:36:45 PM It is Clinton and Sanders people who disrupted my rally in Chicago - and then they say I must talk to my people. Phony politicians!

- Mar 12, 2016 03:21:30 PM Just finished my second speech. 20K in Dayton & 25K in Cleveland- perfectly behaved crowd. Thanks- I love you, Ohio! https://t.co/IDmwG5FQsw
- Mar 12, 2016 05:21:43 PM #EndCommonCore #Trump2016 Video: https://t.co/krYK2DiAlh https://t.co/RAH45igqJI
- Mar 12, 2016 05:47:59 PM Do the people of Ohio know that John Kasich is STRONGLY in favor of Common Core! In other words, education of your children from D.C. No way
- Mar 12, 2016 06:41:57 PM USSS did an excellent job stopping the maniac running to the stage. He has ties to ISIS. Should be in jail! https://t.co/tkzbHg7wyD?ssr=true
- Mar 12, 2016 09:41:33 PM RT @GovMikeHuckabee: Trump says the chaos in Chicago was a planned attack. But Hillary insists it was a spontaneous reaction to an internet…
- Mar 12, 2016 10:30:04 PM Wow, Kasich didn't qualify to run in the state of Pennsylvania, not enough signatures. Big problem!

- Mar 13, 2016 06:35:46 AM "@alextrent4: It is repulsive that Trump was assaulted+politicians used that 2 further themselves+2 further victimize Trump! DISGUSTING!!"
- Mar 13, 2016 06:48:44 AM Bernie Sanders is lying when he says his disruptors aren't told to go to my events. Be careful Bernie, or my supporters will go to yours!
- Mar 13, 2016 06:58:17 AM Ohio Gov.Kasich voted for NAFTA, from which Ohio has never recovered. Now he wants TPP, which will be even worse. Ohio steel and coal dying!
- Mar 13, 2016 09:49:44 AM Gov.Kasich of Ohio just stated on a morning show that he doesn't watch politics or anything on television, he only watches the @GolfChannel
- Mar 13, 2016 12:06:31 PM Thank you Kevin. With unification of the party, Republican wins will be massive! https://t.co/1rmyCGSlsV
- Mar 13, 2016 12:07:00 PM Carly Fiorina- I agree! Ted Cruz is just another politician. All talk- no action! https://t.co/08xkEBD8Be
- Mar 13, 2016 01:26:20 PM Because Gov. Kasich cannot run in the state of Pennsylvania-he cannot win the nomination- & should not be allowed to compete in Ohio on Tue.

- Mar 13, 2016 01:53:07 PM The failing @nytimes is truly one of the worst newspapers. They knowingly write lies and never even call to fact check. Really bad people!
- Mar 13, 2016 03:32:48 PM LYIN' TED https://t.co/Q0qXDGCN1l
- Mar 13, 2016 07:04:26 PM RT @RSBNetwork: LIVE Stream: Donald Trump about to speak in Boca Raton, FL. Protesters already before Trump speaks. #TrumpTrain https://t...
- Mar 13, 2016 07:13:41 PM Just received from @PeteRose_14. Thank you Pete! #VoteTrump on Tuesday Ohio! #Trump2016 #MakeAmericaGreatAgain https://t.co/UvP03n7dQq

- Mar 14, 2016 07:55:28 AM We don't have a country- if we don't have borders. #VoteTrump Video: https://t.co/wG4RgOi1bW https://t.co/oAXBvcKIsr
- Mar 14, 2016 10:24:15 AM Look forward to being in Tampa this afternoon. Wonderful crowds. Thank you, Florida!
- Mar 14, 2016 11:56:06 AM Leaving the great people of North Carolina. Amazing event. Heading to Tampa now! #VoteTrump
- Mar 14, 2016 11:59:19 AM Gov Kasich voted for NAFTA, which devastated Ohio and is now pushing TPP hard- bad for American workers!
- Mar 14, 2016 11:59:52 AM Kasich has helped decimate the coal and steel industries in Ohio. I will bring them back! #MakeAmericaGreatAgain
- Mar 14, 2016 07:48:09 PM THANK YOU - Youngstown, Ohio! I love you! Get out & #VoteTrump tomorrow. #Trump2016 https://t.co/OReGiIS6TF
- Mar 14, 2016 08:11:17 PM Sadly, this kind of stuff even happened to Ronald Reagan. There is nothing nice about it! #MakeAmericaGreatAgain https://t.co/jC7cn1v18u
- Mar 14, 2016 10:22:21 PM "@BrazielCarol: @FoxNews @realDonaldTrump Who started this mess, the protesters of course . And media made it worse."
- Mar 14, 2016 10:24:41 PM "@realwwshelton: @loudobbsnews I believe that @realDonaldTrump will be the big winner tomorrow." Thank you!
- Mar 14, 2016 10:44:11 PM "@wh: https://t.co/AZmCErLKCn WOW people are so misinformed on DonaldTrump character! Watch this video! Hillary and Bernie don't come close
- Mar 14, 2016 10:46:39 PM "@mazzei48: @realDonaldTrump @BrazielCarol @FoxNews Listening to interview on replay of @A Savage Nation #GO DONALD TRUMP !!!!!" Thanks.

- Mar 14, 2016 11:10:00 PM Kasich voted for NAFTA, a disaster for Ohio, and now wants the even worse TPP approved. Vote Trump and end this madness!
- Mar 14, 2016 11:21:20 PM Rubio is weak on illegal immigration, with the worst voting record in the U.S. Senate in many years. He will never MAKE AMERICA GREAT AGAIN!

- Mar 15, 2016 05:25:53 AM I will bring our jobs back to America, fix our military and take care of our vets, end Common Core and ObamaCare, protect 2nd A, build WALL
- Mar 15, 2016 05:39:06 AM Please remember, I am the ONLY candidate who is self-funding his campaign. Kasich, Rubio and Cruz are all bought and paid for by lobbyists!
- Mar 15, 2016 06:31:46 AM Don't reward Mitt Romney, who let us all down in the last presidential race, by voting for Kasich (who voted for NAFTA, open borders etc.).
- Mar 15, 2016 07:10:10 AM Good morning Ohio! Some additional information from my daughter, @IvankaTrump! #VoteTrump #SuperTuesday https://t.co/H7sBEnSpYq
- Mar 15, 2016 07:38:37 AM Just in, big news- I have been declared the winner of the CNMI Rep Caucus with 72.8% of the vote! Thank you! #SuperTuesday #VoteTrump
- Mar 15, 2016 08:24:01 AM RT @EricTrump: Friends in #FL #OH #NC #IL & #MO we would be honored to have your #VOTE! #SuperTuesday #LetsDoThis #MakeAmericaGreatAgain #T…
- Mar 15, 2016 08:37:24 AM North Carolina lost 300,000 manufacturing jobs and Ohio lost 400,000 since 2000. Going to Mexico etc. NO MORE IF I WIN, WE WILL BRING BACK!
- Mar 15, 2016 08:43:25 AM #VoteTrump #SuperTuesday Florida Illinois Missouri North Carolina Ohio #TrumpTrain https://t.co/zyRctsFmSq https://t.co/kxrn0ev4UF
- Mar 15, 2016 09:36:09 AM RT @EricTrump: Mathematically it is statistically impossible for Kasich to get to 1237 - he would need 112% of the remaining delegates to b…
- Mar 15, 2016 09:53:41 AM Watching John Kasich being interviewed - acting so innocent and like such a nice guy. Remember him in second debate, until I put him down.

- Mar 15, 2016 10:03:34 AM Ohio is losing jobs to Mexico, now losing Ford (and many others). Kasich is weak on illegal immigration. We need strong borders now!
- Mar 15, 2016 11:03:57 AM In presidential voting so far, John Kasich is ZERO for 22. So why would he be a good candidate? Hillary would beat him, I will beat Hillary!
- Mar 15, 2016 11:16:16 AM I will bring our jobs back to the U.S., and keep our companies from leaving. Nobody else can do it. Our economy will "sing" again.
- Mar 15, 2016 02:11:12 PM A lot of complaints from people saying my name is not on the ballot in various places in Florida? Hope this is false.
- Mar 15, 2016 06:06:59 PM Word is that, despite a record amount spent on negative and phony ads, I had a massive victory in Florida. Numbers out soon!
- Mar 15, 2016 06:26:54 PM "@BertShad: Was going to watch @Foxnews for the primary results but saw @megynkelly - looks like #CNN tonight"
- Mar 15, 2016 06:34:02 PM "@gregens21: @BertShad @FoxNews @megynkelly She's choking on the results! Call her justifiable Kelly. Justifying everything she says."
- Mar 15, 2016 06:34:55 PM "@jsconlon11: @BertShad @Foxnews @megynkelly I tried to give them a shot tonight, but they have the whole anti Trump cheerleading team."
- Mar 15, 2016 06:37:47 PM "@J_Styborski: @realDonaldTrump @gregens21 @BertShad @FoxNews @megynkelly Hayes is looking depressed as well. https://t.co/wUJacOm32h"
- Mar 15, 2016 06:39:45 PM "@SCNAK45: @megynkelly is trying so hard to bash @realDonaldTrump it's ridiculous" Don't worry, everyone is wise to Crazy Megyn!
- Mar 15, 2016 06:54:29 PM "@DumpFoxNews: @FoxNews @megynkelly If media wasn't so biased against Trump, he would've won all of the delegates.
- Mar 15, 2016 07:05:04 PM Can't watch Crazy Megyn anymore. Talks about me at 43% but never mentions that there are four people in race. With two people, big & over!
- Mar 15, 2016 07:05:11 PM Thank you, Northern Mariana Islands!#SuperTuesday #Trump2016 #MakeAmericaGreatAgain https://t.co/OoP4mls4lp
- Mar 15, 2016 07:05:34 PM Thank you, Florida! #SuperTuesday #MakeAmericaGreatAgain #Trump2016 https://t.co/nzhnLQXrZg

- Mar 15, 2016 07:09:08 PM Watching other networks and local news. Really good night! Crazy @megynkelly is unwatchable.
- Mar 15, 2016 08:33:57 PM Thank you, North Carolina! #Trump2016 #SuperTuesday #MakeAmericaGreatAgain https://t.co/hd4wtDonIB
- Mar 15, 2016 08:48:52 PM Thank you Illinois! #SuperTuesday #MakeAmericaGreatAgain #Trump2016 https://t.co/vcfstc6Wnb
- Mar 15, 2016 09:33:54 PM I only wish my wonderful daughter Tiffany could have been with us at Mar-a-Lago for our great election victory. She is a winner!
- Mar 15, 2016 10:16:09 PM Thank you Marco, I agree! https://t.co/PTfFzFno9p

- Mar 16, 2016 12:35:00 AM "@MaryEH428: @RealBenCarson I thank God you are on board with @realDonaldTrump to help him and us #MakeAmericaGreatAgain Ty!!"
- Mar 16, 2016 12:50:49 AM "@lucyric13835428: @realDonaldTrump @megynkelly That's funny, I switched to other media too, can't stand her"
- Mar 16, 2016 05:28:47 AM Will be interviewed on @GMA at 7:00 A.M. Big wins last night!
- Mar 16, 2016 05:30:14 AM Will be interviewed on @NewDay on @CNN at 7:15 A.M.
- Mar 16, 2016 06:35:33 AM Will be interviewed on @Morning_Joe at 7:40. ENJOY!
- Mar 16, 2016 07:02:01 AM I will be interviewed on @foxandfriends at 8:30 A.M. ENJOY!
- Mar 16, 2016 07:06:10 AM .@pastormarkburns You were great last night and we all very much appreciate it! Thank you!
- Mar 16, 2016 08:34:19 AM "@FoxBusiness: .@RepTomMarino: I think @realDonaldTrump can beat HillaryClinton. And I'm looking forward to Trump being president.
- Mar 16, 2016 08:37:39 AM .@RepTomMarino Great job on television this morning. Glad to have you on my side!
- Mar 16, 2016 11:19:58 AM Is this what we want for a President? https://t.co/2yYy6Nyta9
- Mar 16, 2016 12:04:49 PM Yesterday was amazing—5 victories. Lyin' Ted Cruz had zero. Things are going very well!

- Mar 16, 2016 12:13:17 PM In the last 2 weeks, I had $35M of negative ads against me in Florida & I won in a massive landslide.The establishment should save their $$!
- Mar 16, 2016 12:14:37 PM Thank you to the Governor of Florida, Rick Scott, for your endorsement. I greatly appreciate your support!
- Mar 16, 2016 12:47:07 PM I am making a big speech the night of the @FoxNews debate, but I wish everyone well. Yesterday was a big day for me with 5 wins!
- Mar 16, 2016 01:52:15 PM RT @JohnStossel: I can skate here ONLY b/c @realdonaldtrump fixed this rink after NYC gov't spent $13M, but FAILED! Good for Trump! https:/...
- Mar 16, 2016 01:56:09 PM Wow, just won Missouri!
- Mar 16, 2016 04:21:43 PM Thank you, Missouri! #Trump2016 https://t.co/iOzGtcBbia
- Mar 16, 2016 04:26:40 PM I will be interviewed on The O'Reilly Factor this evening at 8 pm on the Fox News Channel. @oreillyfactor

- Mar 17, 2016 05:09:00 AM Stuart Stevens, the failed campaign manager of Mitt Romney's historic loss, is now telling the Republican Party what to do with Trump. Sad!
- Mar 17, 2016 05:17:00 AM Crazy @megynkelly supposedly had lyin' Ted Cruz on her show last night. Ted is desperate and his lying is getting worse. Ted can't win!
- Mar 17, 2016 05:40:53 AM Great news that @FoxNews has cancelled the additional debate. How many times can the same people ask the same question? I beat Cruz debating
- Mar 17, 2016 07:19:55 AM Crazy @megynkelly is now complaining that @oreillyfactor did not defend her against me - yet her bad show is a total hit piece on me.Tough!
- Mar 17, 2016 07:28:17 AM The reason lyin' Ted Cruz has lost so much of the evangelical vote is that they are very smart and just don't tolerate liars-a big problem!
- Mar 17, 2016 08:08:55 AM .@WSJ Editorial says "Clinton primary vote total is 8,646,551.Trump's is 7,533,692"-a knock. But she had only 3 opponents-I had 16.Apologize

- Mar 17, 2016 08:11:31 AM .@WSJ is bad at math. The good news is, nobody cares what they say in their editorials anymore, especially me!
- Mar 17, 2016 08:22:07 AM Please explain to the dummies at the @WSJ Editorial Board that I love to debate and have won, according to Drudge etc., all 11 of them!
- Mar 17, 2016 11:44:45 AM See you in Arizona on Friday and Saturday. https://t.co/HiOhRaTMbm
- Mar 17, 2016 11:54:21 AM Looking like my 5 victories on Tuesday will be just as good as if I won Ohio. Two more days and Ohio was mine!
- Mar 17, 2016 11:58:04 AM Highly overrated & crazy @megynkelly is always complaining about Trump and yet she devotes her shows to me. Focus on others Megyn!
- Mar 17, 2016 01:33:31 PM Who should star in a reboot of Liar Liar- Hillary Clinton or Ted Cruz? Let me know. https://t.co/ESdiEftWGs
- Mar 17, 2016 03:30:08 PM MAKE AMERICA GREAT AGAIN!
- Mar 17, 2016 07:37:17 PM Hillary Clinton has been involved in corruption for most of her professional life!

- Mar 18, 2016 10:56:16 AM Join us in Salt Lake City, Utah- tonight! #MakeAmericaGreatAgain #Trump2016 https://t.co/1cJ7OFbQiz
- Mar 18, 2016 11:42:29 AM Lyin' Ted Cruz lost all five races on Tuesday-and he was just given the jinx - a Lindsey Graham endorsement. Also backed Jeb. Lindsey got 0!
- Mar 18, 2016 02:03:48 PM Senator @LindseyGrahamSC made horrible statements about @SenTedCruz – and then he endorsed him. No wonder nobody trusts politicians!
- Mar 18, 2016 02:08:05 PM .@EWErickson got fired like a dog from RedState and now he is the one leading opposition against me.
- Mar 18, 2016 02:44:17 PM With millions of dollars of negative and phony ads against me by the establishment, my numbers continue to go up. Can anyone explain this?
- Mar 18, 2016 02:57:35 PM Club For Growth tried to extort $1,000,000 from me. When I said NO, they went hostile with negative ads. Disgraceful!
- Mar 18, 2016 03:05:51 PM Club for Growth letter- trying to extort $1,000,000.00 from me. Remember, I said- NO! https://t.co/suIfdiMg0Q

- Mar 18, 2016 03:07:50 PM Going to Salt Lake City, Utah, for a big rally. Lyin' Ted Cruz should not be allowed to win there - Mormons don't like LIARS! I beat Hillary
- Mar 18, 2016 03:18:14 PM Failed presidential candidate Mitt Romney, the man who "choked" and let us all down, is now endorsing Lyin' Ted Cruz. This is good for me!
- Mar 18, 2016 03:21:17 PM Failed Presidential Candidate Mitt Romney was campaigning with John Kasich & Marco Rubio, and now he is endorsing Ted Cruz. 1/2
- Mar 18, 2016 03:37:31 PM Mitt Romney is a mixed up man who doesn't have a clue. No wonder he lost!
- Mar 18, 2016 03:39:05 PM Join me tomorrow! #Trump2016 #MakeAmericaGreatAgain https://t.co/1Yak4I5B7b
- Mar 18, 2016 03:41:53 PM Thank you Arizona- I love you! #MakeAmericaGreatAgain #Trump2016 https://t.co/fTzaIvTX9b
- Mar 18, 2016 04:55:11 PM Everybody should boycott the @megynkelly show. Never worth watching. Always a hit on Trump! She is sick, & the most overrated person on tv.
- Mar 18, 2016 07:40:10 PM Do you believe that Hillary Clinton now wants Obamacare for illegal immigrants? She should spend more time taking care of our great Vets!
- Mar 18, 2016 08:05:55 PM I guess I have reached yet another "ceiling" - 49.7%, with four people. My highest Reuters poll yet! Thank you! https://t.co/k5Ft585Arp
- Mar 18, 2016 08:53:57 PM Why haven't they released the final Missouri victory for us yet? Could it be because Cruz's guy runs Missouri?
- Mar 18, 2016 08:54:24 PM RT @MarkHalperin: Utah Speaker of the House announces endorsement of @realDonaldTrump. Says @DonaldJTrumpJr played a big role
- Mar 18, 2016 10:43:42 PM Just leaving Salt Lake City, Utah- fantastic crowd with no interruptions. Love Utah- will be back!
- Mar 18, 2016 10:45:23 PM Watching @loudobbsnews- fantastic show! Has very interesting take on Paul Ryan.
- Mar 18, 2016 11:05:20 PM Heading to Phoenix. Will be arriving soon. Tomorrow a big day. Tremendous crowds expected! #Trump2016 #MakeAmericaGreatAgain

- Mar 18, 2016 11:11:18 PM While I have never met @nytdavidbrooks of the NY Times, I consider him one of the dumbest of all pundits- he has no sense of the real world!
- Mar 18, 2016 11:25:54 PM Reading @nytdavidbrooks of the NY Times is a total waste of time, he is a clown with no awareness of the world around him- dummy!
- Mar 18, 2016 11:28:43 PM Landing in Phoenix now. Tomorrow's events will be amazing! #Trump2016
- Mar 18, 2016 11:40:27 PM Thank you- New York! I love you! #MakeAmericaGreatAgain #Trump2016 https://t.co/wyjV9DgdQA
- Mar 18, 2016 11:48:35 PM "@ileanabarkus: @nytdavidbrooks I totally agree! @nytdavidbrooks is strictly conceptual and theoretical and has NO COMMONSENSE!"

- Mar 19, 2016 01:58:13 AM "@cmichaeld2004: Realistic Trump Poll Numbers translate to the 70 percentile range in a two-man race. Gee, what happened to that 30% ceiling
- Mar 19, 2016 02:00:56 AM "@WesleyRickard: Sheriff Joe Arpaio AZ Endorses Donald J Trump for President of the United States #AZ #UT https://t.co/4FzcTZIGqE"
- Mar 19, 2016 02:09:18 AM "@Veteran4Trump: Vets For A Strong America Endorses Donald Trump for president; "We've Endorsed Him, We Believe In Him" #Trump2016
- Mar 19, 2016 02:11:26 AM "@grammy620: 1st time I heard #Trump I said "wow". I liked him! I then became a closet #Trump fan. Today? He's the ONLY 1 I will vote for!
- Mar 19, 2016 02:12:48 AM "@AshleyEdam: It's great to see supporters like you along the way...watching Americans come together the past 8 months #voteTrump
- Mar 19, 2016 07:11:56 AM "@Ma1973sk: Actually, no @FoxNews, @megynkelly has a sick obsession with Trump. Every day, every show, trashing, negative, hate.
- Mar 19, 2016 07:15:16 AM "@DonaldJTrumpJr: Honored to be in #Utah with retired General Robert C. Oaks. We are so thankful for his support and endorsement here in SLC

- Mar 19, 2016 07:16:26 AM "@TeamTrumpAZ: Check out "HANNITY EXCLUSIVE EVENT WITH TRUMP IN PHOENIX, AZ" https://t.co/fj2j9Lf2vH @Eventbrite"
- Mar 19, 2016 07:59:31 AM "@saneplanet: after tonight it is clear! Utah is #TrumpCountry #Utah #Mormon #UtahPrimary #Utah4Trump https://t.co/8e14RE6YJo"
- Mar 19, 2016 10:14:32 AM Crazy @megynkelly says I don't (won't) go on her show and she still gets good ratings. But almost all of her shows are negative hits on me!
- Mar 19, 2016 10:16:55 AM If crazy @megynkelly didn't cover me so much on her terrible show, her ratings would totally tank. She is so average in so many ways!
- Mar 19, 2016 10:40:55 AM Great to be back in Arizona! #MakeAmericaGreatAgain #Trump2016 https://t.co/uo287ZGvvQ
- Mar 19, 2016 10:50:59 AM Wow, @CNN ratings are up 75% because it's "all Trump, all the time." The networks are making a fortune off of me! MAKE AMERICA GREAT AGAIN!
- Mar 19, 2016 02:38:11 PM THANK YOU ARIZONA! 20,000 amazing supporters! Get out and #VoteTrump on Tuesday. I love you! #MakeAmericaGreatAgain https://t.co/pU5vB1pBO5
- Mar 19, 2016 07:31:50 PM .@DiamondandSilk- Just watched you on #WattersWorld with a large group of people. Everybody loves you- two amazing people! #Trump2016
- Mar 19, 2016 07:34:31 PM .@jessebwatters- Watching your show from Arizona where we just had a big rally. It is fantastic- everybody loves it! #MakeAmericaGreatAgain
- Mar 19, 2016 07:48:06 PM .@AndreaTantaros- You are a true journalistic professional. I so agree with what you say. Keep up the great work! #MakeAmericaGreatAgain
- Mar 19, 2016 08:39:20 PM Thank you- Tucson, Arizona! A great afternoon with 6,000 supporters! #VoteTrump on Tuesday! #MakeAmericaGreatAgain https://t.co/CTgYrLnAWV
- Mar 19, 2016 10:06:21 PM THANK YOU ARIZONA! Get out and #VoteTrump on Tuesday! #AZPrimary #MakeAmericaGreatAgain #Trump2016 https://t.co/5itxkQxrLF

- Mar 19, 2016 11:51:59 PM "@jojo2foxy: TRUMP IS NOT AFRAID OF ANYTHING OR ANYONE - THAT'S THE PRESIDENT USA NEEDS TO UNITE US & KNOCK THE SOCKS OFF OUR ENEMIES!

- Mar 20, 2016 12:05:04 AM The rallies in Utah and Arizona were great! Tremendous crowds and spirit. Just returned but will be going back soon.
- Mar 20, 2016 06:51:21 AM "@GStephanopoulos: What's @realDonaldTrump's strategy to secure the GOP nomination? I'll talk to the Republican front-runner. @ThisWeekABC."
- Mar 20, 2016 06:55:27 AM Will be interviewed on @ThisWeekABC this morning. Enjoy!
- Mar 20, 2016 11:13:50 AM Why is it that the horrendous protesters, who scream, curse punch, shut down roads/doors during my RALLIES, are never blamed by media? SAD!
- Mar 20, 2016 01:52:32 PM The protesters blocked a major highway yesterday, delaying entry to my RALLY in Arizona by hours, and the media blames my supporters!
- Mar 20, 2016 02:10:55 PM So the highly overrated anchor, @megynkelly, is allowed to constantly say bad things about me on her show, but I can't fight back? Wrong!
- Mar 20, 2016 02:39:27 PM "@gamzorz: @megynkelly Dont worry Trump, They are losing thousands of viewers and money. Roger Ailes will be telling Megyn to stop"
- Mar 20, 2016 02:45:33 PM Big Republican Dinner tonight at Mar-a-Lago in Palm Beach. I will be there!
- Mar 20, 2016 03:41:03 PM Wow, President Obama just landed in Cuba, a big deal, and Raul Castro wasn't even there to greet him. He greeted Pope and others. No respect
- Mar 20, 2016 09:34:26 PM "@BarronG510: @realDonaldTrump The media is corrupt! We The People are fighting with you."

- Mar 22, 2016 06:11:53 AM "@MyPresidentme: Here's Trump #AIPAC2016 in case anyone missed it. It is a must watch. https://t.co/cGCIYE7yZB"
- Mar 22, 2016 07:04:43 AM Do you all remember how beautiful and safe a place Brussels was. Not anymore, it is from a different world! U.S. must be vigilant and smart!

- Mar 22, 2016 09:53:34 AM President Obama looks and sounds so ridiculous making his speech in Cuba, especially in the shadows of Brussels. He is being treated badly!
- Mar 22, 2016 09:54:32 AM MAKE AMERICA GREAT AGAIN!
- Mar 22, 2016 10:08:32 AM RT @EricTrump: #Arizona: We made it easy to find your polling location for today's primary! Simply visit https://t.co/uJFqD4yTlF US https:/...
- Mar 22, 2016 10:32:36 AM I have proven to be far more correct about terrorism than anybody- and it's not even close. Hopefully AZ and UT will be voting for me today!
- Mar 22, 2016 11:16:10 AM Watch this clip from earlier this year. Time & time again I have been right about terrorism. It's time to get tough! https://t.co/8mnY3GFRzw
- Mar 22, 2016 01:21:24 PM My heart & prayers go out to all of the victims of the terrible #Brussels tragedy. This madness must be stopped, and I will stop it.
- Mar 22, 2016 01:52:55 PM #VoteTrump video: https://t.co/NauXRQ2Q91 #AZPrimary #ArizonaPrimary #UtahCaucus #UTCaucus #AmericanSamoa https://t.co/bKruyYHFma
- Mar 22, 2016 02:04:07 PM #ArizonaPrimary message from @IvankaTrump! #AZPrimary #MakeAmericaGreatAgain #Trump2016 https://t.co/WzTDekWJAQ
- Mar 22, 2016 02:16:42 PM #UtahCaucus message from @IvankaTrump! #UTCaucus #MakeAmericaGreatAgain #Trump2016 https://t.co/kHigCSUnFC
- Mar 22, 2016 02:17:41 PM Obama, and all others, have been so weak, and so politically correct, that terror groups are forming and getting stronger! Shame.
- Mar 22, 2016 05:41:46 PM Pres. Obama should leave the baseball game in Cuba immediately & get home to Washington- where a #POTUS, under a serious emergency belongs!
- Mar 22, 2016 08:53:05 PM Lyin' Ted Cruz just used a picture of Melania from a G.Q. shoot in his ad. Be careful, Lyin' Ted, or I will spill the beans on your wife!
- Mar 22, 2016 09:59:29 PM Incompetent Hillary, despite the horrible attack in Brussels today, wants borders to be weak and open-and let the Muslims flow in. No way!
- Mar 22, 2016 10:30:10 PM Thank you, Arizona! #Trump2016 #WesternTuesday #TrumpTrain https://t.co/VMCzxrryG8

- Mar 22, 2016 10:43:50 PM Much bigger win than anticipated in Arizona. Thank you, I will never forget!
- Mar 22, 2016 11:04:34 PM Hopefully the Republican Party can come together and have a big WIN in November, paving the way for many great Supreme Court Justices!

- Mar 23, 2016 09:22:51 AM Lyin' Ted Cruz denied that he had anything to do with the G.Q. model photo post of Melania. That's why we call him Lyin' Ted!
- Mar 23, 2016 01:35:50 PM Thank you, Arizona! #Trump2016 #MakeAmericaGreatAgain #TrumpTrain https://t.co/MMPR0Omwog https://t.co/Dgqky0JiHO
- Mar 23, 2016 02:45:44 PM Lyin' Ted Cruz steals foreign policy from me, and lines from Michael Douglas— just another dishonest politician.
- Mar 23, 2016 02:49:49 PM Low energy Jeb Bush just endorsed a man he truly hates, Lyin' Ted Cruz. Honestly, I can't blame Jeb in that I drove him into oblivion!
- Mar 23, 2016 02:53:39 PM Just watched Hillary deliver a prepackaged speech on terror. She's been in office fighting terror for 20 years- and look where we are!
- Mar 23, 2016 02:54:59 PM I will be the best by far in fighting terror. I'm the only one that was right from the beginning, & now Lyin' Ted & others are copying me.
- Mar 23, 2016 03:02:29 PM I think having Jeb's endorsement hurts Lyin' Ted. Jeb spent more than $150,000,000 and got nothing. I spent a fraction of that and am first!
- Mar 23, 2016 04:12:54 PM While I believe I will clinch before Cleveland and get more than 1237 delegates, it is unfair in that there have been so many in the race!
- Mar 23, 2016 04:44:44 PM I want to thank @RealSheriffJoe for all of his help in our historic Arizona win. Could not have done it without you Joe!
- Mar 23, 2016 06:25:00 PM MAKE AMERICA GREAT AGAIN!
- Mar 23, 2016 09:33:15 PM "@DebraRakestraw: You have over 2M followers more than than @HillaryClinton. This says something about how America feels. #Trump2016 US"
- Mar 23, 2016 10:03:33 PM "@tcsorr: @jphilman0206 @realDonaldTrump self-funded and media loves him. Not beholden to masters like @tedcruz. Who owns Ted?"

- Mar 23, 2016 10:35:21 PM "@Kj11100Me: @realDonaldTrump Donald Trump will be greater president than Ragan. Trump will set the button for morality,Christianity.
- Mar 23, 2016 10:55:00 PM "@Don_Vito_08: "A picture is worth a thousand words" @realDonaldTrump #LyingTed #NeverCruz @MELANIATRUMP https://t.co/5bvVEwMVF8"

- Mar 24, 2016 06:47:26 AM N.A.T.O. is obsolete and must be changed to additionally focus on terrorism as well as some of the things it is currently focused on!
- Mar 24, 2016 06:59:06 AM We pay a disproportionate share of the cost of N.A.T.O. Why? It is time to renegotiate, and the time is now!
- Mar 24, 2016 08:40:26 AM "@missi51: .@realDonaldTrump thank God is not a politician, but he's one heck of a fighter who will fight for us, the people."
- Mar 24, 2016 09:02:27 AM It is amazing how @LindseyGrahamSC gets on so many T.V. shows talking negatively about me when I beat him so badly (ZERO) in his pres run!
- Mar 24, 2016 09:07:07 AM .@LindseyGrahamSC and Lyin' Ted Cruz are two politicians who are very much alike - ALL TALK AND NO ACTION! Both talk about ISIS, do nothing!
- Mar 24, 2016 09:14:14 AM These politicians like Cruz and Graham, who have watched ISIS and many other problems develop for years, do nothing to make things better!
- Mar 24, 2016 09:17:57 AM Remember when I recently said that Brussels is a "hell hole" and a mess and the failing @nytimes wrote a critical article. I was so right!
- Mar 24, 2016 09:38:13 AM It is amazing how often I am right, only to be criticized by the media. Illegal immigration, take the oil, build the wall, Muslims, NATO!
- Mar 24, 2016 09:41:46 AM "@TimVincent56: @LindseyGrahamSC Talkers think about the future, Doers are already building it" #VoteTrump2016 https://t.co/OoB38jypsD"
- Mar 24, 2016 09:46:29 AM Hillary Clinton has been working on solving the terrorism problem for years. TIME FOR A CHANGE, I WILL SOLVE - AND FAST!

- Mar 24, 2016 10:33:34 AM .@TheView T.V. show, which is failing so badly that it will soon be taken off thr air, is constantly asking me to go on. I TELL THEM "NO"
- Mar 24, 2016 10:39:16 AM Explain how the women on The View, which is a total disaster since the great Barbara Walters left, ever got their jobs. @abc is wasting time
- Mar 24, 2016 10:49:02 AM "@Doctor_S_Freud: @TheView They're all brain-dead puppets with skeletons in their closet. I say you go on and destroy them all" A dead show
- Mar 24, 2016 10:52:11 AM Just announced that as many as 5000 ISIS fighters have infiltrated Europe. Also, many in U.S. I TOLD YOU SO! I alone can fix this problem!
- Mar 24, 2016 10:55:32 AM Europe and the U.S. must immediately stop taking in people from Syria. This will be the destruction of civilization as we know it! So sad!
- Mar 24, 2016 10:59:13 AM "@NeilTurner_: @realDonaldTrump Cruz & Rubio are scared! WATCH -> https://t.co/pWjLW1QBKo https://t.co/W2r6mOzgkb"
- Mar 24, 2016 11:02:06 AM Endorsements for Lyin' Ted Cruz- https://t.co/c3QEbexOwT
- Mar 24, 2016 01:14:18 PM MAKE AMERICA GREAT AGAIN! https://t.co/PHgrT1Nl27
- Mar 24, 2016 04:48:17 PM Just won a big federal lawsuit similar in certain ways to the Trump U case but the press refuses to write about it. If I lost-monster story!
- Mar 24, 2016 05:31:17 PM I didn't start the fight with Lyin'Ted Cruz over the GQ cover pic of Melania, he did. He knew the PAC was putting it out - hence, Lyin' Ted!
- Mar 24, 2016 05:42:27 PM Wow, just released that $67 million in negative ads was spent on me. How am I still number one - by a lot?
- Mar 25, 2016 04:03:32 PM "@11phenomenon: #LyingTed blames @realDonaldTrump for so many things I am starting to think he is having a mental health crisis."
- Mar 25, 2016 09:43:18 PM Top suspect in Paris massacre, Salah Abdeslam, who also knew of the Brussels attack, is no longer talking. Weak leaders, ridiculous laws!

- Mar 25, 2016 09:47:47 PM "@theAgeofLeo: Your instincts on foreign policy & terrorism have been better than all of these so called experienced politicians combined."
- Mar 25, 2016 09:51:23 PM "@stanColtrane: Turns out @glennbeck was wrong. @realDonaldTrump had nothing to do with it https://t.co/svSKfiDkdf"

- Mar 26, 2016 05:36:09 AM "@SpartanMaker: Let me help you Trumpophobes with math: Trump: ($10.3B-$1.2M 74' equity)/1.2M = 858,233%. S&P: 1314.5% #Derp"
- Mar 26, 2016 05:40:04 AM "@Tytan01: Dear @CNN, after doing a quick Google & Twitter search there are over 15,000 women's groups supporting DonaldTrump. Stop Lying."
- Mar 26, 2016 06:24:00 AM "@pattiandsammi: @gullakhta99 @realDonaldTrump @Tytan01 @CNN WOMEN LOVE TRUMP. TRUMP'S EXECS PREDOMINANTLY FEMALE. #WOMEN4TRUMP"
- Mar 26, 2016 10:19:31 AM The media is so after me on women Wow, this is a tough business. Nobody has more respect for women than Donald Trump!
- Mar 26, 2016 02:01:42 PM The press is going out of their way to convince people that I do not like or respect women, when they know that it is just the opposite!
- Mar 26, 2016 02:13:48 PM Lyin' Ted Cruz is now trying to convince prople that his problems with The National Enq.were caused by me. I had NOTHING to do with story!
- Mar 26, 2016 02:20:33 PM Nobody will protect our Nation like Donald J. Trump. Our military will be greatly strengthened and our borders will be strong. Illegals out!
- Mar 26, 2016 02:27:56 PM Wisconsin's economy is doing poorly and like everywhere else in U.S., jobs are leaving. I will make our economy strong again - bring in jobs
- Mar 26, 2016 03:12:01 PM Don't believe the @FoxNews Polls, they are just another phony hit job on me. I will beat Hillary Clinton easily in the General Election.
- Mar 26, 2016 03:16:02 PM Remember, I am the only candidate who is self-funding. While I am given little credit for this by the voters, I am not bought like others!

- Mar 27, 2016 08:02:06 AM I am interviewed on This Week on @ABC this morning. Enjoy!
- Mar 27, 2016 09:14:05 AM Wow, sleepy eyes @chucktodd is at it again. He is do totally biased. The things I am saying are correct. - far better vision than the others
- Mar 27, 2016 09:23:51 AM My statement on NATO being obsolete and disproportionately too expensive (and unfair) for the U.S. are now, finally, receiving plaudits!
- Mar 27, 2016 02:41:16 PM Happy Easter to all, have a great day!
- Mar 27, 2016 03:37:17 PM Another radical Islamic attack, this time in Pakistan, targeting Christian women & children. At least 67 dead,400 injured. I alone can solve
- Mar 27, 2016 03:55:59 PM Why can't the pundits be honest? Hopefully we are all looking for a strong and great country again. I will make it strong and great! JOBS!
- Mar 27, 2016 04:11:43 PM Just to show you how unfair Republican primary politics can be, I won the State of Louisiana and get less delegates than Cruz- Lawsuit coming
- Mar 27, 2016 05:16:52 PM See Lyin' Ted, even the @DailyBeast (no fan of mine) says this story came from Rubio, not Trump! https://t.co/Okc8XajVnz
- Mar 27, 2016 08:17:57 PM The United States cannot continue to make such bad, one-sided trade deals. There are only so many jobs we can give up. No more!
- Mar 27, 2016 08:36:28 PM "@VictorConkle: #WIPrimary @realDonaldTrump will defeat ISIS and #MakeAmericaGreatAgain https://t.co/VWIJ7jUTaV"

- Mar 28, 2016 06:18:50 AM I will be interviewed on @foxandfriends at 7:30. Things are looking good, had a great Easter-look forward to spending the week in Wisconsin!
- Mar 28, 2016 07:05:54 AM "@nellalda: @realDonaldTrump We stand by Trump 100%" Thank you!
- Mar 28, 2016 09:45:44 AM "Kirsten Powers: Anti- Trump Operative was Aggressively Shopping Cruz Story" via the Gateway Pundit: https://t.co/batAmur1FD
- Mar 28, 2016 12:25:23 PM A detainee released from Gitmo has killed an American. When will our so-called "leaders" ever learn!

- Mar 28, 2016 05:18:21 PM Ted Cruz is incensed that I want to refocus NATO on terrorism, as well as current mission, but also want others to PAY FAIR SHARE, a must!
- Mar 28, 2016 05:22:11 PM "@wolfblitzer: Campaign-to-date popular GOP totals: @realDonaldTrump 7,546,980; @tedcruz 5,481,737; @JohnKasich 2,724,749" A BIG DIFFERENCE
- Mar 28, 2016 05:34:11 PM Just released that international gangs are all over our cities. This will end when I am President!
- Mar 28, 2016 05:34:40 PM "@PaulaDuvall2: Cruz will say anything that is contrary to what you have to say. If you're for Motherhood, he'll be against it!"
- Mar 28, 2016 06:13:27 PM After the way I beat Gov. Scott Walker (and Jeb, Rand, Marco and all others) in the Presidential Primaries, no way he would ever endorse me!
- Mar 28, 2016 07:57:35 PM Lyin'Ted Cruz is weak & losing big, so now he wants to debate again. But, according to Drudge,Time and on-line polls, I have won all debates
- Mar 28, 2016 08:04:06 PM Lyin' Ted, I have already beaten you in all debates, and am way ahead of you in votes and delegates. You should focus on jobs & illegal imm!
- Mar 28, 2016 08:07:23 PM We need to secure our borders ASAP. No games, we must be smart, tough and vigilant. MAKE AMERICA GREAT AGAIN & MAKE AMERICA STRONG AGAIN!

- Mar 29, 2016 08:34:36 AM Wow, @CNN has nothing but my opponents on their shows. Really one-sided and unfair reporting. Maybe I shouldn't do their town-hall tonight!
- Mar 29, 2016 09:16:19 AM I have millions more votes/hundreds more dels than Cruz or Kasich, and yet am not being treated properly by the Republican Party or the RNC.
- Mar 29, 2016 09:45:37 AM How come the @TODAYshow & @chucktodd show the new @NBCNews Poll for Hillary vs Bernie but do not show the SAME poll where I am killing Cruz?
- Mar 29, 2016 11:41:33 AM Wow, Corey Lewandowski, my campaign manager and a very decent man, was just charged with assaulting a reporter. Look at tapes-nothing there!

- Mar 29, 2016 11:44:36 AM Why aren't people looking at this reporters earliest statement as to what happened, that is before she found out the episode was on tape?
- Mar 29, 2016 02:05:15 PM Victory press conference was over. Why is she allowed to grab me and shout questions? Can I press charges? https://t.co/qbW2RjkINX
- Mar 29, 2016 02:18:53 PM This was the reporters statement- when she found out there was tape from my facility, she changed her tune. https://t.co/N5815RS1At
- Mar 29, 2016 02:35:20 PM Why is this reporter touching me as I leave news conference? What is in her hand?? https://t.co/HQB8dl0fhn
- Mar 29, 2016 02:38:03 PM MAKE AMERICA GREAT AGAIN! https://t.co/0w4ldD7dW3
- Mar 29, 2016 03:24:25 PM Thank you! #MakeAmericaGreatAgain https://t.co/sVUWI7JoGn
- Mar 29, 2016 04:19:56 PM Trump defends campaign manager charged for bruising a reporter: https://t.co/EKU5QMgjd4
- Mar 29, 2016 04:25:44 PM Thank you! #Trump2016 https://t.co/ZWZkHrtRQN
- Mar 29, 2016 07:07:20 PM Final #'s just announced in the GREAT State of MO. TRUMP WINS! New certified #'s show a 365 vote increase for me- @ least 12 more delegates!
- Mar 29, 2016 10:10:20 PM .@DavidGregory got thrown off of TV by NBC, fired like a dog! Now he is on @CNN being nasty to me. Not nice!

- Mar 30, 2016 11:32:22 AM RT @DonaldJTrumpJr: Nice piece and video today in the Wall Street Journal: Trump's three eldest children jump into campaign https://t.co/35…
- Mar 30, 2016 11:35:57 AM THANK YOU, NEW YORK! #MakeAmericaGreatAgain #Trump2016 https://t.co/PuqiM93zOS https://t.co/fSgpKjwk2q
- Mar 30, 2016 12:05:51 PM Please keep your thoughts & prayers with Melissa Young- Miss Wisconsin 2005. https://t.co/D8RBfufIwH
- Mar 30, 2016 04:17:43 PM Congratulations to @CNN for having the wisdom to pick TRUMP! #MakeAmericaGreatAgain #Trump2016 https://t.co/Up8DhQulZ4

- Mar 30, 2016 04:35:14 PM Thank you- Appleton, Wisconsin! #WIPrimary #Trump2016 https://t.co/XkbTWHpEvy https://t.co/klUNUV2J5S
- Mar 30, 2016 09:47:51 PM "@Gearssuxs: @loudobbsnews @realDonaldTrump I'm a democrat and switch over to republican just to vote for trump in the primary." Great!
- Mar 30, 2016 09:57:50 PM "@susanbirchfiel1: Nothing you say will change my mind! Woman for @realDonaldTrump https://t.co/MIq1iF2097"

- Mar 31, 2016 08:48:20 AM The Trump Doctrine: Peace Through Strength. #Trump2016 https://t.co/2GD1TT8fXc https://t.co/tr1ILOoLUb
- Mar 31, 2016 02:05:59 PM Just had a very nice meeting with @Reince Priebus and the @GOP. Looking forward to bringing the Party together --- and it will happen!
- Mar 31, 2016 03:27:40 PM THANK YOU, WISCONSIN! #VoteTrump next Tuesday, April 5th! #WIPrimary https://t.co/4tymy651ZP https://t.co/IOBhOXeBiN
- Mar 31, 2016 05:16:30 PM THANK YOU, AMERICA! #Trump2016 #MakeAmericaGreatAgain https://t.co/09hTbBgPHf https://t.co/uJnmDnvkUv
- Mar 31, 2016 05:33:09 PM THANK YOU, NEW YORK! #Trump2016 https://t.co/ONDROBrDwr
- Mar 31, 2016 09:21:02 PM #MakeAmericaGreatAgain #Trump2016 https://t.co/aANxirUJJD https://t.co/VlMynYN3sd
- Mar 31, 2016 11:23:25 PM The Club For Growth,which asked me for $1,000,000 in an extortion attempt, just put up a Wisconsin ad with incorrect math.What a dumb group!
- Mar 31, 2016 11:29:49 PM The Club For Growth said in their ad that 465 delegates (Cruz) plus 143 delegates (Kasich) is more than my 739 delegates. Try again!

April, 2016

- Apr 1, 2016 09:24:46 AM The National Border Patrol Council (NBPC) said that our open border is the biggest physical & economic threat facing the American people!
- Apr 1, 2016 09:25:17 AM For the 1st time in American history, America's 16,500 border patrol agents have issue a presidential primary endorsement—me! Thank you.
- Apr 1, 2016 01:45:18 PM Does anybody like Lyin' Ted? https://t.co/h78ESEgEYg
- Apr 1, 2016 02:12:58 PM My new radio ad, airing today in Wisconsin! See you soon! #WIPrimary #Trump2016 https://t.co/iEbcYqyk3i
- Apr 1, 2016 04:49:47 PM We must build a great wall between Mexico and the United States! https://t.co/05SjuRJFbf
- Apr 1, 2016 04:52:14 PM Can you believe that Ted Cruz, who has been killing our country on trade for so long, just put out a Wisconsin ad talking about trade?

- Apr 1, 2016 05:36:39 PM MAKE AMERICA GREAT AGAIN! https://t.co/SULeDE2PYp
- Apr 1, 2016 08:44:00 PM Is it possible for @megynkelly to cover anyone but Donald Trump on her terrible show. She totally misrepresents my words and positions! BAD.
- Apr 1, 2016 09:09:29 PM If @megynkelly stopped covering me on her show, her ratings would drop like a rock! My h to h interview with @AC360 beat her by millions!
- Apr 1, 2016 09:21:56 PM I will be in Wisconsin until the election. Jobs, trade and immigration will be big factors. I will bring jobs back home - make great deals!

- Apr 2, 2016 06:15:20 AM Wisconsin has suffered a great loss of jobs and trade, but if I win, all of the bad things happening in the U.S. will be rapidly reversed!
- Apr 2, 2016 02:18:14 PM Join me on Monday, April 4th in Milwaukee! #WIPrimary #Trump2016 Tickets: https://t.co/L0PmEwdRxn https://t.co/F7P4s6oAzN
- Apr 2, 2016 03:19:05 PM Great honor to have @GOP General Counsel, #JohnRyder as a Trump delegate in TN. RNC meeting well worth it! Unifying the party!
- Apr 2, 2016 03:30:25 PM .@HeyTammyBruce- Thank you for your nice words on Fox today. They never use my full statements on nuclear, which you would agree with!
- Apr 2, 2016 03:31:12 PM .@FoxNews should be ashamed for allowing experts to explain how to make a nuclear attack!
- Apr 2, 2016 06:51:08 PM A GREAT DAY IN WISCONSIN! Thank you #Racine & #Wausau! Just arrived in #EauClaire! #Trump2016 #WIPrimary #TrumpTrain https://t.co/a0iKqNepD5
- Apr 2, 2016 10:09:48 PM I will be interviewed by @jdickerson on @FaceTheNation tomorrow morning. Enjoy! #Trump2016
- Apr 2, 2016 10:15:09 PM Thank you Eau Claire, Wisconsin. #VoteTrump on Tuesday, April 5th! MAKE AMERICA GREAT AGAIN! https://t.co/JI5JqwHnMC

- Apr 3, 2016 06:36:30 AM "@FaceTheNation: Tune in for our sit-down interview with Republican frontrunner @realDonaldTrump! https://t.co/oVm8ozIC8h"
- Apr 3, 2016 07:16:28 AM I will be on @FoxNewsSunday with Chris Wallace this morning. Enjoy!
- Apr 3, 2016 08:37:37 AM "@Wheels155:@CNN is reviewing the week,but majority of the show about @realDonaldTrump cuz there would be 0.0 ratings if not. Media's a JOKE
- Apr 3, 2016 08:40:39 AM "@Margee11: #WISCONSIN VOTE SMART @tedcruz RECORDS R SEALED.. WHAT IS HE HIDING? SAVE AMERICA W/ @realDonaldTrump https://t.co/kMuAoGF99S"
- Apr 3, 2016 08:41:27 AM "@007cigarjoe: #MakeAmericaGreatAgain #Trump2016 @realDonaldTrump IS THE ONLY DEAL !!! https://t.co/PQHIM7AbvK"
- Apr 3, 2016 08:46:39 AM Thank you! #Trump2016 #WIPrimary https://t.co/alx0AY6E8J
- Apr 3, 2016 09:53:01 AM "@GOPjenna: "I don't care about the game, I care about the PEOPLE." And that's exactly why WE THE PEOPLE love you so much! #Trump2016"
- Apr 3, 2016 12:48:16 PM Thank you New York, and Pennsylvania! #MakeAmericaGreatAgain #Trump2016 https://t.co/sziCGsvGbz
- Apr 3, 2016 01:05:32 PM Thank you Miss Katie's Diner! #MakeAmericaGreatAgain #Trump2016 https://t.co/oYpUYJmpKI https://t.co/uTSIiVqPkT
- Apr 3, 2016 03:43:32 PM I will be in Milwaukee, Wisconsin- tomorrow at 7pmE with @MELANIATRUMP. Join us! #WIPrimary #Trump2016 https://t.co/L0PmEwdRxn
- Apr 3, 2016 06:48:11 PM Congratulations to @gohermie for winning the @ShellHouOpen. We are all proud of you @TNGCBedminster & all @TrumpGolf clubs! Great going!
- Apr 3, 2016 07:14:13 PM I am on @FoxNews with @greta doing a town hall, from Wisconsin- now! Enjoy! #MakeAmericaGreatAgain #Trump2016
- Apr 3, 2016 09:16:34 PM A great night in West Allis, Wisconsin! Thank you! #VoteTrumpWI #WIPrimary https://t.co/4x9gw1RhWS https://t.co/syGyqtOebs

- Apr 3, 2016 10:13:47 PM A great day in Wisconsin, many stops, many great people! Melania is joining me on Monday. Big crowds. MAKE AMERICA GREAT AGAIN!

- Apr 4, 2016 09:57:15 AM This Tweet from @realDonaldTrump has been withheld in response to a report from the copyright holder.
- Apr 4, 2016 11:34:21 AM Just departing La Crosse, Wisconsin. Thank you! #Trump2016 #WIPrimary https://t.co/xk2cVAz0eY https://t.co/7umXgUjEzi
- Apr 4, 2016 01:03:52 PM Congratulations Jim Herman! We are all proud of you @TrumpGolf! https://t.co/RuuTippjw1
- Apr 4, 2016 03:35:52 PM Will be interviewed on @SeanHannity on @FoxNews from #Wisconsin tonight. My wife, Melania, will join me for the entire show.
- Apr 4, 2016 03:53:46 PM Wow, great news from Wisconsin. Just made two speeches there with a big one coming tonight. Thank you! https://t.co/Bf95GysWDN
- Apr 4, 2016 04:07:04 PM Leaving Superior, Wisconsin now. Thank you! #Trump2016 #WIPrimary https://t.co/AoTBAQgcZr https://t.co/2C4HEwrTQF
- Apr 4, 2016 07:02:54 PM MAKE AMERICA GREAT AGAIN! https://t.co/yypR5snYBC
- Apr 4, 2016 08:14:09 PM I will be on @SeanHannity @FoxNews- tonight at 10pmE w/ @MELANIATRUMP, from Wisconsin. Enjoy! #WIPrimary #Trump2016 https://t.co/znfxf2wyrr
- Apr 4, 2016 09:00:43 PM "@vikkideiter: Something VERY close to my heart. I'm a NAVY VET! I love @realDonaldTrump's VETERANS ADMINISTRATION REFORMS.
- Apr 4, 2016 10:16:32 PM "@FoxNews: @ScottBaio: "#DonaldTrump is the only guy, I think, that has the will & the nerve to attack & to fight." https://t.co/DjkdAzT3WV
- Apr 4, 2016 10:29:30 PM MAKE AMERICA GREAT AGAIN! https://t.co/iiXHgM7aA2

- Apr 5, 2016 07:00:35 AM Good morning Wisconsin! The polls are now open! #VoteTrump today & we will MakeAmericaGreatAgain! https://t.co/cXvX5SCF3c

- Apr 5, 2016 11:56:54 AM Wisconsin, we will MAKE AMERICA GREAT AGAIN!
- Apr 5, 2016 12:15:12 PM "@roadsho: Challenge to all WI gun owners. Vote @realDonaldTrump.The only candidate that will protect your rights! https://t.co/qjTYLj8bxM
- Apr 5, 2016 12:19:52 PM RT @EricTrump: #Wisconsin: To find your voting location visit https://t.co/9VgGcAJDkK #MakeAmericaGreatAgain #TrumpTrain USUSUS https:/…
- Apr 5, 2016 02:25:58 PM Wow, @Politico is in total disarray with almost everybody quitting. Good news -- bad, dishonest journalists! https://t.co/xTvGLDXY5O
- Apr 5, 2016 03:56:50 PM RT @DonaldJTrumpJr: Last chance #Wisconsin: Find your polling location for today's primary & go vote! Visit https://t.co/LC20hcigoQ USUS #T…
- Apr 5, 2016 05:47:28 PM Still time to get out and VOTE! #WIPrimary #Trump2016 #MAGA https://t.co/HjnGrR25Vf

- Apr 6, 2016 11:40:53 AM It is so great to be back home! Looking forward to a great rally tonight in Bethpage, Long Island!
- Apr 6, 2016 07:30:39 PM I was not scheduled to be on the @oreillyfactor. Pure fiction!
- Apr 6, 2016 07:31:02 PM Unbelievable evening. Just made a speech in front 17,000 amazing New Yorkers in Bethpage, Long Island--- great to be home!
- Apr 6, 2016 10:02:28 PM #MakeAmericaGreatAgain #Trump2016 https://t.co/hjygbNsxee

- Apr 7, 2016 02:31:50 PM Ted Cruz attacked New Yorkers and New York values- we don't forget! https://t.co/83ur9C1qhB
- Apr 7, 2016 09:08:59 PM "@gracefulme3: @seanhannity @tedcruz @realDonaldTrump Cruz is hated in New York. He should go home - no place for a phony"
- Apr 7, 2016 09:45:59 PM "@Genie115: #MakeAmericaGreatAgain we can only do that with @realDonaldTrump RT https://t.co/RViAgxoa4t"
- Apr 7, 2016 09:47:06 PM "@Keeblerqueen: @RealRudyGiulian @realDonaldTrump Thanks Rudy!!! Trump will be a great president!!"

- Apr 7, 2016 09:48:30 PM "@DiCristo13: @realDonaldTrump let's have the policy speeches on immigration, economy, foreign policy, and NATO! https://t.co/Uuit2hWmhW"
- Apr 7, 2016 09:50:00 PM "@iamDaveK: @realDonaldTrump first WWE Hall of Famer to become president?"

- Apr 8, 2016 07:03:23 AM So great to be in New York. Catching up on many things (remember, I am still running a major business while I campaign) and loving it!
- Apr 8, 2016 07:05:56 AM "@WPayton344: @PaulManafort Great Interview on CNN-Being from CT- I am thrilled you are part of this Team-GO TRUMP!"
- Apr 8, 2016 07:08:45 AM "@glozee1: Great interview with @PaulManafort on @CNN regarding @realDonaldTrump path to victory #NewDay #MakeAmericaGreatAgain @DanScavino"
- Apr 8, 2016 07:11:29 AM "@R_U_OK_UK: @realDonaldTrump @glozee1 @PaulManafort @CNN @DanScavino Vote trump to save the west. Don't become like Europe - #WakeUpAmerica
- Apr 8, 2016 02:12:12 PM Jennifer is a terrific person. https://t.co/EHL702civ5
- Apr 8, 2016 02:17:12 PM Looks like I was right about NATO. I had no doubt. https://t.co/x6Ne3sjAWz
- Apr 8, 2016 03:06:21 PM Nobody beats me on National Security. https://t.co/sCrj4Ha1I5
- Apr 8, 2016 04:09:44 PM "Donald Trump—The Disrupter" will air on @FoxNews Saturday night and Sunday night at 8 PM ET. Anchored by @BretBaier. @johnrobertsFox
- Apr 8, 2016 08:51:16 PM "@Cam: Reports are RNC has received +1 million postcards so far! If I get more info on ## I'll post @AnnCoulter https://t.co/yhyWihDdMq"
- Apr 8, 2016 08:54:31 PM "@kirstiealley: HELLO BOYS! this is my formal endorsement of @realDonaldTrump & I'm a woman! (last I checked) And Rudy, U R amazing!
- Apr 8, 2016 09:28:16 PM "@RepMartinDaniel: We support you #HaileyPuckett. You will go far in life. Smart and courageous!
- Apr 8, 2016 09:32:07 PM "@redneckgp: All you haters out there, STOP trashing the only candidate @realDonaldTrump that will put ALL OF YOU & AMERICA FIRST #trump"

- Apr 8, 2016 09:33:07 PM "@RepaloneLori: @realDonaldTrump @kirstiealley we love you and know you will do an awesome job! Saw you in bethpage !!" Thank you.
- Apr 8, 2016 09:35:06 PM "@lilrachiepoo: @realDonaldTrump Thank you, Mr. Trump, for your personal and financial sacrifices in this journey to #MAKEAMERICAGREATAGAIN"
- Apr 8, 2016 09:52:33 PM "@AlexNightrasor: @realDonaldTrump @lilrachiepoo Trump will be our best president since Reagan!
- Apr 8, 2016 09:58:52 PM "@DnGLax: Yes! Thank U 4 coming to LI! It was a thrill 2 B part of it! U will get the job done! #MakeAmericaGreatAgain #trump2016 US"
- Apr 8, 2016 10:07:00 PM Isn't it a shame that the person who will have by far the most delegates and many millions more votes than anyone else, me, still must fight

- Apr 9, 2016 06:22:32 AM Bernie Sanders says that Hillary Clinton is unqualified to be president. Based on her decision making ability, I can go along with that!
- Apr 9, 2016 06:44:24 AM "@gene70: @realDonaldTrump Fugedaboudit!!! The woman in New York love Donald Trump!!! https://t.co/ZcfT90hGEX"
- Apr 9, 2016 07:02:59 AM "@gene70: @realDonaldTrump The Real Person Of The Year! https://t.co/3yFUZALNVn" Wow!
- Apr 9, 2016 04:29:18 PM A great honor to visit the 9/11 Memorial Museum with my wife, @MELANIATRUMP, today. #NewYorkValues https://t.co/eKCEWRD0Ro
- Apr 9, 2016 09:44:11 PM "@vivhall3: @realDonaldTrump here your delegate replaced at CO GOP convention. https://t.co/NxYhzdcMS0" Very sad!
- Apr 9, 2016 09:45:46 PM "@Theresa_Cali: Poll shows @realDonaldTrump leads among registered Republican women with 44%. # https://t.co/yQmh3iSPBY" Thank you!
- Apr 9, 2016 09:47:20 PM "@PennyHicks13: @Carolde @kisster1 @FoxNews Your tax and economic plans are second to none! https://t.co/Q08Kp4esxl Media shld report.
- Apr 9, 2016 10:00:04 PM "@Kids123Nicholas: @gqforbes @RepTomMarino @realDonaldTrump.Lets get it done Philadelphia Pa.Make Trump your pick for president now.

- Apr 9, 2016 10:02:23 PM "@Mutual408Grace: @realDonaldTrump @gene70 California women love Mr Trump too. Will make it happen in New York on April 19. Go out & vote."
- Apr 9, 2016 10:02:59 PM "@governor_savage: @realDonaldTrump is the only person who can save us from this corrupt political mess. #MakeAmericaGreatAgain"
- Apr 9, 2016 10:04:56 PM "@AnnCoulter: GOP is trying to steal nomination from the winner (Trump) not block an insurgent catching up 2 frontrunner (Sanders).
- Apr 9, 2016 10:05:28 PM "@metalmom888: @Theresa_Cali If the GOP screws Trump, his millions will walk from the GOP never to return! They better think long and hard"
- Apr 9, 2016 10:10:16 PM "@becker_berta: @vivhall3 @Reince Millions more will burn their Republican registration if GOP continues to subvert the will of the people."
- Apr 9, 2016 10:17:30 PM "@jlopez05391: @realDonaldTrump Rochester loves you! See you tomorrow! #MakeAmericaGreatAgain #Trump2016 #TrumpTrain" A big crowd!

- Apr 10, 2016 06:25:38 AM "@getreal1234: @realDonaldTrump @Kids123Nicholas @gqforbes @RepTomMarino let's go Pa he has my vote Go Trump"
- Apr 10, 2016 06:29:49 AM "@agentvf: New Jersey Man Joseph Hornick Willing to Go to Jail for Flying Trump Flag - Breitbart https://t.co/zky3vlOJu4 @Q102Philly"
- Apr 10, 2016 08:40:23 AM The @nytimes purposely covers me so inaccurately. I want other nations to pay the U.S. for our defense of them. We are the suckers-no more!
- Apr 10, 2016 08:47:57 AM I win a state in votes and then get non-representative delegates because they are offered all sorts of goodies by Cruz campaign. Bad system!
- Apr 10, 2016 02:23:50 PM #MakeAmericaGreatAgain #Trump2016 https://t.co/TvFgM4TqKj
- Apr 10, 2016 07:28:54 PM How is it possible that the people of the great State of Colorado never got to vote in the Republican Primary? Great anger - totally unfair!

- Apr 10, 2016 07:50:56 PM The people of Colorado had their vote taken away from them by the phony politicians. Biggest story in politics. This will not be allowed!

- Apr 11, 2016 05:45:01 AM I will be interviewed on @foxandfriends at 7:00 A.M. Enjoy!
- Apr 11, 2016 06:17:16 AM "@TimeHasCome1: @WayneDupreeShow @ThePatriot143 Trump needs to hold a massive protest rally in Colorado. He'd get 100k & own the news cycle"
- Apr 11, 2016 06:18:17 AM "@autoprofessor17: @realDonaldTrump Great job on Fox n Friends this morning. Very well spoken and presidential. #TrumpTrain"
- Apr 11, 2016 06:18:43 AM "@WVTTS1017: @realDonaldTrump just listened to you on fox. I love you so much." Thank you!
- Apr 11, 2016 07:21:11 AM "@AnnesLimo: @realDonaldTrump @WVTTS1017 Thanks for Rochester rally." Great people, thank you!
- Apr 11, 2016 10:29:51 AM This is happening all over our country—great people being disenfranchised by politicians. Repub party is in trouble! https://t.co/wNXRqVl9Uu
- Apr 11, 2016 03:40:53 PM Colorado Trump Delegates Scratched from Ballots at GOP Convention https://t.co/WLkmYjJJR9
- Apr 11, 2016 03:58:42 PM Why does the liberal media think Bill O'Reilly (@oreillyfactor) is a complete and total vulgarian? I don't think so!
- Apr 11, 2016 03:58:59 PM Leaving for Albany, New York now, massive crowd expected. Very exciting!
- Apr 11, 2016 05:07:39 PM A very interesting piece, by a very good writer, @KirstenPowers of @USATODAY and @FoxNews. https://t.co/gLuMitRitg
- Apr 11, 2016 05:49:25 PM Tune in & join me live in Albany, New York! 7pmE start time! I love you New York! #Trump2016 #TrumpTrain https://t.co/rY5zqUX9Wu
- Apr 11, 2016 06:02:54 PM Join me in Rome, NY- tomorrow! #Trump2016 #NYPrimary Tickets available: https://t.co/VGCdQubia1
- Apr 11, 2016 08:31:23 PM Thank you Albany, New York! #MakeAmericaGreatAgain #Trump2016 https://t.co/IAOuSY5VDC https://t.co/WcItUuxej8

- Apr 12, 2016 05:13:02 AM WOW, great new poll- New York! Thank you for your support! #Trump2016 #NewYorkValues https://t.co/kuvCXJXjcr https://t.co/WSVmdI8vfZ
- Apr 12, 2016 11:02:54 AM Missouri just confirmed #Trump2016 as the official winner- with an additional 12 delegates. #MakeAmericaGreatAgain https://t.co/AVTkCAne5w
- Apr 12, 2016 11:10:23 AM THANK YOU California, Maryland, New York, and Pennsylvania! See you soon! #MakeAmericaGreatAgain #Trump2016 https://t.co/2lyqnMRIGq
- Apr 12, 2016 05:15:28 PM I LOVE NEW YORK! #NewYorkValues https://t.co/dbTDhYAX1v
- Apr 12, 2016 10:53:39 PM Great to be on @andersoncooper tonight with my wonderful family. Will be rebroadcast at 12:00 A.M. (EASTERN).

- Apr 13, 2016 12:10:07 AM #MakeAmericaGreatAgain #Trump2016 https://t.co/l5TyL8U4e8
- Apr 13, 2016 12:11:41 AM #MakeAmericaGreatAgain #Trump2016 https://t.co/249n3yLQxS
- Apr 13, 2016 08:48:43 AM Join me in Pittsburgh- tonight at 7pmE! #Trump2016 #TrumpTrain Tickets: https://t.co/TrKj5lGXup
- Apr 13, 2016 08:06:25 PM Will be interviewed by @SeanHannity on @FoxNews tonight at 10pm from Pennsylvania. Enjoy! #Trump2016 https://t.co/8IJ40zKS90
- Apr 13, 2016 10:46:29 PM Biggest story in politics is now happening in the great State of Colorado where over one million people have been precluded from voting!
- Apr 13, 2016 10:53:59 PM The rules DID CHANGE in Colorado shortly after I entered the race in June because the pols and their bosses knew I would win with the voters
- Apr 13, 2016 11:11:46 PM Big protest march in Colorado on Friday afternoon! Don't let the bosses take your vote!
- Apr 13, 2016 11:47:21 PM Thank you Pittsburgh, Pennsylvania! #MakeAmericaGreatAgain #Trump2016 https://t.co/7WHS3vbXSw

- Apr 14, 2016 12:55:23 PM Join me on Saturday- in Syracuse, New York! #NYPrimary #Trump2016 https://t.co/F6JkPKb1hn https://t.co/yfJZUlDdCM

- Apr 14, 2016 10:50:37 PM MAKE AMERICA GREAT AGAIN! https://t.co/VxVOG3c5RZ

- Apr 15, 2016 04:12:00 PM Thank you America! #Trump2016 https://t.co/PTKkrLeuCB
- Apr 15, 2016 04:52:38 PM Thank you, @NYPost! #Trump2016 https://t.co/KzGweIxaEo
- Apr 15, 2016 07:59:09 PM Join me this weekend! #NYPrimary 4/16: SYRACUSE - NOON https://t.co/Eu43S1wJN9 4/16: WATERTOWN - 3pm https://t.co/UdOZzisJhA #Trump2016
- Apr 15, 2016 08:14:26 PM "@Bubble709_: @realDonaldTrump Praying for your family and your win in New York." Thank you!
- Apr 15, 2016 08:15:29 PM "@wdct8110: @realDonaldTrump We love you Donald ! Finally someone who actually cares about us .. !! https://t.co/BKoQu1mm4A"
- Apr 15, 2016 08:17:55 PM "@herb_stamper: @JackoffJosh711 @SenFrankNiceley @FoxNews @WSJ we are becoming a third world country because of jerks like him" Great!

- Apr 16, 2016 06:56:11 AM "@dmharvey89: @realDonaldTrump @wdct8110 I just voted for @realDonaldTrump in Indiana. Everyone I talk to was following suit!" Fantastic!
- Apr 16, 2016 07:00:26 AM I will be interviewed on @foxandfriends at 9:00 A.M. I will be talking about the rigged and boss controlled Republican primaries!
- Apr 16, 2016 09:28:39 AM #ICYMI: @foxandfriends this morning. https://t.co/s5pUEdCWI0
- Apr 16, 2016 11:16:13 AM Just arrived in Syracuse, NY. Big crowd, great place! We will bring back the desperately needed jobs. #NYPrimary https://t.co/vOEQDsEAKC
- Apr 16, 2016 01:16:01 PM THANK YOU, SYRACUSE! #NYPrimary https://t.co/9oHimG204Y https://t.co/agy5p8NCox
- Apr 16, 2016 04:27:48 PM "@Trump_Supporter: "Trump Holds 66% Favorable Rating in New York – Leads Hillary Clinton by 19pts in Empire... https://t.co/sGAS3bFpCy

- Apr 16, 2016 04:28:30 PM "@Trumptbird: Dear I'm starting to believe that you're actually going to WIN! #Trump2016 #presidenttrump #primary https://t.co/l7IcxN64gz"
- Apr 16, 2016 04:30:09 PM "@AshleyEdam: New CBS Poll shows defections from Cruz's core supporters & increased support for @realDonaldTrump ...Not surprising."
- Apr 16, 2016 05:02:55 PM "@Ollie_621: @FoxNews @realDonaldTrump I think it's more like 64%. #VoteTrumpNY #MakeAmericaGreatAgain!"
- Apr 16, 2016 06:49:01 PM Will be on Hannity tonight. Rebroadcast of town hall from Pittsburgh, PA. 8:00pm on FOX. Enjoy! #Trump2016 https://t.co/ZhaxXnAohm
- Apr 16, 2016 07:13:34 PM See you tomorrow Dutchess County, New York! #NYPrimary #TrumpTrain https://t.co/z9LOIkEyOq https://t.co/caMLixZfda
- Apr 16, 2016 07:27:45 PM Thank you California, Connecticut, Maryland, and Pennsylvania! #MakeAmericaGreatAgain #Trump2016 https://t.co/pwFFHyzSE6
- Apr 16, 2016 09:50:24 PM #MakeAmericaGreatAgain #NYPrimary https://t.co/x0smlMCWau

- Apr 17, 2016 08:28:41 AM I'll be in one of my favorite places this morning, Staten Island. Big crowd, will be fun!
- Apr 17, 2016 08:34:25 AM Lyin' Ted Cruz will never be able to beat Hillary. Despite a rigged delegate system, I am hundreds of delegates ahead of him.
- Apr 17, 2016 08:38:31 AM Lyin' Ted Cruz can't get votes (I am millions ahead of him) so he has to get his delegates from the Republican bosses. It won't work!
- Apr 17, 2016 08:41:38 AM Crooked Hillary Clinton is spending a fortune on ads against me. I am the one person she doesn't want to run against. Will be such fun!
- Apr 17, 2016 09:34:12 AM I would have millions of votes more than Hillary except for the fact that I had 17 opponents and she just had a socialist named Bernie!
- Apr 17, 2016 04:01:04 PM Thank you, California! Will see you soon! #MakeAmericaGreatAgain https://t.co/VyxSXUEkZn https://t.co/5rk1U4dQ7r
- Apr 17, 2016 06:04:53 PM Thank you for today's endorsement, New York Veteran Police Association! #NewYorkValues https://t.co/AMFBymUXuZ https://t.co/ZQHmkBDUnA

- Apr 18, 2016 04:02:13 AM "@DiamondandSilk: .@realDonaldTrump is who we need 2 fix this corrupted, rigged system. 4 no Profit, Under budget & ahead of schedule.
- Apr 18, 2016 05:58:00 AM Lyin' Ted Cruz can't win with the voters so he has to sell himself to the bosses-I am millions of VOTES ahead! Hillary would destroy him & K
- Apr 18, 2016 06:02:24 AM Kasich only looks O.K. in polls against Hillary because nobody views him as a threat and therefore have placed ZERO negative ads against him
- Apr 18, 2016 12:50:31 PM New York, we will make America great again! https://t.co/KyxbaW4fsL
- Apr 18, 2016 04:54:52 PM Lyin' Ted Cruz even voted against Superstorm Sandy aid and September 11th help. So many New Yorkers devastated. Cruz hates New York!
- Apr 18, 2016 10:25:06 PM #MakeAmericaGreatAgain #NYPrimary https://t.co/awow5pyn7n
- Apr 18, 2016 10:32:02 PM Thank you Buffalo! #NYPrimary https://t.co/Z9QphVlZft https://t.co/4ujDuOvLPj

- Apr 19, 2016 06:01:10 AM I am on @foxandfriends at 7:00 A.M. ENJOY!
- Apr 19, 2016 07:13:34 AM A big day for New York and for our COUNTRY! MAKE AMERICA GREAT AGAIN!
- Apr 19, 2016 10:17:06 AM Thank you Eric! https://t.co/pu1vDiQlrV
- Apr 19, 2016 11:01:54 AM Join me in Indianapolis, Indiana tomorrow at 3pm! #Trump2016 #MakeAmericaGreatAgain Tickets: https://t.co/36c7PLAqyq https://t.co/JBNYtk3FyE
- Apr 19, 2016 12:04:54 PM #ICYMI: #Trump2016 closing speech in Buffalo, New York! #VoteTrumpNY https://t.co/tS6mWn2oth
- Apr 19, 2016 12:53:08 PM LETS GO AMERICA! Time to take back our country, and #MakeAmericaGreatAgain Watch video & go #VoteTrump! https://t.co/lsKdqGFyvQ
- Apr 19, 2016 01:18:52 PM #MakeAmericaGreatAgain #Trump2016 https://t.co/awow5pyn7n
- Apr 19, 2016 02:04:15 PM Who did the House Task Force on Urgent Fiscal Issues call- when America needed HELP? https://t.co/Q1NErOtW9V

- Apr 19, 2016 02:46:32 PM 1988 with Oprah- discussing why I would never rule out a run for #POTUS. #Trump2016 #VoteTrumpNY #PrimaryDay https://t.co/9rup33Rl29
- Apr 19, 2016 03:53:40 PM Discussing #NewYorkValues in Buffalo last night- on the eve of the #NYPrimary. LETS GO NY! #VoteTrump https://t.co/6x8Dag7REA
- Apr 19, 2016 04:40:25 PM RT @DonaldJTrumpJr: A message from Donald J. Trump to NEW YORK! https://t.co/FMosFLn8yq
- Apr 19, 2016 05:00:15 PM Polls close in 3 hours! Everyone get out and VOTE! #Trump2016 #MakeAmericaGreatAgain https://t.co/EuFxefFu0D
- Apr 19, 2016 06:50:09 PM "@kdk144: @realDonaldTrump Everybody is "In A New York State of Mind" now!"
- Apr 19, 2016 06:51:21 PM "@keksec__org: @realDonaldTrump Your policies will make this state and country great again! #MakeAmericaGreatAgain https://t.co/SWxV3YCbqb"
- Apr 19, 2016 07:03:37 PM "@GreenSkyDeb: Look everybody, DonaldTrump will win it on the first ballot so keep praying!!! #TrumpTrain #Trump2016 #MakeAmericaGreatAgain"
- Apr 19, 2016 07:54:52 PM .@CNN is so negative it is impossible to watch. Terrible panel, angry haters. Bill O @oreillyfactor said such an amazing thing about me!
- Apr 19, 2016 08:08:36 PM Thank you New York! I love you! #MakeAmericaGreatAgain #Trump2016 https://t.co/T1J0aUwMXl
- Apr 19, 2016 10:22:19 PM Thank you New York, I will never forget!
- Apr 19, 2016 10:31:23 PM "@bigop1: @realDonaldTrump @CNN @oreillyfactor https://t.co/vXiQru6HIE" Wow, really nice!
- Apr 19, 2016 10:58:30 PM MAKE AMERICA GREAT AGAIN! https://t.co/tK6mKZpFBl

- Apr 20, 2016 07:42:59 AM Ted Cruz is mathematically out of winning the race. Now all he can do is be a spoiler, never a nice thing to do. I will beat Hillary!
- Apr 20, 2016 10:03:10 AM Off to Indiana! #Trump2016 https://t.co/zqUdaaSaXD
- Apr 20, 2016 11:05:36 AM #Trump360 Watch this 360 video of my speech last night at Trump Tower- https://t.co/2YT2Kxly9t

- Apr 20, 2016 05:50:04 PM Thank you Indiana! Will be back soon! #Trump2016 #MakeAmericaGreatAgain https://t.co/pxvSL8cs3B
- Apr 20, 2016 08:58:17 PM Had a meeting with the terrific @GovPenceIN of Indiana. So excited to campaign in his wonderful state! https://t.co/73uCyV6ql4
- Apr 20, 2016 08:58:27 PM We are going to bring steel and manufacturing back to Indiana!
- Apr 20, 2016 09:26:19 PM Thank you Maryland- what a great way to conclude the day! Will be back soon. #Trump2016 https://t.co/dNeTdMENdV https://t.co/JbJYYpEsmo

- Apr 21, 2016 05:14:48 AM I will be doing the @TODAYshow with my wife, Melania, and the rest of my family in a major Town Hall. Hopefully, it will be fun! Enjoy.7A.M.
- Apr 21, 2016 05:22:03 AM Senator Ted Cruz has been MATHEMATICALLY ELIMINATED from race. He said Kasich should get out for same reason. I think both should get out!
- Apr 21, 2016 04:47:21 PM Both Ted Cruz and John Kasich have no path to victory. They should both drop out of the race so that the Republican Party can unify!
- Apr 21, 2016 05:16:27 PM Cruz said Kasich should leave because he couldn't get to 1237. Now he can't get to 1237. Drop out LYIN' Ted.

- Apr 22, 2016 10:00:11 AM I met Prince on numerous occasions. He was an amazing talent and wonderful guy. He will be greatly missed!
- Apr 22, 2016 12:35:37 PM Thank you for the incredible support, Maryland! This is a movement! #MakeAmericaGreatAgain #Trump2016 https://t.co/Uyq4sTYb0l
- Apr 22, 2016 05:21:03 PM Thank you, @DonaldJTrumpJr! #Trump2016 #MakeAmericaGreatAgain https://t.co/FJXjkZAAQf https://t.co/0NQLzbwuFo
- Apr 22, 2016 06:33:20 PM Thank you California! See you soon! #MakeAmericaGreatAgain #Trump2016 https://t.co/uJCqbQYYWR https://t.co/8rqI4mQ3Tw
- Apr 22, 2016 07:03:07 PM Thank you Indiana! Was great seeing everyone on Wednesday! I will be back soon! #Trump2016 https://t.co/mWfLxYKPbk https://t.co/62DKEm5XVm

- Apr 22, 2016 08:17:58 PM Thank you Pennsylvania! #Trump2016 https://t.co/Y3UBsxBQmg https://t.co/ie23QdsVTe

- Apr 23, 2016 07:37:16 AM Will be spending the day campaigning in Connecticut, another state where jobs are being stolen by other countries. I will stop this fast!
- Apr 23, 2016 08:58:30 AM Pennsylvania: Cast your vote for Trump for POTUS & ALSO vote for the TRUMP DELEGATES in your congressional district! https://t.co/1utaLLMfUa
- Apr 23, 2016 09:44:49 AM #MakeAmericaGreatAgain Video: https://t.co/Dsa2v9X3ol https://t.co/aGUHmO98Xm
- Apr 23, 2016 11:10:15 AM Thank you Waterbury, Connecticut! #MakeAmericaGreatAgain #Trump2016 https://t.co/5eZ5nVQbE9 https://t.co/OoQAAKWUUq
- Apr 23, 2016 02:04:43 PM The Establishment and special interests are absolutely killing our country. Stop them now: https://t.co/cLUCrZ2hde https://t.co/zUmuW5WPrk
- Apr 23, 2016 02:27:18 PM Thank you Bridgeport, Connecticut! #MakeAmericaGreatAgain #Trump2016 https://t.co/GCtTKnNq06 https://t.co/qcuDCyBzCN
- Apr 23, 2016 02:30:58 PM Thank you Delaware! #Trump2016 #MakeAmericaGreatAgain #TrumpTrain https://t.co/qLXTzQPbEj https://t.co/ofhbM9bcOI
- Apr 23, 2016 03:29:50 PM Lynne Ryan -- just read your great story in the NY Times -- I am proud of you. Thanks! https://t.co/zVmhYsd4ir
- Apr 23, 2016 07:55:43 PM Congratulations to @seanhannity on his great ratings and ratings increase as reported by the @AP today. Amazing job!
- Apr 23, 2016 08:41:57 PM I had a great day campaigning in Connecticut. Looking for a big vote on Tuesday!
- Apr 23, 2016 08:48:17 PM As soon as John Kasich is hit with negative ads, he will drop like a rock in the polls against Crooked Hillary Clinton. I will win!
- Apr 23, 2016 09:01:25 PM .@Borisep was great on @JudgeJeanine tonight. Very smart commentary that will prove to be correct!

- Apr 24, 2016 08:58:53 AM .@AndreBauer Great job and advice on @CNN @jaketapper Thank you!

- Apr 24, 2016 09:01:37 AM I will be in Maryland this afternoon for a major rally. Things are looking good for Tuesday!
- Apr 24, 2016 09:03:48 AM "@newtgingrich: #NYPrimary turned Trump from frontrunner into presumptive #GOP nominee https://t.co/oLC7mGgnZ9 https://t.co/iNolBfFFRF"
- Apr 24, 2016 09:05:43 AM "@DiamondandSilk: .@DonaldJTrumpJr awesome job on @CNNSotu. DonaldTrump has integrity & he refuses 2 play the game call "Delegate Bribery"
- Apr 24, 2016 08:27:12 PM I am happy to hear how badly the @nytimes is doing. It is a seriously failing paper with readership which is way down. Becoming irrelevant!
- Apr 24, 2016 10:39:58 PM Wow, just announced that Lyin' Ted and Kasich are going to collude in order to keep me from getting the Republican nomination. DESPERATION!
- Apr 24, 2016 10:49:17 PM Lyin' Ted and Kasich are mathematically dead and totally desperate. Their donors & special interest groups are not happy with them. Sad!

- Apr 25, 2016 06:54:21 AM Lyin' Ted Cruz and 1 for 38 Kasich are unable to beat me on their own so they have to team up (collusion) in a two on one. Shows weakness!
- Apr 25, 2016 06:59:06 AM Shows how weak and desperate Lyin' Ted is when he has to team up with a guy who openly can't stand him and is only 1 win and 38 losses.
- Apr 25, 2016 11:15:58 AM Kasich just announced that he wants the people of Indiana to vote for him. Typical politician - can't make a deal work.
- Apr 25, 2016 11:16:27 AM On the way to the great state of Rhode Island- big rally. Then to Pennsylvania for rest of day and night!
- Apr 25, 2016 01:11:08 PM RT @DRUDGE_REPORT: DEAD HEAT: CLINTON VS TRUMP https://t.co/wqfQMEMQOj
- Apr 25, 2016 04:54:55 PM Thank you Warwick, Rhode Island! #RIPrimary #VoteTrump https://t.co/V0d4CuS1xf https://t.co/GU3p28VMe0
- Apr 25, 2016 05:06:26 PM Thank you West Chester, Pennsylvania! #PAPrimary #VoteTrump https://t.co/Qva1QtmhpS https://t.co/CF9SYBqka7
- Apr 25, 2016 05:11:06 PM Passing what was once a vibrant manufacturing area in Pennsylvania. So sad! #MakeAmericaGreatAgain https://t.co/RYWjgPh9Ja

- Apr 25, 2016 08:28:08 PM Get out and VOTE tomorrow! We will MAKE AMERICA GREAT AGAIN! #CTPrimary #DEPrimary #MDPrimary #PAPrimary #RIPrimary https://t.co/ndi8sZI1Gt
- Apr 25, 2016 08:52:16 PM Thank you Wilkes-Barre, Pennsylvania! #MakeAmericaGreatAgain #Trump2016 https://t.co/FJbNlidwJF

- Apr 26, 2016 05:42:39 AM The Cruz-Kasich pact is under great strain. This joke of a deal is falling apart, not being honored and almost dead. Very dumb!
- Apr 26, 2016 07:47:24 AM MAKE AMERICA GREAT AGAIN! https://t.co/xhwhJuV3aa https://t.co/2XWN52IpH2
- Apr 26, 2016 08:33:24 AM Thank you @DonaldJTrumpJr & @EricTrump. #Trump2016 https://t.co/CMfcrZjHgM
- Apr 26, 2016 11:07:35 AM Bernie Sanders has been treated terribly by the Democrats—both with delegates & otherwise. He should show them, and run as an Independent!
- Apr 26, 2016 11:18:18 AM Thank you for the incredible support- Melania, Barron, Ivanka, Jared, Tiffany, Don, Vanessa, Eric, and Lara! https://t.co/mPGpPFiDl8
- Apr 26, 2016 12:43:15 PM How bad is the New York Times—the most inaccurate coverage constantly. Always trying to belittle. Paper has lost its way!
- Apr 26, 2016 01:02:10 PM Lets go Pennsylvania! #VoteTrump https://t.co/TWQM8AV9p4
- Apr 26, 2016 01:03:39 PM Six hours left to #VoteTrump Connecticut! https://t.co/U1kbLMwhNI
- Apr 26, 2016 01:05:25 PM Thank you for a great day yesterday, Rhode Island! #VoteTrump https://t.co/nAlgNIIdyo
- Apr 26, 2016 01:12:06 PM You have until 8pm to #VoteTrump, Delaware! https://t.co/GYeV6m1qOn
- Apr 26, 2016 01:12:15 PM Lets #MakeAmericaGreatAgain, Maryland! #VoteTrump https://t.co/ZttNAmk1QS
- Apr 26, 2016 02:55:15 PM Thank you America! #Trump2016 https://t.co/KL7VZbM1jP
- Apr 26, 2016 07:08:20 PM Thank you Maryland! #Trump2016 https://t.co/hH3h6bRMIs
- Apr 26, 2016 07:14:19 PM Thank you Pennsylvania! #Trump2016 https://t.co/mucxspuHnV

- Apr 26, 2016 07:18:57 PM Thank you Connecticut! #Trump2016 https://t.co/3GGoVXSZSf
- Apr 26, 2016 07:28:31 PM Thank you Rhode Island! #Trump2016 https://t.co/EzCvm7yc0Y
- Apr 26, 2016 08:02:47 PM Thank you Delaware! #Trump2016 https://t.co/FeXThmUWuo

- Apr 27, 2016 12:35:19 PM Thank you! https://t.co/aYbOob1kiT
- Apr 27, 2016 12:38:27 PM Thank you! WE will MAKE AMERICA GREAT AGAIN! https://t.co/aKxoD24IN9
- Apr 27, 2016 12:44:18 PM Thanks! https://t.co/5jiSyvQiNj
- Apr 27, 2016 12:46:35 PM Thanks Dave! https://t.co/NaPPQNjVi2
- Apr 27, 2016 12:57:48 PM RT @AnnCoulter: GREATEST FOREIGN POLICY SPEECH SINCE WASHINGTON'S FAREWELL ADDRESS.
- Apr 27, 2016 01:35:37 PM Thank you Newt! https://t.co/FOh7qEnKUF
- Apr 27, 2016 01:51:08 PM Agreed! https://t.co/biyldP3CIw
- Apr 27, 2016 03:22:25 PM THANK YOU Connecticut, Delaware, Maryland, Pennsylvania, and Rhode Island! #MakeAmericaGreatAgain https://t.co/MGKh77wQt8
- Apr 27, 2016 05:06:11 PM RT @DonaldJTrumpJr: An Honor to be in #Indiana w @realDonaldTrump @greta & the legend, Bobby Knight! I like our secret weapon better!!! htt…
- Apr 27, 2016 05:14:51 PM Join me on @greta- from Indianapolis, Indiana at 7pmE! Enjoy! #Trump2016 https://t.co/gTyn8GLGil
- Apr 27, 2016 08:47:39 PM Thank you for the endorsement, Coach Bobby Knight! I will never forget it! https://t.co/FchYdKY4F8 https://t.co/MpRtRwv51u
- Apr 27, 2016 08:50:05 PM Thank you Laura! https://t.co/C1GHUJazn0
- Apr 27, 2016 10:17:17 PM I am in Indiana where we just had a great rally. Fantastic people! Staying at a Holiday Inn Express - new and clean, not bad!
- Apr 27, 2016 10:49:52 PM Getting the strong endorsement of the great coach, Bobby Knight, has been a highlight of my stay in Indiana. Big speech tomorrow with Bobby!
- Apr 27, 2016 11:01:16 PM "@AnnetteJeanne: I cried when they said you made a clean sweep of all 5 states. I was SO HAPPY! I really adore you Mr. Trump, so much."

- Apr 28, 2016 05:41:35 AM Thank you to all for the wonderful reviews of my foreign policy speech. I will soon be speaking in great detail on numerous other topics!
- Apr 28, 2016 05:47:06 AM I will be interviewed on the @TODAYshow at 7:00 A.M. this morning. Enjoy!
- Apr 28, 2016 06:31:48 AM Lyin' Ted Cruz, who can never beat Hillary Clinton and has NO path to victory, has chosen a V.P.candidate who failed badly in her own effort
- Apr 28, 2016 07:14:37 AM I will be in Evansville, Indiana, with the great Bobby Knight (who last night endorsed me) at 12:00 this afternoon. See you there!
- Apr 28, 2016 08:25:54 AM So many false and phony T.V. commercials being broadcast in Indiana. Reminds me of Florida where thousands were put up-I won in a landslide!
- Apr 28, 2016 11:23:09 AM Heading to rally with Bobby now! See you soon! https://t.co/dWSSOEctZn
- Apr 28, 2016 04:18:26 PM Thank you Evansville, Indiana! #MakeAmericaGreatAgain https://t.co/Fn8ClNjUtr
- Apr 28, 2016 05:41:21 PM #MakeAmericaGreatAgain https://t.co/53qHBKs7yA
- Apr 28, 2016 06:11:58 PM #MakeAmericaGreatAgain #Trump2016 https://t.co/ZHM5w7jnss
- Apr 28, 2016 07:32:22 PM RT @AdrianaCohen16: Carly Fiorina no lifeboat for a fast-sinking @tedcruz campaign https://t.co/nHhENzFBck via @bostonherald @realdonaldtru…
- Apr 28, 2016 07:35:12 PM RT @newtgingrich: Seems out of touch w/ reality to announce a VP nominee before securing 1237 delegates. https://t.co/Hqx8MRyAjR https://t.…
- Apr 28, 2016 07:40:56 PM I will be interviewed on @foxandfriends with the legendary Coach Bobby Knight- tomorrow morning. Enjoy! #INDPrimary https://t.co/c9WVhfyMzs
- Apr 28, 2016 11:08:34 PM New York Yankees President, Randy Levine: 'End of the Republican Party' If Donald Trump Not Nominated. https://t.co/HEXBZeejBc

- Apr 28, 2016 11:24:09 PM Thank you Costa Mesa, California! 31,000 people tonight with thousands turned away. I will be back! #Trump2016 https://t.co/4P0tzvZn0e

- Apr 29, 2016 06:22:04 AM Wow, the ridiculous deal made between Lyin'Ted Cruz and 1 for 42 John Kasich has just blown up. What a dumb deal - dead on arrival!
- Apr 29, 2016 08:46:49 AM Crooked Hillary Clinton, perhaps the most dishonest person to have ever run for the presidency, is also one of the all time great enablers!
- Apr 29, 2016 11:04:46 AM Thank you Indiana! #Trump2016 https://t.co/WAuI0nRNzX
- Apr 29, 2016 01:28:05 PM We are now at 1001 delegates. We will win on the first ballot and are not wasting time and effort on other ballots because system is rigged!
- Apr 29, 2016 10:07:59 PM .@AC360 Anderson, so amazing. Your mother is, and always has been, an incredible woman!

- Apr 30, 2016 08:31:13 AM The "protesters" in California were thugs and criminals. Many are professionals. They should be dealt with strongly by law enforcement!
- Apr 30, 2016 10:53:30 AM "@LexingtonBobby: @FoxNews @tedcruz @realDonaldTrump https://t.co/uhDlyi82Ua"
- Apr 30, 2016 12:21:35 PM The economy is bad and getting worse-almost ZERO growth this quarter. Nobody can beat me on the economy (and jobs). MAKE AMERICA GREAT AGAIN
- Apr 30, 2016 03:50:42 PM Trump locks down Delaware GOP delegates. #Trump2016 #MAGA https://t.co/sto7CYV1fw
- Apr 30, 2016 06:33:19 PM Thank you @MikeOzanian for the nice comments on @FoxNews today. Great job!
- Apr 30, 2016 10:10:35 PM I will be in Indiana on Sunday and Monday at four MAKE AMERICA GREAT AGAIN rallies. See you there!

May, 2016

- May 1, 2016 08:59:20 AM Thank you Indiana! #Trump2016 https://t.co/shPWexfkVX
- May 1, 2016 10:47:29 AM I watched Sen. Graham @FaceTheNation. Why don't they say that I ran him out of the race like a little boy, and in the end he had no support?
- May 1, 2016 11:10:45 AM Will be in Terre Haute, Indiana in a short while -- big rally! See you soon!
- May 1, 2016 11:29:26 AM I am on @FoxNewsSunday with Chris Wallace- his 20th year anniversary with #FNS, throughout the day. Enjoy! https://t.co/hDzdDpZiRx
- May 1, 2016 03:06:16 PM .@KarlRove is a failed Jeb Bushy. Never says anything good & never will, even after I beat Hillary. Shouldn't be on the air!
- May 1, 2016 04:29:09 PM Thank you Terre Haute, Indiana! #MakeAmericaGreatAgain https://t.co/O6ELhlae3h

- May 1, 2016 04:31:05 PM Thank you Fort Wayne, Indiana! #Trump2016 #INPrimary https://t.co/mDGrmMmk5T
- May 1, 2016 06:37:17 PM Join me in Carmel, Indiana- tomorrow at 4pm! #INPrimary https://t.co/tfW6B0eZDm https://t.co/ZiofZ2D6ck

- May 2, 2016 05:42:59 AM I will be interviewed on @CNN @NewDay at 7:30 A.M. Enjoy!
- May 2, 2016 06:12:40 AM Crooked Hillary Clinton said she is used to "dealing with men who get off the reservation." Actually, she has done poorly with such men!
- May 2, 2016 06:21:02 AM Gov Mike Pence has just stated that Donald Trump has taken a strong stance on Hoosier jobs, and he thanks me! I will bring back jobs to USA.
- May 2, 2016 09:06:30 AM Everybody is talking about the protesters burning the American flags and proudly waving Mexican flags. I want America First - so do voters!
- May 2, 2016 09:27:51 AM I will be campaigning in Indiana all day. Things are looking great, and the support of Bobby Knight has been so amazing. Today will be fun!
- May 2, 2016 11:16:14 AM I will defeat Crooked Hillary Clinton on 11/8/2016. #Trump2016 #MakeAmericaGreatAgain https://t.co/HtwD1FGn9e
- May 2, 2016 02:57:55 PM Honored to have received the endorsement of Lou Holtz - a great guy! #INPrimary #Trump2016 https://t.co/AeGyODb37O
- May 2, 2016 04:42:54 PM Thank you Carmel, Indiana! Get out & #VoteTrump tomorrow! #INPrimary #MakeAmericaGreatAgain https://t.co/j07c4oYryG
- May 2, 2016 04:47:59 PM RT @DonaldJTrumpJr: Donald Trump Jr. On The Record: Why Trump International Hotels And Residences Are Still Winning via @forbes https://t.c…
- May 2, 2016 04:50:17 PM THANK YOU AMERICA! #MakeAmericaGreatAgain https://t.co/PvhGP2HmbN
- May 2, 2016 04:56:36 PM Will be interviewed on @seanhannity tonight at 10pmE. Enjoy! #INPrimary
- May 2, 2016 05:24:06 PM Will be in South Bend, Indiana in a short while -- big rally! See you soon!

- May 2, 2016 09:09:00 PM RT @EricTrump: Wow! I am speechless! Thank you to my sidekick @LynnePatton who keeps me & the @EricTrumpFdn in line! https://t.co/L7Y2pjIl6...
- May 2, 2016 09:11:22 PM Thank you South Bend, Indiana! Everyone get out & #VoteTrump tomorrow! #INPrimary https://t.co/rj11BPzqDI https://t.co/xEBlvGrny1

- May 3, 2016 06:23:58 AM MAKE AMERICA GREAT AGAIN! #INPrimary #VoteTrump https://t.co/nMqeKxccv6
- May 3, 2016 09:22:18 AM MAKE AMERICA GREAT AGAIN! #INPrimary #VoteTrump https://t.co/MBgGXSYluW https://t.co/YPwDZ8Irch
- May 3, 2016 10:21:33 AM MAKE AMERICA GREAT AGAIN! #Trump2016 #VoteTrump https://t.co/OKaL5UI4oJ
- May 3, 2016 10:31:51 AM Thank you America! #Trump2016 https://t.co/tiExz8YhFT https://t.co/Hkt3YNccb0
- May 3, 2016 11:50:10 AM Polls close at 6pm! #INPrimary #Trump2016 #VoteTrump https://t.co/DT9WkYAGEK
- May 3, 2016 01:29:03 PM MAKE AMERICA GREAT AGAIN! #INPrimary #VoteTrump https://t.co/TI27thMZEI
- May 3, 2016 06:02:55 PM Wow, Lyin' Ted Cruz really went wacko today. Made all sorts of crazy charges. Can't function under pressure - not very presidential. Sad!
- May 3, 2016 06:08:44 PM Lyin' Ted Cruz consistently said that he will, and must, win Indiana. If he doesn't he should drop out of the race-stop wasting time & money
- May 3, 2016 06:14:30 PM Thank you Indiana! #Trump2016 #MakeAmericaGreatAgain https://t.co/G4JlShRA6I
- May 3, 2016 06:38:34 PM Thank you Indiana, we were just projected to be the winner. We have won in every category. You are very special people-I will never forget!
- May 3, 2016 11:00:46 PM .@oreillyfactor Please correct, I WON Virginia!

- May 4, 2016 04:25:10 AM What a great evening we had. So interesting that Sanders beat Crooked Hillary. The dysfunctional system is totally rigged against him!

- May 4, 2016 04:44:28 AM I would rather run against Crooked Hillary Clinton than Bernie Sanders and that will happen because the books are cooked against Bernie!
- May 4, 2016 05:04:23 AM I will be interviewed on @Morning_Joe at 6:15 A.M. Enjoy!
- May 4, 2016 05:09:36 AM I will be interviewed on @TODAYshow and Good Morning America at 7:00 A.M.
- May 4, 2016 05:12:54 AM I will be interviewed on @foxandfriends at 7:30 A.M. Enjoy!
- May 4, 2016 11:31:05 AM Join me in Charleston, WV - tomorrow! https://t.co/kv624y9UOm

- May 5, 2016 09:29:40 AM Many reports that I will be attending the Alvarez/Khan fight this weekend in Vegas. Totally untrue! Unfortunately I have other plans.
- May 5, 2016 01:37:47 PM I will be interviewed by @BretBaier @SpecialReport at 6pm ET tonight @FoxNews
- May 5, 2016 01:57:30 PM Happy #CincoDeMayo! The best taco bowls are made in Trump Tower Grill. I love Hispanics! https://t.co/ufoTeQd8yA https://t.co/k01Mc6CuDI
- May 5, 2016 02:30:32 PM Bernie Sanders has been treated terribly by the Democrats—both with delegates & otherwise. He should show them, & run as an Independent.
- May 5, 2016 06:28:31 PM Join me tomorrow! #Trump2016 #MakeAmericaGreatAgain Omaha, Nebraska: https://t.co/2OWQIlNutu Eugene, Oregon: https://t.co/oroTbvsNdQ
- May 5, 2016 08:57:05 PM Can you believe Crooked Hillary said, "We are going to put a whole lot of coal miners&coal companies out of business." She then apologized.
- May 5, 2016 10:19:09 PM Thank you West Virginia. Let's keep it going. Go out and vote on Tuesday - we will win big. #Trump2016

- May 6, 2016 05:14:56 AM Unlike crooked Hillary Clinton, who wants to destroy all miners, I want wages to go up in America. We will do so by bringing back jobs!

- May 6, 2016 05:19:08 AM Governor Rick Perry said "Donald Trump is one of the most talented people running for the Presidency I've ever seen." Thank you Rick!
- May 6, 2016 05:26:43 AM So many great endorsements yesterday, except for Paul Ryan! We must put America first and MAKE AMERICA GREAT AGAIN!
- May 6, 2016 06:50:19 AM "@Ausbiz: Many would say that you are the only talented person running for the top job this time! #MakeAmericaGreatAgain #TrumpTrain"
- May 6, 2016 07:08:37 AM Paul Ryan said that I inherited something very special, the Republican Party. Wrong, I didn't inherit it, I won it with millions of voters!
- May 6, 2016 07:38:38 AM Crooked Hillary has ZERO leadership ability. As Bernie Sanders says, she has bad judgement. Constantly playing the women's card - it is sad!
- May 6, 2016 11:08:23 AM Thank you to teachers across America! When I become POTUS we will make education a far more important component of our life than it is now.
- May 6, 2016 01:03:34 PM Joe Scarborough initially endorsed Jeb Bush and Jeb crashed, then John Kasich and that didn't work. Not much power or insight!
- May 6, 2016 01:25:27 PM I hear @JoeNBC of rapidly fading @Morning_Joe is pushing hard for a third party candidate to run. This will guarantee a Crooked Hillary win.
- May 6, 2016 04:01:44 PM Response to @LindseyGrahamSC: https://t.co/lSDE7LHc95
- May 6, 2016 06:15:58 PM I hope corrupt Hillary Clinton chooses goofy Elizabeth Warren as her running mate. I will defeat them both.
- May 6, 2016 06:16:17 PM Let's properly check goofy Elizabeth Warren's records to see if she is Native American. I say she's a fraud!
- May 6, 2016 06:16:36 PM Goofy Elizabeth Warren, Hillary Clinton's flunky, has a career that is totally based on a lie. She is not Native American.
- May 6, 2016 07:14:54 PM Just met with courageous family of Sarah Root in Nebraska. Sarah was horribly killed by illegal immigrant, but leaves behind amazing legacy.
- May 6, 2016 07:16:31 PM Crooked Hillary Clinton wants completely open borders. Millions of Democrats will run from her over this and support me.

- May 6, 2016 09:44:44 PM Goofy Elizabeth Warren and her phony Native American heritage are on a Twitter rant. She is too easy! I'm driving her nuts.
- May 6, 2016 09:44:54 PM Goofy Elizabeth Warren is weak and ineffective. Does nothing. All talk, no action -- maybe her Native American name?

- May 7, 2016 10:36:17 AM Join me in Washington today! Spokane tickets: https://t.co/McBZgICMgs Lynden tickets: https://t.co/MTu0GEM7Dx https://t.co/C7HhNvO01T
- May 7, 2016 10:47:00 AM I am going to keep our jobs in the U.S., and totally rebuild our crumbling infrastructure. Crooked Hillary has no clue! @Teamsters
- May 7, 2016 10:53:38 AM I am honored that the great men and women of the @Teamsters have created a movement from within called Teamsters for Trump! Thank you.
- May 7, 2016 12:46:46 PM Remember when the two failed presidential candidates, Lindsey Graham and Jeb Bush, signed a binding PLEDGE? They broke the deal, no honor!
- May 7, 2016 08:29:54 PM .@EdGoeas thank you for your support tonight on @JudgeJeanine.

- May 8, 2016 12:57:54 AM "@matandsher: I want a leader that will shoot straight with us. The politicians can't. @realDonaldTrump will give his all for us!
- May 8, 2016 07:46:07 AM #HappyMothersDay! https://t.co/T35f2y5YxR https://t.co/BVSHiG2iPA
- May 8, 2016 08:25:28 AM I will be interviewed on This Week with George S this morning. Enjoy!
- May 8, 2016 08:28:04 AM I will be interviewed on @meetthepress this morning. Enjoy!
- May 8, 2016 10:30:47 AM .@KellyannePolls Kellyanne, you were fantastic on @meetthepress today. Keep going - I will win for the people. MAKE AMERICA GREAT AGAIN!
- May 8, 2016 03:15:20 PM Crooked Hillary just can't close the deal with Bernie. It will be the same way with ISIS, and China on trade, and Mexico at the border. Bad!
- May 8, 2016 09:04:03 PM On @seanhannity show @FoxNews now. ENJOY!

- May 9, 2016 04:32:05 AM I will win the election against Crooked Hillary despite the people in the Republican Party that are currently and selfishly opposed to me!
- May 9, 2016 04:34:48 AM I will be interviewed on @NewDay @CNN at 7:00 A.M.
- May 9, 2016 04:49:25 AM "@mathewjmari: On @FaceTheNation #MattSchlapp was on the ball & #jenniferrubin is in a time warped stupor. @realDonaldTrump will EXPAND #GOP
- May 9, 2016 05:05:49 AM .@drmoore Russell Moore is truly a terrible representative of Evangelicals and all of the good they stand for. A nasty guy with no heart!
- May 9, 2016 05:27:02 AM I will be interviewed on @CNN at 7:00 A.M.
- May 9, 2016 05:39:12 AM Wow, I hear @Morning_Joe has gone really hostile ever since I said I won't do or watch the show anymore.They misrepresent my positions!
- May 9, 2016 06:24:42 AM "@RichBooth6: @realDonaldTrump @CNN good interview Mr. Trump. You set the facts straight." Thank you.
- May 9, 2016 06:33:14 AM Will be interviewed by @MariaBartiromo on @FoxBizAlert at 7:30 A.M. Enjoy!
- May 9, 2016 07:05:45 AM "@NathanDWilsonFL: @MariaBartiromo you had a great interview with Donald today! I started watching your show due to Donald Trump.
- May 9, 2016 07:15:04 AM "@daybastrop @foxandfriends @BretBaier The liars that signed the pledge and now won't support @realDonaldTrump IS the reason they are losers
- May 9, 2016 07:17:41 AM "@Valdosta_Monkey: @ChrisCuomo @realDonaldTrump Is Chris serious, lying or misinformed? Bill Clinton signed NAFTA https://t.co/dFDvYQrN1v"
- May 9, 2016 10:13:26 AM #WVPrimary #VoteTrump #Trump2016 https://t.co/ihDWRMdy98 https://t.co/VSStoanoDb
- May 9, 2016 10:15:28 AM #NEPrimary #VoteTrump #Trump2016 https://t.co/ygD2z6EnhY https://t.co/Z2yVlmHl8o
- May 9, 2016 11:56:36 AM Crooked Hillary Clinton says that she got more primary votes than Donald Trump. But I had 17 people to beat—she had one!

- May 9, 2016 11:57:46 AM If I only had 1 person running against me in the primaries like Hillary Clinton, I would have gotten 10 million more votes than she did!
- May 9, 2016 11:59:00 AM I will have set the all time record in primary votes in the Republican party --despite having to compete against 17 other people!
- May 9, 2016 12:21:21 PM I am lowering taxes far more than any other candidate. Any negotiated increase by Congress to my proposal would still be lower than current!
- May 9, 2016 03:35:13 PM RT @greta: interesting poll results so far (and go vote on https://t.co/0Zv2YvEdRX) https://t.co/BnsRf9GSxC
- May 9, 2016 03:50:01 PM Thank you Jason Greenblatt @JasonDovEsq "For Our Children: Let's Elect Donald Trump" https://t.co/3diVyaiw2Q
- May 9, 2016 09:15:41 PM "@RedRising11: US I am a woman & I JUST VOTED FOR @realDonaldTrump #NebraskaPrimary #Trump2016 #TrumpForPresident https://t.co/zgzwxQ92wZ"

- May 10, 2016 05:20:40 AM Get out and vote West Virginia, we will MAKE AMERICA GREAT AGAIN!
- May 10, 2016 05:27:51 AM Get out and vote Nebraska, we will MAKE AMERICA GREAT AGAIN!
- May 10, 2016 06:31:57 AM . #RepMikeKelly Great job on @foxandfriends this morning. Thank you for the nice words!
- May 10, 2016 07:57:08 AM Why does the media, with a strong push from Crooked Hillary, keep pushing the false narrative that I want to raise taxes. Exactly opposite!
- May 10, 2016 08:57:33 AM It was Rosie O'Donnell who ate the cake in the vicious Hillary commercial about me, not Crooked Hillary! @marthamaccallum
- May 10, 2016 09:03:51 AM It is only the people that were never asked to be VP that tell the press that they will not take the position.
- May 10, 2016 10:19:11 AM NEBRASKA #VoteTrump TODAY! #MakeAmericaGreatAgain #Trump2016 https://t.co/hGbesTbQci
- May 10, 2016 10:20:24 AM WEST VIRGINIA #VoteTrump TODAY! #MakeAmericaGreatAgain #Trump2016 https://t.co/pndaZjsruy
- May 10, 2016 10:40:23 AM Via @JTAnews and Jason Greenblatt "Donald Trump is a Visionary With Talents Our Country Needs" @JasonDovEsq https://t.co/lEGJyAinUh

- May 10, 2016 11:18:41 AM I look very much forward to meeting w/Paul Ryan & the GOP Party Leadership on Thurs in DC. Together, we will beat the Dems at all levels!
- May 10, 2016 12:13:49 PM It was so great being in Nebraska last week. Today is the big day--get out and vote!
- May 10, 2016 12:39:34 PM Hillary has bad judgment! https://t.co/LhcIU6kmxs
- May 10, 2016 02:31:30 PM The Clintons spend millions on negative ads on me & I can't tell the truth about her husband? Don't feel sorry for crooked Hillary!
- May 10, 2016 03:09:36 PM RT @DanScavino: OHIO GENERAL ELECTION Donald Trump vs. Hillary Clinton #MakeAmericaGreatAgain #Trump2016 https://t.co/0yXQ4SFSLO
- May 10, 2016 03:15:16 PM RT @DanScavino: LOUISIANA GENERAL ELECTION Donald Trump vs. Hillary Clinton #MakeAmericaGreatAgain #Trump2016 https://t.co/74vYOx7dKz
- May 10, 2016 07:05:31 PM Thank you West Virginia! #MakeAmericaGreatAgain #Trump2016 https://t.co/iCGcF21fWY
- May 10, 2016 08:04:26 PM Thank you Nebraska! #MakeAmericaGreatAgain #Trump2016 https://t.co/RRma61oisz

- May 11, 2016 05:22:54 AM Big wins in West Virginia and Nebraska. Get ready for November - Crooked Hillary, who is looking very bad against Crazy Bernie, will lose!
- May 11, 2016 05:26:37 AM I don't want to hit Crazy Bernie Sanders too hard yet because I love watching what he is doing to Crooked Hillary. His time will come!
- May 11, 2016 09:18:21 AM Goofy Elizabeth Warren has been one of the least effective Senators in the entire U.S. Senate. She has done nothing!
- May 11, 2016 12:12:06 PM Goofy Elizabeth Warren didn't have the guts to run for POTUS. Her phony Native American heritage stops that and VP cold.
- May 11, 2016 12:41:43 PM RT @dmartosko: 'Duck Dynasty' star Phil Robertson says he'll back Trump for president https://t.co/WPJjMPYjlK via @MailOnline
- May 11, 2016 12:43:33 PM #MakeAmericaGreatAgain #Trump2016 https://t.co/CLhqgybbYR
- May 11, 2016 02:09:07 PM Thanks Piers. https://t.co/hiDDT9hV0j

- May 11, 2016 02:18:11 PM If the people of Massachusetts found out what an ineffective Senator goofy Elizabeth Warren has been, she would lose!
- May 11, 2016 02:37:51 PM Goofy Elizabeth Warren is now using the woman's card like her friend crooked Hillary. See her dumb tweet "when a woman stands up to you…"
- May 11, 2016 03:03:35 PM Our Native American Senator, goofy Elizabeth Warren, couldn't care less about the American worker…does nothing to help!
- May 11, 2016 03:22:28 PM Goofy Elizabeth Warren lied when she says I want to abolish the Federal Minimum Wage. See media—asking for increase!
- May 11, 2016 03:41:51 PM Isn't it funny when a failed Senator like goofy Elizabeth Warren can spend a whole day tweeting about Trump & gets nothing done in Senate?
- May 11, 2016 03:51:20 PM In interview I told @AP that my taxes are under routine audit and I would release my tax returns when audit is complete, not after election!
- May 11, 2016 04:07:02 PM If it were up to goofy Elizabeth Warren, we'd have no jobs in America—she doesn't have a clue.

- May 12, 2016 01:12:38 PM Great day in D.C. with @SpeakerRyan and Republican leadership. Things working out really well! #Trump2016 https://t.co/hfHY9MdAc7
- May 12, 2016 02:22:18 PM Great meeting with @SenateMajLdr Mitch McConnell and Republican leaders in D.C. #Trump2016 https://t.co/R0NuOrZISX
- May 12, 2016 09:32:52 PM Senator Lindsey Graham called me yesterday, very much to my surprise, and we had a very interesting talk about national security, and more!

- May 13, 2016 01:40:19 PM .@thehill Your story about me & the carbon tax is absolutely incorrect—it is just the opposite. I will not support or endorse a carbon tax!
- May 13, 2016 03:31:52 PM An incredible honor to receive the endorsement of a person I have such tremendous respect for. Thank you, Sheldon! https://t.co/nW0N3OO4mw

- May 13, 2016 08:03:02 PM If Crooked Hillary Clinton can't close the deal on Crazy Bernie, how is she going to take on China, Russia, ISIS and all of the others?

- May 14, 2016 10:09:49 AM Great new poll- thank you! https://t.co/ytzesbCZas
- May 14, 2016 10:16:06 AM Wow, @CNN is really working hard to make me look as bad as possible. Very unprofessional. Hurting in ratings - bad television!
- May 14, 2016 09:06:11 PM "@stranahan: Sheldon Adelson Pledges $100 Million to Elect Trump President - Breitbart https://t.co/aRXPHAlCLC"

- May 15, 2016 05:49:31 AM Thank you for the nice words this morning @KellyRiddell. Well delivered and totally logical! @CNN @FoxNews
- May 15, 2016 05:55:39 AM The failing @nytimes wrote yet another hit piece on me. All are impressed with how nicely I have treated women, they found nothing. A joke!
- May 15, 2016 06:00:18 AM "@QueenCharlotteO: @realDonaldTrump @nytimes I'm a women & I 100% support @realDonaldTrump & I have since the beginning. Thank you!
- May 15, 2016 06:02:27 AM "@MrTohNey: Leicester & DonaldTrump seem to have the same trajectory, both were written off, but they keep scaling the heights. History?
- May 15, 2016 06:04:06 AM "@DistlerJoyce: @realDonaldTrump @nytimes OHIO WOMEN FOR TRUMP https://t.co/wpxojJnjbb"
- May 15, 2016 06:13:17 AM Everyone is laughing at the @nytimes for the lame hit piece they did on me and women.I gave them many names of women I helped- refused to use
- May 15, 2016 06:14:59 AM "@tzard000: @realDonaldTrump @nytimes Everyone continues to pile onto Donald, but they can NEVER take away our votes!" Thank you!
- May 15, 2016 06:16:01 AM "@TakingIt_Back: @nytimes keep shining....the ppl will not let the media dim your light...we no longer believe them! #Trump2016" Thanks.
- May 15, 2016 06:32:14 AM Why doesn't the failing @nytimes write the real story on the Clintons and women? The media is TOTALLY dishonest!

- May 15, 2016 02:06:18 PM Wow, I have had so many calls from high ranking people laughing at the stupidity of the failing @nytimes piece. Massive front page for that!
- May 15, 2016 02:11:30 PM Why did the failing @nytimes refuse to use any of the names given to them that I was so proud to have helped with their careers. DISHONEST!
- May 15, 2016 02:26:45 PM The media is really on a witch-hunt against me. False reporting, and plenty of it - but we will prevail!
- May 15, 2016 04:26:39 PM Thank you Georgia! See you soon! #Trump2016 https://t.co/8yFd6qA4rD
- May 15, 2016 08:25:54 PM The @washingtonpost report on potential VP candidates is wrong. Marco Rubio and most others mentioned are NOT under consideration.
- May 15, 2016 09:23:06 PM Great new poll- thank you! #MakeAmericaGreatAgain #Trump2016 https://t.co/SZyZ8GkF23

- May 16, 2016 05:00:52 AM Bernie Sanders is being treated very badly by the Dems. The system is rigged against him. He should run as an independent! Run Bernie, run.
- May 16, 2016 06:00:58 AM That was an amazing interview on @foxandfriends - I hope the rest of the media picks it up to show how totally dishonest the @nytimes is!
- May 16, 2016 08:09:26 AM The @nytimes is so dishonest. Their hit piece cover story on me yesterday was just blown up by Rowanne Brewer, who said it was a lie!
- May 16, 2016 08:12:38 AM Wow, Rowanne Brewer, the most prominently depicted woman in the failing @nytimes story yesterday, was on @foxandfriends saying Times lied
- May 16, 2016 08:24:21 AM A political commentator for @cnn, which I no longer watch, said "Trump showed some weakness in the Repub Primaries." I set all-time record!
- May 16, 2016 10:25:02 AM With the coming forward today of the woman central to the failing @nytimes hit piece on me, we have exposed the article as a fraud!
- May 16, 2016 01:19:42 PM Thank you, Anthony @Scaramucci @WSJ "The Entrepreneur's Case for Trump" https://t.co/xm45Ia1GTu

- May 16, 2016 04:50:40 PM Rowanne Brewer, the most prominently depicted woman in the failing @nytimes story yesterday joined @foxandfriends. https://t.co/qkK3LJPoQQ
- May 16, 2016 05:12:53 PM The failing @nytimes is greatly embarrassed by the totally dishonest story they did on my relationship with women.
- May 16, 2016 05:13:20 PM No wonder the @nytimes is failing—who can believe what they write after the false, malicious & libelous story they did on me.
- May 16, 2016 05:14:19 PM Over 50 women were interviewed by the @nytimes yet they only wrote about 6. That's because there were so many positive statements.
- May 16, 2016 05:15:52 PM The writer of the now proven false story in the @nytimes, Michael Barbaro, who was interviewed on CBS this morning, was unable to respond.
- May 16, 2016 08:08:17 PM "In politics, and in life, ignorance is not a virtue." This is a primary reason that President Obama is the worst president in U.S. history!
- May 16, 2016 08:08:17 PM "In politics, and in life, ignorance is not a virtue." This is a primary reason that President Obama is the worst president in U.S. history!
- May 16, 2016 11:02:45 PM What Barbara Res does not say is that she would call my company endlessly, and for years, trying to come back. I said no.
- May 16, 2016 11:40:38 PM "@AprilLaJune: OREGON votes today! Go vote for @realDonaldTrump and kick it BIG TIME! https://t.co/SLYwyM8w1D"

- May 17, 2016 06:29:09 AM Wow, 30,000 e-mails were deleted by Crooked Hillary Clinton. She said they had to do with a wedding reception. Liar! How can she run?
- May 17, 2016 06:37:03 AM The pathetic new hit ad against me misrepresents the final line. "You can tell them to go BLANK themselves" - was about China, NOT WOMEN!
- May 17, 2016 06:46:22 AM Crooked Hillary Clinton put out an ad where I am misquoted on women. Can't believe she would misrepresent the facts! My hit was on China
- May 17, 2016 06:52:00 AM Oregon is voting today. Keep the big numbers going - VOTE TRUMP! MAKE AMERICA GREAT AGAIN!

- May 17, 2016 06:58:10 AM Amazing that Crooked Hillary can do a hit ad on me concerning women when her husband was the WORST abuser of woman in U.S. political history
- May 17, 2016 07:31:53 AM Crooked Hillary can't close the deal with Bernie Sanders. Will be another bad day for her!
- May 17, 2016 08:58:08 AM #VoteTrump at clerk's offices & 185 ballot drop boxes in #ORPrimary! Closes at 8pm! https://t.co/ESGg1Qu68S https://t.co/TqcNAWjP5l
- May 17, 2016 09:17:07 AM Crooked Hillary said her husband is going to be in charge of the economy.If so, he should run,not her.Will he bring the "energizer" to D.C.?
- May 17, 2016 09:21:55 AM How can Crooked Hillary put her husband in charge of the economy when he was responsible for NAFTA, the worst economic deal in U.S. history?
- May 17, 2016 10:25:41 AM I look forward to watching @megynkelly tonight, 8 PM ET. It will be interesting to see how she treats me—I think she will be very fair.
- May 17, 2016 04:19:17 PM I will be live tweeting my interview with @megynkelly on the Fox Network tonight at 8! Enjoy! https://t.co/nlJssZeIWm
- May 17, 2016 06:37:06 PM Do you think Crooked Hillary will finally close the deal? If she can't win Kentucky, she should drop out of race. System rigged!
- May 17, 2016 06:42:33 PM Wall Street paid for ad is a fraud, just like Crooked Hillary! Their main line had nothing to do with women, and they knew it. Apologize?
- May 17, 2016 06:49:47 PM I will be live tweeting @megynkelly Show in 10 minutes. Should be interesting. Will be on Fox Network! ENJOY!
- May 17, 2016 07:06:45 PM "@TrumpTrainRider: .@realDonaldTrump Watching you on Fox with @megynkelly now. Can't wait to hear what you two talked about."
- May 17, 2016 07:14:51 PM "@xGodfatherxzx: @realDonaldTrump amazing on Megan Kelly" Thanks.
- May 17, 2016 07:15:47 PM "@ragdollive: @megynkelly @realDonaldTrump what's with the soft wimpy questions?!? It's not a therapy session ..!!" Not really soft at all!

- May 17, 2016 07:26:43 PM "@manakoa:DonaldTrump, you are fearless! This interview shows you are the Leader we need. @megynkelly is a tough interview! Respect to both"
- May 17, 2016 07:27:41 PM "@wesleyfelixpsi: @realDonaldTrump speaks from the heart 4 all of America.His intention is for a positive future 4 all. @FoxNews @megynkelly
- May 17, 2016 07:28:49 PM "@HFFoundation4: @realDonaldTrump One thing we know for sure @BernieSanders supporters will turn to #Trump - absolutely not @HillaryClinton"
- May 17, 2016 07:29:19 PM "@longbyfive: @realDonaldTrump great interview with @megynkelly !" Thanks.
- May 17, 2016 07:32:10 PM "@SandraR67758219: @realDonaldTrump You are a fighter and we LOVE that about you! Don't listen to these people who want you to change!"
- May 17, 2016 07:32:39 PM "@gerriweth: @megynkelly @realDonaldTrump Made me feel good to hear you both so gracious. Great job"
- May 17, 2016 07:33:40 PM "@curtandkaren: Kudos to @megynkelly and @realDonaldTrump for rising above the drama and coming together. Very respectful and classy "
- May 17, 2016 07:34:55 PM "@LADYJOANNE: @megynkelly @realDonaldTrump we need Trump more then ever Megan Please don't lose it for America for us!"
- May 17, 2016 07:35:40 PM "@LADYJOANNE: @megynkelly @realDonaldTrump we need Trump more then ever Megyn. Thanks.
- May 17, 2016 07:37:13 PM "@FrankDallasAgg: @megynkelly @realDonaldTrump Trump is a great man and is FIGHTING for We The People!"
- May 17, 2016 07:40:41 PM "@jlund04: @megynkelly @realDonaldTrump it was refreshing to see you both in a different light. Well done."
- May 17, 2016 07:41:06 PM "@johnkirtley: @megynkelly @realDonaldTrump #MakeAmericaGreatAgain Thank you for this discourse. Wounds have been healed. Great job!"
- May 17, 2016 07:41:23 PM "@KaceyIlliot1669: @realDonaldTrump We actually really do love you!" Great!

- May 17, 2016 07:42:29 PM "@Janik1968: @realDonaldTrump @SpeakerRyan Watched the Megan Kelly special and I must say..it was very well done on both their parts"
- May 17, 2016 07:43:27 PM "@ladytsbrug: Lovely interview, Mr. Trump! @realDonaldTrump" Thanks.
- May 17, 2016 07:43:47 PM "@markgruber1960: @megynkelly @realDonaldTrump That's why he is so successful. He is driven to succeed" True!
- May 17, 2016 07:45:13 PM "@johnjohnlacca: Donald u have done a terrific job so far on the interview. Cannot wait until u r president #MegynKellyPresents
- May 17, 2016 07:47:01 PM "@svhlevi: @DiamondandSilk @realJeffreyLord @realDonaldTrump @CNN and we love you Diamond and Silk" I do also!
- May 17, 2016 07:47:51 PM "@CostaKenneth: @megynkelly @realDonaldTrump Great interview Megyn"
- May 17, 2016 07:48:42 PM "@thydanielflores: .@megynkelly @realDonaldTrump Best interview that I have ever seen.
- May 17, 2016 07:53:14 PM I like Michael Douglas!
- May 17, 2016 07:56:06 PM "@mai_Ttag: Great interview! Happy you had a chance to show the other side of you. Never change, never forget you are our messenger!"
- May 17, 2016 07:56:35 PM "@jrector34: @realDonaldTrump Amazing job"
- May 17, 2016 07:57:16 PM Will go back on for a final question now!
- May 17, 2016 08:04:23 PM Well, that is it. Well done Megyn --- and they all lived happily ever after! Now let us all see how "THE MOVEMENT" does in Oregon tonight!
- May 17, 2016 08:37:33 PM "@COWBOYSFORTRUMP: @ChristiChat @Rockprincess818 @realDonaldTrump That man is a pillar of strength and will be perfect as our next president
- May 17, 2016 08:49:32 PM I can't believe that @CNN would allow the very nice Jeffrey Lord to be savaged by a panel of seven Trump haters. 7 to 1 - Don't watch CNN!
- May 17, 2016 08:53:58 PM I look so forward to debating Crooked Hillary Clinton! Democrat Primaries are rigged, e-mail investigation is rigged - so time to get it on!

- May 17, 2016 09:14:51 PM "@michael_favreau: @JIS3 @realDonaldTrump He will destroy Hillary but why give CNN record breaking ratings CNN can go to hell. Trump 2016"
- May 17, 2016 09:38:07 PM Michael Barbaro, the author of the now discredited @nytimes hit piece on me with women, has in past tweeted badly about me. He should resign
- May 17, 2016 09:40:34 PM "@sandrajeanne48: No way I believe Trump at 70% disapproval with women. Went to 3 rallies. At least 1/2 women. MSM LIES @TheFive"
- May 17, 2016 09:41:22 PM "@LouDobbs: Hillary Just Handed @realDonaldTrump a Huge Gift: Promising to Put Bubba in Charge of the Economy! #MakeAmericaGreatAgain!
- May 17, 2016 10:15:07 PM Thank you Oregon! #Trump2016 #MakeAmericaGreatAgain https://t.co/hK1yqlp9ca
- May 17, 2016 10:24:48 PM Congratulations to THE MOVEMENT, we have just won THE GREAT STATE OF OREGON. The vote percentage is even higher than anticipated! Thank you.
- May 17, 2016 10:46:26 PM "@MagicMetalNinja: The Trump movement will not be stopped. We support Trump because he is a true American looking out for #AmericaFIRST."
- May 17, 2016 11:03:08 PM "@ShoneeP: @realDonaldTrump Trump for President! Bernie is a joke, knows nothing - and Hillary is yesterday's and today's nightmare"
- May 17, 2016 11:22:01 PM Paul Begala, the dopey @CNN flunky and head of the Pro-Hillary Clinton Super PAC, has knowingly committed fraud in his first ad against me.

- May 18, 2016 06:20:19 AM Bernie Sanders is being treated very badly by the Democrats - the system is rigged against him. Many of his disenfranchised fans are for me!
- May 18, 2016 11:39:07 AM Why did Clinton supporter @AlisonForKY declare Crooked Hillary winner in KY when AP hasn't even called the race?
- May 18, 2016 12:38:20 PM Thank you Arizona! See you soon! #MakeAmericaGreatAgain https://t.co/IC3pe5lRAS
- May 18, 2016 12:47:19 PM Thank you Louisiana! #Trump2016 https://t.co/u8hhrRRFMp

- May 18, 2016 06:14:39 PM #MakeAmericaGreatAgain #Trump2016 https://t.co/kXhc2j94YF https://t.co/YZAdAndKXv
- May 18, 2016 08:54:08 PM Some low-life journalist claims that I "made a pass" at her 29 years ago. Never happened! Like the @nytimes story which has become a joke!
- May 18, 2016 09:52:29 PM My list of potential U.S. Supreme Court Justices was very well recieved. During the next number of weeks I may be adding to the list!

- May 19, 2016 05:27:48 AM Looks like yet another terrorist attack. Airplane departed from Paris. When will we get tough, smart and vigilant? Great hate and sickness!
- May 19, 2016 12:29:36 PM How quality a woman is Rowanne Brewer Lane to have exposed the @nytimes as a disgusting fraud? Thank you Rowanne.
- May 19, 2016 02:36:58 PM Thank you @LtStevenLRogers. We will respond to terrorism with strength in 2017! https://t.co/Mk4YuuRf4s

- May 20, 2016 04:40:37 AM I said that Crooked Hillary Clinton is "not qualified" to be president because she has "very bad judgement" - Bernie said the same thing!
- May 20, 2016 04:47:09 AM Crooked Hillary has zero imagination and even less stamina. ISIS, China, Russia and all would love for her to be president. 4 more years!
- May 20, 2016 04:58:47 AM Look where the world is today, a total mess, and ISIS is still running around wild. I can fix it fast, Hillary has no chance!
- May 20, 2016 05:08:49 AM Crooked Hillary Clinton looks presidential? I don't think so! Four more years of Obama and our country will never come back. ISIS LAUGHS!
- May 20, 2016 05:26:20 AM Crooked Hillary can't even close the deal with Bernie - and the Dems have it rigged in favor of Hillary. Four more years of this? No way!
- May 20, 2016 09:30:06 AM "A Call for Unity" by Jason Greenblatt @JasonDovEsq https://t.co/dQi3Cydckp
- May 20, 2016 10:15:08 AM I am on my way! See you all soon! https://t.co/Arw19Antpj

- May 20, 2016 10:36:44 AM Crooked Hillary Clinton- discussing the #SecondAmendment at a private event. #2A cc: @NRA https://t.co/vV31Pbpkmn
- May 20, 2016 11:09:16 AM Thanks @piersmorgan! "Trump is the most unpredictable, extraordinary, entertaining&massively popular candidate this country has ever seen."
- May 20, 2016 11:11:21 AM Failing @NYTimes will always take a good story about me and make it bad. Every article is unfair and biased. Very sad!
- May 20, 2016 03:06:48 PM Thank you! An honor to be the first candidate ever endorsed by the @NRA- prior to @GOPconvention! #Trump2016 #2A https://t.co/ygLUAl7gzx
- May 20, 2016 04:55:40 PM Great day in Kentucky with Wayne LaPierre, Chris Cox & the @NRA! #MakeAmericaGreatAgain #Trump2016 https://t.co/aJ7s0aqqj0
- May 20, 2016 05:50:18 PM Thank you for your wonderful endorsement today @TGowdySC. It means a great deal to me. We will not disappoint! #Trump2016
- May 20, 2016 06:27:38 PM "@montgomeriefdn: @TrumpTurnberry Best Links Course in Britain. Ailsa Course opens June '16 Can't wait to play it https://t.co/HnQbj3ipuS"
- May 20, 2016 06:36:17 PM @montgomeriefdn Colin, great to have you at Trump Turnberry. So proud of you and your GREAT playing! You made winning MAJORS look easy!
- May 20, 2016 07:44:43 PM Thank you @TheTodaysGolfer for the wonderful statement that "the new par 3 9th hole @Trump Turnberry could be the most dramatic in Britain."
- May 20, 2016 08:51:57 PM Crooked Hillary Clinton wants to essentially abolish the 2nd Amendment. No gun owner can ever vote for Clinton!
- May 20, 2016 08:56:44 PM Crooked Hillary is spending tremendous amounts of Wall Street money on false ads against me. She is a very dishonest person!

- May 21, 2016 05:56:20 AM While our wonderful president was out playing golf all day, the TSA is falling apart, just like our government! Airports a total disaster!
- May 21, 2016 07:49:59 AM Crooked Hillary wants to get rid of all guns and yet she is surrounded by bodyguards who are fully armed. No more guns to protect Hillary!

- May 21, 2016 08:34:02 AM "@RBacliff: Hillary wants to rip the guns out of America's hands. No guns = no protection. Get on #TrumpTrain & join @NRA to stop her."
- May 21, 2016 11:08:26 AM .@CNN is so negative, getting even worse as I get closer. Just had two anti-Trump losers with zero rebuttal from my team. Turning off!
- May 21, 2016 12:00:42 PM MAKE AMERICA GREAT AGAIN! https://t.co/MAZK5bdZuD
- May 21, 2016 12:02:41 PM Crooked Hillary Clintons foreign interventions unleashed ISIS in Syria, Iraq and Libya. She is reckless and dangerous!
- May 21, 2016 03:13:08 PM Thank you to all of the men and women who have served our country. You are our true heroes! #ArmedForcesDay https://t.co/A3Wus0cRIO
- May 21, 2016 10:44:05 PM "@dubilujane: I trust @realDonaldTrump more anyone ever to protect America.He WILL do the right thing for the U.S.A, without a doubt.
- May 21, 2016 10:55:39 PM Crooked Hillary said that I want guns brought into the school classroom. Wrong!

- May 22, 2016 07:47:48 AM Hillary Clinton is not qualified to be president because her judgement has been proven to be so bad! Would be four more years of stupidity!
- May 22, 2016 09:47:45 AM Why do the networks continue to put dopey @BillKristol on panels when he has called every single shot about me wrong for 2 yrs?
- May 22, 2016 10:28:44 AM RT @gatewaypundit: BREAKING POLL: Trump Gains 11 Points on Clinton Since March =>Now Leads Crooked Hillary 46-44 https://t.co/y3BGy15Erb vi…
- May 22, 2016 02:37:05 PM How can Crooked Hillary say she cares about women when she is silent on radical Islam, which horribly oppresses women?
- May 22, 2016 02:38:18 PM Crooked Hillary wants a radical 500% increase in Syrian refugees. We can't allow this. Time to get smart and protect America!
- May 22, 2016 02:46:57 PM Join me on Wednesday, May 25th at the Anaheim Convention Center! #Trump2016 #MAGA Tickets: https://t.co/mmPck1HYrC https://t.co/xGkVbxTamz

- May 22, 2016 03:32:33 PM Bernie Sanders is continuing his quest because he believes that Crooked Hillary Clinton will be forced out of the race - e-mail scandal!
- May 22, 2016 03:44:48 PM The American people are sick and tired of not being able to lead normal lives and to constantly be on the lookout for terror and terrorists!
- May 22, 2016 05:54:48 PM Thank you America! #Trump2016 https://t.co/xfINxdRNiQ

- May 23, 2016 08:46:57 AM In trade, military and EVERYTHING else, it will be AMERICA FIRST! This will quickly lead to our ultimate goal: MAKE AMERICA GREAT AGAIN!
- May 23, 2016 10:32:11 AM Is Hillary really protecting women? https://t.co/8ZtEIWNqz4
- May 23, 2016 12:15:20 PM Obama's VA Secretary just said we shouldn't measure wait times. Hillary says VA problems are not 'widespread.' I will take care of our vets!
- May 23, 2016 06:42:39 PM I will be interviewed on @oreillyfactor at 8:00 P.M. Enjoy!
- May 23, 2016 07:25:41 PM Join me in California or Montana! 5/25/16: Anaheim, California https://t.co/mmPck1HYrC 5/26/16: Billings, Montana https://t.co/atvrCgjFDe
- May 23, 2016 09:38:48 PM While under no obligation to do so, I have raised between 5 & 6 million dollars, including 1million dollars from me, for our VETERANS. Nice!
- May 23, 2016 09:46:08 PM Much of the money I have raised for our veterans has already been distributed, with the rest to go shortly to various other veteran groups.
- May 23, 2016 09:50:48 PM Amazingly, with all of the money I have raised for the vets, I have got nothing but bad publicity from the dishonest and disgusting media.

- May 24, 2016 05:41:44 AM I just released my financial disclosure forms, the largest numbers in the history of the F.E.C. Even the dishonest media thinks great!

- May 24, 2016 06:42:35 AM Crooked Hillary Clinton overregulates, overtaxes and doesn't care about jobs. Most importantly, she suffers from plain old bad judgement!
- May 24, 2016 09:35:32 AM A great new book has been written about Crooked Hillary. Read it & you will never be able to vote for her. @Ed_Klein https://t.co/ujDwSSFhbx
- May 24, 2016 10:03:39 AM A wonderfully written article concerning Israel by @JasonDovEsq https://t.co/LZ9qWRYzdj
- May 24, 2016 10:09:24 AM A suggestion for the dishonest media- https://t.co/zKyRwEaLmz
- May 24, 2016 04:00:07 PM Thank you @DailyMail- for setting the failing @NYTimes story straight. This is what the NYT's should have written! https://t.co/Feb6dhctQo
- May 24, 2016 07:32:47 PM After raising, w/ no obligation, almost $6M for Vets, I couldn't believe protesters formed @ Trump Tower. JUST OUT- SENT BY CROOKED HILLARY!
- May 24, 2016 07:33:27 PM Great honor to receive today's endorsement of @RickSantorum. Really nice! #Trump2016
- May 24, 2016 10:26:20 PM Thank you Washington! #Trump2016 #MakeAmericaGreatAgain https://t.co/v9glTwj6gy

- May 25, 2016 12:12:44 AM Great rally in New Mexico, amazing crowd! Now in L.A. Big rally in Anaheim.
- May 25, 2016 12:37:29 AM @elizabethforma Goofy Elizabeth Warren, sometimes referred to as Pocahontas because she faked the fact she is native American, is a lowlife!
- May 25, 2016 12:41:30 AM "@tcloer11: @realDonaldTrump Great job! Make America Great Again!"
- May 25, 2016 12:41:38 AM "@jknatter: @realDonaldTrump #TrumpTrain"
- May 25, 2016 12:42:49 AM "@oasisupernova: @realDonaldTrump UP TO 8.4 MILLION FOLLOWERS. CAN'T STOP THE #TrumpTrain #MakeAmericaGreatAgain"
- May 25, 2016 12:42:59 AM "@DeepakS76435750: @realDonaldTrump congratulations from India"
- May 25, 2016 12:45:11 AM "@PiperSul: Great speech tonight Mr.Trump! Good Luck in California! Thank you.

- May 25, 2016 12:45:19 AM "@buildthewall: @realDonaldTrump high energy!"
- May 25, 2016 12:47:45 AM "@gordonsr1052: Washington, BIG Thank You for supporting Trump! We are all going to help Trump Make America Great Again! Trump2016!"
- May 25, 2016 07:17:40 AM @elizabethforma Goofy Elizabeth Warren, sometimes known as Pocahontas, bought foreclosed housing and made a quick killing. Total hypocrite!
- May 25, 2016 07:31:56 AM Goofy Senator Elizabeth Warren @elizabethforma has done less in the U.S. Senate than practically any other senator. All talk, no action!
- May 25, 2016 08:14:58 AM Crooked Hillary Clinton just can't close the deal with Bernie. I had to knock out 16 very good and smart candidates. Hillary doesn't have it
- May 25, 2016 08:39:38 AM The protesters in New Mexico were thugs who were flying the Mexican flag. The rally inside was big and beautiful, but outside, criminals!
- May 25, 2016 01:42:55 PM Thank you Washington! Honored to say, on behalf of our great movement, we have broken the all time record for votes in GOP primary history.
- May 25, 2016 06:18:54 PM Thank you Anaheim, California! #Trump2016 https://t.co/AEShamhNVS

- May 26, 2016 08:18:27 AM The Inspector General's report on Crooked Hillary Clinton is a disaster. Such bad judgement and temperament cannot be allowed in the W.H.
- May 26, 2016 11:35:00 AM .@kimguilfoyle- just watched you on @OutnumberedFNC- thank you!
- May 26, 2016 01:59:12 PM Thank you Mr. & Mrs. @TomBarrackJr for the wonderful and magical evening last night. It will not be forgotten. #Trump2016
- May 26, 2016 04:15:16 PM I find it offensive that Goofy Elizabeth Warren, sometimes referred to as Pocahontas, pretended to be Native American to get in Harvard.
- May 26, 2016 04:28:22 PM Thank you! #Trump2016 https://t.co/SPJfMFyPjU
- May 26, 2016 04:30:31 PM Celebrating 1237! #Trump2016 https://t.co/hPQJc7eor0

- May 26, 2016 05:22:50 PM My wife @MELANIATRUMP, and my children will be featured on @FoxNews with @Greta- 7pmE. Enjoy! #MeetTheTrumps #Trump2016
- May 26, 2016 05:57:39 PM Today we, together, won the Republican Nomination for President! https://t.co/82l6TjA2lk
- May 26, 2016 09:09:03 PM Poll data shows that @marcorubio does by far the best in holding onto his Senate seat in Florida. Important to keep the MAJORITY. Run Marco!

- May 27, 2016 09:10:07 AM AN AMERICA FIRST ENERGY PLAN #MakeAmericaGreatAgain #Trump2016 https://t.co/kTi6e1zyNI https://t.co/WjI8Rx11no
- May 27, 2016 12:35:56 PM Bill O'Reilly doing a major special on @OreillyFactor tonight- @FoxNews at 8pmE. Watch it, should be good! #Trump2016
- May 27, 2016 06:19:20 PM I am on @oreillyfactor tonight, a big special. @FoxNews at 8:00 P.M. ENJOY!
- May 27, 2016 06:20:01 PM Wow- 25,000 in San Diego, California! Thank you!! #Trump2016 https://t.co/1NRj3zCuui
- May 27, 2016 09:19:19 PM Thank you @BillyJoel- many friends just told me you gave a very kind shoutout at MSG. Appreciate it- love your music!
- May 27, 2016 09:48:22 PM .@SanDiegoPD- Fantastic job on handling the thugs who tried to disrupt our very peaceful and well attended rally. Greatly appreciated!
- May 27, 2016 11:13:54 PM Obama administration fails to screen Syrian refugees' social media accounts: https://t.co/MMa07nwa44

- May 28, 2016 01:19:54 AM Great rally in Fresno, California- great crowd! Thank you! #Trump2016 https://t.co/TVSPvxOmve
- May 28, 2016 08:47:10 AM The U.S. has 69 treaties with other countries where we would have to defend them and their borders. How nice, but what do we get? NOT ENOUGH
- May 28, 2016 09:47:16 AM I (we) broke the all-time record for most votes gotten in a Republican Primary - by a lot - and with many states left to go! Thank you.

- May 28, 2016 03:28:22 PM The failing @nytimes wrote a story about my management style & that I don't have many people. I have 73, Hillary has 800- & I'm beating her.
- May 28, 2016 03:28:40 PM The media is on a new phony kick about my management style. I spend much less money & get much better results! What we need as Prez!
- May 28, 2016 03:28:48 PM I am always on the front page of the failing @nytimes, but when I won the GOP nomination, I'm in the back of the paper. Very dishonest!
- May 28, 2016 04:33:58 PM Don't believe the biased and phony media quoting people who work for my campaign. The only quote that matters is a quote from me!
- May 28, 2016 04:34:55 PM Does President Obama ever discuss the sneak attack on Pearl Harbor while he's in Japan? Thousands of American lives lost. #MDW

- May 29, 2016 06:04:47 AM Honor Memorial Day by thinking of and respecting all of the great men and women that gave their lives for us and our country! We love them.
- May 29, 2016 11:45:44 AM Heading to D.C. to see and hear ROLLING THUNDER. Amazing people that LOVE OUR COUNTRY. Great spirit!
- May 29, 2016 04:43:15 PM Good news is that my campaign has perhaps more cash than any campaign in the history of politics- b/c I stand 100% behind everything we do.
- May 29, 2016 05:53:16 PM Bill Kristol has been wrong for 2yrs-an embarrassed loser, but if the GOP can't control their own, then they are not a party. Be tough, R's!
- May 29, 2016 05:58:27 PM The Republican Party has to be smart & strong if it wants to win in November. Can't allow lightweights to set up a spoiler Indie candidate!
- May 29, 2016 06:02:01 PM If dummy Bill Kristol actually does get a spoiler to run as an Independent, say good bye to the Supreme Court!

- May 30, 2016 05:41:49 AM Obama says a WALL at our southern border won't enhance our security (wrong) and yet he now wants to build a much bigger wall (fence) at W.H.

- May 30, 2016 06:00:47 AM In getting the endorsement of the 16,500 Border Patrol Agents (thank you), the statement was made that the WALL was very necessary!
- May 30, 2016 06:05:34 AM The endorsement of me by the 16,500 Border Patrol Agents was the first time that they ever endorsed a presidential candidate. Nice!
- May 30, 2016 06:10:12 AM "@TeaPartyNevada: #Trump2016 "Illegals are taken care of better than our veterans." https://t.co/KKIgM4rNma https://t.co/1cEZ8wG7Cy"
- May 30, 2016 06:17:04 AM "@ScottWRasmussen: Donald Trump and Bikers Share Affection at Rolling Thunder Rally https://t.co/ZZl2sc29dn" A great day in D.C.!
- May 30, 2016 06:19:29 AM "@MariaErnandez3b: Trump Supports Rolling Thunder Rally #TRUMP STRONG https://t.co/pfVXQ8NdZu" So true, and remember the M.I.A.'s!
- May 30, 2016 06:20:09 AM "@FrankyLamouche: how many of donald's rolling thunder brigade will sign up and go to war for him in the middle east."
- May 30, 2016 06:20:38 AM "@NBCDFW: Trump rallies veterans at annual Rolling Thunder Gathering https://t.co/b08FcMlgkr https://t.co/RCDeLvHQqD"
- May 30, 2016 06:26:47 AM Have a great Memorial Day and remember that we will soon MAKE AMERICA GREAT AGAIN!
- May 30, 2016 03:13:17 PM I would have had millions of votes more in the primaries (than Crooked Hillary) if I only had one opponent, instead of sixteen. Broke record
- May 30, 2016 03:15:04 PM I hope everyone had a great Memorial Day!
- May 30, 2016 04:45:09 PM I have a judge in the Trump University civil case, Gonzalo Curiel (San Diego), who is very unfair. An Obama pick. Totally biased-hates Trump
- May 30, 2016 04:55:41 PM I should have easily won the Trump University case on summary judgement but have a judge, Gonzalo Curiel, who is totally biased against me.

- May 31, 2016 05:48:49 AM So many great things happening - new poll numbers looking good! News conference at 11:00 A.M. today, Trump Tower!

- May 31, 2016 06:42:20 AM I have raised/given a tremendous amount of money to our great VETERANS, and have got nothing but bad publicity for doing so. Watch!
- May 31, 2016 11:53:58 AM Just finished a press conference in Trump Tower wherein I gave information on which VETERANS groups got the $5,600,000 that I raised/gave!
- May 31, 2016 11:57:17 AM So many veterans groups are beyond happy with all of the money I raised/gave! It was my great honor - they do an amazing job.
- May 31, 2016 04:12:07 PM Join me in Sacramento, California-tomorrow evening @ 7pm! #Trump2016 https://t.co/W7xy7eXcii https://t.co/km0rRYSDnO
- May 31, 2016 05:51:56 PM I will be interviewed on @seanhannity tonight at 10pmE on @FoxNews. Enjoy!
- May 31, 2016 06:14:42 PM Katie Couric, the third rate reporter, who has been largely forgotten, should be ashamed of herself for the fraudulent editing of her doc.
- May 31, 2016 06:17:33 PM I am getting great credit for my press conference today. Crooked Hillary should be admonished for not having a press conference in 179 days.
- May 31, 2016 06:18:28 PM Congratulations to @seanhannity on his tremendous increase in television ratings. Speaking of ratings- I will be on his show tonight @ 10pE.

June, 2016

- Jun 1, 2016 08:17:58 AM So I raised/gave $5,600,000 for the veterans and the media makes me look bad! They do anything to belittle - totally biased.
- Jun 1, 2016 03:46:38 PM Join me in San Jose, California- tomorrow evening at 7pm! #MakeAmericaGreatAgain #Trump2016 https://t.co/jLQukR550J https://t.co/Uds8OdH3A4
- Jun 1, 2016 05:16:36 PM Crooked Hillary Clinton is a fraud who has put the public and country at risk by her illegal and very stupid use of e-mails. Many missing!
- Jun 1, 2016 07:21:01 PM Same failing @nytimes "reporter" who wrote discredited women's story last week wrote another terrible story on me today- will never learn!
- Jun 1, 2016 11:58:34 PM Thank you Sacramento, California! #MakeAmericaGreatAgain https://t.co/t75Zxn9L6f

- Jun 2, 2016 12:11:16 AM "@SCPioneer: @stockdaleism @JamesRosenFNC @FoxNews @realDonaldTrump Not for slackers! Happy w/courses I took." Thanks.
- Jun 2, 2016 12:12:45 AM "@HaloDad22: @realDonaldTrump I already voted for you! My wife did as well! I represent #Teachers4Trump! We represent #CA4Trump! #NeverDems
- Jun 2, 2016 10:03:21 AM Crooked Hillary Clinton has zero natural talent - she should not be president. Her temperament is bad and her decision making ability-zilch!
- Jun 2, 2016 10:10:22 AM Bernie Sanders was right when he said that Crooked Hillary Clinton was not qualified to be president because she suffers from BAD judgement!
- Jun 2, 2016 10:57:14 AM Do you ever notice that @CNN gives me very little proper representation on my policies. Just watched-nobody knew anything about my foreign P
- Jun 2, 2016 11:31:52 AM Wow, USA Today did todays cover story on my record in lawsuits. Verdict: 450 wins, 38 losses. Isn't that what you want for your president?
- Jun 2, 2016 11:37:24 AM Join me in San Jose, California- tonight! #MakeAmericaGreatAgain #Trump2016 Tickets: https://t.co/jLQukR550J https://t.co/OrEhKJZ5Rd
- Jun 2, 2016 11:48:50 AM With all of the Crooked Hillary Clinton's foreign policy experience, she has made so many mistakes - and I mean real monsters! No more HRC.
- Jun 2, 2016 11:54:21 AM Even though I have a very biased and unfair judge in the Trump U civil case in San Diego, I have thousands of great reviews & will win case!
- Jun 2, 2016 12:02:38 PM After the litigation is disposed of and the case won, I have instructed my execs to open Trump U(?), so much interest in it! I will be pres.
- Jun 2, 2016 12:06:29 PM Crooked Hillary Clinton, who I would love to call Lyin' Hillary, is getting ready to totally misrepresent my foreign policy positions.
- Jun 2, 2016 02:15:33 PM Crooked Hillary no longer has credibility - too much failure in office. People will not allow another four years of incompetence!
- Jun 2, 2016 02:18:14 PM Bad performance by Crooked Hillary Clinton! Reading poorly from the telepromter! She doesn't even look presidential!

- Jun 2, 2016 04:12:54 PM So great to have the endorsement and support of Paul Ryan. We will both be working very hard to Make America Great Again!
- Jun 2, 2016 05:16:50 PM A 60% increase in Texas Blue Cross/Blue Shield through ObamaCare. I told you so, there is panic and anger as healthcare costs explode!
- Jun 2, 2016 05:18:50 PM "@free_SA_BD: @realDonaldTrump A vote for Trump is a vote to restore our great country."
- Jun 2, 2016 05:20:29 PM "@TaylorEdwards99: THIS IS @POTUS'S LEGACY! AN ABSOLUTE DISASTER!!! WE NEED @realDonaldTrump NOW!! #MAGA #TRUMP2016 https://t.co/lBgZJg0zd1
- Jun 2, 2016 05:22:20 PM "@Valenti317: @realDonaldTrump she's a criminal and you're the only person that can stop her."
- Jun 2, 2016 05:24:12 PM "@RobertMordica: @realDonaldTrump Only Trump can save America. Right leader at the right time." THANK YOU!
- Jun 2, 2016 08:12:12 PM RT @IvankaTrump: Beautiful article about @realDonaldTrump written by my friend, the incredibly talented golfer Natalie Gulbis: https://t.co…
- Jun 2, 2016 08:13:19 PM .@Natalie_Gulbis- Thank you for the nice piece in @SInow / @Golf_com. Keep up the great work! https://t.co/JCZPCFx10X
- Jun 2, 2016 10:38:56 PM Join me in Redding, California- tomorrow at 1:00pm. #Trump2016 Tickets: https://t.co/tyllhxJHC7
- Jun 2, 2016 10:39:40 PM On June 22- I will be going to Scotland to celebrate the opening of the newly renovated @TrumpTurnberry Resort, the worlds best.
- Jun 2, 2016 10:41:05 PM After @TrumpTurnberry I will be visiting Aberdeen, the oil capital of Europe, to see my great club, @TrumpScotland.
- Jun 2, 2016 10:42:27 PM After @TrumpScotland, I will visit @TrumpDoonbeg in Ireland, the magnificent resort fronting on the Atlantic Ocean.
- Jun 2, 2016 10:42:51 PM Then, on June 25th- back to the USA to MAKE AMERICA GREAT AGAIN!

- Jun 3, 2016 12:11:27 AM "@Crz4basball: @JudgeJeanine @realDonaldTrump Looks like several legal Hispanics supporting Trump! They know he will be good for them too."
- Jun 3, 2016 12:14:36 AM "@angeloftruth11: Clinton says Trump is dangerous. Who's the one who killed 4 Americans in Benghazi? https://t.co/ZV5ehm6NKR"

- Jun 3, 2016 12:17:45 AM "@LunsfordWhitney: This is rich coming from her. She tweeted you will be president! #Women4Ttump #Trump2016 https://t.co/2GSGfLS1yT"
- Jun 3, 2016 12:23:18 AM "@LiliannyLeebou: I think the first female president of the USA will be @IvankaTrump a beautiful intelligent young genuine successful lady!"
- Jun 3, 2016 12:24:28 AM "@fivestarr6028: Yes! Hubby and I voted 4 @realDonaldTrump already! https://t.co/h1iHiJNUjm" Thank you.
- Jun 3, 2016 07:37:03 AM Terrible jobs report just reported. Only 38,000 jobs added. Bombshell!
- Jun 3, 2016 07:43:51 AM Rally last night in San Jose was great. Tremendous love and enthusiasm in the hall. Big crowd. Outside, small group of thugs burned Am flag!
- Jun 3, 2016 08:05:53 AM I don't watch or do @Morning_Joe anymore. Small audience, low ratings! I hear Mika has gone wild with hate. Joe is Joe. They lost their way!
- Jun 3, 2016 08:13:50 AM In Crooked Hillary's telepromter speech yesterday, she made up things that I said or believe but have no basis in fact. Not honest!
- Jun 3, 2016 11:01:47 AM "I'm a former chief of police in a border town. I'm Hispanic, I'm proud to be Hispanic and I'm 100% behind Trump." https://t.co/8YtBU7j17m
- Jun 3, 2016 02:03:17 PM So much interest in my visit to Scotland! I greatly look forward to attending the opening event @TrumpTurnberry- taking place on June 24th.
- Jun 3, 2016 02:07:26 PM Great evening in San Jose other than the thugs. My supporters are far tougher if they want to be, but fortunately they are not hostile.
- Jun 3, 2016 05:20:52 PM Thank you Redding, California! #MakeAmericaGreatAgain #CAPrimary https://t.co/nFiydpTpPn
- Jun 3, 2016 08:14:50 PM RT @CBSNews: WATCH NOW: The @realDonaldTrump supporters you'd never expect https://t.co/jKeVJX5u73 https://t.co/pbft0Eq3Y1
- Jun 3, 2016 11:29:03 PM Muhammad Ali is dead at 74! A truly great champion and a wonderful guy. He will be missed by all!

- Jun 4, 2016 07:47:47 AM "@rapidcraft: Here's The HILLARY UNIVERSITY Scandal No One In The Media Is Talking About https://t.co/suHERIUHo4 @realDonaldTrump"
- Jun 4, 2016 07:49:18 AM "@Don_Vito_08: Thank You Mr. Trump for Standing up for Our Country! #VoteTrump2016 JOIN ME ON THE #TrumpTrain https://t.co/zgopGvSEen"
- Jun 4, 2016 08:04:33 AM Many of the thugs that attacked the peaceful Trump supporters in San Jose were illegals. They burned the American flag and laughed at police
- Jun 4, 2016 08:11:09 AM The Mayor of San Jose did a terrible job of ordering the protection of innocent people. The thugs were lucky supporters remained peaceful!
- Jun 4, 2016 08:14:26 AM We just had the worst jobs report since 2010.
- Jun 4, 2016 04:24:13 PM Thank you Attorney General Gonzales, so many people feel this way. https://t.co/fMR8YYiiMz
- Jun 4, 2016 06:49:35 PM "@sareed59: Our ineffective #POTUS has to make a speech in #Elkhart to make everything look great. Mr. Trump #MakeAmericaGreatAgain"

- Jun 5, 2016 04:36:48 PM The Clinton News Network, sometimes referred to as @CNN, is getting more and more biased.They act so indignant-hear them behind closed doors
- Jun 5, 2016 04:56:01 PM I am watching @CNN very little lately because they are so biased against me. Shows are predictable garbage! CNN and MSM is one big lie!
- Jun 5, 2016 05:15:01 PM Hillary Clinton is unfit to be president. She has bad judgement, poor leadership skills and a very bad and destructive track record. Change!

- Jun 6, 2016 06:23:54 AM People like @KatyTurNBC report on my campaign, but have zero access. They say what they want without any knowledge.True of so much of media!
- Jun 6, 2016 07:56:07 AM Just like I have been able to spend far less money than others on the campaign and finish #1, so too should our country. We can be great!

- Jun 6, 2016 08:15:19 AM Crooked Hillary Clinton has not held a news conference in more than 7 months. Her record is so bad she is unable to answer tough questions!
- Jun 6, 2016 08:23:54 AM Crooked Hillary is being badly criticized (for a Wall Street paid for ad) by PolitiFact for a false ad on me on women. She is a total fraud!
- Jun 6, 2016 08:42:53 AM A massive blow to Obama's message - only 38,000 new jobs for month in just issued jobs report. That's REALLY bad!
- Jun 6, 2016 08:51:31 AM I am getting bad marks from certain pundits because I have a small campaign staff. But small is good, flexible, save money and number one!
- Jun 6, 2016 09:29:47 AM Remembering the fallen heroes on #DDay - June 6, 1944. https://t.co/od7vsDMlHY
- Jun 6, 2016 11:30:58 AM Thank you Diamond and Silk! https://t.co/qdsLUy2hqD
- Jun 6, 2016 11:34:08 AM RT @IvankaTrump: My next project is pretty amazing…! xx, Ivanka https://t.co/Ucq3dz20sQ https://t.co/f60biSURQ7
- Jun 6, 2016 04:36:49 PM See, when I said NATO was obsolete because of no terrorism protection, they made the change without giving me credit.https://t.co/sRCF1H3rjg
- Jun 6, 2016 08:51:12 PM A former Secret Service Agent for President Clinton excoriates Crooked Hillary describing her as ERRATIC & VIOLENT. Bad temperament for pres
- Jun 6, 2016 09:21:08 PM In just out book, Secret Service Agent Gary Byrne doesn't believe that Crooked Hillary has the temperament or integrity to be the president!

- Jun 7, 2016 05:45:26 PM Thank you! Together we will #MakeAmericaGreatAgain! https://t.co/7Jk6voyzue
- Jun 7, 2016 06:52:38 PM I will be interviewed tonight on @seanhannity - Enjoy! 10:00 P.M.
- Jun 7, 2016 07:41:42 PM I will be speaking about our great journey to the Republican nomination at 9:00 P.M. The movement toward a country that WINS again continues
- Jun 7, 2016 10:12:29 PM Thank you Montana! #Trump2016 https://t.co/rOvTapLnWG https://t.co/PyHiy7vjO6

- Jun 7, 2016 10:21:44 PM Thank you New Jersey! #Trump2016 https://t.co/PgIYkHLGtI https://t.co/MyJMOKdpJ9
- Jun 7, 2016 10:32:02 PM Thank you South Dakota! #Trump2016 https://t.co/GbRTQdxIj4 https://t.co/pNqwOrY0ZB
- Jun 7, 2016 10:39:37 PM Thank you New Mexico! #Trump2016 https://t.co/wNOY8Pc2kM https://t.co/osWzVxNkJx
- Jun 7, 2016 10:59:25 PM Thank you California! #Trump2016 https://t.co/GusL2UPrX2 https://t.co/H6D25S1TR5

- Jun 8, 2016 06:43:19 AM "@DjD_Thunder: Standing by @realDonaldTrump all the way to the White House! https://t.co/z4X1o5xHBh"
- Jun 8, 2016 06:45:33 AM "@WolfStopper: Gee ... Does this make @realDonaldTrump right one more time? https://t.co/zjWKGMDgzi"
- Jun 8, 2016 06:52:13 AM Thank you to all for your wonderful comments on my speech. I could feel the electricity in thr air. Great reviews - most votes ever recieved
- Jun 8, 2016 07:00:55 AM "@southpaw816: @SenSanders fans, greatest way to get even with her Highness - vote for @realDonaldTrump, at least you'll have a job.
- Jun 8, 2016 07:08:55 AM Nobody is watching @Morning_Joe anymore. Gone off the deep end - bad ratings. You won't believe what I am watching now!
- Jun 8, 2016 07:10:17 AM "@JoeDeFranco: Top RINO hack for MSNBC Joey Scarborough on the air and calling the next President Trump a racist and bigot. Shame on you"
- Jun 8, 2016 07:11:52 AM "@jimhewitt: . @FrankCaliendo doing @realDonaldTrump on @MikeAndMike is awesome. "Number one presidency of all time"
- Jun 8, 2016 07:13:39 AM "@sara_wejesa: @realDonaldTrump Great speach!!!!!!!" Thanks!
- Jun 8, 2016 07:14:32 AM "@mariadaq: HISTORIC!! what's historic is OUR national debt, record unemployment, &pocketbook crisis!THE PEOPLE NEED TRUMP2 make USA RICH!"
- Jun 8, 2016 07:44:26 AM "@lovusa4: @RichardWeaving Why @foxandfriends @NewDay WHERE IS THE REPORTING @realDonaldTrump <MOST VOTES FOR PRESIDENT IN HISTORY OF USA"

- Jun 8, 2016 03:27:28 PM MAKE AMERICA GREAT AGAIN! #AmericaFirst #Trump2016 https://t.co/42OpVsjXjp
- Jun 8, 2016 04:22:36 PM RT @seanhannity: Graph: @RealDonaldTrump's Historic 13 Million Primary Votes Compared To Every GOP Nominee Since 1908 https://t.co/vNpfaSZ8…
- Jun 8, 2016 07:49:01 PM "@setfire2flames: Senator Sanders spent more than @realDonaldTrump yet lost."
- Jun 8, 2016 07:49:22 PM "@nauthizjane: @realDonaldTrump Congratulations Mr. Trump." Thank you!
- Jun 8, 2016 07:54:44 PM I would have had many millions of votes more than Crooked Hillary Clinton except for the fact that I had 16 opponents, she had one!
- Jun 8, 2016 07:56:58 PM "@Dale_Dangler: @realDonaldTrump You will be the greatest president the world has ever seen" Thanks.
- Jun 8, 2016 08:00:03 PM "@mabynshingleton: JohnKasich, the VOTERS have spoken. We want @realDonaldTrump. You AGREED to support NOMINEE. Get on board or leave @GOP"
- Jun 8, 2016 08:46:03 PM Bernie Sanders must really dislike Crooked Hillary after the way she played him. Many of his supporters, because of trade, will come to me.
- Jun 8, 2016 08:49:25 PM "@KathyCeurter: @realDonaldTrump please Mr.Trump make @SenatorJeffSessions your VP. He is a perfect running mate." He is a great guy!

- Jun 9, 2016 07:11:55 AM As expected, the media is very much against me. Their dishonesty is amazing but, just like our big wins in the primaries, we will win!
- Jun 9, 2016 07:29:24 AM Crooked Hillary Clinton will be a disaster on jobs, the economy, trade, healthcare, the military, guns and just about all else. Obama plus!
- Jun 9, 2016 01:22:21 PM Obama just endorsed Crooked Hillary. He wants four more years of Obama—but nobody else does!
- Jun 9, 2016 02:26:49 PM A message of condolences and support regarding the terrorist attacks in Tel Aviv: https://t.co/iulXLEANei
- Jun 9, 2016 03:40:32 PM How long did it take your staff of 823 people to think that up--and where are your 33,000 emails that you deleted? https://t.co/gECLNtQizQ

- Jun 9, 2016 04:15:11 PM Thank you Roseanne, very much appreciated. https://t.co/COXEJ1In8D
- Jun 9, 2016 09:29:27 PM Join me! #Trump2016 6/10: Richmond https://t.co/I2CJSqAlyl 6/11: Tampa https://t.co/6jk33orxXG 6/11: Pittsburgh https://t.co/bwgL1ZXtC7
- Jun 9, 2016 09:31:06 PM "@FreemarketSara: Trump's Historic 13 Million Primary Votes - A Record ... Congratulations @realDonaldTrump https://t.co/zdOEle8wOL"

- Jun 10, 2016 07:07:49 AM Pocahontas is at it again! Goofy Elizabeth Warren, one of the least productive U.S. Senators, has a nasty mouth. Hope she is V.P. choice.
- Jun 10, 2016 07:20:01 AM "@FoxNews: .@JamesRosenFNC: "Never before has a president endorsed someone under investigation by @TheJusticeDept." https://t.co/fX5bs8fzac
- Jun 10, 2016 07:23:53 AM "@Ausbiz: RECORD 14 million primary votes/beat 16 opponents/financed own campaign. You will be a great POTUS & #MakeAmericaGreatAgain"
- Jun 10, 2016 08:13:42 AM Join me! 6/10: Richmond, VA - 8pm 6/11: Tampa, FL - 11am 6/11: Pittsburgh, PA - 3pm 6/13: Portsmouth, NH - 2:30pm https://t.co/kv624y9UOm
- Jun 10, 2016 10:10:22 AM The great boxing promoter, Don King, just endorsed me. Nice!
- Jun 10, 2016 10:36:17 AM "Donald Trump Plans To Continue GOP Legacy Of Leading On Women's, Civil Rights Against Racist, Sexist Democrats" https://t.co/nEPqAYw1G5
- Jun 10, 2016 10:55:55 AM Heading to D.C. to speak at Faith and Freedom Coalition and visit OPO.
- Jun 10, 2016 11:12:13 AM 2004 VIDEO: Pocahontas describing Crooked Hillary Clinton as a Corporate Donor Puppet. Time for change! #Trump2016 https://t.co/rZ1MqUzpKU
- Jun 10, 2016 11:49:14 AM I rarely agree with President Obama- however he is 100% correct about Crooked Hillary Clinton. Great ad! https://t.co/aOvVsZfAW3
- Jun 10, 2016 02:27:13 PM #FlashbackFriday #CrookedHillary https://t.co/pvrBb7v4NG

- Jun 10, 2016 03:39:41 PM Heading to Richmond, Virginia now. Join me tonight! #Trump2016 Tickets: https://t.co/I2CJSqiKGN
- Jun 10, 2016 04:24:38 PM Thank you @FaithandFreedom Coalition! An honor joining you today- to discuss our shared values. #RTM2016 #Trump2016 https://t.co/Ye6IhOW6ZM
- Jun 10, 2016 11:30:44 PM Thank you Richmond, Virginia! #Trump2016 https://t.co/SxU4yzCLQf

- Jun 11, 2016 06:18:19 AM Mitt Romney had his chance to beat a failed president but he choked like a dog. Now he calls me racist-but I am least racist person there is
- Jun 11, 2016 07:00:26 AM Don King, and so many other African Americans who know me well and endorsed me, would not have done so if they thought I was a racist!
- Jun 11, 2016 09:58:18 AM In Tampa, Florida- thank you to all of our outstanding volunteers who want to #MakeAmericaGreatAgain! https://t.co/04qqpGylT7
- Jun 11, 2016 01:21:15 PM Sad case- @USATODAY did article saying I don't pay bills- false, only don't pay when work is shoddy, bad, or not done! They should do same!
- Jun 11, 2016 04:29:46 PM Thank you Tampa, Florida! #AmericaFirst #TrumpTrain https://t.co/fY4QVoSSfj
- Jun 11, 2016 04:32:24 PM Thank you to our amazing law enforcement officers! #AmericaFirst https://t.co/qWaTT9jsQD
- Jun 11, 2016 05:10:40 PM Thank you Pittsburgh, Pennsylvania! Will be back soon! #AmericaFirst https://t.co/ttLMgInkdA
- Jun 11, 2016 05:35:53 PM Join me on Tuesday- in Greensboro, North Carolina! #Trump2016 #AmericaFirst https://t.co/iaL5IGTfV3
- Jun 11, 2016 05:35:57 PM Riley Rone was a great young man. We will miss him dearly. https://t.co/R0tm44nMao
- Jun 11, 2016 06:28:13 PM Goofy Elizabeth Warren, sometimes referred to as Pocahontas, pretended to be a Native American in order to advance her career. Very racist!

- Jun 12, 2016 07:07:22 AM Really bad shooting in Orlando. Police investigating possible terrorism. Many people dead and wounded.

- Jun 12, 2016 08:39:47 AM Clinton made a false ad about me where I was imitating a reporter GROVELING after he changed his story. I would NEVER mock disabled. Shame!
- Jun 12, 2016 10:45:19 AM Horrific incident in FL. Praying for all the victims & their families. When will this stop? When will we get tough, smart & vigilant?
- Jun 12, 2016 11:43:17 AM Appreciate the congrats for being right on radical Islamic terrorism, I don't want congrats, I want toughness & vigilance. We must be smart!
- Jun 12, 2016 12:58:00 PM Is President Obama going to finally mention the words radical Islamic terrorism? If he doesn't he should immediately resign in disgrace!
- Jun 12, 2016 01:52:13 PM Reporting that Orlando killer shouted "Allah hu Akbar!" as he slaughtered clubgoers. 2nd man arrested in LA with rifles near Gay parade.
- Jun 12, 2016 02:02:42 PM "@WandaWalls20: @realDonaldTrump Please make us safe. We cannot have Hillary as president. We will be in so much trouble.
- Jun 12, 2016 03:47:36 PM What has happened in Orlando is just the beginning. Our leadership is weak and ineffective. I called it and asked for the ban. Must be tough

- Jun 13, 2016 09:59:25 AM I have been hitting Obama and Crooked Hillary hard on not using the term Radical Islamic Terror. Hillary just broke-said she would now use!
- Jun 13, 2016 10:03:29 AM I will be going to New Hampshire today, home of my first primary victory, to discuss terror and the horrible events of yesterday. 2:30 P.M.
- Jun 13, 2016 10:08:20 AM I am watching @FoxNews and how fairly they are treating me and my words, and @CNN, and the total distortion of my words and what I am saying
- Jun 13, 2016 01:08:38 PM Congratulations to the 2016 #StanleyCup Champions, Pittsburgh @Penguins!
- Jun 13, 2016 02:26:07 PM TERRORISM, IMMIGRATION, AND NATIONAL SECURITY SPEECH- TRANSCRIPT: https://t.co/WD1LGFKx3M https://t.co/T7yHSdCeU8

- Jun 13, 2016 02:43:54 PM RT @AnnCoulter: Anyone who plans to talk about Trump ever again has to see this speech. Your opinion is irrelevant unless you listened to…
- Jun 13, 2016 03:35:11 PM I am no fan of President Obama, but to show you how dishonest the phony Washington Post is: https://t.co/cITm8BPixD
- Jun 13, 2016 03:38:59 PM Based on the incredibly inaccurate coverage and reporting of the record setting Trump campaign, we are hereby: https://t.co/THKJwjNkaz
- Jun 13, 2016 04:10:26 PM In my speech on protecting America I spoke about a temporary ban, which includes suspending immigration from nations tied to Islamic terror.
- Jun 13, 2016 04:12:21 PM I thought people weren't celebrating? They were cheering all over, even this savage from Orlando. I was right. https://t.co/DrVa65X9rI
- Jun 13, 2016 04:32:44 PM Saudi Arabia and many of the countries that gave vast amounts of money to the Clinton Foundation- cont'd: https://t.co/t31ReRSzzy
- Jun 13, 2016 04:35:30 PM Crooked Hillary says we must call on Saudi Arabia and other countries to stop funding hate. I am calling on- cont'd: https://t.co/T1fVcu3mEC
- Jun 13, 2016 07:20:57 PM Join me in Atlanta on Wednesday- at noon! #Trump2016 Tickets: https://t.co/1JJ2Kn0ani https://t.co/cyARlHSEFU

- Jun 14, 2016 07:26:49 AM American must now get very tough, very smart and very vigilant. We cannot admit people into our country without extraordinary screening.
- Jun 14, 2016 07:28:16 AM AMERICA FIRST!
- Jun 14, 2016 12:31:58 PM Thank you to the LGBT community! I will fight for you while Hillary brings in more people that will threaten your freedoms and beliefs.
- Jun 14, 2016 01:09:57 PM HAPPY 241st BIRTHDAY to the @USArmy! THANK YOU! https://t.co/mXsxkfcstC
- Jun 14, 2016 01:10:18 PM RT @realDonaldTrump: HAPPY 241st BIRTHDAY to the @USArmy! THANK YOU! https://t.co/mXsxkfcstC
- Jun 14, 2016 01:28:48 PM TONIGHT! NORTH CAROLINA: https://t.co/UolRS3aT6W WEDNESDAY! GEORGIA: https://t.co/1JJ2Kn0ani SATURDAY! NEVADA: https://t.co/x3w1PHtLXP

- Jun 14, 2016 09:40:32 PM Thank you Greensboro, North Carolina! Will be back soon! #AmericaFirst https://t.co/R29WMGNLGG

- Jun 15, 2016 08:38:17 AM An: Media fell all over themselves criticizing what DonaldTrump "may have insinuated about @POTUS." But he's right: https://t.co/bIIdYtvZYw
- Jun 15, 2016 08:44:14 AM The press is so totally biased that we have no choice but to take our tough but fair and smart message directly to the people!
- Jun 15, 2016 08:50:31 AM I will be meeting with the NRA, who has endorsed me, about not allowing people on the terrorist watch list, or the no fly list, to buy guns.
- Jun 15, 2016 03:04:47 PM Thank you Atlanta, Georgia! Will be back soon! #AmericaFirst https://t.co/cVJvfcoGOt
- Jun 15, 2016 03:52:45 PM Join me in Dallas, Texas on Thursday! #AmericaFirst #Trump2016 https://t.co/fX0kXZUNqz https://t.co/c7sCbHDAQh
- Jun 15, 2016 04:25:14 PM Finally an accurate story from the Washington Post! https://t.co/0nNKEBSd73
- Jun 15, 2016 05:49:53 PM I will be interviewed on @greta at 7:00 P.M. @FoxNews
- Jun 15, 2016 05:57:49 PM RT @AnnCoulter: Trump's speech today was Churchillian, only better. You can tell by the spluttering hysteria on TV about @realDonaldTrump.
- Jun 15, 2016 09:36:46 PM "@realericjallen: @realDonaldTrump is a Common Sense Conservative! President Trump=Competence, Safety, Unity, & US JOBS, JOBS, JOB.

- Jun 16, 2016 11:50:00 AM McAllen, Texas- 8 miles from U.S. - Mexico border. #Trump2016 Video: https://t.co/pQ4nSTnVrK https://t.co/dKBTP1QjH3
- Jun 16, 2016 11:54:39 AM The trade deficit rose to a 7yr high thanks to horrible trade policies Clinton supports. I will fix it fast- JOBS! https://t.co/jaGeN4u50U
- Jun 16, 2016 11:59:00 AM "Donald Trumps Speech Is a Game Changer." https://t.co/VXjtSivvuU https://t.co/J777QHdYa3
- Jun 16, 2016 02:07:45 PM RT @Reince: Flying to Dallas now with @realDonaldTrump...Reports of discord are pure fiction. Great events lined up all over Texas. Rs wil…

- Jun 16, 2016 02:16:23 PM Join me in Houston, Texas tomorrow night at 7pm! Tickets: https://t.co/nvHRnfzEbH https://t.co/Yd3f8xLpPl
- Jun 16, 2016 03:38:38 PM Houston, TX: https://t.co/nvHRnfi2N7 Las Vegas, NV https://t.co/ksU8AGrFBS Phoenix, AZ: https://t.co/PVB6QX7VpK https://t.co/2ToWwthEeF
- Jun 16, 2016 09:16:21 PM Thank you Dallas, Texas! https://t.co/ui9tSfMcS8 https://t.co/2iYArmM7oN

- Jun 17, 2016 05:09:42 AM "@VoteTrumpMAGA: The media attack on @realDonaldTrump is relentless. They are desperate. But, they keep #Trump in the news - a good thing.
- Jun 17, 2016 06:04:58 AM Amazing crowd last night in Dallas - more spirit and passion than ever before. Today, all over the great State of Texas!
- Jun 17, 2016 06:20:36 AM People very unhappy with Crooked Hillary and Obama on JOBS and SAFETY! Biggest trade deficit in many years! More attacks will follow Orlando
- Jun 17, 2016 06:24:04 AM MAKE AMERICA GREAT AGAIN! MAKE AMERICA SAFE AGAIN!
- Jun 17, 2016 10:27:37 AM RT @robertjeffress: Honored to pray for my friend, @realDonaldTrump, at tonight's Dallas rally. #TrumpDallas c: @DanScavino https://t.co/Bc…
- Jun 17, 2016 12:07:23 PM THANK YOU! #AmericaFirst https://t.co/qp07UfnnjM
- Jun 17, 2016 04:14:59 PM Join me in Phoenix, Arizona tomorrow at 4pm! #Trump2016 #AmericaFirst https://t.co/PVB6QX7VpK https://t.co/B51r30Mazd
- Jun 17, 2016 06:24:13 PM Thank you @DallasPD! https://t.co/ORJyN4FsNI
- Jun 17, 2016 06:51:43 PM Thank you- on my way! https://t.co/uTCXPbWpve
- Jun 17, 2016 06:55:29 PM The convention in Cleveland will be amazing! https://t.co/NlF2Gcr915
- Jun 17, 2016 06:56:54 PM Thank you! #AmericaFirst https://t.co/TZf8uwQO4L
- Jun 17, 2016 09:44:21 PM Thank you Houston, Texas! #AmericaFirst #Trump2016 https://t.co/593p8uRPhq

- Jun 18, 2016 12:22:31 PM Join me in Phoenix, Arizona today at 4pm! #Trump2016 #AmericaFirst https://t.co/PVB6QX7VpK https://t.co/hSaIurAfvD

- Jun 18, 2016 12:51:08 PM In Las Vegas, getting ready to speak!
- Jun 18, 2016 02:39:17 PM Thank you Las Vegas, Nevada! #Trump2016 #AmericaFirst https://t.co/vhGwmhGCVR https://t.co/m1EIra7YMU
- Jun 18, 2016 03:08:18 PM MAKE AMERICA GREAT AGAIN! MAKE AMERICA SAFE AGAIN! #Trump2016 #AmericaFirst https://t.co/vN4K8FvQNT
- Jun 18, 2016 08:10:55 PM I love you Arizona! Thank you! #Trump2016 #AmericaFirst https://t.co/QuTsSmeVdO
- Jun 18, 2016 08:28:32 PM See you soon Arizona! #Trump2016 https://t.co/W4z2eW5ay4
- Jun 18, 2016 09:24:56 PM Donald Trump's Speech Is a Game Changer. #Trump2016 https://t.co/VXjtSivvuU https://t.co/dIK3IyrYGC
- Jun 18, 2016 09:57:51 PM How can the NY Times show an empty room hours before my speech even started when they knew it was going to be packed? So totally dishonest!
- Jun 18, 2016 10:01:15 PM Yesterday's failing @NYTimes fraudulently shows an empty room prior to my speech, when in fact, it was packed! https://t.co/iFuf8MdTEH

- Jun 19, 2016 08:17:35 AM "@bfraser747: Watch out HillaryClinton Support @realDonaldTrump USUS #MakeAmericaGreatAgain US https://t.co/UTYOLo7wGF"
- Jun 19, 2016 08:22:16 PM .@DJohnsonPGA We are so proud of you Dustin. Your reaction under pressure was amazing. First of many Majors. You are a true CHAMPION!

- Jun 20, 2016 05:24:12 AM When I said that if, within the Orlando club, you had some people with guns, I was obviously talking about additional guards or employees

- Jun 21, 2016 05:38:49 AM Crooked Hillary Clinton is totally unfit to be our president-really bad judgement and a temperament, according to new book, which is a mess!
- Jun 21, 2016 09:22:08 AM I will be making a big speech tomorrow to discuss the failed policies and bad judgment of Crooked Hillary Clinton.

- Jun 21, 2016 11:36:40 AM Hillary says this election is about judgment. She's right. Her judgement has killed thousands, unleashed ISIS and wrecked the economy.
- Jun 21, 2016 11:38:07 AM Hillary Clinton surged the trade deficit with China 40% as Secretary of State, costing Americans millions of jobs.
- Jun 21, 2016 11:42:47 AM How can Hillary run the economy when she can't even send emails without putting entire nation at risk?
- Jun 21, 2016 11:44:28 AM Hillary Clinton's open borders immigration policies will drive down wages for all Americans - and make everyone less safe.
- Jun 21, 2016 11:53:07 AM Obama-Clinton inherited $10T in debt and turned it into nearly $20T. They have bankrupted... https://t.co/1COtt0RPY7
- Jun 21, 2016 11:55:41 AM I am "the king of debt."That has been great for me as a businessman, but is bad for the country. I made a fortune off of debt, will fix U.S.
- Jun 21, 2016 12:16:14 PM Hillary took money and did favors for regimes that enslave women and murder gays.
- Jun 21, 2016 12:17:49 PM If you want to know about Hillary Clinton's honesty & judgment, ask the family of Ambassador Stevens.
- Jun 21, 2016 12:19:22 PM Hillary defrauded America as Secy of State. She used it as a personal hedge fund to get herself rich! Corrupt, dangerous, dishonest.
- Jun 21, 2016 03:44:00 PM I will be interviewed by @LouDobbs tonight on @FoxBusiness 7pm ET
- Jun 21, 2016 10:16:27 PM Crooked Hillary refuses to say that she will be raising taxes beyond belief! She will be a disaster for jobs and the economy!
- Jun 21, 2016 10:48:27 PM "@chrisboydbrew: @LouDobbs @realDonaldTrump @FoxBusiness.. Saw your interview.You are the best! Great questions, great answers" Lou is great

- Jun 22, 2016 02:00:47 PM Hillary says things can't change. I say they have to change. It's a choice between Americanism and her corrupt globalism. #Imwithyou
- Jun 22, 2016 02:01:09 PM #Imwithyou https://t.co/iY4K7Wcw3C
- Jun 22, 2016 04:39:43 PM #Imwithyou https://t.co/tan8BmAuR8 https://t.co/5EZ7X1ZZKh

- Jun 22, 2016 09:24:01 PM "@justininglv: @realDonaldTrump great speech today!! It's all about America and that's why you will become president!!!!" Thank you.
- Jun 22, 2016 09:26:09 PM "@1lion: brilliant 3 word response to Hillary's 'I'm With You' slogan https://t.co/dJL71jwK0g @realDonaldTrump https://t.co/Audi8h85qu"
- Jun 22, 2016 10:29:50 PM "@AllegrettiVicki: You have great children, future presidents...and we all see were raised right and out there for their father." Thank you.

- Jun 23, 2016 08:13:22 AM Thank you to Donald Rumsfeld for the endorsement. Very much appreciated. Clinton's conduct has been "disqualifying."
- Jun 23, 2016 08:17:35 AM "Hillary Clinton may be the most corrupt person ever to seek the presidency." -- Donald J. Trump
- Jun 23, 2016 08:20:29 AM ISIS threatens us today because of the decisions Hillary Clinton has made along with President Obama." -- Donald J. Trump
- Jun 23, 2016 12:07:28 PM Hillary Lies to Benghazi Families #CrookedHillary https://t.co/YWd5lk5skG
- Jun 23, 2016 12:43:17 PM RT @FoxBusiness: .@JerryJrFalwell: "I was so impressed by [@realDonaldTrump's] speech yesterday. He was the best I've ever seen him." https…
- Jun 23, 2016 01:07:46 PM SC has kept us safe from exec amnesty--for now. But Hillary has pledged to expand it, taking jobs from Hispanic & African-American workers.
- Jun 23, 2016 01:18:18 PM Hillary Clinton's open borders are tearing American families apart. I am going to make our country Safe Again for all Americans. #Imwithyou
- Jun 23, 2016 01:30:08 PM Obama & Clinton should stop meeting with special interests, & start meeting with the victims of illegal immigration.
- Jun 23, 2016 01:48:20 PM On immigration, I'm consulting with our immigration officers & our wage-earners. Hillary Clinton is consulting with Wall Street.
- Jun 23, 2016 02:10:45 PM Our inner cities have been left behind. We will never have the resources to support our people if we have an open border.

- Jun 23, 2016 02:18:26 PM RT @ScottAdamsSays: Trump's speech today is the best persuasion I have ever seen. Game over. Now running unopposed: https://t.co/P7fHEMP6U...
- Jun 23, 2016 02:34:35 PM CNN, which is totally biased in favor of Clinton, should apologize. They knew they were wrong. https://t.co/KR7OnS8h6s
- Jun 23, 2016 02:35:45 PM Here is another CNN lie. The Clinton News Network is losing all credibility. I'm not watching it much anymore. https://t.co/pNSgSjD5gW
- Jun 23, 2016 03:08:38 PM Read my full statement here on the Supreme Court's executive amnesty decision #imwithyou https://t.co/sb1Ag1Eb27
- Jun 23, 2016 04:36:06 PM Meet the amazing mother whose letter I read during my speech. She lost her son to policies supported by Clinton. https://t.co/NdGQI6Dnji
- Jun 23, 2016 07:52:53 PM Leaving now for a one night trip to Scotland in order to be at the Grand Opening of my great Turnberry Resort. Will be back on Sat. night!
- Jun 23, 2016 07:58:06 PM Congratulations to my son, Eric, on the fantastic job he has done in rebuilding Turnberry, and its great Ailsa Course. Always support kids!

- Jun 24, 2016 04:21:55 AM Just arrived in Scotland. Place is going wild over the vote. They took their country back, just like we will take America back. No games!
- Jun 24, 2016 04:28:49 AM Statement Regarding British Referendum on E.U. Membership https://t.co/GwWRxT3BVp
- Jun 24, 2016 04:28:54 AM Getting ready to open the magnificent Turnberry in Scotland. What a great day, especially when added to the brave & brilliant vote.
- Jun 24, 2016 05:30:31 AM Self-determination is the sacred right of all free people's, and the people of the UK have exercised that right for all the world to see.
- Jun 24, 2016 05:32:00 AM America is proud to stand shoulder-to-shoulder w/a free & ind UK. We stand together as friends, as allies, & as a people w/a shared history.
- Jun 24, 2016 01:48:50 PM New Government data by the Center for Immigration Studies shows more than 3M new legal & illegal immigrants settled..https://t.co/hMFyZc1kAM

- Jun 24, 2016 01:50:57 PM I want all Americans to succeed together. President Obama's illegal executive amnesty undermines job prospects for...https://t.co/dpIDejXzJw
- Jun 24, 2016 04:23:40 PM Crooked Hillary called it totally wrong on BREXIT - she went with Obama - and now she is saying we need her to lead. She would be a disaster
- Jun 24, 2016 04:34:48 PM The opening of Trump Turnberry in Scotland was a big success. Good timing, I was here for BREXIT. Very exciting news conference today!
- Jun 24, 2016 04:43:17 PM Many people are equating BREXIT, and what is going on in Great Britain, with what is happening in the U.S. People want their country back!
- Jun 24, 2016 05:12:13 PM "@DarrenWaggener: @realDonaldTrump What has happened in the UK in the last 12 hours is exactly what will happen in November..vote TRUMP 2016
- Jun 24, 2016 05:31:14 PM "@Jolena3: @realDonaldTrump And we will get it back once we have President Trump! Can't wait!"
- Jun 24, 2016 11:29:41 PM Thoughts and prayers are with everyone in West Virginia- dealing with the devastating floods. #ImWithYou

- Jun 25, 2016 07:00:29 AM So funny, Crooked Hillary called BREXIT so incorrectly, and now she says that she is the one to deal with the U.K. All talk, no action!
- Jun 25, 2016 09:55:11 AM Arriving @TrumpScotland with @DonaldJTrumpJr & @EricTrump. Back to New York tonight. Video: https://t.co/2GUKqOTHS5
- Jun 25, 2016 10:07:32 AM On the 13th tee box @TrumpScotland with my grand daughter, Kai! @DonaldJTrumpJr https://t.co/7ii4KUfsab
- Jun 25, 2016 11:00:18 AM Thank you to everyone who came out & joined us @TrumpTurnberry yesterday! @EricTrump @IvankaTrump @DonaldJTrumpJr https://t.co/hQ1JTMrUtG
- Jun 25, 2016 09:37:14 PM We must suspend immigration from regions linked with terrorism until a proven vetting method is in place.
- Jun 25, 2016 09:37:59 PM We only want to admit those who love our people and support our values. #AmericaFirst
- Jun 25, 2016 09:39:23 PM I have never liked the media term 'mass deportation' -- but we must enforce the laws of the land!

- Jun 25, 2016 09:40:06 PM Obama has blocked ICE officers and BP from doing their jobs. That ends when I am President!
- Jun 25, 2016 10:32:05 PM Just landed in New York - a one night stay in Scotland. Turnberry came out magnificently. My son, Eric, did a great job - under budget!

- Jun 26, 2016 06:24:00 AM George Will, one of the most overrated political pundits (who lost his way long ago), has left the Republican Party.He's made many bad calls
- Jun 26, 2016 06:33:17 AM Crooked Hillary Clinton, who called BREXIT 100% wrong (along with Obama), is now spending Wall Street money on an ad on my correct call.
- Jun 26, 2016 06:36:14 AM Clinton is trying to wash away her bad judgement call on BREXIT with big dollar ads. Disgraceful!
- Jun 26, 2016 11:06:23 AM Crooked Hillary just took a major ad of me playing golf at Turnberry. Shows me hitting shot, but I never did = lie! Was there to support son
- Jun 26, 2016 11:21:15 AM The @ABC poll sample is heavy on Democrats. Very dishonest - why would they do that? Other polls good!
- Jun 26, 2016 11:31:38 AM Top 50 Facts About Crooked Hillary Clinton From Trump 'Stakes Of The Election' Address: https://t.co/lfUdXYnsgJ
- Jun 26, 2016 04:21:50 PM People in our country want borders, and without them the old line pols like Crooked Hillary will not win. It is time for CHANGE - - and JOBS!
- Jun 26, 2016 05:09:30 PM Hillary Clinton is not a change agent, just the same old status quo! She is spending a fortune, I am spending very little. Close in polls!
- Jun 26, 2016 05:15:40 PM Crooked Hillary Clinton got Brexit wrong. I said LEAVE will win. She has no sense of markets and such bad judgement. Only a question of time
- Jun 26, 2016 05:28:32 PM Crooked Hillary Attacks Foreign Government Donations - While Ignoring Her Own: https://t.co/pr3BSHJSxL
- Jun 26, 2016 06:13:25 PM The "dirty" poll done by @ABC @washingtonpost is a disgrace. Even they admit that many more Democrats were polled. Other polls were good.

- Jun 26, 2016 06:24:35 PM "@JimVitari: @ABC @washingtonpost we know they're fake just like poles during primary. I'm sure u will crush #CrookedHillary in general"
- Jun 26, 2016 07:38:14 PM "@brazosboys: Hillary read "sigh" off the Teleprompter, She's so fake she has to be told how to feel: https://t.co/ENXliW2m77 @FoxNews
- Jun 26, 2016 08:31:40 PM "@w4djt: "Under a Trump presidency, America will make brilliant new trade deals!" —Donald Trump #dtmag https://t.co/NpYI9i4iSG"
- Jun 26, 2016 08:33:10 PM "@LindaSuhler: Trump voters don't scare or back down. Our numbers are growing & we're taking our country BACK. #Trump2016 US #MAGA

- Jun 27, 2016 08:07:04 AM Crooked Hillary is wheeling out one of the least productive senators in the U.S. Senate, goofy Elizabeth Warren, who lied on heritage.
- Jun 27, 2016 08:18:12 AM The media is unrelenting. They will only go with and report a story in a negative light. I called Brexit (Hillary was wrong), watch November
- Jun 27, 2016 08:39:12 AM .@CNN is all negative when it comes to me. I don't watch it anymore.

- Jun 28, 2016 02:20:15 PM "@GovBrewer: I'll be a guest today on Making Money with @cvpayne on @ Fox Business 6 PM ET / 3 PM PT Discussing @realDonaldTrump. Tune in!"
- Jun 28, 2016 02:23:18 PM "@vegas_sports: Good for @realDonaldTrump he's smart on business. Maybe If corporations weren't overtaxed they would stay. Voting for #Trump
- Jun 28, 2016 02:24:26 PM "@Patricia_Graf: @GovBrewer @cvpayne let's get Trump supporters out in massive numbers and make America Great Again - create jobs"
- Jun 28, 2016 02:24:43 PM "@arnold_ziffel: @AnnCoulter also can't help but notice the stock market's reaction as @realDonaldTrump was speaking. #UPUPUP"

- Jun 28, 2016 02:26:42 PM "@bluedogdemky: @CWAUnion @iowa_trump @RichardTrumka @AFLCIO This is why I would think the unions would support @realDonaldTrump for #POTUS"
- Jun 28, 2016 02:28:13 PM "@kridan1: Canceled cable - sick of their bad coverage of you and the fawning over Clinton ... Listened to your great speech on YouTube"
- Jun 28, 2016 02:30:35 PM Check it out - 2nd video on Lying Crooked Hillary is now online! Watch it here: https://t.co/5mtwkOvQnd #CrookedHillary #Trump2016
- Jun 28, 2016 03:24:13 PM Benghazi is just another Hillary Clinton failure. It just never seems to work the way it's supposed to with Clinton.
- Jun 28, 2016 03:26:22 PM Hillary Clinton's Presidency would be catastrophic for the future of our country. She is ill-fit with bad judgment.
- Jun 28, 2016 04:08:51 PM Yet another terrorist attack, this time in Turkey. Will the world ever realize what is going on? So sad.
- Jun 28, 2016 04:10:57 PM We must do everything possible to keep this horrible terrorism outside the United States.
- Jun 28, 2016 07:31:48 PM "@jtsbk: @AllenWest thanks for sharing Eric we need @realDonaldTrump now as this administration is incapable of keeping our country safe"
- Jun 28, 2016 09:55:50 PM Iron Mike Tyson was not asked to speak at the Convention though I'm sure he would do a good job if he was. The media makes everything up!

- Jun 29, 2016 08:09:49 AM The @USCHAMBER must fight harder for the American worker. China, and many others, are taking advantage of U.S. with our terrible trade pacts
- Jun 29, 2016 08:14:56 AM Why would the USChamber be upset by the fact that I want to negotiate better and stronger trade deals or that I want penalties for cheaters?
- Jun 29, 2016 09:37:37 AM Just watched Senator John Barrasso on @FoxNews - He was great! Thank you John.
- Jun 29, 2016 09:39:13 AM New Q poll out- we are going to win the whole deal- and MAKE AMERICA GREAT AGAIN! #Trump2016 https://t.co/dL5ahNcwZb

- Jun 29, 2016 09:48:24 AM Will be in Bangor, Maine today! Join me- 4pmE at the Cross Insurance Center! https://t.co/y4n4nERPFr https://t.co/7LAPewxE05
- Jun 29, 2016 01:21:38 PM ISIS exploded on Hillary Clinton's watch- she's done nothing about it and never will. Not capable!
- Jun 29, 2016 05:57:44 PM I will be on @oreillyfactor at 8:00 P.M. Enjoy!
- Jun 29, 2016 08:46:50 PM "@Gengm7: @jakeda @realDonaldTrump As of April this year, Hillary had spent $264,000,000 on her campaign Mr.Trump $55,000,000. self funding"
- Jun 29, 2016 09:30:59 PM Tremendous day in Massachusetts and Maine. Thank you to everyone for making it so special!
- Jun 29, 2016 09:39:36 PM For reasons only they can explain, the @USChamber wants to continue our bad trade deals rather than renegotiating and making them better.

- Jun 30, 2016 09:35:39 AM RT @DRUDGE_REPORT: 43-39 https://t.co/TkQYb6V2do
- Jun 30, 2016 09:48:18 AM The story with Hillary will never change. https://t.co/h0Av3TAIiM
- Jun 30, 2016 12:32:20 PM New book by @ericbolling is absolutely terrific and a must read! #WakeUpAmerica
- Jun 30, 2016 01:53:11 PM Why would college graduates want Crooked Hillary as their President? She will destroy them! https://t.co/S80xxdeHfG
- Jun 30, 2016 02:28:27 PM One of the reasons Hillary hid her emails was so the public wouldn't see how she got rich- selling out America. https://t.co/mO9QrmYXRD
- Jun 30, 2016 02:29:48 PM The very dishonest @NBCNews refuses to accept the fact that I have forgiven my $50 million loan to my campaign. Done deal!
- Jun 30, 2016 02:30:20 PM I have self funded my winning primary campaign with an approx. $50 million loan. I have totally terminated the loan!
- Jun 30, 2016 02:30:54 PM The reason I put up approximately $50 million for my successful primary campaign is very simple, I want to MAKE AMERICA GREAT AGAIN!
- Jun 30, 2016 05:41:28 PM I will be interviewed by @SeanHannity tonight at 10pm on FOX! Enjoy!
- Jun 30, 2016 09:59:43 PM #ThrowbackThursday #Trump2016 https://t.co/gFtspBViXe

July, 2016

- Jul 1, 2016 07:11:41 AM As Bernie Sanders said, Hillary Clinton has bad judgement. Bill's meeting was probably initiated and demanded by Hillary!
- Jul 1, 2016 07:12:06 AM Bill Clinton's meeting was a total secret. Nobody was to know about it but he was caught by a local reporter.
- Jul 1, 2016 07:12:48 AM Take a look at what happened w/ Bill Clinton. The system is totally rigged. Does anybody really believe that meeting was just a coincidence?
- Jul 1, 2016 08:24:14 AM .@TraceAdkins great job on FOX this morning. Keep up the good work!
- Jul 1, 2016 08:32:19 AM Horrible killing of a 13 year old American girl at her home in Israel by a Palestinian terrorist. We must get tough. https://t.co/zauQ6kb9Hj
- Jul 1, 2016 10:51:46 AM Yet another terrorist attack today in Israel -- a father, shot at by a Palestinian terrorist, was killed while: https://t.co/Cv1HzKVbiT

- Jul 1, 2016 11:43:56 AM These crimes won't be happening if I'm elected POTUS. Killer should have never been here. #AmericaFirst https://t.co/XDGKaj0ico
- Jul 1, 2016 12:07:52 PM Thank you for your support! We will MAKE AMERICA SAFE AND GREAT AGAIN! #ImWithYou #AmericaFirst https://t.co/ravfFT5UBE
- Jul 1, 2016 02:47:04 PM Thank you for inviting me to the Western Conservative Summit in Colorado! #ImWithYou #WCS16 https://t.co/lK3UW4fY2q https://t.co/QDQhRRuBbG
- Jul 1, 2016 08:19:46 PM Just returned from Colorado. Amazing crowd!
- Jul 1, 2016 08:29:25 PM When you can't say it - or see it -- you can't fix it. We will MAKE AMERICA SAFE AGAIN! #ImWithYou #AmericaFirst https://t.co/Vd2A747L29

- Jul 2, 2016 06:48:18 AM Just read in the failing @nytimes that I was not aware "the event had to be held in Cleveland" - a total lie. These people are sick!
- Jul 2, 2016 06:55:14 AM The speakers slots at the Republican Convention are totally filled, with a long waiting list of those that want to speak - Wednesday release
- Jul 2, 2016 08:45:16 AM #AmericaFirst #ImWithYou https://t.co/iEcnnlJ728
- Jul 2, 2016 08:55:45 AM The #2A to our Constitution is clear. The right of the people to keep & bear Arms shall not be infringed upon. https://t.co/sqe12D0MBJ
- Jul 2, 2016 10:19:19 AM Crooked Hillary -- Makes History! #ImWithYou #AmericaFirst https://t.co/PKQhYhMmIX
- Jul 2, 2016 10:19:35 AM If I become the next POTUS- they will not be ignoring! #AmericaFirst https://t.co/97R0cQdnGI
- Jul 2, 2016 10:23:25 AM Thank you! #AmericaFirst https://t.co/MYG45LxGmH
- Jul 2, 2016 10:29:38 AM RT @GOP: Reminder: last year, Clinton pledged she had turned over all work-related email under penalty of perjury https://t.co/X4R7LnsSoy
- Jul 2, 2016 10:32:04 AM Thank you for your support! #AmericaFirst #LeadRight2016 https://t.co/a6f6xZNrym
- Jul 2, 2016 10:33:19 AM Thank you @greta. #ImWithYou https://t.co/SLdqNhD4Tm

- Jul 2, 2016 03:39:39 PM It is impossible for the FBI not to recommend criminal charges against Hillary Clinton. What she did was wrong! What Bill did was stupid!
- Jul 2, 2016 04:13:02 PM It was just announced-by sources-that no charges will be brought against Crooked Hillary Clinton. Like I said, the system is totally rigged!

- Jul 3, 2016 12:40:49 PM Just watched @meetthepress and how totally biased against me Chuck Todd, and the entire show, is against me.The good news-the people get it!
- Jul 3, 2016 03:16:23 PM Only a fool would believe that the meeting between Bill Clinton and the U.S.A.G. was not arranged or that Crooked Hillary did not know.
- Jul 3, 2016 03:20:20 PM Crooked Hillary Clinton knew that her husband wanted to meet with the U.S.A.G. to work out a deal. The system is totally rigged & corrupt!
- Jul 3, 2016 03:47:51 PM On Saturday a great man, Elie Wiesel, passed away.The world is a better place because of him and his belief that good can triumph over evil!
- Jul 3, 2016 04:00:39 PM "THE SYSTEM IS RIGGED!"
- Jul 3, 2016 04:38:20 PM Does anybody really believe that Bill Clinton and the U.S.A.G. talked only about "grandkids" and golf for 37 minutes in plane on tarmac?
- Jul 3, 2016 04:43:25 PM The SECRET meeting between Bill Clinton and the U.S.A.G. in back of closed plane was heightened with FBI shouting "go away, no pictures."
- Jul 3, 2016 04:46:58 PM I believe that Crooked Hillary sent Bill to have the meeting with the U.S.A.G. So Bill is not in trouble with H except that he got caught!

- Jul 4, 2016 06:35:16 AM In Bangladesh, hostages were immediately killed by ISIS terrorists if they were unable to cite a verse from the Koran. 20 were killed!
- Jul 4, 2016 06:54:40 AM The third mass attack (slaughter) in days by ISIS. 200 dead in Baghdad, worst in many years. We do not have leadership that can stop this!

- Jul 4, 2016 07:00:11 AM Crooked Hillary will NEVER be able to handle the complexities and danger of ISIS - it will just go on forever. We need change!
- Jul 4, 2016 08:32:35 AM Happy 4th of July! #Trump2016 #AmericaFirst https://t.co/Ndb3AQrLtY https://t.co/YhHyQjwJW6
- Jul 4, 2016 08:42:16 AM Dishonest media is trying their absolute best to depict a star in a tweet as the Star of David rather than a Sheriff's Star, or plain star!
- Jul 4, 2016 08:56:34 AM Senator Tom Cotton was great on Meet the Press yesterday. Despite a totally one-sided interview by Chuck Todd, the end result was solid!
- Jul 4, 2016 09:11:09 AM Spent time with Indiana Governor Mike Pence and family yesterday. Very impressed, great people!
- Jul 4, 2016 09:19:13 AM I look forward to meeting @joniernst today in New Jersey. She has done a great job as Senator of Iowa!
- Jul 4, 2016 09:25:04 AM The only people who are not interested in being the V.P. pick are the people who have not been asked!
- Jul 4, 2016 10:26:56 AM Crooked Hillary Clinton is "guilty as hell" but the system is totally rigged and corrupt! Where are the 33,000 missing e-mails?
- Jul 4, 2016 10:34:15 AM With Hillary and Obama, the terrorist attacks will only get worse. Politically correct fools, won't even call it what it is - RADICAL ISLAM!
- Jul 4, 2016 05:30:15 PM Why is President Obama allowed to use Air Force One on the campaign trail with Crooked Hillary? She is flying with him tomorrow. Who pays?
- Jul 4, 2016 05:59:46 PM On @FoxNews at 7:00 P.M. "Special: Meet the Trumps" Hope you enjoy!

- Jul 5, 2016 06:14:58 AM Taxpayers are paying a fortune for the use of Air Force One on the campaign trail by President Obama and Crooked Hillary. A total disgrace!
- Jul 5, 2016 07:05:46 AM It was great spending time with @joniernst yesterday. She has done a fantastic job for the people of Iowa and U.S. Will see her again!
- Jul 5, 2016 10:37:23 AM The system is rigged. General Petraeus got in trouble for far less. Very very unfair! As usual, bad judgment.
- Jul 5, 2016 10:39:06 AM FBI director said Crooked Hillary compromised our national security. No charges. Wow! #RiggedSystem

- Jul 5, 2016 01:36:15 PM Looking forward to meeting with @SenBobCorker in a little while. We will be traveling to North Carolina together today.
- Jul 5, 2016 07:52:40 PM My son, @EricTrump will be interviewed by @SeanHannity tonight at 10pm on @FoxNews. Enjoy!
- Jul 5, 2016 09:21:20 PM I will be interviewed by @oreillyfactor tonight on @FoxNews at 11pm. Enjoy!
- Jul 5, 2016 11:23:03 PM Raised a lot of money for the Republican Party. There will be a big gasp when the figures are announced in the morning. Lots of support! Win
- Jul 5, 2016 11:30:04 PM I don't think the voters will forget the rigged system that allowed Crooked Hillary to get away with "murder." Come November 8, she's out!
- Jul 5, 2016 11:36:31 PM Crooked Hillary Clinton is unfit to serve as President of the U.S. Her temperament is weak and her opponents are strong. BAD JUDGEMENT!

- Jul 6, 2016 06:12:45 AM Crooked Hillary Clinton and her team "were extremely careless in their handling of very sensitive, highly classified information." Not fit!
- Jul 6, 2016 06:21:34 AM Crooked Hillary has once again been proven to be a person who is dishonest, incompetent and of very bad judgement.
- Jul 6, 2016 07:11:03 AM The rigged system may have helped Hillary Clinton escape criminal charges, but...https://t.co/KO64IAMDgj https://t.co/8CBSfNpl2l
- Jul 6, 2016 07:31:27 AM Crooked Hillary Clinton lied to the FBI and to the people of our country. She is sooooo guilty. But watch, her time will come!
- Jul 6, 2016 08:08:44 AM I made a lot of money in Atlantic City and left 7 years ago, great timing (as all know). Pols made big mistakes, now many bankruptcies.
- Jul 6, 2016 08:12:43 AM Hillary Clinton should ask why the Democrat pols in Atlantic City made all the wrong moves - Convention Center, Airport - and destroyed City
- Jul 6, 2016 08:24:50 AM Even the once great Caesars is bankrupt in A.C. Others to follow. Ask the Democrat City Council what happened to Atlantic City.
- Jul 6, 2016 09:01:09 AM Sleepy eyes Chuck Todd, a man with so little touch for politics, is at it again.He could not have watched my standing ovation speech in N.C.

- Jul 6, 2016 09:06:38 AM I have over seven million hits on social media re Crooked Hillary Clinton. Check it out Sleepy Eyes, @MarkHalperin @NBCPolitics
- Jul 6, 2016 10:32:35 AM Convention speaker schedule to be released tomorrow. Let today be devoted to Crooked Hillary and the rigged system under which we live.
- Jul 6, 2016 04:58:50 PM To all of my twitter followers, please contribute whatever you can to the campaign. We must beat Crooked Hillary. https://t.co/Xv8Q1GuWiH
- Jul 6, 2016 08:34:20 PM Where is the outrage for this Disney book? Is this the 'Star of David' also? Dishonest media! #Frozen https://t.co/4LJBpSm8xa

- Jul 7, 2016 06:33:49 AM Great being in Cincinnati, Ohio last night- thank you! Off to Washington D.C. now. #Trump2016 #AmericaFirst https://t.co/sryJgRyd56
- Jul 7, 2016 01:07:28 PM Just leaving D.C. Had great meetings with Republicans in the House and Senate. Very interesting day! These are people who love our country!
- Jul 7, 2016 03:04:58 PM Thank you Rep. Collins! #Trump2016 https://t.co/zkmPywMDxg
- Jul 7, 2016 03:06:17 PM #MakeAmericaGreatAgain https://t.co/fxlVgfAA1l
- Jul 7, 2016 03:09:59 PM Thank you Speaker @PRyan! #AmericaFirst #Trump2016 https://t.co/PPsyxGPdFc
- Jul 7, 2016 08:52:04 PM After today, Crooked Hillary can officially be called Lyin' Crooked Hillary.

- Jul 8, 2016 06:02:41 AM Prayers and condolences to all of the families who are so thoroughly devastated by the horrors we are all watching take place in our country
- Jul 8, 2016 08:20:47 AM Last night's horrific execution-style shootings of 12 Dallas law enforcement officers...https://t.co/mwzYU98yTt
- Jul 8, 2016 09:32:15 AM Due to the horrific events taking place in our country, I have decided to postpone my speech on economic opportunity- today in Miami.
- Jul 8, 2016 04:31:01 PM Isn't it sad that on a day of national tragedy Hillary Clinton is answering softball questions about her email lies on @CNN?
- Jul 8, 2016 06:26:56 PM MAKE AMERICA SAFE AGAIN! https://t.co/m0AJWlV8nm https://t.co/P0GleHEmJy

- Jul 9, 2016 10:18:58 AM Way to go @serenawilliams - you are a true champion. Proud of you!
- Jul 9, 2016 04:22:25 PM New poll - thank you! #Trump2016 https://t.co/Mi87Vmw06H https://t.co/WmqvcYG4r3

- Jul 10, 2016 07:02:02 AM Look what is happening to our country under the WEAK leadership of Obama and people like Crooked Hillary Clinton. We are a divided nation!
- Jul 10, 2016 01:27:58 PM President Obama thinks the nation is not as divided as people think. He is living in a world of the make believe!
- Jul 10, 2016 01:42:32 PM The media is so dishonest. If I make a statement, they twist it and turn it to make it sound bad or foolish.They think the public is stupid!
- Jul 10, 2016 01:58:10 PM I heard that the underachieving John King of @CNN on Inside Politics was one hour of lies. Happily, few people are watching - dead network!

- Jul 11, 2016 06:57:45 AM Join me in Westfield, Indiana- tomorrow night at 7:30pm! #Trump2016 Tickets: https://t.co/Jj9TmSEoOd https://t.co/Rq6YRHlpib
- Jul 11, 2016 02:51:29 PM Thoughts and prayers with the victims, and their families- along with everyone at the Berrien County Courthouse in St. Joseph, Michigan.
- Jul 11, 2016 04:40:30 PM Great poll- Florida! Thank you! https://t.co/4FuPpL5WOM
- Jul 11, 2016 05:18:22 PM Speech on Veterans' Reform: https://t.co/XB7RMwesMK
- Jul 11, 2016 07:56:29 PM Senior United States District Judge Robert E. Payne today ruled in favor of Trump campaign delegates who had argued..https://t.co/qVwfjgCHU7
- Jul 11, 2016 09:12:19 PM #MakeAmericaGreatAgain #ImWithYou https://t.co/lb5ViCDH0g https://t.co/roVn7pAVfy

- Jul 12, 2016 06:58:58 AM Crime is out of control, and rapidly getting worse. Look what is going on in Chicago and our inner cities. Not good!

- Jul 12, 2016 07:55:29 AM For too many years, our inner cities have been left behind. I am going to deliver jobs, safety and protection for those in need.
- Jul 12, 2016 07:57:18 AM This election is a choice between law, order & safety - or chaos, crime & violence. I will make America safe again for everyone. #ImWithYou
- Jul 12, 2016 08:36:47 AM Bernie Sanders, who has lost most of his leverage, has totally sold out to Crooked Hillary Clinton. He will endorse her today - fans angry!
- Jul 12, 2016 08:39:56 AM I am somewhat surprised that Bernie Sanders was not true to himself and his supporters. They are not happy that he is selling out!
- Jul 12, 2016 11:45:45 AM #CrookedHillary is not qualified! https://t.co/6qi7KTW43O
- Jul 12, 2016 12:01:51 PM Bernie Sanders endorsing Crooked Hillary Clinton is like Occupy Wall Street endorsing Goldman Sachs.
- Jul 12, 2016 12:03:44 PM Bernie sanders has abandoned his supporters by endorsing pro-war pro-TPP pro-Wall Street Crooked Hillary Clinton.
- Jul 12, 2016 12:04:19 PM To all the Bernie voters who want to stop bad trade deals & global special interests, we welcome you with open arms. People first.
- Jul 12, 2016 04:10:03 PM The American people agree. No free pass for #CrookedHillary! https://t.co/lTjLVKkzh1
- Jul 12, 2016 04:59:45 PM I will be interviewed by @oreillyfactor tonight on @FoxNews at 8pm. Enjoy!
- Jul 12, 2016 05:19:52 PM Thank you Iowa- see you soon! #Trump2016 #ImWithYou https://t.co/gva0MbgnuO https://t.co/PE1jdqZysc
- Jul 12, 2016 10:08:58 PM THANK YOU INDIANA! #Trump2016 https://t.co/Jmkah9wGaA
- Jul 12, 2016 11:54:40 PM Justice Ginsburg of the U.S. Supreme Court has embarrassed all by making very dumb political statements about me. Her mind is shot - resign!

- Jul 13, 2016 07:33:15 AM Thank you! #ImWithYou https://t.co/6XkUQ0W4QS
- Jul 13, 2016 07:50:04 AM Thank you Florida, Ohio, and Pennsylvania! #CrookedHillary is not qualified. #ImWithYou https://t.co/M1yzgyeEdY

- Jul 13, 2016 04:22:44 PM #CrookedHillary is outspending me by a combined 31 to 1 in Florida, Ohio, & Pennsylvania. I haven't started yet! https://t.co/BcoPrwqFMe
- Jul 13, 2016 04:56:42 PM New GOP platform now includes language that supports the border wall. We will build the wall and MAKE AMERICA SAFE AGAIN!
- Jul 13, 2016 05:05:22 PM The Republican platform is most pro-Israel of all time!
- Jul 13, 2016 05:06:30 PM Is President Obama trying to destroy Israel with all his bad moves? Think about it and let me know!
- Jul 13, 2016 05:11:04 PM Lyin' Crooked Hillary's email stories all have one thing in common. https://t.co/teoVCYXKOR
- Jul 13, 2016 05:19:48 PM Despite spending $500k a day on TV ads alone #CrookedHillary falls flat in nationwide @QuinnipiacPoll. Having ZERO impact. Sad!!
- Jul 13, 2016 05:22:20 PM Voters understand that Crooked Hillary's negative ads are not true- just like her email lies and her other fraudulent activity.
- Jul 13, 2016 05:23:40 PM On my way to San Diego to raise money for the Republican Party. I am spending a lot myself and also helping others.
- Jul 13, 2016 05:26:20 PM Is Supreme Court Justice Ruth Bader Ginsburg going to apologize to me for her misconduct? Big mistake by an incompetent judge!
- Jul 13, 2016 05:27:45 PM Even the @NYTimes and @WashingtonPost Editorial Boards condemned Justice Ginsburg for her ethical and legal breach. What was she thinking?
- Jul 13, 2016 05:28:44 PM If I win the Presidency, we will swamp Justice Ginsburg with real judges and real legal opinions!
- Jul 13, 2016 08:19:51 PM I will be making the announcement of my Vice Presidential pick on Friday at 11am in Manhattan. Details to follow.

- Jul 14, 2016 08:21:48 AM Great new poll- thank you America! #Trump2016 #ImWithYou https://t.co/aVH9c5QRwc
- Jul 14, 2016 09:53:46 AM Another new poll. Thank you for your support! Join the MOVEMENT today! #ImWithYou https://t.co/3KWOl2ibaW https://t.co/miT4atHxQz

- Jul 14, 2016 12:23:58 PM I employ many people in the State of Virginia - JOBS, JOBS, JOBS! Crooked Hillary will sell us out, just like her husband did with NAFTA.
- Jul 14, 2016 05:40:31 PM Another horrific attack, this time in Nice, France. Many dead and injured. When will we learn? It is only getting worse.
- Jul 14, 2016 06:09:57 PM In light of the horrible attack in Nice, France, I have postponed tomorrow's news conference concerning my Vice Presidential announcement.
- Jul 14, 2016 07:39:27 PM My prayers and condolences to the victims and families of the terrible tragedy in Nice, France. We are with you in every way!

- Jul 15, 2016 09:31:18 AM #NeverTrump is never more. They were crushed last night in Cleveland at Rules Committee by a vote of 87-12. MAKE AMERICA GREAT AGAIN!
- Jul 15, 2016 09:41:20 AM Four more years of weakness with a Crooked Hillary Administration is not acceptable. Look what has happened to the world with O & Hillary!
- Jul 15, 2016 09:50:55 AM I am pleased to announce that I have chosen Governor Mike Pence as my Vice Presidential running mate. News conference tomorrow at 11:00 A.M.
- Jul 15, 2016 09:12:13 PM Look forward to Governor Mike Pence V.P. introduction tomorrow in New York City.

- Jul 16, 2016 07:29:43 AM Look forward to introducing Governor Mike Pence (who has done a spectacular job in the great State of Indiana). My first choice from start!
- Jul 16, 2016 08:08:43 AM Crooked Hillary is spending big Wall Street money on ads saying I don't have foreign policy experience, yet look what her policies have done
- Jul 16, 2016 08:13:56 AM Crooked Hillary, who embarrassed herself and the country with her e-mail lies, has been a DISASTER on foreign policy. Look what's happening!
- Jul 16, 2016 08:19:11 AM Very sad that a person who has made so many mistakes, Crooked Hillary Clinton, can put out such false and vicious ads with her phony money!

- Jul 16, 2016 08:23:17 AM Crooked Hillary Clinton is bought and paid for by Wall Street, lobbyists and special interests. She will sell our country down the tubes!
- Jul 16, 2016 11:13:29 AM Thank you! #TrumpPence16 https://t.co/RHprMCsGT6
- Jul 16, 2016 03:44:37 PM Donate Today To Help Make America Great Again! You Can Help Stop Crooked Hillary Clinton! https://t.co/VlObaDG4eR https://t.co/mBDwW5orrd
- Jul 16, 2016 04:01:31 PM Donate Today To Help Make America Great Again! You Can Help Stop Crooked Hillary Clinton! https://t.co/swzCe5PiNI https://t.co/0fmgNBuAcc
- Jul 16, 2016 10:15:22 PM Thank you to Chris Cox and Bikers for Trump - Your support has been amazing. I will never forget. MAKE AMERICA GREAT AGAIN!
- Jul 16, 2016 10:21:14 PM "@TrumpDoonbeg: Great news! We've been nominated for Ireland's Best Golf Hotel 2016. We would appreciate your vote! https://t.co/5uEBphqdG9"
- Jul 16, 2016 10:39:09 PM Thank you to Jack Morgan, Tamara Neo, Cheryl Ann Kraft and all of my friends and supporters in Virginia. GREAT JOB!
- Jul 16, 2016 11:15:49 PM Goofy Elizabeth Warren, who may be the least productive Senator in the U.S. Senate, must prove she is not a fraud. Without the con it's over
- Jul 16, 2016 11:19:05 PM We are going to have a great time in Cleveland. Will lead to special results for our country. We will Make America Great Again!

- Jul 17, 2016 06:55:21 AM As the days and weeks go by, we see what a total mess our country (and world) is in - Crooked Hillary Clinton led Obama into bad decisions!
- Jul 17, 2016 07:06:18 AM It doesn't matter that Crooked Hillary has experience, look at all of the bad decisions she has made. Bernie said she has bad judgement!
- Jul 17, 2016 07:14:46 AM I hope that Crooked Hillary picks Goofy Elizabeth Warren, sometimes referred to as Pocahontas, as her V.P. Then we can litigate her fraud!

- Jul 17, 2016 07:24:04 AM If Goofy Elizabeth Warren, a very weak Senator, didn't lie about her heritage (being Native American) she would be nothing today. Pick her H
- Jul 17, 2016 08:04:10 AM .@FoxNews is much better, and far more truthful, than @CNN, which is all negative. Guests are stacked for Crooked Hillary! I don't watch.
- Jul 17, 2016 08:09:02 AM The ratings at @FoxNews blow away the ratings of @CNN - not even close. That's because CNN is the Clinton News Network and people don't like
- Jul 17, 2016 12:30:42 PM We grieve for the officers killed in Baton Rouge today. How many law enforcement and people have to... https://t.co/pPNrzG8kEa
- Jul 17, 2016 01:26:51 PM We are TRYING to fight ISIS, and now our own people are killing our police. Our country is divided and out of control. The world is watching
- Jul 17, 2016 01:39:36 PM I will be on @60Minutes tonight at 7:00 P.M. with Mike Pence talking about LAW AND ORDER and many other subjects! Bad times for divided USA!
- Jul 17, 2016 01:41:24 PM "@60Minutes: DonaldTrump and his running mate @Mike_Pence to appear on #60Minutes in first joint interview. CBS https://t.co/lZH7qw9qmu"
- Jul 17, 2016 04:22:23 PM Our country is totally divided and our enemies are watching. We are not looking good, we are not looking smart, we are not looking tough!
- Jul 17, 2016 04:26:50 PM President Obama just had a news conference, but he doesn't have a clue. Our country is a divided crime scene, and it will only get worse!

- Jul 18, 2016 05:53:55 AM RT @foxandfriends: STILL AHEAD: @realDonaldTrump joins us at 7am/et! #RNCinCLE https://t.co/TzGbDs88b3
- Jul 18, 2016 12:10:39 PM Thank you Mahoning County, Ohio! See you soon! #MakeAmericaSafeAgain https://t.co/TNJMUKImpK https://t.co/iFdqRvaL3q
- Jul 18, 2016 12:28:04 PM Looking forward to being at the convention tonight to watch all of the wonderful speakers including my wife, Melania. Place looks beautiful!

- Jul 18, 2016 03:48:00 PM .@CNN is the worst.They go to their dumb, one-sided panels when a podium speaker is for Trump! VAST MAJORITY want: Make America Great Again!
- Jul 18, 2016 03:51:55 PM Networks other than low ratings @CNN have been very fair and exciting!
- Jul 18, 2016 06:04:11 PM #MakeAmericaSafeAgain! #GOPConvention #RNCinCLE https://t.co/QniZIsGrG8 https://t.co/Kvq6r6WkQ1
- Jul 18, 2016 07:21:49 PM Will be on @OreillyFactor tonight at 8:30pm @FoxNews- prior to Melania's speech at the #GOPConvention. Tune in- she will do great! #RNCinCLE
- Jul 18, 2016 11:14:11 PM It was truly an honor to introduce my wife, Melania. Her speech and demeanor were absolutely incredible. Very proud! #GOPConvention

- Jul 19, 2016 08:36:43 AM "@RoxaneTancredi: Democrats are coming to TRUMP. I used to be proud of the dem party. No more It is crooked and not for the people."
- Jul 19, 2016 02:34:40 PM #MakeAmericaWorkAgain #TrumpPence16 #RNCinCLE https://t.co/xlB2C1cpKp https://t.co/5Kv03luMZW
- Jul 19, 2016 03:38:20 PM #MakeAmericaWorkAgain #TrumpPence16 #RNCinCLE https://t.co/bsUp4MSysD https://t.co/mYBjp03XYf
- Jul 19, 2016 05:12:56 PM The ROLL CALL is beginning at the Republican National Convention. Very exciting!
- Jul 19, 2016 06:52:59 PM Such a great honor to be the Republican Nominee for President of the United States. I will work hard and never let you down! AMERICA FIRST!

- Jul 20, 2016 05:18:17 AM Congratulations to my children, Don and Tiffany, on having done a fantastic job last night. I am very proud of you!
- Jul 20, 2016 07:47:56 AM Bill Hemmer of @FoxNews was very nice in explaining the excitement and energy in the arena. More than in past years.
- Jul 20, 2016 07:51:58 AM In November, I think the people of Ohio will remember that the Republicans picked Cleveland instead of going to another state. Jobs!

- Jul 20, 2016 10:31:15 AM Good news is Melania's speech got more publicity than any in the history of politics especially if you believe that all press is good press!
- Jul 20, 2016 10:36:06 AM The media is spending more time doing a forensic analysis of Melania's speech than the FBI spent on Hillary's emails.
- Jul 20, 2016 12:02:19 PM STATEMENT ON MELANIA SPEECH https://t.co/uzBOm21Pug
- Jul 20, 2016 01:41:29 PM URGENT: we've just announced a $2 million fundraising goal tonight. Please stand with us! https://t.co/Ssrh55C6hW https://t.co/2KjT4TJ07Y
- Jul 20, 2016 01:48:11 PM John Kasich was never asked by me to be V.P. Just arrived in Cleveland - will be a great two days!
- Jul 20, 2016 06:49:18 PM Watching the #GOPConvention #AmericaFirst #RNCinCLE
- Jul 20, 2016 07:50:21 PM #AmericaFirst #RNCinCLE https://t.co/PvdTA8HTCC
- Jul 20, 2016 08:08:33 PM Thank you @IngrahamAngle! #AmericaFirst https://t.co/cv3I3xRSOK
- Jul 20, 2016 08:24:26 PM Thank you to Governor @ScottWalker for such warm support. Great speech!
- Jul 20, 2016 08:52:25 PM #TextTrump88022 for exclusive @realDonaldTrump updates! We will Make America Great Again!
- Jul 20, 2016 08:56:56 PM Thank you @ScottWalker! #AmericaFirst #RNCinCLE https://t.co/k2Poy3gGvQ
- Jul 20, 2016 09:06:13 PM Limited opportunity to get your OFFICIAL Trump gear! Shop now! https://t.co/LQMDdNkUwR https://t.co/KSAv65FuiD
- Jul 20, 2016 09:19:28 PM Limited opportunity to get your OFFICIAL Trump gear! Shop now! https://t.co/3lUaSztKYx https://t.co/ssNVgF7PTt
- Jul 20, 2016 09:35:23 PM Great job @EricTrump! Proud of you! #AmericaFirst #RNCinCLE https://t.co/EE7C6XKDkt https://t.co/946U6bgREQ
- Jul 20, 2016 10:45:48 PM Wow, Ted Cruz got booed off the stage, didn't honor the pledge! I saw his speech two hours early but let him speak anyway. No big deal!
- Jul 20, 2016 10:49:38 PM Our next Vice President of the United States of America, Gov. @Mike_Pence! #GOPinCLE #GOPConvention #AmericaFirst https://t.co/TZT3XcKp1c

- Jul 20, 2016 10:53:28 PM .@mike_pence was fantastic tonight. Will be a great V.P.
- Jul 20, 2016 10:56:28 PM Arena was packed, totally electric!
- Jul 20, 2016 11:00:25 PM MAKE AMERICA GREAT AGAIN! https://t.co/qL9rjb7OsD
- Jul 20, 2016 11:32:03 PM Great job @EricTrump! Proud of you! #AmericaFirst #RNCinCLE https://t.co/S7IHXDrmsJ

- Jul 21, 2016 07:37:53 AM I am soooo proud of my children, Don, Eric and Tiffany - their speeches, under enormous pressure, were incredible. Ivanka intros me tonight!
- Jul 21, 2016 09:12:45 AM Ted Cruz talks about the Constitution but doesn't say that if the Dems win the Presidency, the new JUSTICES appointed will destroy us all!
- Jul 21, 2016 09:16:20 AM Limited opportunity to get your OFFICIAL Trump gear! Shop now! https://t.co/3lUaSztKYx
- Jul 21, 2016 09:49:19 AM Other than a small group of people who have suffered massive and embarrassing losses, the party is VERY united. Great love in the arena!
- Jul 21, 2016 09:56:49 AM Great job @IvankaTrump! #RNCinCLE https://t.co/swsAKE11F0
- Jul 21, 2016 11:45:23 AM We've just set a new goal: raise $4 million from our grassroots supporters by MIDNIGHT! https://t.co/Ssrh55C6hW https://t.co/9Hd6dRcojF
- Jul 21, 2016 11:47:02 AM We've just set a new goal: raise $4 million from our grassroots supporters by MIDNIGHT! https://t.co/Ssrh55C6hW https://t.co/8E0LiC8wYE
- Jul 21, 2016 12:00:24 PM Thank you @DonaldJTrumpJr. Proud of you! #RNCinCLE #TrumpPence2016 https://t.co/gobSNWughP
- Jul 21, 2016 01:49:27 PM I'm with you! I will work hard and never let you down. Make America Great Again! https://t.co/V92PkdHbG6 https://t.co/SQs6ERk6El
- Jul 21, 2016 02:55:31 PM I'm with you! I will work hard and never let you down. Make America Great Again! https://t.co/V92PkdHbG6 https://t.co/FhWHekyU4Q

- Jul 21, 2016 02:56:45 PM This is a MOVEMENT! #RNCinCLE https://t.co/bdox6JcrAp
- Jul 21, 2016 09:02:18 PM You can watch 360 video live from the podium! https://t.co/yqcIsBUdAi #RNCinCLE #TrumpIsWithYou #MakeAmericaGreatAgain
- Jul 21, 2016 11:01:07 PM FORMAL ACCEPTANCE OF THE NOMINATION! #TrumpPence16 https://t.co/E6ZtVjSQZa

- Jul 22, 2016 12:11:10 AM MAKE AMERICA SAFE AND GREAT AGAIN! #RNCinCLE https://t.co/KH2ZFHUHGP
- Jul 22, 2016 08:07:51 AM What a great four days in Cleveland. So proud of the great job done by the RNC and all. The police and Secret Service were fantastic!
- Jul 22, 2016 08:13:02 AM Thank you Cleveland. We love you and will be back many times!
- Jul 22, 2016 09:06:01 AM One of the best produced, including the incredible stage & set, in the history of conventions. Great unity! Big T.V. ratings! @KarlRove
- Jul 22, 2016 06:03:19 PM Another attack, this time in Germany. Many killed. God bless the people of Munich.
- Jul 22, 2016 10:23:15 PM Is it the same Kaine that took hundreds of thousands of dollars in gifts while Governor of Virginia and didn't get indicted while Bob M did?
- Jul 22, 2016 10:49:04 PM I highly recommend the just out book - THE FIELD OF FIGHT - by General Michael Flynn. How to defeat radical Islam.
- Jul 22, 2016 10:56:38 PM "@Theresa_Cali: @realDonaldTrump General Michael Flynn will make a great Secretary of Defense when you become POTUS! #MakeAmericaSafeAgain"

- Jul 23, 2016 05:31:18 AM The Bernie Sanders supporters are furious with the choice of Tim Kaine, who represents the opposite of what Bernie stands for. Philly fight?
- Jul 23, 2016 05:35:37 AM Tim Kaine is, and always has been, owned by the banks. Bernie supporters are outraged, was their last choice. Bernie fought for nothing!

- Jul 23, 2016 05:42:10 AM Pocahontas wanted V.P. slot so badly but wasn't chosen because she has done nothing in the Senate. Also, Crooked Hillary hates her!
- Jul 23, 2016 05:55:20 AM Leaked e-mails of DNC show plans to destroy Bernie Sanders. Mock his heritage and much more. On-line from Wikileakes, really vicious. RIGGED
- Jul 23, 2016 09:51:32 AM Crooked Hillary Clinton has destroyed jobs and manufacturing in Pennsylvania. Against steelworkers and miners. Husband signed NAFTA.
- Jul 23, 2016 10:01:48 AM Funny that the Democrats would have their convention in Pennsylvania where her husband and her killed so many jobs. I will bring jobs back!
- Jul 23, 2016 10:36:41 AM Tim Kaine has been praising the Trans Pacific Partnership and has been pushing hard to get it approved. Job killer!
- Jul 23, 2016 11:06:15 AM I will bring jobs back and get wages up. People haven't had a real wage increase in almost twenty years. Clinton killed jobs!
- Jul 23, 2016 03:43:33 PM Just saw Crooked Hillary and Tim Kaine together. ISIS and our other enemies are drooling. They don't look presidential to me!
- Jul 23, 2016 04:20:58 PM The Wikileaks e-mail release today was so bad to Sanders that it will make it impossible for him to support her, unless he is a fraud!
- Jul 23, 2016 05:05:55 PM Thank you to everyone for the wonderful reviews of my speech on Thursday night. From the heart!
- Jul 23, 2016 05:11:11 PM "@OliMauritania: @realDonaldTrump Kaine supported the stupidest deal in the history of deals https://t.co/0FFeKTsuJn #HillaryKaine2016"
- Jul 23, 2016 05:13:39 PM "@NancyNielsenn: @realDonaldTrump Dinesh D'Sousa Hillary's America. see it"
- Jul 23, 2016 07:38:47 PM #MakeAmericaGreatAgain #TrumpPence16 https://t.co/gCzHX1nyxD

- Jul 24, 2016 06:16:15 AM The Crooked Hillary V.P. choice is VERY disrespectful to Bernie Sanders and all of his supporters. Just another case of BAD JUDGEMENT by H!
- Jul 24, 2016 06:25:06 AM Bernie Sanders started off strong, but with the selection of Kaine for V.P., is ending really weak. So much for a movement! TOTAL DISRESPECT

- Jul 24, 2016 06:56:43 AM Wow, President Obama's brother, Malik, just announced that he is voting for me. Was probably treated badly by president-like everybody else!
- Jul 24, 2016 07:15:51 AM Looks like the Bernie people will fight. If not, their BLOOD, SWEAT AND TEARS was a total waste of time. Kaine stands for opposite!
- Jul 24, 2016 07:30:15 AM An analysis showed that Bernie Sanders would have won the Democratic nomination if it were not for the Super Delegates.
- Jul 24, 2016 08:27:56 AM There is no longer a Bernie Sanders "political revolution." He is turning out to be a weak and somewhat pathetic figure,wants it all to end!
- Jul 24, 2016 08:30:59 AM Sorry folks, but Bernie Sanders is exhausted, just can't go on any longer. He is trying to dismiss the new e-mails and DNC disrespect. SAD!
- Jul 24, 2016 03:20:57 PM Today proves what I have always known, that @Reince Priebus is the tough one and the smart one, not Debbie Wasserman Shultz (@DWStweets.)
- Jul 24, 2016 03:30:06 PM I always said that Debbie Wasserman Schultz was overrated. The Dems Convention is cracking up and Bernie is exhausted, no energy left!
- Jul 24, 2016 03:45:31 PM The @CNN panels are so one sided, almost all against Trump. @FoxNews is so much better and the ratings are much higher. Don't watch CNN!
- Jul 24, 2016 04:53:29 PM If the Republican Convention had blown up with e-mails, resignation of boss and the beat down of a big player. (Bernie), media would go wild
- Jul 24, 2016 05:02:42 PM Crooked Hillary Clinton was not at all loyal to the person in her rigged system that pushed her over the top, DWS. Too bad Bernie flamed out
- Jul 24, 2016 05:07:49 PM Even though Bernie Sanders has lost his energy and his strength, I don't believe that his supporters will let Crooked Hillary off the hook!
- Jul 24, 2016 05:16:59 PM The Democrats are in a total meltdown but the biased media will say how great they are doing! E-mails say the rigged system is alive & well!

- Jul 24, 2016 05:33:42 PM The highly neurotic Debbie Wasserman Schultz is angry that, after stealing and cheating her way to a Crooked Hillary victory, she's out!
- Jul 24, 2016 06:47:08 PM The ratings for the Republican National Convention were very good, but for the final night, my speech, great. Thank you!
- Jul 24, 2016 06:59:10 PM Watched Crooked Hillary Clinton and Tim Kaine on 60 Minutes. No way they are going to fix America's problems. ISIS & all others laughing!

- Jul 25, 2016 06:31:22 AM The new joke in town is that Russia leaked the disastrous DNC e-mails, which should never have been written (stupid), because Putin likes me
- Jul 25, 2016 06:57:17 AM How much BAD JUDGEMENT was on display by the people in DNC in writing those really dumb e-mails, using even religion, against Bernie!
- Jul 25, 2016 07:02:01 AM Hillary was involved in the e-mail scandal because she is the only one with judgement so bad that such a thing could have happened!
- Jul 25, 2016 07:26:56 AM Thank you! #MakeAmericaGreatAgain https://t.co/Pzs9uwgzam
- Jul 25, 2016 07:27:35 AM If Bernie Sanders, after seeing the just released e-mails, continues to look exhausted and done, then his legacy will never be the same.
- Jul 25, 2016 08:19:18 AM Crooked Hillary Clinton knew everything that her "servant" was doing at the DNC - they just got caught, that's all! They laughed at Bernie.
- Jul 25, 2016 08:42:55 AM Here we go again with another Clinton scandal, and e-mails yet (can you believe). Crooked Hillary knew the fix was in, B never had a chance!
- Jul 25, 2016 08:47:45 AM Wow, the Republican Convention went so smoothly compared to the Dems total mess. But fear not, the dishonest media will find a good spinnnn!
- Jul 25, 2016 09:01:25 AM The State of Florida is so embarrassed by the antics of Crooked Hillary Clinton and Debbie Wasserman Schultz that they will vote for CHANGE!

- Jul 25, 2016 09:05:27 AM Great POLL numbers are coming out all over. People don't want another four years of Obama, and Crooked Hillary would be even worse. #MAGA
- Jul 25, 2016 11:46:33 AM #MakeAmericaGreatAgain https://t.co/EXsoUOsEP4 https://t.co/3ji7a14GSw
- Jul 25, 2016 01:57:06 PM MAKE AMERICA SAFE AND GREAT AGAIN! #TrumpPence16 https://t.co/4O4yjh7X4O https://t.co/cptBaZbV1v
- Jul 25, 2016 04:24:28 PM Thank you Roanoke, Virginia- be back soon! #TrumpPence16 https://t.co/rwxXhfFsn1 https://t.co/HwqI2iGPDu
- Jul 25, 2016 04:25:50 PM Thank you OHIO! #TrumpPence16 https://t.co/NOF9Td9BHs https://t.co/WPMBkYjuIm
- Jul 25, 2016 04:32:59 PM Clinton betrayed Bernie voters. Kaine supports TPP, is in pocket of Wall Street, and backed Iraq War.
- Jul 25, 2016 04:33:49 PM While Bernie has totally given up on his fight for the people, we welcome all voters who want a better future for our workers.
- Jul 25, 2016 04:45:54 PM Hard to believe that Bernie Sanders has done such a complete fold. He got NOTHING for all of the time, energy and money. The V.P. a joke!
- Jul 25, 2016 04:57:14 PM I was at @FoxNews and met Juan Williams in passing. He asked if he could have pictures taken with me. I said fine. He then trashes on air!
- Jul 25, 2016 09:14:29 PM If Cory Booker is the future of the Democratic Party, they have no future! I know more about Cory than he knows about himself.
- Jul 25, 2016 10:04:56 PM Sad to watch Bernie Sanders abandon his revolution. We welcome all voters who want to fix our rigged system and bring back our jobs.
- Jul 25, 2016 10:12:57 PM Elizabeth Warren, often referred to as Pocahontas, just misrepresented me and spoke glowingly about Crooked Hillary, who she always hated!
- Jul 25, 2016 10:19:38 PM Bernie Sanders totally sold out to Crooked Hillary Clinton. All of that work, energy and money, and nothing to show for it! Waste of time.

- Jul 26, 2016 07:34:19 AM Funny, if you listen to @FoxNews, the Democrats did not have a good day. If you listen to the other two, they are fawning. What a difference

- Jul 26, 2016 07:38:27 AM Why aren't the Democrats speaking about ISIS, bad trade deals, broken borders, police and law and order. The Republican Convention was great
- Jul 26, 2016 07:42:33 AM Pocahontas bombed last night! Sad to watch.
- Jul 26, 2016 12:43:45 PM Join us tomorrow in Scranton, Pennsylvania at 3pm! #TrumpPence16 #MAGA Tickets: https://t.co/4FTydj8s9U https://t.co/7zMKhhMmhp
- Jul 26, 2016 12:53:40 PM Join us in Toledo, Ohio- tomorrow night at 8pm! #TrumpPence16 #MAGA Tickets: https://t.co/ERNRrksikq https://t.co/zmGZauCnQF
- Jul 26, 2016 01:20:48 PM Thank you New Hampshire! #MakeAmericaGreatAgain https://t.co/KRCdV77BQp
- Jul 26, 2016 02:27:43 PM The invention of email has proven to be a very bad thing for Crooked Hillary in that it has proven her to be both incompetent and a liar!
- Jul 26, 2016 02:27:58 PM Bernie's exhausted, he just wants to shut down and go home to bed!
- Jul 26, 2016 02:48:08 PM Dems don't want to talk ISIS b/c Hillary's foreign interventions unleashed ISIS & her refugee plans make it easier for them to come here.
- Jul 26, 2016 05:47:28 PM In order to try and deflect the horror and stupidity of the Wikileakes disaster, the Dems said maybe it is Russia dealing with Trump. Crazy!
- Jul 26, 2016 05:50:12 PM For the record, I have ZERO investments in Russia.
- Jul 26, 2016 06:34:19 PM I'm with you! I will work hard and never let you down. Make America Great Again! https://t.co/ajAJ13xQvr
- Jul 26, 2016 06:41:07 PM I'm with you! I will work hard and never let you down. Make America Great Again! https://t.co/LwxMIAn0kK
- Jul 26, 2016 06:42:38 PM I'm with you! I will work hard and never let you down. Make America Great Again! https://t.co/CWfECeUSSq
- Jul 26, 2016 08:51:45 PM You have no idea what my strategy on ISIS is, and neither does ISIS (a good thing). Please get your facts straight - thanks. @megynkelly
- Jul 26, 2016 09:02:24 PM No matter what Bill Clinton says and no matter how well he says it, the phony media will exclaim it to be incredible. Highly overrated!

- Jul 26, 2016 09:08:50 PM I hate to say it, but the Republican Convention was far more interesting (with a much more beautiful set) than the Democratic Convention!
- Jul 26, 2016 09:11:47 PM Many of Bernie's supporters have left the arena. Did Bernie go home and go to sleep?
- Jul 26, 2016 10:01:04 PM Just like I have warned from the beginning, Crooked Hillary Clinton will betray you on the TPP. https://t.co/eoNTWK6I8y

- Jul 27, 2016 04:33:52 AM As I have been saying, Crooked Hillary will approve the job killing TPP after the election, despite her statements to the contrary: top adv.
- Jul 27, 2016 04:43:16 AM Funny how the failing @nytimes is pushing Dems narrative that Russia is working for me because Putin said "Trump is a genius." America 1st!
- Jul 27, 2016 04:50:55 AM The Democratic Convention has paid ZERO respect to the great police and law enforcement professionals of our country. No recognition - SAD!
- Jul 27, 2016 05:01:39 AM Hopefully the violent and vicious killing by ISIS of a beloved French priest is causing people to start thinking rationally. Get tough!
- Jul 27, 2016 05:08:35 AM Crooked Hillary Clinton wants to flood our country with Syrian immigrants that we know little or nothing about. The danger is massive. NO!
- Jul 27, 2016 07:57:20 AM Our not very bright Vice President, Joe Biden, just stated that I wanted to "carpet bomb" the enemy. Sorry Joe, that was Ted Cruz!
- Jul 27, 2016 08:01:03 AM Not one American flag on the massive stage at the Democratic National Convention until people started complaining-then a small one. Pathetic
- Jul 27, 2016 11:03:07 AM Join our next Vice President, @Mike_Pence in Wisconsin tonight & Michigan Thursday! MI: https://t.co/daR2xIhCEs WI: https://t.co/LKc7e4VZkB
- Jul 27, 2016 11:16:02 AM If Russia or any other country or person has Hillary Clinton's 33,000 illegally deleted emails, perhaps they should share them with the FBI!
- Jul 27, 2016 12:16:56 PM Great new poll - thank you! #MakeAmericaGreatAgain https://t.co/mXovx0TLPC

- Jul 27, 2016 01:23:14 PM "Trump right: Illegal families crossing border set to double, 51,152 so far" https://t.co/1noCe9W6Ru
- Jul 27, 2016 02:15:42 PM Thank you to our amazing law enforcement officers! #MAGA https://t.co/UEZorOQhTw
- Jul 27, 2016 04:01:22 PM As President, I will bring jobs back and get wages up for Americans who need it most. https://t.co/rSEcsjiNFb https://t.co/ybFOV3gh0l
- Jul 27, 2016 04:58:43 PM Thank you Pennsylvania! #MakeAmericaGreatAgain https://t.co/bbv3EhGs5x https://t.co/bbroAGTdMw
- Jul 27, 2016 05:01:40 PM #CrookedHillary https://t.co/lwi9gqDEHE
- Jul 27, 2016 07:01:31 PM Join me live in Toledo, Ohio! #MakeAmericaGreatAgain https://t.co/ruEvMGx4C9
- Jul 27, 2016 09:39:07 PM Shooting deaths of police officers up 78% this year. We must restore law and order and protect our great law enforcement officers!
- Jul 27, 2016 09:42:13 PM Our country does not feel 'great already' to the millions of wonderful people living in poverty, violence and despair.
- Jul 27, 2016 10:56:47 PM "@DavidWohl: Barack is offended that @realDonaldTrump will demand that #NATO allies pay their fair share. #DemsInPhilly"
- Jul 27, 2016 11:00:23 PM "@trumplican2016: @realDonaldTrump @DavidWohl stay the course mr trump your message is resonating with the PEOPLE"

- Jul 28, 2016 10:09:11 AM President Obama spoke last night about a world that doesn't exist. 70% of the people think our country is going in the wrong direction. #DNC
- Jul 28, 2016 10:10:35 AM RT @DRUDGE_REPORT: Obama Refers to Himself 119 Times During Hillary Nominating Speech... https://t.co/TyJI2DuqEk
- Jul 28, 2016 10:30:06 AM RT @piersmorgan: Trump makes a funny, obvious joke about Russia going after Hillary's emails & U.S. media goes insane with fury. He plays t…
- Jul 28, 2016 10:48:56 AM RT @mike_pence: Good morning! Join me in Lima, Ohio - tomorrow evening at 7pm. #MAGA Tickets: https://t.co/sNfhyGeaAH
- Jul 28, 2016 01:32:31 PM "@LallyRay: Poll: Donald Trump Sees 17-Point Positive Swing in Two Weeks - Breitbart https://t.co/bVAj52fA3Y @realdonaldtrump" Great!
- Jul 28, 2016 01:36:06 PM Bernie caved! https://t.co/xtcOnA8cw1

- Jul 28, 2016 03:30:18 PM AMERICA'S FUTURE https://t.co/xymiA0Az7x
- Jul 28, 2016 03:31:59 PM A vote for Clinton-Kaine is a vote for TPP, NAFTA, high taxes, radical regulation, and massive influx of refugees.
- Jul 28, 2016 03:56:09 PM Median household income is down for the middle class since Obama took office. It will only go further down under Clinton.
- Jul 28, 2016 04:08:32 PM Great to be back in Iowa! #TBT with @JerryJrFalwell joining me in Davenport- this past winter. #MAGA https://t.co/A5IF0QHnic
- Jul 28, 2016 04:38:12 PM "Dems warn not to underestimate Trump's potential win" https://t.co/X3xHtjhHpB
- Jul 28, 2016 04:56:33 PM As President, I WILL fix this rigged system and only answer to YOU, the American people! https://t.co/aE4cuEQBFQ https://t.co/hjYzQvwMaC
- Jul 28, 2016 06:13:55 PM #CrookedHillary https://t.co/JeXFnO6e3s
- Jul 28, 2016 09:04:26 PM I will once again write a $1 MILLION check to our campaign if we hit our million-dollar end-of-month goal! https://t.co/CgHp1CqPSp
- Jul 28, 2016 09:26:27 PM Departing now - thank you Cedar Rapids, Iowa. This is a MOVEMENT! https://t.co/ezrqVqPtta
- Jul 28, 2016 10:18:23 PM I will once again write a $1 MILLION check to our campaign if we hit our million-dollar end-of-month goal! https://t.co/fUTugI2R2k
- Jul 28, 2016 10:47:56 PM Hillary's refusal to mention Radical Islam, as she pushes a 550% increase in refugees, is more proof that she is unfit to lead the country.
- Jul 28, 2016 10:50:59 PM Our way of life is under threat by Radical Islam and Hillary Clinton cannot even bring herself to say the words.
- Jul 28, 2016 10:52:46 PM Hillary will never reform Wall Street. She is owned by Wall Street!
- Jul 28, 2016 10:54:22 PM Hillary's vision is a borderless world where working people have no power, no jobs, no safety.
- Jul 28, 2016 10:57:06 PM Hillary's wars in the Middle East have unleashed destruction, terrorism and ISIS across the world.
- Jul 28, 2016 10:59:04 PM No one has worse judgement than Hillary Clinton - corruption and devastation follows her wherever she goes.

- Jul 29, 2016 07:40:10 AM The media coverage this morning of the very average Clinton speech and Convention is a joke. @CNN and the little watched @Morning_Joe = SAD!
- Jul 29, 2016 07:51:13 AM Crooked Hillary Clinton made up facts about me, and "forgot" to mention the many problems of our country, in her very average scream!
- Jul 29, 2016 08:13:07 AM Two policemen just shot in San Diego, one dead. It is only getting worse. People want LAW AND ORDER!
- Jul 29, 2016 08:13:16 AM CAMPAIGN STATEMENT: https://t.co/RNW3ED2ifR
- Jul 29, 2016 08:16:22 AM "@AnnCoulter: "I believe in science" Dem code for "we're shutting down coal mines, steel plants and any other remaining manufacturing""
- Jul 29, 2016 08:27:24 AM Join @mike_pence at the University of Northwestern Ohio- tonight at 7pm. Tickets: https://t.co/DvP8p7ueNU
- Jul 29, 2016 08:44:54 AM Crooked Hillary Clinton mentioned me 22 times in her very long and very boring speech. Many of her statements were lies and fabrications!
- Jul 29, 2016 08:53:31 AM General John Allen, who I never met but spoke against me last night, failed badly in his fight against ISIS. His record = BAD #NeverHillary
- Jul 29, 2016 08:59:42 AM "Little" Michael Bloomberg, who never had the guts to run for president, knows nothing about me. His last term as Mayor was a disaster!
- Jul 29, 2016 09:06:38 AM If Michael Bloomberg ran again for Mayor of New York, he wouldn't get 10% of the vote - they would run him out of town! #NeverHillary
- Jul 29, 2016 09:14:25 AM Crooked Hillary said that I "couldn't handle the rough and tumble of a political campaign." Really,I just beat 16 people and am beating her!
- Jul 29, 2016 11:34:22 AM Thank you! Facebook: https://t.co/nmlRJqzA7S Instagram: https://t.co/5gDeluaBXG https://t.co/Pw7GS8R9Gg
- Jul 29, 2016 11:56:30 AM The dishonest media didn't mention that Bernie Sanders was very angry looking during Crooked's speech. He wishes he didn't make that deal!

- Jul 29, 2016 11:59:58 AM In Hillary Clinton's America - things get worse. #TrumpPence16 https://t.co/WdHbnhhCbW
- Jul 29, 2016 12:03:56 PM Wow, my campaign is hearing from more and more Bernie supporters that they will NEVER support Crooked Hillary. She sold them out, V.P. pick!
- Jul 29, 2016 12:43:52 PM I am watching Crooked Hillary speak. Same old stuff, our country needs change!
- Jul 29, 2016 12:53:47 PM What Bernie Sanders really thinks of Crooked Hillary Clinton. https://t.co/VgMaAsZBep
- Jul 29, 2016 01:10:58 PM Join me in Colorado Springs at 2pm- or in Denver tonight at 7pm! Colorado Springs: https://t.co/HgFW7IRtz9 Denver: https://t.co/aE5P9jNcFC
- Jul 29, 2016 01:30:25 PM Even Bill is tired of the lies, SAD! https://t.co/LPk1OkwH9P
- Jul 29, 2016 03:04:03 PM "Only a Reagan or a Trump-like figure in the White House will achieve this goal." https://t.co/6a7Ef12giZ
- Jul 29, 2016 05:25:29 PM Thank you Colorado Springs. Get out & VOTE #TrumpPence16 in November! https://t.co/wK02fWzJey
- Jul 29, 2016 07:34:52 PM Thank you to the amazing law enforcement officers in Colorado! #MakeAmericaGreatAgain #LESM https://t.co/glxTQYAQiN
- Jul 29, 2016 07:57:57 PM Hillary Clinton should not be given national security briefings in that she is a lose cannon with extraordinarily bad judgement & insticts.
- Jul 29, 2016 08:01:43 PM #CrookedHillary Job Application https://t.co/CKXkAlGSiV
- Jul 29, 2016 10:03:43 PM As usual, Hillary & the Dems are trying to rig the debates so 2 are up against major NFL games. Same as last time w/ Bernie. Unacceptable!
- Jul 29, 2016 10:22:57 PM Thank you Denver, Colorado! #MakeAmericaGreatAgain! https://t.co/1KHrLdkOyW

- Jul 30, 2016 01:59:41 AM "@patrioticpepe: @realDonaldTrump ONLY TRUMP CAN UNITE AMERICA AND FIX OBAMA'S MISTAKES!!! #Trump2016 https://t.co/yB72Bm2muM"

- Jul 30, 2016 07:53:39 AM Colorado was amazing yesterday! So much support. Our tax, trade and energy reforms will bring great jobs to Colorado and the whole country.
- Jul 30, 2016 07:54:44 AM Hillary can never win over Bernie supporters. Her foreign wars, NAFTA/TPP support & Wall Street ties are driving away millions of votes.
- Jul 30, 2016 07:57:48 AM We are suffering through the worst long-term unemployment in the last 70 years. I want change - Crooked Hillary Clinton does not.
- Jul 30, 2016 08:35:20 AM American homeownership rate in Q2 2016 was 62.9% - lowest rate in 51yrs. WE will bring back the 'American Dream!' https://t.co/yI4Q8FHRjp
- Jul 30, 2016 09:05:54 AM Join me Monday in Columbus, Ohio & Harrisburg, Pennsylvania! #MAGA 3pm in OH: https://t.co/DDg0AUsqRq 7pm in PA: https://t.co/VmSLBvL43l
- Jul 30, 2016 09:19:56 AM While I am in OH & PA - you can also join @Mike_Pence in Nevada on Mon! Carson City: https://t.co/28G3RVbFsn Reno: https://t.co/4nLjRGyFYw
- Jul 30, 2016 11:29:17 AM Just got back from Colorado. The love and enthusiasm at two rallies was incredible. Big crowds!
- Jul 30, 2016 12:45:32 PM I will write a $2 MILLION check to our campaign if we hit our million-dollar end-of-month goal! https://t.co/fUTugI2R2k
- Jul 30, 2016 01:06:17 PM Violent crime is rising across the United States, yet the DNC convention ignored it. Crime reduction will be one of my top priorities.
- Jul 30, 2016 01:07:07 PM Crooked Hillary Clinton is soft on crime, supports open borders, and wants massive tax hikes. A formula for disaster!
- Jul 30, 2016 01:34:54 PM #CrookedHillary https://t.co/xyoPFJmByp
- Jul 30, 2016 02:55:26 PM Why doesn't the media want to report that on the two "Big Thursdays" when Crooked Hillary and I made our speeches - Republican's won ratings
- Jul 30, 2016 03:01:32 PM I turned down a meeting with Charles and David Koch. Much better for them to meet with the puppets of politics, they will do much better!
- Jul 30, 2016 04:51:25 PM Word is that Crooked Hillary has very small and unenthusiastic crowds in Pennsylvania. Perhaps it is because her husband signed NAFTA?

- Jul 30, 2016 04:55:48 PM #CrookedHillary = Obama's third term, which would be terrible news for our economic growth - seen below. https://t.co/y9WJoUaaql
- Jul 30, 2016 05:04:14 PM Crooked's stop in Johnstown, Pennsylvania, where jobs have been absolutely decimated by dumb politicians, drew less than 200 - with Bill, VP
- Jul 30, 2016 05:12:36 PM The "Rust Belt" was created by politicians like the Clintons who allowed our jobs to be stolen from us by other countries like Mexico. END!
- Jul 30, 2016 05:18:58 PM Wow, NATO's top commander just announced that he agrees with me that alliance members must PAY THEIR BILLS. This is a general I will like!
- Jul 30, 2016 05:24:40 PM NATO commander agrees members should pay up via @dcexaminer: https://t.co/VZLDFy707K
- Jul 30, 2016 05:28:22 PM Can you imagine if I had the small crowds that Hillary is drawing today in Pennsylvania. It would be a major media event! @CNN @FoxNews
- Jul 30, 2016 06:00:07 PM Thank you to all of the television viewers that made my speech at the Republican National Convention #1 over Crooked Hillary and DEMS.
- Jul 30, 2016 10:32:40 PM Nielson Media Research final numbers on ACCEPTANCE SPEECH: TRUMP 32.2 MILLION. CLINTON 27.8 MILLION. Thank you!

- Jul 31, 2016 12:30:51 AM We crushed the original goal! I will write a $2 MILLION check to our campaign if we hit our end-of-month goal! https://t.co/n6W9Dm6FqY
- Jul 31, 2016 07:57:21 AM Captain Khan, killed 12 years ago, was a hero, but this is about RADICAL ISLAMIC TERROR and the weakness of our "leaders" to eradicate it!
- Jul 31, 2016 08:32:55 AM I was viciously attacked by Mr. Khan at the Democratic Convention. Am I not allowed to respond? Hillary voted for the Iraq war, not me!
- Jul 31, 2016 03:09:00 PM The dishonest media is fawning over the Democratic Convention. I wonder why, then, my speech had millions of more viewers than Crooked H?

- Jul 31, 2016 03:31:06 PM "@RealJamesWoods: Without absolutely OWNING the liberal media, HillaryClinton wouldn't stand a chance. #VoterFraud and #MSM her only hope."
- Jul 31, 2016 07:57:15 PM Wow, it is unbelievable how distorted, one-sided and biased the media is against us. The failing @nytimes is a joke. @CNN is laughable!

August, 2016

- Aug 1, 2016 06:10:51 AM Mr. Khan, who does not know me, viciously attacked me from the stage of the DNC and is now all over T.V. doing the same - Nice!
- Aug 1, 2016 06:27:43 AM This story is not about Mr. Khan, who is all over the place doing interviews, but rather RADICAL ISLAMIC TERRORISM and the U.S. Get smart!
- Aug 1, 2016 07:50:32 AM When I said in an interview that Putin is "not going into Ukraine, you can mark it down," I am saying if I am President. Already in Crimea!
- Aug 1, 2016 08:03:02 AM So with all of the Obama tough talk on Russia and the Ukraine, they have already taken Crimea and continue to push. That's what I said!
- Aug 1, 2016 09:48:22 AM #CrookedHillary https://t.co/oHI6xrDJU0
- Aug 1, 2016 09:52:50 AM Join Governor Mike Pence in Reno, Nevada- tonight at 7pm! Tickets available at: https://t.co/4nLjRGyFYw

- Aug 1, 2016 01:42:50 PM CNN will soon be the least trusted name in news if they continue to be the press shop for Hillary Clinton.
- Aug 1, 2016 01:43:25 PM CNN anchors are completely out of touch with everyday people worried about rising crime, failing schools and vanishing jobs.
- Aug 1, 2016 01:44:04 PM When will we see stories from CNN on Clinton Foundation corruption and Hillary's pay-for-play at State Department?
- Aug 1, 2016 01:45:22 PM Will CNN send its cameras to the border to show the massive unreported crisis now unfolding -- or are they worried it will hurt Hillary?
- Aug 1, 2016 01:46:58 PM The people who support Hillary sit behind CNN anchor chairs, or headline fundraisers - those disconnected from real life.
- Aug 1, 2016 01:47:54 PM People believe CNN these days almost as little as they believe Hillary....that's really saying something!
- Aug 1, 2016 03:40:27 PM Thank you Oklahoma & Virginia! #MakeAmericaGreatAgain #ImWithYou https://t.co/WUdY7feRvV
- Aug 1, 2016 03:42:50 PM Thank you Columbus, Ohio! I will be back soon. #ImWithYou #MAGA https://t.co/vMf1EPJp4r
- Aug 1, 2016 04:42:57 PM Crooked Hillary Clinton is 100% owned by her donors. #ImWithYou #MAGA https://t.co/iYM3CCWS2z
- Aug 1, 2016 05:46:28 PM Hillary, whose decisions have led to the deaths of many, accepted $ from a business linked to ISIS. Silence at CNN. https://t.co/gJYSSXtpaz
- Aug 1, 2016 05:52:00 PM Hillary Clinton raked in money from regimes that horribly oppress women and gays & refuses to speak out against Radical Islam.
- Aug 1, 2016 05:52:39 PM When will CNN do a segment on Hillary's plan to increase Syrian refugees 550% and how much it will cost?
- Aug 1, 2016 05:54:27 PM During the GOP convention, CNN cut away from the victims of illegal immigrant violence. They don't want them heard. https://t.co/EHRiLkQDWD
- Aug 1, 2016 06:02:59 PM Join me in Florida on Wednesday! Daytona & Jacksonville: Daytona | 3pm- https://t.co/rJjYUbwiLL Jacksonville | 7pm- https://t.co/zfxeNbr1nq
- Aug 1, 2016 06:25:11 PM Thanks to @pnehlen for your kind words, very much appreciated.
- Aug 1, 2016 08:33:45 PM Vast numbers of manufacturing jobs in Pennsylvania have moved to Mexico and other countries. That will end when I win!

- Aug 1, 2016 08:40:37 PM RT @DanScavino: .@realDonaldTrump stops by overflow room in Mechanicsburg, Pennsylvania- prior to main rally. #TrumpMovement #MAGA US https:…
- Aug 1, 2016 08:58:48 PM Just leaving Mechanicsburg, PA. Incredible crowd-- so enthusiastic! Will be back soon. #MAGA https://t.co/RbuXfDZ5w9
- Aug 1, 2016 09:22:42 PM Great afternoon in Ohio & a great evening in Pennsylvania - departing now. See you tomorrow Virginia! https://t.co/jQTQYBFpdb

- Aug 2, 2016 05:24:03 AM The Washington Post calls out #CrookedHillary for what she REALLY is. A PATHOLOGICAL LIAR! Watch that nose grow! https://t.co/FsrUGByuuD
- Aug 2, 2016 10:07:48 AM LIMITED EDITION signed copies of my book "The Art of the Deal" for your donation of $184 or more. Get YOURS today! https://t.co/NNOM5GANxD
- Aug 2, 2016 10:10:26 AM LIMITED EDITION signed copies of my book "The Art of the Deal" for your donation of $184 or more. Get YOURS today! https://t.co/KpVEN635SH
- Aug 2, 2016 10:11:15 AM LIMITED EDITION signed copies of my book "The Art of the Deal" for your donation of $184 or more. Get YOURS today! https://t.co/4LnzfKRsqZ
- Aug 2, 2016 11:57:16 AM Thank you Virginia! #ImWithYou https://t.co/9inCh1BVwM
- Aug 2, 2016 12:47:19 PM STATEMENT IN RESPONSE TO PRESIDENT OBAMA'S FAILED LEADERSHIP: https://t.co/SPgFIFuSO7
- Aug 2, 2016 01:00:06 PM Join me in Florida tomorrow! #MakeAmericaGreatAgain Daytona | 3pm- https://t.co/jbOS2s4qGI Jacksonville | 7pm- https://t.co/XSF1kp7R54
- Aug 2, 2016 01:13:10 PM #CrookedHillary https://t.co/xe0I0EmxMa
- Aug 2, 2016 01:27:51 PM #ICYMI: John Podesta's Brother Pocketed $180,000 from Putin's Uranium Company: https://t.co/d0LfyiBlvX https://t.co/I5fF3didZs
- Aug 2, 2016 02:00:04 PM RT @gatewaypundit: Democrat Fire Marshal Turns THOUSANDS of Trump Supporters Away at Columbus Rally https://t.co/TO8oE5cv8Z via @gatewaypun…
- Aug 2, 2016 02:07:25 PM President Obama will go down as perhaps the worst president in the history of the United States!

- Aug 2, 2016 02:38:16 PM Report raises questions about 'Clinton Cash' from Russians during 'reset' https://t.co/vVcAzY2zcp
- Aug 2, 2016 04:52:32 PM My daughter @IvankaTrump will be on @Greta tonight at 7pm. Enjoy! https://t.co/QySC5PLFMy
- Aug 2, 2016 09:51:00 PM Great day in Virginia. Crowd was fantastic!

- Aug 3, 2016 04:14:40 AM There is great unity in my campaign, perhaps greater than ever before. I want to thank everyone for your tremendous support. Beat Crooked H!
- Aug 3, 2016 05:23:27 AM Our incompetent Secretary of State, Hillary Clinton, was the one who started talks to give 400 million dollars, in cash, to Iran. Scandal!
- Aug 3, 2016 12:20:29 PM RT @mike_pence: Join me in Colorado, today! Look forward to seeing you! Denver- 2pm https://t.co/8VbvJYDa4F Colorado Springs- 6pm https:/…
- Aug 3, 2016 04:57:07 PM THANK YOU Daytona Beach, Florida! #MakeAmericaGreatAgain https://t.co/IAcLfXe463
- Aug 3, 2016 05:10:11 PM Thank you to the amazing law enforcement officers today- in Daytona Beach, Florida! #LESM #MAGA https://t.co/QoxJf4Xzbc
- Aug 3, 2016 06:10:41 PM Thank you for your support of my candidacy! #MAGA #ImWithYou https://t.co/Al5bZlRFYk
- Aug 3, 2016 09:27:52 PM Thank you Jacksonville, Florida! #MakeAmericaGreatAgain https://t.co/xrTQjt9WOC https://t.co/VSnBoQYoZs

- Aug 4, 2016 10:17:01 AM Looking forward to IA & WI with Gov. Pence, tomorrow. Join us! #MAGA https://t.co/3Hcnzj0Slx https://t.co/sEwLWkn1Sz https://t.co/0Ei3EdQdXB
- Aug 4, 2016 02:16:00 PM Great meeting all of you. This group knocked on 50K doors & counting here in Maine, thank you! @MaineGOP https://t.co/Iui1F2z9ca
- Aug 4, 2016 02:23:41 PM Happy 226th Birthday to the United States Coast Guard. Thank you @USCG! #CoastGuardDay https://t.co/hr4O8Xgq2R [
- Aug 4, 2016 05:42:13 PM Thank you Portland, Maine! #MakeAmericaGreatAgain https://t.co/oVfF28rWL5 https://t.co/RhblAXkNPw

- Aug 4, 2016 09:16:20 PM See you tomorrow w/ Gov. @Mike_Pence, Iowa & Wisconsin! 3pm- https://t.co/3Hcnzj0Slx 7pm- https://t.co/sEwLWkn1Sz https://t.co/UODSMp0oTo
- Aug 4, 2016 09:18:18 PM President Obama should ask the DNC about how they rigged the election against Bernie.
- Aug 4, 2016 09:19:08 PM Obama's disastrous judgment gave us ISIS, rise of Iran, and the worst economic numbers since the Great Depression!
- Aug 4, 2016 09:19:22 PM President Obama refuses to answer question about Iran terror funding. I won't dodge questions as your President. https://t.co/jsAMGO3s4P

- Aug 5, 2016 05:39:27 AM The plane I saw on television was the hostage plane in Geneva, Switzerland, not the plane carrying $400 million in cash going to Iran!
- Aug 5, 2016 08:08:35 AM Hillary Clinton has bad judgment and is unfit to serve as President. https://t.co/3EzG620fpT
- Aug 5, 2016 10:26:41 AM I am counting on your help to defeat Hillary Clinton and her cronies. Let's Make America Great Again! https://t.co/z3pzKBfP0U
- Aug 5, 2016 11:41:28 AM I'm with YOU. I will work hard and never let you down. Make America Great Again! https://t.co/wotYvx6Prz
- Aug 5, 2016 11:46:17 AM I'm with YOU. I will work hard and never let you down. Make America Great Again! https://t.co/im2J6xXq1u
- Aug 5, 2016 11:46:28 AM I'm with YOU. I will work hard and never let you down. Make America Great Again! https://t.co/Eb6jr4nbj3
- Aug 5, 2016 11:52:06 AM We need your support to get to the White House and defeat #CrookedHillary. Let's Make America Great Again! https://t.co/J7ICZN3Bus
- Aug 5, 2016 11:58:55 AM The Establishment and special interests are absolutely killing our country. We must put #AmericaFirst. https://t.co/jMgAETgW6U
- Aug 5, 2016 12:00:41 PM As President, I WILL fix this rigged system and only answer to YOU, the American people! https://t.co/98Vtqu4i7n
- Aug 5, 2016 12:49:38 PM I am counting on your help to defeat Hillary Clinton and her cronies. Let's Make America Great Again! https://t.co/0KL9McborU
- Aug 5, 2016 12:57:59 PM I'm with YOU. I will work hard and never let you down. Make America Great Again! https://t.co/k1ZvNC3YAC

- Aug 5, 2016 12:59:21 PM We need your support to get to the White House and defeat #CrookedHillary. Let's Make America Great Again! https://t.co/u2WQondgqm
- Aug 5, 2016 01:02:41 PM The Establishment and special interests are absolutely killing our country. We must put #AmericaFirst. https://t.co/GMYEWngo2y
- Aug 5, 2016 01:04:13 PM As President, I WILL fix this rigged system and only answer to YOU, the American people! https://t.co/laUdwGO1aX
- Aug 5, 2016 01:15:02 PM I am counting on your help to defeat Hillary Clinton and her cronies. Let's Make America Great Again! https://t.co/c7Ekrgn9jx
- Aug 5, 2016 01:16:55 PM We need your support to get to the White House and defeat #CrookedHillary. Let's Make America Great Again! https://t.co/FgPFo1NWiC
- Aug 5, 2016 01:18:09 PM I'm with YOU. I will work hard and never let you down. Make America Great Again! https://t.co/NTDm6xfREg
- Aug 5, 2016 01:19:22 PM The Establishment and special interests are absolutely killing our country. We must put #AmericaFirst. https://t.co/XcqwGHAUue
- Aug 5, 2016 01:20:22 PM As President, I WILL fix this rigged system and only answer to YOU, the American people! https://t.co/4GWAHgf8us
- Aug 5, 2016 01:33:58 PM We need your support to get to the White House and defeat #CrookedHillary. Let's Make America Great Again! https://t.co/bwxirLtPXY
- Aug 5, 2016 01:34:44 PM I'm with YOU. I will work hard and never let you down. Make America Great Again! https://t.co/DGMxQYUm7s
- Aug 5, 2016 01:35:33 PM The Establishment and special interests are absolutely killing our country. We must put #AmericaFirst. https://t.co/IBt9JpYh7p
- Aug 5, 2016 01:36:42 PM As President, I WILL fix this rigged system and only answer to YOU, the American people! https://t.co/pteWtMjXVO
- Aug 5, 2016 02:28:58 PM RT @DRUDGE_REPORT: 'Win-lose deal that benefits Iran and hurts United States'... https://t.co/zqpeNCouXc
- Aug 5, 2016 02:29:02 PM RT @DRUDGE_REPORT: FORMER HOSTAGE SAYS PLANE WAITED UNTIL MONEY ARRIVED... https://t.co/Uo0MS6w9OQ
- Aug 5, 2016 03:03:29 PM #MakeAmericaSafeAgain https://t.co/5yuLKyh8Q6

- Aug 5, 2016 04:12:00 PM As President, I WILL fix this rigged system and only answer to YOU, the American people! https://t.co/r1ySXDJ1Wq
- Aug 5, 2016 04:14:32 PM I'm with YOU! I will work hard and never let you down. Make America Great Again! https://t.co/XT3U5mY0oc
- Aug 5, 2016 04:16:02 PM The Establishment and special interests are absolutely killing our country. We must put #AmericaFirst. https://t.co/Q96e1Npa5d
- Aug 5, 2016 05:42:08 PM Thank you Des Moines, Iowa! Governor @Mike_Pence and I appreciate your support! #MAGA #TrumpTrain https://t.co/gr6tGqqmcm
- Aug 5, 2016 06:53:53 PM DON'T LET HILLARY CLINTON DO IT AGAIN! #TrumpPence16 https://t.co/1mGkPNZPKF
- Aug 5, 2016 09:44:55 PM Thank you Green Bay, Wisconsin! Governor @Mike_Pence and I will be back soon. #TrumpPence16 #MAGA https://t.co/qsYbyrm3UR
- Aug 5, 2016 09:57:11 PM 'Trump is right about violent crime: It's on the rise in major cities' https://t.co/XbnZ5vktGk
- Aug 5, 2016 10:59:08 PM Good luck #TeamUSA #OpeningCeremony #Rio2016 https://t.co/mS8qsQpJPh

- Aug 6, 2016 06:53:00 AM Hillary Clinton is being badly criticized for her poor performance in answering questions. Let us all see what happens!
- Aug 6, 2016 09:24:43 AM Crooked Hillary said loudly, and for the world to see, that she "SHORT CIRCUITED" when answering a question on her e-mails. Very dangerous!
- Aug 6, 2016 09:48:14 AM Anybody whose mind "SHORT CIRCUITS" is not fit to be our president! Look up the word "BRAINWASHED."
- Aug 6, 2016 01:05:41 PM LIMITED EDITION signed copies of my book "The Art of the Deal" for your donation of $184 or more. Get YOURS today! https://t.co/pvNwKWlFy1
- Aug 6, 2016 01:08:19 PM LIMITED EDITION signed copies of my book "The Art of the Deal" for your donation of $184 or more. Get YOURS today! https://t.co/wzsE7SoGUG
- Aug 6, 2016 01:11:50 PM Heading to New Hampshire - will be talking about Hillary saying her brain SHORT CIRCUITED, and other things!

- Aug 6, 2016 03:04:08 PM #CrookedHillary is not fit to be our next president! #TrumpPence16 https://t.co/I0zJO2sZKk
- Aug 6, 2016 08:53:45 PM I am not just running against Crooked Hillary Clinton, I am running against the very dishonest and totally biased media - but I will win!
- Aug 6, 2016 09:03:39 PM .@Larry_Kudlow - 'Donald Trump Is the middle-class growth candidate' https://t.co/YbqkhWNm0g
- Aug 6, 2016 09:19:37 PM Thank you Windham, New Hampshire! #TrumpPence16 #MAGA https://t.co/ZL4Q01Q49s

- Aug 7, 2016 08:49:29 AM I see where Mayor Stephanie Rawlings-Blake of Baltimore is pushing Crooked hard. Look at the job she has done in Baltimore. She is a joke!
- Aug 7, 2016 04:25:58 PM RT @DRUDGE_REPORT: CLINTON EMAIL LED TO EXECUTION IN IRAN? https://t.co/4rY1faptL6
- Aug 7, 2016 04:31:46 PM The media is going crazy. They totally distort so many things on purpose. Crimea, nuclear, "the baby" and so much more. Very dishonest!
- Aug 7, 2016 06:09:08 PM Michael Morell, the lightweight former Acting Director of C.I.A., and a man who has made serious bad calls, is a total Clinton flunky!
- Aug 7, 2016 07:05:54 PM #ICYMI: "Will Media Apologize to Trump?" https://t.co/ia7rKBmioA

- Aug 8, 2016 08:28:20 AM Join me in Fayetteville, North Carolina tomorrow evening at 6pm. Tickets now available at: https://t.co/Z80d4MYIg8
- Aug 8, 2016 10:20:44 AM My economic policy speech will be carried live at 12:15 P.M. Enjoy!
- Aug 8, 2016 03:14:57 PM RT @NFIB: .@NFIB encouraged by @realDonaldTrump's #taxplan, says #smallbiz would benefit from lower tax rate: https://t.co/JCQCvXj9WC
- Aug 8, 2016 05:06:25 PM Thank you Alex! https://t.co/c2uIa7mndP
- Aug 8, 2016 05:12:21 PM Thank you! https://t.co/4p0hzpkVWF
- Aug 8, 2016 05:15:44 PM Thank you @NFIB- together we will #MakeAmericaGreatAgain! https://t.co/wQQIHQKsdK

- Aug 8, 2016 05:20:31 PM Thank you @RepLouBarletta! https://t.co/bre8u93vac https://t.co/eKtSXUw51R
- Aug 8, 2016 05:24:09 PM Thank you Senator David Perdue! https://t.co/d0dCUZ20jf https://t.co/LmfiGByFPb
- Aug 8, 2016 05:27:02 PM Thank you Congressman Steven Palazzo! https://t.co/R5Z4CGfjqJ https://t.co/XGSIJJQiGJ
- Aug 8, 2016 05:43:56 PM Thank you Newt! https://t.co/Acg0hMvrpr
- Aug 8, 2016 05:45:33 PM Many people are saying that the Iranians killed the scientist who helped the U.S. because of Hillary Clinton's hacked emails.
- Aug 8, 2016 06:18:42 PM 'As Senator Clinton promised 200,000 jobs in Upstate New York - her efforts fell flat.' https://t.co/I2WqZb5N8P https://t.co/i5S3mtJWpe
- Aug 8, 2016 08:00:23 PM RT @FieldofFight: We Can Do Better, We Must Do Better, We Will Do Better By LTG (R) Keith Kellogg and LTG (R) Michael Flynn @GenFlynn http…
- Aug 8, 2016 09:45:10 PM Being in Detroit today was wonderful. Quick stop in Ohio to meet with some of our great supporters. Just got back home!

- Aug 9, 2016 06:32:43 AM Will be interviewed on @foxandfriends now!
- Aug 9, 2016 06:59:25 AM I am running against the Washington insiders, just like I did in the Republican Primaries. These are the people that have made U.S. a mess!
- Aug 9, 2016 07:01:33 AM "@sprts08: @realDonaldTrump @foxandfriends great interview.....all solid points on our economy TRUMP2016"
- Aug 9, 2016 07:02:25 AM "@LinHen23: @foxandfriends Loved Trump's answers to voters questions this morning! Trump's economic plan will help #MAGA #NeverHillary"
- Aug 9, 2016 10:07:45 AM Act NOW for your chance to have a private lunch with Eric Trump & tour of campaign HQ at Trump Tower in NYC. https://t.co/dDA0CZWdYF
- Aug 9, 2016 10:08:35 AM Act NOW for your chance to have a private lunch with Eric Trump & tour of campaign HQ at Trump Tower in NYC. https://t.co/4ccXAY5ZNo
- Aug 9, 2016 10:09:17 AM Act NOW for your chance to have a private lunch with Eric Trump & tour of campaign HQ at Trump Tower in NYC. https://t.co/J3NzuVpruI

- Aug 9, 2016 10:18:18 AM Act NOW for your chance to have a private lunch with Eric Trump & tour of campaign HQ at Trump Tower in NYC. https://t.co/szAygwbchK
- Aug 9, 2016 10:18:46 AM Act NOW for your chance to have a private lunch with Eric Trump & tour of campaign HQ at Trump Tower in NYC. https://t.co/fwU0jMcB1m
- Aug 9, 2016 10:19:21 AM Act NOW for your chance to have a private lunch with Eric Trump & tour of campaign HQ at Trump Tower in NYC. https://t.co/RBLII8rIfo
- Aug 9, 2016 03:15:14 PM RT @Carl_C_Icahn: 1/2 Believe Trump gave a great speech.
- Aug 9, 2016 03:15:16 PM RT @Carl_C_Icahn: 2/2 How many of our presidents, even our great presidents, would have handled the antics that went on in that auditorium…
- Aug 9, 2016 03:49:38 PM RT @NRA: .@RealDonaldTrump is right. If @HillaryClinton gets to pick her anti-#2A #SCOTUS judges, there's nothing we can do. #NeverHillary
- Aug 9, 2016 03:49:42 PM RT @NRA: But there IS something we will do on #ElectionDay: Show up and vote for the #2A! #DefendtheSecond #NeverHillary
- Aug 9, 2016 04:07:38 PM Thank you Wilmington, North Carolina! #MakeAmericaGreatAgain https://t.co/ZnnaSPF5or
- Aug 9, 2016 07:17:28 PM Thank you @SenatorFischer! #TrumpPence16 https://t.co/RMtU6aRZTQ
- Aug 9, 2016 07:18:46 PM Thank you Senator @ChuckGrassley! #TrumpPence16 https://t.co/YmdH3fcaeW
- Aug 9, 2016 08:11:39 PM When is the media going to talk about Hillary's policies that have gotten people killed, like Libya, open borders, and maybe her emails?
- Aug 9, 2016 09:21:12 PM Media desperate to distract from Clinton's anti-2A stance. I said pro-2A citizens must organize and get out vote to save our Constitution!

- Aug 10, 2016 09:43:30 AM "@dbongino: 'Now cut off my mic!' Bongino refuses to be bullied by Don Lemon over Trump, 2nd Amendment – HEATED! https://t.co/UgtfaUXzcr"

- Aug 10, 2016 10:08:01 AM .@dbongino You were fantastic in defending both the Second Amendment and me last night on @CNN. Don Lemon is a lightweight - dumb as a rock
- Aug 10, 2016 10:36:31 AM Morning Joe's weakness is its low ratings. I don't watch anymore but I heard he went wild against Rudy Giuliani and #2A - sad & irrelevant!
- Aug 10, 2016 12:43:26 PM My thoughts and prayers are with the two police officers shot in Sebastian County, Arkansas. #LESM
- Aug 10, 2016 12:54:53 PM I will be interviewed on @greta tonight at 7pm. Enjoy! https://t.co/9yicUxd87D
- Aug 10, 2016 03:37:58 PM Great meeting w/ coal miners & leaders from the Virginia coal industry- thank you! #MAGA https://t.co/wnpVlq6oe4 https://t.co/32gdX684ew
- Aug 10, 2016 03:49:33 PM No such meeting or conversation ever happened - a made up story by "low ratings" @CNN.
- Aug 10, 2016 04:07:01 PM Thank you Abingdon, Virginia! #MakeAmericaGreatAgain https://t.co/g7ivluiyF2 https://t.co/RQUKD6sjno
- Aug 10, 2016 06:24:51 PM #MakeAmericaGreatAgain! https://t.co/8rWz6p1Ged
- Aug 10, 2016 06:36:35 PM "@DSF2020: Really admire your determination: Working so hard for all Americans n daily having to defend yourself from a biased Media."
- Aug 10, 2016 06:38:15 PM Reuters just announced that Secret Service never spoke to me or my campaign. Made up story by @CNN is a hoax. Totally dishonest.
- Aug 10, 2016 09:07:07 PM Great job today by the NYPD in protecting the people and saving the climber.
- Aug 10, 2016 09:12:01 PM Thank you Fort Lauderdale, Florida. #MakeAmericaGreatAgain https://t.co/cjivzdRpU1

- Aug 11, 2016 09:15:40 AM This is no surprise. Constant phony reporting from failing @CNN turns everyone off. The American people get it! https://t.co/a1A6XMfYx1
- Aug 11, 2016 05:01:30 PM Will be doing @oreillyfactor tonight at 8pm. Enjoy!

- Aug 11, 2016 05:10:59 PM I am counting on your help to defeat Hillary Clinton and her cronies. Let's Make America Great Again! https://t.co/fSKOf0Jz9K
- Aug 11, 2016 10:59:11 PM "@SheriffClarke: https://t.co/G9R9CGhf8q Everything coming from this administration is a lie. Only @realDonaldTrump will change it"
- Aug 11, 2016 11:06:22 PM "@elsolarverde: THE CORRUPT MEDIA CREATS CONTROVERSY AGAINST @realDonaldTrump TO AVOID ISSUES ABOUT HillaryClinton https://t.co/RW5UcWLfA8"
- Aug 11, 2016 11:10:25 PM "@EnemyWithinn: @realDonaldTrump @elsolarverde @nytimes People gotta stop believing media lies about Trump." That would indeed be nice!

- Aug 12, 2016 12:16:13 AM I'm with YOU. I will work hard and never let you down. Make America Great Again! https://t.co/uHiGJ6Pe3E
- Aug 12, 2016 05:26:20 AM Ratings challenged @CNN reports so seriously that I call President Obama (and Clinton) "the founder" of ISIS, & MVP. THEY DON'T GET SARCASM?
- Aug 12, 2016 05:57:34 AM "@laurencristmann: Thank you for coming to Pennsylvania today. I will be there with @C_Lynne_Ryan your 3rd CD delegate at 2 pm"
- Aug 12, 2016 06:07:51 AM A massive tax increase will be necessary to fund Crooked Hillary Clinton's agenda. What a terrible (and boring) rollout that was yesterday!
- Aug 12, 2016 06:43:43 AM I love watching these poor, pathetic people (pundits) on television working so hard and so seriously to try and figure me out. They can't!
- Aug 12, 2016 08:01:06 AM ISIS gained tremendous strength during Hillary Clinton's term as Secretary of State. When will the dishonest media report the facts!
- Aug 12, 2016 11:09:35 AM The Establishment and special interests are absolutely killing our country. We must put #AmericaFirst. https://t.co/R751UfHQ0A
- Aug 12, 2016 11:12:56 AM I'm with YOU! I will work hard and never let you down. Make America Great Again! https://t.co/xI4qjds5fP

- Aug 12, 2016 12:12:37 PM I'm with YOU. I will work hard and never let you down. Make America Great Again! https://t.co/vzZZ6M5K9t
- Aug 12, 2016 12:13:22 PM The Establishment and special interests are absolutely killing our country. We must put #AmericaFirst. https://t.co/mjTScP4sZ2
- Aug 12, 2016 12:14:30 PM We need your support to get to the White House and defeat #CrookedHillary. Let's Make America Great Again! https://t.co/AKIHQW4ljd
- Aug 12, 2016 12:36:31 PM Unbelievable support in Florida last night - thank you! #MAGA https://t.co/WNDAagFRRS
- Aug 12, 2016 02:48:18 PM Thank you Erie, Pennsylvania! Together we will #MakeAmericaGreatAgain! https://t.co/5hZp7PnRoT
- Aug 12, 2016 07:17:38 PM Will be on @seanhannity tonight at 10pm, hosted by @GovMikeHuckabee. Enjoy!

- Aug 13, 2016 01:29:23 PM The failing @nytimes has become a newspaper of fiction. Their stories about me always quote non-existent unnamed sources. Very dishonest!
- Aug 13, 2016 01:39:26 PM I am truly enjoying myself while running for president. The people of our country are amazing - great numbers on November 8th!
- Aug 13, 2016 02:39:23 PM "@willspeakout: Thank you for all that you are doing for us! You campaign endlessly and have spent millions.We love you! #TrumpTrain" Thanks
- Aug 13, 2016 03:02:38 PM We now have confirmation as to one reason Crooked H wanted to be sure that nobody saw her e-mails - PAY-FOR-PLAY. How can she run for Pres.
- Aug 13, 2016 03:03:55 PM "@need2knowu: @willspeakout yes you are my hero I admire you for laying down your glorious luxurious life to get beat up for America!!!"
- Aug 13, 2016 03:06:38 PM "@PaulaDuvall2: We're all enjoying you, as well, Mr. T.! You've inspired Hope and a Positive Spirit throughout America! God bless you!" Nice
- Aug 13, 2016 03:08:01 PM "@zulu_out: You are a man for the people because you know what it is like to be among the people #MakeAmericaGreatAgain #USA Loves U" Thanks

- Aug 14, 2016 07:24:48 AM The failing @nytimes talks about anonymous sources and meetings that never happened. Their reporting is fiction. The media protects Hillary!
- Aug 14, 2016 07:31:23 AM The failing @nytimes, which never spoke to me, keeps saying that I am saying to advisers that I will change. False, I am who I am- never said
- Aug 14, 2016 07:37:37 AM If the disgusting and corrupt media covered me honestly and didn't put false meaning into the words I say, I would be beating Hillary by 20%
- Aug 14, 2016 07:46:17 AM My rallies are not covered properly by the media. They never discuss the real message and never show crowd size or enthusiasm.
- Aug 14, 2016 11:50:51 AM Crooked Hillary Clinton is being protected by the media. She is not a talented person or politician. The dishonest media refuses to expose!
- Aug 14, 2016 11:55:07 AM I am not only fighting Crooked Hillary, I am fighting the dishonest and corrupt media and her government protection process. People get it!
- Aug 14, 2016 12:06:20 PM It is not "freedom of the press" when newspapers and others are allowed to say and write whatever they want even if it is completely false!
- Aug 14, 2016 06:57:37 PM I have always been the same person-remain true to self.The media wants me to change but it would be very dishonest to supporters to do so!
- Aug 14, 2016 07:07:43 PM "Stay on message" is the chant. I always do - trade, jobs, military, vets, 2nd A, repeal Ocare, borders, etc - but media misrepresents!
- Aug 14, 2016 08:34:25 PM Certain Republicans who have lost to me would rather save face by fighting me than see the U.S.Supreme Court get proper appointments. Sad!

- Aug 15, 2016 02:29:09 PM #MakeAmericaSafeAgain https://t.co/bgBGPaKaqI
- Aug 15, 2016 03:26:17 PM "CLINTON REFUGEE PLAN COULD BRING IN 620,000 REFUGEES IN FIRST TERM AT LIFETIME COST OF OVER $400 BILLION." https://t.co/COZQNt6KVs
- Aug 15, 2016 03:28:30 PM #AmericasMerkel https://t.co/QFRs4bEUC1

- Aug 16, 2016 01:59:14 PM Another health insurer is pulling back due to 'persistent financial losses on #Obamacare plans.' Only the beginning! https://t.co/YqfaEvg8c3
- Aug 16, 2016 02:22:57 PM 'It's just a 2-point race, Clinton 38%, Trump 36%' https://t.co/EzDzJ4EzIN
- Aug 16, 2016 05:38:57 PM This is my pledge to the American people: https://t.co/Jb21oyNfxt
- Aug 16, 2016 06:17:18 PM Just as we won the Cold War, in part, by exposing the evils of communism and the virtues of free markets.... Cont: https://t.co/SXp7efXEZU
- Aug 16, 2016 08:48:16 PM Will be on @SeanHannity tonight at 10pmE - delivering an important speech live from Wisconsin. #MakeAmericaGreatAgain
- Aug 16, 2016 11:22:01 PM #LawandOrder #ImWithYou Transcript: https://t.co/YlATGI2Ph6
- Aug 16, 2016 11:39:04 PM #LawandOrder #ImWithYou Video: https://t.co/AIa2Z9po2h https://t.co/qqSfOfgdap

- Aug 17, 2016 08:24:41 AM Join me in North Carolina - tomorrow at 7:30pm! #ImWithYou Tickets: https://t.co/vDag45zrDc
- Aug 17, 2016 11:36:37 AM Thank you Governor @ScottWalker & @GOP Chairman @Reince Priebus. #MakeAmericaGreatAgain #ImWithYou https://t.co/IdJBuaKMwK
- Aug 17, 2016 11:46:57 AM #MakeAmericaSafeAgain #ImWithYou https://t.co/N9XNoGNcqc
- Aug 17, 2016 11:57:58 AM A vote for Hillary Clinton is a vote for another generation of poverty, high crime, & lost opportunities. #ImWithYou https://t.co/Eph6qy7zyB
- Aug 17, 2016 03:05:08 PM We will repeal & replace #Obamacare, which has caused soaring double-digit premium increases. It is a disaster! https://t.co/NNMyTJo6i6
- Aug 17, 2016 04:44:48 PM We are going to make this a government of the people once again! #MakeAmericaGreatAgain #ImWithYou https://t.co/Fi7yEb2XQb
- Aug 17, 2016 05:25:02 PM Will be participating in a town hall event- hosted by @SeanHannity tonight at 10pmE on @FoxNews. Enjoy! https://t.co/7nReqYM7FF

- Aug 17, 2016 08:21:30 PM I will be doing a Town Hall tonight at 10:00 P.M. on @seanhannity - @FoxNews

- Aug 18, 2016 07:11:48 AM They will soon be calling me MR. BREXIT!
- Aug 18, 2016 03:55:33 PM #CrookedHillary #ThrowbackThursday https://t.co/v8J0r64J7h
- Aug 18, 2016 07:33:54 PM Together, we will MAKE AMERICA GREAT AGAIN! https://t.co/aENuIvrUrS
- Aug 18, 2016 07:52:35 PM Thank you Charlotte, North Carolina! #MakeAmericaGreatAgain https://t.co/Y19nUKkYTc

- Aug 19, 2016 05:40:15 AM We are one nation. When one state hurts, we all hurt. We must all work together - to lift each other up. https://t.co/XoDkW5X3Wy
- Aug 19, 2016 07:42:38 AM Thank you to NC for last evenings great reception. The speech was a great success. Heading now to Louisiana & another speech tonight in MI.
- Aug 19, 2016 07:43:37 AM The reporting at the failing @nytimes gets worse and worse by the day. Fortunately, it is a dying newspaper.
- Aug 19, 2016 08:27:10 AM Thank you to everyone for all of the nice comments, by Twitter, pundits and otherwise for my speech last night.
- Aug 19, 2016 08:34:54 AM Great job by @EricTrump on interview with @BillHemmer on @FoxNews. #ImWithYou #TrumpTrain
- Aug 19, 2016 05:16:16 PM Thank you Michigan. This is a MOVEMENT. We are going to MAKE AMERICA SAFE AND GREAT AGAIN! #TrumpPence16 https://t.co/vP3eqF3Zbb
- Aug 19, 2016 07:17:09 PM #WheresHillary? Sleeping!!!!!
- Aug 19, 2016 08:00:12 PM We are one nation. When one hurts, we all hurt. We must all work together-to lift each other up. #StandWithLouisiana https://t.co/Ob7J2oBWhq
- Aug 19, 2016 08:14:08 PM .@Franklin_Graham @BillyNungesser @SamaritansPurse- so humbled by my time w/ you. You are in our thoughts & prayers. https://t.co/I6xGsEzlwv

- Aug 20, 2016 12:02:57 AM "@CatOnGlass: 200,000 new followers for @realDonaldTrump. From 10,800,000 to 11,000,000, All in the last ten days or so! #MAGA #AlwaysTrump
- Aug 20, 2016 12:35:11 PM Thank you @JerryJrFalwell- will see you soon. #TrumpPence16 https://t.co/epfSJckcKq
- Aug 20, 2016 05:57:23 PM Just leaving Virginia - really big crowd, great enthusiasm!
- Aug 20, 2016 06:02:37 PM Will be interviewed on @JudgeJeanine at 9:00 P.M. Enjoy!
- Aug 20, 2016 06:04:02 PM Will be back soon Virginia. We are going to MAKE AMERICA GREAT AGAIN! #TrumpPence16 https://t.co/IU4JPSi0rZ
- Aug 20, 2016 06:11:51 PM We will bring America together as ONE country again – united as Americans in common purpose and common dreams. #MAGA
- Aug 20, 2016 07:02:05 PM "@J58golf: @realDonaldTrump been a great week. More of the same will get you in the white house!"
- Aug 20, 2016 07:02:41 PM "@EyeCandyTMGayle: @realDonaldTrump please oh please take the CHARLOTTE NC speech ACROSS the swing states .... sooo powerful" Good!
- Aug 20, 2016 07:04:28 PM Together, we are going to MAKE AMERICA SAFE AND GREAT AGAIN! https://t.co/pUtN4kFhDK

- Aug 21, 2016 06:35:17 PM I have been drawing very big and enthusiastic crowds, but the media refuses to show or discuss them. Something very big is happening!
- Aug 21, 2016 07:33:38 PM Crooked Hillary is flooding the airwaves with false and misleading ads - all paid for by her bosses on Wall Street. Media is protecting her!
- Aug 21, 2016 08:08:08 PM I heard that @Morning_Joe was very nice on Friday but that little Donny D, a big failure in TV (& someone I helped), was nasty. Irrelevant!
- Aug 21, 2016 08:19:06 PM "@Jimbos2002: @Morning_Joe Video: Hillary referring to blacks as super predators that need to be brought to heel. https://t.co/pMIHWayMRw"
- Aug 21, 2016 08:23:16 PM "@SinAbunz_TM: @realDonaldTrump TRUMP VICTORY IN NOVEMBER! #MAGA #TrumpPence16"

- Aug 21, 2016 08:25:00 PM "@55Lidsville: #TeamTrump @KellyannePolls You need to show the crowds at the rallies use Periscope! Show HC's 139 YT viewers vs DT 38K"
- Aug 21, 2016 08:40:42 PM "@Brainykid2010: @shl @realDonaldTrump The ad was actually very good!"

- Aug 22, 2016 06:06:36 AM "@realbill2016: @realDonaldTrump @Brainykid2010 @shl Trump leading LA Times poll https://t.co/908uLXCIWz"
- Aug 22, 2016 06:21:53 AM Tried watching low-rated @Morning_Joe this morning, unwatchable! @morningmika is off the wall, a neurotic and not very bright mess!
- Aug 22, 2016 06:29:13 AM Some day, when things calm down, I'll tell the real story of @JoeNBC and his very insecure long-time girlfriend, @morningmika. Two clowns!
- Aug 22, 2016 07:31:39 AM Will be interviewed on @foxandfriends at 8:30 A.M. Eastern. ENJOY!
- Aug 22, 2016 07:55:40 AM Statement on Clinton Foundation: https://t.co/2twuzrB9om
- Aug 22, 2016 04:06:42 PM Great meeting with active & retired law enforcement officers- at the Fraternal Order of Police lodge in Akron, Ohio. https://t.co/EUWhDC644R
- Aug 22, 2016 06:46:42 PM Just leaving Akron, Ohio, after a packed rally. Amazing people! Going now to Texas.
- Aug 22, 2016 07:56:51 PM .@AnnCoulter's new book, 'In Trump We Trust, comes out tomorrow. People are saying it's terrific - knowing Ann I am sure it is!
- Aug 22, 2016 08:02:19 PM The @WashingtonPost quickly put together a hit job book on me- comprised of copies of some of their inaccurate stories. Don't buy, boring!

- Aug 23, 2016 07:56:46 AM I am now in Texas doing a big fundraiser for the Republican Party and a @FoxNews Special on the BORDER and with victims of border crime!
- Aug 23, 2016 08:53:11 AM It is being reported by virtually everyone, and is a fact, that the media pile on against me is the worst in American political history!

- Aug 23, 2016 09:46:58 AM Hillary Clinton strongly stated that there was "absolutely no connection" between her private work and that of The State Department. LIE!
- Aug 23, 2016 11:15:25 AM President Obama should have gone to Louisiana days ago, instead of golfing. Too little, too late!
- Aug 23, 2016 11:37:38 AM Join me in Tampa, Florida- tomorrow at 1pmE! Tickets: https://t.co/iwEAiWKgtR https://t.co/lLyaW6nxsP
- Aug 23, 2016 04:21:59 PM In Austin, Texas with some of our amazing Border Patrol Agents. I will not let them down! https://t.co/U28HNPtjm9 https://t.co/7ImVH69fNb
- Aug 23, 2016 07:13:49 PM Will be participating in a Town Hall tonight on @SeanHannity at 10pmE from Austin, Texas. Enjoy! https://t.co/8ZBneb0pGk
- Aug 23, 2016 09:56:21 PM Thank you Travis County, Texas! #MakeAmericaGreatAgain https://t.co/ZBnYzNb0eo

- Aug 24, 2016 09:01:46 AM My thoughts and prayers are with the victims and families of those affected by two powerful earthquakes in Italy and Myanmar.
- Aug 24, 2016 10:19:24 AM I will not let the families of The Remembrance Project down! #MakeAmericaSafeAgain https://t.co/EMuSftG6RP https://t.co/FHPR44WixX
- Aug 24, 2016 11:42:04 AM Great new poll Florida - thank you! #MakeAmericaGreatAgain https://t.co/7TKpe388Bc
- Aug 24, 2016 12:24:13 PM New national poll released. Join the MOVEMENT & together we will #MakeAmericaGreatAgain! https://t.co/3KWOl2ibaW https://t.co/rnU1fkn274
- Aug 24, 2016 04:32:46 PM A great afternoon in Tampa, Florida. Thank you! #TrumpPence16 https://t.co/K5MBAcnfR1
- Aug 24, 2016 05:39:23 PM Thank you for your support! #AmericaFirst #ImWithYou https://t.co/N8FShwYt2g
- Aug 24, 2016 07:05:24 PM Will be on #Hannity @ 10pE @FoxNews- discussing various subjects including immigration-if elected, we will #BuildTheWall & enforce our laws!
- Aug 24, 2016 08:40:08 PM Great Governor @Mike_Pence is in Indiana to help lead the relief efforts after tornadoes struck. True leadership.
- Aug 24, 2016 08:41:53 PM Thoughts and prayers to the great people of Indiana. You will prevail!

- Aug 24, 2016 11:34:00 PM "@Trump_Videos: .@Nigel_Farage of the #brexit fame - We CAN do this! We can #MAGA with @realDonaldTrump https://t.co/1qyuc8ZykJ"

- Aug 25, 2016 07:34:58 AM Poll numbers are starting to look very good. Leading in Florida @CNN Arizona and big jump in Utah. All numbers rising, national way up. Wow!
- Aug 25, 2016 07:44:55 AM So many in the African-American community are doing so badly, poverty and crime way up, employment and jobs way down: I will fix it, promise
- Aug 25, 2016 03:11:41 PM Just watched recap of #CrookedHillary's speech. Very short and lies. She is the only one fear-mongering!
- Aug 25, 2016 03:14:20 PM Hillary Clinton's short speech is pandering to the worst instincts in our society. She should be ashamed of herself!
- Aug 25, 2016 03:45:38 PM Hillary Clinton is using race-baiting to try to get African-American voters- but they know she is all talk and NO ACTION!
- Aug 25, 2016 04:25:15 PM HRC is using the oldest play in the Dem playbook- when their policies fail, they are left w/this one tired argument! https://t.co/FNbCMmwLTn
- Aug 25, 2016 09:40:04 PM Hillary Clinton only knows how to make a speech when it is a hit on me. No policy, and always very short (stamina). Media gives her a pass!
- Aug 25, 2016 09:45:11 PM CLINTON CORRUPTION AND HER SABOTAGE OF THE INNER CITIES. Full speech transcript: https://t.co/npswT6lbg3
- Aug 25, 2016 09:46:34 PM "@foxnation: Flashback: Hillary Clinton Praised Former KKK Member Robert Byrd as 'Friend and Mentor': https://t.co/e0Hb2rLb1X"
- Aug 25, 2016 09:47:34 PM "@DonaldJTrumpJr: Company Gouging Price Of EpiPens Is A Clinton Foundation Donor And Partner https://t.co/HHlNGnlGMN via dailycaller"
- Aug 25, 2016 09:58:51 PM "Hillary Clinton needs to address the racist undertones of her 2008 campaign." #FlashbackFriday https://t.co/MJQp0rcnzH
- Aug 25, 2016 10:59:54 PM "@Lewenskimo: Your opponent has run out of ideas, now resorts to personal attacks on you. Every Amercan knows, you represent HOPE!!"

- Aug 26, 2016 07:05:57 AM The Clinton's are the real predators... https://t.co/Fr0gFtZVVz
- Aug 26, 2016 08:50:42 AM Crooked Hillary will NEVER be able to solve the problems of poverty, education and safety within the African-American & Hispanic communities
- Aug 26, 2016 09:20:55 AM What do African-Americans and Hispanics have to lose by going with me. Look at the poverty, crime and educational statistics. I will fix it!
- Aug 26, 2016 09:50:06 AM Wonderful @pastormarkburns was attacked viciously and unfairly on @MSNBC by crazy @morningmika on low ratings @Morning_Joe. Apologize!
- Aug 26, 2016 11:01:03 AM I am very proud to have brought the subject of illegal immigration back into the discussion. Such a big problem for our country-I will solve
- Aug 26, 2016 12:14:09 PM How quickly people forget that Crooked Hillary called African-American youth "SUPER PREDATORS" - Has she apologized?
- Aug 26, 2016 02:18:15 PM "Hillary Clinton Deleted Emails Using Program Intended To Prevent Recovery" #CrookedHillary https://t.co/D0MeBJXBwN
- Aug 26, 2016 02:21:22 PM Meet the 'Trumpocrats': Lifelong Democrats Breaking w/ Party Over Hillary to Support Donald Trump for President: https://t.co/g2N3JJWV8a
- Aug 26, 2016 02:26:16 PM Army training slide lists Hillary Clinton as insider threat: https://t.co/CQTSo2ETJF
- Aug 26, 2016 05:59:30 PM I will be interviewed by @kimguilfoyle at 7pm on @FoxNews. #Enjoy!
- Aug 26, 2016 06:11:22 PM Thank you @TeamTrump Florida. Keep me updated, and lets get those 100,000 registered voters! #MakeAmericaGreatAgain https://t.co/lseAAqxjA9
- Aug 26, 2016 06:54:09 PM Will be in Phoenix, Arizona on Wednesday. Changing venue to much larger one. Demand is unreal. Polls looking great! #ImWithYou
- Aug 26, 2016 06:59:43 PM Join us via our new #AmericaFirst APP! #TrumpPence16 https://t.co/FccLQSCkDY https://t.co/0angXB2BrI
- Aug 26, 2016 07:32:59 PM New polls - join the MOVEMENT today. https://t.co/3KWOl20zMm #ImWithYou https://t.co/numII7W99T

- Aug 27, 2016 09:17:14 AM Heroin overdoses are taking over our children and others in the MIDWEST. Coming in from our southern border. We need strong border & WALL!
- Aug 27, 2016 10:10:10 AM "@DiamondandSilk: Crooked Hillary getting desperate. On TV bashing Trump. @CNN, she forgot how she said a KKK member was her mentor.
- Aug 27, 2016 10:18:52 AM "@GoldJazz559: #BlackMenForBernie Leader: #Hillary2016 'No Regard For Black Race' https://t.co/m8952Ly3Jb via @dailycaller #BlacksForTrump
- Aug 27, 2016 11:26:08 AM Dwyane Wade's cousin was just shot and killed walking her baby in Chicago. Just what I have been saying. African-Americans will VOTE TRUMP!
- Aug 27, 2016 12:48:47 PM My condolences to Dwyane Wade and his family, on the loss of Nykea Aldridge. They are in my thoughts and prayers.
- Aug 27, 2016 01:47:50 PM Just landed in Iowa to attend a great event in honor of wonderful Senator @JoniErnst. Look forward to being with all of my friends.
- Aug 27, 2016 04:27:08 PM Thank you Iowa! #ImWithYou https://t.co/3BIF6jBTkk
- Aug 27, 2016 09:08:10 PM It was an honor to have the amazing Root family join me in Iowa. I have been so inspired by their courage & bravery. https://t.co/P4qVGGUYVZ
- Aug 27, 2016 09:33:29 PM NATIONAL DEBT January 2009 = $10.6 TRILLION August 2016 = $19.4 TRILLION https://t.co/dKAVaLfGAJ
- Aug 27, 2016 10:37:21 PM "@LindaHarden: @realDonaldTrump America loves Trump and @mike_pence -- praying for you every day. Stay strong. #TrumpPence2016 #NeverHillary

- Aug 28, 2016 09:01:53 AM Join me Tuesday in Everett, Washington at the Xfinity Arena! Tickets: https://t.co/ABQGySdcYt https://t.co/sn08gnd0lq
- Aug 28, 2016 09:04:46 AM Thank you Arizona! #VoteTrump https://t.co/v8VLxdd0fO
- Aug 28, 2016 02:29:15 PM RT @FoxNews: Poll: @realDonaldTrump vs. @HillaryClinton among white Evangelicals. https://t.co/6ohwIh1Q24

- Aug 28, 2016 05:12:27 PM Today is the 53rd anniversary of the March on Washington - today we honor the enduring fight for justice, equality and opportunity.
- Aug 28, 2016 06:24:14 PM I think that both candidates, Crooked Hillary and myself, should release detailed medical records. I have no problem in doing so! Hillary?
- Aug 28, 2016 06:27:59 PM I will be making a major speech on ILLEGAL IMMIGRATION on Wednesday in the GREAT State of Arizona. Big crowds, looking for a larger venue.

- Aug 29, 2016 08:02:47 AM Look how bad it is getting! How much more crime, how many more shootings, will it take for African-Americans and Latinos to vote Trump=SAFE!
- Aug 29, 2016 08:09:52 AM Inner-city crime is reaching record levels. African-Americans will vote for Trump because they know I will stop the slaughter going on!
- Aug 29, 2016 08:14:12 AM "@Patrici: Crowd at Trump Rally in Akron, Ohio is a Sea of Women, Minorities, Independents, Dems https://t.co/wm7HV8WPGk via @gatewaypundit
- Aug 29, 2016 08:15:39 AM "@RhondaR: Thank-You Clarence Henderson for telling @cnn you know racism & it's not DonaldTrump https://t.co/fSBPxZU8Gu via @BreitbartNews"
- Aug 29, 2016 08:17:47 AM "@PMNOrlando: @realDonaldTrump I know of NO ONE voting for Crooked Hillary! Her rallies are held in (blank) & she still has room.
- Aug 29, 2016 08:23:02 AM Does anyone know that Crooked Hillary, who tried so hard, was unable to pass the Bar Exams in Washington D.C. She was forced to go elsewhere
- Aug 29, 2016 08:30:04 AM Crooked Hillary's brainpower is highly overrated.Probably why her decision making is so bad or, as stated by Bernie S, she has BAD JUDGEMENT
- Aug 29, 2016 08:35:31 AM Now that African-Americans are seeing what a bad job Hillary type policy and management has done to the inner-cities, they want TRUMP!
- Aug 29, 2016 01:41:49 PM #CrookedHillary https://t.co/vXhcC8PaPy

- Aug 29, 2016 05:03:53 PM We will repeal and replace the horrible disaster known as #Obamacare! https://t.co/YzRTPrqrNC
- Aug 29, 2016 06:24:42 PM #MakeAmericaGreatAgain #ImWithYou https://t.co/IoYMdjvWHf
- Aug 29, 2016 07:15:51 PM Join me this Wednesday in Phoenix, Arizona at 6pm! #ImWithYou Tickets: https://t.co/1jATILh2k7 https://t.co/VwKnxo1TNQ
- Aug 29, 2016 07:27:21 PM Join me this Thursday in Wilmington, Ohio at noon! #ImWithYou Tickets: https://t.co/66bfVtIwf1 https://t.co/fDAJl5wVGe

- Aug 30, 2016 05:27:21 AM From day one I said that I was going to build a great wall on the SOUTHERN BORDER, and much more. Stop illegal immigration. Watch Wednesday!
- Aug 30, 2016 05:46:19 AM "@meequalsfree: Looking forward to seeing you again! Everett to be a packed house! @realDonaldTrump @mike_pence"
- Aug 30, 2016 03:47:05 PM Thank you America! #MAGA https://t.co/FljBVvbwKr https://t.co/ePJW9jLckM
- Aug 30, 2016 06:54:36 PM Thank you North Carolina! #MAGA https://t.co/1oWrFnHe0u
- Aug 30, 2016 09:14:10 PM RT @DRUDGE_REPORT: REUTERS POLL: CLINTON, TRUMP ALL TIED UP... https://t.co/htCXcTA5T7
- Aug 30, 2016 09:17:40 PM RT @RSBNetwork: We are ALREADY LIVE in Everett, WA for the Trump Rally. Come join us- our cameras tonight! #TrumpinEverett https://t.co/R...
- Aug 30, 2016 09:33:22 PM I have accepted the invitation of President Enrique Pena Nieto, of Mexico, and look very much forward to meeting him tomorrow.
- Aug 30, 2016 10:56:43 PM Thank you Washington! Together, WE will MAKE AMERICA SAFE AND GREAT AGAIN! #ImWithYou #AmericaFirst https://t.co/CWDQnISYH4

- Aug 31, 2016 08:07:38 AM Former President Vicente Fox, who is railing against my visit to Mexico today, also invited me when he apologized for using the "f bomb."
- Aug 31, 2016 07:40:07 PM Hillary Clinton didn't go to Louisiana, and now she didn't go to Mexico. She doesn't have the drive or stamina to MAKE AMERICA GREAT AGAIN!

- Aug 31, 2016 07:43:00 PM Great trip to Mexico today - wonderful leadership and high quality people! Look forward to our next meeting.
- Aug 31, 2016 07:57:54 PM Just arrived in Arizona! #ImWithYou https://t.co/MT3wW61YS5
- Aug 31, 2016 11:40:26 PM RT @AnnCoulter: I hear Churchill had a nice turn of phrase, but Trump's immigration speech is the most magnificent speech ever given.
- Aug 31, 2016 11:40:54 PM RT @LouDobbs: We are Watching A Leader Who for the First Time in Three Presidencies Will Put America and Americans First! @realDonaldTrump…
- Aug 31, 2016 11:58:19 PM Mexico will pay for the wall - 100%! #MakeAmericaGreatAgain #ImWithYou https://t.co/pSFuPZz0xP
- Aug 31, 2016 11:58:53 PM There will be no amnesty! #MakeAmericaGreatAgain #ImWithYou https://t.co/vVhzSdCblA

September, 2016

- Sep 1, 2016 12:06:52 AM Hillary Clinton doesn't have the strength or the stamina to MAKE AMERICA GREAT AGAIN! #AmericaFirst https://t.co/G1MuLrjhW9
- Sep 1, 2016 12:07:04 AM Under a Trump administration, it's called #AmericaFirst! #ImWithYou https://t.co/QfHfCQg0Wa
- Sep 1, 2016 05:31:17 AM Mexico will pay for the wall!
- Sep 1, 2016 05:40:13 AM Thank you to @foxandfriends for the great review of the speech on immigration last night. Thank you also to the great people of Arizona!
- Sep 1, 2016 05:46:44 AM Poll numbers way up - making big progress!
- Sep 1, 2016 09:22:26 AM Thank you for having me this morning @AmericanLegion. I enjoyed my time with everyone! #ALConvention2016 https://t.co/19TZEi6EbB

- Sep 1, 2016 12:05:25 PM I am promising you a new legacy for America. We're going to create a new American future. Thank you OHIO! #ImWithYou https://t.co/TUgccsxvoy
- Sep 1, 2016 05:53:52 PM I will be interviewed by @ericbolling tonight at 8pm on the @oreillyfactor. Enjoy!

- Sep 2, 2016 07:28:58 AM Just heard that crazy and very dumb @morningmika had a mental breakdown while talking about me on the low ratings @Morning_Joe. Joe a mess!
- Sep 2, 2016 07:32:31 AM People will be very surprised by our ground game on Nov. 8. We have an army of volunteers and people with GREAT SPIRIT! They want to #MAGA!
- Sep 2, 2016 07:35:44 AM I visited our Trump Tower campaign headquarters last night, after returning from Ohio and Arizona, and it was packed with great pros - WIN!
- Sep 2, 2016 11:55:57 AM Great new poll Iowa - thank you! #MakeAmericaGreatAgain #ImWithYou https://t.co/7hupah1RQN
- Sep 2, 2016 06:35:14 PM #AmericaFirst #ImWithYou https://t.co/Gtl7DyQkzt

- Sep 3, 2016 06:39:03 AM #ImWithYou https://t.co/I8dHzezmY4
- Sep 3, 2016 12:27:53 PM Thank you Great Faith Ministries International, Bishop Wayne T. Jackson, and Detroit! https://t.co/4Ucx678ZCC
- Sep 3, 2016 03:15:15 PM I am returning to the Pensacola Bay Center in Florida- Friday, 9/9/16 at 7pm. Join me! https://t.co/L8Ui56dcrJ https://t.co/wAePlfS0JL
- Sep 3, 2016 03:33:36 PM Great visit to Detroit church, fantastic reception, and all @CNN talks about is a small protest outside. Inside a large and wonderful crowd!
- Sep 3, 2016 03:36:39 PM .@CNN is so disgusting in their bias, but they are having a hard time promoting Crooked Hillary in light of the new e-mail scandals.

- Sep 4, 2016 07:55:58 AM Wow, the failing @nytimes has not reported properly on Crooked's FBI release. They are at the back of the pack - no longer a credible source

- Sep 4, 2016 11:04:21 AM Crooked Hillary's V.P. pick said this morning that I was not aware that Russia took over Crimea. A total lie - and taken over during O term!
- Sep 4, 2016 11:11:27 AM "@AnneBellar: @realDonaldTrump @CNN CNN is so biased. Never ever watch them. Trump 2016!!"
- Sep 4, 2016 11:35:36 AM RT @DanScavino: Doesn't fit the MSM narrative - so they wont share what @realDonaldTrump did for Jesse Jackson in 1999 - so I will! https:/…
- Sep 4, 2016 05:05:29 PM The Republican Party needs strong and committed leaders, not weak people such as @JeffFlake, if it is going to stop illegal immigration.
- Sep 4, 2016 06:05:24 PM The Great State of Arizona, where I just had a massive rally (amazing people), has a very weak and ineffective Senator, Jeff Flake. Sad!
- Sep 4, 2016 06:17:38 PM The polls are close so Crooked Hillary is getting out of bed and will campaign tomorrow.Why did she hammer 13 devices and acid-wash e-mails?
- Sep 4, 2016 06:26:41 PM To the African-American community: The Democrats have failed you for fifty years, high crime, poor schools, no jobs. I will fix it, VOTE "T"
- Sep 4, 2016 06:49:48 PM Lyin' Hillary Clinton told the FBI that she did not know the "C" markings on documents stood for CLASSIFIED. How can this be happening?
- Sep 4, 2016 08:24:26 PM "@CherNuna: @realDonaldTrump It defies belief the Web of Lies Hillary is spinning! One excuse after another. Then it's this, then it's that.
- Sep 4, 2016 08:28:02 PM "@lblackvelvet: @realDonaldTrump We need to show Americans that Hillary will KILL our Country !! Vote for Trump !!"
- Sep 4, 2016 08:30:36 PM "@ronnieclemmons: @ChrisCJackson @TakouiS @realDonaldTrump Trump now leads her by 2 - get real, she will lose big"
- Sep 4, 2016 10:58:39 PM "@tweak626: I'm at a biker rally in Perry, Kansas...and everyone is a @realDonaldTrump fan. Love it."
- Sep 4, 2016 10:59:58 PM "@OSPREY675: @Miami4Trump I followed you because you are a patriot & support @realDonaldTrump, as do I. #MAGA by sticking together.

- Sep 5, 2016 08:49:00 AM President Obama & Putin fail to reach deal on Syria - so what else is new? Obama is not a natural deal maker. Only makes bad deals!
- Sep 5, 2016 09:03:05 AM Can you believe that the Chinese would not give Obama the proper stairway to get off his plane - fight on tarmac! https://t.co/FAldS5zZi5
- Sep 5, 2016 09:09:28 AM #LaborDay #AmericaFirst Video: https://t.co/RNl7cfzkmN https://t.co/ZqRtbV4KRI
- Sep 5, 2016 11:55:19 AM Thank you American Legion Post 610- for hosting @Mike_Pence & I for a roundtable with labor leaders. #LaborDay #MAGA https://t.co/r0cwJlV38L
- Sep 5, 2016 01:26:10 PM Heading to Youngstown, Ohio now- some great polls. #AmericaFirst https://t.co/cGwDLSOFUt
- Sep 5, 2016 05:46:00 PM Thank you Ohio! #AmericaFirst https://t.co/p68GAJdhwu

- Sep 6, 2016 06:00:56 AM The truly great Phyllis Schlafly, who honored me with her strong endorsement for president, has passed away at 92. She was very special!
- Sep 6, 2016 06:12:11 AM China wouldn't provide a red carpet stairway from Air Force One and then Philippines President calls Obama "the son of a whore." Terrible!
- Sep 6, 2016 07:48:02 AM As a tribute to the late, great Phyllis Schlafly, I hope everybody can go out and get her latest book, THE CONSERVATIVE CASE FOR TRUMP.
- Sep 6, 2016 07:49:02 AM Thank you! #AmericaFirst https://t.co/6v4C8ykDVl
- Sep 6, 2016 08:05:12 AM "@Ler: Message for undecided voters: Please wake up and vote DonaldTrump now! Trump/Pence very important save our America before too late!"
- Sep 6, 2016 10:31:09 AM Mainstream media never covered Hillary's massive "hacking" or coughing attack, yet it is #1 trending. What's up?
- Sep 6, 2016 12:08:51 PM Thank you! #VoteTrump #ImWithYou https://t.co/SCEq9LqTTj
- Sep 6, 2016 12:57:59 PM Join me in Pensacola, Florida this Friday at 7pm! #VoteTrump https://t.co/L8Ui56dcrJ https://t.co/0ciDCuoFeO
- Sep 6, 2016 03:02:26 PM Thank you to all of our amazing military families, service members, and veterans. #ImWithYou https://t.co/RmQJt0Wxcq

- Sep 6, 2016 05:09:01 PM Great meeting with military spouses in Virginia-joined by @IvankaTrump, @LaraLeaTrump, @GenFlynn & @MayorRGiuliani. https://t.co/00GNH9nLet
- Sep 6, 2016 07:32:58 PM Thank you North Carolina- get out & #VoteTrump on 11/8/2016! #MakeAmericaGreatAgain https://t.co/HX2LRYs4Vq
- Sep 6, 2016 08:20:48 PM I will be interviewed on @oreillyfactor tonight at 11pmE @FoxNews. Enjoy!
- Sep 6, 2016 11:22:37 PM "@adhd_fa:Kudos to @PARISDENNARD for standing up to CNN's attempt to bully you and shout you down for defending @realDonaldTrump #media bias

- Sep 7, 2016 10:11:59 AM 'Donald Trump leads Hillary Clinton by 19 points among military, veteran voters: poll' #AmericaFirst #MAGA https://t.co/5FmxGtLkwt
- Sep 7, 2016 01:12:26 PM #AmericaFirst! https://t.co/fQGxwAjXD7
- Sep 7, 2016 03:23:56 PM Wow - thank you Pensacola, FL. See you Friday at 7pm -- join me! https://t.co/JCO7Za78tV https://t.co/LYmpRyY0Hq
- Sep 7, 2016 05:07:20 PM Thank you Peter - if elected, I will think big for our country & never let the American people down! #AmericaFirst https://t.co/6Nwu7EMJ9d
- Sep 7, 2016 11:02:15 PM Thank you to our fantastic veterans. The reviews and polls from almost everyone of my Commander-in-Chief presentation were great. Nice!

- Sep 8, 2016 04:59:36 AM Thank you America - great #CommanderInChiefForum polls! https://t.co/Rcu6KaRGCB
- Sep 8, 2016 05:39:04 AM Thank you to @foxandfriends for the nice reviews of last night.
- Sep 8, 2016 05:43:12 AM COMING UP @GenFlynn @newtgingrich on @foxandfriends
- Sep 8, 2016 05:52:27 AM Wow, reviews are in - THANK YOU!
- Sep 8, 2016 07:10:13 AM "A rough night for Hillary Clinton" ABC News.
- Sep 8, 2016 10:09:13 AM RT @DanScavino: Last nights winner was clear & it will be proven time & time again - lets #MAGA!! Lets WIN!! #TrumpTrain https://t.co/sGqp9...

- Sep 8, 2016 10:17:47 AM Hillary just gave a disastrous news conference on the tarmac to make up for poor performance last night. She's being decimated by the media!
- Sep 8, 2016 11:25:36 AM Hillary Clinton answered email questions differently last night than she has in the past. She is totally confused. Unfit to serve as #POTUS.
- Sep 8, 2016 01:16:25 PM Mexico has lost a brilliant finance minister and wonderful man who I know is highly respected by President Peña Nieto.
- Sep 8, 2016 01:17:01 PM With Luis, Mexico and the United States would have made wonderful deals together - where both Mexico and the US would have benefitted.
- Sep 8, 2016 02:52:32 PM Last nights results - in poll taken by NBC. #AmericaFirst #ImWithYou https://t.co/sCOnny1fl3
- Sep 8, 2016 06:56:22 PM More poll results from last nights Commander-in-Chief Forum. #AmericaFirst #TrumpTrain https://t.co/FxyBL6fO1h
- Sep 8, 2016 07:39:36 PM It wasn't Matt Lauer that hurt Hillary last night. It was her very dumb answer about emails & the veteran who said she should be in jail.
- Sep 8, 2016 09:00:32 PM Final poll results from NBC on last nights Commander-in-Chief Forum. Thank you! #ImWithYou #MAGA https://t.co/C5ipaxUN7B
- Sep 8, 2016 11:10:49 PM The documentary of me that @CNN just aired is a total waste of time. I don't even know many of the people who spoke about me. A joke!

- Sep 9, 2016 09:37:53 AM .@CNN is unwatchable. Their news on me is fiction. They are a disgrace to the broadcasting industry and an arm of the Clinton campaign.
- Sep 9, 2016 09:42:56 AM Jeff Zucker failed @NBC and he is now failing @CNN.
- Sep 9, 2016 11:20:55 AM RT @EricTrump: Join @TeamTrump on Saturday for National Day of Action as we work to #MakeAmericaGreatAgain! https://t.co/hyclkzPoBR https:/...
- Sep 9, 2016 12:32:36 PM Henry McMaster, Lt. Governor of South Carolina who endorsed me, beat failed @CNN announcer Bakari Sellers, so badly. Funny!

- Sep 9, 2016 04:10:51 PM MAKE AMERICA GREAT AGAIN! #AmericaFirst #ImWithYou https://t.co/JIlNW7myEN
- Sep 9, 2016 06:13:34 PM Great honor to be endorsed by popular & successful @gov_gilmore of VA. A state that I very much want to win-THX Jim! https://t.co/x4Y1TAFHvn
- Sep 9, 2016 06:19:33 PM Thank you Ohio. Together, we will MAKE AMERICA GREAT AGAIN! https://t.co/3KWOl20zMm https://t.co/n026nE4XIp
- Sep 9, 2016 07:11:22 PM Will be delivering a major speech tonight - live on @oreillyfactor at 8:10pm from Pensacola, Florida.
- Sep 9, 2016 09:31:43 PM Thank you Florida - we are going to MAKE AMERICA GREAT AGAIN! Join us: https://t.co/3KWOl2ibaW. #AmericaFirst https://t.co/vzKtRxzvwv

- Sep 10, 2016 12:47:11 AM Dummy writer @tonyschwartz, who wanted to do a second book with me for years (I said no), is now a hostile basket case who feels jilted!
- Sep 10, 2016 12:57:59 AM I havn't seen @tonyschwartz in many years, he hardly knows me. Never liked his style. Super lib, Crooked H supporter. Irrelevant dope!
- Sep 10, 2016 01:15:08 AM Just returned from Pensacola, Florida, where the crowd was incredible.
- Sep 10, 2016 07:30:40 AM "@Stvzbnk: Just Watched @tonyschwartz. Obviously Tony is a Total Whack Job @realDonaldTrump"
- Sep 10, 2016 07:43:08 AM Will be in Missouri today with Melania for the funeral of a wonderful and truly respected woman, Phyllis S!
- Sep 10, 2016 07:47:18 AM Wow, Hillary Clinton was SO INSULTING to my supporters, millions of amazing, hard working people. I think it will cost her at the Polls!
- Sep 10, 2016 10:54:27 AM Really sad that Republicans would allow themselves to be used in a Clinton ad. Lindsey Graham, Romney, Flake, Sass. SUPREME COURT, REMEMBER!
- Sep 10, 2016 01:18:37 PM While Hillary said horrible things about my supporters, and while many of her supporters will never vote for me, I still respect them all!

- Sep 10, 2016 03:46:30 PM RT @BarackObama: RT if you agree: We need a President who is fighting for all Americans, not one who writes off nearly half the country.
- Sep 10, 2016 06:37:06 PM Hillary Clinton just had her 47% moment. What a terrible thing she said about so many great Americans!
- Sep 10, 2016 08:14:10 PM The seriously failing @nytimes, despite so much winning and poll numbers that will soon put me in first place, only writes dishonest hits!

- Sep 11, 2016 12:34:30 PM #NeverForget https://t.co/G5TMAUzy0z

- Sep 12, 2016 05:09:36 AM I will be interviewed on @foxandfriends at 7:00 A.M.
- Sep 12, 2016 06:21:08 AM Will be on @CNBC at @7:22. Enjoy!
- Sep 12, 2016 10:51:45 AM Stopped by @TrumpDC to thank all of the tremendous men & women for their hard work! https://t.co/oGcJL4N454
- Sep 12, 2016 07:35:11 PM Just got back from Asheville, North Carolina, where we had a massive rally. The spirit of the crowd was unbelievable. Thank you! #MAGA
- Sep 12, 2016 07:49:01 PM "@brimyers813: Saw ur speech on Twitter. U give me hope and optimism. I feel as though I am in the room with u. I pray 4 ur/our success."
- Sep 12, 2016 10:19:53 PM Join me in Clive, Iowa tomorrow at noon! #AmericaFirst #MAGA Tickets: https://t.co/TEY6BbCyxt https://t.co/l17uzRPyLs

- Sep 13, 2016 08:14:02 AM Heading to Iowa- join me today at noon! #MakeAmericaGreatAgain Tickets: https://t.co/TEY6BbCyxt https://t.co/QyR2MDYYbZ
- Sep 13, 2016 10:00:23 AM Join us today! Together, we will #MakeAmericaGreatAgain! https://t.co/v40n8RXgti https://t.co/e3KQfBR2K8
- Sep 13, 2016 02:40:53 PM Thank you Clive, Iowa! https://t.co/tuZ35BkD9J
- Sep 13, 2016 03:04:31 PM RT @IvankaTrump: Ivanka is joining @realDonaldTrump to outline an innovative new child care policy to support American families. Tune in to…

- Sep 13, 2016 05:09:30 PM #ImWithYou #AmericaFirst
https://t.co/Ne4pI7FyU7
- Sep 13, 2016 05:42:08 PM RT @IvankaTrump: Ivanka penned an Op-Ed that
ran in the @WSJ this afternoon, read it here. https://t.co/3QE4nRXzLZ
@realDonaldTrump https:/...
- Sep 13, 2016 09:24:59 PM CHILD CARE REFORMS THAT WILL MAKE
AMERICA GREAT AGAIN! Transcript: https://t.co/rntyxBSb9J
https://t.co/5SWmxfVfto https://t.co/j389Quo4bg
- Sep 13, 2016 09:40:12 PM RT @LouDobbs: Trump outlines new child-care
policy proposals via the @FoxNews App @realDonaldTrump seems a candidate
of destiny https://t.c...
- Sep 13, 2016 09:43:01 PM Thank you @RepReneeEllmers!
https://t.co/1DrZpfa6je https://t.co/rzEw8pQhds
- Sep 13, 2016 09:44:55 PM Thank you Rep. @MarshaBlackburn!
https://t.co/vxEk0X4ntS https://t.co/9gAk0FWqZ8
- Sep 13, 2016 09:47:14 PM Thank you Rep. @CynthiaLummis!
https://t.co/4S4pnx4Q6r https://t.co/PLUKlsPXPR
- Sep 13, 2016 10:09:37 PM Why isn't President Obama working instead of
campaigning for Hillary Clinton?
- Sep 13, 2016 10:21:34 PM Russia took Crimea during the so-called Obama
years. Who wouldn't know this and why does Obama get a free pass?

- Sep 14, 2016 08:44:02 AM Thank you Ohio - see you tonight!
https://t.co/0DyHkzzWvj
- Sep 14, 2016 09:02:28 AM Great poll Florida - thank you! #ImWithYou
#AmericaFirst https://t.co/6Odle7j1hd
- Sep 14, 2016 11:54:41 AM Thank you @ATFD17! #ImWithYou Video:
https://t.co/z9Yg83VTF4
- Sep 14, 2016 03:46:23 PM Thank you Florida- can't wait to see you Friday in
Miami! Join me: https://t.co/rsx313493u https://t.co/JxsWXz05T9
- Sep 14, 2016 04:24:01 PM Thank you Ohio! Just landed in Canton for a rally at
the Civic Center. Join me at 7pm: https://t.co/s0XVVNyBKf
https://t.co/UtCRxykurW
- Sep 14, 2016 07:16:21 PM Honor to have been interviewed by the very
wonderful @bishopwtjackson in Detroit last week - tune in at 9pmE. Enjoy!
https://t.co/9ahPnfhQ5N

- Sep 14, 2016 07:57:20 PM Great evening in Canton, Ohio-thank you! We are going to MAKE AMERICA GREAT AGAIN! Join us: https://t.co/3KWOl2ibaW https://t.co/4MvwUj9eX9
- Sep 14, 2016 09:33:39 PM Great poll out of Nevada- thank you! See you soon. #MAGA #AmericaFirst https://t.co/3KWOl2ibaW https://t.co/27sR3MjjXc
- Sep 14, 2016 10:00:37 PM I will be interviewed on @foxandfriends tomorrow at 7am. Enjoy!
- Sep 14, 2016 10:59:01 PM I was never a fan of Colin Powell after his weak understanding of weapons of mass destruction in Iraq = disaster. We can do much better!
- Sep 14, 2016 11:04:14 PM "@ghfanlovessonny: @realDonaldTrump you have my vote in Pennsylvania. Trump 2016" Thank you!

- Sep 15, 2016 05:48:25 AM Will be on @foxandfriends at 7:00 A.M. Enjoy!
- Sep 15, 2016 09:34:13 AM Thank you for having me! I enjoyed the tour and spending time with everyone. See you soon. #MAGA https://t.co/eNtS7IBPDo
- Sep 15, 2016 09:50:08 AM Thank you to all of our law enforcement officers - across America! #LESM #MAGA https://t.co/Mcbc2JzhN2 https://t.co/4MTmR8kXVb
- Sep 15, 2016 10:39:10 AM Thank you @JerryJrFalwell! https://t.co/jzUQxkW4tB
- Sep 15, 2016 12:12:03 PM Full transcript of economic plan- delivered to the Economic Club of New York. #MAGA https://t.co/xiu9AUiSSD https://t.co/Fsy1diPWjU
- Sep 15, 2016 04:11:47 PM I will be interviewed by @jessebwatters on @oreillyfactor tonight at 8pm. Enjoy!
- Sep 15, 2016 05:23:48 PM RT @EricTrump: What a scary statistic! Americans are working harder and making less! We need competent leadership! https://t.co/jcGCbVOf6v
- Sep 15, 2016 05:41:13 PM Will be joining @jimmyfallon on @FallonTonight at 11:35pmE tonight. Enjoy!
- Sep 15, 2016 05:46:11 PM Instead of driving jobs and wealth away, AMERICA will become the WORLD'S great magnet for innovation & job creation! https://t.co/cvu20ZQSVJ

- Sep 15, 2016 09:37:51 PM "@jimmyfallon: Tonight: @realDonaldTrump, @normmacdonald, a performance by Kiiara,and your funniest #MyTeacherIsWeird tweets. #FallonTonight
- Sep 15, 2016 09:43:07 PM "@AK_TWEET: #TheDonald's hair gets the #JimmyFallon treatment on #TheTonightShow #TrumpPence16 https://t.co/0RRPbfIgXH" So true!
- Sep 15, 2016 10:31:28 PM Thank you for a great evening - Laconia, New Hampshire -- will be back soon! #AmericaFirst https://t.co/3KWOl2ibaW https://t.co/QWbYm2lY7B

- Sep 16, 2016 08:23:00 AM I am now going to the brand new Trump International, Hotel D.C. for a major statement.
- Sep 16, 2016 12:58:14 PM I am truly honored and grateful for receiving SO much support from our American heroes...https://t.co/S9bvbysiOr https://t.co/JJQncd3zhf
- Sep 16, 2016 04:01:27 PM Great parade in The Villages- I love you all. We will #MAGA. Thank you for the incredible support-I will not forget! https://t.co/5qTDijU3hn
- Sep 16, 2016 08:13:18 PM Just leaving Miami for Houston, Oklahoma and Colorado. Miami crowd was fantastic!
- Sep 16, 2016 11:15:53 PM Just arrived in Texas - have been informed two @fortworthpd officers have been shot. My thoughts and prayers are with them.
- Sep 16, 2016 11:43:14 PM A very interesting take from @KatiePavlich: https://t.co/XaM9yEYCHL

- Sep 17, 2016 12:15:44 AM "Donald Trump's birther event is the greatest trick he's ever pulled" https://t.co/zvVQnxeiQ9
- Sep 17, 2016 12:25:48 AM My thoughts and prayers go out to the @PhillyPolice & @Penn police officers- in Philadelphia. https://t.co/eyC3W1mweY
- Sep 17, 2016 12:53:09 AM Crooked Hillary wants to take your 2nd Amendment rights away. Will guns be taken from her heavily armed Secret Service detail? Maybe not!
- Sep 17, 2016 06:51:41 AM I never met former Defense Secretary Robert Gates. He knows nothing about me. But look at the results under his guidance - a total disaster!

- Sep 17, 2016 08:13:43 AM .@CNN just doesn't get it, and that's why their ratings are so low - and getting worse. Boring anti-Trump panelists, mostly losers in life!
- Sep 17, 2016 12:28:43 PM Wacky @NYTimesDowd, who hardly knows me, makes up things that I never said for her boring interviews and column. A neurotic dope!
- Sep 17, 2016 12:29:26 PM Crazy Maureen Dowd, the wacky columnist for the failing @nytimes, pretends she knows me well--wrong!
- Sep 17, 2016 04:38:50 PM The failing @nytimes has gone nuts that Crooked Hillary is doing so badly. They are willing to say anything, has become a laughingstock rag!
- Sep 17, 2016 05:57:09 PM My lawyers want to sue the failing @nytimes so badly for irresponsible intent. I said no (for now), but they are watching. Really disgusting
- Sep 17, 2016 06:03:47 PM Heading to Colorado for a big rally. Massive crowd, great people! Will be there soon - the polls are looking good.
- Sep 17, 2016 06:14:58 PM Never met but never liked dopey Robert Gates. Look at the mess the U.S. is in. Always speaks badly of his many bosses, including Obama.

- Sep 18, 2016 08:06:56 AM I would like to express my warmest regards, best wishes and condolences to all of the families and victims of the horrible bombing in NYC.
- Sep 18, 2016 04:07:05 PM RT @KellyannePolls: more media #polls showing @realDonaldTrump ahead in states Pres Obama won twice. https://t.co/EGySAz6Am1
- Sep 18, 2016 04:11:48 PM HAPPY BIRTHDAY - to the United States Air Force!! https://t.co/5Gwi1M5R2t
- Sep 18, 2016 09:30:34 PM Under the leadership of Obama & Clinton, Americans have experienced more attacks at home than victories abroad. Time to change the playbook!
- Sep 18, 2016 09:32:03 PM Terrible attacks in NY, NJ and MN this weekend. Thinking of victims, their families and all Americans! We need to be strong!

- Sep 19, 2016 06:02:30 AM Will be on @foxandfriends at 7:02 A.M. Enjoy.

- Sep 19, 2016 07:14:59 AM "@AngPiazza: @foxandfriends @realDonaldTrump he's the ONLY candidate that will keep us safe!"
- Sep 19, 2016 07:27:28 AM "@TarukMatuk: @CNN @FoxNews @realDonaldTrump @RogerRice10 Refugees from Syria over 10k plus more coming. Lots young males, poorly vetted.
- Sep 19, 2016 11:32:32 AM Great job once again by law enforcement! We are proud of them and should embrace them - without them, we don't have a country!
- Sep 19, 2016 11:41:15 AM Once again someone we were told is ok turns out to be a terrorist who wants to destroy our country & its people- how did he get thru system?
- Sep 19, 2016 11:53:42 AM Hillary Clinton's weakness while she was Secretary of State, has emboldened terrorists all over the world..cont: https://t.co/E5BdTiwlur
- Sep 19, 2016 02:52:00 PM Philly FOP Chief On Presidential Endorsement: Clinton 'Blew The Police Off' https://t.co/ATBY343pS1
- Sep 19, 2016 07:14:56 PM I will be interviewed on the @oreillyfactor - tonight from Florida, now. Enjoy!
- Sep 19, 2016 07:19:00 PM Together, we will MAKE AMERICA SAFE AND GREAT AGAIN! #ImWithYou #AmericaFirst https://t.co/XhwUGw0v2H
- Sep 19, 2016 07:26:50 PM Amazing rally in Florida - this is a MOVEMENT! Join us today at https://t.co/3KWOl2ibaW. https://t.co/BF1IqPXNho

- Sep 20, 2016 07:02:35 AM Crooked Hillary has been fighting ISIS, or whatever she has been doing, for years. Now she has new ideas. It is time for change.
- Sep 20, 2016 08:49:50 AM Thank you Georgia! #AmericaFirst #MakeAmericaGreatAgain https://t.co/3KWOl2ibaW https://t.co/y01qpON7h7
- Sep 20, 2016 08:50:56 AM Thank you Nevada! #AmericaFirst #MakeAmericaGreatAgain https://t.co/3KWOl2ibaW https://t.co/RJqHgq2Rn0
- Sep 20, 2016 09:20:50 AM Do people notice Hillary is copying my airplane rallies - she puts the plane behind her like I have been doing from the beginning.
- Sep 20, 2016 09:22:02 AM Heading to North Carolina for two big rallies. Will be there soon. We will bring jobs back where they belong!
- Sep 20, 2016 09:23:59 AM Hillary Clinton is taking the day off again, she needs the rest. Sleep well Hillary - see you at the debate!

- Sep 20, 2016 03:33:08 PM Thank you High Point, NC! I will fight for every neglected part of this nation & I will fight to bring us together… https://t.co/DSaUpSptBz
- Sep 20, 2016 07:07:51 PM Thank you Kenansville, North Carolina! Remember- on November 8th, that special interest gravy train is coming to a… https://t.co/AysJRMzvKw

- Sep 21, 2016 06:17:43 AM It is a MOVEMENT - not a campaign. Leaving the past behind, changing our future. Together, we will MAKE AMERICA SAF… https://t.co/Lt2L3NKzyi
- Sep 21, 2016 08:20:15 AM The situations in Tulsa and Charlotte are tragic. We must come together to make America safe again.
- Sep 21, 2016 08:23:13 AM Hopefully the violence & unrest in Charlotte will come to an immediate end. To those injured, get well soon. We need unity & leadership.
- Sep 21, 2016 01:01:51 PM RT @GMA: WATCH: @IvankaTrump on "women who work;" empowering campaign celebrates modern women. https://t.co/rMFe9o6WcL
- Sep 21, 2016 04:02:56 PM Thank you Toledo, Ohio! It is so important for you to get out and VOTE on November 8, 2016! Lets MAKE AMERICA SAFE… https://t.co/MQdp4GgLIE
- Sep 21, 2016 05:35:19 PM Great new polls! Thank you Nevada, North Carolina & Ohio. Join the MOVEMENT today & lets #MAGA!… https://t.co/Y8Sb8MNyXA
- Sep 21, 2016 07:49:24 PM .@YoungDems4Trump Thank you!
- Sep 21, 2016 07:54:26 PM "@ThAllenSBoucher: @DiamondandSilk @realDonaldTrump @seanhannity I love those beautiful gals." D + S = Two amazing women!
- Sep 21, 2016 07:58:03 PM I will be interviewed from Cleveland, Ohio, on @seanhannity - Tonight at 10:00 P.M. Enjoy!

- Sep 22, 2016 06:02:01 AM Will be on @foxandfriends now.
- Sep 22, 2016 09:45:45 AM Join me in Roanoke, Virginia on Saturday evening at 6pm! #MAGA https://t.co/uKG55Pznwu

- Sep 22, 2016 08:17:50 PM This is more than a campaign- it is a movement. #MakeAmericaGreatAgain SIGN UP TODAY & WE WILL WIN! https://t.co/2XBs5SSRC3
- Sep 22, 2016 09:09:13 PM Spoke with Governor @PatMcCroryNC of North Carolina today. He is doing a tremendous job under tough circumstances.

- Sep 23, 2016 10:55:55 AM RT @dcexaminer: EXCLUSIVE: How Donald Trump's 30 million followers are crashing the Internet https://t.co/hV2z4yrTU7 https://t.co/lWkjmdyQ7Q
- Sep 23, 2016 10:57:47 AM Tomorrow's the day! Knock on doors and make calls with us on National Day of Action! #TrumpTrain #MAGA… https://t.co/05NY0wJHkL
- Sep 23, 2016 12:26:56 PM Hillary Clinton just lost every Republican she ever had, including Never Trump, all farmers & sm. biz, by saying she'll tax estates at 65%.
- Sep 23, 2016 12:32:20 PM 'How Trump Would Stimulate the U.S. Economy' https://t.co/jU3HHglnIu
- Sep 23, 2016 03:13:49 PM Join me in Roanoke, Virginia tomorrow at the Berglund Center- Coliseum ~ 6pm! Tickets available at:… https://t.co/bnEE6NX41Z
- Sep 23, 2016 09:09:56 PM Crooked Hillary's bad judgement forced her to announce that she would go to Charlotte on Saturday to grandstand. Dem pols said no way, dumb!

- Sep 24, 2016 06:06:32 AM Today is the day! Knock on doors and make calls with us on National Day of Action! #TrumpTrain #MAGA… https://t.co/4iW06ROvsT
- Sep 24, 2016 07:35:02 AM The @SenTedCruz endorsement was a wonderful surprise. I greatly appreciate his support! We will have a tremendous victory on November 8th.
- Sep 24, 2016 07:43:52 AM "@KellyannePolls: Trump is headed for a win, says professor who has predicted 30 years of presidential outcomes https://t.co/68WEMcuHSO"
- Sep 24, 2016 09:10:37 AM Will be back in Virginia tonight- for a 6pm rally at the Berglund Center in Roanoke. Join me! Tickets:… https://t.co/6pQMSgPWuN

- Sep 24, 2016 12:08:17 PM If dopey Mark Cuban of failed Benefactor fame wants to sit in the front row, perhaps I will put Gennifer Flowers right alongside of him!
- Sep 24, 2016 06:39:02 PM Thank you Roanoke, Virginia - this a MOVEMENT - join us today! Sign up: https://t.co/NQEgRxQN2m #AmericaFirst… https://t.co/Rz3DkpBQJu

- Sep 25, 2016 07:30:28 AM Many on the team and staff of Bernie Sanders have been treated badly by the Hillary Clinton campaign - and they like Trump on trade, a lot!
- Sep 25, 2016 08:04:46 AM Bernie Sanders gave Hillary the Dem nomination when he gave up on the e-mails. That issue has only gotten bigger!
- Sep 25, 2016 08:20:56 AM Looking forward to my meeting with Benjamin Netanyahu in Trump Tower at 10:00 A.M.
- Sep 25, 2016 01:15:11 PM Readout of my meeting with Israeli Prime Minister Benjamin Netanyahu: https://t.co/VHuyE65hgi https://t.co/6KDPrQxSED
- Sep 25, 2016 07:18:40 PM Five people killed in Washington State by a Middle Eastern immigrant. Many people died this weekend in Ohio from drug overdoses. N.C. riots!
- Sep 25, 2016 08:13:40 PM Really sad news: The great Arnold Palmer, the "King," has died. There was no-one like him - a true champion! He will be truly missed.

- Sep 26, 2016 07:02:48 AM New national Bloomberg poll just released - thank you! Join the MOVEMENT: https://t.co/3KWOl2ibaW. #TrumpTrain… https://t.co/xDGCwYVK0Q
- Sep 26, 2016 11:29:31 AM RT @KellyannePolls: #Polls showing @realDonaldTrump surging, @hillaryclinton #slipping, have HER camp on defense/lowering expectations, goi…
- Sep 26, 2016 05:31:53 PM My team of deplorables will be managing my Twitter account for this evenings debate. Tune in! #DebateNight #TrumpPence16
- Sep 26, 2016 06:30:40 PM RT @DanScavino: Join @realDonaldTrump on his official social media platforms during tonight's debate ~ as @TeamTrump manages rapid response…
- Sep 26, 2016 07:47:05 PM Why isn't Hillary Clinton 50 points ahead? #DebateNight https://t.co/iux7icIkaT

- Sep 26, 2016 08:14:09 PM RT @TeamTrump: A @realDonaldTrump Administration will bring JOBS BACK! #Debates2016 https://t.co/4O3rIyycyW
- Sep 26, 2016 08:18:55 PM .@HillaryClinton and Obama policies increased debt by $9trillion over the last 8 years
- Sep 26, 2016 08:23:43 PM .@HillaryClinton channels John Kerry on trade: she was for bad trade deals before she was against them. #TPP #Debates2016
- Sep 26, 2016 08:28:04 PM Instead of driving jobs and wealth away, AMERICA will become the world's great magnet for innovation and job creati... https://t.co/02NMQn3ZNQ
- Sep 26, 2016 08:28:50 PM .@HillaryClinton has been part of the rigged DC system for 30 years? Why would we take policy advice from her? #Debates2016
- Sep 26, 2016 08:32:25 PM A Clinton economy = more taxes and more spending! #DebateNight https://t.co/oFlaAhrwe5
- Sep 26, 2016 08:33:59 PM HILLARY'S BAD TAX HABIT! https://t.co/x3FBy8Hdq2
- Sep 26, 2016 08:36:50 PM This is the simple fact about @HillaryClinton: she is a typical politician - all talk, no action. #Debates2016
- Sep 26, 2016 08:44:01 PM RT @TeamTrump: WATCH: @realDonaldTrump on the stakes in this election #Debates2016 https://t.co/l7DSbPXDGh
- Sep 26, 2016 08:50:01 PM RT @TeamTrump: When @realDonaldTrump is POTUS, families are going to be safe and secure. Law and order will be RESTORED! #MAGA #Debates #De...
- Sep 26, 2016 08:51:58 PM I will stand with police and protect ALL Americans! #Debates2016 #MAGA https://t.co/CX4oEWgEMp
- Sep 26, 2016 09:10:30 PM RT @DanScavino: Jesse Jackson on @realDonaldTrump - when he donated space for the Rainbow/Push Coalition. #DebateNight https://t.co/JTbqO0...
- Sep 26, 2016 09:19:20 PM RT @TeamTrump: Hillary's policies have made America less safe, that's why 200+ general and military leaders have endorsed @realDonaldTrump!...
- Sep 26, 2016 09:19:47 PM .@HillaryClinton's 2008 Campaign And Supporters Trafficked In Rumors About Obama's Heritage #DebateNight https://t.co/6EEOAaCiNv
- Sep 26, 2016 09:21:59 PM Hillary Clinton is the only candidate on stage who voted for the Iraq War. #Debates2016 #MAGA https://t.co/Um5WJXEEKr

- Sep 26, 2016 09:22:12 PM RT @TeamTrump: 100% TRUE --> @realDonaldTrump is right - @HillaryClinton did call TPP 'the gold standard' #Debates2016 https://t.co/W7L7a9...
- Sep 26, 2016 09:26:13 PM Hillary Clinton failed all over the world. X LIBYA X SYRIA X IRAN X IRAQ X ASIA PIVOT X RUSSIAN RESET X BENGHAZI... https://t.co/OoakXs2rij
- Sep 26, 2016 09:28:26 PM Russia has more warheads than ever, N Korea is testing nukes, and Iran got a sweetheart deal to keep theirs. Thanks, @HillaryClinton.
- Sep 26, 2016 09:33:59 PM RT @TeamTrump: .@realDonaldTrump calling out @HillaryClinton's support for NAFTA = most searched moment during tonight's debate. #Debates20...
- Sep 26, 2016 09:36:11 PM .@HillaryClinton - Obama #ISIS Strategy Has Allowed It To Expand To Become A Global Threat #DebateNight https://t.co/f7PctDE31L
- Sep 26, 2016 09:40:26 PM Nothing on emails. Nothing on the corrupt Clinton Foundation. And nothing on #Benghazi. #Debates2016 #debatenight
- Sep 26, 2016 09:42:49 PM .@HillaryClinton's Nuclear Agreement Paved The Way For The $400 Million Ransom Payment #DebateNight https://t.co/qfZTx6aKYs
- Sep 26, 2016 10:58:24 PM Thank you Senator @TedCruz! #Debates2016 #MAGA https://t.co/cgO6109USJ
- Sep 26, 2016 11:01:32 PM Thank you Governor @Mike_Pence! Lets MAKE AMERICA SAFE AND GREAT AGAIN with the American people. #AmericaFirst... https://t.co/6k7qP9X8nC
- Sep 26, 2016 11:02:51 PM Thank you Governor @TerryBranstad! #AmericaFirst #Debates2016 https://t.co/yIeZctdQy8
- Sep 26, 2016 11:34:09 PM Wow, did great in the debate polls (except for @CNN - which I don't watch). Thank you!

- Sep 27, 2016 12:18:10 AM .@newtgingrich just said "a historic victory for Trump." NICE!
- Sep 27, 2016 12:36:33 AM TIME #DebateNight poll - over 800,000 votes. Thank you! #AmericaFirst #MAGA https://t.co/bTPX9E0wKu

- Sep 27, 2016 12:44:02 AM Thank you! CNBC #DebateNight poll with over 400,000 votes. Trump 61% Clinton 39% #AmericaFirst #ImWithYou… https://t.co/MJ3NwA98op
- Sep 27, 2016 12:54:42 AM .@DRUDGE_REPORT's First Presidential Debate Poll: Trump: 80% Clinton: 20% Join the MOVEMENT today & lets #MAGA!… https://t.co/B12lgC97tn
- Sep 27, 2016 01:32:29 AM Thank you! Four new #DebateNight polls with the MOVEMENT winning. Together, we will MAKE AMERICA SAFE & GREAT AGAIN… https://t.co/39FCnUf8Pb
- Sep 27, 2016 05:44:58 AM Great debate poll numbers - I will be on @foxandfriends at 7:00 to discuss. Enjoy!
- Sep 27, 2016 07:53:42 AM I really enjoyed the debate last night.Crooked Hillary says she is going to do so many things.Why hasn't she done them in her last 30 years?
- Sep 27, 2016 07:55:31 AM 'How Trump won over a bar full of undecideds and Democrats' https://t.co/WWO39kxn8Y
- Sep 27, 2016 08:14:55 AM I won every poll from last nights Presidential Debate - except for the little watched @CNN poll.
- Sep 27, 2016 08:17:40 AM The #1 trend on Twitter right now is #TrumpWon - thank you!
- Sep 27, 2016 08:49:07 AM 'True blue-collar billionaire Donald Trump shows Hillary Clinton is out of touch' https://t.co/NHO1OicfVm
- Sep 27, 2016 09:49:09 AM Hillary's been failing for 30 years in not getting the job done - it will never change.
- Sep 27, 2016 09:51:25 AM Thank you! #TrumpWon #MAGA https://t.co/a5rr1i38km
- Sep 27, 2016 09:55:57 AM 'U.S. Murders Increased 10.8% in 2015' via @WSJ: https://t.co/CIJMQJhLqp
- Sep 27, 2016 10:47:29 AM Such a great honor. Final debate polls are in - and the MOVEMENT wins! #AmericaFirst #MAGA #ImWithYou… https://t.co/DV1BKMwHEM
- Sep 27, 2016 11:58:58 AM Thank you for your endorsement, @GovernorSununu. #MAGA https://t.co/8BEeQPsuyd
- Sep 27, 2016 12:47:36 PM Well, now they're saying that I not only won the NBC Presidential Forum, but last night the big debate. Nice!

- Sep 27, 2016 02:37:22 PM In the last 24 hrs. we have raised over $13M from online donations and National Call Day, and we're still going! Thank you America! #MAGA
- Sep 27, 2016 02:59:04 PM Great afternoon in Little Havana with Hispanic community leaders. Thank you for your support! #ImWithYou https://t.co/vxWZ2tyJTF
- Sep 27, 2016 03:06:25 PM 'CNBC, Time magazine online polls say Donald Trump won the first presidential debate' via @WashTimes. #MAGA https://t.co/PGimqYKPoJ
- Sep 27, 2016 03:14:33 PM Hillary Clinton's Campaign Continues To Make False Claims About Foundation Disclosure: https://t.co/zhkEfUouHH
- Sep 27, 2016 03:31:14 PM RT @GOP: On National #VoterRegistrationDay, make sure you're registered to vote so we can #MakeAmericaGreatAgain https://t.co/GKcaLkx8C8 ht...
- Sep 27, 2016 04:08:22 PM Once again, we will have a government of, by and for the people. Join the MOVEMENT today! https://t.co/lWjYDbPHav https://t.co/uYwJrtZkAe
- Sep 27, 2016 05:13:24 PM Join me for a 3pm rally - tomorrow at the Mid-America Center in Council Bluffs, Iowa! Tickets:... https://t.co/dfzsbICiXc
- Sep 27, 2016 08:03:03 PM Unbelievable evening in Melbourne, Florida w/ 15,000 supporters- and an additional 12,000 who could not get in. Tha... https://t.co/VU5wh2zXBU
- Sep 27, 2016 09:17:06 PM My supporters are the best! $18 million from hard-working people who KNOW what we can be again! Shatter the record: https://t.co/8ZHGyOth0f

- Sep 28, 2016 07:41:03 AM Every on-line poll, Time Magazine, Drudge etc., has me winning the debate. Thank you to Fox & Friends for so reporting!
- Sep 28, 2016 11:20:01 AM Join me in Council Bluffs, Iowa- today at 3pm! #MakeAmericaGreatAgain Tickets: https://t.co/iRL3xh37gF
- Sep 28, 2016 12:26:26 PM Melania and I extend our deepest condolences to the family of Shimon Peres...https://t.co/xeGYL2IzUP
- Sep 28, 2016 12:40:10 PM An honor to meet with the Polish American Congress in Chicago this morning! #ImWithYou Video:... https://t.co/lBFHoWRqox

- Sep 28, 2016 04:42:43 PM RT @TeamTrump: "She put the office of Sec of State up for sale. If she ever got the chance, she'd put the Oval Office up for sale too." #Fo…
- Sep 28, 2016 05:54:59 PM Thank you Council Bluffs, Iowa! Will be back soon. Remember- everything you need to know about Hillary -- just… https://t.co/45kIHxdX83
- Sep 28, 2016 06:54:08 PM Join me live in Waukesha, Wisconsin for an 8pmE rally! #AmericaFirst #MAGA https://t.co/G8kGLSFy6S
- Sep 28, 2016 07:01:35 PM Joining @oreillyfactor from Waukesha, Wisconsin - now, live! Enjoy!
- Sep 28, 2016 09:51:57 PM Thank you Waukesha, Wisconsin! Full transcript of my speech, #FollowTheMoney: https://t.co/Xb1yyDSNNf https://t.co/WdKK6nJCZW
- Sep 28, 2016 10:23:07 PM Join me in Bedford, New Hampshire- tomorrow at 3:00pm. Can't wait to see everyone! #AmericaFirst #MAGA… https://t.co/oeOJFAS7it
- Sep 28, 2016 10:42:03 PM Will be in Novi, Michigan this Friday at 5:00pm. Join the MOVEMENT! Tickets available at: https://t.co/Q6APf0ZFYA… https://t.co/6WAyO9eQHN

- Sep 29, 2016 01:05:56 PM My condolences to those involved in today's horrible accident in NJ and my deepest gratitude to all of the amazing first responders.
- Sep 29, 2016 02:16:40 PM Join me in Manheim, Pennsylvania on Saturday at 7pm! #TrumpRally Tickets: https://t.co/ADOGW34ctF https://t.co/LNWQZ9yUJy
- Sep 29, 2016 04:34:57 PM Thank you for joining me this afternoon, New Hampshire! Will be back soon. #FollowTheMoney Speech transcript:… https://t.co/VtUkDgF4vs
- Sep 29, 2016 05:17:55 PM While Hillary profits off the rigged system, I am fighting for you! Remember the simple phrase: #FollowTheMoney… https://t.co/8mVInc82E9
- Sep 29, 2016 09:16:00 PM Wow, did you see how badly @CNN (Clinton News Network) is doing in the ratings. With people like @donlemon, who could expect any more?

- Sep 30, 2016 02:20:02 AM Anytime you see a story about me or my campaign saying "sources said," DO NOT believe it. There are no sources, they are just made up lies!
- Sep 30, 2016 04:14:03 AM Wow, Crooked Hillary was duped and used by my worst Miss U. Hillary floated her as an "angel" without checking her past, which is terrible!
- Sep 30, 2016 04:19:25 AM Using Alicia M in the debate as a paragon of virtue just shows that Crooked Hillary suffers from BAD JUDGEMENT! Hillary was set up by a con.
- Sep 30, 2016 04:30:11 AM Did Crooked Hillary help disgusting (check out sex tape and past) Alicia M become a U.S. citizen so she could use her in the debate?
- Sep 30, 2016 07:50:48 AM Remember, don't believe "sources said" by the VERY dishonest media. If they don't name the sources, the sources don't exist.
- Sep 30, 2016 09:21:54 AM The people are really smart in cancelling subscriptions to the Dallas & Arizona papers & now USA Today will lose readers! The people get it!
- Sep 30, 2016 01:24:21 PM Why isn't Hillary 50 points ahead? Maybe it's the email scandal, policies that spread ISIS, or calling millions of… https://t.co/yKz9vCz8O1
- Sep 30, 2016 01:37:48 PM For those few people knocking me for tweeting at three o'clock in the morning, at least you know I will be there, awake, to answer the call!
- Sep 30, 2016 03:03:41 PM Join me in Pueblo, Colorado on Monday afternoon at 3pm! #TrumpRally https://t.co/3P3QZxzSPJ
- Sep 30, 2016 03:10:54 PM Thank you for your support - on my way now! See you soon. #TrumpTrain https://t.co/SYuRpzosb5
- Sep 30, 2016 06:01:50 PM Thank you Novi, Michigan! Get out and VOTE #TrumpPence16 on 11/8. Together, WE WILL MAKE AMERICA GREAT AGAIN!… https://t.co/n7Gd6Xc18H
- Sep 30, 2016 07:52:15 PM I believe in #AmericaFirst and that means FAMILY FIRST! My childcare plan reflects the needs of modern working-clas… https://t.co/RCnZZtTk4c

October, 2016

- Oct 1, 2016 12:01:31 PM Crooked H is nasty to Sanders supporters behind closed doors. Owned by Wall St and Politicians, HRC is not with you. https://t.co/WN1lyCDXla
- Oct 1, 2016 03:16:05 PM I won the debate if you decide without watching the totally one-sided "spin" that followed. This despite the really bad microphone.
- Oct 1, 2016 03:47:45 PM The so-called Commission on Presidential Debates admitted to us that the DJT audio & sound level was very bad. So why didn't they fix it?
- Oct 1, 2016 04:25:52 PM Wow, just saw the really bad @CNN ratings. People don't want to watch bad product that only builds up Crooked Hillary.
- Oct 1, 2016 04:29:56 PM Heading to Pennsylvania for a big rally tonight. We will MAKE AMERICA GREAT AGAIN!

- Oct 2, 2016 06:22:41 AM I know our complex tax laws better than anyone who has ever run for president and am the only one who can fix them. #failing@nytimes
- Oct 2, 2016 06:35:00 AM I have created tens of thousands of jobs and will bring back great American prosperity. Hillary has only created jobs at the FBI and DOJ!
- Oct 2, 2016 07:10:33 AM "@trumplican2016: .@realDonaldTrump There will be MASSIVE turnout for you, Mr. Trump - These polls don't register the pulse of the PEOPLE!
- Oct 2, 2016 04:48:21 PM Bernie should pull his endorsement of Crooked Hillary after she decieved him and then attacked him and his supporters.
- Oct 2, 2016 04:59:07 PM Melania and I extend our warmest greetings to those observing Rosh Hashanah here in the United States, in Israel, and around the world.
- Oct 2, 2016 06:45:40 PM Just announced that Iraq (U.S.) is preparing for battle to reclaim Mosul. Why do they have to announce this? Makes mission much harder!

- Oct 3, 2016 09:10:52 AM Join me in Henderson, Nevada on Wednesday at 11:30am! #MAGA Tickets: https://t.co/pWTYv9BbUE
- Oct 3, 2016 04:41:35 PM Thank you Pueblo, Colorado! #TrumpRally #AmericaFirst https://t.co/3KWOl20zMm https://t.co/rFAf7xYNhy
- Oct 3, 2016 05:03:46 PM We must bring the truth directly to hard-working Americans who want to take our country back. #BigLeagueTruth… https://t.co/0iAeiPYEhO
- Oct 3, 2016 09:20:21 PM Thank you Colorado! #MAGA https://t.co/3KWOl20zMm https://t.co/M7QhdCgRzw https://t.co/wIGNtKPA2X
- Oct 3, 2016 10:39:42 PM Join me in Reno, Nevada on Wednesday at 3:30pm at the Reno-Sparks Convention Center! #MAGA Tickets:… https://t.co/G0NvFLQWgS

- Oct 4, 2016 02:36:19 PM Join me in Reno, Nevada tomorrow at 3:30pm! #AmericaFirst #MAGA Tickets: https://t.co/DJ7JJUkkz7
- Oct 4, 2016 02:40:44 PM I will be watching the great Governor @Mike_Pence and live tweeting the VP debate tonight starting at 8:30pm est! Enjoy!

- Oct 4, 2016 02:48:15 PM My childcare plan makes a difference for working families - more money, more freedom. #AmericaFirst means… https://t.co/X3Yn3FZphf
- Oct 4, 2016 05:38:18 PM Thank you ARIZONA! This is a MOVEMENT like nobody has ever seen before. Together, we are going to MAKE AMERICA SAFE… https://t.co/EwP4hnaeoE
- Oct 4, 2016 06:44:28 PM Join the MOVEMENT! https://t.co/3KWOl20zMm https://t.co/BS5JLelPJd
- Oct 4, 2016 06:55:55 PM Wow, did you just hear Bill Clinton's statement on how bad ObamaCare is. Hillary not happy. As I have been saying, REPEAL AND REPLACE!
- Oct 4, 2016 07:12:59 PM Wow, @CNN is so negative. Their panel is a joke, biased and very dumb. I'm turning to @FoxNews where we get a fair shake! Mike will do great
- Oct 4, 2016 07:18:38 PM I will be live-tweeting the V.P. Debate. Very exciting! MAKE AMERICA GREAT AGAIN!
- Oct 4, 2016 08:01:12 PM Here we go - Enjoy!
- Oct 4, 2016 08:05:53 PM Both are looking good! Now we begin!
- Oct 4, 2016 08:06:02 PM .@megynkelly- I am in Nevada. Sorry to inform you Kellyanne is in the audience. Better luck next time.
- Oct 4, 2016 08:12:45 PM "@RoadkingL: @mike_pence Wow, Kaine couldn't go 12 seconds without a lie. Marines and military are scared of the liar running. #bengazi"
- Oct 4, 2016 08:15:22 PM "@lainey34210: @realDonaldTrump Great opening Pence"
- Oct 4, 2016 08:16:00 PM "@Susiesentinel: #pence is so much more likeable than Kaine #cbsnews @realDonaldTrump"
- Oct 4, 2016 08:21:25 PM RT @joshrogin: Pence is right. Clinton & Obama tried to negotiate an Iraq troop extension but failed. Bush admin always anticipated such an…
- Oct 4, 2016 08:21:57 PM RT @mike_pence: There's one clear choice in this election to create jobs and grow the American economy. #VPDebate https://t.co/cvv0cK6Fbt
- Oct 4, 2016 08:22:08 PM "@bigdog_joey: @realDonaldTrump @timkaine is so angry. Our @mike_pence looks great. kaine can't defend all those lies #makeamericagreatagain

- Oct 4, 2016 08:24:38 PM RT @TeamTrump: .@timkaine has a pay-to-play problem just like Crooked @HillaryClinton #VPDebates #BigLeagueTruth https://t.co/SPOIn8AN8m
- Oct 4, 2016 08:26:09 PM "@elisac006: @nycmia @realDonaldTrump I agree. Kaine looks like a fool!!"
- Oct 4, 2016 08:28:25 PM "@Jnelson52722: @realDonaldTrump @Susiesentinel Kaine looks like an evil crook out of the Batman movies"
- Oct 4, 2016 08:29:13 PM "@TeamTrump: .@mike_pence & @realDonaldTrump are PROVEN job creators and are prepared to bring JOBS BACK to the American people!
- Oct 4, 2016 08:30:39 PM .@mike_pence is doing a great job - so far, no contest!
- Oct 4, 2016 08:33:17 PM "@ARSenMissyIrvin: I want a "you're fired" president with people in Govt who are WASTING my tax $'s. @realDonaldTrump"
- Oct 4, 2016 08:33:50 PM "@carol_lcnixon67: @realDonaldTrump Kaine says Hillary and he have plans. She could care less what Kaine thinks."
- Oct 4, 2016 08:34:46 PM "@ifdanyt: @realDonaldTrump Loving @mike_pence he's so likeable and sensible. Kaine is just talking bull!
- Oct 4, 2016 08:35:06 PM "@bcuzimdamomma: @FreeDavidKing No she only gets #Americans killed #Benghazi - we need @realDonaldTrump #MAGA"
- Oct 4, 2016 08:35:25 PM "@aldonturnaolco1: @FrankLuntz @marthamaccallum @realDonaldTrump good!!"
- Oct 4, 2016 08:35:45 PM .@timkaine oversaw unemployment INCREASE by 179,249 while @mike_pence DECREASED unemployment in Indiana by 113,826…. https://t.co/wFQM8kg287
- Oct 4, 2016 08:36:09 PM RT @seanspicer: .@timkaine wants to tough on crime - fails to talk about defending rapists and murders #VPDebate
- Oct 4, 2016 08:37:00 PM RT @TeamTrump: Law enforcement officers bring communities together & keep us safe. @mike_pence & @realDonaldTrump RESPECT & stand by them!…
- Oct 4, 2016 08:37:38 PM "@GeeVeeM: @realDonaldTrump @Susiesentinel Pence is so prepared! He did his homework to outperform Kaine."
- Oct 4, 2016 08:40:09 PM RT @TeamTrump: "Police officers are the BEST of us. Law enforcement in this country is a force for GOOD." - @mike_pence #VPDebate #BigLeagu…

- Oct 4, 2016 08:46:08 PM .@HillaryClinton Sneers At Millions Of Average Americans. https://t.co/gEfURjRCfu #VPDebate #BigLeagueTruth
- Oct 4, 2016 08:50:48 PM I agree Mike - thank you to all of our law enforcement officers! #VPDebate "Police officers are the best of us..." @Mike_Pence
- Oct 4, 2016 08:52:36 PM WHAT THEY ARE SAYING ABOUT MIKE PENCE "DOMINATING" THE DEBATE: https://t.co/mUw9S5GgNM #VPDebate
- Oct 4, 2016 08:54:08 PM .@mike_pence and I will defeat #ISIS. https://t.co/oCIIDwtptV #VPDebate
- Oct 4, 2016 08:54:48 PM RT @GOP: In @timkaine's own words #Debates2016 https://t.co/PMngoKHUjA
- Oct 4, 2016 09:05:58 PM CLINTON'S FLAILING SYRIA POLICY WAS JUDGED A FAILURE: https://t.co/ICZxn7Q3vZ #VPDebate
- Oct 4, 2016 09:06:12 PM RT @TeamTrump: We need STRONG, BROAD-SHOULDERED leadership like @mike_pence & @realDonaldTrump in the White House! #VPDebate #BigLeagueTrut...
- Oct 4, 2016 09:09:58 PM .@timkaine is the ANTI-DEFENSE SENATOR. #VPDebate #BigLeagueTruth https://t.co/qWkvGFARA1
- Oct 4, 2016 09:12:23 PM ICYMI: PENCE: I RAN A STATE THAT WORKED; KAINE RAN A STATE THAT FAILED. https://t.co/XuWaueNkH0
- Oct 4, 2016 09:13:40 PM .@timkaine is wrong for defense: https://t.co/QN9qqoq1kH #BigLeagueTruth #VPDebate
- Oct 4, 2016 09:15:21 PM Sanctions Relief From Clinton-Obama Iran Nuclear Deal Likely Go to Terrorists: https://t.co/lM80JriF9k #BigLeagueTruth #VPDebate
- Oct 4, 2016 09:16:15 PM CLINTON'S CLOSE TIES TO PUTIN DESERVE SCRUTINY: https://t.co/wPYm5vQoyt #VPDebate
- Oct 4, 2016 09:17:20 PM RT @TeamTrump: .@HillaryClinton & @timkaine think you're #Deplorables & #BasementDwellers. @realDonaldTrump & @mike_pence think you're PATR...
- Oct 4, 2016 09:17:30 PM RT @TeamTrump: Obama-Clinton FAILED foreign policy: -Bad nuclear deal -Ransom payment to leading state sponsor of terror - Sharing classifie...
- Oct 4, 2016 09:19:54 PM CLINTON IS WEAK ON NORTH KOREA: https://t.co/8pRednmnFX #VPDebate

- Oct 4, 2016 09:22:24 PM .@HillaryClinton's Careless Use Of A Secret Server Put National Security At Risk: https://t.co/OiAEMnrGcy #VPDebate #BigLeagueTruth
- Oct 4, 2016 09:23:01 PM "@FLifeforce: @_CFJ_ @vine That is a reason to NOT Vote for Hillary Clinton. Vote for Liberty! Vote for @realDonaldTrump"
- Oct 4, 2016 09:26:41 PM Clinton's Top Aides Were Mired In Conflict Of Interest At The State Department: https://t.co/wWfdaECtVu #VPDebate #BigLeagueTruth
- Oct 4, 2016 09:27:18 PM "@Gsimmons03Ginny: @realDonaldTrump ..Kaine is awful, Trump and Pence are the ticket..no more lies, we are ready to see America Great Again!
- Oct 4, 2016 09:28:24 PM "@AnyoneTennis: @timkaine Cannot believe how often the moderator interrupts #Pence vs the other guy...so obvious @FoxNews" So true!
- Oct 4, 2016 09:30:59 PM RT @TeamTrump: .@timkaine's Abortion Flip-Flops: From Valuing The Sanctity of Life --> Pro-Abortion Demagogue #VPdebate https://t.co/aK4061...
- Oct 4, 2016 09:31:22 PM RT @TeamTrump: RT if you agree - @HillaryClinton & @timkaine are WRONG for America! #VPDebate #MAGA https://t.co/2MZfFzCo6c
- Oct 4, 2016 09:32:12 PM RT @mike_pence: History teaches us that weakness arouses evil. America needs to be strong on the world stage. #VPDebate https://t.co/FJ59o5...
- Oct 4, 2016 09:36:02 PM Mike Pence won big. We should all be proud of Mike!

- Oct 5, 2016 08:28:52 AM The constant interruptions last night by Tim Kaine should not have been allowed. Mike Pence won big!
- Oct 5, 2016 01:40:17 PM Beautiful morning- thank you @ICLV! https://t.co/xzJhrLgjHP
- Oct 5, 2016 01:53:09 PM About to begin a rally here in Henderson, Nevada. New Reuters poll just out- thank you! Join the MOVEMENT:... https://t.co/uvbntNsxGl
- Oct 5, 2016 04:11:34 PM Thank you Henderson, NV. This is a MOVEMENT like never seen before! Watch some of the rally via my Facebook page:... https://t.co/dNF8G4VUqY

- Oct 5, 2016 04:19:48 PM Bill Clinton is right: Obamacare is 'crazy', 'doesn't work' and 'doesn't make sense'. Thanks Bill for telling the truth.
- Oct 5, 2016 04:22:52 PM Thank you @SenJohnMcCain for your kind remarks on the important issue of PTSD and the dishonest media. Great to be in Arizona yesterday!
- Oct 5, 2016 05:02:58 PM 'Small business says Trump is their pick for president' https://t.co/tzVN9QgPFS
- Oct 5, 2016 05:57:42 PM EARLY VOTING: MN & IA already underway, more states coming up in the next week: OH, ME, AZ, IN — check w/local officials for details & VOTE!
- Oct 5, 2016 05:59:52 PM Thank you South Carolina! Everyone has to get out and VOTE on 11/8/16. #MakeAmericaGreatAgain... https://t.co/os7EmRCdPf
- Oct 5, 2016 06:19:43 PM Reuters polling just out- thank you! #MakeAmericaGreatAgain https://t.co/UMY6kOiSTu
- Oct 5, 2016 08:15:20 PM Amazing rally in Reno, Nevada- thank you. Make sure you get out on 11/8 & VOTE #TrumpPence16. Together, we will put... https://t.co/6gPJhb29xk
- Oct 5, 2016 08:32:48 PM Such a great honor! https://t.co/vt4AmLdkeP
- Oct 5, 2016 08:53:05 PM Nation's Immigration And Customs Enforcement Officers (ICE) Make First-Ever Presidential Endorsement: https://t.co/eO1UY5N9J1
- Oct 5, 2016 11:02:19 PM Pennsylvania poll just released. Two rallies there on Mon- join me! Ambridge: https://t.co/TujWDWcgd3 Wilkes-Barre:... https://t.co/TeIeCttUpP
- Oct 5, 2016 11:08:23 PM New Virginia poll- thank you! We are going to show the whole world that America is back – BIGGER, and BETTER, and S... https://t.co/2CikEXb0G7
- Oct 5, 2016 11:24:43 PM Praying for everyone in Florida. Hoping the hurricane dissipates, but in any event, please be careful.

- Oct 6, 2016 01:39:41 PM RT @IvankaTrump: Thank you Angie Phillips for inviting me to tour your plant Middletown Tube Works. #Ohio https://t.co/fUKiiEIBXT
- Oct 6, 2016 01:41:46 PM RT @DonaldJTrumpJr: Great group at our Victory Office in Columbus, Ohio. I'm incredibly grateful to have so many... https://t.co/rLJWCAGRlW

- Oct 6, 2016 03:45:38 PM Volunteer to be a Trump Election Observer. Sign up today! #MakeAmericaGreatAgain https://t.co/ZzFHlsWnh4
- Oct 6, 2016 03:47:49 PM 'Donald Trump: A President for All Americans' https://t.co/3lU2vrUE3t
- Oct 6, 2016 04:51:58 PM VOTE #TrumpPence16 on 11/8/16! https://t.co/12zAk8VmgK
- Oct 6, 2016 04:57:35 PM Thank you Tennessee! #MAGA https://t.co/OoDFmerQ5B
- Oct 6, 2016 05:54:16 PM New National Rasmussen Poll: https://t.co/BnAveA5OuP
- Oct 6, 2016 09:18:06 PM "@kevcirilli: Trump speaking in exact same tone he did in Waterville Valley on 12/1. The night I first realized he was gonna be GOP nominee"
- Oct 6, 2016 10:03:48 PM Thoughts & prayers with the millions of people in the path of Hurricane Matthew. Look out for neighbors, and listen… https://t.co/JqjyTiKicD

- Oct 7, 2016 11:19:43 PM Here is my statement. https://t.co/WAZiGoQqMQ

- Oct 8, 2016 09:48:22 AM Certainly has been an interesting 24 hours!
- Oct 8, 2016 02:40:48 PM The media and establishment want me out of the race so badly - I WILL NEVER DROP OUT OF THE RACE, WILL NEVER LET MY SUPPORTERS DOWN! #MAGA
- Oct 8, 2016 05:40:30 PM RT @atensnut: How many times must it be said? Actions speak louder than words. DT said bad things!HRC threatened me after BC raped me.
- Oct 8, 2016 05:41:10 PM RT @atensnut: Hillary calls Trump's remarks "horrific" while she lives with and protects a "Rapist". Her actions are horrific.
- Oct 8, 2016 07:38:52 PM Thank you to my great supporters in Wisconsin. I heard that the crowd and enthusiasm was unreal!

- Oct 9, 2016 08:00:51 AM Tremendous support (except for some Republican "leadership"). Thank you.
- Oct 9, 2016 08:17:02 AM EXCLUSIVE — Video Interview: Bill Clinton Accuser Juanita Broaddrick Relives Brutal Rapes: https://t.co/9j7f8VK9Md

- Oct 9, 2016 09:01:33 AM "@Jodygirl1010: @realDonaldTrump I am a woman who continues to support & stand with #Trump! #dtmag https://t.co/nFmY3FJuEf" Thank you.
- Oct 9, 2016 09:02:28 AM "@eericmyers: @realDonaldTrump "Republican leadership" should have only one job: Help elect the nominee we voted for, Donald J. Trump."
- Oct 9, 2016 09:03:24 AM "@CharleneOsbor17: @realDonaldTrump politicians don't count. It's the people. We are behind trump all the way to White House."
- Oct 9, 2016 09:04:28 AM "@maidaa17: @realDonaldTrump GOP traitors! Not supporting U is voting for her, destroying America.
- Oct 9, 2016 09:05:17 AM "@HenryLeledog: @realDonaldTrump This Black Democrat is on the "TRUMP TRAIN"!!"
- Oct 9, 2016 09:12:23 AM So many self-righteous hypocrites. Watch their poll numbers - and elections - go down!
- Oct 9, 2016 11:02:35 AM LA Times- USC Dornsife Sunday Poll: Donald Trump Retains 2 Point Lead Over Hillary: https://t.co/n05rul4Ycw
- Oct 9, 2016 12:16:50 PM Exclusive Video–Broaddrick, Willey, Jones to Bill's Defenders: 'These Are Crimes,' 'Terrified' of 'Enabler' Hillary https://t.co/DMfLsIbtU1
- Oct 9, 2016 05:26:27 PM The Palestinian terror attack today reminds the world of the grievous perils facing Israeli citizens....continued: https://t.co/d2Upx5FitC
- Oct 9, 2016 06:26:24 PM Join me on #FacebookLive as I conclude my final #debate preparations. https://t.co/gAbNvI8Fd7
- Oct 9, 2016 07:24:46 PM My team of deplorables will be taking over my Twitter account for tonight's #debate #MakeAmericaGreatAgain
- Oct 9, 2016 08:08:45 PM RT @TeamTrump: .@HillaryClinton just claimed she has a "positive, optimistic view" for America. #Debates https://t.co/hOWJYZbD7v
- Oct 9, 2016 08:11:26 PM It's this simple. "Make America Great Again." #debate #BigLeagueTruth
- Oct 9, 2016 08:11:51 PM RT @TeamTrump: .@realDonaldTrump is here to talk about the REAL issues #BigLeagueTruth #Debates2016 https://t.co/C5OF7HdJz6
- Oct 9, 2016 08:13:03 PM I'm not proud of my locker room talk. But this world has serious problems. We need serious leaders. #debate #BigLeagueTruth

- Oct 9, 2016 08:16:36 PM RT @TeamTrump: Quite simply, @HillaryClinton mistreats women. #BigLeagueTruth #Debate2016 https://t.co/zhgrulIctf https://t.co/wHtwtnCxxQ
- Oct 9, 2016 08:23:22 PM There's never been anyone more abusive to women in politics than Bill Clinton.My words were unfortunate-the Clintons' actions were far worse
- Oct 9, 2016 08:24:47 PM Donald J. Trump's History Of Empowering Women #BigLeagueTruth https://t.co/oY2YSPz7nB
- Oct 9, 2016 08:24:50 PM RT @TeamTrump: RT if you believe @HillaryClinton is the one who owes America an apology! #BigLeagueTruth #Debates https://t.co/KcmDedSUTw
- Oct 9, 2016 08:27:04 PM If I win-I am going to instruct my AG to get a special prosecutor to look into your situation bc there's never been anything like your lies.
- Oct 9, 2016 08:28:36 PM Basically nothing Hillary has said about her secret server has been true. #CrookedHillary
- Oct 9, 2016 08:29:17 PM Hillary's 33,000 deleted emails about her daughter's wedding. That's a lot of wedding emails. #debate
- Oct 9, 2016 08:29:45 PM ATTN: @HillaryClinton - Why did five of your staffers need FBI IMMUNITY?! #BigLeagueTruth #Debates
- Oct 9, 2016 08:32:10 PM Obama and Clinton told the same lie to sell #ObamaCare. #Debates2016 https://t.co/vhOLtHrR66
- Oct 9, 2016 08:35:26 PM We must repeal Obamacare and replace it with a much more competitive, comprehensive, affordable system. #debate #MAGA
- Oct 9, 2016 08:36:24 PM .@HillaryClinton : Bill "clarified" what he meant when calling Obamacare a "disaster." Actually "disaster" is pretty clear. #Debate
- Oct 9, 2016 08:36:40 PM RT @TeamTrump: We agree with Bill, ObamaCare is "the craziest thing in the world." #BigLeagueTruth #Debates2016 https://t.co/v2yo6pSYoB
- Oct 9, 2016 08:37:50 PM .@HillaryClinton is NOT above the law! #Debates2016 https://t.co/4arYZcGgYZ
- Oct 9, 2016 08:40:11 PM RT @realDonaldTrump: ATTN: @HillaryClinton - Why did five of your staffers need FBI IMMUNITY?! #BigLeagueTruth #Debates
- Oct 9, 2016 08:43:04 PM #CrookedHillary has FAILED all over the world! □ #BigLeagueTruth #Debates2016 https://t.co/dalk9JKcFg

- Oct 9, 2016 08:44:29 PM RT @TeamTrump: ONLY @realDonaldTrump will end what even @BillClinton called a CRAZY SYSTEM. #BigLeagueTruth #Debate https://t.co/cgoqZLDXDV
- Oct 9, 2016 08:45:16 PM .@HillaryClinton #ICYMI- "WE ARE NOT IN A NARRATIVE FIGHT." @Mike_Pence #MAGA https://t.co/FUQzXlyPwY
- Oct 9, 2016 08:48:19 PM .@HillaryClinton - ITS CALLED EXTREME VETTING! #Debates2016 https://t.co/ueq7cbOg9Y
- Oct 9, 2016 08:49:56 PM I hope when the MSM runs its "interruption counters" they consider the # of times the moderators interrupted me com… https://t.co/pHEjp8bZVP
- Oct 9, 2016 08:50:45 PM Hypocrite! @HillaryClinton claims she needs a "public and a private stance" in discussions with Wall Street banks. #Debate
- Oct 9, 2016 08:51:33 PM "YOU NEED BOTH A PUBLIC AND A PRIVATE POSITION" @HillaryClinton #Debates2016 https://t.co/oI2qi2HAdO
- Oct 9, 2016 08:57:38 PM We're going to cut taxes BIG LEAGUE for the middle class. She's raising your taxes and I'm lowering your taxes! https://t.co/ZwIkqNH2FX
- Oct 9, 2016 09:00:31 PM History lesson: There's a big difference between Hillary Clinton and Abraham Lincoln. For one, his nickname is Hone… https://t.co/A5JDkz1eCE
- Oct 9, 2016 09:02:28 PM RT @TeamTrump: .@HillaryClinton is RAISING your taxes to a disastrous level. @realDonaldTrump is going to LOWER your taxes - BIG LEAGUE! #D…
- Oct 9, 2016 09:03:01 PM RT @TeamTrump: #RattledHillary wants to talk about her 30 years in service. How about her 30 years of FLOPS↔FLOPS?! #BigLeagueTruth #Debat…
- Oct 9, 2016 09:06:41 PM Here are Hillary Clinton's "accomplishments" at the State Department. #Debates2016 #RattledHillary https://t.co/iouuqXYAdq
- Oct 9, 2016 09:07:58 PM The world is most peaceful, and most prosperous when America is strongest. https://t.co/Y2Dx7xyBBs
- Oct 9, 2016 09:08:51 PM RT @JasonMillerinDC: Is @realDonaldTrump debating Crooked @HillaryClinton or the moderators, @AC360 and @MarthaRaddatz? #rattledhillary
- Oct 9, 2016 09:09:51 PM This is the definition of ransom https://t.co/370piI2JLp

- Oct 9, 2016 09:11:26 PM We cannot let this evil continue! #Debates2016 https://t.co/f6BxYyRJID
- Oct 9, 2016 09:12:38 PM RT @TeamTrump: "We are going to be THRIVING again." - @realDonaldTrump #BigLeagueTruth #Debates2016 https://t.co/CaFOF7jS7k
- Oct 9, 2016 09:12:56 PM RT @TeamTrump: .@HillaryClinton had her chance and she BLEW IT. #BigLeagueTruth #Debates https://t.co/d2MI0DCg5Y
- Oct 9, 2016 09:14:59 PM RT @TeamTrump: It's hard to fight terrorism when you're making cash payments to the world's LARGEST state sponsor of TERROR. Under Trump: N…
- Oct 9, 2016 09:15:24 PM In my administration, EVERY American will be treated equally, protected equally, and honored equally #Debate #BigLeagueTruth
- Oct 9, 2016 09:18:37 PM FACT [check] on "red line" in Syria: HRC "I wasn't there." Fact: line drawn in Aug '12. HRC Secy of State til Feb '13. https://t.co/4yZjH3TR5B
- Oct 9, 2016 09:19:35 PM If @HillaryClinton is president, she'll be all talk and nothing will get done. #Debate #BigLeagueTruth
- Oct 9, 2016 09:20:35 PM We agree @POTUS- "SHE'LL (Hillary Clinton) SAY ANYTHING & CHANGE NOTHING. IT'S TIME TO TURN THE PAGE" -President Obama
- Oct 9, 2016 09:21:50 PM This country cannot take four more years of Barack Obama! #Debate
- Oct 9, 2016 09:23:21 PM @AC360: "How can you unite a country if you've written off tens of millions of Americans?" #Deplorables #BigLeagueTruth #Debate
- Oct 9, 2016 09:24:29 PM RT @DanScavino: WE LOVE OUR DEPLORABLES!!! #TrumpTrain #Debates2016 https://t.co/2Nt9ID3tV7
- Oct 9, 2016 09:24:50 PM Our country has the slowest growth since 1929. #BigLeagueTruth #debate
- Oct 9, 2016 09:25:04 PM RT @KellyannePolls: After a decent first debate, @HillaryClinton is back to form: pedantic, lawyerly, technocratic, (woefully untruthful) r…
- Oct 9, 2016 09:25:20 PM RT @TeamTrump: "She calls our people deplorable and irredeemable. I will be a president for ALL of our people." - @RealDonaldTrump #BigLeag…

- Oct 9, 2016 09:30:02 PM RT @DonaldJTrumpJr: Ironic since Hillary has gotten a lot more of that "dark unaccountable money" into her campaign. #debates
- Oct 9, 2016 09:30:17 PM Hypocrite: @HillaryClinton is the single biggest beneficiary of Citizens United in history, by far. #debate #bigleaguetruth
- Oct 9, 2016 09:31:41 PM MY PRO-GROWTH Econ Plan: Eliminate excessive regulations! Lean government! Lower taxes! #Debates … https://t.co/OchcnuSAgR
- Oct 9, 2016 09:41:32 PM RT @TeamTrump: It's US vs. them! @realDonaldTrump will fight for you! #BigLeagueTruth #Debates
- Oct 9, 2016 09:42:40 PM RT @DonaldJTrumpJr: Someone please fact check her coal comments. Give me a break. #debates
- Oct 9, 2016 09:55:25 PM RT @TeamTrump: RT if you agree @realDonaldTrump WON the #Debate- BIG LEAGUE! #MAGA https://t.co/EmwDZ32uAZ
- Oct 9, 2016 10:01:22 PM RT @mike_pence: Congrats to my running mate @realDonaldTrump on a big debate win! Proud to stand with you as we #MAGA.
- Oct 9, 2016 10:39:21 PM Thank you St. Louis, Missouri! #MakeAmericaGreatAgain https://t.co/2llBltf0mE https://t.co/wBmVxf1a9D

- Oct 10, 2016 12:08:21 PM Thank you for all of the great comments on the debate last night. Very exciting!
- Oct 10, 2016 12:22:22 PM Paul Ryan should spend more time on balancing the budget, jobs and illegal immigration and not waste his time on fighting Republican nominee
- Oct 10, 2016 02:14:00 PM CNN is the worst - fortunately they have bad ratings because everyone knows they are biased. https://t.co/oFRfNY2rUY
- Oct 10, 2016 02:22:56 PM Debate polls look great - thank you! #MAGA #AmericaFirst https://t.co/4peQ3Sswdz
- Oct 10, 2016 02:31:04 PM Wow, @CNN got caught fixing their "focus group" in order to make Crooked Hillary look better. Really pathetic and totally dishonest!
- Oct 10, 2016 05:31:52 PM Is this really America? Terrible! https://t.co/WiwC61PIFu
- Oct 10, 2016 08:33:32 PM Thank you Pennsylvania. This is a MOVEMENT like we have never seen before! #VoteTrumpPence16 on 11/8/16- together,… https://t.co/x0197JL5RU

- Oct 11, 2016 07:16:57 AM Despite winning the second debate in a landslide (every poll), it is hard to do well when Paul Ryan and others give zero support!
- Oct 11, 2016 08:05:53 AM Our very weak and ineffective leader, Paul Ryan, had a bad conference call where his members went wild at his disloyalty.
- Oct 11, 2016 09:00:38 AM It is so nice that the shackles have been taken off me and I can now fight for America the way I want to.
- Oct 11, 2016 09:15:10 AM With the exception of cheating Bernie out of the nom the Dems have always proven to be far more loyal to each other than the Republicans!
- Oct 11, 2016 09:48:29 AM Disloyal R's are far more difficult than Crooked Hillary. They come at you from all sides. They don't know how to win - I will teach them!
- Oct 11, 2016 10:25:11 AM Wow. Unbelievable. https://t.co/RcBPCcmwnD
- Oct 11, 2016 11:11:41 AM 13 states have voter registration deadlines TODAY: FL, OH, PA, MI, GA, TX, NM, IN, LA, TN, AR, KY, SC. Register: https://t.co/wAtnFpN6wL
- Oct 11, 2016 11:52:28 AM The very foul mouthed Sen. John McCain begged for my support during his primary (I gave, he won), then dropped me over locker room remarks!
- Oct 11, 2016 12:12:35 PM In Texas now, leaving soon for BIG rally in Florida!
- Oct 11, 2016 12:43:06 PM I hope people are looking at the disgraceful behavior of Hillary Clinton as exposed by WikiLeaks. She is unfit to run.
- Oct 11, 2016 01:29:59 PM Crooked's State Dept gave special attention to "Friends of Bill" after the Haiti Earthquake. Unbelievable! https://t.co/opP2l8ln0J
- Oct 11, 2016 01:43:35 PM DON'T LET HER FOOL US AGAIN. https://t.co/3QSoADFh7S
- Oct 11, 2016 03:56:33 PM VOTER REGISTRATION DEADLINES TODAY. You can register now at: https://t.co/HfihPEA3Sp and get out to… https://t.co/LlFdF0DRX4
- Oct 11, 2016 04:35:41 PM Thank you Texas! If you haven't registered to VOTE- today is your last day. Go to: https://t.co/HfihPEA3Sp & get ou… https://t.co/gxbDRD4x2k
- Oct 11, 2016 06:04:25 PM Wow, @CNN Town Hall questions were given to Crooked Hillary Clinton in advance of big debates against Bernie Sanders. Hillary & CNN FRAUD!

- Oct 11, 2016 07:56:06 PM Join me Thursday in Florida & Ohio! West Palm Beach, FL at noon: https://t.co/jwbZnQhxg9 Cincinnati, OH this 7:30pm: https://t.co/5w2UhalPIx
- Oct 11, 2016 11:04:47 PM Thank you Florida- a MOVEMENT that has never been seen before and will never be seen again. Lets get out &… https://t.co/t9XM9wFDZI

- Oct 12, 2016 07:59:05 AM Crooked Hillary Clinton likes to talk about the things she will do but she has been there for 30 years - why didn't she do them?
- Oct 12, 2016 08:46:43 AM Very little pick-up by the dishonest media of incredible information provided by WikiLeaks. So dishonest! Rigged system!
- Oct 12, 2016 09:00:48 AM PAY TO PLAY POLITICS. #CrookedHillary https://t.co/wjsl8ITVvk
- Oct 12, 2016 02:20:48 PM The people of Cuba have struggled too long. Will reverse Obama's Executive Orders and concessions towards Cuba until freedoms are restored.
- Oct 12, 2016 04:01:31 PM The MOVEMENT in Lakeland, Florida. Voter registration extended to 10/18. REGISTER ASAP @ https://t.co/HfihPERFgZ &… https://t.co/PygIlshrgv
- Oct 12, 2016 05:59:48 PM I will be in Cincinnati, Ohio tomorrow night at 7:30pm- join me! #OhioVotesEarly #VoteTrumpPence16 Tickets:… https://t.co/Bp5iHKbT2d

- Oct 13, 2016 08:09:45 AM Why didn't the writer of the twelve year old article in People Magazine mention the "incident" in her story. Because it did not happen!
- Oct 13, 2016 08:35:12 AM The phony story in the failing @nytimes is a TOTAL FABRICATION. Written by same people as last discredited story on women. WATCH!
- Oct 13, 2016 08:52:14 AM Join me in Ohio & Maine! Cincinnati, Ohio- tonight @ 7:30pm: https://t.co/XlHGD1VrMo Bangor, Maine - Saturday @ 3pm… https://t.co/DYHPQYBwpK
- Oct 13, 2016 10:27:27 AM Thank you! #MAGA #AmericaFirst https://t.co/fG313wjlKm
- Oct 13, 2016 10:28:34 AM I am making a major speech in West Palm Beach, Florida at noon. Tune in!

- Oct 13, 2016 03:04:14 PM Just left a great rally in Florida - now heading to Ohio for two more. Will be there soon.
- Oct 13, 2016 05:14:56 PM Great event in Columbus- taking off for Cincinnati now. Great new Ohio poll out- thank you! OHIO NBC/WSJ/MARIST POLL Trump 42% Clinton 41%
- Oct 13, 2016 05:50:04 PM "This is a crossroads in the history of our civilization that will determine whether or not We The People reclaim c... https://t.co/a84WMHpSYy
- Oct 13, 2016 05:51:17 PM Dem Gov. of MN. just announced that the Affordable Care Act (Obamacare) is no longer affordable. I've been saying this for years- disaster!
- Oct 13, 2016 06:28:02 PM Join me in Greensboro, North Carolina tomorrow at 2:00pm! #TrumpRally https://t.co/vpLryxCyoq https://t.co/dRra2AqayJ
- Oct 13, 2016 06:53:56 PM Join me live in Cincinnati, Ohio! #TrumpRally #MAGA https://t.co/MzqgNNVfZb
- Oct 13, 2016 08:18:07 PM Thank you to our U.S. Navy for protecting our country, both in times of peace & war. Together, WE WILL MAKE AMERICA... https://t.co/v23jCl4tEQ

- Oct 14, 2016 10:23:38 AM WHAT THEY ARE SAYING ABOUT THE CLINTON CAMPAIGN'S ANTI-CATHOLIC BIGOTRY: https://t.co/oRUlaT4zbn
- Oct 14, 2016 02:28:18 PM Thank you for your support Greensboro, North Carolina. Next stop - Charlotte! #MAGA https://t.co/3KWOl2ibaW https://t.co/jjde4W1hz2
- Oct 14, 2016 03:21:25 PM Make sure you're registered to vote! Let's #MakeAmericaGreatAgain! We can't afford more years of FAILURE! All info:... https://t.co/MgV5urLhB0
- Oct 14, 2016 08:14:08 PM Thank you Charlotte, North Carolina! We are going to have an AMAZING victory on November 8th...because this is all... https://t.co/A7Ql7KuMfT
- Oct 14, 2016 10:05:29 PM Thank you @TrumpWomensTour! #MakeAmericaGreatAgain https://t.co/R4oxaHpsAB

- Oct 15, 2016 05:51:40 AM 100% fabricated and made-up charges, pushed strongly by the media and the Clinton Campaign, may poison the minds of the American Voter. FIX!
- Oct 15, 2016 06:45:58 AM This election is being rigged by the media pushing false and unsubstantiated charges, and outright lies, in order to elect Crooked Hillary!
- Oct 15, 2016 07:17:06 AM Will be in Bangor, Maine today at 3pm- join me! #MAGA Tickets: https://t.co/NY7E1FBOB7 https://t.co/5TN2wvnR7J
- Oct 15, 2016 07:23:08 AM Hillary Clinton should have been prosecuted and should be in jail. Instead she is running for president in what looks like a rigged election
- Oct 15, 2016 10:37:39 AM Mr. Trump removing the broken teleprompter in North Carolina-in front of a massive crowd. He goes on&delivers the b... https://t.co/dyNxc1HDTW
- Oct 15, 2016 10:52:48 AM The truth is a beautiful weapon. https://t.co/P7FrFhicvw
- Oct 15, 2016 10:55:19 AM Landing in New Hampshire soon to talk about the massive drug problem there, and all over the country.
- Oct 15, 2016 01:11:06 PM The MOVEMENT in Portsmouth, New Hampshire w/ 7K supporters. THANK YOU! This is the biggest election of our lifetime... https://t.co/4otZyjYLc2
- Oct 15, 2016 01:29:22 PM Nothing ever happened with any of these women. Totally made up nonsense to steal the election. Nobody has more respect for women than me!
- Oct 15, 2016 05:49:18 PM The failing @nytimes reporters don't even call us anymore, they just write whatever they want to write, making up sources along the way!
- Oct 15, 2016 06:11:27 PM Thank you Bangor, Maine! Get out & #VoteTrumpPence16 on 11/8/16- and together we will MAKE AMERICA SAFE AND GREAT A... https://t.co/sUSh8v07MW
- Oct 15, 2016 07:03:06 PM A great day in New Hampshire and Maine. Fantastic crowds and energy! #MAGA
- Oct 15, 2016 07:03:33 PM Thank you for sharing Amy. https://t.co/StfzCeaQgH
- Oct 15, 2016 07:06:08 PM "@davidshiloach: @realDonaldTrump Go Mr. Trump! Israel is behind you!"

- Oct 16, 2016 06:14:00 AM Watched Saturday Night Live hit job on me.Time to retire the boring and unfunny show. Alec Baldwin portrayal stinks. Media rigging election!
- Oct 16, 2016 06:36:28 AM Polls close, but can you believe I lost large numbers of women voters based on made up events THAT NEVER HAPPENED. Media rigging election!
- Oct 16, 2016 07:31:40 AM Election is being rigged by the media, in a coordinated effort with the Clinton campaign, by putting stories that never happened into news!
- Oct 16, 2016 08:12:17 AM They let Crooked & the Gang off the hook for the crime, but it looks like the cover-up is just as bad. Unbelievable! https://t.co/eWjHoq20Dw
- Oct 16, 2016 08:15:03 AM A country that Crooked Hillary says has funded ISIS also gave Wild Bill $1 million for his birthday? SO CORRUPT! https://t.co/00s5tgsXrM
- Oct 16, 2016 11:07:08 AM Hillary's staff thought her email scandal might just blow over. Who would trust these people with national security? https://t.co/EvBCQoZRG2
- Oct 16, 2016 11:07:58 AM We've all wondered how Hillary avoided prosecution for her email scheme. Wikileaks may have found the answer. Obama! https://t.co/xF0wv8Oa8q
- Oct 16, 2016 12:01:12 PM The election is absolutely being rigged by the dishonest and distorted media pushing Crooked Hillary - but also at many polling places - SAD
- Oct 16, 2016 02:26:11 PM "The vast majority felt she should be prosecuted..." -- even senior FBI officials thought Crooked was guilty. https://t.co/AFtDs7HVlt
- Oct 16, 2016 03:13:36 PM Join me in Wisconsin tomorrow or Colorado on Tuesday! Green Bay- 6pm https://t.co/9L917nvCBX Colorado Springs- 1pm… https://t.co/972GWZDGEp
- Oct 16, 2016 03:47:23 PM The Democrats have a corrupt political machine pushing crooked Hillary Clinton. We have Paul Ryan, always fighting the Republican nominee!
- Oct 16, 2016 03:54:37 PM Paul Ryan, a man who doesn't know how to win (including failed run four years ago), must start focusing on the budget, military, vets etc.

- Oct 16, 2016 04:02:34 PM Finally, in the new ABC News/Washington Post Poll, Hillary Clinton is down 11 points with WOMEN VOTERS and the election is close at 47-43!
- Oct 16, 2016 05:15:33 PM Wow, interview released by Wikileakes shows "quid pro quo" in Crooked Hillary e-mail probe.Such a dishonest person - & Paul Ryan does zilch!
- Oct 16, 2016 05:29:46 PM Animals representing Hillary Clinton and Dems in North Carolina just firebombed our office in Orange County because we are winning @NCGOP
- Oct 16, 2016 05:34:35 PM ALL SAFE IN ORANGE COUNTY, NORTH CAROLINA. With you all the way, will never forget. Now we have to win. Proud of you all! @NCGOP

- Oct 17, 2016 07:15:50 AM Can't believe these totally phoney stories, 100% made up by women (many already proven false) and pushed big time by press, have impact!
- Oct 17, 2016 07:19:33 AM "@MarkSimoneNY: Watch Joe Biden's Long History Of Grabbing, Kissing and Groping Women Who Are Cringing: https://t.co/1iQCMd25Dz"
- Oct 17, 2016 07:24:47 AM "@PrisonPlanet: Trump accuser praised him in an email as recently as April! This is all yet another hoax. https://t.co/tcKzmIKpfS" Terrible
- Oct 17, 2016 07:28:57 AM "@RosieGray: Peter Thiel chooses now to give $1.25mil in support of Trump https://t.co/sNEEB2n2TE"
- Oct 17, 2016 07:33:48 AM Of course there is large scale voter fraud happening on and before election day. Why do Republican leaders deny what is going on? So naive!
- Oct 17, 2016 07:35:45 AM We have all got to come together and win this election. We can't have four more years of Obama (or worse!).
- Oct 17, 2016 09:58:32 AM WikiLeaks proves even the Clinton campaign knew Crooked mishandled classified info, but no one gets charged? RIGGED! https://t.co/FgGxDsS0a1
- Oct 17, 2016 10:12:51 AM BREAKING: "State Department's Kennedy pressured FBI to unclassify Clinton emails: FBI documents" https://t.co/GYYaneeysA
- Oct 17, 2016 10:20:17 AM Unbelievable. https://t.co/D7kpxlQPwU

- Oct 17, 2016 10:24:31 AM Voter fraud! Crooked Hillary Clinton even got the questions to a debate, and nobody says a word. Can you imagine if I got the questions?
- Oct 17, 2016 10:50:00 AM CORRUPTION CONFIRMED: FBI confirms State Dept. offered 'quid pro quo' to cover up classified emails https://t.co/A3mCNBLCsO
- Oct 17, 2016 11:12:24 AM Wow, new polls just came out from @CNN Great numbers, especially after total media hit job. Leading Ohio 48 - 44.
- Oct 17, 2016 12:50:57 PM Our thoughts are with the forces fighting ISIS in Iraq. We must never back down against this extreme radical Islami... https://t.co/oEoFIA8Rym
- Oct 17, 2016 02:11:28 PM "State Department official accused of offering 'quid pro quo' in Clinton email scandal" https://t.co/XkmcKeyRPJ
- Oct 17, 2016 02:23:15 PM "Journalists shower Hillary Clinton with campaign cash" https://t.co/qZPPX0LO4X https://t.co/NsWbJN01Uu
- Oct 17, 2016 02:31:22 PM New polls are good because the media has deceived the public by putting women front and center with made-up stories and lies, and got caught
- Oct 17, 2016 04:03:16 PM Crooked Hillary colluded w/FBI and DOJ and media is covering up to protect her. It's a #RiggedSystem! Our country d... https://t.co/kuinRTImVJ
- Oct 17, 2016 04:38:13 PM Join me in Colorado Springs, Colorado tomorrow at 1:00pm! #MAGA Tickets: https://t.co/ktFk8RuaUK
- Oct 17, 2016 04:44:31 PM Trump Virginia Office Announces Statewide TV Ad Strategy and Leadership Team: https://t.co/wVJZTjY8bA https://t.co/JUBRu4mqCE
- Oct 17, 2016 05:02:11 PM I will sign the first bill to repeal #Obamacare and give Americans many choices and much lower rates!
- Oct 17, 2016 05:27:00 PM My wife, Melania, will be interviewed tonight at 8:00pm by Anderson Cooper on @CNN. I have no doubt she will do very well. Enjoy!
- Oct 17, 2016 05:46:12 PM Yet more evidence of a media-rigged election: https://t.co/rVh4ocgx3r
- Oct 17, 2016 05:51:31 PM Get rich quick! Crooked Hillary Clinton's pay to play guide: https://t.co/uKh5sCFfrv

- Oct 17, 2016 08:42:15 PM EXCLUSIVE: FBI Agents Say Comey 'Stood In The Way' Of Clinton Email Investigation: https://t.co/6n63fHVvNo
- Oct 17, 2016 08:43:34 PM Donald J. Trump Ethics Reform Plan For Washington D.C. https://t.co/lKzas1SqUA
- Oct 17, 2016 09:07:55 PM Great night in WI. I'm going to fight for every person in this country who believes government should serve the PEO... https://t.co/UIKwWNmwR7

- Oct 18, 2016 06:32:52 AM "@THEREALMOGUL: 41% of American voters believe the election could be "stolen" from DonaldTrump due to widespread voter fraud. - Politico"
- Oct 18, 2016 10:33:18 AM I will Make Our Government Honest Again -- believe me. But first, I'm going to have to #DrainTheSwamp in DC. https://t.co/m1lMAQPnIb
- Oct 18, 2016 10:34:06 AM Pay-to-play. Collusion. Cover-ups. And now bribery? So CROOKED. I will #DrainTheSwamp. https://t.co/FNzMit7mD8
- Oct 18, 2016 10:36:44 AM If we let Crooked run the govt, history will remember 2017 as the year America lost its independence. #DrainTheSwamp https://t.co/VpYiO8CnXQ
- Oct 18, 2016 11:15:20 AM Nevada: A quick reminder that today is your last day to register to vote! https://t.co/ZnPgnu8vCS https://t.co/gF8ErCzTC1
- Oct 18, 2016 01:05:45 PM Hillary's Aides Urged Her to Take Foreign Lobbyist Donation And Deal With Attacks: https://t.co/o2qvr1myIZ
- Oct 18, 2016 01:25:42 PM It is time to #DrainTheSwamp in Washington, D.C! Vote Nov. 8th to take down the #RIGGED system! https://t.co/Ox9hH13Q9I
- Oct 18, 2016 01:43:15 PM FL, KS, ME, MD, MN, NJ, OR & WV! It's the LAST DAY to mail in voter reg forms. Get the forms at... https://t.co/CbpgL6wynY
- Oct 18, 2016 02:53:23 PM Thank you Colorado Springs. If I'm elected President I am going to keep Radical Islamic Terrorists out of our count... https://t.co/N74UK73RLK
- Oct 18, 2016 04:42:34 PM 'Trump rally disrupter was once on Clinton's payroll' https://t.co/75oLLuD4SI
- Oct 18, 2016 07:31:25 PM 'Clinton Campaign Tried to Limit Damage From Classified Info on Email Server' #DrainTheSwamp https://t.co/5j8WuKLL5o

- Oct 18, 2016 07:34:21 PM Hillary is the most corrupt person to ever run for the presidency of the United States. #DrainTheSwamp https://t.co/xA3YO8YzCq
- Oct 18, 2016 07:53:43 PM Time to #DrainTheSwamp in Washington, D.C. and VOTE #TrumpPence16 on 11/8/2016. Together, we will MAKE AMERICA SAFE… https://t.co/rVcjXdWxzp
- Oct 18, 2016 08:00:40 PM #DrainTheSwamp https://t.co/wqqPjxfBoJ
- Oct 18, 2016 08:28:27 PM 'Food Groups' – Emails Show Clinton Campaign Organized Potential VPs By Race And Gender: https://t.co/Qk1fOm1t8L

- Oct 19, 2016 10:34:12 AM It is time to #DrainTheSwamp! https://t.co/U2XeM2vDJK
- Oct 19, 2016 11:57:44 AM More Anti-Catholic Emails From Team Clinton: https://t.co/KYirBbYjp2 https://t.co/f8Z7olUvlM
- Oct 19, 2016 12:00:22 PM The State Department's 'shadow government' #DrainTheSwamp https://t.co/UtbqlGrYJh
- Oct 19, 2016 01:05:18 PM 'Scandals surround Clinton's gatekeeper at State' #DrainTheSwamp https://t.co/xxTTZeMYAc
- Oct 19, 2016 01:06:23 PM 'State works hard, and illegally, for Clinton' #DrainTheSwamp https://t.co/zXvUnJTKhF
- Oct 19, 2016 01:10:41 PM 'Dem Operative Who Oversaw Trump Rally Agitators Visited White House 342 Times' #DrainTheSwamp https://t.co/MO4SJaQMzo
- Oct 19, 2016 02:09:28 PM 'Top Hillary Adviser Mocked, Plotted Attacks on Pro-Sanders Civil Rights Leader' #DrainTheSwamp https://t.co/ER5FtjZgjw
- Oct 19, 2016 02:31:10 PM Join me in Delaware, Ohio tomorrow at 12:30pm! #DrainTheSwamp Tickets: https://t.co/TWRFY1ryY8 https://t.co/Zd1KjzlCtJ
- Oct 19, 2016 02:57:03 PM 'Hillary Clinton Deleted Emails With Her Email Server Technician' https://t.co/VvO4lTKsaj
- Oct 19, 2016 04:22:26 PM Obamacare premiums increasing 33% in Pennsylvania - a complete disaster. It must be repealed and replaced!… https://t.co/aDZEfcI7SM
- Oct 19, 2016 04:26:25 PM I am going to expand the definition of LOBBYIST - so we close all the LOOPHOLES! #DrainTheSwamp https://t.co/PBPrrEnfSK
- Oct 19, 2016 04:28:45 PM I will issue a lifetime ban against senior executive branch officials lobbying on behalf of a FOREIGN GOVERNMENT!… https://t.co/GQizTdCdFC

- Oct 19, 2016 05:14:24 PM Join my team tonight at 8:30pmE! https://t.co/ZqJmf4yB87 https://t.co/ncJXn6fURF
- Oct 19, 2016 05:16:07 PM 'Over 250,000 to Lose Health Insurance in Battleground North Carolina Due to #Obamacare' https://t.co/18McSKO2AY
- Oct 19, 2016 05:57:24 PM UNBELIEVABLE! Clinton campaign contractor caught in voter-fraud video is a felon who visited White House 342 times: https://t.co/qQdsMHAtkT
- Oct 19, 2016 07:48:32 PM I will be handing over my Twitter account to my team of deplorables for tonight's #debate #MakeAmericaGreatAgain
- Oct 19, 2016 07:57:04 PM Tune in at https://t.co/Q08Kp4w3oT and get the word out #BigLeagueTruth #Debate Help us spread the TRUTH, stop the… https://t.co/GS9YQYzF6x
- Oct 19, 2016 07:58:56 PM This is an incredible MOVEMENT- WE are going to take our country BACK! #November8th #BigLeagueTruth #Debate https://t.co/BT4VgYTkBr
- Oct 19, 2016 08:04:57 PM Ready to lead. Ready to Make America Great Again. #Debate #MAGA
- Oct 19, 2016 08:07:40 PM Hillary Clinton wants to create the most liberal Supreme Court in history #debate #DrainTheSwamp https://t.co/fKJBNXvluh
- Oct 19, 2016 08:10:23 PM The 2nd Amendment is under siege. We need SCOTUS judges who will uphold the US Constitution. #Debate #BigLeagueTruth
- Oct 19, 2016 08:11:14 PM .@realDonaldTrump will PROTECT and DEFEND the Constitution #Debate #BigLeagueTruth #DrainTheSwamp https://t.co/mNTio22WK8
- Oct 19, 2016 08:13:09 PM .@HillaryClinton lists litany of ways she plans to restrict gun rights. 2A will not survive a Hillary presidency. #Debate #BigLeagueTruth
- Oct 19, 2016 08:14:12 PM It is so imperative that we have the right justices. #DrainTheSwamp #Debates #BigLeagueTruth https://t.co/RHryqijTlu
- Oct 19, 2016 08:17:32 PM .@realDonaldTrump is PRO-LIFE, PRO-FAMILY #BigLeagueTruth #Debates2016 https://t.co/nOqbDBMQFM
- Oct 19, 2016 08:18:09 PM #SecondAmendment #2A #Debates https://t.co/QbOaf8Dlhs
- Oct 19, 2016 08:22:19 PM Drugs are pouring into this country. If we have no border, we have no country. That's why ICE endorsed me. #Debate #BigLeagueTruth

- Oct 19, 2016 08:22:56 PM Hillary Clinton will use American tax dollars to provide amnesty for thousands of illegals. I will put... https://t.co/ZpV33TfbR6
- Oct 19, 2016 08:23:45 PM One of my first acts as President will be to deport the drug lords and then secure the border. #Debate #MAGA
- Oct 19, 2016 08:24:20 PM Plain & Simple: We should only admit into this country those who share our VALUES and RESPECT our people. https://t.co/TlJo8dtVjZ
- Oct 19, 2016 08:27:37 PM .@RealDonaldTrump wants a SAFE America w/ stronger borders, no amnesty, and an END to sanctuary cities. He is... https://t.co/7Ha00c77Gb
- Oct 19, 2016 08:28:08 PM Hillary is too weak to lead on border security-no solutions, no ideas, no credibility.She supported NAFTA, worst deal in US history. #Debate
- Oct 19, 2016 08:28:41 PM TRUMP & CLINTON ON IMMIGRATION #Debate #BigLeagueTruth https://t.co/OP4c7Jc8Ad
- Oct 19, 2016 08:29:22 PM Moderator: Hillary paid $225,000 by a Brazilian bank for a speech that called for "open borders." That's a quote! #Debate #BigLeagueTruth
- Oct 19, 2016 08:32:46 PM Hey @POTUS - WE AGREE! #BigLeagueTruth #DrainTheSwamp https://t.co/WnofYy60fc
- Oct 19, 2016 08:34:49 PM Hillary has called for 550% more Syrian immigrants, but won't even mention "radical Islamic terrorists." #Debate... https://t.co/Rf48XkZWbu
- Oct 19, 2016 08:37:37 PM .@HillaryClinton- you have failed, failed, and failed. #BigLeagueTruth Time to #DrainTheSwamp! https://t.co/c2EiyU8XKK
- Oct 19, 2016 08:38:47 PM Moderator: Hillary plan calls for more regulation and more government spending. #Debate #BigLeagueTruth
- Oct 19, 2016 08:39:29 PM .@HillaryClinton has been a foreign policy DISASTER for the American people. I will #MakeAmericaStrongAgain #Debate... https://t.co/tj6PWM5r1J
- Oct 19, 2016 08:39:40 PM .@HillaryClinton talking about jobs? Remember what she promised upstate New York. #BigLeagueTruth #Debates https://t.co/SmjNuHi7XB
- Oct 19, 2016 08:42:53 PM .@HillaryClinton's tax hikes will CRUSH our economy. I will cut taxes -- BIG LEAGUE. https://t.co/EtA1tBnrNG https://t.co/NgMDP4wilI

- Oct 19, 2016 08:44:31 PM #BigLeagueTruth https://t.co/jhDLwFez3v
- Oct 19, 2016 08:44:36 PM This is what we can expect from #CrookedHillary. More Taxes. More Spending. #BigLeageTruth #DrainTheSwamp #Debates https://t.co/5yxnt0gNUF
- Oct 19, 2016 08:45:17 PM #CrookedHillary's plan will add $1.15 TRILLION in new taxes. We cannot afford her! #DrainTheSwamp #Debate https://t.co/jpjKY1IiQh
- Oct 19, 2016 08:45:45 PM I will renegotiate NAFTA. If I can't make a great deal, we're going to tear it up. We're going to get this economy running again. #Debate
- Oct 19, 2016 08:46:54 PM THE CHOICE IS CLEAR! #BigLeagueTruth #DrainTheSwamp https://t.co/kGx88PEpmX
- Oct 19, 2016 08:49:00 PM #CrookedHillary gives Obama an "A" for an economic recovery that's the slowest since WWII... #BigLeagueTruth... https://t.co/wVMFHdyCu2
- Oct 19, 2016 08:50:20 PM .@HillaryClinton has been doing this for THIRTY YEARS....where has she been? #BigLeagueTruth
- Oct 19, 2016 08:51:15 PM Crooked Hillary has never created a job in her life. We will create 25 million jobs. Think she can do that? Not a c... https://t.co/64Kll0Dl7K
- Oct 19, 2016 08:51:49 PM Our country is stagnant. We've lost jobs and business. We don't make things anymore b/c of the bill Hillary's husband signed and she blessed
- Oct 19, 2016 08:53:57 PM .@realDonaldTrump will do more in the first 30 days in office than Hillary has done in the last 30 years! #Debate... https://t.co/GunaVggS0N
- Oct 19, 2016 08:55:42 PM Brought to you by @HillaryClinton & her campaign- in Chicago, Illinois. #BigLeagueTruth #DrainTheSwamp https://t.co/10iUBOcECp
- Oct 19, 2016 08:56:01 PM #CrookedHillary is nothing more than a Wall Street PUPPET! #BigLeagueTruth #Debate https://t.co/skhBWG6AQ3
- Oct 19, 2016 08:56:54 PM Crooked's camp incited violence at my rallies. These incidents weren't "spontaneous" - like she claimed in Benghazi! https://t.co/aCzOgFIfZ2

- Oct 19, 2016 08:57:00 PM I will do more in the first 30 days in office than Hillary has done in the last 30 years! #Debate #BigLeagueTruth https://t.co/tuNQePu8Vk
- Oct 19, 2016 08:58:34 PM She'll say anything and change NOTHING! #MAGA #BigLeagueTruth https://t.co/6E767Uw6Dj
- Oct 19, 2016 08:59:07 PM .@HillaryClinton loves to lie. America has had enough of the CLINTON'S! It is time to #DrainTheSwamp! Debates https://t.co/3Mz4T7qTTR
- Oct 19, 2016 09:02:15 PM Moderator: "Respectfully, you won't answer the pay-to-play question." #Debate #BigLeagueTruth
- Oct 19, 2016 09:02:53 PM Crooked @HillaryClinton's foundation is a CRIMINAL ENTERPRISE. Time to #DrainTheSwamp! https://t.co/89eOMTsIjt #BigLeagueTruth #Debate
- Oct 19, 2016 09:06:52 PM LIVE FACT-CHECK: Trump's RIGHT. The Clinton Foundation has taken MILLIONS from the Middle East. #DrainTheSwamp https://t.co/Kgcaf5tdTM
- Oct 19, 2016 09:08:08 PM Crooked's top aides were MIRED in massive conflicts of interests at the State Dept. We MUST #DrainTheSwamp https://t.co/a4p7q9jZde #Debate
- Oct 19, 2016 09:11:33 PM You should give the money back @HillaryClinton! #DrainTheSwamp https://t.co/m0LKHRUoHz
- Oct 19, 2016 09:14:29 PM Hillary says "take back Mosul?" We would have NEVER lost Mosul- if it wasn't for #CrookedHillary. #DrainTheSwamp https://t.co/TmsY0ApFLQ
- Oct 19, 2016 09:16:25 PM HILLARY FAILED ALL OVER THE WORLD. #BigLeagueTruth X LIBYA X SYRIA X IRAN X IRAQ X ASIA PIVOT X RUSSIAN RESET X BENGHAZI… https://t.co/H1UH0svtt2
- Oct 19, 2016 09:19:22 PM Bernie Sanders on HRC: Bad Judgement. John Podesta on HRC: Bad Instincts. #BigLeagueTruth #Debate
- Oct 19, 2016 09:21:19 PM #BigLeagueTruth #DrainTheSwamp https://t.co/eoBiXFPc5f
- Oct 19, 2016 09:21:32 PM I opposed going into Iraq. Hillary voted for it. As with everything else she's supported, it was a DISASTER. https://t.co/Um5WJXWfBZ
- Oct 19, 2016 09:22:13 PM "Her instincts are suboptimal." https://t.co/PRCHvRtPVA

- Oct 19, 2016 09:24:44 PM What They Are Saying About @realDonaldTrump's GREAT Debate and @HillaryClinton's Bad Performance… https://t.co/1O86a49vJZ
- Oct 19, 2016 09:26:24 PM After Crooked @HillaryClinton allowed ISIS to rise, she now claims she'll defeat them? LAUGHABLE! Here's my plan: https://t.co/FzRMObNQVn
- Oct 19, 2016 09:27:31 PM I WILL DEFEAT ISIS. THEY HAVE BEEN AROUND TOO LONG! What has our leadership been doing? #DrainTheSwamp https://t.co/tU0iW3Gi9v
- Oct 19, 2016 09:28:17 PM USA has the greatest business people in the world but we let political hacks negotiate our deals. We need change! #BigLeagueTruth #Debate
- Oct 19, 2016 09:29:29 PM Together we can save American JOBS, American LIVES, and AMERICAN FUTURES! #Debates https://t.co/2Yfd0Omn4X
- Oct 19, 2016 09:31:07 PM The economy cannot take four more years of these same failed policies. #BigLeagueTruth #DrainTheSwamp https://t.co/o8g2E5xXy6
- Oct 19, 2016 09:31:45 PM ISIS has infiltrated countries all over Europe by posing as refugees, and @HillaryClinton will allow it to happen h… https://t.co/MmeW2qsTQh
- Oct 19, 2016 09:32:37 PM .@realDonaldTrump is going to cut taxes BIG LEAGUE -- Crooked is going to raise taxes BIG LEAGUE! #DrainTheSwamp… https://t.co/41X9Qjy0RJ
- Oct 19, 2016 09:32:57 PM We have to repeal & replace #Obamacare! Look at what is doing to people! #DrainTheSwamp https://t.co/fsv7P11mWV
- Oct 19, 2016 09:34:01 PM HILLARY'S HEALTH CARE POLICIES #DrainTheSwamp #Debate https://t.co/t1Sr8dk2Xi
- Oct 19, 2016 09:39:25 PM I started this campaign to Make America Great Again. That's what I'm going to do. #MAGA #debate
- Oct 19, 2016 09:40:23 PM We cannot take four more years of Barack Obama and that's what you'll get if you vote for Hillary. #BigLeagueTruth
- Oct 19, 2016 09:47:21 PM The era of division is coming to an end. We will create a new future of #AmericanUnity. First, we need to… https://t.co/mZUFP24Bgh
- Oct 19, 2016 09:51:39 PM Join my team over on my Facebook page- live now! #Debates https://t.co/vpDVQfO58A https://t.co/5v1tWzHrxq

- Oct 19, 2016 09:59:26 PM That was really exciting. Made all of my points. MAKE AMERICA GREAT AGAIN!
- Oct 19, 2016 11:06:44 PM Great poll - thank you America! Once we #DrainTheSwamp, together we will #MAGAUS#Debate https://t.co/SvcjmrsHKD
- Oct 19, 2016 11:10:06 PM Join the MOVEMENT to #MAGA! https://t.co/3KWOl2ibaW https://t.co/V84qfN4oz1
- Oct 19, 2016 11:18:06 PM The Washington Times Presidential Debate Poll: TRUMP 77% (18,290) CLINTON 17% (4,100) #DrainTheSwamp #Debate https://t.co/wsgsf5nv6H
- Oct 19, 2016 11:27:27 PM Totally dishonest Donna Brazile chokes on the truth. Highly illegal! Watch: https://t.co/Rs5brj31bA https://t.co/FYoRo6MUjX

- Oct 20, 2016 02:14:05 AM Just landed in Ohio. Thank you America- I am honored to win the final debate for our MOVEMENT. It is time to… https://t.co/ivdjRzL6wZ
- Oct 20, 2016 08:27:41 AM Thank you America! #MAGA Rasmussen National Poll Donald Trump 43% Hillary Clinton 40% https://t.co/n4eZ3qpcjg
- Oct 20, 2016 09:55:50 AM Why didn't Hillary Clinton announce that she was inappropriately given the debate questions - she secretly used them! Crooked Hillary.
- Oct 20, 2016 10:52:38 AM If elected POTUS - I will stop RADICAL ISLAMIC TERRORISM in this country! In order to do this, we need to… https://t.co/45Vyk6z18m
- Oct 20, 2016 12:33:10 PM Thank you Delaware County, Ohio! Remember- either we WIN this election, or we are going to LOSE this country!… https://t.co/ntDRTzYOqi
- Oct 20, 2016 01:25:34 PM Want access to Crooked Hillary? Don't forget - it's going to cost you! #DrainTheSwamp #PayToPlay https://t.co/qjMBZkEnK9
- Oct 20, 2016 02:27:22 PM On behalf of the entire family, we would truly be honored to have your vote! Let's #MakeAmericaGreatAgain #EarlyVote https://t.co/tv7ihuvmfS
- Oct 20, 2016 02:51:39 PM #ICYMI - OHIO RALLY! Watch here: https://t.co/0qAjfOcu6Y https://t.co/fpShHiXI31
- Oct 20, 2016 02:51:59 PM UPCOMING RALLIES - JOIN ME! TOMORROW Fletcher, NC @ 12pm. https://t.co/uASvA4Gd4r SATURDAY Cleveland, OH @ 7pm. https://t.co/hre7Foxqpo

- Oct 20, 2016 03:06:18 PM 'Trump won the third debate'
https://t.co/Wh52fyLNRz
- Oct 20, 2016 03:26:01 PM Crooked took MILLIONS from oppressive ME
countries. Will she give the $$$ back? Probably not. Don't forget her slog...
https://t.co/esLgql0Gg8
- Oct 20, 2016 03:30:01 PM Crooked Hillary promised 200k jobs in NY and
FAILED. We'll create 25M jobs when I'm president, and I will DELIVER!
https://t.co/NgyCkEH7Xn
- Oct 20, 2016 03:52:15 PM When Obama took office in 2009 employer-
provided premiums cost $13,375. Today they are $18,142. Thanks, Obama.
- Oct 20, 2016 04:59:48 PM In addition to those without health coverage- those
that have disastrous #Obamacare are seeing MASSIVE PREMIUM INCR...
https://t.co/J7ldXmUmJm
- Oct 20, 2016 05:08:15 PM Hillary & Obama's Broken Promises.
#RepealObamacare https://t.co/oz24r2xW7G

- Oct 21, 2016 10:23:39 AM Huma calls it a "MESS," the rest of us call it
CORRUPT! WikiLeaks catches Crooked in the act - again. #DrainTheSwamp
https://t.co/juvdLIJPWu
- Oct 21, 2016 12:34:35 PM The results are in on the final debate and it is almost
unanimous, I WON! Thank you, these are very exciting times.
- Oct 21, 2016 12:43:39 PM Great crowd in Fletcher, North Carolina- thank you!
Heading to Johnstown, Pennsylvania now! Get out on November 8th...
https://t.co/IG5KhKIz3W
- Oct 21, 2016 01:54:00 PM #CrookedHillary "was at center of negotiating
$12M commitment from King Mohammed VI of Morocco" to Clinton Fdn.
https://t.co/HWOQ7jQWY2
- Oct 21, 2016 01:58:20 PM A top Clinton Foundation official said he could
name "500 different examples" of conflicts of interest. https://t.co/rtWhdYOyq7
- Oct 21, 2016 04:07:54 PM Great crowd in Johnstown, Pennsylvania- thank
you. Get out & VOTE on 11/8! Watch the MOVEMENT in PA. this afternoon...
https://t.co/DUMlbSkVeY
- Oct 21, 2016 05:10:57 PM VERY IRONIC: "In 2010 video, Clinton lectured
underlings on cybersecurity and guarding 'sensitive information'"
https://t.co/dL7VDMqSLy

- Oct 21, 2016 05:14:47 PM 'Clinton Campaign And Harry Reid Worked With New York Times To Smear State Dept Watchdog' Time to #DrainTheSwamp! https://t.co/0VDdGdpCTg
- Oct 21, 2016 05:30:14 PM "{Crooked Hillary Clinton} created this mess, and she knows it." #DrainTheSwamp https://t.co/3cBNYjl5CD https://t.co/sjwkuq3nkk
- Oct 21, 2016 05:36:04 PM Donna Brazile Shreds Obama Economy - Acting DNC chair says 'people are more in despair about how things are' https://t.co/LQNbISSoX0
- Oct 21, 2016 05:46:37 PM WikiLeaks reveals Clinton camp's work with 'VERY friendly and malleable reporters' #DrainTheSwamp #CrookedHillary https://t.co/bcYLslrxi0
- Oct 21, 2016 05:50:00 PM #CrookedHillary sending U.S. intelligence info. to Podesta's hacked email is 'unquestionably an OPSEC violation' https://t.co/z58aeo4CO7
- Oct 21, 2016 07:58:02 PM Thank you to the great crowd of supporters in Newtown, Pennsylvania. Get out & VOTE on 11/8/16. Lets #MAGA! Watch:… https://t.co/eb6XuMlbFW
- Oct 21, 2016 09:41:07 PM Governor @Mike_Pence and I will be in Cleveland, Ohio tomorrow night at 7pm - join us! #MAGA Tickets:… https://t.co/kfJv5Po0x6
- Oct 21, 2016 10:23:34 PM Just returned from Pennsylvania where we will be bringing back their jobs. Amazing crowd. Will be going back tomorrow, to Gettysburg!
- Oct 21, 2016 10:33:54 PM The media refuses to talk about the three new national polls that have me in first place. Biggest crowds ever - watch what happens!

- Oct 22, 2016 06:35:18 AM "@jensen4law: Best way to pay Hillary back for what she did to @BernieSanders #DNCleak is a DonaldTrump LANDSLIDE https://t.co/Ha8o5wCyGh"
- Oct 22, 2016 06:37:58 AM "@AZTRUMPTRAIN: I #Voted for DonaldTrump! #Arizona #Economy #Immigration #Jobs #Veterans #BorderControl #Trade… https://t.co/0BJk9BwkfW"

- Oct 22, 2016 09:01:18 AM Will be in Cleveland, Ohio w/ @mike_pence tonight- join us: https://t.co/hre7FofPxQ Naples, Florida-tomorrow @ 6pm: https://t.co/Oax06JVzv1
- Oct 22, 2016 09:20:56 AM Landing in Pennsylvania now. Great new poll this morning, thank you. Lets #DrainTheSwamp and #MakeAmericaGreatAgain… https://t.co/BV2RFavG84
- Oct 22, 2016 12:49:56 PM Thank you Gettysburg, Pennsylvania! #DrainTheSwamp https://t.co/jWgLcxDji7
- Oct 22, 2016 12:54:11 PM Crooked Hillary Clinton Tops Middle East Forum's 'Islamist Money List' https://t.co/JC25rNtx6G
- Oct 22, 2016 01:18:43 PM Change has to come from outside our very broken system. #MAGA https://t.co/OH9Lvo3R7K
- Oct 22, 2016 02:54:40 PM In order to #DrainTheSwamp & create a new GOVERNMENT of, by, & for the PEOPLE, I need your VOTE! Go to https://t.co/HfihPERFgZ- LET'S #MAGA!
- Oct 22, 2016 01:40:31 PM Today I introduced my Contract with the American Voter - our economy will be STRONG & our people will be SAFE.… https://t.co/Sa6XUfueU4
- Oct 22, 2016 04:09:56 PM Unbelievable crowd of supporters in Virginia Beach, Virginia. Thank you! Next stop - Cleveland, Ohio.… https://t.co/CN3sdX5ft1
- Oct 22, 2016 04:34:44 PM Hillary Clinton: 'Architect of failure' #DrainTheSwamp #CrookedHillary https://t.co/b5HqsGrc7N
- Oct 22, 2016 06:08:25 PM Just arrived in Cleveland, Ohio- join Governor @Mike_Pence and I now, LIVE via: https://t.co/SS58ChFTNy
- Oct 22, 2016 09:05:01 PM 'Huma Abedin told Clinton her secret email account caused problems' https://t.co/i4zN2QzKnf
- Oct 22, 2016 09:21:32 PM 'Trump lays out policies for first 100 days in White House' https://t.co/OrwOIFJuSz
- Oct 22, 2016 09:26:32 PM WikiLeaks: 'Clinton-Kaine Even Lied About Timing of Veep Pick' https://t.co/e1NVdpSfNr
- Oct 22, 2016 10:00:32 PM Thank you for the massive turnout tonight- Cleveland, Ohio! Get out & VOTE #TrumpPence16 on 11/8. Watch rally here:… https://t.co/XuJZeJwSGk

- Oct 23, 2016 07:53:51 AM "If you can't run your own house you certainly can't run the White House" A statement made by Mrs. Obama about Crooked Hillary Clinton
- Oct 23, 2016 09:04:01 AM Well, Iran has done it again. Taken two of our people and asking for a fortune for their release. This doesn't happen if I'm president!
- Oct 23, 2016 11:23:50 AM Thank you Las Vegas Review Journal! EDITORIAL: 'Donald Trump for president' https://t.co/uH5GH7Bhe0 via @reviewjournal
- Oct 23, 2016 11:30:03 AM Former Prosecutor: The Clintons Are So Corrupt, Everything 'They Touch Turns To Molten Lead' https://t.co/5Eyfi092vn
- Oct 23, 2016 11:34:32 AM Remember - get out on November 8th & VOTE #TrumpPence16. It is time to #DrainTheSwamp -- this is our last chance! https://t.co/bnGcJUt7UL
- Oct 23, 2016 12:56:43 PM Join me in Naples, Florida this evening at 6:00pm! Tickets: https://t.co/Oax06JVzv1 https://t.co/g9LBxI1dJ8
- Oct 23, 2016 02:08:42 PM #CrookedHillary #PayToPlay https://t.co/BT1Nv0ZMYg
- Oct 23, 2016 06:40:14 PM The attack on Mosul is turning out to be a total disaster. We gave them months of notice. U.S. is looking so dumb. VOTE TRUMP and WIN AGAIN!
- Oct 23, 2016 07:05:36 PM Thank you Naples, Florida! Get out and VOTE #TrumpPence16 on 11/8. Lets #MakeAmericaGreatAgain! Full Naples rally… https://t.co/5ZbteSJ00K
- Oct 23, 2016 07:07:47 PM 'Clinton Charity Got Up To $56 Million From Nations That Are Anti-Women, Gays' #CrookedHillary https://t.co/eHsuBdi8XM
- Oct 23, 2016 09:25:05 PM 'Clinton Ally Aided Campaign of FBI Official's Wife' https://t.co/U0w99gfyKE

- Oct 24, 2016 07:00:02 AM Wow, just came out on secret tape that Crooked Hillary wants to take in as many Syrians as possible. We cannot let this happen - ISIS!
- Oct 24, 2016 07:44:29 AM Major story that the Dems are making up phony polls in order to suppress the the Trump . We are going to WIN!

- Oct 24, 2016 08:05:36 AM Why has nobody asked Kaine about the horrible views emanated on WikiLeaks about Catholics? Media in the tank for Clinton but Trump will win!
- Oct 24, 2016 09:17:35 AM We are winning and the press is refusing to report it. Don't let them fool you- get out and vote! #DrainTheSwamp on November 8th!
- Oct 24, 2016 09:46:16 AM Get out to VOTE on 11/8/2016- and we will #DrainTheSwamp! RASMUSSEN NATIONAL Trump 43% Clinton 41% https://t.co/jIOR7Bq816
- Oct 24, 2016 10:55:44 AM Departing Farmers Round Table in Boynton Beach, Florida. Get out & VOTE- lets #MAGA! EARLY VOTING BY FL. COUNTY:… https://t.co/MgJxNbxRga
- Oct 24, 2016 11:04:52 AM 'The Clinton Foundation's Most Questionable Foreign Donations' #PayToPlay #DrainTheSwamp https://t.co/IkeqMRjX5z
- Oct 24, 2016 11:35:59 AM Leaving West Palm Beach, Florida now - heading to St. Augustine for a 3pm rally. Will be in Tampa at 7pm - join me:… https://t.co/eLunEQRxZq
- Oct 24, 2016 11:37:58 AM 'Hillary Clinton Had Gun Control Supporters Planted In Town Hall Audience' https://t.co/1GVq74iW8a
- Oct 24, 2016 01:30:43 PM Honored to receive an endorsement from @SJSOPIO - thank you! Together, we are going to MAKE AMERICA SAFE & GREAT AG… https://t.co/PSTcOei5t1
- Oct 24, 2016 02:01:18 PM Join me LIVE on my Facebook page in St. Augustine, Florida! Lets #DrainTheSwamp & MAKE AMERICA GREAT AGAIN!… https://t.co/mPzVrcaR9L
- Oct 24, 2016 03:39:38 PM THANK YOU St. Augustine, Florida! Get out and VOTE! Join the MOVEMENT - and lets #DrainTheSwamp! Off to Tampa now!… https://t.co/zgwqhy2jBX
- Oct 24, 2016 04:15:23 PM Join me tomorrow in Sanford or Tallahassee, Florida! Sanford at 3pm: https://t.co/PZENw9Kheg Tallahassee at 6pm: https://t.co/WKI69e1bqD
- Oct 24, 2016 04:50:25 PM 'Democratic operative caught on camera: Hillary PERSONALLY ordered 'Donald Duck' troll campaign that broke the law' https://t.co/sTreHAfYUH
- Oct 24, 2016 04:52:36 PM Peter Navarro: 'Trump the Bull vs. Clinton the Bear' #DrainTheSwamp https://t.co/mQRkfMG80j

- Oct 24, 2016 07:33:07 PM My contract with the American voter will restore honesty, accountability & CHANGE to Washington! #DrainTheSwamp https://t.co/sbVwctT1Sj
- Oct 24, 2016 08:27:16 PM Thank you Bobby Bowden for the intro tonight and your support! I hope I can do as well for Florida as you have done! https://t.co/Vx5iltoaXj
- Oct 24, 2016 08:43:26 PM Record crowd in Tampa, Florida- thank you! We will WIN FLORIDA, #DrainTheSwamp in Washington D.C. and MAKE AMERICA… https://t.co/IpSUYnXcp6

- Oct 25, 2016 09:31:19 AM As election looms, some bad news for Clinton, Democrats: https://t.co/7aWWVQPjTo
- Oct 25, 2016 09:33:57 AM #Obamacare premiums are about to SKYROCKET --- again. Crooked H will only make it worse. We will repeal & replace! https://t.co/fY1REYV4rK
- Oct 25, 2016 09:39:09 AM Key Obamacare premiums to jump 25% next year: https://t.co/TCdHEdPQDG
- Oct 25, 2016 09:44:51 AM Get out and vote! I am your voice and I will fight for you! We will make America great again! https://t.co/XXvLRlhSaz
- Oct 25, 2016 10:20:18 AM #ObamacareFail https://t.co/Mb0YW1rg6g
- Oct 25, 2016 10:21:37 AM #ObamacareFail https://t.co/5Zvsys8j5w
- Oct 25, 2016 10:22:35 AM Obamacare is a disaster! Time to repeal & replace! #ObamacareFail https://t.co/xDPhVczf1g
- Oct 25, 2016 11:10:59 AM #ObamacareFail https://t.co/90Aixp25Oc
- Oct 25, 2016 11:20:43 AM Obamacare is a disaster - as I've been saying from the beginning. Time to repeal & replace! #ObamacareFail https://t.co/5CvoMbVceT
- Oct 25, 2016 01:27:06 PM Truly honored to receive the first ever presidential endorsement from the Bay of Pigs Veterans Association. #MAGA… https://t.co/aRdlFkVjAx
- Oct 25, 2016 03:43:45 PM Obamacare is a disaster. Rates going through the sky - ready to explode. I will fix it. Hillary can't! #ObamacareFailed
- Oct 25, 2016 04:03:40 PM 'Obama Warned Of Rigged Elections In 2008.' Time to #DrainTheSwamp https://t.co/AkczH8l0FJ https://t.co/7mIkwAHTuV
- Oct 25, 2016 04:36:51 PM Get your ballots in Colorado - I will see you soon -- and we will win! #MakeAmericaGreatAgain https://t.co/oDLvZg7MLk

- Oct 25, 2016 04:54:05 PM I have met & spent a lot of time with families @ The Remembrance Project. I will fight for them everyday!... https://t.co/Ot6vQGqVW0
- Oct 25, 2016 05:01:50 PM REPEAL AND REPLACE!!! #ObamaCareInThreeWords
- Oct 25, 2016 05:28:43 PM Thank you Sanford, Florida. Get out & VOTE #TrumpPence16! #ICYMI- watch this afternoons rally here:... https://t.co/zVXrScClfd
- Oct 25, 2016 06:31:58 PM Thank you Tallahassee, Florida! A beautiful evening with the MOVEMENT! Get out & VOTE! #ICYMI- watch here: https://t.co/GDKhwrCa9R

- Oct 26, 2016 06:02:53 AM REPEAL AND REPLACE OBAMACARE!
- Oct 26, 2016 01:49:49 PM JOIN ME IN OHIO TOMORROW! Springfield-1pm: https://t.co/YcbpSigtva Toledo-4pm: https://t.co/BOJH0l1CZz Geneva-7pm... https://t.co/7qbIRel33u
- Oct 26, 2016 04:59:15 PM Hillary said she was under sniper fire (while surrounded by USSS.) Turned out to be a total lie. She is not fit to... https://t.co/hBIrGj2ll6
- Oct 26, 2016 08:52:45 PM Thank you Charlotte, North Carolina. Great afternoon! #ICYMI - I delivered a speech on urban renewal. Full speech:... https://t.co/ga6DQZrIR0
- Oct 26, 2016 08:57:51 PM Beautiful evening in Kinston, North Carolina - thank you! Get out and VOTE!! You can watch tonight's rally here:... https://t.co/x7wtERl55d

- Oct 27, 2016 07:16:35 AM RT @EricTrump: Tune into @GMA right now to catch a great interview with my father & the entire family! US #VoteTrumpPence16 https://t.co/Sa...
- Oct 27, 2016 07:17:57 AM Obamacare is a disaster. We must REPEAL & REPLACE. Tired of the lies, and want to #DrainTheSwamp? Get out & VOTE... https://t.co/jOelj829Pg
- Oct 27, 2016 08:01:12 AM A lot of call-ins about vote flipping at the voting booths in Texas. People are not happy. BIG lines. What is going on?

- Oct 27, 2016 09:08:15 AM 'WikiLeaks Drip-Drop Releases Prove One Thing: There's No Nov. 8 Deadline on Clinton's Dishonesty and Scandals' https://t.co/MfRy3Nvd4F
- Oct 27, 2016 09:10:38 AM Ron Fournier: "Clinton Used Secret Server To Protect #CircleOfEnrichment" https://t.co/4OGP3tPxyp
- Oct 27, 2016 09:12:42 AM "Clinton Foundation's Fundraisers Pressed Donors to Steer Business to Former President" https://t.co/PlFILR6JCn
- Oct 27, 2016 09:32:59 AM I agree, @MMFlint- To all Americans, I see you & I hear you. I am your voice. Vote to #DrainTheSwamp w/ me on 11/8. https://t.co/D7nBwkogBb
- Oct 27, 2016 09:44:46 AM JOIN ME! #MAGA TODAY: Springfield, OH Toledo, OH Geneva, OH FRIDAY: Manchester, NH Lisbon, ME Cedar Rapids, IA https://t.co/kv624y9UOm
- Oct 27, 2016 09:49:59 AM Inside 'Bill Clinton Inc.': Hacked memo reveals intersection of charity and personal income. #DrainTheSwamp! https://t.co/UfDVzeSDfd
- Oct 27, 2016 12:45:20 PM Join me live in Springfield, Ohio! https://t.co/LREA7WRmOx
- Oct 27, 2016 02:26:05 PM Thank you Springfield, Ohio. Get out and #VoteTrumpPence16! #ICYMI - watch here: https://t.co/dEoXV6oS3b... https://t.co/RNgCUUqO4X
- Oct 27, 2016 03:27:44 PM #ICYMI: I agree- To all Americans, I see you & I hear you. I am your voice. Vote to #DrainTheSwamp with me on 11/8.... https://t.co/P2edj2MoXy
- Oct 27, 2016 04:02:09 PM Join me in Cedar Rapids, Iowa tomorrow at 7:00pm! #MAGA https://t.co/QWaEJpzvKN https://t.co/CniHGkjp0v
- Oct 27, 2016 04:07:48 PM Join me live in Toledo, Ohio. Time to #DrainTheSwamp & #MAGA! https://t.co/NU39Mmlh1T
- Oct 27, 2016 05:05:00 PM I delivered a speech in Charlotte, North Carolina yesterday. I appreciate all of the feedback & support. Lets #MAGA... https://t.co/aI2HtiRUzr
- Oct 27, 2016 05:23:56 PM I will be interviewed on @oreillyfactor tonight at 8:00 P.M. Enjoy!
- Oct 27, 2016 05:27:20 PM "@KeithRowland: People in Arizona just got a taste of Obamacare with a 116% increase in premiums. @realDonaldTrump" Repeal and replace!

- Oct 27, 2016 05:37:22 PM Crooked Hillary launched her political career by letting terrorists off the hook. #DrainTheSwamp… https://t.co/BLMkZQ8svK
- Oct 27, 2016 07:14:46 PM Join @TeamTrump on Facebook & watch tonight's rally from Geneva, Ohio- our 3rd rally of the day. #AmericaFirst #MAGA https://t.co/ZqJmf4QcwH
- Oct 27, 2016 08:47:08 PM Thank you Geneva, Ohio. If I am elected President, I am going to keep RADICAL ISLAMIC TERRORISTS OUT of our countr… https://t.co/a7t5QN2iqW

- Oct 28, 2016 09:48:59 AM RT @DRUDGE_REPORT: WSJ: Grifters-in-Chief… https://t.co/mPFocMuBgu
- Oct 28, 2016 10:27:05 AM "@Jmoschetti1363: @Johnatsrs1949 FBI must be outraged that their hands r tied she has no regard or t secret service, FBI, or (Dallas)police"
- Oct 28, 2016 10:39:01 AM Join me tonight in Cedar Rapids, Iowa at 7pm: https://t.co/QWaEJpR79n Phoenix, Arizona tomorrow night at 3pm: https://t.co/0LjE9qbNLh
- Oct 28, 2016 10:53:19 AM If my people said the things about me that Podesta & Hillary's people said about her, I would fire them out of self respect. "Bad instincts"
- Oct 28, 2016 12:04:59 PM Heading to New Hampshire. Will be talking about the disaster known as ObamaCare!
- Oct 28, 2016 12:23:39 PM RT @DRUDGE_REPORT: WSJ: The Cold Clinton Reality… https://t.co/udWj5mXcA6
- Oct 28, 2016 12:24:08 PM Just out: Neera Tanden, Hillary Clinton adviser said, "Israel is depressing." I think Israel is inspiring!
- Oct 28, 2016 02:20:22 PM We must not let #CrookedHillary take her CRIMINAL SCHEME into the Oval Office. #DrainTheSwamp https://t.co/GtPkj4xIz6
- Oct 28, 2016 08:28:46 PM Just landed in Iowa - speaking soon!
- Oct 28, 2016 08:30:55 PM "@piersmorgan: BOMBSHELL: FBI reopening its investigation into HillaryClinton's email server after new discovery!
- Oct 28, 2016 11:04:25 PM Thank you Maine, New Hampshire and Iowa. The waiting is OVER! The time for change is NOW! We are going to… https://t.co/HVPjw6qeQ2

- Oct 28, 2016 11:11:17 PM Join me in Colorado at 12pm tomorrow - or Arizona at 3pm! TICKETS: Golden: https://t.co/Eix7SspO2Z Phoenix:… https://t.co/pheYCksxq0

- Oct 29, 2016 08:08:22 AM I am in Colorado - big day planned - but nothing can be as big as yesterday!
- Oct 29, 2016 10:37:26 AM "@DeplorableCBTP: "In my mind, #DonaldTrump is the only way out of this mess." - #PhilRobertson of TV's #DuckDynasty" Thank you Phil!
- Oct 29, 2016 11:54:54 AM Tomorrow! Las Vegas, NV- 11a: https://t.co/KluudKImvn Greeley, CO- 4p: https://t.co/JYimiIbqKB Albuquerque, NM- 7p: https://t.co/7SCol4vQlM
- Oct 29, 2016 12:02:04 PM #ObamacareFail https://t.co/iusXk4n9w7
- Oct 29, 2016 02:56:49 PM Departing Golden, CO. for Arizona now - after an unbelievable rally. Watch here: https://t.co/zNzmWuZPiV Overflow: https://t.co/93L7JfdmXJ
- Oct 29, 2016 03:02:16 PM So nice - great Americans outside Trump Tower right now. Thank you! https://t.co/34ATTgICTz
- Oct 29, 2016 08:23:28 PM THANK YOU Phoenix, Arizona! Time for new POWERFUL leadership. Just imagine what WE can accomplish in our first 100… https://t.co/gqZLLxcenk
- Oct 29, 2016 08:36:25 PM Great day in Colorado & Arizona. Will be in Nevada, Colorado and New Mexico tomorrow - join me! Tickets:… https://t.co/vMPTsLXsCT

- Oct 30, 2016 08:55:06 AM We are now leading in many polls, and many of these were taken before the criminal investigation announcement on Friday - great in states!
- Oct 30, 2016 09:04:06 AM Hillary and the Dems loved and praised FBI Director Comey just a few days ago. Original evidence was overwhelming, should not have delayed!
- Oct 30, 2016 09:26:30 AM Wow, Twitter, Google and Facebook are burying the FBI criminal investigation of Clinton. Very dishonest media!
- Oct 30, 2016 12:58:52 PM See you tomorrow Michigan! Grand Rapids, MI tomorrow at noon: https://t.co/xFPRNEPNZ5 Warren, MI tomorrow at 3pm:… https://t.co/UHRTgS88B5

- Oct 30, 2016 02:05:31 PM Thank you Las Vegas, Nevada- I love you! Departing for Greeley, Colorado now. Get out & VOTE! #ICYMI- watch here:… https://t.co/uIloPRtEn9
- Oct 30, 2016 06:19:09 PM Thank you Greeley, CO! REAL change means restoring honesty to the govt. Our plan will END govt. corruption! Watch:… https://t.co/qz5AL7zvp4
- Oct 30, 2016 06:23:26 PM "@slh: I follow Mr.Trump at all of his rallies by watching them on https://t.co/biseaBESvS. He is a lion-hearted warrior, who inspires hope
- Oct 30, 2016 09:52:08 PM Beautiful rally in Albuquerque, New Mexico this evening - thank you. Get out & VOTE! #DrainTheSwamp Watch rally:… https://t.co/K2RSgt2Zh5
- Oct 30, 2016 10:59:48 PM Join me tomorrow in Michigan! Grand Rapids at 12pm: https://t.co/xFPRNF7pnF Warren at 3pm: https://t.co/DREwbH7ZVd https://t.co/iyXwiP0rvd

- Oct 31, 2016 11:00:19 AM 'Hillary's Two Official Favors To Morocco Resulted In $28 Million For Clinton Foundation' #DrainTheSwamp https://t.co/6qOO7FZSvF
- Oct 31, 2016 11:38:13 AM Legendary basketball coach Bobby Knight who has 900+ wins, many championships and a gold medal will be introducing… https://t.co/aHltfG7U4I
- Oct 31, 2016 01:20:00 PM $25 Million+ raised online in just one week! RECORD WEEK. #DrainTheSwamp Today we set a bigger record. Contribute >https://t.co/CZ1QmzCxwO
- Oct 31, 2016 02:00:42 PM Thank you Grand Rapids, Michigan! #ICYMI- watch: https://t.co/2mDQCs6coB https://t.co/gN7BYfLD9K
- Oct 31, 2016 02:08:25 PM #ObamacareFail #HillarycareFail https://t.co/gaXOWVI0Xa
- Oct 31, 2016 03:49:56 PM Wow! I hear you Warren, Michigan. Streaming live - join us America. It is time to DRAIN THE SWAMP! Watch: https://t.co/pjXELwc5E1

November, 2016

- Nov 1, 2016 05:31:46 AM Look at the way Crooked Hillary is handling the e-mail case and the total mess she is in. She is unfit to be president. Bad judgement!
- Nov 1, 2016 06:55:47 AM Wow, now leading in @ABC /@washingtonpost Poll 46 to 45. Gone up 12 points in two weeks, mostly before the Crooked Hillary blow-up!
- Nov 1, 2016 07:01:11 AM Crooked Hillary should not be allowed to run for president. She deleted 33,000 e-mails AFTER getting a subpoena from U.S. Congress. RIGGED!
- Nov 1, 2016 08:35:47 AM JOIN ME TOMORROW IN FLORIDA! MIAMI•12pm https://t.co/A3X71Q6sG2 ORLANDO•4pm https://t.co/6BqTVoty5C PENSACOLA•7p... https://t.co/kNzrAeuLZO
- Nov 1, 2016 09:14:09 AM So terrible that Crooked didn't report she got the debate questions from Donna Brazile, if that were me it would have been front page news!

- Nov 1, 2016 12:24:18 PM #ICYMI: Governor @mike_pence and I were in Valley Forge, Pennsylvania today. You can watch it here:... https://t.co/6GWgmCV23Z
- Nov 1, 2016 01:44:44 PM .@DarrellIssa is a very good man. Help him win his congressional seat in California.
- Nov 1, 2016 04:15:42 PM 'Kept me out of jail': Top DOJ official involved in Clinton probe represented her campaign chairman: https://t.co/QUZn97CEOq
- Nov 1, 2016 04:16:57 PM Trump promises special session to repeal Obamacare: https://t.co/wTCd108yrV
- Nov 1, 2016 04:20:04 PM Hillary Advisers Wanted Her To Avoid Supporting Israel When Talking To Democrats: https://t.co/y7m8iVU173
- Nov 1, 2016 04:28:55 PM Mika Brzezinski: Dem Criticism of Comey Reinforcing Idea 'There's Something There' https://t.co/EvBp0xESPN https://t.co/QIDBiDpat8
- Nov 1, 2016 04:46:18 PM 'Podesta urged Clinton team to hand over emails after use of private server emerged' https://t.co/NYvVmoA8wl
- Nov 1, 2016 04:57:54 PM WikiLeaks emails reveal Podesta urging Clinton camp to 'dump' emails. Time to #DrainTheSwamp! https://t.co/P3ajiACiXK
- Nov 1, 2016 06:07:25 PM RT @DanScavino: Join @realDonaldTrump LIVE in Wisconsin with Gov. @ScottWalker, @MayorRGiuliani, @Reince & Coach Bobby Knight! LIVE: https:...
- Nov 1, 2016 07:32:51 PM Thank you for your incredible support Wisconsin and Governor @ScottWalker! It is time to #DrainTheSwamp & #MAGA!... https://t.co/gKBkKmTudn
- Nov 1, 2016 10:43:15 PM Join me in Florida tomorrow! MIAMI•12pm https://t.co/A3X71Q6sG2 ORLANDO•4pm https://t.co/6BqTVoty5C PENSACOLA•7p... https://t.co/kEQuuJeO1B

- Nov 2, 2016 05:35:56 AM You can change your vote in six states. So, now that you see that Hillary was a big mistake, change your vote to MAKE AMERICA GREAT AGAIN!
- Nov 2, 2016 06:00:30 AM I am going to repeal and replace ObamaCare. We will have MUCH less expensive and MUCH better healthcare. With Hillary, costs will triple!

- Nov 2, 2016 07:47:48 AM Crooked Hillary Clinton deleted 33,000 e-mails AFTER they were subpoenaed by the United States Congress. Guilty - cannot run. Rigged system!
- Nov 2, 2016 08:11:06 AM "@Ravenrantz: #Billygraham's grand daughter #SupportsTrump https://t.co/sKz1SPHzDZ" So nice, thank you Cissy Graham Lynch!!!!
- Nov 2, 2016 08:18:39 AM "@PYNance: Evangelical women live at #trumptower @pdpryor1 @CissieGLynch @SaysGabrielle https://t.co/k5kGXPR2WA"
- Nov 2, 2016 09:37:03 AM Praying for the families of the two Iowa police who were ambushed this morning. An attack on those who keep us safe is an attack on us all.
- Nov 2, 2016 12:15:30 PM Thank you Miami! In 6 days, we are going to WIN the GREAT STATE of FLORIDA - and we are going to win back the White… https://t.co/MKYPOp0MeD
- Nov 2, 2016 01:57:07 PM "It pays to have friends in high places- like the Justice Department. Clearly the Clintons do." #DrainTheSwamp! https://t.co/KZXB4B156M
- Nov 2, 2016 01:58:34 PM Clinton camp fumed when surrogate told supporters Clinton planned to betray labor on TPP post-election: https://t.co/ZZjbGDZP7e
- Nov 2, 2016 02:09:28 PM After decades of lies and scandal, Crooked Hillary's corruption is closing in. #DrainTheSwamp! https://t.co/YivCacmkKq
- Nov 2, 2016 04:30:24 PM Thank you Orlando, Florida! We are just six days away from delivering justice for every forgotten man, woman and ch… https://t.co/LPXBQZ5AXt
- Nov 2, 2016 06:34:23 PM #MakeAmericaGreatAgain #6Days https://t.co/eHTGIEpFsm
- Nov 2, 2016 10:44:39 PM RT @T_Lineberger: Thanks @IvankaTrump for coming to help win Michigan! More people here than a Hillary rally with less than 24 hours notice…
- Nov 2, 2016 10:55:49 PM Thank you Arlene! We will MAKE AMERICA SAFE AND GREAT AGAIN! #ImWithYou #DrainTheSwamp https://t.co/tSI0YP2LL9

- Nov 3, 2016 07:27:27 AM My wife, Melania, will be speaking in Pennsylvania this afternoon. So exciting, big crowds! I will be watching from North Carolina.

- Nov 3, 2016 07:34:14 AM ObamaCare is a total disaster. Hillary Clinton wants to save it by making it even more expensive. Doesn't work, I will REPEAL AND REPLACE!
- Nov 3, 2016 10:19:12 AM Looking at Air Force One @ MIA. Why is he campaigning instead of creating jobs & fixing Obamacare? Get back to work for the American people!
- Nov 3, 2016 02:25:37 PM Watching my beautiful wife, Melania, speak about our love of country and family. We will make you all very proud.... https://t.co/DiKmSnTlC2
- Nov 3, 2016 03:52:52 PM Thank you Concord, North Carolina! When WE win on November 8th, we are going to Washington, D.C. and we are going t... https://t.co/7j4MBn1Waf
- Nov 3, 2016 03:55:36 PM #CrookedHillary is unfit to serve. https://t.co/bSuGvInNF1
- Nov 3, 2016 04:28:01 PM Join me in Wilmington, Ohio tomorrow at 4:00pm! It is time to #DrainTheSwamp! Tickets: https://t.co/eCLECM3nmW https://t.co/sb5irRxjxJ
- Nov 3, 2016 06:30:17 PM RT @PaulaReidCBS: .@CBSNews confirms FBI found emails on #AnthonyWeiner computer, related to Hillary Clinton server, that are "new" & not p...
- Nov 3, 2016 09:35:08 PM There is no challenge too great, no dream outside of our reach! Thank you Selma, North Carolina! #ICYMI, watch here... https://t.co/8uIrhgYRsl

- Nov 4, 2016 10:32:31 AM Join me today in Wilmington, Ohio at 4pm: https://t.co/eCLECMkYLw Tomorrow- Tampa, Florida at 10am: https://t.co/N9380pVmuM
- Nov 4, 2016 11:17:22 AM "The Clinton Campaign at Obama Justice" #DrainTheSwamp https://t.co/LZkvFc071z
- Nov 4, 2016 11:26:19 AM RT @TeamTrump: Mrs. Saucier's son is in prison for having classified info on an unsecured device. @HillaryClinton did FAR WORSE & is runnin...
- Nov 4, 2016 11:28:36 AM Clinton Aides: 'Definitely' Not Releasing Some HRC Emails: https://t.co/GY5pGKaDoW

- Nov 4, 2016 01:46:42 PM Thank you NH! We will end illegal immigration, stop the drugs, deport all criminal aliens&save American lives! Watc… https://t.co/uxcazVkb32
- Nov 4, 2016 01:56:15 PM 'ICE OFFICERS WARN HILLARY IMMIGRATION PLAN WILL UNLEASH GANGS, CARTELS & DRUG VIOLENCE NATIONWIDE'… https://t.co/09aSrBwQrv
- Nov 4, 2016 02:07:20 PM If Obama worked as hard on straightening out our country as he has trying to protect and elect Hillary, we would all be much better off!
- Nov 4, 2016 03:33:12 PM Join me live in Wilmington, Ohio! https://t.co/nQ2p4EulLu
- Nov 4, 2016 06:14:59 PM Thank you Ohio! VOTE so we can replace Obamacare and save healthcare for every family in the United States! Watch:… https://t.co/7CH8ZnGdOa
- Nov 4, 2016 06:31:28 PM The only thing that can stop this corrupt machine is YOU. The only force strong enough to save our country is US.… https://t.co/7dcSHOkuzc
- Nov 4, 2016 06:50:57 PM Join me live in Hershey, Pennsylvania! #MakeAmericaGreatAgain LIVE: https://t.co/xEj6sZpb12 https://t.co/JWfGI1vlwW
- Nov 4, 2016 06:57:37 PM Join me in Denver, Colorado tomorrow at 9:30pm! Tickets: https://t.co/LJYGIK7Mri
- Nov 4, 2016 09:52:56 PM Thank you Hershey, Pennsylvania. Get out & VOTE on November 8th & we will #MAGA! #RallyForRiley #ICYMI, watch here… https://t.co/maWukVBTr8

- Nov 5, 2016 08:33:10 AM MAKE AMERICA GREAT AGAIN!
- Nov 5, 2016 11:45:05 AM Join me in Denver, Colorado tonight at 9:30pm: https://t.co/LJYGIK7Mri NEW- Scranton, Pennsylvania Monday @ 5:30pm: https://t.co/BcErCtsPdF
- Nov 5, 2016 03:06:21 PM Thank you for the incredible support this morning Tampa, Florida! #ICYMI- watch here: https://t.co/q43kHf7MoE https://t.co/1GscFNaV4L
- Nov 5, 2016 03:13:34 PM Thank you Wilmington, North Carolina. We are 3 days away from the CHANGE you've been waiting for your entire life!… https://t.co/6ZJZRBfLST

- Nov 5, 2016 04:27:32 PM Watch Coach Mike Ditka- a great guy and supporter tonight at 8pmE on #WattersWorld with @jessebwatters @FoxNews.
- Nov 5, 2016 04:38:01 PM 'Must Act Immediately': Clinton Charity Lawyer Told Execs They Were Breaking The Law https://t.co/hsi4qhqTV1
- Nov 5, 2016 04:39:44 PM Top Clinton Aides Bemoan Campaign 'All Tactics,' No Vision: https://t.co/mHYvQtIq78
- Nov 5, 2016 04:46:34 PM #DrainTheSwamp! https://t.co/z68vGp9Bvf
- Nov 5, 2016 07:19:18 PM JOIN ME TOMORROW! MINNESOTA • 2pm https://t.co/WcgLh4prS7 MICHIGAN • 6pm https://t.co/9BqGVKNNrt VIRGINIA • 9:30p... https://t.co/A1oVhCrT6t
- Nov 5, 2016 07:20:16 PM Join me live in Reno, Nevada! https://t.co/T4bf1hrxaA https://t.co/EPqRXHa1CM
- Nov 5, 2016 09:03:20 PM Thank you Reno, Nevada. NOTHING will stop us in our quest to MAKE AMERICA SAFE AND GREAT AGAIN! #AmericaFirst... https://t.co/A4eeHoCbGS
- Nov 5, 2016 11:27:00 PM RT @DanScavino: Join @realDonaldTrump LIVE in Denver, Colorado via his #Facebook page- we are here!! #MakeAmericaGreatAgain US https://t.c...

- Nov 6, 2016 01:08:32 AM Great night in Denver, Colorado- thank you! Together, we will MAKE AMERICA GREAT AGAIN! #ICYMI watch rally here:... https://t.co/LbvNHo6T2k
- Nov 6, 2016 12:06:08 PM Van Jones: 'There Is A Crack in the Blue Wall' — It Has to Do With Trade: https://t.co/BvEF9cC7o7
- Nov 6, 2016 01:09:44 PM RT @IvankaTrump: Thank you New Hampshire!US https://t.co/pdnxXq2jgy
- Nov 6, 2016 02:26:58 PM Thank you Iowa - Get out & #VoteTrumpPence16! https://t.co/HfihPERFgZ https://t.co/QsukELQmKb
- Nov 6, 2016 06:08:58 PM MONDAY - 11/7/2016 Scranton, Pennsylvania at 5:30pm. https://t.co/BcErCtsPdF Grand Rapids, Michigan at 11pm.... https://t.co/pgFMLp0173
- Nov 6, 2016 06:42:28 PM Thank you Minnesota! It is time to #DrainTheSwamp & #MAGA! #ICYMI- watch: https://t.co/fVThC7yIL6 https://t.co/e8SaXiJrxj

- Nov 6, 2016 07:09:41 PM Our American comeback story begins 11/8/16. Together, we will MAKE AMERICA SAFE & GREAT again for everyone! Watch:… https://t.co/ek8Cn3CgTr
- Nov 6, 2016 08:52:18 PM Thank you Michigan! This is a MOVEMENT that will never be seen again- it's our last chance to #DrainTheSwamp! Watch… https://t.co/cSdGkCFYRL
- Nov 6, 2016 11:14:31 PM Thank you Pennsylvania- I am forever grateful for your amazing support. Lets MAKE AMERICA GREAT AGAIN! #MAGA… https://t.co/qbcJZAzw6z

- Nov 7, 2016 01:35:39 AM Thank you for you support Virginia! In ONE DAY - get out and #VoteTrumpPence16! #ICYMI: https://t.co/Nid8qcFTwY https://t.co/WOsEcjM8sm
- Nov 7, 2016 12:10:20 PM Starting tomorrow it's going to be #AmericaFirst! Thank you for a great morning Sarasota, Florida! Watch here:… https://t.co/ig62Kjkkvl
- Nov 7, 2016 02:30:12 PM Just landed in North Carolina- heading to the J.S. Dorton Arena. See you all soon! Lets #MakeAmericaGreatAgain! https://t.co/EUo0keWX1Y
- Nov 7, 2016 02:31:54 PM On my way! https://t.co/6L2ILD6r8h
- Nov 7, 2016 04:03:13 PM I love you North Carolina- thank you for your amazing support! Get out and https://t.co/HfihPERFgZ tomorrow! Watch:… https://t.co/jZzfqUZNYh
- Nov 7, 2016 04:32:26 PM 'Why Trump' https://t.co/RpwIYB7aOV
- Nov 7, 2016 04:35:14 PM 'What I Like About Trump ... and Why You Need to Vote for Him' https://t.co/6rVuDUehZq
- Nov 7, 2016 04:37:25 PM 'America must decide between failed policies or fresh perspective, a corrupt system or an outsider' https://t.co/ll8QIW9SqW
- Nov 7, 2016 05:21:53 PM Hey Missouri let's defeat Crooked Hillary & @koster4missouri! Koster supports Obamacare & amnesty! Vote outsider Navy SEAL @EricGreitens!
- Nov 7, 2016 06:28:48 PM LIVE on #Periscope: Join me for a few minutes in Pennsylvania. Get out & VOTE tomorrow. LETS #MAGA!! https://t.co/Ej0LmMK3YU

- Nov 7, 2016 07:08:28 PM Thank you Pennsylvania! Going to New Hampshire now and on to Michigan. Watch PA rally here: https://t.co/d29DLINGst… https://t.co/zcH9crFIKM
- Nov 7, 2016 07:16:15 PM Today in Florida, I pledged to stand with the people of Cuba and Venezuela in their fight against oppression- cont: https://t.co/8eELqk2wUw
- Nov 7, 2016 07:17:57 PM Big news to share in New Hampshire tonight! Polls looking great! See you soon.
- Nov 7, 2016 10:43:54 PM Unbelievable evening in New Hampshire - THANK YOU! Flying to Grand Rapids, Michigan now. Watch NH rally here:… https://t.co/hP88anrfgk
- Nov 7, 2016 11:27:18 PM RT @detroitnews: .@IvankaTrump in Michigan: 'This is your movement' https://t.co/0Sa7huoOP1 @realDonaldTrump https://t.co/cMXEqSHuDj
- Nov 7, 2016 11:29:10 PM RT @DonaldJTrumpJr: Thanks New Hampshire!!! #NH #NewHampshire #MAGA https://t.co/JDgcyJvJpk

- Nov 8, 2016 01:42:36 AM Today we are going to win the great state of MICHIGAN and we are going to WIN back the White House! Thank you MI!… https://t.co/onRpEvzHrW
- Nov 8, 2016 06:43:14 AM TODAY WE MAKE AMERICA GREAT AGAIN!
- Nov 8, 2016 11:39:36 AM VOTE TODAY! Go to https://t.co/MXrAxYnTjY to find your polling location. We are going to Make America Great Again!… https://t.co/KPQ5EY9VwQ
- Nov 8, 2016 01:03:49 PM We need your vote. Go to the POLLS! Let's continue this MOVEMENT! Find your poll location: https://t.co/VMUdvi1tx1… https://t.co/zGOx74Ebhw
- Nov 8, 2016 01:23:39 PM #ElectionDay https://t.co/MXrAxYnTjY https://t.co/FZhOncih21
- Nov 8, 2016 04:18:04 PM I will be watching the election results from Trump Tower in Manhattan with my family and friends. Very exciting!
- Nov 8, 2016 04:28:24 PM Just out according to @CNN: "Utah officials report voting machine problems across entire country"
- Nov 8, 2016 04:31:20 PM Don't let up, keep getting out to vote - this election is FAR FROM OVER! We are doing well but there is much time left. GO FLORIDA!

- Nov 8, 2016 06:03:42 PM Still time to #VoteTrump! #iVoted #ElectionNight https://t.co/UZtYAY1Ba6
- Nov 8, 2016 06:20:09 PM RT @DonaldJTrumpJr: FINAL PUSH! Eric and I doing dozens of radio interviews. We can win this thing! GET OUT AND VOTE! #MAGA #ElectionDay ht…
- Nov 8, 2016 06:20:39 PM RT @EricTrump: Join my family in this incredible movement to #MakeAmericaGreatAgain!! Now it is up to you! Please #VOTE for America! https:…
- Nov 8, 2016 08:35:15 PM RT @IvankaTrump: Such a surreal moment to vote for my father for President of the United States! Make your voice heard and vote! #Election2…
- Nov 8, 2016 09:48:27 PM Watching the returns at 9:45pm. #ElectionNight #MAGA US https://t.co/HfuJeRZbod

November 9, 2016

The Day After the Election

- Nov 9, 2016 06:36:58 AM Such a beautiful and important evening! The forgotten man and woman will never be forgotten again. We will all come together as never before

- Nov 10, 2016 02:31:27 PM Happy 241st birthday to the U.S. Marine Corps! Thank you for your service!! https://t.co/Lz2dhrXzo4
- Nov 10, 2016 09:10:46 PM A fantastic day in D.C. Met with President Obama for first time. Really good meeting, great chemistry. Melania liked Mrs. O a lot!
- Nov 10, 2016 09:19:44 PM Just had a very open and successful presidential election. Now professional protesters, incited by the media, are protesting. Very unfair!

- Nov 11, 2016 06:14:20 AM Love the fact that the small groups of protesters last night have passion for our great country. We will all come together and be proud!
- Nov 11, 2016 08:33:35 AM Busy day planned in New York. Will soon be making some very important decisions on the people who will be running our government!

- Nov 11, 2016 10:26:37 AM Today we express our deepest gratitude to all those who have served in our armed forces. #ThankAVet https://t.co/wPk7QWpK8Z

- Nov 12, 2016 10:05:33 AM This will prove to be a great time in the lives of ALL Americans. We will unite and we will win, win, win!

- Nov 13, 2016 09:16:46 AM Wow, the @nytimes is losing thousands of subscribers because of their very poor and highly inaccurate coverage of the "Trump phenomena"
- Nov 13, 2016 09:43:09 AM The @nytimes sent a letter to their subscribers apologizing for their BAD coverage of me. I wonder if it will change - doubt it?
- Nov 13, 2016 09:45:28 AM Mitt Romney called to congratulate me on the win. Very nice!
- Nov 13, 2016 10:23:28 AM Jeb Bush, George W and George H.W. all called to express their best wishes on the win. Very nice!
- Nov 13, 2016 10:28:52 AM Governor John Kasich of the GREAT, GREAT, GREAT State of Ohio called to congratulate me on the win. The people of Ohio were incredible!
- Nov 13, 2016 11:03:21 AM The @nytimes states today that DJT believes "more countries should acquire nuclear weapons." How dishonest are they. I never said this!
- Nov 13, 2016 11:33:26 AM I will be interviewed on @60Minutes tonight after the NFL game - 7:00 P.M. Enjoy!
- Nov 13, 2016 01:46:36 PM The debates, especially the second and third, plus speeches and intensity of the large rallies, plus OUR GREAT SUPPORTERS, gave us the win!

- Nov 15, 2016 08:34:43 AM If the election were based on total popular vote I would have campaigned in N.Y. Florida and California and won even bigger and more easily
- Nov 15, 2016 08:40:29 AM The Electoral College is actually genius in that it brings all states, including the smaller ones, into play. Campaigning is much different!
- Nov 15, 2016 09:55:34 PM Very organized process taking place as I decide on Cabinet and many other positions. I am the only one who knows who the finalists are!

- Nov 16, 2016 06:28:57 AM I am not trying to get "top level security clearance" for my children. This was a typically false news story.
- Nov 16, 2016 07:12:30 AM The failing @nytimes story is so totally wrong on transition. It is going so smoothly. Also, I have spoken to many foreign leaders.
- Nov 16, 2016 07:17:12 AM I have recieved and taken calls from many foreign leaders despite what the failing @nytimes said. Russia, U.K., China, Saudi Arabia, Japan,
- Nov 16, 2016 07:25:21 AM Australia, New Zealand, and more. I am always available to them. @nytimes is just upset that they looked like fools in their coverage of me.

- Nov 17, 2016 07:46:23 AM My transition team, which is working long hours and doing a fantastic job, will be seeing many great candidates today. #MAGA
- Nov 17, 2016 09:01:52 PM Just got a call from my friend Bill Ford, Chairman of Ford, who advised me that he will be keeping the Lincoln plant in Kentucky - no Mexico
- Nov 17, 2016 09:15:28 PM I worked hard with Bill Ford to keep the Lincoln plant in Kentucky. I owed it to the great State of Kentucky for their confidence in me!

- Nov 18, 2016 11:52:39 AM RT @transition2017: President-elect Trump announces selections for Attorney General, National Security Advisor, CIA Director. More here: ht…
- Nov 18, 2016 05:35:27 PM Will be working all weekend in choosing the great men and women who will be helping to MAKE AMERICA GREAT AGAIN!

- Nov 19, 2016 08:34:38 AM I settled the Trump University lawsuit for a small fraction of the potential award because as President I have to focus on our country.
- Nov 19, 2016 08:39:34 AM The ONLY bad thing about winning the Presidency is that I did not have the time to go through a long but winning trial on Trump U. Too bad!
- Nov 19, 2016 08:48:31 AM Our wonderful future V.P. Mike Pence was harassed last night at the theater by the cast of Hamilton, cameras blazing.This should not happen!

- Nov 19, 2016 08:56:30 AM The Theater must always be a safe and special place.The cast of Hamilton was very rude last night to a very good man, Mike Pence. Apologize!
- Nov 20, 2016 06:22:34 AM The cast and producers of Hamilton, which I hear is highly overrated, should immediately apologize to Mike Pence for their terrible behavior
- Nov 20, 2016 06:44:23 AM Numerous patriots will be coming to Bedminster today as I continue to fill out the various positions necessary to MAKE AMERICA GREAT AGAIN!
- Nov 20, 2016 08:26:04 AM I watched parts of @nbcsnl Saturday Night Live last night. It is a totally one-sided, biased show - nothing funny at all. Equal time for us?
- Nov 20, 2016 08:39:05 AM General James "Mad Dog" Mattis, who is being considered for Secretary of Defense, was very impressive yesterday. A true General's General!
- Nov 20, 2016 09:05:01 AM I have always had a good relationship with Chuck Schumer. He is far smarter than Harry R and has the ability to get things done. Good news!

- Nov 21, 2016 06:58:06 PM .@transition2017 update and policy plans for the first 100 days. https://t.co/HTgPXfPWeJ
- Nov 21, 2016 09:14:21 PM Prior to the election it was well known that I have interests in properties all over the world.Only the crooked media makes this a big deal!
- Nov 21, 2016 09:22:16 PM Many people would like to see @Nigel_Farage represent Great Britain as their Ambassador to the United States. He would do a great job!

- Nov 22, 2016 06:16:45 AM I cancelled today's meeting with the failing @nytimes when the terms and conditions of the meeting were changed at the last moment. Not nice
- Nov 22, 2016 06:31:18 AM Perhaps a new meeting will be set up with the @nytimes. In the meantime they continue to cover me inaccurately and with a nasty tone!
- Nov 22, 2016 06:36:46 AM The failing @nytimes just announced that complaints about them are at a 15 year high. I can fully understand that - but why announce?

- Nov 22, 2016 06:46:57 AM Great meetings will take place today at Trump Tower concerning the formation of the people who will run our government for the next 8 years.
- Nov 22, 2016 08:38:17 AM 'President-elect Donald J. Trump's CIA Director Garners Praise' https://t.co/UFdLWtwBEQ https://t.co/MrPaG7OziQ
- Nov 22, 2016 08:39:46 AM 'Jeff Sessions, a Fitting Selection for Attorney General' https://t.co/LjKTkAZSFy
- Nov 22, 2016 10:40:31 AM The meeting with the @nytimes is back on at 12:30 today. Look forward to it!
- Nov 22, 2016 12:10:47 PM I am seriously considering Dr. Ben Carson as the head of HUD. I've gotten to know him well--he's a greatly talented person who loves people!
- Nov 22, 2016 07:24:46 PM Bus crash in Tennessee so sad & so terrible. Condolences to all family members and loved ones. These beautiful children will be remembered!

- Nov 23, 2016 09:17:26 PM Let us give thanks for all that we have, and let us boldly face the exciting new frontiers that lie ahead. Happy Th... https://t.co/RY9mGGjrXm
- Nov 23, 2016 10:30:36 PM Happy Thanksgiving to everyone. We will, together, MAKE AMERICA GREAT AGAIN!

- Nov 24, 2016 10:11:58 AM I am working hard, even on Thanksgiving, trying to get Carrier A.C. Company to stay in the U.S. (Indiana). MAKING PROGRESS - Will know soon!

- Nov 26, 2016 08:08:11 AM Fidel Castro is dead!
- Nov 26, 2016 07:31:32 PM The Green Party scam to fill up their coffers by asking for impossible recounts is now being joined by the badly defeated & demoralized Dems
- Nov 26, 2016 10:59:52 PM The Democrats, when they incorrectly thought they were going to win, asked that the election night tabulation be accepted. Not so anymore!

- Nov 27, 2016 07:19:31 AM Hillary Clinton conceded the election when she called me just prior to the victory speech and after the results were in. Nothing will change
- Nov 27, 2016 07:55:03 AM Hillary's debate answer on delay: "That is horrifying. That is not the way our democracy works. Been around for 240 years. We've had free --
- Nov 27, 2016 08:01:08 AM and fair elections. We've accepted the outcomes when we may not have liked them, and that is what must be expected of anyone standing on a -
- Nov 27, 2016 08:08:05 AM during a general election. I, for one, am appalled that somebody that is the nominee of one of our two major parties would take that kind --
- Nov 27, 2016 08:18:06 AM of position." Then, separately she stated, "He said something truly horrifying ... he refused to say that he would respect the results of --
- Nov 27, 2016 08:23:18 AM this election. That is a direct threat to our democracy." She then said, "We have to accept the results and look to the future, Donald --
- Nov 27, 2016 08:29:30 AM Trump is going to be our President. We owe him an open mind and the chance to lead." So much time and money will be spent - same result! Sad
- Nov 27, 2016 03:30:43 PM In addition to winning the Electoral College in a landslide, I won the popular vote if you deduct the millions of people who voted illegally
- Nov 27, 2016 03:34:18 PM It would have been much easier for me to win the so-called popular vote than the Electoral College in that I would only campaign in 3 or 4--
- Nov 27, 2016 03:41:32 PM states instead of the 15 states that I visited. I would have won even more easily and convincingly (but smaller states are forgotten)!
- Nov 27, 2016 07:31:54 PM Serious voter fraud in Virginia, New Hampshire and California - so why isn't the media reporting on this? Serious bias - big problem!

- Nov 28, 2016 09:02:06 AM If Cuba is unwilling to make a better deal for the Cuban people, the Cuban/American people and the U.S. as a whole, I will terminate deal.

- Nov 28, 2016 04:01:47 PM Just met with General Petraeus--was very impressed!
- Nov 28, 2016 09:14:04 PM "@HighonHillcrest: @jeffzeleny what PROOF do u have DonaldTrump did not suffer from millions of FRAUD votes? Journalist? Do your job! @CNN"
- Nov 28, 2016 09:15:54 PM "@JoeBowman12: @jeffzeleny just another generic CNN part time wannabe journalist !" @CNN still doesn't get it. They will never learn!
- Nov 28, 2016 09:19:53 PM "@Filibuster: @jeffzeleny Pathetic - you have no sufficient evidence that Donald Trump did not suffer from voter fraud, shame! Bad reporter.
- Nov 28, 2016 09:21:04 PM "@sdcritic: @HighonHillcrest @jeffzeleny @CNN There is NO QUESTION THAT #voterfraud did take place, and in favor of #CorruptHillary !"
- Nov 28, 2016 10:03:59 PM .@CNN is so embarrassed by their total (100%) support of Hillary Clinton, and yet her loss in a landslide, that they don't know what to do.

- Nov 29, 2016 06:15:49 AM The Great State of Michigan was just certified as a Trump WIN giving all of our MAKE AMERICA GREAT AGAIN supporters another victory - 306!
- Nov 29, 2016 06:34:42 AM I thought that @CNN would get better after they failed so badly in their support of Hillary Clinton however, since election, they are worse!
- Nov 29, 2016 06:55:13 AM Nobody should be allowed to burn the American flag - if they do, there must be consequences - perhaps loss of citizenship or year in jail!
- Nov 29, 2016 03:08:12 PM My thoughts and prayers are with the great people of Tennessee during these terrible wildfires. Stay safe!
- Nov 29, 2016 03:45:55 PM RT @DanScavino: Back to Cincinnati, Ohio this Thursday (12/1/16) at 7pm for #PEOTUS @realDonaldTrump's #ThankYouTour2016! Join us! https://…
- Nov 29, 2016 03:59:10 PM 'President-Elect Donald J. Trump Intends to Nominate Congressman Tom Price and Seema Verma.' https://t.co/ZTh5cuY26Z https://t.co/twIgAKJs3s

- Nov 29, 2016 06:37:40 PM 'President-Elect Donald J. Trump Nominates Elaine Chao as Secretary of the Department of Transportation' https://t.co/5FMGdhAZxB
- Nov 29, 2016 10:40:16 PM I will be going to Indiana on Thursday to make a major announcement concerning Carrier A.C. staying in Indianapolis. Great deal for workers!
- Nov 29, 2016 10:50:44 PM Big day on Thursday for Indiana and the great workers of that wonderful state.We will keep our companies and jobs in the U.S. Thanks Carrier

- Nov 30, 2016 06:20:01 AM ISIS is taking credit for the terrible stabbing attack at Ohio State University by a Somali refugee who should not have been in our country.
- Nov 30, 2016 06:39:45 AM I will be holding a major news conference in New York City with my children on December 15 to discuss the fact that I will be leaving my ...
- Nov 30, 2016 06:44:52 AM great business in total in order to fully focus on running the country in order to MAKE AMERICA GREAT AGAIN! While I am not mandated to ....
- Nov 30, 2016 06:54:40 AM do this under the law, I feel it is visually important, as President, to in no way have a conflict of interest with my various businesses..
- Nov 30, 2016 06:59:38 AM Hence, legal documents are being crafted which take me completely out of business operations. The Presidency is a far more important task!
- Nov 30, 2016 10:23:43 AM Join me in Cincinnati, Ohio tomorrow evening at 7:00pm. I am grateful for all of your support. THANK YOU! Tickets:… https://t.co/51Emq7Tffa
- Nov 30, 2016 11:21:26 AM 'President-elect Donald J. Trump today announced his intent to nominate Steven Mnuchin, Wilbur Ross & Todd Ricketts… https://t.co/cEBxoWsnYp
- Nov 30, 2016 02:51:16 PM RT @DanScavino: Great interview on @foxandfriends by @SteveDoocy w/ Carrier employee- who has a message for #PEOTUS @realDonaldTrump & #VPE…
- Nov 30, 2016 03:00:14 PM 'Donald Trump is already helping the working class' https://t.co/GTuNcQhLYx

- Nov 30, 2016 10:48:35 PM Look forward to going to Indiana tomorrow in order to be with the great workers of Carrier. They will sell many air conditioners!

December, 2016

- Dec 1, 2016 09:37:57 AM My thoughts and prayers are with those affected by the tragic storms and tornadoes in the Southeastern United States. Stay safe!
- Dec 1, 2016 09:38:09 AM Getting ready to leave for the Great State of Indiana and meet the hard working and wonderful people of Carrier A.C.
- Dec 1, 2016 05:52:10 PM Heading to U.S. Bank Arena in Cincinnati, Ohio for a 7pm rally. Join me! Tickets: https://t.co/HiWqZvHv6M
- Dec 1, 2016 09:45:18 PM Thank you Ohio! Together, we made history – and now, the real work begins. America will start winning again!… https://t.co/sVNSNJE7Uf

- Dec 2, 2016 07:44:20 PM The President of Taiwan CALLED ME today to wish me congratulations on winning the Presidency. Thank you!
- Dec 2, 2016 08:41:30 PM Interesting how the U.S. sells Taiwan billions of dollars of military equipment but I should not accept a congratulatory call.
- Dec 2, 2016 10:06:41 PM Rexnord of Indiana is moving to Mexico and rather viciously firing all of its 300 workers. This is happening all over our country. No more!

- Dec 3, 2016 11:37:27 AM "@TigerWoods: Can't wait to get back out there and mix it up with the boys. –TW #heroworldchallenge" Great to have you back Tiger - Special!
- Dec 3, 2016 02:09:40 PM State Treasurer John Kennedy is my choice for US Senator from Louisiana. Early voting today; election next Saturday.
- Dec 3, 2016 02:13:01 PM Our great VPE, @mike_pence, is in Louisiana campaigning for John Kennedy for US Senate. John will be a tremendous help to us in Washington.

- Dec 4, 2016 12:13:58 AM Just tried watching Saturday Night Live - unwatchable! Totally biased, not funny and the Baldwin impersonation just can't get any worse. Sad
- Dec 4, 2016 06:41:47 AM The U.S. is going to substantialy reduce taxes and regulations on businesses, but any business that leaves our country for another country,
- Dec 4, 2016 06:49:06 AM fires its employees, builds a new factory or plant in the other country, and then thinks it will sell its product back into the U.S. ......
- Dec 4, 2016 06:57:41 AM without retribution or consequence, is WRONG! There will be a tax on our soon to be strong border of 35% for these companies ......
- Dec 4, 2016 07:05:35 AM wanting to sell their product, cars, A.C. units etc., back across the border. This tax will make leaving financially difficult, but.....
- Dec 4, 2016 07:21:01 AM these companies are able to move between all 50 states, with no tax or tariff being charged. Please be forewarned prior to making a very ...
- Dec 4, 2016 07:23:27 AM expensive mistake! THE UNITED STATES IS OPEN FOR BUSINESS
- Dec 4, 2016 01:58:43 PM The Green Party just dropped its recount suit in Pennsylvania and is losing votes in Wisconsin recount. Just a Stein scam to raise money!
- Dec 4, 2016 04:47:21 PM .@FoxNews will be re-running "Objectified: Donald Trump," the ratings hit produced by the great Harvey Levin of TMZ, at 8:00 P.M. Enjoy!

- Dec 4, 2016 05:23:55 PM Did China ask us if it was OK to devalue their currency (making it hard for our companies to compete), heavily tax our products going into..
- Dec 4, 2016 05:30:22 PM their country (the U.S. doesn't tax them) or to build a massive military complex in the middle of the South China Sea? I don't think so!

- Dec 5, 2016 08:53:11 AM I am thrilled to nominate Dr. @RealBenCarson as our next Secretary of the US Dept. of Housing and Urban Development... https://t.co/OJKuDFhP3r
- Dec 5, 2016 11:00:27 AM If the press would cover me accurately & honorably, I would have far less reason to "tweet." Sadly, I don't know if that will ever happen!
- Dec 5, 2016 06:06:43 PM #ThankYouTour2016 12/6- North Carolina https://t.co/79AHq3NC0v 12/8- Iowa https://t.co/1IuRTVwMSx 12/9- Michiga... https://t.co/vcQaIJ8qoB

- Dec 6, 2016 08:52:35 AM Boeing is building a brand new 747 Air Force One for future presidents, but costs are out of control, more than $4 billion. Cancel order!
- Dec 6, 2016 11:45:27 AM Join me tonight in Fayetteville, North Carolina at 7pm! #ThankYouTour2016 Tickets: https://t.co/79AHq3NC0v https://t.co/KoZCE7JeG7
- Dec 6, 2016 02:09:49 PM Masa (SoftBank) of Japan has agreed to invest $50 billion in the U.S. toward businesses and 50,000 new jobs....
- Dec 6, 2016 02:10:27 PM Masa said he would never do this had we (Trump) not won the election!
- Dec 6, 2016 04:17:45 PM Departing New York with General James 'Mad Dog' Mattis for tonight's rally in Fayetteville, North Carolina! See you... https://t.co/Z8sgJBWI09
- Dec 6, 2016 10:33:20 PM A great night in Fayetteville, North Carolina. Thank you! #ICYMI watch here: https://t.co/ZAuTgxKPpb https://t.co/EF9xRWmciA

- Dec 7, 2016 07:18:56 AM I will be interviewed on the @TODAYshow at 7:30. Enjoy!

- Dec 7, 2016 01:38:00 PM We pause today to remember the 2,403 American heroes who selflessly gave their lives at Pearl Harbor 75 years ago... https://t.co/r5eRLR24Q3
- Dec 7, 2016 02:37:32 PM Join me tomorrow in Des Moines, Iowa with Vice President-Elect @mike_pence - at 7:00pm! #ThankYouTour2016 #MAGA... https://t.co/Geq6sT70IT
- Dec 7, 2016 07:41:48 PM Chuck Jones, who is President of United Steelworkers 1999, has done a terrible job representing workers. No wonder companies flee country!
- Dec 7, 2016 08:56:40 PM If United Steelworkers 1999 was any good, they would have kept those jobs in Indiana. Spend more time working-less time talking. Reduce dues

- Dec 8, 2016 04:15:52 PM Today we lost a great pioneer of air and space in John Glenn. He was a hero and inspired generations of future explorers. He will be missed.
- Dec 8, 2016 05:55:24 PM On my way to Des Moines, Iowa- will see you soon with @mike_pence. Join us! Tickets: https://t.co/1IuRTVwMSx #ThankYouTour2016
- Dec 8, 2016 06:12:11 PM Join me tomorrow! #MAGA 10am- Baton Rouge, LA. Tickets: https://t.co/rvIQ6Yq45P 7pm- Grand Rapids, MI. Tickets: https://t.co/2UTwAg5V87
- Dec 8, 2016 10:02:04 PM THANK YOU IOWA! #ThankYouTour2016 https://t.co/v6EB2OQMeO

- Dec 9, 2016 02:42:30 PM Join me live in Louisiana! Tomorrow, we need you to go to the polls & send John Kennedy to the U.S. Senate. https://t.co/O0jtz0BKeL
- Dec 9, 2016 05:13:21 PM Thank you Louisiana! Get out & vote for John Kennedy tomorrow. Electing Kennedy will help enact our agenda on behal... https://t.co/sHXeyreEZI
- Dec 9, 2016 10:30:50 PM Thank you Michigan. We are going to bring back your jobs & together, we will MAKE AMERICA GREAT AGAIN! Watch:... https://t.co/EyLOo26FqW

- Dec 10, 2016 06:19:24 AM .@RudyGiuliani, one of the finest people I know and a former GREAT Mayor of N.Y.C., just took himself out of consideration for "State".
- Dec 10, 2016 06:27:22 AM I have NOTHING to do with The Apprentice except for fact that I conceived it with Mark B & have a big stake in it. Will devote ZERO TIME!
- Dec 10, 2016 07:38:24 AM As a show of support for our Armed Forces, I will be going to The Army-Navy Game today. Looking forward to it, should be fun!
- Dec 10, 2016 09:11:49 AM Reports by @CNN that I will be working on The Apprentice during my Presidency, even part time, are ridiculous & untrue - FAKE NEWS!
- Dec 10, 2016 09:14:23 AM A very interesting read. Unfortunately, so much is true. https://t.co/ER2BoM765M
- Dec 10, 2016 01:41:12 PM RT @TrumpInaugural: Counting down the days until the swearing in of @realDonaldTrump & @mike_pence. Check in here for the latest updates. #…
- Dec 10, 2016 02:09:13 PM October 2015 - thanks Chris Wallace @FoxNewsSunday! https://t.co/VEsgPcWq7z
- Dec 10, 2016 02:09:28 PM RT @FoxNewsSunday: Sunday-- our exclusive interview with President-elect @realDonaldTrump Watch on @FoxNews at 2p/10p ET Check your local…

- Dec 11, 2016 07:56:18 AM I will be interviewed today on Fox News Sunday with Chris Wallace at 10:00 (Eastern) Network. ENJOY!
- Dec 11, 2016 08:12:06 AM Being at the Army - Navy Game was fantastic. There is nothing like the spirit in that stadium. A wonderful experience, and congrats to Army!
- Dec 11, 2016 08:51:47 AM I spent Friday campaigning with John Kennedy, of the Great State of Louisiana, for the U.S.Senate. The election is over - JOHN WON!
- Dec 11, 2016 10:29:10 AM Whether I choose him or not for "State"- Rex Tillerson, the Chairman & CEO of ExxonMobil, is a world class player and dealmaker. Stay tuned!
- Dec 11, 2016 07:32:28 PM Will be interviewed on @FoxNews at 10:00 P.M. Enjoy!

- Dec 11, 2016 08:02:14 PM Just watched @NBCNightlyNews - So biased, inaccurate and bad, point after point. Just can't get much worse, although @CNN is right up there!

- Dec 12, 2016 08:17:54 AM Can you imagine if the election results were the opposite and WE tried to play the Russia/CIA card. It would be called conspiracy theory!
- Dec 12, 2016 08:21:20 AM Unless you catch "hackers" in the act, it is very hard to determine who was doing the hacking. Why wasn't this brought up before election?
- Dec 12, 2016 08:26:13 AM The F-35 program and cost is out of control. Billions of dollars can and will be saved on military (and other) purchases after January 20th.
- Dec 12, 2016 05:25:52 PM #ThankYouTour2016 Tue: West Allis, WI. Thur: Hershey, PA. Fri: Orlando, FL. Sat: Mobile, AL. Tickets:… https://t.co/OJ8S7iVzFx
- Dec 12, 2016 06:40:48 PM The final Wisconsin vote is in and guess what - we just picked up an additional 131 votes. The Dems and Green Party can now rest. Scam!
- Dec 12, 2016 07:33:05 PM I will be making my announcement on the next Secretary of State tomorrow morning.
- Dec 12, 2016 11:26:13 PM Even though I am not mandated by law to do so, I will be leaving my businesses before January 20th so that I can focus full time on the......
- Dec 12, 2016 11:32:01 PM Presidency. Two of my children, Don and Eric, plus executives, will manage them. No new deals will be done during my term(s) in office.
- Dec 12, 2016 11:41:33 PM I will hold a press conference in the near future to discuss the business, Cabinet picks and all other topics of interest. Busy times!

- Dec 13, 2016 06:43:38 AM I have chosen one of the truly great business leaders of the world, Rex Tillerson, Chairman and CEO of ExxonMobil, to be Secretary of State.
- Dec 13, 2016 06:57:35 AM Wisconsin and Pennsylvania have just certified my wins in those states. I actually picked up additional votes!

- Dec 13, 2016 07:44:06 AM The thing I like best about Rex Tillerson is that he has vast experience at dealing successfully with all types of foreign governments.
- Dec 13, 2016 04:33:53 PM Join me this Saturday at Ladd–Peebles Stadium in Mobile, Alabama! #ThankYouTour2016 Tickets:… https://t.co/1RFmKCMgyw
- Dec 13, 2016 07:52:40 PM RT @DanScavino: Join #PEOTUS Trump & #VPEOTUS Pence live in West Allis, Wisconsin! #ThankYouTour2016 #MAGA https://t.co/vU5EPIYKUc https:/…
- Dec 13, 2016 10:48:55 PM Thank you Wisconsin! My Administration will be focused on three very important words: jobs, jobs, jobs! Watch:… https://t.co/iEGWZLuiFE

- Dec 14, 2016 01:07:55 PM .@BillGates and @JimBrownNFL32 in my Trump Tower office yesterday- two great guys! https://t.co/4PjSOEU5y9

- Dec 15, 2016 08:05:55 AM Has anyone looked at the really poor numbers of @VanityFair Magazine. Way down, big trouble, dead! Graydon Carter, no talent, will be out!
- Dec 15, 2016 08:09:14 AM Thank you to Time Magazine and Financial Times for naming me "Person of the Year" - a great honor!
- Dec 15, 2016 08:28:54 AM The media tries so hard to make my move to the White House, as it pertains to my business, so complex - when actually it isn't!
- Dec 15, 2016 09:24:29 AM If Russia, or some other entity, was hacking, why did the White House wait so long to act? Why did they only complain after Hillary lost?
- Dec 15, 2016 05:27:16 PM Join me in Mobile, Alabama on Sat. at 3pm! #ThankYouTour2016 Tickets: https://t.co/GGgbjl8Zo6 https://t.co/opKrWO4k0C
- Dec 15, 2016 08:32:56 PM Thank you Pennsylvania! Together, we are going to MAKE AMERICA GREAT AGAIN! Watch here: https://t.co/7R382qWfWS… https://t.co/yB6u5FEfHq

- Dec 16, 2016 06:09:19 AM Are we talking about the same cyberattack where it was revealed that head of the DNC illegally gave Hillary the questions to the debate?
- Dec 16, 2016 11:03:09 AM Well, we all did it, together! I hope the "MOVEMENT" fans will go to D.C. on Jan 20th for the swearing in. Let's set the all time record!

- Dec 16, 2016 11:54:28 AM #ThankYouTour2016 Tonight- Orlando, Florida Tickets: https://t.co/JwQeccp79N Tomorrow- Mobile, Alabama Tickets:... https://t.co/Cq5AwcuzT9
- Dec 16, 2016 10:52:01 PM Thank you Florida. My Administration will follow two simple rules: BUY AMERICAN and HIRE AMERICAN! #ICYMI-Watch:... https://t.co/3vgtzSJsFu

- Dec 17, 2016 08:05:02 AM Last night in Orlando, Florida, was incredible - massive crowd - THANK YOU FLORIDA! Today at 3:00 P.M. I will be in Alabama for last rally!
- Dec 17, 2016 08:07:22 AM "@EazyMF_E: @realDonaldTrump Many people are now saying you will be an extremely successful president! #MakeAmericaGreatAgain" Thank you!
- Dec 17, 2016 08:20:23 AM Mobile, Alabama today at 3:00 P.M. Last rally of the year - "THANK YOU ALABAMA AND THE SOUTH" Biggest of all crowds expected, see you there!
- Dec 17, 2016 08:57:20 AM China steals United States Navy research drone in international waters - rips it out of water and takes it to China in unprecedented act.
- Dec 17, 2016 04:17:39 PM RT @DanScavino: Join President-elect Trump LIVE from Mobile, Alabama via his #Facebook page! #ThankYouTour2016 Watch: https://t.co/btzN080...
- Dec 17, 2016 07:12:05 PM Thank you Alabama! From now on, it's going to be #AmericaFirst. Our goal is to bring back that wonderful phrase:... https://t.co/4UAazd7TmF
- Dec 17, 2016 07:59:25 PM We should tell China that we don't want the drone they stole back.- let them keep it!

- Dec 18, 2016 04:54:40 PM If my many supporters acted and threatened people like those who lost the election are doing, they would be scorned & called terrible names!

- Dec 19, 2016 06:21:11 PM Today there were terror attacks in Turkey, Switzerland and Germany - and it is only getting worse. The civilized world must change thinking!

- Dec 19, 2016 06:51:41 PM We did it! Thank you to all of my great supporters, we just officially won the election (despite all of the distorted and inaccurate media).
- Dec 19, 2016 08:31:21 PM RT @DanScavino: #TrumpTrain USUSUS https://t.co/qAQdBGEwSv
- Dec 19, 2016 09:46:01 PM "@Franklin_Graham: Congratulations to President-elect @realDonaldTrump--the electoral votes are in and it's official." Thank you Franklin!
- Dec 19, 2016 09:50:25 PM "@mike_pence: Congratulations to @RealDonaldTrump; officially elected President of the United States today by the Electoral College!"

- Dec 20, 2016 08:03:59 AM Bill Clinton stated that I called him after the election. Wrong, he called me (with a very nice congratulations). He "doesn't know much" ...
- Dec 20, 2016 08:09:18 AM especially how to get people, even with an unlimited budget, out to vote in the vital swing states (and more). They focused on wrong states
- Dec 20, 2016 03:27:57 PM Yes, it is true - Carlos Slim, the great businessman from Mexico, called me about getting together for a meeting. We met, HE IS A GREAT GUY!

- Dec 21, 2016 08:15:14 AM Campaigning to win the Electoral College is much more difficult & sophisticated than the popular vote. Hillary focused on the wrong states!
- Dec 21, 2016 08:24:29 AM I would have done even better in the election, if that is possible, if the winner was based on popular vote - but would campaign differently
- Dec 21, 2016 08:29:38 AM I have not heard any of the pundits or commentators discussing the fact that I spent FAR LESS MONEY on the win than Hillary on the loss!
- Dec 21, 2016 10:39:33 PM I met some really great Air Force GENERALS and Navy ADMIRALS today, talking about airplane capability and pricing. Very impressive people!

- Dec 22, 2016 08:37:04 AM The resolution being considered at the United Nations Security Council regarding Israel should be vetoed....cont: https://t.co/s8rXKKZNF1
- Dec 22, 2016 11:41:52 AM Someone incorrectly stated that the phrase "DRAIN THE SWAMP" was no longer being used by me. Actually, we will always be trying to DTS.
- Dec 22, 2016 11:50:30 AM The United States must greatly strengthen and expand its nuclear capability until such time as the world comes to its senses regarding nukes
- Dec 22, 2016 05:26:05 PM Based on the tremendous cost and cost overruns of the Lockheed Martin F-35, I have asked Boeing to price-out a comparable F-18 Super Hornet!
- Dec 22, 2016 08:59:58 PM The so-called "A" list celebrities are all wanting tixs to the inauguration, but look what they did for Hillary, NOTHING. I want the PEOPLE!

- Dec 23, 2016 06:53:05 AM My wonderful son, Eric, will no longer be allowed to raise money for children with cancer because of a possible conflict of interest with...
- Dec 23, 2016 06:58:36 AM my presidency. Isn't this a ridiculous shame? He loves these kids, has raised millions of dollars for them, and now must stop. Wrong answer!
- Dec 23, 2016 03:14:34 PM As to the U.N., things will be different after Jan. 20th.
- Dec 23, 2016 04:17:42 PM The terrorist who killed so many people in Germany said just before crime, "by God's will we will slaughter you pigs, I swear, we will......
- Dec 23, 2016 04:23:00 PM slaughter you. This is a purely religious threat, which turned into reality. Such hatred! When will the U.S., and all countries, fight back?
- Dec 23, 2016 07:13:02 PM Vladimir Putin said today about Hillary and Dems: "In my opinion, it is humiliating. One must be able to lose with dignity." So true!

- Dec 24, 2016 03:59:30 PM .@NBCNews purposely left out this part of my nuclear qoute: "until such time as the world comes to its senses regarding nukes." Dishonest!

- Dec 24, 2016 04:33:27 PM The big loss yesterday for Israel in the United Nations will make it much harder to negotiate peace.Too bad, but we will get it done anyway!
- Dec 24, 2016 04:44:32 PM Happy #Hanukkah https://t.co/UvZwtykV1E
- Dec 24, 2016 07:21:08 PM .@FoxNews - "Objectified" tonight at 10:00 P.M. Enjoy!

- Dec 25, 2016 07:46:41 AM #MerryChristmas https://t.co/5GgDmJrGMS
- Dec 25, 2016 12:48:48 PM Merry Christmas and a very, very, very , very Happy New Year to everyone!

- Dec 26, 2016 04:36:28 PM President Obama said that he thinks he would have won against me. He should say that but I say NO WAY! - jobs leaving, ISIS, OCare, etc.
- Dec 26, 2016 04:41:58 PM The United Nations has such great potential but right now it is just a club for people to get together, talk and have a good time. So sad!
- Dec 26, 2016 06:32:28 PM The world was gloomy before I won - there was no hope. Now the market is up nearly 10% and Christmas spending is over a trillion dollars!
- Dec 26, 2016 09:53:20 PM I gave millions of dollars to DJT Foundation, raised or recieved millions more, ALL of which is given to charity, and media won't report!
- Dec 26, 2016 10:06:59 PM The DJT Foundation, unlike most foundations, never paid fees, rent, salaries or any expenses. 100% of money goes to wonderful charities!

- Dec 27, 2016 04:52:29 PM President Obama campaigned hard (and personally) in the very important swing states, and lost.The voters wanted to MAKE AMERICA GREAT AGAIN!
- Dec 27, 2016 10:10:07 PM The U.S. Consumer Confidence Index for December surged nearly four points to 113.7, THE HIGHEST LEVEL IN MORE THAN 15 YEARS! Thanks Donald!

- Dec 28, 2016 09:07:13 AM Doing my best to disregard the many inflammatory President O statements and roadblocks.Thought it was going to be a smooth transition - NOT!
- Dec 28, 2016 09:19:46 AM We cannot continue to let Israel be treated with such total disdain and disrespect. They used to have a great friend in the U.S., but.......
- Dec 28, 2016 09:25:11 AM not anymore. The beginning of the end was the horrible Iran deal, and now this (U.N.)! Stay strong Israel, January 20th is fast approaching!
- Dec 28, 2016 05:06:28 PM 'Economists say Trump delivered hope' https://t.co/SjGBgglIuQ

- Dec 29, 2016 09:54:21 AM My Administration will follow two simple rules: https://t.co/ZWk0j4H8Qy

- Dec 30, 2016 02:41:33 PM Great move on delay (by V. Putin) - I always knew he was very smart!
- Dec 30, 2016 02:46:55 PM Join @AmerIcan32, founded by Hall of Fame legend @JimBrownNFL32 on 1/19/2017 in Washington, D.C.... https://t.co/9WJZ8iTCQV
- Dec 30, 2016 05:18:18 PM Russians are playing @CNN and @NBCNews for such fools - funny to watch, they don't have a clue! @FoxNews totally gets it!

- Dec 31, 2016 08:17:21 AM Happy New Year to all, including to my many enemies and those who have fought me and lost so badly they just don't know what to do. Love!
- Dec 31, 2016 01:58:12 PM Happy Birthday @DonaldJTrumpJr! https://t.co/uRxyCD3hBz
- Dec 31, 2016 01:59:04 PM RT @realDonaldTrump: Happy Birthday @DonaldJTrumpJr! https://t.co/uRxyCD3hBz

January, 2017

- Jan 1, 2017 12:00:10 AM TO ALL AMERICANS- #HappyNewYear & many blessings to you all! Looking forward to a wonderful & prosperous 2017 as we... https://t.co/1asdMAL4iy
- Jan 1, 2017 12:39:13 AM RT @DanScavino: On behalf of our next #POTUS & @TeamTrump- #HappyNewYear AMERICA US https://t.co/Y6XDdijXea https://t.co/D8plL7xHql https:...
- Jan 1, 2017 12:43:23 AM RT @Reince: Happy New Year + God's blessings to you all. Looking forward to incredible things in 2017! @realDonaldTrump will Make America...
- Jan 1, 2017 12:44:17 AM RT @EricTrump: 2016 was such an incredible year for our entire family! My beautiful wife @LaraLeaTrump made it even better! USUS https://t....
- Jan 1, 2017 01:49:33 AM RT @DonaldJTrumpJr: Happy new year everyone. #newyear #family #vacation #familytime https://t.co/u9fJIKNoZq
- Jan 1, 2017 01:49:49 AM RT @IvankaTrump: 2016 has been one of the most eventful and exciting years of my life. I wish you peace, joy, love and laughter. Happy New...

- Jan 2, 2017 09:40:10 AM Well, the New Year begins. We will, together, MAKE AMERICA GREAT AGAIN!
- Jan 2, 2017 12:31:17 PM Chicago murder rate is record setting - 4,331 shooting victims with 762 murders in 2016. If Mayor can't do it he must ask for Federal help!
- Jan 2, 2017 01:32:29 PM @CNN just released a book called "Unprecedented" which explores the 2016 race & victory. Hope it does well but used worst cover photo of me!
- Jan 2, 2017 01:37:10 PM Various media outlets and pundits say that I thought I was going to lose the election. Wrong, it all came together in the last week and.....
- Jan 2, 2017 01:44:04 PM I thought and felt I would win big, easily over the fabled 270 (306). When they cancelled fireworks, they knew, and so did I.
- Jan 2, 2017 06:05:44 PM North Korea just stated that it is in the final stages of developing a nuclear weapon capable of reaching parts of the U.S. It won't happen!
- Jan 2, 2017 06:47:12 PM China has been taking out massive amounts of money & wealth from the U.S. in totally one-sided trade, but won't help with North Korea. Nice!

- Jan 3, 2017 07:30:05 AM General Motors is sending Mexican made model of Chevy Cruze to U.S. car dealers-tax free across border. Make in U.S.A.or pay big border tax!
- Jan 3, 2017 07:46:33 AM People must remember that ObamaCare just doesn't work, and it is not affordable - 116% increases (Arizona). Bill Clinton called it "CRAZY"
- Jan 3, 2017 07:51:15 AM The Democrat Governor.of Minnesota said "The Affordable Care Act (ObamaCare) is no longer affordable!" - And, it is lousy healthcare.
- Jan 3, 2017 10:03:29 AM With all that Congress has to work on, do they really have to make the weakening of the Independent Ethics Watchdog, as unfair as it
- Jan 3, 2017 10:07:41 AM ....may be, their number one act and priority. Focus on tax reform, healthcare and so many other things of far greater importance! #DTS
- Jan 3, 2017 11:44:13 AM "@DanScavino: Ford to scrap Mexico plant, invest in Michigan due to Trump policies" https://t.co/137nUo03Gl

- Jan 3, 2017 12:00:11 PM Instead of driving jobs and wealth away, AMERICA will become the world's great magnet for INNOVATION & JOB CREATION. https://t.co/siXrptsOrt
- Jan 3, 2017 12:20:43 PM There should be no further releases from Gitmo. These are extremely dangerous people and should not be allowed back onto the battlefield.
- Jan 3, 2017 01:44:47 PM "Trump is already delivering the jobs he promised America" https://t.co/11spTMa6Tm
- Jan 3, 2017 06:58:31 PM I will be having a general news conference on JANUARY ELEVENTH in N.Y.C. Thank you.
- Jan 3, 2017 08:14:52 PM The "Intelligence" briefing on so-called "Russian hacking" was delayed until Friday, perhaps more time needed to build a case. Very strange!

- Jan 4, 2017 07:22:38 AM Julian Assange said "a 14 year old could have hacked Podesta" - why was DNC so careless? Also said Russians did not give him the info!
- Jan 4, 2017 08:10:05 AM "@FoxNews: Julian Assange on U.S. media coverage: "It's very dishonest." #Hannity https://t.co/ADcPRQifH9" More dishonest than anyone knows
- Jan 4, 2017 08:19:09 AM Thank you to Ford for scrapping a new plant in Mexico and creating 700 new jobs in the U.S. This is just the beginning - much more to follow
- Jan 4, 2017 08:27:03 AM Somebody hacked the DNC but why did they not have "hacking defense" like the RNC has and why have they not responded to the terrible......
- Jan 4, 2017 08:31:32 AM things they did and said (like giving the questions to the debate to H). A total double standard! Media, as usual, gave them a pass.
- Jan 4, 2017 08:55:53 AM Republicans must be careful in that the Dems own the failed ObamaCare disaster, with its poor coverage and massive premium increases......
- Jan 4, 2017 09:01:53 AM like the 116% hike in Arizona. Also, deductibles are so high that it is practically useless. Don't let the Schumer clowns out of this web...

- Jan 4, 2017 09:26:45 AM massive increases of ObamaCare will take place this year and Dems are to blame for the mess. It will fall of its own weight - be careful!
- Jan 4, 2017 01:52:09 PM Jackie Evancho's album sales have skyrocketed after announcing her Inauguration performance.Some people just don't understand the "Movement"

- Jan 5, 2017 06:57:57 AM The Democrats, lead by head clown Chuck Schumer, know how bad ObamaCare is and what a mess they are in. Instead of working to fix it, they..
- Jan 5, 2017 07:01:33 AM ...do the typical political thing and BLAME. The fact is ObamaCare was a lie from the beginning."Keep you doctor, keep your plan!" It is....
- Jan 5, 2017 07:06:42 AM ...time for Republicans & Democrats to get together and come up with a healthcare plan that really works - much less expensive & FAR BETTER!
- Jan 5, 2017 08:25:30 AM The dishonest media likes saying that I am in Agreement with Julian Assange - wrong. I simply state what he states, it is for the people....
- Jan 5, 2017 08:45:57 AM to make up their own minds as to the truth. The media lies to make it look like I am against "Intelligence" when in fact I am a big fan!
- Jan 5, 2017 01:14:30 PM Toyota Motor said will build a new plant in Baja, Mexico, to build Corolla cars for U.S. NO WAY! Build plant in U.S. or pay big border tax.
- Jan 5, 2017 07:24:34 PM How did NBC get "an exclusive look into the top secret report he (Obama) was presented?" Who gave them this report and why? Politics!
- Jan 5, 2017 07:30:15 PM The Democratic National Committee would not allow the FBI to study or see its computer info after it was supposedly hacked by Russia......
- Jan 5, 2017 07:40:03 PM So how and why are they so sure about hacking if they never even requested an examination of the computer servers? What is going on?

- Jan 6, 2017 06:19:49 AM The dishonest media does not report that any money spent on building the Great Wall (for sake of speed), will be paid back by Mexico later!
- Jan 6, 2017 06:39:35 AM Hillary and the Dems were never going to beat the PASSION of my voters. They saw what was happening in the last two weeks before the......
- Jan 6, 2017 06:45:47 AM and knew they were in big trouble - which is why they cancelled their big fireworks at the last minute.THEY SAW A MOVEMENT LIKE NEVER BEFORE
- Jan 6, 2017 07:05:01 AM Hopefully, all supporters, and those who want to MAKE AMERICA GREAT AGAIN, will go to D.C. on January 20th. It will be a GREAT SHOW!
- Jan 6, 2017 07:34:37 AM Wow, the ratings are in and Arnold Schwarzenegger got "swamped" (or destroyed) by comparison to the ratings machine, DJT. So much for....
- Jan 6, 2017 07:42:53 AM being a movie star-and that was season 1 compared to season 14. Now compare him to my season 1. But who cares, he supported Kasich & Hillary
- Jan 6, 2017 09:18:51 AM Anna Wintour came to my office at Trump Tower to ask me to meet with the editors of Conde Nast & Steven Newhouse, a friend. Will go this AM.
- Jan 6, 2017 11:51:37 AM I am asking the chairs of the House and Senate committees to investigate top secret intelligence shared with NBC prior to me seeing it.
- Jan 6, 2017 02:30:09 PM Monitoring the terrible situation in Florida. Just spoke to Governor Scott. Thoughts and prayers for all. Stay safe!
- Jan 6, 2017 07:07:09 PM Happy Birthday @EricTrump! https://t.co/bJaEY7qFSn
- Jan 6, 2017 10:53:38 PM Gross negligence by the Democratic National Committee allowed hacking to take place.The Republican National Committee had strong defense!

- Jan 7, 2017 06:56:29 AM Intelligence stated very strongly there was absolutely no evidence that hacking affected the election results. Voting machines not touched!

- Jan 7, 2017 07:03:31 AM Only reason the hacking of the poorly defended DNC is discussed is that the loss by the Dems was so big that they are totally embarrassed!
- Jan 7, 2017 10:02:20 AM Having a good relationship with Russia is a good thing, not a bad thing. Only "stupid" people, or fools, would think that it is bad! We.....
- Jan 7, 2017 10:10:46 AM have enough problems around the world without yet another one. When I am President, Russia will respect us far more than they do now and....
- Jan 7, 2017 10:21:42 AM both countries will, perhaps, work together to solve some of the many great and pressing problems and issues of the WORLD!
- Jan 7, 2017 06:54:05 PM Congratulation to Jane Timken on her major upset victory in becoming the Ohio Republican Party Chair. Jane is a loyal Trump supporter & star
- Jan 7, 2017 09:07:09 PM I look very much forward to meeting Prime Minister Theresa May in Washington in the Spring. Britain, a longtime U.S. ally, is very special!

- Jan 8, 2017 11:36:46 AM "@KellyannePolls: Welcome to President and Mrs. Bush. https://t.co/I1K4nj1gVu" Very nice!
- Jan 8, 2017 11:39:14 AM "@FoxNews: "We certainly don't want intelligence interfering with politics and we don't want politics interfe... https://t.co/bwDjEg1d7S"
- Jan 8, 2017 11:46:07 AM Kellyanne Conway went to @MeetThePress this morning for an interview with @chucktodd. Dishonest media cut out 9 of her 10 minutes. Terrible!
- Jan 8, 2017 11:57:46 AM RT @MeetThePress: Watch our interview with @KellyannePolls: Russia "did not succeed" in attempts to sway election https://t.co/EZhgUIUbYx #...
- Jan 8, 2017 01:56:20 PM Before I, or anyone, saw the classified and/or highly confidential hacking intelligence report, it was leaked out to @NBCNews. So serious!
- Jan 8, 2017 11:05:31 PM Dishonest media says Mexico won't be paying for the wall if they pay a little later so the wall can be built more quickly. Media is fake!

- Jan 9, 2017 06:17:40 AM Rupert Murdoch is a great guy who likes me much better as a very successful candidate than he ever did as a very successful developer!
- Jan 9, 2017 06:27:50 AM Meryl Streep, one of the most over-rated actresses in Hollywood, doesn't know me but attacked last night at the Golden Globes. She is a.....
- Jan 9, 2017 06:36:02 AM Hillary flunky who lost big. For the 100th time, I never "mocked" a disabled reporter (would never do that) but simply showed him.......
- Jan 9, 2017 06:43:26 AM "groveling" when he totally changed a 16 year old story that he had written in order to make me look bad. Just more very dishonest media!
- Jan 9, 2017 09:14:10 AM It's finally happening - Fiat Chrysler just announced plans to invest $1BILLION in Michigan and Ohio plants, adding 2000 jobs. This after...
- Jan 9, 2017 09:16:34 AM Ford said last week that it will expand in Michigan and U.S. instead of building a BILLION dollar plant in Mexico. Thank you Ford & Fiat C!
- Jan 9, 2017 05:32:33 PM An old picture with Nancy and Ronald Reagan. https://t.co/8kvQ1PzPAf
- Jan 9, 2017 09:20:01 PM Thank you to all of the men and women who protect & serve our communities 24/7/365! #LawEnforcementAppreciationDay… https://t.co/aqUbDipSgv

- Jan 10, 2017 10:26:22 AM 'U.S. Small-Business Optimism Index Surges by Most Since 1980' https://t.co/X22x1BttdG
- Jan 10, 2017 03:50:31 PM 'Small business optimism soars after Trump election' https://t.co/WjBaTp824U
- Jan 10, 2017 05:30:53 PM 'Trump Helps Lift Small Business Confidence to 12-Yr. High' https://t.co/MhbABREhzt https://t.co/CWAvJ4fRdx
- Jan 10, 2017 08:19:23 PM FAKE NEWS - A TOTAL POLITICAL WITCH HUNT!
- Jan 10, 2017 08:35:41 PM RT @MichaelCohen212: I have never been to Prague in my life. #fakenews https://t.co/CMil9Rha3D
- Jan 10, 2017 09:00:11 PM 'BuzzFeed Runs Unverifiable Trump-Russia Claims' #FakeNews https://t.co/d6daCFZHNh

- Jan 11, 2017 07:13:40 AM Russia just said the unverified report paid for by political opponents is "A COMPLETE AND TOTAL FABRICATION, UTTER NONSENSE." Very unfair!
- Jan 11, 2017 07:31:31 AM Russia has never tried to use leverage over me. I HAVE NOTHING TO DO WITH RUSSIA - NO DEALS, NO LOANS, NO NOTHING!
- Jan 11, 2017 07:44:05 AM I win an election easily, a great "movement" is verified, and crooked opponents try to belittle our victory with FAKE NEWS. A sorry state!
- Jan 11, 2017 07:48:52 AM Intelligence agencies should never have allowed this fake news to "leak" into the public. One last shot at me.Are we living in Nazi Germany?
- Jan 11, 2017 11:01:38 PM We had a great News Conference at Trump Tower today. A couple of FAKE NEWS organizations were there but the people truly get what's going on
- Jan 11, 2017 11:24:52 PM "@zhu_amy3: @realDonaldTrump It's Morning in America again!!! Thank you President-Elect Donald Trump!!! So proud of you!!!!" THANKS!

- Jan 12, 2017 07:23:45 AM James Clapper called me yesterday to denounce the false and fictitious report that was illegally circulated. Made up, phony facts.Too bad!
- Jan 12, 2017 08:50:13 AM Thank you to Linda Bean of L.L.Bean for your great support and courage. People will support you even more now. Buy L.L.Bean. @LBPerfectMaine
- Jan 12, 2017 09:22:21 AM .@CNN is in a total meltdown with their FAKE NEWS because their ratings are tanking since election and their credibility will soon be gone!
- Jan 12, 2017 12:41:11 PM Congrats to the Senate for taking the first step to #RepealObamacare- now it's onto the House!

- Jan 13, 2017 05:49:34 AM All of my Cabinet nominee are looking good and doing a great job. I want them to be themselves and express their own thoughts, not mine!

- Jan 13, 2017 06:05:55 AM It now turns out that the phony allegations against me were put together by my political opponents and a failed spy afraid of being sued....
- Jan 13, 2017 06:11:13 AM Totally made up facts by sleazebag political operatives, both Democrats and Republicans - FAKE NEWS! Russia says nothing exists. Probably...
- Jan 13, 2017 06:16:54 AM released by "Intelligence" even knowing there is no proof, and never will be. My people will have a full report on hacking within 90 days!
- Jan 13, 2017 06:22:38 AM What are Hillary Clinton's people complaining about with respect to the F.B.I. Based on the information they had she should never.....
- Jan 13, 2017 06:25:54 AM have been allowed to run - guilty as hell. They were VERY nice to her. She lost because she campaigned in the wrong states - no enthusiasm!
- Jan 13, 2017 06:33:24 AM The "Unaffordable" Care Act will soon be history!
- Jan 13, 2017 12:42:42 PM A beautiful funeral today for a real NYC hero, Detective Steven McDonald. Our law enforcement community has my complete and total support.

- Jan 14, 2017 07:50:26 AM Congressman John Lewis should spend more time on fixing and helping his district, which is in horrible shape and falling apart (not to......
- Jan 14, 2017 08:07:12 AM mention crime infested) rather than falsely complaining about the election results. All talk, talk, talk - no action or results. Sad!
- Jan 14, 2017 08:14:13 AM INTELLIGENCE INSIDERS NOW CLAIM THE TRUMP DOSSIER IS "A COMPLETE FRAUD!" @OANN
- Jan 14, 2017 07:22:01 PM Congressman John Lewis should finally focus on the burning and crime infested inner-cities of the U.S. I can use all the help I can get!
- Jan 14, 2017 08:58:57 PM Inauguration Day is turning out to be even bigger than expected. January 20th, Washington D.C. Have fun!

- Jan 15, 2017 08:59:29 AM The Democrats are most angry that so many Obama Democrats voted for me. With all of the jobs I am bringing back to our Nation, that number..

- Jan 15, 2017 09:02:41 AM will only get higher. Car companies and others, if they want to do business in our country, have to start making things here again. WIN!
- Jan 15, 2017 02:00:21 PM For many years our country has been divided, angry and untrusting. Many say it will never change, the hatred is too deep. IT WILL CHANGE!!!!
- Jan 15, 2017 03:04:38 PM Thank you to Bob Woodward who said, "That is a garbage document...it never should have been presented...Trump's right to be upset (angry)...
- Jan 15, 2017 03:13:00 PM about that...Those Intelligence chiefs made a mistake here, & when people make mistakes, they should APOLOGIZE." Media should also apologize
- Jan 15, 2017 05:46:33 PM .@NBCNews is bad but Saturday Night Live is the worst of NBC. Not funny, cast is terrible, always a complete hit job. Really bad television!
- Jan 15, 2017 07:16:20 PM .@FoxNews "Outgoing CIA Chief, John Brennan, blasts Pres-Elect Trump on Russia threat. Does not fully understand." Oh really, couldn't do...
- Jan 15, 2017 07:29:05 PM much worse - just look at Syria (red line), Crimea, Ukraine and the build-up of Russian nukes. Not good! Was this the leaker of Fake News?

- Jan 16, 2017 08:54:52 AM Celebrate Martin Luther King Day and all of the many wonderful things that he stood for. Honor him for being the great man that he was!
- Jan 16, 2017 08:42:18 PM "@levisteveholt: @realDonaldTrump I appreciate your use of Twitter to keep us informed and maintain transparency." Very dishonest media!
- Jan 16, 2017 08:49:38 PM At 9:00 P.M. @CNN, of all places, is doing a Special Report on my daughter, Ivanka. Considering it is CNN, can't imagine it will be great!
- Jan 16, 2017 09:08:21 PM "@drgoodspine: @realDonaldTrump @Ivanka Trump is great, a woman with real character and class."

- Jan 17, 2017 08:05:10 AM People are pouring into Washington in record numbers. Bikers for Trump are on their way. It will be a great Thursday, Friday and Saturday!

- Jan 17, 2017 08:11:56 AM The same people who did the phony election polls, and were so wrong, are now doing approval rating polls. They are rigged just like before.
- Jan 17, 2017 09:30:19 AM With all of the jobs I am bringing back into the U.S. (even before taking office), with all of the new auto plants coming back into our.....
- Jan 17, 2017 09:36:26 AM country and with the massive cost reductions I have negotiated on military purchases and more, I believe the people are seeing "big stuff."
- Jan 17, 2017 09:46:27 AM John Lewis said about my inauguration, "It will be the first one that I've missed." WRONG (or lie)! He boycotted Bush 43 also because he...
- Jan 17, 2017 09:52:39 AM "thought it would be hypocritical to attend Bush's swearing-in....he doesn't believe Bush is the true elected president." Sound familiar! WP
- Jan 17, 2017 12:36:45 PM "How Trump Won--And How The Media Missed It" https://t.co/Hfab41h65X
- Jan 17, 2017 12:55:38 PM Thank you to General Motors and Walmart for starting the big jobs push back into the U.S.!
- Jan 17, 2017 02:36:21 PM RT @MoskowitzEva: .@BetsyDeVos has the talent, commitment, and leadership capacity to revitalize our public schools and deliver the promise…
- Jan 17, 2017 02:58:10 PM RT @EricTrump: Thank you to @GolfDigest for this incredible feature! "Golfer-in-Chief" @RealDonaldTrump https://t.co/vpdY4jNbI4 https://t.c…

- Jan 18, 2017 06:53:24 AM Will be interviewed by @ainsleyearhardt on @foxandfriends - Enjoy!
- Jan 18, 2017 07:34:09 AM Totally biased @NBCNews went out of its way to say that the big announcement from Ford, G.M., Lockheed & others that jobs are coming back...
- Jan 18, 2017 07:44:03 AM to the U.S., but had nothing to do with TRUMP, is more FAKE NEWS. Ask top CEO's of those companies for real facts. Came back because of me!

- Jan 18, 2017 08:00:51 AM "Bayer AG has pledged to add U.S. jobs and investments after meeting with President-elect Donald Trump, the latest in a string..." @WSJ
- Jan 18, 2017 08:06:58 AM No wonder the Today Show on biased @NBC is doing so badly compared to its glorious past. Little credibility!
- Jan 18, 2017 09:03:53 AM .@TheAlabamaBand was great last night in D.C. playing for 147 Diplomats and Ambassadors from countries around the world. Thanks Alabama!
- Jan 18, 2017 12:33:25 PM Writing my inaugural address at the Winter White House, Mar-a-Lago, three weeks ago. Looking forward to Friday.... https://t.co/J0ojOXjrga
- Jan 18, 2017 05:21:02 PM Looking forward to a speedy recovery for George and Barbara Bush, both hospitalized. Thank you for your wonderful letter!
- Jan 18, 2017 08:54:13 PM Great seeing @TheLeeGreenwood and Kimberly at this evenings VP dinner! #GodBlessTheUSA https://t.co/SxVmaWvOFT
- Jan 18, 2017 11:01:40 PM Thank you to our amazing Wounded Warriors for their service. It was an honor to be with them tonight in D.C.... https://t.co/Qj5cpfaykD

- Jan 19, 2017 07:52:22 AM "It wasn't Donald Trump that divided this country, this country has been divided for a long time!" Stated today by Reverend Franklin Graham.
- Jan 19, 2017 08:00:13 AM Getting ready to leave for Washington, D.C. The journey begins and I will be working and fighting very hard to make it a great journey for..
- Jan 19, 2017 08:02:18 AM the American people. I have no doubt that we will, together, MAKE AMERICA GREAT AGAIN!
- Jan 19, 2017 03:13:57 PM On my way! #Inauguration2017 https://t.co/hOuMbxGnpe
- Jan 19, 2017 03:18:32 PM Great Concert at 4:00 P.M. today at Lincoln Memorial. Enjoy!
- Jan 19, 2017 03:21:36 PM Join me at 4pm over at the Lincoln Memorial with my family! #Inauguration2017 https://t.co/GQeQpJOgWz
- Jan 19, 2017 07:40:51 PM Thank you for joining us at the Lincoln Memorial tonight- a very special evening! Together, we are going to MAKE AM... https://t.co/OSxa3BamHs

- Jan 19, 2017 11:24:33 PM Thank you for a wonderful evening in Washington, D.C. #Inauguration https://t.co/a6xpFQTHj5

#

INDEX

@_bri 12
@_BScarb 298
@_CFJ_ 545
@_EOD 58
@_fly_on_wall_ 32
@_GOLD4MONEY 14
@_HankRearden 316
@_Holly_Renee 235
@_John_Handel 72
@_JoshBishop 41
@_Just_Mads_ 127
@_laurenharding 13
@_MSFL_ 273
@_Snurk 2
@_trump4potus 86
@_Tsac_More 35
@_Tsac_ 34
@007cigarjoe 395
@007lLisav 158-9
@00patriot 109
@0Nonsense 159
@10inchpolitics 250
@11phenomenon 90,387
@1776Pirate 97
@1Barbara1 61,186
@1lion 457
@1ns1de_J9b 114
@1rdgreenberg 263
@1sonny12 345
@2009softail 60
@2014_vince 30,57
@2big2bereal 37
@2bigj 185
@2ndVoter: 100
@2timeslucky 226,228,244,268
@3462727 150

@3DOT 253
@3rdedit 66
@4mostcoach 148,188
@4udirtyrat 146
@55Lidsville 510
@5SOS_jrt1d 119
@60Minutes 131,133-6,156,216,475,589
@678b4612a62641f 91
@700club 140
@760_831 220
@8723g 189
@93101Dianne 323
@97Musick 57-8,123,169
@9News 188
@aaron_athman 175
@AB1132 212
@ABC 144,176,179-80,196,210,224-6,229
         237,242,254,262,265,268,292,328
               387,289,460-1,579
@ABC2020 225-6
@ABCFamily 140
@ABCinSC 217
@ABCNetwork 227
@ABCnews 60
@ABCPolitics 99,328-9
@AbishurPrakash 10
@about_life 73
@absabella 38
@AC360 43,66,123,302,325,327,358,394,413
               550-1
@AceofSpadesHQ 297
@Achilarre 161
@adair_ariel 83
@AdamBlickstein 169
@adamscottnow 159
@adeeasthope 13

@adenunzio 202
@adhd_fa 522
@AdiosLiberty 135
@AdrianaCohen16 412
@AdriannaMarie 103
@adriparsonss 371
@aduanebrown 98
@aews 246
@afievoli 115
@AFLCIO 462
@agcaddauan 91
@Agent_54 73
@agentvf 189,400
@agirland3boys 19
@agreatimage 180
@AgsEliza 241
@ahernandez85a 351
@AhmedBawazir 61
@ainsleyyearhardt 619
@airforce2100 33
@AJ_Nix 147
@AJDelgado13 205
@Ajdx4Sdesq 256
@ajodom60 263
@AK_TWEET 528
@akawhit1 66
@alarae37 43
@Alaskan_Gypsy 9
@AlbertoMarsano 184
@AlbertoZambrano 61
@Albusinvogue 208
@ALConvention2016 518
@aldeguer_elsa 173
@AlexNightrasor 399
@AlexPagliano 74
@alextrent4 373
@AliasHere 83
@AliceCarozza 176
@AliceEngle3 154,205
@AlisaApps 152
@AlisonForKY 430
@AlisynCamerota 304
@alivelutheran 127,128
@AllegrettiVicki 457
@AllenWest 462
@AlleyKat2 61
@Allibiis 237
@AllRepublicans 129
@almy23841665 123
@Alwaleed_Talal 259,261

@AlWaleedbinT 20
@alyssathgreat 59
@amandajoan40 54
@amazon 251
@amd9890 160
@america_trump 135
@American1st 170,173
@AmerIcan32 608
@AmericanAsPie 247,304
@americanhowl 117
@AmericanLegion 518
@ameriflames 298
@AmesMoreno 208
@AmFree 336
@amit_ 58
@Ammoland 40
@amrightnow 203
@amsardina 56
@AmSpec 27,77,107
@amstaffbru 20,21
@AmyMek 76,80,100
@ananavarro 148,149
@and_is_w 197
@AndersonCooper 24,64,66,163,191,219,297
.... 342,358,401
@AndreaTantaros 145,272,382
@AndreaWeslien 69
@AndreBauer 408
@andres_3v 57
@AndrewMillerKC 85
@AndrewStilesUSA 58
@andrewwagner29 7
@AndyBran 4
@andydean2014 50,264
@AngelaDale143 147
@AngelaTribble 130
@angeloftruth11 138,443
@Angie58493041 162
@AngieSteinberg 364
@AngPiazza 530
@ANHQDC 46
@AniesiODaniels 270
@AnnCoulter ... 7,21,26,29,39,49,60,76,78,91,146
..... 149,153,170,173,177,206,232,243,262
..... 265,304,308-9,311,343,398,400,411
.... 452-3,461,488,510,517
@AnneBellar 520
@AnnesLimo 401
@AnnetteJeanne 411
@AnnieClarkCole 138

@AnonymouSyndica 193
@anotherTRUMPvot 88
@ansun_sayavong 175
@Antonio92692 238
@antSTACKSgrieco 195
@AnyoneTennis 545
@aoldonturnaolcol 543
@AP 38,53,62,96,221,229-30,408,423
@apalmerdc 361
@Apipwhisperer 135
@ApolloBohono69 190
@ApprenticeNBC 3
@AppSame 2,27
@AprilLaJune 426
@AProudRebel 49
@arappeport 308
@ARealSuperMan 127
@Arful1dodger 74
@ARGOP 53
@ariannahuff 54,70
@AriEmanuel 271
@ArkaysDesign 290
@arnold_ziffel 461
@ARSenMissyIrvin 543
@ArthurOHara 120
@ArtistdeeDd 37
@ArtNGonzalez 27
@ArtPar17 237
@ASA_Patriot 104
@ASAQ_3 283
@ASavageNation 374
@Ashevillelaura 222
@AshleyEdam 189,381,404
@AshlieJuliard 175
@Asmurfinmypants 237
@aspiesmom 167
@ASwoyer 8,27,51
@atensnut 547
@ATFD17 526
@AtheistWWonka 189
@Auburnfan2155 8
@Ausbiz 351,418,449
@autoprofessor17 401
@autumnandews08 177,270,327,337
@aviv1818 180
@AWRHawkins 46
@AY4WEB 226
@AynsFriend 313
@azblonde2015 236
@AZTRUMPTRAIN 569

@azuriterealtor 60
@b_ranzetta 209
@babo_sirin 240
@BabyPhatRox 37
@babyylissa 30
@back2reason 252
@BackOnTrackUSA 28,156
@BADfundraisers 87
@BAM4AU 64
@Bane1349 179
@BannermanJack 97
@BarackObama 126,525
@Barbara_NC 263
@BarbaraDeStasio 187
@BarbaraGarro 51
@BarbaraJensen1 185
@BarbaraJWalters 222,224-6,230,254,292
@barbaraslavin1 288
@Barbavh 103
@Barber2012Jeff 238
@barbgee68 13
@BarbMuenchen 152,230
@barreto_eugenio 140
@BarronG510 383
@Bass705 15
@batchelorshow 144
@bawl 184
@BB1959_ 65
@BBCARKING 169
@bcuzimdamomma 543
@bdckool 9
@bdean1468 35,37-8,47,57,72,74,80,83-4,154
@bdevil89 41
@BDubLasVegas 84
@beck_coulter 105
@becker_berta 290,400
@BeckyOmz 238
@bedard_nancy 86
@BeezakaMrB 235
@beingmesuzieeJ 231
@BelAirCA 109
@Belizediver88 312
@BellicWolf 197
@ben_techpro 49,247
@BenFergusonShow 106
@BenKissel 301
@BenSasse 319
@benshapiro 341
@BentleyforTrump 171,190,283
@bentomchik 112

@beny_bensn 18
@BernardGoldberg 258
@BernieSanders 18,170,262,279,428,569
@BertShad 376
@BetseyDeVos 619
@Betsy_McCaughey 211
@BettyeBear 26
@BeverlySimcic 179
@bewhatjesuswas 128
@bfb123456 282
@BfgBobgrant 74
@bfraser747 455
@bhill3333 65
@big_carsonrocks 327
@BigBrett45 84
@BigBrotherKat 121
@bigdog_joey 542
@bigg_ritch 61
@BigGstory 31
@bigmikeobrien 164
@bigop1 304,406
@bigpaulfla 103
@bigsampolkcoga 206
@BigStick2013 140
@BillAndMoShow 54
@billboard 193
@BillClinton 550
@Billd111 62-3
@BillDaley1 266
@BilldeBlasio 224
@BillGates 603
@BillHemmer 508
@BillKristol 66,105,184,206,238,433
@BillLester651 79
@billmaher 16
@BillOreilly 3,325
@BillPwr1 144
@billrey16929057 327
@billsupdates 141
@BillyGraham 206
@BillyJoel 437
@billyjowiggins 73
@BillyNungesser 508
@BillyParker03 54
@Biracial_Chick 193
@BirgitOlsen1 344
@bishopwjackson 526
@bitchpuuuhlease 65
@bjmgraphics 247
@BJSeastoneAMP 60

@BK00023 8
@bk2seattle 168
@Blackan 343-4
@blackrepublican 142,144
@Blacks4Trump16 243
@blayne_troy 114
@blewthebigone 128,175-6,191
@blindtotheruth 81
@bloggerjulie 230
@blondesforjesus 168
@bloombergtv 164
@blt21muttrades 363
@bluedogdemky 462
@blueeyd2020 270
@bluegirlvi 148
@bluestarwindow 72,74
@BMW_e38forever 208
@Boazziz 290
@BOB_EWASHINGTON 114-5
@bob_forbes2 206
@bobby990r_1 130
@bobbybnews 6-7
@bobbyjindal 67,270
@BobD746847 184
@BobPriceBBTX 64
@bobvanderplaats 227,313-4,320
@BoDiet 259
@bollweevil51 74
@Bonfiredesigns 298,335
@BonnieKit 32
@BooBooBear4U2 35
@boogiefinger 238
@BorderWall 152,195
@boreed615 228
@Borisep 408
@Born2RunJosh 238
@BornToBeGOP 189,192,198-9,206,208,214
.... 226,252,267,279,305,312,351
@BOSSYtxmar55 243
@BostonGlobe 231
@bostonherald 412
@bperez733 30
@bpolitics 11,199,202
@BradANGSA 130
@BradCross4 316
@BradPaisley 232
@BradSaidWhat 34
@BradSteinle 49-50
@brady2edelman 83
@Brainbow_Bite 38

@Brainykid2010... 510
@Brammz3 72
@BrandenHarvey 12
@BrandenRoderick 94
@brandongordy1 165
@BrandonSawyer84 336
@brandonstinney 287
@BrandyDianeK2 120
@bravehart60 179
@BraveLad.. 194
@BrazielCarol 374
@brazosboys.. 461
@breadman28 87
@BreitbartNews ... 8,16,27,34-5,42-3,46,51,53,62
            64,69,78,107,157,179,199,212,227,242
            515

@BreitbartVideo... 7
@BrentBozell 40,307
@brentcfritz.. 1
@BretBaier 91,111,148-50,171,216,225,283
            398,417,420
@BretEastonEllis.. 345
@BrianBl43802294 249
@BrianCraigShow.. 91
@BrianCstandsup 59
@brimyers813 525
@brithume 111,169,171,339,347
@Britinnv 49
@BrittainShannon 20
@broewads 114
@BrookslawBrooks... 249
@brucedhendrix.. 200
@btodd539 175
@Bubbachitchat1... 207
@Bubble709_ 403
@buckleybro40.. 187,236
@bucwaas.. 17
@buildthewall 436
@burgettn 212
@business... 92,241
@businessinsider 40,166
@bxldgxng 60
@ByronYork 181-2
@bzocash.. 32
@C_Archaeology 21
@C_Lynne_Ryan 504
@C4Constitution 310
@cadigirl13 114
@califortrump... 80
@Cam   398

@CandyThomas3583... 8
@CaptainMark_.. 205
@CaptTimScrim 92
@Carl_C_Icahn 137,148,502
@CarlHigbie 264
@CarlRove 164
@CarlyFiorina 216
@CarmineZozzora.. 241
@carol_lcnixon67 543
@CarolBurnett3 309
@Carolde 174,182,250,297,315,399
@Carolin42539648 265
@Carolyn82471448 344
@carrillo_pete.............................. 142,144,177
@CarrollKuykend2 344
@carsonbonner 10
@CaseyBierer 40
@CASuperrunner.. 146,286
@cathyspartanj 189
@catisbetter666 35
@CatOnGlass 509
@cb_beach_bum... 174
@CBNNews 44,65,105,208,295
@CBS 133-5,212,339
@CBSNews 11,180-3,196,210,248,309-10,444
            582

@ccakul 209
@ccorreia401 176
@cecki 232
@celestefick... 130
@Centaur6D 71
@CFT1   138,155
@ChaddRyann... 5
@ChadR73 148
@ChadRowland3 367
@ChadSchiebler 89
@chained111 268
@ChanRogers 51
@CharleneOsbor17... 548
@charlescwcooke 130
@CharlesGKoch 201
@CharlesHodgson1 356
@CharlesHurt 6,46,191,280,282
@CharlesMarino8 253
@CharlesMBlow 199
@charlierose 42,305
@charlottepturn 239
@chaseelliott... 359
@ChateauEmissary...243-4
@ChatteringTeef.. 351

@chazermann26 169
@ChefMama32................................. 172
@Cher 178
@CheriJacobus 229,324,326
@CherNuna 520
@CherokeeShaman2 65
@ChezVachon 329
@chgardens1 316
@ChipB 21
@chipman88.................................... 28
@ChJLuc91 340
@CHM1321 164
@Chocolate3Way 176
@Chr 64
@Chris_D2...................................... 16
@Chris0u24 117
@chrisboydbrew 456
@ChrisChristie 92,189,354,356
@ChrisCJackson............................... 520
@chriscoxb2b 123
@ChrisCuomo 58,97,147,313,420
@chriskyleband 204
@chrislhayes................................... 60
@Chrisofficer23 119
@ChrisRuddyNMX 39
@ChrisStirewalt 92
@christa_dorsett 117
@ChristianInst................................. 51
@Christianlord12.............................. 214
@ChristiChat................................... 429
@ChristineMMoran............................ 209
@Christo20722105 241
@christotepis 179
@ChuckGrassley 502
@ChuckLane1 41,45
@ChuckTodd........ 46-7,62,64,112,143-4,154,210
.... 237-8,244,250,258,276,278,288,294
.... 367,389-90,614
@CindyBl....................................... 183
@CindyBlackwel12............................ 236,249
@CissieGLynch................................ 581
@Citizens4Trump............................. 241
@CJCboi 315
@clar 171
@claramarks.................................... 29
@Clare_OC 42
@classyexplorer................... 276,319,351
@ClassySnobbb 226,277
@clayaiken 155
@ClaytonMorris................................ 168

@CleopattraUSA 210
@clew136 29
@CLewandowski_ 253,296,298,310,321,325,360
.... 371
@CliffShep 4
@Clint_Goodrich............................... 155
@club4growth............................. 114-5,122,147
@cmichaeld2004 381
@cmrose111 186
@CNBC 164-5,183,186-7,190-1,199,525
@CNN ... 20,43,47,54-5,64,76,78,99,105-6,112
. 117,119,121,123-5,132,137-8,140,142
. 144,146-9,157-9,178,180-2,191,206-7
. 210-2,214,217,227,236-9,241-2,246-9
.....252-6,258,261,264-7,274-8,285,293
. 295,297,302,304,311-3,316,324-6,329
.333,335,339,342,350,353,355,358,362
. 382,388,390-1,395,398,406,408-9,415
420,424-5,429-30,433,442,445,451,461
469-70,475-6,481,488,491-2,503-4,512
.... 514-5,519-20,523,529-30,535-6,538
. 540,542,552-3,559,586,594,601-2,608
.... 610,616,618
@CNNOpinion 241
@CNNPolitics 32,40,43,46,54-5,78,147,155
.... 158-9,181,229,231,238,246,315
@CNNSitRoom 291,311-12
@CNNSotu....................................... 18
@CNNTonight................................... 138
@Co 244
@CoachAbda.............................. 71,72
@CoachJMan.................................... 38
@CoachZachCooper........................... 83
@codyave 157
@codyraymille.................................. 286
@CodyShirk 105
@Cola0531 162
@colbertlateshow................... 117,131-2,339
@ColeHudson68................................ 103
@ColinCavall 120
@ColinCowherd 194,200
@ColinSWood.................................. 81
@collegestump 142,144
@coloradojoe2001 184
@coltsfan322 210
@colvinj 62,229
@ComatoseJeb 259
@CommissarOfGG............................. 93
@CompresPhyllis 290
@concerningtimes 181

@connie_lee1 156
@ConnieHegel 69-70
@ConnieMackIV 109
@ConnorBaldwin21 61
@ConradMBlack 266-7
@conservativevin 351
@ConserveCast 172
@constant4change 270
@contrarian11 58
@cookingdoll 87
@coolgirl6978 128,188
@cospy8 182
@CostaKenneth 429
@costareports 196
@cota2012 10
@COWBOYSFORTRUMP 429
@CPO_Mark_2010 147
@crainsdetroit 183
@CreativeXwalk 363
@creta_r 315
@CRinQC 253
@Crowebar_67 172
@crstin0516 101
@Crusade4Honesty 312
@CrystalPrebola 40
@Crz4basball 443
@cs1racefan 140
@cspan 57
@ctmommy 86
@cu_mr2ducks 146
@currentlyFeed 188
@curtandkaren 428
@curtiscraven76 247
@curtismuddog 182,203,213
@customwww 42
@cvpayne 26,461
@CWAUnion 462
@CWilliams_Rltr 12
@CwiseCwise1 247
@CyberCiety 306
@CynthiaLummis 526
@d_seaman 169
@Daaahawks 86
@dabeard 18
@Dad_Trump 189
@DagnyRed 26,28
@DailyBeast 389
@DailyCaller 31,40,237,264,514
@DailyMail 435
@Dale_Dangler 448

@dallasmavs 77,79
@DallasPD 454
@dalva1616 193
@DAMRON88 199
@Dan__Crocker 85-6
@DanaPerino 6,11,33,67
@DanaWhite 260,262
@dancriscuolo 62
@danforc 51
@DanHenninger 80
@DanielaMarino 14
@DanielGenseric 196
@danielhalper 277
@DanielleBoussel 120
@danlifting 169,195
@DannyBo4455 45
@danpfeiffer 361
@danpgabriel 316
@DanSaltsman 183,220
@DanScavino 39,58,69,79-80,82-4,92,101
.......146,151,192,201,241,243,247,252,262
.......290,315,325,344,360,389,422,454,495
.......520,522,533-4,551,580,584,594-5,603
.... 604-5,609-10
@DanSondhelm 228
@dantegtmeyer 290
@Darci51 34
@darcy027027 149
@Dark_Red_Hair 59
@Dark_Red_Hair2 82
@DarrellIssa 580
@DarrenJJordan 150,325
@DarrenWaggener 459
@DashMan18 27
@DattiJulia 18
@daveandlouanns 273
@DaveInKeno 121
@Davejager1 315
@davenorthYV 219
@DavesBigWife 38
@David_A_Hurd 25
@David_Gergen 329
@David360NC 202,209,231,236
@davidaxelrod 164,267,353
@DavidBougs 41,83
@davidco71875026 17
@DavidDCarpenter 28
@DavidFoody 152
@DavidGregory 391
@DavidHerjavec 96

@DavidJMadeira 343
@DavidKyleOnline 73
@DavidRagan 359
@davidrwoods 31
@DavidSBaldwin 2
@davidshiloach 556
@DavidWohl 312,486
@davist19 119-20
@daybastrop 420
@dblack15nc 192
@dboiarsky 250
@dbongino 502-3
@DBottenhagen 87
@dc1a7ce3d7f7402 71,77
@dcexaminer 176,491,532
@dcfoodsafety 5
@DCnumerology 34,35
@DDietlin3 200
@DDiTarant 73
@ddpick18 283,350
@deacon6375 309
@deadeyemadoc 192
@Deaf_Dwayne 18
@DeanAllen12 114
@DeanDesign101 17
@deannecox777 56
@debateless 162
@debdew2 339
@DeborahCroce5 144
@debra0155 119
@DebraRakestraw 385
@deedeegop 278
@deedeesorvino 277
@DeeMcNa 204
@DeepakS76435750 435
@Def 140
@DefendingtheUSA 135,170,206,325
@deggow 284
@deneenborelli 10
@DennisDMZ 105
@DennisRodman 69
@DeplorableCBTP 577
@DeptVetAffairs 58
@deqwik2 157
@derekcarlson 189-90
@derektheeight 244
@Desheay 2,182
@DesignerDeb3 118,151,208
@Destiny 203
@detnews 183

@detroitnews 586
@deucecrew 281-2
@DeusVultGeorgia 235
@DeusVultUSMC 192
@DGrant39107133 145
@DHarley187 29
@DharmaBum77 326
@DiamondandSilk 247,287,339,382,405,409,429
.... 514,531
@DianeHauschildt 200
@diannrr 129
@DiCristo13 398
@DillyDoesIt 62
@Diplomt 91
@Diplomtc_Immnty 91
@directorblue 180
@Dis_labeledVet 126
@DistlerJoyce 424
@DittoPost 312
@dixierhilton 127
@dj4k4000 335
@DjD_Thunder 447
@djf123 59
@DJohnsonPGA 455
@DJTrump2016 201
@djw11223 289
@DLake66675 243-4
@DLoesch 59
@DISCORD 123
@dlt912 217
@Dlund22226523 104
@dlustv 211
@dmartosko 422
@dmharvey89 403
@DMRegister 71
@Dmsrcmc12Bob 238
@DnGLax 399
@dnmiller2000 343
@DNorrell 161
@Doctor_S_Freud 387
@Doctr__Wang 121
@DoDFiredawg78 141
@dojiedojie 101
@Dollfinish 241
@Domenclature 91
@DomineekSmith 270
@Don_Vito_08 386,445
@DonaldJTrumpJr.... 212,284,298,321-2,330,346
347,366,380-1,391,397,406,409-11,415
.... 459,478,512,552,587,608-9

@DonaldTrumpFink 267
@donell27743094 353
@DONJUBBER 1
@donlemon 26,111,137-40,146,255-6,295,324
.... 339,538
@donnieboysmith 354
@DonnySmith557 231,233
@DottieandBogey 85
@DougDWiley 202
@dpdax 177
@dphilbs 290
@dr_tweedy 248-9
@dragonian3333 262
@Drake4444444 59
@drdoucette 271
@drewcarter49 64
@drewtheg 229
@drgoodspine 618
@DrHawk12 184
@DRJAMESCABOT 297,315
@drmoore 420
@DrRPSmall 243
@DRUDGE 319
@DRUDGE_REPORT 89-92,111,124,142,144
...156,189-90,216,245,266,272,297,314
.316,318,409,463,486,498,500,516,536
.... 576
@DSF2020 503
@dsherfinski 53,64
@dubilujane 433
@dukeofbc 316
@DumpFoxNews 376
@dunn_cheri 56
@DWStweets 481
@DynamyteBeats 19
@earredondo 27
@eastevens54 26
@eastonelliott22 35
@EasyEarl 180
@EazyMF_E 604
@ebalky 57
@echump 21
@Ecsullie 129
@Ed_Klein 435
@eddiebrognano 73
@eddiern 192
@EdGoeas 419
@EdRollins 348
@Edward1 121
@EdwardChelednik 130-1

@EdwardFrancisII 61
@edwards_cristy 258
@EdwinRo47796972 289
@EEGRC98 209
@eericmyers 548
@ehShaun 25
@Einsteinrevisit 22
@elisac006 543
@EliseChristine 127
@elizabethforma 435-6
@elizwatkins 5
@elkay14 142
@ellenEspence 129,214,323
@ElliekeMary 149
@elsolarverde 504
@ElviNichols 157-8
@Elvisfan1976 335
@ElvisFever 92
@elvisknievil 184
@EmaGabi23 357
@EmitteLucemTuam 210
@emtitus 11
@EndlessMike03 268
@EnemyWithinn 504
@energy43 263
@energypryde 70
@Enlighten2881 327
@Entrepreneur 105
@EOetzel 72
@ept_rudyru 90,153
@eric_wagaman94 206
@ericbolling ...3,11,38-9,41,82-4,95,221,282,299
.... 463,519
@EricCantor 106
@EricGreitens 585
@ericnlin 327
@EricShawnonFox 210
@EricSjursen 175
@EricTrump 82-4,164-6,246,287,290,297-8
.... 302,322,328,330,336,345,348-9,355
.. 360,365,369-70,375,384,397,410,416
.... 459,462,468,477-8,508,523,527,574
.... 587,609,613,619
@ErinBurnett 136,216,302,322
@ErinEdwards001 42
@ErinSiegal 27
@erintighe_ 60
@essygalloway 207
@EthaBrooke 140
@ethanolbyPOET 216

@ethansimmons111................................. 129,201
@Eugene_Scott 46
@eva_rider 36
@eVDefuse... 189
@eventbrite... 353,382
@EveWicked... 261
@EWErickson 28,42,94,151-2,379
@EyeCandyTMGayle.................................. 509
@faagifts 185
@facebook... 85
@FacetheNation .152-3,155,366-7,394-5,414,420
@facingeast52 68
@fackinpeter... 8
@fairess369 356
@fairy_tabibi 185
@FaithandFreedom 450
@Faithful_USA 72
@FallonTonight................... 118-20,173,295,527
@FamilyRedsFans.. 343
@fanodale... 135
@farrightgregy 157
@FBeadon 206
@FEDEnergy 160
@fedupwithgovern 66
@Felix_Clay... 61
@fernandocarnal... 38
@Fieldoffight 501
@FieldRoamer... 249
@Figlo7 22
@Filibuster 594
@FireFlyFury 315
@fitsnews 12,16,55
@fivestarr6028 444
@FL_GIRL979... 11
@flanny1971 68
@FLifeforce 545
@FLTrumpTeam 346
@Foosball38... 149
@fooschamp95 241
@ForAmerica 25-6,28
@Forbes 42,146,215,415
@Ford 183
@Forrestben94 63
@FortuneMagazine 196,228
@fortworthpd 528
@Foshay504 71
@Fox 155,261
@Fox411 212
@foxandfriends 10,33,63,68,76,83-6,102,111
120,126,144,148,165-6,200,209-10,212

. 229,240-1,257,260,320,329,330-1,355
.... 358,377,389,401,405,412,417,420-1
.... 425-6,447,475,501,510,518,522,525
............................527,529-31,536,619
@FoxBizAlert...420
@FoxBusiness 184,205-6,214,312-3,377,456-7
@FoxGotTrumped 164
@foxnation 63,213,228,512
@FoxNews 3,8-10,14-5,43-4,49-51,77,80
.......82-86,89-94,97,103,106,108,110-2
...... 115-6,118,124,126,128-33,142,144
...146,148,156,162-4,166-72,174-5,181
.... 185,187,192,198,200,203-4,206-7
....211-2,217,221-2,226,228,230,232-3
....242-3,246,249,256,258-9,262-6,270
275,277,280-2,284,288-90,293-4,298-9
....314-7,319,324,337,340-3,347-9,356
.362,366,368,370,374,376,378,381,388
....394-6,398-9,401-4,413,417,419,424
... 428,437,440,442,449,451,453,461-2
....467-8,471,475-6,481,483,491,507-8
.......510-1,513-4,522,526,530,542,545
.... 584,598,601,607-8,611,614,618
@FoxNewsInsider 12,102,258
@foxnewspolitics............................. 146,180,351
@FoxNewsSunday.. 155,168-72,232,249,395,414
....601
@frank_lemoine 45
@FrankCaliendo 447
@FrankDallasAgg 428
@frankdimauro 30
@FrankGuaragna 162
@FrankieEMT_B..34
@frankieguy85 214
@Franklin_Graham 53,258,260,508,605
@FrankLuntz 65,88-92,134,258,267,299,543
@FrankyLamouche...439
@FranMFarber 233
@free_SA_BD 443
@freebird_Pepper 201
@FreeDavidKing...543
@FreedomHaawk 17
@Freedomr 201
@Freedomrings22...201
@freedoms411..212
@FreeJesseJames...302
@freelancer1787...200
@FreemarketSara..449
@FreeStateYank 134,191
@FS1 200

@FSMtweet 51
@ftimewifenmomma 25
@fubaglady 73
@funtravel777 32
@futureicon 36
@g_pluth 71
@Gabigayle 3
@gamzorz 383
@GardiBates 148-9
@GarethBale22 70
@GarettWadekempe 36
@GaryGaryt52 151
@garyinlv01 208
@garyplayer 192
@GaryT212 245
@gatewaypundit 34,63,248,276,433,495,515
@gawker 86,87
@Gearssuxs 392
@gedion_t 140
@GeeVeeM 543
@Gemgm7 463
@gene70 65-6,315,399-400
@genemarks 105
@GeneMcGee6 253
@genesimmons 53-4
@GenFlynn 501,522
@Genie115 397
@gentlemanirish 135
@GeoffEarle 44
@george_frye 93
@georgehenryw 286
@georgeokc 116
@GeorgeWill 97,171-2,249,266
@GeraldoRivera 22,299,311,319
@GeraldSoelz 225
@gerardtbaker 214
@gerriweth 428
@getreal1234 400
@ghfanlovessonny 527
@GhostDancer_2 58
@ghosthunter_lol 289
@ghostofnicky 20
@giatny 191
@gigglcmitz 319
@GinaandersonRN 57
@GinHay 118-9
@girl_iowagirl20 169
@GirlDayTrader 175
@GlendaAhrens 233
@glendabelle_11 102,130

@glennbeck 151,190,268,299,304,307-9,337,388
@Glitter_alex 169
@glozee1 398
@GMA 111,175-6,200,213,312,377,531,574
@Gman0623 217
@GmoneyRainmaker 316
@gneumann 15
@gohermie 395
@GoldJazz559 514
@Golf_com 443
@GolfChannel 39-40,373
@GolfDigest 619
@gomrunner 42
@Good2bqueen67 231,339
@Google 328
@GOP 36,40,60,65,72,123,146,164,198-9
       217,229,231,247,249,392,394,448
        465,507,537,544
@GOP_Left_Me 328
@GOPconvention 432
@GOPjenna 395
@gordonsr1052 436
@GotMade 53,92
@gov_gilmore 524
@GovBrewer 461
@GovChristie 205-6
@governor_savage 400
@GovernorPataki 25,104,266
@GovernorPerry 29,52,64,118
@GovernorSununu 76,536
@GovMikeHuckabee 192,267,373,505
@GovPenceIN 407
@GovtsTheProblem 17
@gpavlik7 68
@gqforbes 71,83,399-400
@gracefulme3 397
@Gracematters 225
@GraggQuinton 150
@grammies28 335
@grammy620 381
@Granite_Hope 287
@granitttg 93
@grant_hose 67
@GravisMarketing 185,188-9,297
@greengolf56 60
@GreenSkyDeb 406
@Greg39529063 226
@GregAbbott_TX 55
@gregens21 376
@greggutfeld 3,301

@GregGutfeldShow 3,301
@gregusp61 345
@GregWescott 156
@greta 40,48,71,85,103,112,115,117,128,135
.159,164,204,206,211,233,278,297,305
.319,324,362,371,395,411,421,437,453
.... 465,496,503
@gretawire 12
@GriceCindy 350
@grindingdude 152
@GroverWindham 29
@GrundleMan27 205
@GSamUSA1 174
@gse_says 142
@Gsimmons03Ginny 545
@GSRPygmies 225
@GStephanopoulos 8,143-4,155,180,191,210
.... 213,228-9,270,295,312,321,383
@gulfportedd 110
@GulfWarVet123 236
@gullakhta99 388
@gump6363 45
@guthrie_kelley 72
@GZervs 17
@HalangManok 64
@HallieJackson 277
@hallmarkm1 38
@HaloDad22 442
@HaloOneForTrump 217,315
@hamishjoy 45
@HamishP95 119
@hammetjohn 69,74,282
@Hanan_Khan2 203-4,206
@HankCampbell 179
@hapearce1 159
@happyjack225 289
@hardball_chris 264
@HardcoreRepub 113,170
@HarpAmyStabler 200
@HARyder 332
@Hashtag1USA 121,137,282
@HavBat22 362
@hbtc23 88
@HCannonball 18
@heavenlyitalian 156
@HeinzFGuderian 61
@heiressarts 229
@helendhughes 36
@Hell0ThereLydia 162
@HenryLeledog 548

@HenryOray 315
@HenryTheZebra 198
@herb_stamper 403
@Heritage 232
@HerschelWalker 272
@HeyTammyBruce 394
@heytana 105,228
@HFFoundation4 428
@hiddenspeed42 226
@Highlander6700 28-9
@HighonHillcrest 594
@HighSock_Sunday 127
@highwayhopper66 109
@HillaryClinton 47,49,53,76,86,143,162,167
.176,189,208,225,229,280,385,428,514
.... 533-5,543-5,548-52,562-6,582
@HillsGypsydad05 210
@hillx123 195,334
@HL3tweets 56,71,159,167
@HMaewest 186
@hofmannken 292
@Hohummm 165
@hollyammon 5,20
@hollywoodJV 316
@HolySelena 5
@homefreeee 250
@hookjan 87
@hoosierclinger 183
@Hopeisalive66 129,193
@HorseShort 156,188
@HosierN 351
@Hot_Steam_ 245
@hotroddergirl 226
@HouseCracka 207
@HoustonGunn 29-30
@HoustonWelder 50
@HowardJax50 89
@HowardKurtz 21,37,142,153,155,243
@HowardStern 94,302
@howddyd 171
@hrkbenowen 97
@Hturne 72,219
@HuffingtonPost 48,54,70,96
@HuffPostEnt 178
@HuffPostPol 185
@HuffPostUKPol 73
@hufseyg 5
@hughhewitt 283
@hunterw 40
@HuskerPower811 130

@hyannis1952 9-10
@hyatt1942 187
@HyperbolicX 241
@i_am__tyler 162,177
@I_Dont_Know_Her 7
@iamapatsfan 119
@iamDaveK 398
@iAmerican 63
@IAmFreedomMan 144
@Iamnewhere 161
@IanHanchett 7
@ibemoshing 104
@ibleedcoffee 25
@IBTimes 173
@icareeguns 288
@iceblink62 242
@Iceman0921 30
@icenycbx 19
@ICLV 545
@idawhannadoyou 233
@ifdanyt 543
@IgnatiusGReilly 130
@ihatematt 275-6
@IJNIPGM 280
@ilduce2016 356
@ileadliberty 62
@ileanabarkus 381
@iliveamongyou 229,231,244,247
@iLoveiDevices 289
@iluvbks1 241
@IMG 271
@imprimis310 20
@Incazzato2015 134
@incorrectpoliti 16,18
@Indies4Trump 353
@IngrahamAngle 116,161,323,477
@InsideGym 283
@Insides4Trump 185
@insighter007 205
@instapundit 25
@insuradude 63,267
@insuraider 1
@InsureRetire 87
@iowa_trump 462
@IowaCentral 216
@Ir0nSpirit 178
@irisodle 106
@IsaacNewYorker 9
@isabelsimon80 1
@iStandWithUSA 188

@IsupportTrump16 164
@italy2320 91
@itsblakec 134,354
@itsEmilyshine 18
@itsjoeco 362
@iuhoops2015 88
@IvankaTrump 132,151,159,164,191,220,298
        .301,321,333,342,347,366,375,384,443
        444,446,459,478,496,522,525-6,531
        581,584,586-7,609,618
@IvoryRymes 83
@J_Styborski 376
@J58golf 509
@jaazee1 227
@JackBurtonReflx 312
@JackDix03868724 193
@jackie4545890 36
@jackmarchione 209
@jacknicklaus 304
@JackoffJosh711 403
@jackson3pack 114
@JacobKamarasJNS 20
@jacobmathews 21
@Jacobsac2015 277
@JacoH 237
@Jaguar11d 19
@jak00seven 208
@JakeAwK 10
@jakeda 463
@JakeKonczyk 8
@jaketapper 2,178,180,217,248-9,261,263,305
        329,408
@jakistheman 189
@jakub_lisa 229
@jallenaip 285
@jamalwms45 21
@james_artherton 30
@jamesdschulzejr 166
@jamesgo31991021 17
@Jameslauer6 236
@Jamesppierce 162
@JamesPWilson1 225
@JamesRosenFNC 442,449
@Jamgrigs 154
@jan102345678 78
@janetaylorann 57
@Janetlarose1 367
@JaniBetancoirt 266
@JaniceTaylor912 298
@janienorris22 273

@janik1968.. 429
@JaredChristophr.. 179
@JaredWyand.. 371
@Jarod_Pitmon10.. 2
@jaslohr 218
@jasondhorowitz.. 98
@JasonDovEsq 421,431,435
@JasonKoster17 17
@JasonMillerinDC 550
@jasonusmc2017.. 114
@jasthompcountry.. 247
@javonniandjeno.. 96
@jaxsiete 187
@jaxx613 146
@Jaybaby63 67
@jaycatalyst1 138
@JayJohnsonLikes 201
@JayknightJay.. 186
@JayMichaelsProd 153
@JayRHaw 139
@jazztheelf.. 31
@jbclemson.. 233
@JBOD2001.. 153
@JCippy 54
@jcooper75.. 218
@jdanielmoore 129
@jdenino1 312
@JDiamond1 43,231
@JDickerson.................. 155,295,321,366-7,394
@jdwarren12 103
@jeanne_mazzotta.. 29
@JebBush 15,33,35,102,104,110,117,157,160
           165-6,170-1,173,178,181-2,255,269-71
          273,276-7,280,283-4,286,288,291-2
          304,306,330,334,337,348
@JEDTHEFISH7 84
@Jeff_Gabe.. 160
@JeffBezos.. 251
@JeffFlake.. 520
@JeffHorwitz 230
@JeffJlpa1 27,77,317
@JeffPage5.. 231
@jeffpaine 337
@jeffraykovich 121
@jeffzeleny.. 594
@jenilynn1001 118-9
@Jenism101 58
@JennaLeeUSA.. 135
@jennasnowy69 160
@Jennifer75AR 80

@JenniferJJacobs.. 260
@jensen4law.. 569
@JereeGeeStavich 79
@JeremyHL.. 163
@JeriHyatt 102,104
@jerome_corsi.. 86
@JerryJrFalwell 302,354,457,487,509,527
@jessebwatters 100,281,382,527,584
@Jessi_Libertad.. 245
@jessicarnewman.. 89
@Jessyandcandy 10
@jesuspacheco58.. 84
@JetRanger69.. 91
@JewNamedLew 25
@JezzaK 213
@jfgrcar 182
@JFK4701.. 250
@jharwood14.. 30
@jheil 199
@jimbos2002.. 509
@JimBrownNFL32............................ 603,608
@JimClarkFarrier 130
@JimHarbaugh49 200
@jimhewitt 447
@jimlibertarian 40,54,63,65,86,115
@jimmcvey1 192
@jimmy_jkmorgan 166
@jimmyfallon 118-21,295,527-8
@JimmyForTrump.. 205
@JimmyGould07 212
@jimmykimmel 268
@JimmyTheSaint09.. 356
@jimparkey.. 256
@JimShellenback.. 131
@JimStaricha.. 25-6
@JimVitari.. 461
@jinx510 63
@JIS3 340
@jjhrkel 19
@jknatter 435
@jlangdale 47
@jlopez05391 400
@jlund04 428
@jmartNYT 207
@Jmoschetti1363.. 576
@Jnelson52722.. 543
@JNSworldnews.. 20
@JodiL792.................... 130,135,195,278,285
@Jodygirl1010.. 548
@JoeBowman12.. 594

@JoeDeFranco 447
@JoeDurak 88
@joeearle 121
@joehos18 107,120
@JOELMENTUM 31
@JoeMarzocco 133
@JoeNBC 4,142,157,188,292,310,323,328-9
.... 344,361,418,510
@joeoh89 129
@JoethomasSmith 159
@joetoohey 144
@JoeTrippi 169,198
@JoeWeissnmb 98
@JoeyCarna 54
@JoeyL3rd 165-6
@john_dipaolo 129
@john_franco 102
@John832TheTruth 92
@Johnatsrs1949 576
@JohnBerman 98
@johncook4189 95
@johndickerson 152
@johnjcarp61 58
@JohnJHarwood 190
@johnjohnlacca 429
@JohnKasich 92,248-9,251,390
@johnkirtley 428
@johnkurkosky 297
@JohnLegere 220
@johnmarzan 17
@JohnMcCain 53,58
@JohnNew2015 165
@JohnnnnyT 119
@johnnydollar01 21
@JohnnyG__62 57
@JohnRiversToo 25
@johnrobertsFox 398
@Johnsmi01433966 362
@JohnSte38475254 126
@JohnStossel 378
@johnwilson12511 238
@jojo2foxy 348,383
@JokerzWild_ 134
@Jolena3 459
@JonahNRO 293
@JonathonTrugman 7
@joncford 9
@joniernst 467,514
@jonkarl 270,329
@jonnati77 94

@JoNosuchinsky 301
@jonygitar 157
@jordanallen21 84
@JordanDworaczyk 184
@jordanfax 142
@JordanSpieth 10
@jorgeramosnews 19,106
@joseangelSP500 17
@josemen31 181
@joshdill64 173
@joshdronzek 50
@joshrogin 542
@JoshuaEnglishh 202
@joshuapantoja 91
@JoyCardinShow 139
@joycefinance 127
@joyciej2 241
@JoylynBest 20
@jp_sitles 106
@jphilman0206 385
@JPJAC 9
@jpm05880 147,182
@JPMORGAN2016 262-3
@Jrdavisii 148
@jrector34 429
@jrpantiques 217,230
@Jrprotalker 85
@JRubinBlogger 246
@jsconlon11 376
@JSears68 248
@jspence80 213
@jstaggs362 188
@JTAnews 421
@Jtrink97 162
@jtsbk 462
@JudgeJeanine 309,356,408,419,443,509
@JudgeMoroz 128,202
@judiejudyjudy 35
@JudiLoera 151
@JulesSiscoe 173,202
@julian771177 184
@JuliaTock 160
@julieruot 161
@JuliInkster 131
@JulUSN 25,28
@justdoit377 33
@Justice41ca 172,344
@justin_sellers 368
@JustinBores1 4
@justininglv 457

@justintupper 209
@JUSTTHETRUTHTV 30
@JuvenIle 238
@JWbananastand.. 143
@JWCarrr.. 60
@JWCesare 15
@JYakburger 140
@K1047 164
@Kacee50 245,290
@KaceyIlliot1669.. 428
@Karen05866992 171-2
@Karentalk.............................. 26,28,35,134,147
@karl 233
@KarlRove 8-9,11,40,49-51,110,116,129,165
.... 174-5,215,220,231,233,257,259,261
.... 262,266,275,325,349-50,414,479
@katek104 164
@Kathe56Kat 67
@KathieLGifford... 94
@Kathlee08380944 87
@KathleenLove10 57
@KathyCeurter... 448
@KathyPica1 241
@kathystone1221 106,171,182
@KathyTravels777 342
@KatiePavlich 295,528
@katiesinex 180
@KatrinaCampins 95,105
@KatrinaPierson...........167,177,217,222,288,325
@katygolf 92
@KatyTurNBC...................................... 196,248,445
@kausmickey 155
@kavemanrj 49
@kayleighmcenany 295,324,339
@KazmierskiR 212
@KBrocking.. 41
@kda20151223 57
@kdk144 406
@Keeblerqueen 260,397
@Keeganbcall... 87
@KEEMSTARx 19
@Keeping__Real... 234
@keichri 4
@KeithRowland 575
@keksec_org ..145,150,162,201,204,207,310,406
@KelliHeathman1 141
@KelliKM 39
@Kellmat2... 170
@KellyannePolls 419,510,529,532-3,551,614
@KellyRiddell... 424

@kellyz713 270
@kemper34... 200
@kencampbell66 170
@KenPettigrew... 141
@keraladubai 101
@kerrygold1914 70
@kevcirilli 322,547
@KevinGalyon 19
@KevinHart4real 164
@kevinolearytv 111
@khoges34 262
@kidran1 462
@Kids123Nicholas 399-400
@kilmeade 199
@KimBredesen.. 69
@kimguilfole 3,11,226,282,436,513
@KingAmory 33
@kingjersey1 22
@KingRollinZonez.. 30
@KingSchnabel 72
@kingster73 200
@KingVantes... 146
@KinnardJan 362
@kirkcameronfan... 9
@KirstenPowers 401
@kirstiealley 398-9
@kissmeandrocco 137
@kisster1 399
@kitkat123frank 147
@KittenHoliday 119
@Kj11100Me 386
@KMoriconi 34
@KNDetweiler 97
@kniala 212
@Knight276...................... 2,18,21,61,146,310
@kobuck12 30
@kolbytraveller 12
@koltonbittner 54
@KOsbornSullivan 160
@KosloffM 28
@koster4missouri 585
@Kotcha301 190
@kpdelbridge...60-1
@kpmck63 43,59
@krauthammer 5,41,45,85,92,97,106,214,264
.... 266,289
@KristenCWard 22
@kristopheryan11 290
@KristyWilliams79 21
@kronayne... 62

@KSmith233035 345
@KsRedbirds13 32
@ktd101551 230
@ktmcfarland 267
@ktumulty 98
@KurtSchlichter 312
@kuuleme69 57
@kylesteckel 115
@KyleStephens30 127
@kyredblood 156
@ladycatherinecd 105
@LADYJOANNE 428
@LadyKellLiberty 265
@LadySandersfarm 68
@ladytsbrug 429
@lafrana 26,28
@LAgirlrebelyell 67
@lainey34210 542
@LallyRay 486
@lance_combrink 165
@LandmanMarius 106,180,199
@LaneLynmil 87
@LaraLeaTrump 522,609
@Larry_Kudlow 137,144,500
@LarrySchweikart 146
@lasannewton 80
@Latinos4Trump16 261
@laura_damron 185
@lauralynn1955 9
@LauraRosenCohen 152
@Lauren_Nann 34
@laurencristmann 144,313,316,504
@LaurenDa123 160
@Lawrence 52
@LBabcock2 111
@lblackvelvet 520
@LBPerfectMaine 616
@LeahR77 130
@lee_richter 238
@LeeEllmauerJr 48
@LeeMiracle3 280
@leftfootjustice 143
@LeghanLiptak712 125
@LendonDonna 37
@LepleyAmanda 28
@Ler 521
@LesgartCPA 263
@lesleyclark 89
@LeStudio1 202
@LettyNTX 111

@levisteveholt 618
@Lewenskimo 512
@lewgeraldine 148
@LexingtonBobby 194,253,413
@Lg4Lg 61
@LiberatedCit 292
@libertyladyusa 116
@Libsaredemfools 94
@LifeZette 76
@LiliannyLeebou 444
@lilrachiepoo 399
@lilredfrmkokomo 289
@limbaugh 26,39,42,77,213
@linda_lcarson 104
@LindaHarden 514
@lindaleereyes 144
@LindaRicker6 147
@LindaSuhler 160,461
@lindseygraham 340
@LindseyGrahamSC .. 64,88,97,105,266,283,340
    379,386,418
@LinFlies 58,80
@LinHen23 501
@linley4067_jane 126
@linnie13 112
@LionsTrinityCap 13
@Lisa_Milicaj 306
@Lisa_Steen 147
@lisabrossman 327
@littlebytesnews 21
@Live5News 207
@LivNow 250
@lizaperri 60,119
@lizzym420 203
@LKDUSA 99
@Lking2fly 90
@llambert0207 5
@Lo7us_ 114
@lolabigirl 39
@longbyfive 428
@longtalltexan20 290
@LookerCherry 201
@LoreWestphal 323
@LoriPatriot 261
@LouDobbs 430,456,517,526
@loudobbsnews 37,260,374,380,392
@lovusa4 447
@Loyal2Trump2016 212
@Lrihendry 24
@LtStevenRogers 431

@lucascoon1 69
@Luciano031982 283
@Lucky5713 289
@luckydoginwesty 11
@lucyric13835428 377
@luismp77 73
@LukeBrinker 308
@LukeDillon6 119
@LunsfordWhitney 444
@lvphillies08 189
@lwentzel1 172
@lynn_weiser 84
@LynnePatton 416
@M0ther0f2kids 310
@Ma1973sk 157,228,381
@mabynshingleton 448
@MachadoKirk 181
@Macys 24-6,28-30,34-5,38-41,44-5,50-1
.... 65-6,69-70,220,230,235,247,291
@Maddow 248
@madisongesiotto 97
@madscape 129
@maggieNYT 236
@MagicMetalNinja 430
@magnifier661 162
@mai_Ttag 429
@maidaa17 548
@MailOnline 187,422
@MaineGOP 496
@MajorCBS 295
@MalachiNo. 84
@MalachiNorris 11,19-20,84
@Malibu101834 59
@malski1954 363
@Man_In_The_Hole 73
@ManahawkinMikey 149
@manakoa 428
@Mannamalistic 91
@MANX38 84
@MaraLiasson 40
@MARCMODE 40
@marcoinjersey 174
@marcorubio 32-5,133,146,160,334,351,356
.... 437
@marcthiessen 165
@MargaretCrowth1 235
@Margaretweber48 139
@Margee11 145,395
@MARGIE352 20,21,28
@maria_heck 183

@MariaBartiromo 214,313,420
@mariadaq 447
@MariaErnandez3b 439
@MariaTCardona 238
@mariclaire81 33,167
@marie7777777777 285
@MarieLeff 127,186
@Mario_Posillico 217
@marita1j 35
@Mark60644 131
@Mark98z 289
@MarkAGiarrusso 13
@MarketMavensInc 127
@markg0077 34,36
@markgruber1960 429
@MarkHalperin 199,246-7,267,328,331-2,380
.... 469
@marklevinshow 69,77,92,129,145-6,214,228
@marklindsay78 204
@MarkPavelich 135
@MarkSimoneNY 235,558
@MarkStahlbaum 245
@MarkSteynOnline 99,123,152
@MarshaBlackburn 526
@MarshallFSmith 194
@Marta_AQT4U 48
@marthamaccallum 88,246,421,543
@MarthaRaddatz 8,550
@martinmatishak 18
@martydrinksbeer 209
@MaryAnn1942 310,326
@Maryannzfoster 20
@marybnall01 289
@MaryEH428 377
@marykissel 364
@Maryland4T 232
@matandsher 419
@mathewjmari 420
@mattbai 238
@MatthewJDowd 230
@MattyJack33 100
@mauigirl56 89
@MaxChupailo 57
@Maxinerunner 66,92,99,194
@maxxgadog 160
@Mayor_Nutter 255
@MayorRGiuliani 522,580
@mazzei48 374
@mboyle1 78
@mcgranejt 41,45

@mcjeff42 209-10
@mckee16365 34
@McLaughlinGroup............................ 47
@mcowgerFL 162
@mcuban 77,79,122
@mdavis22569 35
@me_lisa_m 80
@MeaganShamy 12
@MediaBiasAlert 130
@MediaBuzzFNC 243
@Mediaite 143
@meequalsfree 516
@meetthepress.........36,125,143-4,154-5,210,237
...238,250,276,288,309-10,367,466,614
@meganena13 200
@meganweaver321 225
@MeghanMcCain............................... 112
@megliq 4
@megynkelly... 21-2,65,86,90-2,94,102-4,129-31
. 133-4,142,149,172-3,192,199,202,204
.... 208,256,265-6,295,299,308,312-3
.... 315-6,339-40,376-83,394,427-9,484
.... 542
@MELANIATRUMP...142,336,349,358,362,386
.... 395,399,437
@MelindaDC..................................... 269
@melindaross123 298
@MellysModern 29
@melsthemom 22
@MEMEoryHead 286
@MeOnAJourney 63,135
@mercedesschlapp 120
@mesiaindo 169
@metalmom888 400
@Metazip 343
@Mets 48
@metskins10 150
@Mey 121
@mholsbunes 219
@mia_liner 225
@Miami4Trump 520
@MiamiHerald 177
@MiamiNewTimes 306
@micah_micahk 344
@Michael_0000 197
@michael_favreau 194,430
@Michael2014abc 261
@MichaelCohen212 52,58,67,86,98,177,220
..........................232,242,270,325,615
@michaelG4NY 316

@michaelglassner 226
@michaeljohns 62,77,153
@MichaelW56 36
@MichaelPlu 51
@MichaelTribunel 160
@michaelUrso2 256
@michell33841372 29
@MichellePippin 145
@Michelleri 114
@mickelsenkyle 126
@MidOhioMilitia 151
@midwestcaucus 135
@Mike_Beacham................................ 87
@Mike_Pence. 475,485-6,488,490,496-7,499,511
514,516,521,535,541-5,550,552,569-70
.... 580,598,600,605
@Mike05999224 243
@Mike350Zdriver 174
@MikeandDawnNY 190
@MikeAndMike 447
@mikebarnicle 323
@mikeezepek 59
@MikeG_Beats 33
@MikeHuckabeeGOP 205-6
@mikeliberation 344
@MikeNeedham 232
@MikeOG_ 217
@MikeOzanian 413
@mikepetrella17 262
@MikeRaj7...................................... 103
@mikerichterp 161
@mikerotondo86 95
@mikescintoshow 33
@mikiebarb...................................... 361
@MilitaryRosary 40
@mimi_saulino.......................... 156,167
@MingBlueTeaCup 235
@MintzShire 159
@MiriamRoseMc................................ 130
@missi51 386
@misskellyaudrey 142
@misstozak 202
@MissUniverse................................ 15,271
@misterdish69 144,189
@MisterGoldiloxx 256
@mitchellvii 68,165,212,279,316,345
@MitchEPerry 79
@MitchPrefach 74
@Mitestarossa................................. 14,44

@MittRomney 34,36,55,139-40,168,172,350-2
.... 366
@mj_lee 40,46
@mjh811 17
@MJJustus1.. 58
@MJosephSheppard 115
@MJP1370 230,353
@mkhammer 224
@mklloydva 168
@MLauer... 165,183
@MlSSTHOT...119-20
@MMFlint 575
@MMMDigits 287
@mmolina44 182
@MNManstein2 141
@mnrosrnr.. 218
@ModerateMic.. 72
@Modern_Do_Good 127
@MoeHoward86 125
@moekamerow 66
@MollyCBS2 20
@mollymaguires61... 249
@Momfullofhope 152
@MonicaCrowley....................................... 3,175,259
@Montel_Williams 63,64
@MontesKitchen 141
@montgomeriefdn 432
@Moonwkr.. 151
@MorenoDadKC 51
@morg25016893 353
@mormontim... 142
@Morning_Joe ..4,20,79,86,106,112,132,152,157
          184,186,191,199,213-4,233,239,258
          267,312-3,323,332,349,364,377,417
          ...418,420,444,447,488,509-10,513,519
@morningmika 157,188,214,233,349,510,513
.... 519
@MorningsMaria.. 313
@moses11211.. 76
@moshe_mkmdca 159
@MoskowitzEva 619
@mozarttaig1 186
@Mr_Holtzworth... 202
@MrBiggles12345... 29
@MrBrentAllen 8
@mrctv 40
@MrdannyArthur 61
@MrDeuce25 266
@MrJuuon 310
@MrsJRobbins 60

@MrsVanessaTrump 321
@MrTohNey.. 424
@msann43 140
@msbul 181
@msnbc 5,349,513
@mstanish53.. 103
@mstrbass2000 27
@msully65.. 271
@muhfuck 170
@muireb_tpnd 26
@MULawPoll 139
@munciewolves.. 236
@MunichEleven 14
@Mutual408Grace... 400
@mwood_79.. 56
@myGianLuca.. 32
@myhealthcoach1.. 166
@MYKALFURY... 69
@MyPresidentme........................... 154,210,312,383
@mysteriousLoser 255
@N_R_Mandela 197
@namusca... 287,323
@nanaelaine7 15,34
@NancyLLeonard... 107
@NancyNielsenn 480
@NancyRomano17 182
@NASCAR.. 360
@NastiaLiukin 283
@natalie_gulbis 39,443
@Nate_Cohn.. 60
@NathanDWilsonFL 420
@nathanpaul1975 144-5
@nationalrifle 161
@nauthizjane 448
@NauticusNorfolk 194
@Nay_2xTimes 147
@NBC ..20,34,62,96,118,121,125,143,169,188
.... 277,295,523,620
@NBCDFW.. 439
@NBCNews 242,309-10,316,370,390,463,606
.... 608,614,618-9
@NBCNewYork.. 63
@NBCNightlyNews 64,277,602
@NBCPolitics.. 469
@NBCSNL 143,158,202,205-11,591
@NCGOP 558
@NealConan... 274
@NeBonnie...34,36
@nedbello 149
@need2knowu 505

@NeilECollins................................27
@NeilForell...................................143
@Neilleon_....................................27
@NeilTurner_..............304-5,310,355,387
@Neilyoung....................................13
@nellaalda...............................335,389
@nepafortrump...............182,247,269
@neraex.......................................190
@Netanyahu..................................257
@NewDay..........242,289,377,415,420
@Newsmax_Media.................36,39,42
@newtgingrich.......328,409,412,522,535
@NexiaVauxhall..............................161
@NFIB...500
@ngb6060....................................188
@Nick_Da_Slick..............................34
@Nick95B....................................232
@nickcokley...................................14
@NickEgoroff................................200
@nickmichaels12............................174
@NickyFlash2...................................2
@NicolleDWallace............................97
@Nigel_Farage..........................512,591
@NikkiHaley..................................360
@nikkisue69..................................283
@NishantAgg23.................................7
@njoh1234......................................7
@NoahGrayCNN.............................166
@noamscheiber.............................308-9
@nobaddog....................................236
@NobamaDotCom............................97
@nodramahea................................108
@nojoed..11
@nolehace......................................35
@NolteNC.................................16,69
@Non_PC_Guy................................30
@nonstop85716................................54
@NorahODonnell............................361
@norge1956..................................201
@normmacdonald............................528
@Norsu2.......................................150
@NorthStarMF.................................48
@NottaLiberal................................203
@nowandthan................................82-3
@nozzero.......................................69
@npomalley....................................73
@NRA...................161,432-3,502
@nranews......................................161
@NRO.....................................31,306-7
@NRSC...335

@Numerologynow.............................30
@nunyabus1..................................126
@ny_conservative...........................230
@nycmia......................................543
@NYCStadsliv.................................17
@NYDailyNews.........4,19,48,124,331-4,371
@nypost.................7,44,154,212,403
@nytdavidbrooks............................381
@nytimes...7,85,132,167,205,234-5,241,246,252
............254-5,276,303,308,373,386,400,424-6
............430-2,435,438,441,455,465,472,485
............492,504-6,508,519,525,529,541,554
...........................556,589,590-2
@NYTimesDowd..............................529
@nytimesworld................................84
@nytpolitics..................................249
@OAmericanGirl..............................205
@OANN.....185,188-9,191,201-2,206,232-3,251
...........................297,617
@oasisupernova..............................435
@oates_tom....................................17
@ObamaTax..................................162
@ObfuscateClear.............................182
@ofccadjust.............170,173,261,270
@officialjtw....................................95
@OliMauritania..............................480
@Oliviaand24................................218
@Ollie_621..................................404
@OMAROSA..............................94,317
@omgnastygirl.................................32
@onesoldiersmom.......................27,123
@OpenChampionship..........................62
@Operator1975............................70,74
@oreillyfactor......9,22-3,59,60,63-4,85-6,95,100
.........103,110-1,116-7,128-9,164,193,206
.........214,255-6,258,267-8,299,315,319,347
.........378,397,401,406,416,434,437,463,468
.........471,476,503,519,522,524,527,530,538
...........................575
@oshack.......................................178
@OSPREY675................................520
@otto2468......................................71
@OUSoonerManiac...........................175
@OutFrontCNN...........20,136,216
@OutnumberedFNC...........................436
@OUTOF_3_9_0................................93
@Pablo44x....................................237
@paintonmy...................................328
@paintonmyjeans.............................327
@PamelaJaneVP..............................196

@Pandorasandy1 161
@Pappenjazz 170
@PARISDENNARD 522
@Parker_Votes 157,192,220
@pastormarkburns 377,513
@pastormike7 292
@PatMcCroryNC 532
@Patrici 515
@Patricia_Graf 461
@Patrick0215 110
@Patrick92299179 128
@PatrickAnna 244
@PatrickBuchanan 6,264
@PatrickJLavin 29
@PatrickStinard 104
@PATRIOT4657 65
@PatriotByGod 174
@patrioticpepe 489
@PatSheldon10913 232
@pattiandsammi 388
@PattiPav1 172
@PattonDivision 243
@patty_laughlin 233
@PattyDs50 172,247
@Paul_Beiss 61
@PaulaDuvall2 73-4,390,505
@PaulaPedene 196
@PaulaReidCBS 582
@paulferguson17 171
@paulfincher2 97,153
@PaulkDebra 126
@paulkellysr 69
@PaulManafort 398
@PaulRSidneyUK 145
@paulteutulsr! 346
@PauperInAPinch 163
@paysbig 72
@pbralick 301
@pbsgwen 305
@pbstwo 9,51
@pbump 230,236
@pdpryor1 581
@pdxnancy 36
@pearl_brendan 290
@PearlsPolkaDots 209
@peddoc63 72,146
@peg4cats 220
@Peggynoonannyc 261-2
@Penguins 451
@Penn 528

@pennjillette 50,52,169
@pennybishop16 119,247
@PennyHicks13 399
@PennySingletary 151
@periscopeco 3
@PeritusTraining 36
@PerryJames778 29
@PeteNice1976 106
@peter_smells 202
@PeteRose_14 264,374
@pg_rant 57
@Pg1493 45
@PHATWHODAT 45
@PhillyPolice 528
@philmonaco67 273
@PhinsDiehard 206
@PhoenixConvCtr 43
@PHussionWYFF 339
@PhxKen 143-4
@phxladydi 24
@PhyllisA 129
@PianoBecca 1
@piercingshawn 143
@PiersMorgan 176,187,211,213,265,288,329
.... 432,486,576
@Pimpburgh2015 248
@pink_sprnva 292
@PiperSul 435
@Pistol044 121
@PizzaPartyBen 31,84,209
@PJAliveguy 64
@Pjdahling 165
@pjs307 206
@PJTV 59
@PjwJ316 150
@PlatinumRosie 91
@PlaysTrumpCard 282,315
@Plazzmatic 316
@Plruble58 117
@PMgeezer 123,310
@PMNOrlando 515
@pnehlen 494
@pnicastro1 148
@Poetry4Bitcoin 200
@pokeyisme1971 95
@polemicism 144
@polina6 136
@politicalwire 179
@politichick_ 249

@politico 77,101,132-3,149,152,186,188,191
.... 194,206,228,244-5,332,397
@POLITICOMag 27
@Politics_Reddit 157
@PolitiTrends 50
@Polling 186
@pollsterpolls 48
@Port3Star 231
@Portosj81J 174
@POTUS 143,551,563
@PPFA 70
@ppppolls 41
@premuse 2
@PressTV 113
@PrestonsDayOff 63-4
@pretrim10 73
@PrimMrs 97
@princeolivier13 160
@printingsharon 176
@PrisonPlanet 234,558
@prissyalways 161
@Pryan 469
@pthebnyc 235
@puttster71 313
@PValk16 63
@PYNance 581
@Q1776 146
@qbeacademy 274
@QueenCharlotteO 424
@QuinnipiacPoll 349,472
@QuinnLisaq 256
@R_U_OK_UK 398
@racheljoycowley 26
@Raddmom 146
@RadioFreeTom 174
@radioworldsv 183
@ragdollive 427
@RageFelix 104
@RagingCynicism 128-9
@raider8381 233
@raleynicole143 84
@RandPaul 95,120,139
@rapidcraft 445
@RasmussenNews 51
@Ravenrantz 581
@ravila30 119
@RaxsonDFS 83
@ray_aub 213,255
@RBacliff 433
@Rbbrkhd 129

@rbern11162 42
@RD_2008 170
@rdbrewer4 42
@rdpaga 171
@Reagan_Girl 204
@ReaganWorld 16
@Real_Carl_Icahn 146
@real_one23 88
@realArthurSpina 252
@RealBenCarson 92,186,200,324,333,336,363
.... 371,377,599
@realbigstriper 147
@realbill2016 510
@realbobmassi 89
@RealCinders2 208
@RealClearNews 120
@realclearspam 149
@realdctaylor 233
@realericjallen 453
@RealJamesWoods 61,492
@realJeffreyLord 429
@realJoeMurray 1,2
@realkingrobbo 226
@reallyo1 235
@RealMarkCole 82-3
@realmarkjackson 35
@realNevaDie 273
@RealNinjetta 27,161
@realOllieTaylor 195,201,305,328
@RealReagan0503 143,219
@RealRudyGiulian 397
@RealSheriffJoe 385
@realwwshelton 374
@rebamoreland 28
@RebelCapsGal: 171
@red77angelluis 310
@redletter99 209,218,294
@RedNationRising 71
@redneckgp 398
@RedRising11 421
@RedScareBot 165
@RedState 28,93,146,152
@ReevesMH 50
@reganharycki 204
@RegentU 350
@Reid2962 91
@reidepstein 12
@ReillyCarole 35
@Reince 41,43,191,335,392,400,453,481,507
.... 580,609

@releafpen.. 163
@RenaSummersLtd.. 227
@Renhowe 140,146
@RepaloneLori.. 399
@RepBJNikkel 236
@RepChrisCollins 350
@RepDavid 61
@RepLouBarletta 501
@RepMartinDaniel.. 398
@RepMattSalmon 61
@RepReneeEllmers.. 526
@RepTomMarino.......................... 377,399-400
@RepTrentFranks.. 61
@Reryan08 298
@Resi_Diederich... 91
@ResisTyr 343
@restore_US_now.. 57
@restorereality 323,353
@Retrogirl01 38
@Reuters 229
@revdojoe 249
@Reveretoo 32
@ReversingASD 136,241
@reviewjournal 571
@rfscottga 171,187
@rg_radical99 2
@RhatPatriot 184
@RhettRiley1234 288
@rhinostate.. 205
@RhondaR 515
@Rhumeey 2
@RichardTBurnett... 340
@RichardTrumka 462
@RichardWeaving... 447
@RichBooth6 420
@RichLowry 27,129,132,236,282
@RICHMCLOUGHLIN 72
@Rick_Gobbi... 316
@Rick_Sa 204
@RickCanton 146,235
@RickSantorum 435
@RickSt. 185
@RickStans1 165
@rickwtyler... 346
@Ricky_Vaughn99 107
@RickysPlace1 21
@Riggs101 7
@rightside 309
@rikemohome 172
@RinglingBros... 295

@RioSunny3 234
@rjdicksii 160
@Rketeltas......133,135,183,185,195,235,238,310
@rkirchmeyer 316
@RKMCPHERSON2014 89
@rkswaney7 326
@rlbenney 292
@RLHoldenSr 140
@Rmac747 213
@rnull65 115
@RoadkingL... 542
@roadsho 397
@Roadstarr1 192
@robertaritzen 76,190
@robertew2945.. 200
@RobertGBeckel.. 207
@RobertH25937464 266
@robertjeffress 118,454
@RobertMordica 443
@RobertsLiardon... 183
@robmo 198
@robmont777 198-9
@Robostop10 205-6
@RobRucker.. 16
@robstanley79 244
@Rockprincess818 97,130,229,429
@rodsandguitars 33
@RodStewart.. 193
@rogerhartford8 148
@RogerJStoneJr 134,163
@RogerRice10.. 530
@ron_fournier.. 181,303
@RondaRousey 219
@RoniSeale 32,82,85-6,110
@ronnieclemmons 520
@RonnieMemo.. 356
@RonNussbeck.. 66
@ronsirak...39-40
@Roolaloo 160
@roparsons 33
@rosemarylowe105 262
@RosieGray... 558
@RossMahan1952 41
@rox473 66
@RoxaneTancredi 476
@Roy_Propsner.. 95
@rp53pierce.. 74
@rpollockDC 31
@RSan 19
@RSBNetwork 370,374,516

@rtoneff25... 17
@RTylerR4... 67
@rua1ri 54
@Rub 106
@RubenMMoreno 90
@RubenNavarrette 17
@RubinsteinNel 290
@RudyGiuliani.. 601
@RuizSeferino 97
@RunPureMichigan 27
@rupertmurdoch...................................... 249,363
@rushlimbaugh...............79,98,123,144,191,206
@russia890 181
@RussOnPolitics 246
@RustyBlissUSA 227
@RustyOsborne15 71
@RuthMarcus 288
@RW84JR... 58
@rwalkerTennesse... 343
@RWSurferGirl................................... 53,82,92
@ryan_padraic.. 157
@ryanamberwhite... 113
@RyanJNewman 359
@saadvisory 175
@sacquisto23 93
@sadmexi 162
@SahilKapur 184
@SaintPetersblog... 48,79
@SallyAvicii2014 195
@sallyvp 9
@SalRiccobono 289
@salyboy3 211
@SamaritansPurse... 508
@samijs1 166
@samsellars.. 225
@samsondunn.. 40
@SamSteel10 114
@Samstwitch... 18
@samuelghaddad.. 289
@SamuelLJackson..................................... 289,291
@SanchezBrutus.. 66
@SanDiegoPD.. 437
@Sandikay60 150,231
@sandrajeanne48... 430
@SandraJenners... 204
@SandraOpines 193
@sandrapatriot.. 70
@SandraR677582.. 346
@SandraR67758219.. 428
@saneplanet.. 115,382

@santiagos58.. 178
@sara_wejesa 447
@SaraGreenwell 243
@SarahPalinUSA................107,220-1,303-4,344
@SaraMurray 157
@sareed59 445
@Sari_Swensen 235
@sassylassee... 159
@SassyPantsjj 354
@SavannahGuthrie 146
@SaveAmerica15 29
@SaysGabrielle 581
@sburton305 188
@Scaramucci 425
@schnoepoe 263
@schoremis1... 274
@schwartzb... 60
@Schwarzenegger 121
@SCNAK45 376
@ScoodieGolden 76
@scorpio5053 82-3
@ScotMReed... 346
@ScottAdamSays 458
@ScottBaio 396
@scottferson 143
@ScottFordTVGuy 12
@scottienhughes 76,115,166,169,264
@ScottPelley... 135
@ScottWalker...... 70,72,76,128,139,477,507,580
@ScottWRasmussen.. 439
@SCPioneer.. 442
@SCTeamTrump 282
@Scully64 40
@sdcritic 594
@SeaBeeVietN... 87
@sean_in_NH 195
@seanbarakett... 31
@SeanBolza... 115
@seancduarte 158
@seanhannity...........9,43,60-3,65,69,76-7,95,103
.... 115,123-4,129,140,144,156,173-5
. 191,201-3,213,216,222,232,253,258-9
........262,282,290,293,326-7,342,346-7
.... 368,396-7,402,408,415,419,440,446
.... 448,463,468,505,507-8,511,531
@seanmdav.. 190
@SeanSean252 229
@seanspicer 543
@secupp 256,274
@seleti00 129

@SemiNoland.. 88
@sempek1 149
@SenateMajLdr... 423
@SenatorCardin 13
@SenatorFischer.. 502
@SenatorJeffSessions 448
@SenatorReid... 350
@SenatorSessions... 358
@SenBobCorker... 468
@SenFrankNiceley 403
@SenJohnMcCain 52,61,546
@SenSanders............................... 218,284,447
@SenTedCruz..20,38,87,95,116,291,299,314,317
.... 334,379,532
@SenTenCes 60
@SenzuLean.. 7
@serenawilliams 470
@setfire2flames... 448
@sfurnbac 143
@ShahKourosh... 262
@SharNeal...33,41-2
@sharonDay5.. 149
@Sharp_Trident 312-3
@SharylAttkisson 56
@shawncrazyshawn.. 9
@ShawnJohnson.. 70,283
@shawnlivinlife 217
@shawnslawns4u.. 195
@shelbycockaxe 200
@Shelia1965A 89
@Shella_Bella 70
@ShellHouOpen 395
@ShellyLeigh123 249
@ShellyPayne4328.. 253
@ShepherdGarrett 59
@ShepNewsTeam 217
@Sheriapple 26
@SheriffClarke 175,504
@sherrysue66 208
@shl 510
@SHLOMO_ABADDON 165
@shoegoddesss 37
@ShoneeP 430
@shook_stephanie 114
@Sia 207-8
@SilverSharen 74
@simonschuster.. 153
@SinAbunz_TM... 509
@SInow 443
@Sir_Max 279

@SirHatchporch 364
@Sisters4everT 188
@SJavner 202
@sjbatis 57
@sjh2222 81
@SJonesCNS 77
@SJSOPIO 572
@SKennedy1979 151
@skillethead58 190
@skulls2001 123
@SkyeShepard... 135
@skyjones55.. 164,169
@SkylerDeckard.. 353
@Slate 190,266
@slh 578
@slone 68,114,280,290
@sloopjohnb15 56
@slucch24 21
@SlwStdySqueeze..114-5
@Slytle24 353
@smith_jere 225
@smithj1 192
@smr111382 169
@SMW5683 5
@Snapchat! 349
@snoozinglion1 309
@SoCal4Trump 204
@socalmike_SD 109
@SocialInNewYork 207
@SolFusionGreg... 143
@SongBird1154 171
@SopanDeb 248
@sorensen_ao 73
@soupman227 26
@Southern_Anon63 91
@southpaw816 447
@SovAdjEast 10
@soz58 115
@SpacemanChris... 262
@spankemewanke18 36
@sparkey03 111
@SpartanMaker 388
@SpeakerRyan 190,271,423,429
@SpecialKMB1969 147,210
@SpecialReport 111,148,417
@Spen_A_John 30
@spiritofshiloh 203
@splashpoint50... 315
@sprinklermanus 285
@sprivitor 356

@sprts08 501
@SpurrellJulie 136
@squirtlong 83
@sr_stocks 86
@sruhle 164
@ss 312
@ssheaver 255
@stanColtrane 388
@SteelerDan619 268
@StefanVersac 92
@StellaDean 335
@steph93065 228,316
@stephbewitching 323
@StephenAtHome 132,339
@StephenBaldwin7 50
@stephenfhayes 70,148
@StephPrichard1 17,34
@sternbutgreg 138
@steveaustinBSR 88
@SteveBashino 189
@SteveBrainard1 147
@SteveDoocy 595
@SteveHuang68 100
@Stevekwebb 351
@SteveMarz1 61
@SteveMullaney1 54
@Stevenfclifford 12
@stevenkirk 6
@StevenMeyers11 348
@stinger_inc 91
@StJude 355
@stockdaleism 442
@StoneZipper 70
@StraightHand 262
@stranahan 424
@strayamaaaate 94
@StreckerJosh 159
@StreetR77 220
@StrengthenTheUS 181,198-9
@stuartpstevens 150,296
@Stvzbnk 524
@stylin1188 284
@suandres2013 89
@sueinwny 208
@SueSabo 196
@sugarhoney157 7
@sugarofsaturn 150
@Sulli1963 91
@sunnykcollins 115
@sunquist007 280

@SurfPHX 266
@surveyusa 113
@susanadana432 21
@susanbirchfiel1 392
@Susiesentinel 542-3
@suzost 264
@suzyserb 162
@svhlevi 429
@Svingali 172
@svn2hd 202
@swamp_bug 103
@swargcoming 206
@SweetFreedom29 173
@sweetspottrader 102
@swterry91 141
@syoka68 219
@T_Johnson_TJ 190
@T_Lineberger 581
@TadBoikins 18
@TakingIt_Back 424
@TakouiS 520
@Talkersmagazine 295
@talsept58 126
@Tamaralynn212 53
@TamiDurling 297
@tammyhorne19 128
@Tar_Heel_73 198
@tarabernie 65
@TaraHollyFigure 14
@TaranKillam 143
@TarukMatuk 530
@tas0727 227
@tasteofaz 218
@taurus82409 134,199
@tavissmiley 295
@TaylorEdwards99 443
@TaylorWrightAU 188
@tazz53098 207
@TCash78 226
@TCastilonia 60
@tcloer11 435
@tcsorr 385
@TDarbyMitchell 107
@TdavisTonya 200
@tdltdltdltdl 353
@TDsVoice 159
@Tea_Alliance 7
@Tea_Party_Chris 61
@Tea4Freedom 141,147
@TeamBobbyEwing 8,9

@TeamCavuto 67,158,264,298,362
@TeamFallowwBack 83
@TeamSpringsteen.. 203
@Teamsters 292,419
@Teamsters14 162
@TeamTrump...513,523,533-5,538,543-5,548-52
.... 576,582,609
@TeamTrumpAZ 382
@TeaPartyCat... 256
@TeaPartyNevada 439
@teapartynews 107
@Techn9cian1923 97
@tedb75 270
@tedcruz 22,28-9,36,65,258,275,296,300-2
. 315-6,333-4,340,346,351,385,390,395
.... 397,412-3,535
@teddyschleifer... 32
@teed_chris.. 192,212
@tegodreaux... 210
@TejadaDennes.. 218
@TeresaC85469500 270
@TeresaWageman.. 26
@TerryBranstad...................................... 321,535
@terrykimk93 195
@TerryLambert201 220
@TGowdySC 77,281,432
@ThAllenSBoucher... 531
@thatgirlflorida 181
@Thatsalrighty 110
@thatx209xguy 237
@The_Lady_Colors.. 297
@The_Trump_Train 371
@The2ndguardsUS.. 225
@theAgeofLeo 388
@TheAlabamaBand.. 620
@theblaze 51,73,103,129,259
@theBrandonMcKee 200
@TheBrianMo 103
@TheBrodyFile 44,65,76,105,126,140,297,301
.... 302
@TheCarCzarsPage... 256
@TheConnieMoore 148
@TheCRwire 181
@thecybermenace.. 289
@thedemonking18... 36
@TheEconomist 70,187
@theericker... 160
@TheFive 3,41,112
@TheFix 155,167,229,236,293
@thegre8_1... 38
@TheguhMantap 30
@TheHerd 194,200
@theHickMan33 5
@thehill ..18,68,77,97,133,141,154,196,238,253
.... 269,292,423
@TheHolyBreadcat 21
@TheIntellect111 134
@TheJordanHafizi 67
@TheJuanWilliams................................... 32,224
@TheJusticeDept 449
@TheJusticeEngle 184
@TheKrankyGirl 110
@thelastrefuge2~ 36,107,284
@TheLeeGreenwood 620
@TheLongShotzz 106
@themakaylamarie 67
@TheMindWave... 129
@TheMsDlr 196
@Themyamccurry 271
@TheNewsClub_US....................... 141,144,198
@THENORAWILLIAMS 61
@ThePatriot143 14,401
@TheProdigy3D.. 263
@theratzpack 172,243
@TheReadRyder.. 270
@therealbigdt.. 106
@TheRealCamSand 53
@TheReaLJuiCe88 16
@THEREALMOGUL 560
@Theresa_Cali 399-400,479
@TheRevAl 22
@TheRickWilson...256
@THESHARKTANK1...................................... 23
@TheSlyStallone 295
@TheSouthwasRite 307
@thetimes 97
@TheTodaysGolfer 432
@thetylerjames9 227
@TheUSALifeStyle... 29
@TheUSDesigns.. 115
@TheView... 292,387
@TheVotingVenue 45
@thewatcher23579 219
@TheWhiteHatter... 184
@TheWTFTahoe 146,154
@ThisWeekABC 8,143,155,191,228,237,238
.... 295,383
@ThomaOlivia 177
@THR 133,228
@ThtsWhtKelSaid..336

@thumpmomma 242
@thydanielflores 429
@tiarardis 356
@TickerCandy.. 26
@tiffyluck... 38
@TigerWoods... 598
@TimCooperTweets...................................... 161
@TIME 51,90,99,255-6,266
@TimeHasCome1 401
@TIMENOUT........................ 138,140,194,201
@timjcam 90
@timkaine 542-5
@TimVincent56 386
@TINAHILLSTROM1 288
@Tirolian2.. 181
@TitanicQueen.. 68
@tixxannatrix 24
@TJeeyy 34
@TLCastle... 227
@tmautner1211 67
@TMobile... 220
@TMoody 173
@TN_RiverFolk.. 148
@TNGCBedminster 395
@TODAYshow 5,94,105,126-8,146,165,179
.... 183-4,203,390,407,412,417,599
@toddinwichita.. 177
@toddstarnes 44
@toddwmoore01 115
@TomBarrackJr.. 436
@TomLlamasABC 99-100
@TomLydon.. 228
@tommyz63 43
@TomNocera 79,92,245
@TomOdell... 341
@TomRichey.. 218
@toneantone96 103
@Tony_Leers 178
@tonyarolandtr..28-9
@tonyewen 16
@tonykatz.. 26
@tonyparker1981 60
@tonyschiano 18
@tonyschwartz 524
@topcota1SG...143-4
@TopherCarlton 157
@ToTheTanr 88
@tperkins.. 106
@TPFA_KathyA_1 83
@TPInsidr 53

@tr3s3can 160
@TraceAdkins 464
@traceclmbs82 171
@TradingStreetCo 211
@tranerofmonstrs.. 41
@transition2017..590-1
@trapman2000... 18
@Trekwolf164... 174
@TriciaNC1... 71
@tropic20 113
@troubic 11
@troyconway 289
@trscoop 27,43
@TruBluMajority 305
@Trump_in_2016 120
@Trump_Supporter 403
@Trump_Videos.. 512
@trump_world.. 199
@Trump2016Donald 283
@Trump2016online 236
@Trump4potusplz 174
@TrumpAlabama.. 212
@TrumpDC... 525
@TrumpDemocrats... 119
@TrumpDoonbeg 443,474
@TrumpDoral........................... 15,178,264,366
@trumpettes16 243,244
@TrumpFix..163,200
@trumpgasm... 149
@TrumpGolf..264,395-6
@TRUMPHIANT2016 166,243
@TrumpInaugural... 601
@trumpiowa 154,282
@trumpisawinner... 263
@Trumpismyhero 249
@TrumpLasVegas 12
@trumplican2016......................................486,541
@TrumpNewMedia 144,343
@TrumpNV 349
@TrumpScotland 443,459
@TrumpsGucciGirl 86
@TrumpsMyHomeboy 206
@trumpstump2016.. 145
@Trumptbird... 404
@TrumpToronto 176
@TrumpTowerNY 2,111,135,199
@TrumpTrainRider 427
@TrumpTurnberry............85,432,443-4,459
@TrumpUSA16 273
@TRUMPVICTORY16 154

@TrumpWomensTour 555
@trumpy17 290
@TrussElise 241
@Truth_or_Rumor 199,252
@truthinvest 189,333
@TruthisAll1 282
@truthshallbe 135
@tryeye 13
@TS01171980 162
@TSettles14 86
@tudybone4 84
@Tuggers56 310
@turnberrybuzz 80
@Tuvarkz 170
@tvegan 142
@TwallMa 201
@tweak626 520
@tweet2u2 88
@tweet4upatriots 171
@tweetybird2009 236
@twendencyUSA 71,74
@twillnurse 195
@twister2445 270
@twitter 328
@TwitterNYC 127-8
@twlhb 266
@tytan01 388
@tzard000 424
@ukcatwoman52 327
@ultradave1951 61
@umakemeill 280
@UMassAmherst 221
@UncleLouie 50
@UndEngel 170
@Unicurls 225
@UnionLeader 282-3,289,291,293,295
@UnitedCitizen01 192
@Univision 15,27,41,45
@unknown_resist 119
@UrbandaleSchool 125
@USAforDJTRUMP 254
@USARestoring 77
@USArmy 452
@USATODAY 107,117,212,349,401,450
@USATOpinion 56,57
@USATrumpDiva 219
@USATrustTrump 177
@USCG 496
@USCHAMBER 462-3
@usclarry 33

@usplaymoney 18,32
@USSIowa 122
@utwey 8
@V4SA 122
@Valdosta_Monkey 420
@Valenti317 58,443
@ValetaSue57 85
@valmouw 159
@VanityFair 166,219,603
@Vaporcon2015 186
@Variety 211
@VaughnVhalen 235
@vbonina 172
@vdare 29
@vegas_sports 461
@VeneziaMatthew 34-5
@Vermont5girl 188
@VetApologist 58
@Veteran4Trump 381
@vettesetter 57
@VickyBrush 82,84,130,156
@VictorConkle 389
@victoryorbust 191
@videosigninc 282
@vikkideiter 396
@VincentKunicki 226
@vine 545
@Virginia4USA 37
@VisitScotNews 108
@vivhall3 399-400
@vlynpowell 167
@Vogelsong1 348
@Vote_For_Trump 343-4
@Vote_Trump 134
@VoteDonaldTrump 140
@VoteTrumpMAGA 454
@voxdotcom 180
@VRWCTexan 34
@VYlvisaker 262
@w_gorham 154
@w4djt 461
@waite_lane 63
@wakeupfla 209
@wakeuppeopleSOS 212
@wallen_jeanine 130
@WalshFreedom 206
@WalterEKurtzJr 169
@WalterWhfla 72
@WaltSeher 353
@WandaWalls20 451

@Ward_II 350
@WashingtonPost 60,101,225,231,246,251-2
.... 265,275,288,425,460-1,472,510,579
@WashTimes 6,53,64,97,537
@Watchman4the1 211
@WavRidr101 194
@Waxking911 208
@WayneAllynRoot 264
@waynearmstron10 129
@WayneDupreeShow. 45,145,196,228-9,344,401
@WayneNewtonMrLV 147-8
@WayneRoot 253
@wayway71 159
@wbtonyturner 174
@WBUR 305
@wdct8110 403
@Weaverinc31 172
@webster07 22
@weeklystandard 51
@WendyJFluga28 99
@wesleyfelixpsi 428
@WesleyRickard 381
@WesleyRuedy 61
@WETHEPEOPLE65 140
@WFinchner 30
@WGinetta 12,18
@Wheels155 395
@whispers34 284
@WhiteGenocideTM 306
@WhiteJacketPink 312
@Whitejl0111 77
@WhoopiGoldberg 14
@whyWinblo 121
@WiggintonRandy 251
@wildatlanticway 120
@WILDMANBS 22
@WillDangelo 88
@WilliamESammon1 269
@williamonlyrent 5,10,12,41
@williebosshog 68,305,309
@willspeakout 505
@WineChics 210
@winkiechance 82
@wizHether 35
@WKRG 234
@WMikeW 139
@WMikeWood 147
@wmsolomon 284
@WNTonight 222,254
@wolfblitzer 67,266,291,311,390

@WolfStopper 447
@WollmanRink 199
@Women4Trump 88-9,153
@wompol 239
@woodardralph31 66
@woodmank104 164
@Woodsy_gal 67
@woofeous 22,63
@WordgirlSmith 12
@WPayton344 398
@wpjenna 298
@WreckThisPro 83
@Writeintrump 157
@Writeonright 146
@WriteReadRock 97
@WSJ   58-9,80,86-7,194-5,214-5,231.253,345
.... 370,378-9,403,425,526,536,620
@WSJPolitics 12
@WVTTS1017 401
@WWDBLane 93
@WWE 88,143
@wzpd8z 239
@xai7126 159
@XGDesignsNYC 161
@XGNRaging 253
@xGodfatherxzx 427
@xXFlame 313
@xXFlameriumXx 190
@yang_karl 135
@YankeesJC1 103
@yankeeworshiper 22
@yayala19 132-3
@YesMrGilbert 277
@yeswecandeport 29
@YitzySchwartz 254
@Yoel_NY 262
@YomasterJon 340
@YossiGestetner 71-3
@YoungDems4Trump 531
@YoungYoung54 104
@youtube 109,125,202,309,310
@Youxia88 28-9
@ywu510 111
@ZacharySmitty 72
@ZachJohnsonPGA 62
@ZankMatt 191
@ZekeJMiller 51
@zengadfly 34
@ZephyrusMatrix 102
@zhu_amy3 616

@Zimbo251 48
@zulu_out 505
20/20 (tv program) 222,225-6
60 Minutes (tv program) 135,475,482
9/11   . 166,170-1,173,234,239,241-2,244,251
.... 255,399,405
Abbott, Greg 62
ABC News 176,179,196,262,294,313,522,558
ABC 175,181,222-3,226,293-4
Abdeslam, Salah 387
Abedin, Huma 85,108,568,570
Aberdeen, Scotland 108,174,443
Abingdon, VA 503
Abortion 65,545
AC360 (tv program) 180
Access Hollywood 65
Adelson, Sheldon 157,424
Affordable Care Act 555,610,617
Afghanistan 272
Africa 74
African American 69,116,218,237,239,450,457
.... 509,512-5,520,548
AIG 292
Ailes, Roger 94,141,315-6,383
Air Force One 269,467,521,582,599
Airbus 300
Akron, OH 510,515
Alabama 100-1,103,112,225,227-9,355,357-8
.... 361,602-4,620
Alaska 84,355
al-Baghdadi, Abu Bakr 112
Albany, NY 401
Albuquerque, NM 577-8
Aldridge, Nykea 514
Ali, Muhammad 444
Allen, John 488
Al-Shabbab 287,288
Amazon 275
Ambassador 456,591,620
Ambridge, PA 546
Amenia, New York 141
American Airlines Center 112,114,116
American dream 10,11,164,491
American Hunter 68
American Legion 521
American Samoa 384
Ames, Iowa 300
Amnesty 42,48,71,114,130-1,152,197-8,201,212
. 215,279,347,356-7,457-9,517,563,585
Anaheim, CA 433-6

Anchor babies 100,104
Annapolis 52
Apple 342-3
Appleton, WI 392
Apprentice, The 50,52,58,96,123,196,601
Argentina 107
Arizona   39,43,46,66,193,268,379-85,430,454-5
512-20,539,542,545-6,569,575-7,610-1
Arkansas 54,325,355-6,361,503,553
Army 258,513,601
Arpaio, Joe 381
Art of the Deal (book) 200,495,499
Art of War, The by Sun Tzu 175
Asheville, NC 525
Asia 102,104
Assange, Julian 611-2
Assault weapons 40
Associated Press 430
Atkinson, NH 184
Atlanta, GA 93,153-4,344-5,452-3
Atlantic City, NJ 468
Attorney General 77,445,549,590,592
Austin, TX 511
Australia 180,590
Autism 125
Baghdad, Iraq 466
Baja, Mexico 612
Baker, Gerard 214
Baldwin, Alec 557,598
Baltimore, MD 13,160,218,500
Bandon Dunes, Oregon 174
Bangladesh 466
Bangor, ME 463,554,556
Bankrupt 6
Bannon, Steve 51,62,199
Barbaro, Michael 426,430
Barrack, Tom 436
Barrasso, John 462
Baseball 14,48,132,264,384
Batali, Mario 193
Baton Rouge, LA 333,475,600
Bay of Pigs Veterans Assoc 573
Bayer AG 620
Bean, Linda 616
Beck, Elizabeth 78,79
Beck, Glenn 304-5,312
Bedford, MA 538
Bedminster, NJ 591
Begala, Paul 430
Behar, Joy 292

Bell, Jeff 137
Benefits 57,66,71,499
Benghazi .177,208,279,281,285,443,457,462,535
....542-3,564-5
Berlin, Germany 177
Berra, Yogi 132
Bethpage, NY 397,399
Bible 44,336,343,346,348
Biden, Joe 176-7,184,485,558
Billings, MT.................................... 434
Biloxi, MS 287,288
bin Talal, Al-Waleed.................... 259,312
Bipartisan.. 98
Birmingham, AL.............................227-8
Birther 131,528
Black Lives Matter 161-2,193
Black, Leon...................................... 6
Blaze, The...................................268,337
Blitzer, Wolf 67
Bloomberg 92,108,132,152,259,533
Bloomberg, Michael 488
Bluffton, South Carolina.................... 68
Bngino, Dan.................................... 502
Bobic, Igor..................................... 27
Boca Raton, FL................................. 374
Boehner, John 133,151
Boeing 599,606
Boise, Idaho.................................... 202
Booker, Cory 483
Boone, Iowa.................................... 120
Border patrol.....................144,393,439,460,511
Borders 14-16,18,22,24-5,27-33,36-7,39-40
... 43,46-48,52,55,62,64,67-8,78,87,101
. 104,121-3,144,153,170,174,197,214-5
.217,222,224,229,242,277,299,304,308
. 327,334,374-6,384,388,390,393,437-8
.... 453,456-7,460,472,484,487,490,494
.502,506,510,514,516,563,569,598,610
.... 612
Boston 16,76,100,166
Boston Globe........................... 174,234
Boston Herald................................. 176
Bowden, Bobby 573
Boxer, Barbara................................ 125
Boycott 15,24-5,27,44-5,48,50,66,70,130
..............172,215,230,291,343,380,619
Boynton Beach, FL............................ 572
Brady, Tom..............79,111,113,119,123,166,220
Brazile, Donna............................... 567,569,579
Breitbart 17,124,152,155,242,371,424,486

Brennan, John 618
Brewer (Lane), Rowanne 425-6,431
Brexit 458-61,508,512
Bridgeport, CT................................408
Broaddrick, Juanita 547-8
Brody File 102
Brooks, David 246,367
Brown, Jerry..................................157
Bruni, Frank..................................302
Brussels, Belgium 383-4,386-7
Brzezinski, Mika...........................444,580
Buchanan, Pat 38,264,293
Buckley, William F...........................305
Budget 80,372,552,557
Buffalo Bills..................................141
Buffalo, NY 405-6
Burlington, Iowa............................. 175
Burlington, VT...............................291-2
Burnett, Mark.................................601
Bush, Barbara.............. 102,182,327,332,338,620
Bush, George H.W. 182,589,620
Bush, George W...15,41,64,117,129,165-6,168-71
.182,242,259,332,338,342,542,589,614
....619
Bush, Jeb 11,13-5,25,34,37,41,44-6,48,52-3
.....59,72,76-9,84-5,87-8,93-4,98,100-2
...104-5,107,108-10,113,115-7,119,127
...129,131,136,141-3,146,149-50,157-8
. 162-4,167-9,173,176-8,180-3,198,201
.... 203,205,211,216,222,232-3,267,270
.....274,276,281-3,286,292,297-8,305-9
.311,317,323,327-30,332-3,337-40,345
.... 347,350,385,390,414,418-9,589
Business Insider 167
BuzzFeed 615
Byrd, Robert..................................512
Byrne, Gary...................................446
C.I.A. 500,602,618
C.I.A. Director 590,592,618
Cadillac, MI..................................364
Caesars Palace, Atlantic City, NJ..................468
California 39,47,68,82,125,157,172,182,242-3
.246,290,343,400-1,407,413,433-7,440
.... 441,444,447,580,589,593
Cameron, Carl.................................80
Cameron, David 290
Camerota, Alisyn 246
Canada   176,206,210,291,299,305,307-8,310-11
.... 314,316,319-20,338,350,404
Canadians...................................154,299

Canton, OH 32,526-7
Capitol,The 114,116,117
Cardona, Maria 238
Carmel, IN 415
Carrier 336,592,595-7
Carson City, NV 490
Carson, Ben 60,91,103,105,111,117,119,131
.... 149,153,163,165,175-6,178,180-7
..... 192-4,196,201,203-6,212,215-6,222
.... 231,275,297,317,324-5,328,347,354
.... 371,592
Cartels 47,583
Carter, Graydon 166,219,603
Carter, Jimmy 69,255
Castro, Fidel.. 592
Castro, Raul 383
Catholic League.. 335
Catholic 335,555,561,572
Caucus 216,288-9,296-7,305,308,310-5
...317-21,324,328,336,345,347-9,365-6
.... 370,375,384
Cavuto, Neil... 362
CBN News....................................... 102,218,301
CBS   . 131,153,155,181,242,244,248,257,296
.... 314,337-8,341,404,426,475
CBS News 542
Cedar Falls, IA................................. 296,487,576
Cedar Rapids, IA 268,270,321-2,575
Celebrity Apprentice.................................... 121
Chafee, Lincoln.. 160
Chalian, David.. 246
Chao, Elaine... 595
Charleston, SC 167,252,341
Charleston, WV 417
Charlotte, NC................508-9,531-2,555,574-5
Charlottesville.. 48
Chicago Cubs... 346
Chicago, IL 18-20,30,372-3,470,514,537,564,610
Child care..................................... 525-6,539,542
China   4,7,71,96,102,117,157-8,172,192-3
.... 214-5,289,307,419,424,426,431,456
.................462,521,590,599,604,610
Chinese currency manipulation.......................... 5
Chozick, Amy.. 276
Christ   30
Christian Broadcasting Network.................... 105
Christianity 30,236,386
Christians...... 51,125-6,145,236,320,333,341,389
Christie, Chris...... 78,150,189,206,232,239,241-3
.... 317,328

Christmas 213,230,235,247,260,275-8,360,607
Churchill, Winston........................... 162,453,517
Cillizza, Chris 293
Cincinnati, OH..............372,469,554-5,594-5,597
Citibank 299,307
Citizens United 552
Citizenship 53,98,215,270,291,302,307,594-5
Civil rights 449,561
Clapper, James...616
Claremont, CA 290
Classified 108,468,520,558-60,582,614
Clemson University 326,332
Cleveland, OH ... 373,385,454,465,473-4,476,477
.............................479,531,567,569-70
Climate change 155
Clinton emails. 78-9,85,108,138,161,249,279,284
.318,426,429,434,441,448,456,463,465
.... 467-8,472-3,477,482,484-6,499-502
. 505,513,519-20,523,535,539,549,557-
.... -561,570,575-6,579-82
Clinton Foundation 452,494,510,512,535,537
.... 565,568,571-2,575,578,584
Clinton, Bill .. 65,174,244,276,281,286-8,292,420
.422,424,427,430,446,464,466,480,484
489-91,513,542,545,547-9,553,557,564
.... 565,575,581,605,610
Clinton, Hillary 6,7,10,14,22,27,30,40,42-3,46
.... 48,58,76,78-9,85-8,106,108,110,113
.... 126,131,138,145,158-9,161-3,171
.....176-9,182-3,186-7,189,193,198,200
...... 210,213,218-9,229-30,242,244,247
.... 249,252,254-5,257-8,260-2,264-5
.... 267-72,274-81,285-8,290-2,294,298
.304-6,308,310,312,318-20,337-41,349
...... 351,353,356,358,363,371-4,376-80
384-6,388,390,399,403-6,408-9,412-24
426-7,429-36,438,441-2,444-8,451,453
.454-9,460-75,480,482-5,486-92,494-9
.500-1,504-6,509-16,518-20,522-6,528
.... 529-30,532-5,537-45,547-54,556-85
.... 593-4,603,605-6,611,613,615,617
Clive, Iowa..525
Club for Growth...110,113-5,122,334,348,369-70
.... 379,392
CNBC 140,187-190,536-7
CNET 167
CNMI Rep Caucus...375
CNN   .. 18,50,52,67,93,98,106,111,121,124-5
...127-9,133,141,144,147,157-60,162-3
.170,174,181,198,237,246,252,259,261

CNN (cont) 263-4,276,303-4,311,313,315,341
...376,398,429-30,458,475,481,494,520
.... 522,552,594,618
Cnsnews 77
Coal mining 373-4,417,481,488,503,552
Cohen, Michael.. 67
Colbert, Stephen 339
College tuition 162
College 72,89,98,162,224,463
Collins, Chris.. 350,469
Colorado 186,188,355,399,400-2,465,489-90,496
...528-9,539,541,557,559-60,573,577-8
....583-4
Colorado Springs, CO........... 489,496,557,559-60
Columbus, OH 230-1,358,360,490,494-5,546,555
Comey, James................................. 560,577,580
Common Core.......... 43,52,73,101,167,170-1,196
........201,308,313,330,332,356,373,375
CONCACAF Cup.. 153
Conde Nast 613
Conde Nast Traveler....................................... 176
Congress .6,52,66,73,106,156,202,421,580-2,610
Connecticut................... 158,398,404,408,410-11
Conservative 33,39,136,142,170,241,332,334,336
..............................369,372,453,465,521
Constitution 87,252,293,305-6,465-6,478,502
.... 555,562
Consumer Confidence Index........................... 607
Conway, Kellyanne.......................... 419,542,614
Cooper, Anderson 66,161,325,342,559
Corker, Bob 364
Corporate inversion 137
Cosby, Bill.. 292
Costa Mesa, CA 413
Cotton, Tom.. 467
Coulter, Ann 309
Council Bluffs, Iowa............................ 281,537-8
Couric, Katie.. 440
Cox, Chris.. 432,474
CPAC 365
Crime 34,37,39,40,42,47,51,87,95,251,279
.... 291,465-6,470-1,475,490,494,499
.... 507,510,512-3,515,520,536,543,548
.... 557,606,617
Crimea 493,500,520,526,618
Criminals 29,30,32-4,38,99,583
Crippled America (book).... 153,191,198-203,206
...... 209,213,218,227,230,239-42,244-5
.... 247-9,251-3,255,257,269,273,277
Cruz, Ted 36,91,97,103,131,139,163,176,178

.. 181,216,222,228,235,241,253,259-65
274-76,284,291,296-7,299-302,304-11
.313-7,319-20,322-5,327-8,333,336-43
.345-55,357,361-2,368-9,373-5,377-80
.... 384-90,392-3,397,400,404-7,409-10
..............................412-3,416,477-8,485
C-Span 7
Cuba 123,383-4,554,586,593
Cuban, Mark 533
Cuomo, Chris.................................... 147,420
Curiel, Gonzalo.. 439
Cyrus, Miley 210
Czech Republic 615
D'Sousa, Dinesh 480
Daily Beast.. 79,155
Daily Ledger 251
Daily Mail.. 222,255
Dallas, Texas...... 112,114,116,118,122,359,453-4
.... 469,539,576
Database 224,228,230
Davenport, Iowa.................................... 248,487
Davi, Robert.. 158,245
Dayton, OH...372-3
Daytona, FL 494-6
de Blasio, Bill 227,251
Dean, Howard 324
Debate(s) 80,83,85,89-93,95,112,117,120-25
...... 129,131,133,135-6,155,157-65,170
.... 176-7,185-91,193-5,205,213-15,218
.223,231,241,261,264-73,276,291,293-
-295,298,301,306,308,313-8,320,326-9
.....336-9,346,352-4,363-4,371,375,378
.390,489,523,530,533-7,539-45,548-53
.... 559,562-8,579,589,593,603,611
Debt 45,55,68,95
Deerfield 150
Defense 20,33,40,189,264,400,533,544,591
.... 611,613
Deficit 75,80,453,454,456
Delaware 408,410-1,413,561
Delegates 361,375-6,385,389-92,399-402,404
.... 408,410,412-3,417,471,482
Democratic debate 155,157-64,170,177
.... 218,270
Democratic National Convention...... 480-2,485-6
....488,490-1,493
Democrats......17,36,41,45,51,59,66,77,89,91,113
.. 125,129,153,155,177,179-80,193,203
.... 204,207,218,225,227,239,241-2,247
.... 265,270,272,277,279,291,293,296-7

Democrats (cont) 326,339,343,348,355,357-8
.... 361,363,392,410,417-8,422,425
...429-31,442,449,460,468,476,478,481
.....483-9,491,512-3,515,532-3,536,553
. 555,557-8,561,571-3,577,580,592,602
.... 606,610-4,617
Denali 108
Denver, CO 489,496,583-4
Deportation 36,39,168,276-78,459,563,583
Depression 102
Dept. of Housing & Urban Dev. 592
Dept. of Justice 541,559,580-1
Dept. of State 284,494,511,545,550,553
.... 558-9,561,565,569,601
Dept. of Transportation................................ 595
Dept. of Veterans Affairs............................. 196
Des Moines Area Comm. College 224
Des Moines Register................ 62,63,70,259,261
Des Moines, Iowa 125,224,259,499,600
Detroit, MI 501,519,526
Deutsch, Donny 509
Devaney, Jason 42
Diamond and Silk .... see Hardaway, Lynnette
.... & Richardson, Rochelle
Dickerson, John 210,337
Diddy, P. 141
Diller, Barry.................................... 148,155,158
Discrimination 138,145
Disloyal .143,198,203,215,230,235,247,269,291
.... 348,351,553
Disney 191,193
Ditka, Mike.. 123,584
DJT Foundation 607
DNC   162,480-2,486,490,493,497,569,603
....611-4
Dole, Bob.. 303
Donahue, Bill.. 335
Doonbeg, Ireland 120,174
Dossier 616-8
Douglas, Michael................................... 385,429
Dow 100,308-9
Dowd, Maureen 529
Drake University................................. 316
Driver's licenses 68,157
Drudge Report 93,124,133,165,188,213-4,274
...............................318,337,379,390,537
Drugs 6,46-7,237,327,331,364,514,533,556
....562-3,583
Dubuque, IA 318
Duke, David... 357

Durdin, Sabine 44
Dutchess County, New York...................... 141
Eagle Forum..312
Eagle 99
Eastwood, Clint....................................39,96
Eau Claire, WI 394
Economic Club of NY.....................................527
Economist, The 4,69,137,187,608
Economy ... 5,7,11,32-3,44,68,94,97,102,104,160
.189,199,203,205,289,303,338,376,388
.393,398,413,427,430,448,456,501,532
...................534,542,563-4,566,569-70
Education 43,60,80,193,196,201,312,330,332
.... 356,373,418,494,513,520,619
El Chapo 46-7
Eleccion2015 29
Election observer 547
Electoral college........................ 182,589,593,605
Element Electronics 171-2
Elites 27,30,42-3,146
Elliott, Bill 359
Eminent domain 148,305,328,330,337-8
Endorsement 6,106,197,258,263,266,279,289
.... 298,302-4,309,313,321,337,346,350
353,360,363,371-2,378-81,385,387,393
.398,404,411,415,418,423,432,435,439
.443,457,521,530,532,536,541,546,572
....573
Energy 136,206,437,490
Entitlements 135,155,183,189,193,203
Entrepeneurs 11,39
Environment..98,206
Erickson, Erick....................................93
Erie, PA 505
ESPN 42
Establishment........ 7,16,38,45,63-4,75,93,114,132
.... 143,149,152,164-5,172,175,186,215
.227,231,233,236,239,242,245-6,257-8
.....260,303,327,350-1,356-7,362-3,368
.... 378-9,408,497-9,504-5,547
Eugene, OR..417
Europe 54,269,278,387,398,443,566
Evancho, Jackie 612
Evangelicals.102-3,115,117-8,194,252,297,301-2
.... 320,333,345-6,348,354,378,420,514
....581
Evansville, IN 412
Everett, WA 514,516
Executive order 201,458,459,554
Extreme vetting..550

ExxonMobil 601-2
F-18 Super Hornet 606
F-35 602,606
F.B.I.   234,251,466-8,477,485,519-20,541,549
.... 557-60,571,576-7,582,612,617
F.C.C. 132
Face the Nation (tv program) 155,180-1,210
.... 248-9,271,288,295,309,314,321,337
Facebook 242,289,301,314,367-8,488,545,548
.... 566,572,576-7,584,604
Faith & Freedom Coalition 302,449-50
Faith and Freedom Forum............................ 125
Fake news 601,615-9
Fake 10,45,67,143,170,234-35,350
.... 435,461,601,614-9
Fallon, Jimmy 118-9
Falwell, Jerry Jr. 313
Farmers 532,572
Farmington, NH............................ 312
Favorability............................. 52,88,98,108,313
Fayetteville, NC 500,599
Fazio, Tom.................................. 4
Federal Election Comm. (FEC) 434
Feminist 157
Fence 73,104,108,438
Ferrara, America............................ 32
Ferraro, Geraldine.......................... 274
Ferry Point................................. 10
Fiat Chrysler 615
Financial disclosure form................. 300,320,434
Financial markets (US) 102
Financial Times 603
Fiorina, Carly 91,94,125,127,131,133-4,149
.... 163,171,216,373,412
First Amendment 372
Flake, Jeff 520,524
Fletcher, NC............................567-8
Florida 15,79,102,109,116,123,131,136,151
.173,177-8,181,183-4,192,195,200,205
....224,236-7,239,276,282,292,298,303
..306,333-5,345-6,353-4,356-7,361,363
.365-6,368,370,372,374-6,378,412,437
.449-52,469-72,482,494-6,503,505,511
.512-3,519,521-2,524,526,530,537,546
553-5,560,570-4,579-81,583,585-6,589
.... 602,604,613
Flowers, Gennifer 533
Flynn, Michael....................... 479,501
Focus groups................ 65,72,90,92,332,552
Football 169,195,266

Ford Motor Co. .48,182-3,336,376,590,610-1,615
.... 619
Ford, Bill................................. 590
Ford, Henry................................. 81
Foreign policy . 10,74,140,231,385,388,398,411-2
.... 442,473,544,563
Fort Lauderdale, FL 503
Fort Wayne, IN 415
Fort Worth, TX 353-4
Fournier, Ron............................ 575
Fox   32,39,63,64,91,111,126,128,130-3,150
.154,168,172,207,224,233,254,257,261
.... 263,268,271,283,312,318,339
Fox 2 318
Fox and Friends 17,201,401,537
Fox Business Network 311,461
Fox News ..17,45,60,92,103,155,167,169,171,177
.... 202,207,232,261,263,275,293-5,297
307-10,312,315-6,318-9,340,361-2,366
.... 378,394,401,427,463-4,601
Fox, Vicente............................ 352,516
France 105,291,473,485
France, Brian............................359-60
Franklin Pierce 174,176
Franklin, Tennessee 142,144-5
Frederal Reserve 346
Free speech 27,29,35,39,125
Freedom Fest............................ 45
Freeman, James............................ 195
Fresno, CA............................ 437
Fusion 18,51
G.Q. (magazine)............................384-5,387
Gaddafi, Muammar........................... 145
Gang bangers 27,29-30
Gang members 99,390,583
Gang of Eight............................ 39,134,197,214
Garrett, Major............................ 295
Gates, Robert 528-9
Gateway Pundit............................ 389
Gay marriage............................ 300,333
Geist, Willie............................ 3
General Motors 610,619
Geneva, OH............................574-6
Geneva, Switzerland 497
Georgia .148,153,155,162,237,239,243,259,280
302,345,351,355,359-61,425,452-3,530
.... 553
Germany 177,255,290,291,479,604,606,616
Gettysburg, PA............................569-70
Gifford, Frank............................ 94

Gilmore, Jim 524
Gingrich, Newt 264,411,501
Ginsburg, Ruth Bader 471-2
Giuliani, Rudy 397-8,503,601
Glenn, John 600
Global warming 173
Goldberg, Whoopi 292
Golden Globes 295,615
Golden, CO 577
Goldman Sachs 299-300,307,310,471
Golf Odyssey 264
Golf 42,76,108,120,166,264,262,289,291
.... 363,366,368,395-6,432,443,455,460
..........................466,474,511,533,619
Gonzales, Alberto 445
Good Morning America
  (tv program) 175-6
Google 337,388,577
GOP 15-8,20,37-8,41-3,52,54,58-9,62-3
  65,67,69-70,76,82-6,88-9,91,106,110-1
  ... 114-5,130,132,136-7,139-40,150,166
  ..176-8,185-8,190,196,204,221-2,227-8
  . 232-3,235,237,241,243,245-6,253,264
  ....267-8, 272,276,280,296,298,303,306
  ....309-10, 314,316-8,328-30,336-7,352
  354,361363-4,371,383,390,399-401
  ....409,413, 420,422,436,438,448-9,472
  477,547-8
Government housing 58
Gowdy, Trey 279
Grace, Nancy 103
Graham Lynch, Cissie....................... 581
Graham, Ben................................ 40
Graham, Billy 206,581
Graham, Franklin 257,605,620
Graham, Lindsey 104,227,266,298,340,367-9,379
 386,414,419,423,524
Grand Rapids, MI 272,577-8,584,586,600
Gravis 141,153,184
Great Britain 258,432,459,591,614
Great Faith Ministries Intl................ 519
Greeley, CO 577-8
Green Bay, WI 499,557
Green Party, The 592,598,602
Greenberg, Hank 292
Greenblatt, Bob............................ 96
Greenblatt, Jason.......................... 421,431
Greensboro, NC 450,453,555
Greenville, SC 338
Greenwood, Kimberly 620

Guam 372
Guantanamo Bay............................ 389,611
Guardian, The 152
Gucci 2
Guilfole, Kimberly 228
Gulbis, Natalie 443
Gun control 40,149,219
Gun free zones 40,52,53,64
Guns 39,40,48,52-3,64,149,219,270,287
  290,325,397,432-3,448,451,453,455
  528,531,562,572,581
H-1B Visa 98,167
Haberman, Maggie.......................... 254,276
Hacked email .. 501,569,575,602-3,611-4,617,621
Haiti 553
Haley, Nikki.............................. 360
Halperin, Mark............................ 14,353
Hamilton (broadway show).................. 590-1
Hannity, Sean....99,130,176,192,232,258,327,346
  382,404,511,611
Hanukkah................................. 250,607
Hardaway, Lynette........................ 446,531
Harrisburg, PA 490
Harrison, Michael 295
Hart, Kevin............................... 164
Hartford Courant.......................... 335
Harvard University........................ 293,436
Harvey, Matt 48,135
Harwood, John 140,191
Hawaii 269,368-70
Hayes, Stephen........................... 148-9,376
HBO 141,144,198
Healthcare ..55,194,203,223,278,327,331,342,362
  .443,448,549,562,566,568,573,575,580
  583,610-2
Hedge fund............................... 113,300,456
Heilemann, John 14
Hemmer, Bill 476
Henderson, Clarence....................... 515
Henderson, NV 541,545
Henninger, Daniel......................... 195
Herman, Jim............................... 396
Hershey, PA 583,602
Hewitt, Hugh.............................. 112
Hewlett-Packard........................... 94
Higbie, Carl.............................. 199
High Point, NC 531
Highways 149,305,383
Hill, The 49,118,177
Hilton Head, SC........................... 282

Hispanics 67,72,78,88,104,116,143,152-4,163
..... 173-4,185,204,208-9,218,417,443-4
.... 457,513,515,537
Hoft, Jim 276
Hollywood 16,30,144,255,345,615
Holtz, Lou.. 415
Homeless veterans 58
Honolulu, Hawaii... 368
Hopkins, Kate 257
Hornick, Joseph 400
Hostages 111-2,217,255,296-7,467,498-9
House of Representatives.....151,380,405,469,613
.... 616
Houston, TX 454,528
Huckabee, Mike............................... 192,206,286
Huffington Post....... 18,27,31,37,48,53-4,111,128
Hughes, Scottie.. 166
Hunt, Kasie 186
Huntsville, AL 358
Hurricane Matthew 547
Hurt, Harry.. 79
Hussein, Sadam 145
Hvidston, Robin... 44
I.B.D. (Investor's Business Daily) 202
I.C.E. (US Immigration & Customs
Enforcement) 276,357,457,460,546,562
.... 583
Icahn, Carl 6-7,137
Idaho 202,368-9
Illegal alien 21,51,58,61,66,583
Illegal immigrants................16-7,20-2,24-5,27,30
..... 32-4,36-41,43,45,48-9,53,55-6,58-9
.62,66,68-72,78,87,95,100-2,118,133-4
.... 137,144-5,153,157,162,167,180,183
. 197-8,209,215,222,225,230,240,242-3
. 262,277,304,326-7,330,334,343-4,347
.... 357,375-6,380,386,388,390,418,439
. 445,457-8,486,494,513,515-6,520,552
.... 563,583
Illinois .140,211,213,271,284,309,347,352,375
.... 377,564
Immigration 27-8,30,41-3,46,48,51,58,97,103
.123,129,134,170,173,180,189,193,202
..208-9,211-2,214-5,220,252,254-5,327
. 347,353,394,398,451-2,456,458-9,485
.... 517-8,533,539,563,569,583
Inaugural address 620
Inauguration.............. 34,244,606,612,617,619-21
Independents...241,253,279,339,348,357,410,417
.... 425,438,515,610

India 435
Indiana 403,405-7,409,411-6,467,470-1,473
.... 511,543,546,553,592,595-7,600
Indianapolis, IN 405,411
Infectious disease 38
Infrastructure...................... 149,305,328,383,419
Inside Politics (tv program)........................... 470
Inspector General 436
Internal Revenue Service 355
International Business Times 102
Iowa 16,31,55,63,70-1,74,96-7,105,108
...... 111,120-1,125,138,147,149-51,167
.... 175,181,185-6,194,201,216,224,248
.252-54,258-61,264,266,268,270,281-2
.. 288-9,293-7,299-305,307-25,328,346
. 467,471,487,496-7,499,514,519,537-8
.... 546,575-6,581,584,599-600
iPhone 342
IQ 52,219,241,263
Iran 7,18,28,42-3,51-2,66,74,77,96,106
. 111-4,116-7,136,158,198-9,288,296-8
.300,496-8,500-1,535,544,551,565,571
.... 608
Iranians 255,501
Iraq 5,101,131,161,168,171,203,266,338
.344,433,483,491,527,534-5,541-2,559
.... 565,571
Ireland 474
ISIL 217,251
ISIS .84,106,145,193,217,219-22,224-5,251
.. 252,258,260,268-72,277,287,290,307
.... 331,373,386-7,389,419,424,431,433
.....456-7,463,466-7,475,480,482,484-5
.... 487-8,494,497,504,530,535,539,544
.... 557,559,566,571,595,607
Islamic terrorists.....61,104,217-8,224,229,248-52
.254,271,272,299,301,343,389,433,451
........466,479,487,493,560,563,567,576
Israel . 20,74,126,131,193,254,257,285-6,355
.... 435,463-4,472,533,541,548,556,576
................................578,580,606-8
Italy 511
Jack Trice Stadium.. 120
Jackson, Bishop Wayne T.............................. 519
Jackson, Jesse.. 520,534
Jacksonville, Florida 178,181,183,494-6
Jacobus, Cheri...246
Japan 438,590,599
Jeffres, Robert............................... 141,308,354
Jersey City, NJ 244

Jews 250-1
Jillette, Penn................................. 50,169
Jindal, Bobby............................ 117,227,229
Jobs   .8,12-16,22,27,31-2,37,44,48-9,69,71-2
     75,97-8,115,118,123,130,156,171
     179-80,206,208,273,280,292-3,308,326
     ...327,335-6,342,368,375-6,388-90,394
     . 407-8,415,417,423,435,444-6,448,453
     454,456,459-61,471,473,476,480,485-7
     .490,494,501,506,512,520,527,530,534
    541-3,552,563-4,565,568-9,595,599
     600,603,607,611,615-7,619-20
Johnson, Dustin 366,455
Johnson, Shawn 283
Johnson, Woody 288
Johnstown, PA 491,568
Jones, Chuck................................... 600
Jones, Paula 548
Jones, Van....................................... 584
Jordan   254
Journalist 100,165,288,382,397,431,559,594
Judge Jeanine.................................. 303
Kaine, Tim 479-83,487,520,542-5,570,572
Kansas   156,364-6,520,560
Kardashians 226
Kasich, John.... 193,196,216,222-3,227,231-2,236
     238,248,328,347,354,372-6,380,390
     ...392,405,407-10,413,418,448,477,589
     613
Kellogg, Keith 501
Kelly File, The.................................... 86,103,104
Kelly, Megyn 91-3,103-4,111,130,141,165,172
     .256,263,277,312,314,340,376,379,383
    427-9
Kelly, Mike...................................... 421
Kenansville, NC................................ 531
Kennedy, Joe (coach).......................... 194
Kennedy, John (of Louisiana)........... 598,600,601
Kennedy, John F. 195
Kennedy, Patrick................................ 558
Kentucky 95,120,361,365-6,427,430,432,553,590
Kerry, John 74,199,534
Keystone XL Pipeline.............................. 98,206
KGB   135
Khan, Capt. Humayun 491
Khan, Khizr 491-3
Kiawah, SC...................................... 340
Kiiara   528
Kimmel, Jimmy 268
King Mohammed VI......................... 568

King, Don 449-50
King, John.................................... 246,470
King, Martin Luther 618
Kinston, NC 574
Kissel, Ben.................................... 301
Kissel, Mary.................................... 364
Klu Klux Klan (KKK)..................... 512,514
Knight, Bobby............... 123,411-12,415,578,580
Knoxville, TN 220,221
Koch brothers.................... 79,82,356-7,490
Koch, Charles.................................... 490
Koch, David 490
Koran   465
Korean   89
Koster, Chris.................................... 585
Kraft, Cheryl Ann 474
Krauthammer, Charles 41,317,337
Kristol, Bill 66,438
Kudlow, Larry.................................. 137
Kuhner, Jeffrey T............................. 27
Kurtz, Howard 154-5,198
Kushner, Jared 410
L.L. Bean 616
La Crosse, WI 396
Labor   148,193,521,581
Laconia, NH.................................... 528
Lafayette, Louisiana............................ 67
LaGuardia Airport............................ 144
Lakeland, FL.................................... 554
Lane, Charles 170,225,263
Langone, Ken.................................... 362
LaPierre, Wayne 432
Laredo   66,68
Las Vegas.... 25,39,45,52,84,88,150-53,265,345-7
    417,454-5,577-8
Las Vegas Review Journal............................. 571
Late Show w/Stephen Colbert........................339
Latinos   19,79,107,140,284,321,515
Lauer, Matt.................................... 165,523
Law Enforcement...... 228,242-3,256,294,358,372
     413,450,469,475,485-6,489,496,510
    527,530,543-4,617
Leaked emails 480-2,533
Ledger, Graham 251
Left wing 57,100,219
Legere, John.................................... 220
Lehman Brothers.................... 102,116,223
Lemon, Don 502-3
Leppert, Tom 359
LeVell, Bruce.................................... 243

Levin, Harvey 598
Levin, Mark 27,129,146,192
Levine, Randy.................................. 412
Lewandowski, Corey 371,390
Lewinsky, Monica 292
Lewis, John.................................. 617,619
Lexington, SC................................... 315
LGBT 452
Liberal 20,54,56,63,70,71,91,130,186,203
.................233,243,301,336,401,492,562
Libertarians.................................. 64
Liberty Institute 194
Liberty University................................301-2,313
Libya 433,502,535,565
Lima, OH................................... 486
Limbaugh, Rush...............48,97,123,192,307,314
Lincoln Memorial 620
Lincoln, Abraham............................. 550
Lisbon, ME.................................. 575
Little Rock, Arkansas 325
Lobbyists ...9,24,51,78,98,109,113,116,122-3,133
.... 137,190,249,274-5,287,314,334,338
.... 344,351,357,375,474,560-1
Lockheed Martin...................... 606,619
London, England.............................. 255
Londonderry, NH............................. 330
Long Island.................................. 167
Lopez, George 59
Lord, Jeffrey 317,429
Los Angeles Times 510, 548
Los Angeles, California 122-3,451
Louis, Errol.................................. 238
Louisiana 229,333,365-6,389,422,430,508,511
.........................516,553,598,600,601
Louisville, KY 361
Lowell, MA 288-9
Loyalty 25,94,217,225,303,355,481,553,614
Lupica, Mike.................................. 124
MacCallum, Martha........................... 246
Machado, Alicia.............................. 539
Macon, GA 239-40
Macy's 26-8,30,40,48-51,70,215,235
Madison, AL................................. 358
Madison, MS................................. 368
Maine .364-6,463,496,546,554,556,560,575-6
Maitner, Capt. Andrew 339
Major League Baseball 264
Malkin, Michelle.............................. 260
Manassas, VA...............................243-4
Manchester, NH....................37,326,328-9,575

Manheim, PA................................... 538
Mannatech.................................... 194
Manufacturing... 11,27,28,169,171-2,375,407,409
.... 480,488,494,598,618
Mar-a-Lago 5,79,285,377,383,620
March on Washington.......................... 515
Marines 52,542,588
Marist Poll................................... 555
Markley, Andrea 279
Marshall Fields 30
Martin, Jonathan 132
Maryland 12,162,402,404,407,409-10,500,560
Mass deportation............................. 459
Massachusetts 107,166,180,209,223,288-9,347
.... 355,361,423,463
Massi, Bob 89
Mattis, Gen. James "Mad Dog" 591,599
May, Theresa 614
McAllen, TX................................... 453
McCain, John 53,55-6,58-62,65-6,69,71-3,77
.... 140,260,291,299,308,553
McCarthy, Kevin............................... 151
McConnell, Mitch 153,423
McDonald, Steven........................... 617
McEnany, Kayleigh 236
McHugh, Katie............................... 43
McIlroy, Rory 366-7
McManamon, Mary Brigid 305-6
McMaster, Henry 523
McQuaid, Joe 281-3,294
Mechanicsburg, PA.......................... 495
Media ..3,16,24,26,28-30,45,47,59,60,63-4,66
..73-4,98,101,125,127-8,132-3,139,146
........162,176,181,183,187,196,224,227
.....233-6,242-3,248,252,263,265,273-5
.288,290,298,303,355,370-1,376-7,383
.....385-6,388,395,399,401,423-5,434-5
.438,441,445,448,453-4,459,461-2,467
...469-70,477,481-2,484,486,488,490-2
...500,502-4,506,509-10,520-3,529,539
.546-7,550,554,556-9,572,577,588,591
.............593,599,603,605,610-5,618-9
Media Buzz (tv program)........................ 155,198
Media Matters................................ 42
Medicaid 44,57,193
Medicare 183,189,193,203
Meet the Press............ 46-7,144,294,329,419,467
Mek, Amy 88
Melbourne, FL 537
Memphis, TN................................... 355

Menendez, Bob...479
Mercer, Robert...317
Merchandise (Trump) 95-6,98-9,103,120,173
.... 178,189,200,278,477-8,495,499
Mesa, Arizona..268
Mexican government 15,23,31,37
Mexicans 19,22,27,36,46,47
Mexico 6,15,16,22,27,31-2,46-8,71,153,156
. 170,174,181-2,277,308,335-6,352,372
.376,393,415,419,436,453,491,494,516
.... 517-8,523,590,597,605,610-5
MIA 61,439
Miami, FL..123,178,363,366,469,526,528,579-81
Michigan 48,272-74,318,347,354,364,367-70,470
. 485,501,508,526,538-9,553,577-8,581
.... 584-6,594,599-600,610,615
Mickelson, Phil.. 366
Middle class........ 14,60,113,122,130,142,156,170
.... 280,487,500,550
Middle East.......77,168,244,439,487,533,565,568
.... 570
Middletown Tube Works............................... 546
Military . 14,27,43-4,53,58,64-5,68,122,192,217
. 298,309,375,388,433-4,448,506,521-2
.534,542,557,589,597,599-600,602,619
Millennials.. 165,204
Milwaukee, WI..394-5
Minnesota 355,529,546,555,560,584,610
Minorities 281,314,515
Miss Katie's Diner... 395
Miss Universe................................... 36,271,539
Miss USA 19,46
Mississippi......................................286-8,368-70
Missouri .371,375,378,380,391,402,524,552,585
Mnuchin, Steven... 595
Mobile, Alabama 100-1,602-4
Mondale, Walter 274
Monmouth Poll...................................... 174,265
Montana 434,446
Montgomerie, Colin....................................... 432
Moore, Michael... 316
Moore, Russell.. 420
Morell, Michael 500
Moreno, Lupe 44
Morgan, Jack 474
Morgan, Piers............................. 50,211,255,422
Morning Consult.............................. 133,174,258
Morning Joe (tv program)............ 94,157,233,503
Morning's with Maria (tv program)................ 311
Morocco 289,568,578

Morris, Clayton... 168
Mosul, Iraq......................................541,565,571
Mount McKinley.. 108
Mount Pleasant, SC....................................... 252
MSNBC 129,329,345,447
Munich, Germany 479
Murdoch, Rupert.................................63,255,615
Muscatine, Iowa.. 309
Muslim 126,156,228,234,239,242,251,252
.... 255,257,258,284,286,384,386
Myanmar 511
Myrtle Beach, SC... 232
NAFTA 372-5,420,427,473,480,487,490,535
....563-4
Naples, FL...570-1
NASCAR 42,359-60
Nashua, NH..280,318
Nashville, TN............................. 29,107,141,143
Nasrallah, Hassan.. 112
National Black Repub. Assoc. 306
National debt........................... 447,456,514,534
National defense...33
National Enquirer... 388
National Review...........................305-7,309,312
National security advisor 364,590
National security 52,131,319,364,398,423,451
.... 467,489,545,550,557,590
NATO 386,389-90,398,446,486,491
Natural born citizen................... 293,299,306,334
Navarro, Ana... 211
Navarro, Peter... 572
NBC 13,20-2,25,27,58,89,125,127-8,133
.... 174,193,195,262,298,329,340-1,367
.... 391,523,555,612-3,618
NBC News... 87
Nebraska 231,319,417-8,420-2
Neo, Tamara.. 474
Netanyahu, Benjamin...................................... 533
Nevada 163,184,189,265,283-4,294,307,323
.333,336,340,344-9,351,417,452,454-5
.....490,493,527,530-1,541-2,545-6,560
....577-8,584
New Hampshire 4,12-4,42,52-3,76-7,96,98-9,124
.... 132,137-8,150,153,155,158,167,174
.... 176,179,181,183,198,203,213-4,218
......221-23,227,239,241,245,253-4,258
...273,281-2,289-91,294-5,300-1,303-4
....310-12,318,322-32,351,449,451,484
.499-500,528,538,547,556,575-6,583-4
....586,593

New Jersey...... 165,213,234,239,241,242,244,400
...................447,462,467,529,538,560
New Mexico 435-6,447,553,577-8
New Orleans, Louisiana................................. 365
New York (state)....... 141,392,395,397,400-6,409
.... 501,529,568.589
New York Jets 288
New York Police Dept (NYPD).................... 503
New York Post............................... 167,240,321
New York Times.. 93,120,222,235,302-3,367,381
..........................408,410,435,455,569
New York values 397,399,406
New York Yankees.. 412
New York, NY.....3,25,52,63,68,104,110,121,144
.158,167,207,224,227,251,299-301,355
.... 358,378,381,391-2,395,397-400,402
...405-6,459-60,472-3,488,527,529,563
....................586,588,595,599,611,617
New Zealand.. 590
Newhouse, Steven... 613
Newmarket, NH... 273
Newsmax 92-3,107,124,335
Newsweek.. 155
Newton, Wayne 147
Newtown, PA... 569
Nice, France.. 473
Nielsen Media Research 491
No Labels (event) 157
Nolte, John... 227
Noonan, Peggy... 300
Norcross, GA 162
Norfolk, VA.. 194,196
North Augusta... 339
North Carolina 42,185,225,245,247-8,347,368
. 374-5,377,450,452-3,467,500,502,507
. 508,516,522,525,530-3,555-6,558,562
...................567-8,574-5,581-3,585,599
North Korea... 544,610
North Mariana Islands 376
Novi, MI 538-9
NRA 161,453
Nuclear 18,43,77,113,116-7,173,394,500,535
..........................544,589,606,610,618
Nutter, Michael.. 255
NYC Mayor 31
O'Brien, Tim 66
O'Donnell, Lawrence................................. 14,52
O'Donnell, Rosie 92,421
O'Malley, Martin............................. 160,162,218
O'Reilly Factor................................... 59,289,378

O'Reilly, Bill 9,18,116-7,128,206,245,267
.... 317,319,401,406,437
Oaks, Robert C. 381
OAN Network........................... 107,129,141,162
Obama, Barack.......12,18,22,25,27-30,33-5,43,48
.....51,55,61-2,64-5,72,74,77-8,104,108
.111-14,124-5,139-41,146,150,156,168
.... 191,193,199,201-2,206,211,217-8
...220-3,230,240,248-51,269,274,287-8
.... 299,306,310-1,327,333,340,344,351
. 357,362,368,383-4,426,431,434,437-9
...... 446,448-9,451-2,454,456-7,459-60
. 467,470,472-5,481,483,486-7,489,491
.... 493,495,497,504,511,520-1,526,529
.... 534,542,544,549,551,554,557-8,564
.....566,568-9,573,582-3,588,607-8,612
....617
Obama, Malik 481
Obama, Michelle...................................... 571,588
Obamacare .15,162,181,223,231,278,301,320,324
.... 331,338,342,362,375,380,443,506-7
..... 516,542,546,549-50,555,559,561-2
.... 566,568,573-8,580,582-3,585,607
....610-2,616
Obamatrade...8
Occupy Wall Street... 471
Off-shoring......... 280,335,408,595,597-8,600,615
Ohio 108,115,183,185,223,227,230-1,348
.358,360,372-6,379,422,424,469,471-2
.....475-6,483-4,486,490,494-5,501,510
.....515-6,519,521,524,526-7,530-1,533
...546,553-5,559,561,567,569-70,574-6
..............582-3,589,594-5,597,614,615
Ohio Republican Party 614
Ohio State University.....................................595
Oil 20,217,219-20,251,268,288,386,443
Oklahoma State Fair 133
Oklahoma.... 133-4,150,156,304,352,355,494,528
Old Post Office 133,176,244,245,449
Oliver, John.. 196
Olympics 76,499
Omaha, NE.. 417
On the Record (tv program)....... 117,128,226,362
Orange County, NC 558
Oregon 140,417,426-7,429-30,560
Orlando, FL... 365-6,450-2,454-5,579-81,602,604
Oskaloosa, Iowa.. 71
Oval Office 19,154,250,538,576
Padilla, Alejandro Garcia............................... 358
Pakistan 389

Palazzo, Steven 501
Palestine 464,548
Palin, Sarah 202,228,284,302,303
Palm Beach, FL 276,383
Palmer, Arnold 533
Paris, France 217,219-20,222,230,291,387,430
Parlux 42
Pataki, George 121,227,266
Paterson, NJ 239
Patton, Gen. George 192
Paul, Rand 95,136,139,206,276,365,390
Paul, Ron 120
Payne, Robert E 470
Pearl Harbor 438,600
Pegula, Terrence 141
Pella (company) 309
Pella, IA 309
Pelley, Scott 135
Peña Nieto, Enrique 516,523
Pence, Mike 415,467,473,475-8,483,489,491,493
         496,521,528,539,542,544-7,556,561
         571,574,580,585,590-1
Pennsylvania.. 115,259,265,373,395,399-402,404
         ...408-10,449-50,471-2,479-80,484,486
        490-1,494-5,504-5,527,530,538,540
         546,552-3,561,568-70,580-1,583,585-6
        598,602-3
Pennsylvania Avenue 133
Pensacola, FL 298,519,521-2,524,579-80
People Magazine 213,554
Perdue, David 501
Peres, Shimon 537
Periscope 3,96,111,136,242,510,585
Perkins, Tony 106
Perry, KS 520
Perry, Rick 29,37,41,55,62,65,146,418
Petraeus, Gen. David 467,594
Pew 141,147
Philadelpia, PA 255,399,479,486,528,530
Philippines 521
Phillips, Angie 546
Phoenix, AZ..... 40,43-46,52,56,61,101,278,380-2
         454,513,516,576-7
Pierson, Katrina 222
Pitt, Harvey 298
Pittsburgh, PA 265,402,404,449-51
Plaats, Bob 313
Planned Parenthood 70
Pledge 112,129,356,419-20,424,457,465,477
         507,586,620

Plunder and Deceit 69
Plymouth, NH 327,329
Podesta, John 260,495,565,569,576,580,611
Poland 353,537
Police 166,222,242-3,255-258,291,294,328
         . 358,404,444-5,450,475,479,484-6,488
         .. 503,510,527,528,530,534,543-44,576
         581
Political Insider, The 192
Politically correct 18,57,58,67,75,93,104,263
         299,314,317,384,468
Politico 140,222,371,560
PolitiFact 446
Polls 12-15,19,26,29,31,36,43-4,47-49,52
         ... 54,60,62,65,70,76-81,83-8,90-2,97-9
         .102,104,105,107-113,116-8,121,123-5
         ... 127-8,131-5,137,141-2,145-6,149-50
         153-5,157-8,163,165-8,170,174-6
         178-9,191-5,199-207,212-4,218-9
         221-3,229,234-5,239,241-3,246-8
         ...252-4,257-9,261-5,267,269-71,273-4
        276,278,283-4,286,292-4,296-7,302
        306-7,310-3,316-8,320-1,324-5,330
        337-41,345,347-54,360,362,370,381
         . 388,390,402,404-6,408,416,421,424-5
         433,437,439,460-2,470,472,483,485
         507,510-14,516,518-9,522-3,525-7,529
        531,533,536-7,541,545-8,552-3,555
        558-60,567,569-71,577,579,586,619
Pollster 37,52,111,128,235,345
Pope Francis 341,383
Portland, ME 364,496
Portsmouth, NH 300,449,556
Potawatomi 72
POW 61
Powell, Colin 527
Powers, Kirsten 389
PPP .... see Public Policy Polling
Prague, Czech Republic 615
Presbyterian 55
Price, Tom 594
Priebus, Reince 41,392,481,507
Prince 407
Prisoners 136
Progressives 143
Protestant 55
Protesters . 193,210,374,383,413,415,435-6,444-5
         519,560,587,564,588
Public Policy Polling 78,108-9,266,338-9
Puckett, Hailey 398

Pueblo, CO... 539,541
Puerto Rico 358
Putin, Vladimir 7,19,72,121,135,159-60,182
.216,220,307,333,482,485,493,495,521
.... 544,606,608
Quinnipiac University Poll ..118,158,275,276,340
.... 462
Racial profiling 25-6,70,255
Racism 19,516
Radical Islam ... 218,229,248-51,254,299,301,343
.... 389,433,451,467,479,487,491,493-4
.... 559-60,563,567,576
Rainbow/Push Coalition 534
Raleigh, NC 245,247,248
Rally 100-101,118
Rapists 6,33,40
Rasmussen Reports 176,547,567,572
Rather, Dan.. 65,157
Ratings 14-5,47,52,54,92-4,112,119,124,126
.... 133,136,143,151,154-5,159,165,169
...172,177,191,210-13,216,250,263,278
...292,295,313-14,316,320,340,367,382
. 394-5,408,424,430,440,444,447,475-6
. 479,481-2,490,503-4,513,519,529,538
...........................540,552,598,613,616
Rawlings-Blake, Stephanie............................ 500
Reagan, Nancy.. 367,615
Reagan, Ronald...... 6,17,29-31,35,40,52,64,69,77
...... 82-3,135,137,142,176,183,202,207
.... 225-6,253,343,348,374,386,399,489
.... 615
Reaganomics.. 69
RealClear Politics 156,311,380,502,515,544-5
Redding, CA 443-4
Redford, Robert 116
RedState (blog)..................................... 151,379
Reed, Ralph 302
Refugees .221,228-9,255,261-2,369,387,433,437
...............484,487,494,506,530,566,595
Regulation...........................435,487,552,563,598
Reid, Harry 352,357,569,591
Religious freedom..125-6
Remembrance Project, The............... 266,511,574
Reno, NV 184,189,294,490,493,541,546,584
Repeal & replace....223,320,324,331,342,362,506
........507,516,542,549,559,561,566,568
.... 573-5,580,582,616
Republican National Comm. ...42-3,65,260,306-7
.... 335-7,339,346,390,398,479,613
Republican National Convention ... 465,476-8,481
................................482,484-5,491,494
Republican Party.. 8,56,139,165,172,174,279,332
.362,378,385,390,392,394,401,407,421
.......422,438,460,468,472,510,520,611
Republican platform....................................... 472
Republican primary. 88,131,297,309,389,400,425
.... 437,501
Republicans..... 17,31,33,35,41,43-45,52,58,64,78
.......82,88-9,91,106-7,125,129,131,150
.....153-4,169,177-8,180-1,186,192,202
..........204-5,215,219-20,231-2,239,242
.246-7,258,261,265,270,279,281,297-8
.301,309,321,330,333,339,346,348,350
.355-7,362-3,368,373,383,389,392,395
.... 399,400,403-4,409,412,418,420,423
.... 437-8,446,453,469,476,482,490,506
.... 524,532,547-8,553,557-8,612,617
Res, Barbara...426
Reuters .102,141,149,195,205,216,221,259,269
.274,290,297,306-7,380,503,516,545-6
Rhode Island 16,409-11
Richardson, Rochelle 446,531
Richmond, VA 163-4,449-50
Rickets, Todd...595
Ricketts, Thomas.. 346
Ridge, Tom 259
Riehl, Fredy 40
RINO 73,129,143,165,447
Ripa, Kelly 193
Rivera, Geraldo 3,299
Roads 80,305,383
Roanoke, VA 483,531-3
Roberts, Cokie 237-8,328
Roberts, John 15,301,337-8,342
Robertson, Pat... 350
Robertson, Phil... 422,577
Robertson, Willie.. 366
Rochester, NY...400-1
Rockingham County 150
Roff, Peter.. 251
Rome, NY 401
Romney, Mitt 8,9,33,36,39,110,140,145,149
.... 150,165,181,220,232-3,257,260,275
.....296-7,347,350-1,357,360,362-3,366
.... 368-9,375,378,380,450,524,589
Rone, Riley 450
Roosevelt, Franklin D. 173
Roosevelt, Teddy 88
Root, Sarah.. 418,514
Root, Wayne 74,136-7,220

Rorke, Robert..................................212
Rose, Pete 48
Roseburg, Oregon.............................140
Rosenberg, Don 44
Rosh Hashanah 541
Ross, Doug....................................180
Ross, Wilbur 595
Rove, Karl.......110,111,129,165,233,263,302,349
Rubin, Jennifer.............................241,420
Rubio, Marco 33,39,41,87,104,130-1,134,137
........143,146-7,149-50,152,157,167-70
...... 175-6,178,183,185,187,189-91,194
........196-201,203-5,208,211-2,214,216
.218,222,232,246,253,275,279,281,284
.....292,297,306-7,310,317,322-3,327-8
...333,339,341,343-7,349,353-7,359-64
.... 366-70,372,375,377,380,387,389-90
.....................................425
Rule of law....................................28,78
Rumsfeld, Donald 311,457
Russia   157-8,167,193,220,296,298,424,431
... 482,484-6,493,496,520,526,535,565
...............590,602-3,608,611-2,614-8
Ryan, Lynne....................................408
Ryan, Paul....154-5,380,418,422,443,552-3,557-8
Ryder, John....................................394
Saban, Haim...................................255
Sacramento, CA................................440-1
Sadler, Anthony 105
Safety 32
Salem, NH 329
Salt Lake City, UT 379-80
Samsung 342
San Antonio, TX...............................145
San Bernardino, CA............................246
San Diego, CA............................ 437,472,488
San Francisco, CA 32-3,36,48
San Jose, CA..................................441-2,444-5
Sanchez, Felix.................................174
Sanctions 28,43
Sanctuary cities..........................39,153,563
Sanders, Bernie.... 60,101,161-2,218,269,280,284
.... 304,310,325,331,341,349,372-4,390
399-400,404,410,416-9,422,424-5,427
.... 430-1,434,436,442,448,464,471,474
.479-86,488-90,497,515,533,540-1,553
.....................................561,565
Sanford, FL...................................572,574
Sarasota, FL 236,237,239,585
Sasse, Ben....................................524
Saturday Night Live............ 143,158,171,178,202
..............206-13,364,557,591,598,618
Saudi Arabia 20,112,167,261,288,312,452,590
Scalia, Antonin................................336,344
Scaramucci, Anthony 425
Scarborough, Joe.......................418,444,447
Schlafly, Phyllis........... 272,312,357,372,521,524
Schlapp, Matt.....................................420
Schlonged 274
Schools 305,494,520,619
Schreckenger, Ben 244
Schumer, Chuck.........................211,591,611-2
Schwartz, Tony 524
Schwarzenegger, Arnold........................ 123,613
Scotland 76,79-80,108,174,258,443-4,458-60
Scott, Adam 366-8
Scott, Rick....................................15,378,613
Scott, Tamara...................................260
Scott, Tim 179
Scranton, PA....................................484,583-4
Seattle 29
Second Amendment.. 8,124,161,189,250,260,325
........375,397,432,465,502,506,528,562
Secret Service 373,446,479,503,528,576
Secretary of Defense 479,591
Secretary of State .. 108,456,496,504,530,538,551
.....................................602
Security   24,31,33,37,46-7,52,68,108,138,267
........327,331,343,398,423,438,451,466
Self defense.......................................40
Self funding................. 110,116,314,335,336,350
.....................................358,365,463
Sellers, Bakari...................................523
Selma, NC...582
Senate 11,63,125,131,133,137,139,299,327
.353,368,375,422-3,436-7,461,469,474
.....................480,598,600-1,613,616
Senator 11,73,95,120,131,134,137,171,179
.227,291,307,319,324,338,352-3,356-7
.361,363-4,366,368,370,379,407,422-3
. 436,448-9,461-2,467,474-5,501-2,514
.....................................520,535,544,598
Seniors 74
Sessions, Jeff....................................364,592
Sharpton, Al.......................................27
Shaw, Jamiel....................................44,240
Silent majority... 53,79-80,94,98,100,102,106,133
.....................................204,230,275,281
Silicon Valley 98
Sims, Molly.......................................14

Singer, Paul...............197
Sioux City, Iowa...............185
Sioux County, Iowa...............308
Sirius National News...............199
Situation Room (tv program)...............311
Skarlatos, Alex...............105
Slate...............133,165
Slim, Carlos...............605
Sliwa, Curtis...............240
Small Business Optimism Index...............615
Small business...............39,546,615
SNL...............see Saturday Night Live
Social security...............44,135,183,189,203
Socialist...............35,165,404
Softbank...............599
Soloman, Alisa...............196
Somalia...............595
Son, Masayoshi...............599
South Bend, IN...............415-6
South Carolina........4,63,68,105,107,145,163,167
......171-73,181,213,224-6,232-3,252-3
........255,260,281-3,292-3,302,323,326
331-2,334-6,338-48,352,355-6,360,370
...............523,546,553
South Dakota...............447
Spanish...............104
Sparks, Brenda...............44
Sparks, Nevada...............348-9,541
Speaker...............151,380,466,470
Special interest.......28,78,109,113,116,122-3,137
...249,267,273,287,300,304,314,329-30
.334,337-8,342,344,351,361-2,367,405
.....408-9,457,471,474,497-9,504-5,531
Spencer, Iowa...............248
Spencer, Lara...............193
Spokane, WA...............419
Springfield, IL...............211,574-5
Spy Magazine...............219
St. Augustine, FL...............572
St. Joseph, MI...............470
St. Jude's Charity...............153
St. Louis, Missouri...............371,552
Stamina.203,225,242,244,254,262,268,271,274
...............279,286,431,512,516,518
State Department..........284,494,511,545,550,553
...............558-9,561,565,569,601
State of the Union (speech)...............211,296
State of the Union (tv program)........180,261,329
Staten Island, NY...............404
Steel...............373-4,407,480,488,600

Stein, Jill...............598
Steinle, Kathryn...............31,32,48
Stephanopoulos, George...............419
Stern, Howard...............241
Stevens, J. Christopher...............456
Stevens, Stuart.145,149-50,295,297,347,366,378
Stewart, Rod...............193
Stirewalt, Chris...............103,165,207
Stone, Roger...............355
Stone, Spencer...............105
Straw poll...............107,150
Streep, Meryl...............615
Strong, Cecily...............202,208
Suffolk University...............13,137
Suleimani, Qassem...............112
Sun Herald...............294
Sun Sentinel...............369
Sun Tzu...............175
Sununu, John...............305
Super Pacs.......110,162,167,181,183,190,192,194
...............330,430
Superior, WI...............396
Superman...............140
Supreme Court........15,336,338,385,431,438,458
...............471-2,478,502,506,524,562
Switzerland...............497,604
Syracuse, NY...............402-3
Syria.156,202,219,221-2,228-9,261,344,369
.387,433,437,485,494,521,530,535,544
...............551,563,565,571,618
Taiwan...............597
Tallahassee, FL...............572,574
Tampa Bay Times...............92
Tampa, FL.....334-5,374,449-50,511,572-3,582-3
Tanden, Neera...............576
Tapper, Jake...............180,210
Tariffs...............135,598
TARP...............307
Tax returns...............164,350-2,355,360,423
Taxes 80,101,113,122,130,135-7,189,237,251
.275,280,336,421,423,435,456,461,487
.490,500,504,532,534,541,543,550,552
...............563-4,566,598-9,610,612
Tea Party...............107,115,303
Tel Aviv, Israel...............448
Tennessee....107,141-44,220-21,317,346,355,361
...............394,547,553,592,594
Terre Haute, IN...............414
Terris, Ben...............371
Terrorism........105-6,114,217-8,222,224,230,246

Terrorism (cont)........ 268-9,272,278,290,301,384
.... 386-8,390,430,434,446,448,450-1
.459,462,467,473,487,493,497,529,548
.... 551,558,606
Terrorists 170,217,219,222,224,229,272,342
...............430,434,464,466,530,544,576
Texas   29,55,64,112,145,215,219,262,337,344
.....350-1,353-5,357,359,361,443,453-4
.... 510-1,528,553,574,606
Theismann, Joe 266
Thiel, Peter.. 558
Thiessen, Marc.. 103
Third party 95
This Week (tv program)............. 229,321,389,419
Threaten, Marc.. 165
Tillerson, Rex 601-3
Time Magazine 91-3,99,124,133,165,214,256
.... 293-4,337,390,535,537,603
Time to get Tough (book)................................ 152
Timken, Jane.. 614
TMZ   598
Today Show, The (tv program)............. 183-4,620
Todd, Chuck 238-9,250,276,329,466-8
Toledo, OH 484,486,531,574-5
Tonight Show, The 118,295,296,528
Torres, Ralph DLG 372
Toyota Motor Corp 612
TPA   11
TPP   .... see Trans Pacific Partnership
Trade   15-6,22,24,28,31,37,130,134-6,160
. 198,214-5,389,393-4,419,434,448,453
. 454,456,461-3,471,484,490,506,533-4
.... 569,584,610
Traitor   41,114,548
Trans Pacific Partnership (TPP).......28,145,214-5
. 372-5,480,483,485,487,490,534-5,581
Transportation Safety Admin. (TSA) 432
Travel ban............................... 255,286,451-2,459
Treasure Island, Las Vegas............................. 151
Tribe, Laurence.. 293,305
Trippi, Joe... 169
Truman, Harry 41
Trump Barry, Maryanne 98
Trump Hotel, Honolulu.................................... 213
Trump Int'l Golf Links &
    Hotel Doonbeg... 120
Trump Int'l Golf Links.................................... 108
Trump Int'l Hotel & Tower........................ 4,415
Trump Int'l Hotel, DC..................... 176,317,528
Trump Int'l Hotel, Las Vegas........... 151,265,345

Trump Int'l Hotel, Waikiki........................369-70
Trump Nat'l Doral, Miami 178,363,367-8
Trump Nat'l Golf Club Jupiter 370
Trump Nat'l Golf Club Philadelphia 4
Trump Organization....................................... 291
Trump Tower & Hotel,
    Vancouver... 213
Trump Tower Grill... 417
Trump Tower, NYC.... 3,42,191,199-200,237,239
242,302,306,406,435,439-40,501-2,519
.... 533,577,586,592,603,613,616
Trump Turnberry 430,458-60
Trump University...... 358,362-4,367,387,439,442
.... 590
Trump Vineyards 48,51,210
Trump, Ann Marie 141
Trump, Barron 410
Trump, Donald Jr. 165,192,212,227-28,261,309
.329,358,410,415,476,478,574,587,595
.... 602
Trump, Eric 165,192,227-28,246,309,329,358
.... 405,410,458,460,478,501-2,587,595
.... 602,606
Trump, Fred 141,355
Trump, Ivana.. 134,410
Trump, Ivanka...... 13-4,164-5,192,204,227-8,322
.... 446,478,525-6,574,595,618
Trump, Kai...459
Trump, Lara 410
Trump, Mary Anne MacLeod 141
Trump, Melania 94,142,222-3,227-8,320,349
. 384-5,387,396,407,410,475-7,524,537
....................................541,559,581-2,588
Trump, Robert... 141
Trump, Tiffany................ 377,410,476,478,574
Trump, Vanessa 410
Trumpenomics 69
Tucson, AZ 382
Tulsa, Oklahoma..................................... 303,531
Turkey   268,462,604
Turnberry, Scotland 76,79-80,85,174,258,262
Twitter   2,10,50,76,83,90,94,110,129,157-61
.... 174,182,191,235,250,318,344,367-8
.388,419,469,508-9,525,532-3,536,539
.... 548,562,577,618
Tyler, Steven.. 163
Tyngsboro, MA.. 168
Tyson, Mike 184,197,462
U.S. Air Force.. 529,605
U.S. Chamber of Commerce 462

U.S. Navy 199,396,555,585,601,604-5
U.S. News & World Report 251
U.S.S. Iowa... 122-3
U.S.S. Wisconsin 194,196
U.S.S. Yorktown... 252
UFC 260,264
Ukraine 493,618
Undocumented.. 33
Unemployment 146,218,447,490,543
Union Leader (newspaper)....................... 281,294
Unions 148,183,258,292-3,462,600
United Auto Workers..................................... 183
United Kingdom 257,258,458,590
United Nations... 606-8
United States Coast Guard.............................. 496
United Steelworkers 1999.............................. 600
University of Florida...................................... 368
University of Massachusetts 325,328
University of Northwestern Ohio................... 488
Univision 15,17-20,23,51,106-7,138
Uranium 296
Urbandale High School................................. 124
US Men's National Soccer Team................... 153
USA Today 137,340-1,442,539
USC Dornslife/LA Times Poll....................... 548
Utah 379-84,512,586
Vaccine 125
Valley Forge, PA 580
Values Voter Summit..................................... 133
Values . 133,323,325,333,369,397,399,402,404
.... 406,450,459,563
Van Susteren, Greta.............. 74,102,228,315,354
VanderSloot, Frank.. 232
Vanity Fair Magazine 219
Vatican City.. 341
Vega, Paulina... 36
Venezuela 586
Verma, Seema.. 594
Vermont 165,291,292,347,355,361
Veterans 14,27,41,55-61,65-6,68,71,73,77,88
...... 97,102,121-3,130,162,174,177,185
. 192,194,196,201,211,213,217,251,277
283,315,317-20,326,338,344,375,380-1
396,434,439-41,470,521-3,557,569,573
.... 589
Veterans Administration..... 55-6,58,61,64,68,174
.... 196,199,277-78,396,434
Veterans Day 68
Videgaray Caso, Luis..................................... 523
Vietnam veterans 61,89

View, The (tv program,) 14,312,387
Virginia Beach, VA 141,145,570
Virginia . 48,51,141,163-4,194,196,216,244,279
350,355,358,361,416,449-50,473-4,479
. 483,494-6,503,509,521,524,531-3,546
.... 559,570,584-5,593
Visa 167,191,250,257,364
Von Drehle, David 293
Voter registration 80,86,157,184,214
Voters 13,34,57,73,88,91,110,121,123,129
. 148,180,200,214,219,221,237,246,262
.. 266,279-80,286,296,301,308,311,320
.... 323-4,333,344,362,365,388,402,405
.. 415,418,448,461,468,471-72,483,501
. 483,501,512-3,521,522,537,557-8,560
.... 607,613
Wade, Dwyane.. 514
Wages 243,279-80,417,456,480,486
Walding, John Wayne....................................318
Walker, Herschel... 107
Walker, Scott 64,71,73-4,91,98,104,129
.... 146,201,227,253,390
Wall 28,32,38,43,46,48,75,78,87,95,104,108
. 190,222,229,277,286,308,331,341,352
.... 375,386,393,438,472,511,514,516-8
....613-4
Wall Street .. 300,307-9,427,432,446,457,460,471
.... 473-4,483,487,490,509,540,550,564
Wall Street Journal.. 87,170,180,194,262,298,340
.... 341,345,364,391,555,576
Wallace, Chris.....8,155,167-9,171-2,177,232,249
.... 261,263,294,395,414,601
Wallace, Mike 8
Wallace, Nicole... 14
Walmart 619
Walsh, Marty 76
Walters, Barbara 222-3,387
War 6,16-7,28,44,101,103,135,251,471,483
Warren, Elizabeth 418-9,422-3,435-6,449-50,461
.... 474-5,483-4
Warren, MI...577-8
Warwick, Rhode Island................................. 409
Washington & Lee University 336
Washington (state) 419,435-6,514,516,533
Washington Examiner..................................... 148
Washington Post 176,181,185-6,196,241,252
.... 274,306,307,313,316,371,452-3,495
.... 558
Washington Times 566

Washington, DC . 16,28,38,41,60,62,68,74,77,114
.... 116-7,133,151,181,243-4,251,317,336
.... 353,357,367,371,373,384,422-3,427
.... 436,438-9,449,469,501,515,534,560-1
.... 573,582,588,598,603,608,613-4,617-8
....620-1
Washington, George 411
Wasserman Shultz, Debbie 481-2
Waterbury, CT 408
Waterloo, Iowa 149,321
Watertown, NY... 403
Waterville Valley, NH 547
Watson, Bubba.. 366
Watters, Jesse... 382,584
Waukesha, WI 538
Wayne, John 283,302
Weapons of mass destruction..... 168,171,173,527
Webb, Jim.. 159-61
Weekly Standard, The 206
Weiner, Anthony........................ 85,108,292,582
West Allis, Wisconsin........................... 395,602-3
West Chester, PA.. 409
West Hollywood, CA..................................... 345
West Palm Beach, FL 554,572
West Virginia.................. 227,417,420-2,459,560
West, Dr. Cornel 103
Western Conservative Summit 465
Westfield, IN 470
Wharton School, The 216
White House .. 18,30-1,48,68,90,101,108,119,156
.... 178,189,198,217,233,247,285,290,315
.... 370,438,447,489,497-8,505,509,544
.... 548,561-2,570-1,581,586,603,620
White, Dana.. 264
Wichita, Kansas... 364-5
Wiesel, Elie... 466
Wikileaks..... 480,484,553-4,557-8,568-9,570,572
.... 575,580
Wilkes-Barre, PA.................................... 410,546
Will, George 5,64,97,169,172,249,263,460
Willey, Kathleen... 548
Williams, Brian.. 5,22
Williams, Juan 483
Willis, Bruce.. 35,173
Wilmington, NC 502,583
Wilmington, OH 516,582-3
Windham, NH... 500
Winfrey, Oprah... 406
Wintour, Anna 613
Wisconsin 72-3,80,104,121,139,388-9,392-7

.... 485,496-7,499,507,538,547,557,560
....580,598,602-3
WMUR 303
Wollman Rink... 10,200
Women's health 101
Woods, Tiger 598
Woodward, Bob..618
Worcester, MA...223
World News Tonight...99
World Trade Center 166,240,338
World Tribune...27
Wounded Warriors.......................................620
Wrestlemania 9
WWE 398
Wyoming 113
Young, Melissa...391
Youngstown, OH 374,521
Zell, Sam 6
Zogby 127-8,133,136,306-7
Zucker, Jeff..117,523
Zuckerman, Mort 19,331-4,371

www.ingramcontent.com/pod-product-compliance
Lightning Source LLC
Chambersburg PA
CBHW061753260326
41914CB00006B/1090